GARVEY LIBRARY
VERMONT JUNIOR COLLEGE
WITHDRAWN
P9-DNB-069

Methods of PSYCHOLOGY

WILEY PUBLICATIONS IN PSYCHOLOGY

FOUNDATIONS OF PSYCHOLOGY.
By Edwin G. Boring, Herbert S. Langfeld, and Harry P. Weld.
INTRODUCTION TO PSYCHOLOGY.
By Edwin G. Boring, Herbert S. Langfeld, and Harry P. Weld.
SOCIAL PSYCHOLOGY.
By Daniel Katz and Richard L. Schanck.
HEARING—ITS PSYCHOLOGY AND PHYSIOLOGY.
By S. Smith Stevens and Hallowell Davis.
MANUAL OF PSYCHIATRY AND MENTAL HYGIENE. Seventh Edition.
By Aaron J. Rosanoff.
STATISTICAL METHODS IN BIOLOGY, MEDICINE, AND PSYCHOLOGY. Fourth Edition.
By C. B. Davenport and Merle P. Ekas.
MOTIVATION OF BEHAVIOR.
By P. T. Young.
PSYCHOLOGY—A FACTUAL TEXTBOOK.
By Edwin G. Boring, Herbert S. Langfeld, and Harry P. Weld.
PSYCHOLOGY IN BUSINESS AND INDUSTRY.
By John G. Jenkins.

HERBERT S. LANGFELD
Advisory Editor

METHODS OF PSYCHOLOGY.
T. G. Andrews, Editor.
THE PSYCHOLOGY OF EGO-INVOLVEMENTS.
By Muzafer Sherif and Hadley Cantril.
MANUAL OF CHILD PSYCHOLOGY.
Leonard Carmichael, Editor.
EMOTION IN MAN AND ANIMAL.
By P. T. Young.
UNCONSCIOUSNESS.
By James Grier Miller.
THE PSYCHOLOGY OF PERSONAL ADJUSTMENT.
By Fred McKinney.
THE PSYCHOLOGY OF SOCIAL MOVEMENTS.
By Hadley Cantril.

Methods of PSYCHOLOGY

T. G. Andrews, Editor

Scientific Advisor, Research
and Development Group at
the Logistics Division,
General Staff, U. S. Army

1948

JOHN WILEY AND SONS, INC., NEW YORK
CHAPMAN AND HALL, LTD., LONDON

THIRD PRINTING, APRIL, 1949

PRINTED IN THE UNITED STATES OF AMERICA

Contributing Authors

T. G. Andrews
S. Howard Bartley
Arthur G. Bills
Andrew W. Brown
Claude E. Buxton
Herbert S. Conrad
R. C. Davis
James J. Gibson
Harry F. Harlow
Edna Heidbreder
William Leroy Jenkins
W. N. Kellogg
Helen L. Koch
Donald B. Lindsley
W. D. Neff
Theodore M. Newcomb
Carl Pfaffmann
Saul Rosenzweig
L. L. Thurstone
Ernest Glen Wever
Paul Thomas Young
Joseph Zubin

To the memory of

ANDREW WILSON BROWN

November 21, 1890 — December 19, 1946

Editor's Preface

This book has been written in recognition of the need for greater emphasis on methodology in the training of students in psychology. Considerable stress is placed on this type of training, and many of our courses are directed toward this primary objective, but the textbooks and references available to us are mainly devoted to a discussion of investigative results, with only an occasional explanation of methods. These results, the facts and principles of psychology, are always to be tempered and interpreted in terms of the methods used. Actually we spend many hours talking to our students about methodology, but very little time is devoted to writing about this subject for a broader audience.

We hope in this volume to bridge the gap between other textbooks and the objectives of several of our academic courses. Our introduction to the methods of psychology applies this principle especially to the second course, which is usually called *experimental psychology* but which is supposed to serve as a methodological introduction to a large number of more advanced courses. To the extent that methodology is stressed in the first course or in more advanced and specialized courses, our book will help to fill a gap among the available textbooks. It is, then, a book of rather wide application, and it may serve also to introduce a new undergraduate course on methodology into our curricula.

Because of the varieties of approach and the details of research techniques to be represented, a book composed of the writings of many persons was clearly indicated. I have been most fortunate in obtaining the interest and services of as large a number of respected specialists in the various fields as there are chapters in the book. The fact that all these experts readily accepted the heavy responsibility of writing their chapters for our book and entered into the spirit of intensive collaboration on this project must certainly mean that the problem of training in methodology is important to them.

The contributing authors were asked to write their chapters in terms familiar to students who have completed the introductory course in psychology. In assigning work in this book, that basic level should be considered by the instructor. The authors also agreed that there should be a very minimum of involvement in purely historical and theoretical controversies. Some authors have preferred to arrange their chapters so that methods are presented in terms of the major problems. Others have presented the problems in terms of the methods. In no case, however, have the central problems of investigation been omitted from any chapter topic. Methods are always to be understood in their relations to the problems of psychology.

The "content" aspects of general psychology—the investigative results, facts, and principles—are surveyed in brief form in the chapters and in terms of the methods involved in their discoveries. Because the purpose of the book is to discuss the major and representative methods of psychology, these sections on results have been held to a rather minor role. Were we to stress methods and results equally, the text would take on the form of a handbook of psychology. That has not been our purpose, and it is to be understood that the material of this book is organized to supplement other textbooks whose purpose is to present the "content" aspects of general psychology.

The reader who is disposed to seek for a really complete discussion of all aspects of psychological methodology will find many omissions in each chapter and some omissions in the chapter headings. The present limitations of space have forced me to request that each contributing author choose the essential and more representative modern methods for discussion. These are the things we stress in our methodological training of undergraduate students. Some readers may be disappointed to find that there are no chapters on statistical methods or on methods of industrial psychology. Such chapters might be expected to appear in our book. Statistical methods, a very important cornerstone in modern psychological research, are treated more fully than any of our other methods in textbooks and reference works devoted to that subject. Consequently we have elected to have the student referred elsewhere for a discussion of statistics, so that we may have an increased amount of space to devote to the details of other methods and techniques not found in other works. Any course on methods of psychology must devote considerable attention to statistical methods, and it is to be understood that some conversancy with this subject is presumed for a full appreciation of the methods described in our book.

Industrial psychology does not represent a separate discipline, and most of its characteristic methods have been borrowed from other fields of psychology. We have not included a chapter on the methods of industrial psychology because the material of such a chapter would mainly repeat parts of the content of Chapters 16, 17, 18, and 19.

It is impossible to mention all the sources of influence and information to which the authors and the editor are indebted. When the source is apparent, as in the case of quotations and illustrations, appropriate acknowledgment has been made in the text. As the editor, I am deeply grateful to the advisory editor of this series for his many helpful suggestions. I am most grateful, also, to the contributing authors for their grand spirit of cooperation and scholarly advice. I must, however, stand personally responsible for the pattern of organization of this book. If it functions in any way to aid in the directive training of our future psychologists, it will have served its purpose well and offered ample reward to the authors and the editor.

T. G. Andrews

University of Chicago
January, 1948

Table of Contents

Chapter 1

An Introduction to Psychological Methodology

T. G. Andrews[1]

As the student surveys the literature of modern psychology, he is impressed with its wide scope and the extremely varied methods that are employed in its heterogeneous domain. The data that fall within the boundaries of psychology include such diverse subjects as loudness discrimination in dogs, factors of delinquency in urban areas, spinal reflexes, and psychotherapy. Yet all these are psychology. Not only do the data and sources of data show great diversity, but it naturally follows that the methods of the field must also exhibit some similar degree of diversity.

Within the gigantic framework of psychological science there is some system and order among the facts and among the methods. The purpose of this introductory chapter is to search into the bases of methodology and attempt to bring together some of the common features and differentiating features of the sundry methods that are being employed in the advancement of psychological knowledge. The remaining chapters of the book are devoted to the more specific methods and the technical details of their application in the different fields of interest.

The science of psychology faces several rather fundamental difficulties. One of these major difficulties can be appreciated by a comparison with the so-called natural sciences, in which the beginning points—the raw material—are not under great controversy. Man does not ordinarily question the basic subject matter of physics or of chemistry; such raw stuff constitutes the main stimulus objects of his physical environment. On the other hand, historically, psychology has had some difficulty in trying to decide the boundaries of its subject matter, which has ranged from consciousness to the more modern and opera-

[1] Assistant Professor of Psychology, University of Chicago.

tionally definable *discriminatory response* [3]. There are many ways of going about the analysis of the behavior which we call the subject matter. As Professor E. G. Boring has indicated, psychology has settled down to the attempt to account man's functional capacities and describe them [4].

During its historical difficulties concerning subject matter psychology has fostered the growth of several rather divergent points of view, out of which there have arisen several interesting controversies [11, 12]. Certain psychologists have also felt compelled to expend considerable energy in trying to combat the easily made claim that their field should not be classified as a science. Perhaps the older subjects of analysis, such as consciousness, did not appear very scientific, but such a controversy is nevertheless a barren one. In this regard it is best to follow the rule, as stated by Karl Pearson [19], that any field is a science so long as it consistently employs scientific methods.

BACKGROUNDS OF SCIENTIFIC METHOD

Rationalism and Empiricism

If method is to be the major criterion of science, we can easily see the necessity for becoming conversant with the backgrounds and characteristics of scientific method.

The philosophical techniques used to evaluate and investigate behavior and all other things are *rational* in nature. Rationalism is the more speculative philosophy which attempts to arrive at "truths" by reasoning from a few rather broad assumptions in accordance with some principles of correct procedure, rather than by turning directly to experience. It is evident that rationalism presupposes a very strong faith in man's power to reason.

There have been some quite satisfactory procedures and criteria for deduction from propositions [6], but a major criticism of the familiar syllogistic form is that it has never proved of value in obtaining really new information. Demonstrating by syllogistic reasoning such things as "Socrates is mortal" has not been sufficient to satisfy the more spirited and *empirical* truth seekers [16]. Also, the major premise (the large *if*) in such syllogisms is usually an untestable hypothesis. Waiting until the last man has died in order to demonstrate that all men are mortal would not be a fruitful procedure.

Some investigators of a less speculative frame of mind were seeking new information, and so they scrapped most of the techniques of the rationalists and turned directly to nature and experience for the

answers to their questions. These questions took on new forms; they were stated with greater precision and were more closely directed to the world of experience. Rather than remaining satisfied with a statement merely because the rules of logical deduction had been followed in deriving it, these investigators tested the statement by determining whether it concurred with other types of observation.

These newer techniques were carried out in an entirely different spirit. Instead of the syllogistic form, the reverse was applied—that of starting from particulars and going toward generalities. This principle of *induction,* however, did not allow the application of convenient criteria of "truth" that had been developed for a syllogistic deduction. Although a little more troublesome, this lack of complete criteria served a purpose, because it helped science to throw off the cloak of absolutism and become progressive by never feeling too certain about its results [15].

There were many verbal battles and some actual bloodshed before the more inductive and empirical techniques were fully launched on their way toward the development of the body scientific. In the division of the two camps, the more rugged and individualistic empiricists tended toward overcompensation by throwing completely overboard any connections with the despised speculative systems. During more recent years, however, there has been an interesting and profitable reversion to the extent that scientists are becoming more and more concerned about the philosophical bases of their methods and modes of discourse. Philosophy, therefore, is still with us in all our scientific endeavors [5, 17, 20].

For purposes of the description and prediction of natural phenomena, the empirical and inductive methods of science have survived as the fittest. Nevertheless, whenever the scientist poses an hypothesis for investigation, designs an experiment, arranges precision instruments for purposes of recording, statistically analyzes the quantitative results of the investigation, and makes inferences about behavior on the basis of the experimental results, he is making a large number of critical assumptions that are based on some one or another philosophical presupposition. In the following analysis of psychological methodology we shall see how the more abstract tools of science are inextricably mixed with philosophy.

The General Plan of Scientific Method

The scientist selects a tentative explanation as the beginning step in his inquiry, and this tentative suggestion is taken as an *hypothesis,* which directs the search for corroborative or negating facts. The hypothesis is merely a question and is usually quite narrow in scope. These hypotheses are piecemeal but not haphazardly so; each is a question recognized as belonging to a larger family of questions.

An investigation is designed in such a way that it involves a direct analysis of all the major conditions of the hypothesis. Preferably the investigation takes the form of an *experiment,* which is carried out under rigidly controlled conditions during the systematic variation of one of these conditions in particular. These characteristics allow the *reproducibility* of the conditions under which a given experiment is performed. When experimentation is impossible, however, the investigator may employ other methods. Psychological science is founded upon but not limited by the experimental method.

If the results of the investigation are not controversial, the hypothesis may be confirmed (although not proved), and the next step involves tying together the results of a large number of scientifically tested propositions which have some system of relationship. The results of this last step may involve the formulation of a *scientific law,* which is only a type of mental shorthand by which a number of facts or relations are subsumed under one simplified statement. A natural law, then, is merely a résumé of a longer and more detailed description.

Another stage, although not an absolutely necessary one, is the organization of a *theory* to account for the laws. The laws, as well as the theories, represent generalizations from which formal deductions can be made. These deductions are then set up as hypotheses for further scientific investigation. A particular law or theory is thus tested objectively according to whether or not the things which it predicts (which may be deduced from it) are supported or discredited empirically. As more and more correct predictions are added for a particular theory or law, we say that *truth is approached* (not *attained*) by the theory or law.

The process of induction from empirical evidence always involves a treacherous step because the evidence is never complete. In testing a certain hypothesis about human behavior, we can never study *all* humans but must obtain what is believed to be a "representative" sample from the hypothetical population of all humans. Generalizations are thus of necessity made on the basis of partial evidence, and so they are made only as *probable inferences.* The degree of probability—or confidence—that can be attached to scientific inferences differs from one to another, and to this extent the business of science is directed toward diminishing error in the general process of scientific problem solving.

The scientific method becomes more than a mere circular game played by scientists when prediction directs investigation to seek something that has not been previously suspected. Furthermore, some of the most spectacular achievements of science have been produced by the rather straightforward system of inducing a generalization and then deducing from the generalization. Good experimentation, then, is not a hit-or-miss affair or purely random trial and error, and this fact led Darwin to the pregnant statement, "How odd it is that anyone should not see that all observation must be for or against some view, if it is to be of any service."

Theory and experiment are the helpmates of scientific pursuit, theory suggesting the pattern of the maze, and experiment determining the blind alleys and the short cuts. Whenever such a maze is found to be composed only of blind alleys, it is modified or discarded, or at least it should be. To this extent the term *science* should be reserved to describe a body of *verified knowledge,* and the most satisfactory criterion of science is in terms of the method of verification. Knowledge of facts without knowledge of the procedures to discover the facts does not constitute science, and this is especially true in psychology. Knowing about the behavior of people does not qualify one as a psychologist.

Classification of Psychological Methods

When we try to catalog the many methods of investigation in psychology, we find that there are several types of general methods and several types of more specific techniques. The various fields of psychological study have their own specific techniques of research. The more general methods, however, are not peculiar to the separate fields but are used as common property by all psychologists. These general methods of investigation may be broadly classified in several different ways; one classification scheme is as follows:

1. Methods of selecting the individuals to be studied.
2. Methods of controlling extraneous stimulation during the investigation.
3. Methods of instructing or directing the attention of the individuals under investigation.
4. Methods of presenting the stimuli.
5. Methods of registering intermediate bodily changes.
6. Methods of observing and recording overt responses to stimulation.
7. Methods of analyzing and synthesizing the data resulting from an investigation.

Although there is some overlapping among these classes of methods, each class pertains to humans or lower animals, to learning, sensory, motivational, motor, social, abnormal, child, personality, educational, or industrial investigations. This classification of methods is easily seen as depending to a considerable extent on the *stages of the investigation.*

Another and somewhat old-fashioned type of classification is based on a differentiation between *subjective* and *objective methods.* Because of the nature of many psychological phenomena there has always been some concern about this differentiation. In so far as the direct experience of an individual is to some extent a private and subjective phenomenon, many of the methods used to study direct experience and mental processes are called subjective. The general technique for investigating these phenomena—thought, images, feelings, sensations, perceptions—has been to ask the subject to report on these experiences, to introspect. This general type of observation has been distinguished from objective observation, which is not so dependent on the biases or judgments of the individual observer and better permits independent verification. Such a methodological distinction has become of less importance with the growing realization that all the subjective methods can be handled with a considerable degree of objectivity and that all the objective methods have some of the characteristics of subjectivity.

Still another and somewhat more fruitful classification of psychological methods is in terms of the conditions of control and the purposes of the observations. The general methods may be characterized as *experimental, differential,* or *clinical.* These classes overlap only slightly, and a choice between them is usually made on the basis of the specific problem to be solved and the nature of the assumptions that are possible or advisable for a particular investigation.[2]

EXPERIMENTAL METHODS

Experimentation holds the central position in psychological science, as it does in all other sciences, for the reason that it best exemplifies the principles of scientific method [20, 22]. The experiment consists of objective observations of actions performed under rigidly controlled conditions. The hypothesis for investigation is chosen and is stated in such a manner that it can be tested rather completely. One factor,

[2] All three general methods may be used in any one psychological research project. For an example of the joint use of these methods in one series of interesting studies the reader is referred to [18].

the "causal" one, is usually varied through a predetermined range of values. In the more classical scheme, changes are produced in one variable at a time, and the effects of these changes are observed and measured or recorded while all other important variables of influence are held constant in their effects [2, 7].

The Independent and the Dependent Variable

One manner of illustrating a typical design for a psychological experiment is shown in Fig. 1. This diagram indicates that a certain type of specified action, the *dependent variable,* is observed while it is influenced by arbitrarily produced changes in some specified stimulating condition, the *independent variable.* Other stimulating condi-

Fig. 1. A diagram to represent the scheme of a psychological experiment

tions that might influence the dependent variable are not allowed to vary during the course of the experiment; i.e., their influences are held constant. On the other hand, actions other than those of one particular dependent variable are quite naturally being carried on by the organism, and these are indicated by the lines R_1 and R_3. In some experiments measures of these other responses are recorded during the whole process, and under such conditions more than one dependent variable exists in the experiment. Such is the case in an experiment which is designed to determine the effects on both mood and efficiency (two dependent variables) of changes in oxygen content of the air breathed by the subjects in the experiment.

Thus there is only one independent variable in an experiment of the classical design, and so we often hear of the *law of the independent variable.* This law states that we are to keep all causal factors constant except one, which is to be systematically varied while observations of concomitant or successive changes in the dependent variables are made. Such a procedure rules out all other possibilities of producing in the results effects not attributable to the one independent variable. Certain systematic experimental designs are now available that enable the experimenter to employ more than one independent variable in a single experiment. A discussion of this important point will arise later.

The foregoing description is not to be taken as indicating that all the factors involved in any experiment are under the investigator's control. If the observations could be completely controlled, the experimenter would need to make only as many observations as there are degrees of change in the independent variable. This may be the situation in certain physical sciences, but certainly not in the behavioral sciences, where the behavior of the organism is quite variable and is influenced by a multitude of factors, both internal and external. Because of the relatively great variability of behavior, it is necessary for the experimenter to obtain several observations under each condition of the experiment. An average tendency among the observations for each level of the independent variable is then computed, and that average tendency is accepted as a more dependable and representative value for the dependent variable.

Importance of Controls

Many of the factors that would influence and modify the behavior specified by a particular dependent variable must have their influence removed from the experimental situation. Insuring adequate controls is one of the most important problems for the experimentalist to face. The influences of uncontrolled factors may obscure the results of experiments that would otherwise be critical, and yet psychology cannot exert control over all the possible sources of influence that are extraneous to the independent variable. The result of this seeming impasse is that all experiments must be repeated (replicated) and must produce consistency of results under a variety of conditions before they become accepted as demonstrating "facts." The scientist must always be prepared to scrap his results whenever they are demonstrated to be untenable in the light of replication under more precise control.

A Typical Psychological Experiment

Before going further into the logic of experimental design, the reader is referred to Buxton's description of an experiment by Courts.

In Chapter 3, pages 73–75, the experiment is analyzed. Courts tested the hypothesis that there is a functional relationship between the degree of tension on the part of the learner and the efficiency of learning, and the description given of Courts's study forms a good lesson in experimental design. The reader should study this description carefully before proceeding in this introduction.

Functional and Factorial Experiments

As a result of having carried out an experiment, the psychological investigator usually wishes to express a relationship between the independent and a dependent variable. Seeking for such *concomitant variations* is one of the most important endeavors in scientific work [6, 23]. As a result of this type of information science is able to understand causal factors and make predictions.

Through experimentation we wish ultimately to establish statements of scientific law, or at least generalizations which approach the status of laws. The laws, our goal, express relations and thus become the model for an important type of experiment. When the researcher wishes to determine the functional relationship between two experimental variables, he first establishes the range of the independent variable within which he will experiment. As a next step he chooses several values within that range and stimulates his subjects with each of these values (or under the conditions of each of these values) while he observes and records the resulting changes in behavior of a specified sort (the dependent variable). This general procedure identifies the experiment as being of the *functional type,* i.e., one in which a functional relationship is sought. Such was Courts's experiment.

Quite often, however, the researcher must cast about in a more exploratory fashion to determine factors that will offer some chance of showing important and useful relationships. Instead of using several values along the independent variable, the experimenter may use only two, as in the typical experiment wherein a difference is sought between the presence and the absence of a certain feature. The results of such experiments as this do not indicate the functional relations between variables but do show whether the factor which has been changed produces any measurable change in the dependent variable. We may classify experiments of this second type as *factorial.*[3] Experiments of the factorial type are most useful as

[3] The term *factorial,* as used here, is not to be confused with *factorial analysis* (see pages 531–533) or with *factorial design,* a term used in certain kinds of statistical analysis.

preliminary stages in an experimental program; they are used mainly to answer the question *what,* whereas experiments of the functional type are designed to answer the question *how.*

The Control-Test Method

In order further to see how experiments are designed to answer psychological hypotheses, we may make another type of classification of experimental methods.[4] One of these classes may be called the control-test method, which consists in the observation of performance under what may be called normal conditions and then again with one condition changed. The control-test method is an example of the factorial type of experiment at its simplest level. For example, visual acuity might be measured under ordinary conditions of illumination and then under the condition of glare. Actually the measure would be taken several times under each condition, but it would not be necessary to have two different groups of subjects for the experiment. The control-test method is sometimes called the *method of difference.*

The control-test method is used when there is little or no practice effect or transfer from one condition of measurement to the other. Visual acuity is not changed by its measurement, although the process of measurement is usually novel or complex to the degree that it may take the subjects a few practice trials to learn to follow the instructions and to give reliable reports. Such practice trials, of course, are not recorded.

The Control-Group Method

This technique consists in observing two equated groups of subjects who are performing under the same conditions except for the influence of one element. The scale of presence-absence of this one particular element represents the independent variable of the experiment and identifies it as factorial in type. The difference in performance between the two groups is the dependent variable and is a function of the independent variable if all other sources of influence are eliminated.

In this experimental design it is very important that the two groups involved have equal potentialities to begin with. In order to approximate this condition the groups are equated; i.e., they are so chosen as

[4] This classification and analysis of psychological experiments has been suggested by T. A. Jackson [14].

to be at the same level of measured capacity on the variables that may conceivably affect the results, and ideally they should be equated for *all* characteristics which might bear on the investigation at hand. Because perfectly equated groups are a frank impossibility, the investigator is usually content to equate for those characteristics which seem most likely to influence the dependent variable.

An example of the control-group technique may be described in the following manner. The general hypothesis may be that practice in memorizing increases memory ability. Such an hypothesis defies direct experimental test, and so a more particular aspect of the general statement is chosen: practice in memorizing certain prose increases ability to memorize certain poetry. In designing an experiment for an adequate test of this hypothesis, the first step is to select a group of subjects who are reasonably homogeneous in memorizing ability and do not differ from one another very much in intelligence. All the subjects are then given a test (the *fore-test*) to determine their ability to memorize poetry. On the basis of the scores from this fore-test, the subjects are divided into two groups such that the average poetry-memorizing abilities (as measured by the test) are the same. It is also desirable that the variabilities of the two groups be equal. One of the two groups is now chosen as the *experimental group,* and a period of practice in memorizing prose is spent by this group. The other group becomes the *control group* and does not receive any of the practice on prose. Both groups are then given a final test on memorizing poetry.

The following hypothetical data may be used to indicate the expression and treatment of experimental results that might accrue from this investigation:

	Fore-Test (poetry)	Training Period (prose)	Final Test (poetry)
Experimental group	62	——	79
Control group	62	....	66
		Difference =	13

The two groups were equated at 62 (same measure of proficiency) on the fore-test, and the experimental group was 13 points better than the control group on the final test. This difference is now attributable to the effects of the training period on the experimental group, because the two groups were the same in most other important respects. It is to be noted that the control group in this hypothetical experiment became slightly better (by 4 points) at poetry on the final test, presumably due to the practice administered in the very taking of the fore-test. Therefore, we may assume that the experimental group likewise gained 4 of their 17 points as a result of the practice afforded by the fore-test.

The control-group method is used whenever it is possible that the function to be measured (memory in the experiment described) may change every time it is measured. That is, there may be and usually is some practice effect within the fore-test itself, and the only way to determine the amount of this unwanted practice effect is by the use of the control group.

The Matched-Pair Technique

The theory of the control-group method is applied to situations other than those involving growth or learning. When choosing two groups for the purpose of evaluating the effects of an independent variable, the investigator often selects the subjects in *pairs,* and this procedure is known as the *matched-pair technique.* In such cases the independent variable may form the basis of the selection. For example, an investigator may wish to determine whether bright children are more or less suggestible than dull children. This hypothesis is an interesting one and has been tested in a rather precise manner by Simmons [21]. Knowing that suggestibility may be influenced to a considerable extent by age and sex, Simmons chose children in pairs in such a way that the two members of each pair were exactly equal in age and were of the same sex. One member of each pair was dull, with an intelligence quotient below 90, and the other member was bright, with an intelligence quotient above 125. For our purposes we need not be concerned with the way in which suggestibility was measured. It will suffice to say that the groups were treated in exactly the same manner in the investigation and a numerical suggestibility score was obtained on each subject. Interestingly enough, the bright children averaged 30.7, and the dull children averaged 46.3, the latter being definitely the more suggestible. In this factorial type of study by Simmons the independent variable was intelligence, which she "varied" in the manner in which she selected her groups

It is worth pausing for a moment to note that Simmons' investigation does not qualify as a real experiment, which necessarily involves the more purposive manipulation of the independent variable. It is, however, sometimes desirable to turn to nature and find conditions that conform rather closely to what is wanted and so to utilize these conditions without further manipulation. In such cases selection may replace control. After all, intelligence is not a variable which we can easily manipulate and vary, and therefore we must turn to individual differences for a scale, rather than to a physical scale which can be employed in the laboratory.

The Practice Method

This method consists in training the subject or subjects in the function to be used until no more improvement is made as a result of training or practice. After such a level of practice is reached, variations in performance may safely be ascribed to variations in the conditions under which they are made. When a subject is used as his own control in this manner, it is obviously necessary to reach a high practice level before beginning the experiment proper. The practice method is not frequently used in experimentation because a great deal of time is required for each subject, thus making it difficult to obtain a very large number of subjects; also the method is obviously not suitable for studies that pertain to the early stages of the learning process. These factors that weigh against the general use of the practice method clearly indicate a central problem in experimenting on organisms; i.e., the organism is subject to change by the very measurement process itself—a feature especially peculiar to psychological experimentation.

The Rotation Method

The rotation method consists in presenting two or more stimulation situations to the experimental subjects in as many sequences as necessary to control the serial effects of fatigue or practice. For example, if we wished to determine the relative influence of two specified conditions, A and B, on a group of subjects, we would *not* measure all the subjects under condition A and then under condition B. Condition A might so fatigue or train the subjects that the measures under condition B would not be independent of the fatigue or training effects—another case in which the measuring process changes the behavior. We would thus be faced with two alternatives. We might obtain half the measures for condition A, all the measures for condition B, and then the other half of the measures for condition A. This technique is sometimes called the ABBA order or *counterbalancing.* Another alternative is to separate the subjects into two equated groups, one of which receives treatment A and then B, whereas the other group receives treatment B and then A. Both sets of A results and both sets of B results may then be combined, and the difference between them calculated.

The purpose of the rotation method in experimental design is fairly obvious. The advantage or disadvantage of placing one condition first in the sequence is balanced for the two conditions. An assumption is made in this logic, however, to the effect that the transfer effect from condition A to condition B is the same as from B to A. This assumption may or may not be sound, and it is probably made more often than is justified. At any rate, the rotation method should be applied only with some caution, and it is usually a compromise method. Ideally, large groups of carefully equated subjects should be used in an experiment, one for one condition and the other for the other condition. The rotation method, however, is usually resorted to when only a limited number of subjects are available, and with this method all the subjects are measured under all the conditions; the two groups are equated because they are the same persons. This assumption, however, may be a delusion because a subject is not the same after he has had a certain test—he may learn important elements or attitudes for the next test.

Let us briefly go through a typical situation in which the rotation method is employed as a group demonstration for classes in experimental psychology. Using the hypothesis that the three typical methods of measuring retention of verbal material give different results, we choose three lists of nonsense syllables in such a way that the three lists are of equal difficulty. (This equality can be obtained from lists published for the purpose.) Calling these lists A, B, and C, we have a large group of subjects memorize the lists in the order ABC and under standardized conditions. For each subject we obtain a score on each of the three lists, and three scores are then averages for each person. We send the subjects away with the admonition that they should not rehearse the material in any way and that they should return to the laboratory at a designated time in the future.

From the set of scores we equate three groups of subjects, I, II, and III, such that they are equal in their demonstrated ability to memorize the material. When the subjects return for further observations, we instruct them in such a way that the different groups take the retention measures in the following manner:

GROUP I	GROUP II	GROUP III
Recall test on list A	Recognition test on list A	Relearning on list A
Relearning on list B	Recall test on list B	Recognition test on list B
Recognition test on list C	Relearning on list C	Recall test on list C

Note that all three measures of retention occur in all three orders. Thus no method of measurement gets more practice or fatigue effect than any other when we combine the data for analysis. We pool the data simply by taking all the scores on *recall* together, those on *recognition* together, and those on *relearning* together. Remember that the lists were equated before the investigation began.

As a general result, in analyzing the data from such an experiment, we would probably find that methods of measuring retention differed and that recognition produced highest scores, relearning next highest, and recall lowest. In such an experiment the lists might be made up of different types of materials: one list of related words, another of unrelated words, and the third of nonsense syllables. Our retention tests would probably then indicate that the list of related words is retained best and the nonsense syllables least. An additional question of interest would then be whether there was considerable interaction between one of the lists and one of the measures of retention. For example, we might find that recalling the related words was relatively a very easy task, although recall in general did not produce high scores. This problem of interaction can be approached with proper experimental designs and is becoming an important aspect of experimentation in psychology [9].

If the lists of nonsense syllables were not equated in this experiment or if the lists were made up of different materials, a more complicated experimental design would be needed, and we would probably have our groups of subjects do different things. A characteristic to note in such a case as this is the possibility of interaction between a certain type of material and a certain method of measuring retention.

Notice that in the foregoing experiment two independent variables were involved and were active in conjunction with one another. This appears to contradict the statement made earlier to the effect that we employ only one independent variable at a time in an experiment. There are, however, some new types of experimental designs based on concepts that differ rather radically from the classical ones as to the number of inquiries that should be included in a single experiment. In the newer experimental designs all the factors to be tested are varied concurrently in all possible combinations. Such complicated experimental designs are really extensions of the rotation method and are based on a statistical method called analysis of variance [9, 13]. These techniques allow much greater efficiency than the classical technique of the single independent variable.

Artificial Characteristic of Experiments

A meaningless criticism has frequently been directed against experimental methods as used in psychology. This criticism is to the effect that real human behavior, the kind of everyday behavior that we wish to understand, occurs outside of laboratories, and when it is studied in the laboratory under the usual conditions of rigid control and precise measurement, it is not the same behavior. This statement is of course quite true, but the experimentalist does not take it as a serious criticism because he actively seeks for stringent and artificial conditions, rather than attempting to avoid them and study "daily life" behavior as it occurs.

Because of the extreme variety and complexity of behavior and of the forces which influence it, no one would be able to establish a science of behavior by trying to study it under "normal" conditions. Whenever we begin a behavioral investigation, normal conditions do not exist because the measurement situation (even the interview situation) is not "normal." As stated near the beginning of this chapter, scientific hypotheses are necessarily quite limited in scope. It is only by the piecemeal selection of a few very limited aspects of behavior at a time and by carefully planned and intensive analysis of those limited aspects that successive investigations may allow us to construct a picture of behavior such that we may understand it, describe it, predict it, and control it. In all this work there is an obvious *error of fractionation,* but the error is important only when laboratory conditions are incorrectly thought of as counterparts of daily life activities.

Woodworth [24] has stated an analogous situation in the history of physics (the experimental techniques of which science are more easily "acceptable" to the layman). In order to test the law of falling bodies with adequate precision and control, objects of different mass are dropped simultaneously in a vacuum. The counterpart of this situation would be very unusual if it occurred in nature: what is more "unnatural" than a vacuum?

There are, of course, psychological methods of investigation which are not so rigorous nor quite so artificial as experimentation. The psychological investigator therefore must be acquainted with the other techniques that may be applied to problems that temporarily defy laboratory experimentation. The second major class of psychological methods of investigation is called *differential,* and these methods will be seen to meet more nearly some of the objections leveled at the experimental methods.

Non-experimental Variables

The class of methods called differential includes those systems of techniques which employ *individual differences* as variables of investigation. An example of such use has already been described on page 12 in the investigation of Simmons. In such studies there usually is no purposive *manipulation* of the independent variable; the investigator merely chooses his subjects according to certain criteria, and the measurements on the subjects themselves form the variable or variables for the investigation. The criterion of selection of the subjects may become the independent variable for an investigation (intelligence, in Simmons' study), but it is to be noted that this variable is not under the full control of the investigator, to be varied up and down a given scale at will and with full freedom.

At first view the above differentiation between experiments and differential methods may appear quite artificial, and it is true that all psychologists will not agree to such an apparently artificial classification scheme. Nevertheless, it should always be made clear that the independent variables resulting from individual differences are never under the investigator's control to the same degree that experimental variables are. Also the scales are different in kind.

Although the experimental methods are more precise and the inferences made from the results of these methods have greater likelihood of validity and can be more easily verified, it cannot be said that they are always more desirable than the differential methods. Experimental methods establish the model of objectivity for the other methods of psychological investigations, but experiments obviously cannot be devised for all the problems that are raised in the heterogeneous subject matter of psychology, as will be seen in a perusal of the various techniques described later in this book.

Correlational Methods

It is easily seen that most correlation studies in psychology fall into the class of differential methods. The major studies of intelligence and aptitudes (Chapter 17) and personality (Chapter 18) and a large number of those on social behavior (Chapter 22) are therefore classed as differential investigations. In these studies the psychologist takes people as they are and studies what they do, usually without changing the conditions under which they respond to the "tests" or perform the desired tasks. (If the conditions are changed, the situation becomes more like an experiment.) The subjects will naturally differ from one another in their behavior, and the investigator is usually seeking *concomitant variations* in other ways in which they behave.

The importance of this general technique for purposes of prediction can easily be seen from a few simple examples. It is quite important to be able to predict what kind of work each person can do best in order to produce the most efficient matching of workers with jobs. Attempts at solution of this problem are handled mainly by correlational techniques, in which workers are rated in terms of success on the job, and these ratings are correlated with a number of test scores on the same workers. Those tests that produce the highest correlations with the ratings of merit are then employed in the screening of others for the job in question. Other persons may now be given the same tests, and those who score highest on them will be judged as having a higher likelihood of performing efficiently on the specified job. More detailed descriptions of this type of work with aptitude tests will be found in Chapter 17.

The foregoing is an example of the use of correlation procedures in analyzing related scores, and the literature of psychology contains thousands of published studies on these problems. Another general type of application of the correlation method is directed toward the nature-nurture problem in psychology and involves studying pairs of persons who are genetically related. The score of one member of a pair is plotted against the score of the other member, and this is repeated for successive pairs. Most studies of this general sort indicate that in terms of intelligence test scores identical twins correlate quite highly (.90), fraternal twins less (.70), and siblings still less (.50), while relations as remote as grandparent-grandchild correlate hardly at all (.15). Such correlation studies as these on related pairs are really quite inadequate because of the presence of another correlating variable: similarity of environmental conditions during early development. The studies do, however, constitute examples of how correlational analyses are applied for the purpose of testing relations other than between one mental test and another.

The Longitudinal and the Cross-sectional Approaches

The problem of mental growth is a good one to illustrate the differential methods in studying concomitant variations. In investigations on this problem mental progress, as measured by some type of test, is observed and charted. There is no attempt on the part of the investigator to alter the normal course of development because it is the normal trend that is to be discovered. This general technique obviously raises an important issue, in which the investigator must choose whether to retest a group of individuals at successive ages, the *longitudinal approach,* or to test different age groups at the same time, the *cross-sectional approach.* Each of these approaches offers its own peculiar difficulties [1, 10]. It is enough for our purposes here merely to indicate the general nature of the differential technique in contrast to the experimental approach. The experimental approach has no way of giving information on the general problem of mental growth, although certain more limited hypotheses concerning such growth may be studied experimentally. The issue in this case is that both age and mental ability go along without our being able to do much direct manipulation of either of them. The investigator merely takes things as they are and determines the relationship between two specified natural phenomena. In order to study the differences between males and females in terms of certain psychological or physical traits, differential methods must also be applied. We most certainly cannot experimentally vary the sex of the human subject.

The cross-sectional approach has become an extremely important technique in an active democratic society. By its use determinations may be made of such phenomena as the morale effects of certain government policies, of electioneering effects, of food habits during critical shortages.

General Statistical Methods

The differential methods have often been called statistical for the reason that statistical techniques become the major devices for studying individual differences. This fact can be seen from a brief listing of the more important characteristics of statistical methods: (*a*) efficiently describing masses of data in terms of relatively few numerical expressions, (*b*) expressing the relationships between variables, (*c*) allowing the extensions of scientific inferences to be tested under conditions of mathematical exactness.

The commonly noted relation between differential methods and statistical techniques does not mean that statistics are not considered important tools to be applied in experimental methods. The data that result from experiments are expressed in mathematical form, and statistical analyses are applied to these data in order to exhaust all the useful information from them. It is also through statistical methods that the most efficient experimental designs have been derived [8].

CLINICAL METHODS

The clinical methods have a different frame of reference from the experimental and differential methods in psychology. The word clinic originally referred to "something pertaining to a bed," and it has been extended to mean "directed toward the individual." Whereas the experimental and differential methods have been established to ascertain facts which transcend the individual case, the clinical methods are directed less toward investigations of general behavioral facts and more toward individual appraisal and adjustment.

No attempt will be made to elaborate upon clinical methods at this point because these techniques and their applications are thoroughly described in Chapter 19. The reference to clinical methods in this introductory chapter serves mainly to indicate a third and important general class of psychological methods.

ORGANIZATION OF THE CHAPTERS THAT FOLLOW

The plan of organization of the chapters in this book is fairly obvious and seems to represent a logical form. The chapters on acquiring behavior changes—learning and thinking—cover the major types of investigation in these fields and indicate how the central problems have been attacked by properly devised methods and techniques.

The next section of the book is devoted to the topics of reception. Because of the psychological nature of measurement in sensory and perceptual research, this section is introduced by a chapter on psychophysics. The chapter on methods of studying perceptual phenomena was placed next because of the excellent discussion of the methodological relations between perception and sensation. Furthermore, this chapter serves as a bridge between the psychophysics and the psychophysiology of sensation.

The chapter on animal behavior represents a transition of subject matter. It takes its present position because it serves as an indicator of how the learning and reception techniques are applied to lower animals, and it introduces the topic of motivation at a lower level. The next section, containing chapters on motivation and emotion, recording action, neurophysiological and other bodily functions, and motor functions and efficiency, discusses the methods of psychology which have been applied to solving the significant problems of response mechanisms and tendencies.

The last section of the book is devoted to descriptions of the important methods of studying individual differences in the more specialized domains of psychological investigation. Here the non-experimental methods of psychology are seen in their important relations to investigating and appraising various capacities and traits of people classified in different manners.

SUMMARY

In this introduction we indicated some of the causes in the development of the scientific method and also some of the characteristic features of scientific method in the steps intervening between investigation and theory. A rather crude classification of psychological methods was made, and the more important features of each of the three types were described. In experimental methods the characteristic features of the independent and dependent variables were discussed, and the difference between "factorial" and "functional" experimentation was evaluated. Some of the basic forms of psychological experiments were analyzed as (1) the control-test method, (2) the control-group method, (3) the matched-pair method, (4) the practice method, and (5) the rotation method.

Differential methods were characterized by their dependence on individual differences for the variables under investigation, and clinical methods by their individual-centered interests. Some of the interrelationships between the different classes of methods were shown, and it is hoped that the student will become more and more aware of this characteristic of interdependence among the psychological methods as he studies the topical chapters of this book.

REFERENCES

1. ANASTASI, A. *Differential Psychology.* New York: Macmillan, 1939.
2. BENTLEY, M. The nature and uses of experiment in psychology. *Amer. J. Psychol.*, 1937, *50*, 452–469.
3. BORING, E. G. A psychological function is the relation of successive differentiations of events in the organism. *Psychol. Rev.*, 1937, *44*, 445–461.
4. BORING, E. G. Mind and mechanism. *Amer. J. Psychol.*, 1946, *59*, 173–192.
5. CHURCHMAN, C. W. *Theory of Experimental Inference.* University of Pennsylvania, privately distributed.
6. COHEN, M. R., and E. NAGEL. *An Introduction to Logic and Scientific Method.* New York: Harcourt, Brace, 1934.

7. DINGLER, H. *Das Experiment.* Munich: Ernst Reinhardt, 1928.
8. FISHER, R. A. *The Design of Experiments.* London: Oliver and Boyd, 1935.
9. GARRETT, H. E., and J. ZUBIN. The analysis of variance in psychological research. *Psychol. Bull.,* 1943, *40,* 233–267.
10. GREENE, E. B. *Measurements of Human Behavior.* New York: Odyssey Press, 1941.
11. GRIFFITH, C. R. *Principles of Systematic Psychology.* Urbana, Illinois: University of Illinois Press, 1943.
12. HEIDBREDER, E. *Seven Psychologies.* New York: Appleton-Century, 1933.
13. JACKSON, R. W. B. Application of the analysis of variance and covariance method to educational problems. *Univ. Toronto, Dept. Educ. Research, Bull. No. 11,* 1940.
14. JACKSON, T. A. *Principles of Experimentation.* (On file in Psychology Reading Room, Columbia University.)
15. JAFFE, H. The development of the experimental method. In *Philosophical Essays in Honor of Edgar Arthur Singer, Jr.* F. P. Clarke and M. C. Nahm, Eds. Philadelphia: University of Pennsylvania Press, 1942.
16. JEFFREYS, H. *Scientific Inference.* New York: Macmillan, 1937.
17. JOHNSON, H. M. Pre-experimental assumptions as determiners of experimental results. *Psychol. Rev.,* 1940, *47,* 338–346.
18. MURRAY, H. A. *Explorations in Personality, a Clinical and Experimental Study of Fifty Men of College Age.* New York: Oxford University Press, 1938.
19. PEARSON, K. *The Grammar of Science.* London: Adam and Charles Black, 1911.
20. RITCHIE, A. D. *Scientific Method.* New York: Harcourt, Brace, 1923.
21. SIMMONS, R. M. A study of a group of children of exceptionally high intelligence quotients in situations partaking of the nature of suggestion. *Teach. Coll. Contrib. Educ.,* 1940, No. 788.
22. WESTAWAY, F. W. *Scientific Method.* London: Blackie and Sons, 1937.
23. WOLF, A. *Essentials of Scientific Method.* New York: Macmillan, 1925.
24. WOODWORTH, R. S. Successes and failures of experimental psychology. *Science,* 1941, *94,* 265–270.

SUGGESTED READINGS

COHEN, M. R., and E. NAGEL. *An Introduction to Logic and Scientific Method.* New York: Harcourt, Brace, 1934.

PRATT, C. C. *The Logic of Modern Psychology.* New York: Macmillan, 1939.

RITCHIE, A. D. *Scientific Method.* New York: Harcourt, Brace, 1923.

STEVENS, S. S. Psychology and the science of sciences. *Psychol. Bull.,* 1939, *36,* 221–263.

Chapter 2

Conditioning and Motor Learning

By W. N. Kellogg[1]

The ability to modify and improve its behavior with practice is one of the greatest assets of the living organism. In fact, life, as we know it today, would be impossible if man—and other animals—were unable to "benefit by experience." The manner in which the changes in behavior which we call learning take place is consequently of primary importance to the psychologist, and the scientific study of the process of learning is one of the major divisions of experimental psychology. Since new things are likely to be discovered only by accident or chance—unless one knows beforehand just where and how to look for them—it follows that the methods and procedures for revealing the facts of learning are basic to an understanding of the process itself.

THE MOTOR LEARNING EXPERIMENT

The Nature of Motor Learning

A large part of the information which we now possess about learning ability has come from experiments on animals. Rational learning, dealing as it does with verbal or linguistic material, can be studied only in human subjects who are capable of verbal behavior. Motor learning, or perceptual-motor learning, however, since it confines itself to the learning of non-verbal tasks, can be observed not only in adult humans, but also in animals of almost any kind, in babies, and in other humans in which speaking or linguistic ability has not yet developed or for some other reason is lacking. Most of the research on conditioning, although usually treated as a field in itself, belongs properly under the heading of motor learning.

[1] Professor of Psychology, Indiana University.

Even though all learning is fundamentally the same, we can think of motor learning, therefore, as somehow more primary and elementary than rational learning. It is broader or more comprehensive in that (*a*) it deals with any non-linguistic task, and (*b*) it can be demonstrated in a variety of organisms. In a way it underlies the study of other more complex psychological processes.

Preparation for the Learning Experiment

Before any actual experimentation on learning is attempted in the laboratory, the *motivation* of the subject or subjects must be provided for. The learning organism must be given some reason for going to work on the problem to be mastered. An animal may be rewarded in his solution of a problem in learning by food, if he has previously been made hungry, or by water, if he has previously been made thirsty. Or, the apparatus may be heated, cooled, or charged with a weak electric current, and the organism can avoid these difficulties only by solving the problem and escaping the punishment.

In the human subject, the motive is likely to be a social one, although he can also be motivated by concrete incentives. Candy is effective as a reward for young children, and money as a reward for adults. The words "right" or "wrong" may be said by the experimenter when the subject makes correct or incorrect responses. More often, the social approval of a task well done, and the social disapproval of a task poorly done, are sufficient without other special incentives.[2]

A further prerequisite to the study of learning is the matter of preliminary adjustment or *adaptation*. If one intends to observe the learning organism at its best, he must certainly prepare it in some way for the task which lies ahead. Adaptation for the human subject consists in explaining just what he is to do, and in pointing out the essential parts of the apparatus or equipment to be used. In order to hold conditions constant for all subjects, each may perhaps be read or asked to read a printed set of instructions. The subject can hardly be expected to start on a problem without some idea of the nature of the task.

The adaptation of the animal subject is by no means so easy and usually requires considerably more time. Since verbal explanations are out of the question, an effort is made to have the organism familiarize himself with the apparatus and the general situation by repeatedly bringing him into contact with them. Once or more daily, for several days before the learning experiment is begun, the subject

[2] For a more complete discussion of this topic see Chapter 13.

is placed inside the experimental box or other equipment and allowed time to run around and explore it. Throughout these periods of initial adjustment he *is not motivated* as he will later be during the process of actually mastering the problem. In this way he should become well enough adapted to the new surroundings to be willing to work when properly motivated. If some such method is not followed at the beginning, the rate of learning will be slower and less efficient.

Design of the Learning Experiment

After these preliminary conditions have been satisfied, the learning experiment itself can begin. The general procedure of any such experiment is to observe and record the activity of the subject while he practices the task he has been given to master. In order to be capable of quantitative study, the learning task should be of such a nature that the speed or efficiency of performing it can be measured on every trial. The total number of trials or repetitions which are necessary for mastery will depend both on the nature of the task and on the ability of the subject. If the task is difficult and a great many trials are required to learn to perform it skillfully, these trials may be regularly spaced over a period of days, weeks, or even months, as the case may be.

We should distinguish clearly at this point between (*a*) the problem, task, or result which the subject accomplishes on every trial, and (*b*) the method or means by which he performs the task or achieves the result. The former is set by the nature of the experiment. It is the latter which gradually changes in the direction of greater efficiency as the subject learns, and which is observed and recorded by the experimenter.

The dependent variable in the learning experiment is therefore the subject's method of solving the problem or of performing the learning task, measured in terms of his score per trial. The independent variable is the number of trials or the stage of practice. Until the subject has reached the limit of his ability, the more advanced the stage of practice, the better should be his skill in the solution of the problem, except for minor fluctuations.

When he has attained some previously determined level of skill or efficiency in his method of performing the task, the subject is said to have reached the *criterion of mastery*. The criterion of mastery may be in terms of the number of solutions within a given number of attempts, for example, four solutions in five consecutive trials. Or, it may be in terms of time, such as ten consecutive solutions, all under one minute each. The attaining of the criterion of mastery by all the subjects marks the completion of the laboratory work on the experiment. The data are then ready to be analyzed and treated mathematically.

Equivalent Groups in the Learning Experiment

The mere demonstration of whether a particular organism or class of organisms is capable of learning how to perform a given task is not, as a rule, the object of a learning experiment. More often the purpose is to discover the effect of some special condition upon the learning ability of the subject. For example, one may wish to know how great an improvement in the speed of learning will result from giving help, assistance, or guidance during the early trials. Or one's purpose may be to ascertain whether a year of training in playing the piano will facilitate or inhibit the subsequent learning of typewriting. Experiments like these—and, in fact, many investigations in the field of learning—require the use of a control group as well as at least one experimental group of subjects. In order to be certain that an increase or a decrease actually occurs, as well as to measure the extent of the increase or decrease, it is necessary to have a standard or norm of performance, such as the rate of learning without guidance or the rate of learning without previous piano playing, with which to compare the learning of the experimental subjects. The results of different but equivalent groups—one learning under normal or average conditions and the other (or others) learning under special experimental conditions—are then directly comparable.

MAZE LEARNING

The Animal Spatial Maze

Undoubtedly the most widely used device for the study of motor learning is the spatial maze, or labyrinth. The typical maze has a starting point or entrance compartment, an exit point or goal compartment, and from two to twenty blind alleys or cul-de-sacs. The problem of mastering the maze is one of recognizing and avoiding the blind alleys in which the subject may go astray. What the subject learns is how to get from one place (the entrance) to another place (the goal) in the shortest possible time and with the smallest number of unnecessary responses (blind-alley entrances). His method of getting from the entrance to the goal improves upon successive trials by the gradual elimination of the different alleys. A large variety of forms and patterns of mazes have been employed in experimental studies of motor learning. See Fig. 1.

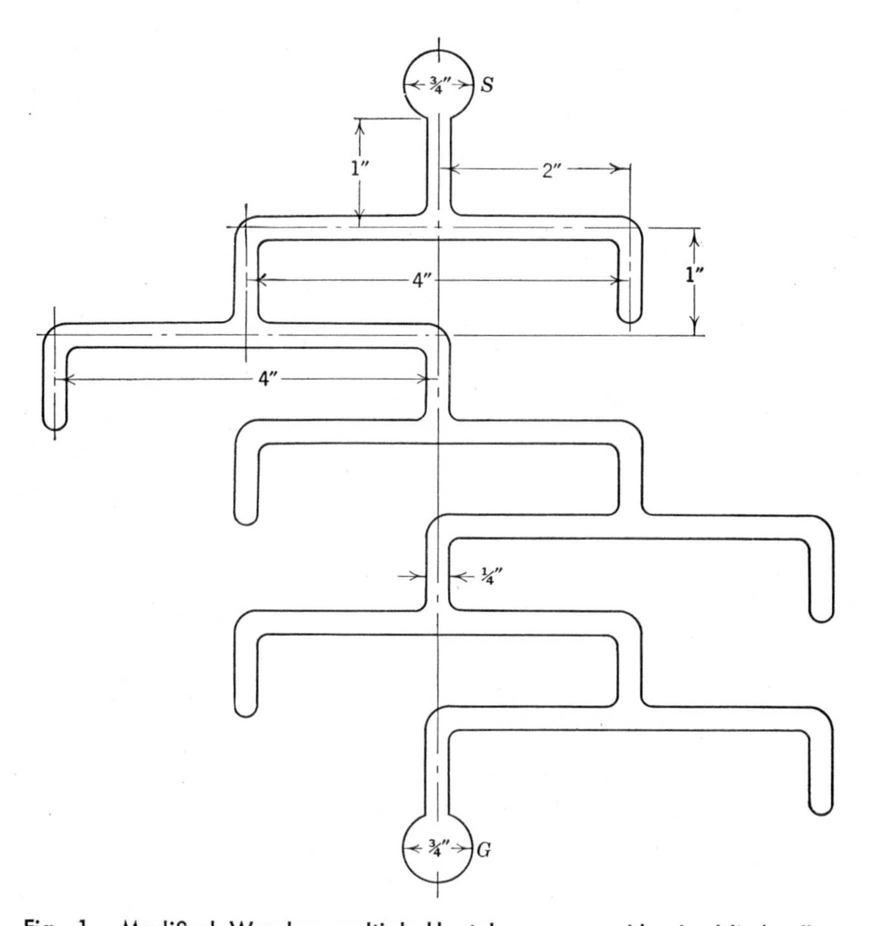

Fig. 1. Modified Warden multiple-U stylus maze with six blind alleys. S is the starting or entrance compartment, and G the goal. (Cf. [42]. Reprinted from *J. Comp. Psychol.*, 1935, *19*, 124, by permission of the editor and publishers.)

With respect to animals, spatial mazes fall naturally into the two general classes of enclosed and elevated. An enclosed maze, as the name implies, has sidewalls and usually a cover of wire mesh or glass to prevent the organism from climbing out over the sides [43]. The elevated maze has no sides or top but is raised from the floor to such a height that the animal will not jump off. An elevated maze can be made by cutting the design from a flat piece of sheetmetal and hanging it by rods from the ceiling. Another way to make an elevated maze is to stand boards on edge or on end. Some mazes of this sort have true pathways and blind alleys supported by a series of posts or columns, not unlike the stanchions of a long bridge [29].

The Spatial Maze for Humans

For human subjects the full-sized (enclosed) maze, although occasionally employed, gives no better results than the smaller stylus maze, the finger maze, or the paper-and-pencil maze, any one of which can be substituted for it. The stylus maze is essentially a slot cut in a piece of plywood or a flat metal plate [42]. The subject sits at a table or desk upon which the maze is laid, places the stylus in the entrance or starting point at one end of the slot, and manipulates the stylus with his hand until he succeeds in finding the goal at the other end of the slot. Unless such a maze is very long and complex, it must be concealed in some way—either by a screen or by blindfolding the subject—in order to force him to discover and remember the movements which are necessary to push the stylus along the true pathway.

The finger maze is like the stylus maze, except that the pathway is raised rather than cut out of a flat surface. Such a maze can be made by fastening wire or small copper tubing, which is bent in the right pattern, to a board. No stylus or other accessory device is necessary with the finger maze. The subject places the end of his index finger on the raised pathway and feels his way along.

In the paper-and-pencil maze, the design is simply printed on a sheet of paper. The subject must be given a new sheet or copy of the maze on every trial. Obviously he cannot work blindfolded in this instance. The pattern or pathway of the paper-and-pencil maze must therefore be considerably more complex than that of other human mazes. If it is not, he will see at a glance where to move the pencil and will not be presented with a genuine problem in learning.

Conditions of Maze Learning

Since maze learning is essentially place learning, or the learning of the position of certain objects in space, the influences which contribute to this learning have a bearing on similar learning of other kinds. Cues of whatever sort, both from inside and from outside the maze itself, are likely to be seized upon by the subject if they can tell him anything about his location. If a maze is rotated through 180 degrees so that the extra-maze stimuli now reach it from a different angle, the animal subject is seriously disturbed and makes more errors on trials immediately after the change than he did on trials before it [4, 40]. Such cues as the position of an electric light within the room may be important in the learning of a particular direction [39]. Removing a bright spot in the field of vision by covering a window, without in any way altering the maze, may similarly affect performance [4].

Long before the subject has eliminated all the blind alleys, he seems to have developed a kind of orientation in the direction of the goal. This is shown by the fact that he tends to turn toward the goal whenever the opportunity presents itself. As a result, the alleys which point goalward are entered more frequently than those which point away from the goal [37]. The subject learns the general direction in which he must go before he learns the details of the pathway.

The tendency to enter any particular blind alley may also be influenced by the shape of the portion of the maze which the subject has passed through before arriving at that alley. If the organism has just made one or more turns to the left, the chances are that at the next choice point he will turn to the right, somewhat as if he were thrown outward by the centrifugal force of the last previous turn. This tendency, known as *centrifugal swing,* further complicates the regular elimination of errors [1, 45].

One theory of the order of elimination of alleys in a maze is the *goal gradient* hypothesis of Hull [14]. This view maintains that the first alleys to be learned (eliminated) are those nearest the goal, and that the order of elimination of the remaining alleys proceeds backward from the goal to the entrance compartment. It has been clearly demonstrated, however, that not all mazes are learned in this manner [42].

Ideally, the alleys in a maze should be of "equal difficulty." This means that they should all point in the same direction, should all be of the same length, and should all leave the true pathway at the same angle. Such requirements are difficult to achieve in actual practice. It is nevertheless clear that modifications of maze designs produce many important effects on the rate of learning and that these modifications can well be used as methodological factors in experimental studies of maze learning.

OTHER MOTOR LEARNING TASKS

Different Kinds of Pathways

A case of learning to follow a pathway quite different from that of the spatial maze is afforded by the so-called *temporal maze.* The temporal maze has no blind alleys, and the pathway is a continuous circuit without a beginning or an end. In this respect it is similar to a figure 8. See Fig. 2. There is a designated place where the subject must start, and he may also end at the same place; i.e., the starting point and the goal are usually one and the same. In order to solve the problem the subject must go over the same portion or portions of the maze more than once, in a certain predetermined order. The essential thing that he learns is the sequence or arrangement in which he must traverse the parts.

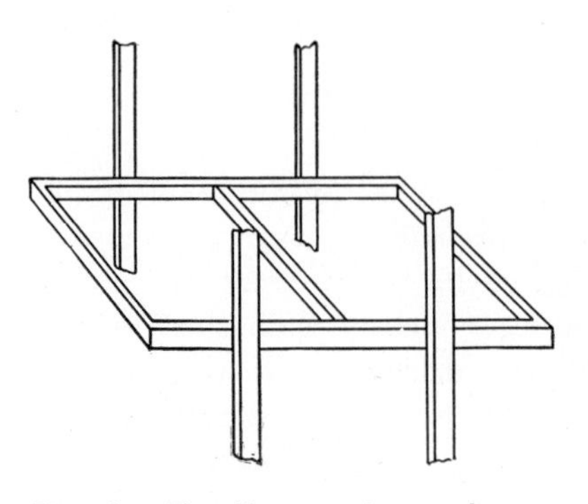

Fig. 2. The Hunter elevated temporal maze.

(From W. S. Hunter. The sensory control of the maze habit in the white rat. *J. Genet. Psychol.,* 1929, *36,* 527. Reprinted by permission of the editor and publishers.)

Hunter [16, 17], who first used the temporal maze, required that his laboratory animals cover a pathway like a rectangular figure 8 with square corners, by going around one half of the 8 twice and the other half of the 8 twice in the order *llrrllrrll.* Until an animal had learned this sequence, he had not mastered the problem. The maze was therefore called a temporal maze, and this particular problem the *double-alternation* problem. It should be obvious that tasks of almost any degree of complexity can be set up with a temporal maze. The difficulty depends upon the number of repetitions which the experimenter requires for each half of the pattern and the order or sequence in which they have to be run.

The Mirror-drawing Task

The mirror-drawing task is still another application of the problem of learning to follow a pathway, but with additional complications [36]. In contrast to the alternation problem, which has been employed mostly with animals, the mirror-drawing method can be used to study learning only with human subjects. It is incidentally a task which is likely to prove particularly baffling to the neophyte. As the problem and cry. In early solutions of the problem he is likely to go first to the door, which closes abruptly before him, then to change direction sharply and circle the barrier in a wide arc. In later solutions his method is to avoid the direct pathway completely, whether it is closed or open. Instead, he will proceed directly from the starting point around the detour by the shortest possible route.

Such a task is strictly a yes-or-no type of problem. It does not lend itself to blind, variable, or clumsy solutions, like early trials in a maze. As a consequence the solution in the detour experiment comes all at once. It is seldom if ever a gradual step-by-step process which slowly improves in efficiency.

Multiple-choice Learning

Another method for the study of sudden learning, which is more adaptable than the detour method, is the *multiple-choice* procedure. With this technique a number of learning problems of varying difficulty can be set. As originally employed by Yerkes [50] with animals, the subject is presented with a series of stalls or feeding boxes, any one of which he can enter. The boxes are arranged in a straight line in front of him, with food contained in only one of the boxes. The subject has to choose which box to enter on any trial. If he chooses the correct box, he obtains the reward; if he enters one of the incorrect boxes, he is punished by a short period of confinement in the box which he has entered.

Different numbers of boxes are used on every trial, but the correct box for any given problem can always be found by applying a principle which carries over from one trial to the next. If the problem set by the experimenter is to discover the principle of "second-from-the-right," the food is always placed in the box second from the right end of the row of boxes presented on each trial. When nine boxes are put before the subject, the correct box is number eight; when six boxes are used, the correct box is number five, and so on. Another similar problem is to discover the principle of middleness. In this case odd numbers of boxes are always used, and the food is placed in the middle box of the row on every trial.

The multiple-choice method, as applied to humans, makes use of a more compact apparatus, which the subject can manipulate from a laboratory desk or table [51]. The experimenter and the subject sit opposite one another and are separated by a screen, which also conceals parts of the apparatus from the subject. On the subject's side of the screen is a row of twelve keys or buttons, any one of which can be

is ordinarily arranged, the subject is required to follow with a pencil a pathway made by two parallel lines in the shape of a six-pointed star. A small screen prevents him from seeing, in direct vision, the star, the pencil, or his hand. He can view these only in indirect vision, through a mirror. As a result, every movement he attempts is reversed, and what appears at first to be ridiculously easy turns out to be a difficult and often an irritating task to learn. The subject must break down his long-established visual-motor habits and move the pencil exactly the opposite from the accustomed responses he would make to such a visual stimulus.

Puzzle Solving

Practically any non-language task can be adapted to the scientific study of motor learning, provided that the performance of the subject from trial to trial can be accurately measured and recorded in some quantitative way. Puzzles of various sorts meet this requirement, since it is always possible to measure the time necessary to solve a puzzle on any given attempt. Animal puzzles, in the form of the *problem box* or *puzzle box,* have proved to be a favorite device with many investigators.

The method of the puzzle-box experiment is to place a hungry animal inside a cage or box and to place food on the outside. Or, the reward may be inside the box and the animal on the outside. The subject must then get out of or into the box in order to solve the problem. The trick or puzzle which it is necessary to learn may consist of uncovering a doorway concealed beneath a pile of sawdust, pulling a string which operates a latch and opens a door, stepping on a little platform or on several platforms in a certain sequence, pressing a lever, turning a knob, or pushing against a vertical rod or pole. As in human puzzle-solving, the quantitative data are the times of solution on the different trials.

The *Skinner box,* a modified version of the traditional problem box, does not permit the animal to escape at all [35]. A little pellet of food is automatically delivered into the box each time the animal presses a lever. Since each of the pellets is much too small to satisfy the subject's hunger, he will learn to make a series of repeated responses over a period of time. What is measured in this instance is usually the rate of responding or the frequency of lever pressing, rather than the time required for each individual response. The Skinner procedure may be thought of as a technique which bridges the gap between the problem-box method as originally devised and the classical conditioned-reflex method [49, p. 107].

Special Human Problems

Among the problems exclusively for human subjects which are of value in the study of motor learning are tasks which develop accuracy in shooting or aiming. Here should be classified archery, dart throwing, and tossing balls at a target. In these cases the performance of the subject is measurable in terms of the distance by which the missiles fail to hit the bull's-eye. Improvement in speed and accuracy can be nicely measured in the card-sorting experiment, where the subject learns to arrange cards into piles according to a predetermined order. Learning to juggle rubber balls is similarly subject to quantitative study, as is the development of skill on the *pursuit-rotor* or *pursuit-meter*. With the latter apparatus the subject follows some sort of a moving object, such as a swinging pendulum or a small spot on the surface of a rotating phonograph disk, with a pointer or stylus. His eye-hand coordination will gradually improve with practice, just as performance does in learning a maze.

SUDDEN OR IMMEDIATE MOTOR LEARNING

The Umweg Method

The methods of studying learning which have thus far been discussed are often described as methods of studying trial-and-error learning. The subject works long and hard at the problem, usually making many mistakes, and achieves efficiency only through dogged persistence. There is never any possibility of a quick or immediate solution.

An entirely different sort of learning situation is one whose solution depends upon some principle or method which the subject seeks to discover. After he has discovered the principle, he can solve the problem or perform the task perfectly upon every attempt. Before the discovery of the principle he may not be able to solve it at all. Mastering the problem consists in grasping the principle or method upon which its solution depends. Usually the understanding of this principle dawns upon the learner suddenly, like a hunch, a bright idea, or insight. Whether a given problem can be solved in this fashion depends primarily upon the nature of the problem itself. Generally speaking, complex tasks cannot be solved abruptly. Easier tasks, if they are of the right sort, stand a greater chance of being solved by insight. They must be suited, however, to the ability of the particular learning organism, whether animal or human.

One of the simpler methods for the study of sudden l *Umweg* or detour method. The essential of this pro placing of some sort of block or barrier between the su goal he is trying to reach [25, 26]. As a result, he can ge only by going under, over, or around the barrier. He mu previously untried roundabout way to reach a place formerly directly accessible to him. It is a case of the l around being the shortest way home. When the subjec

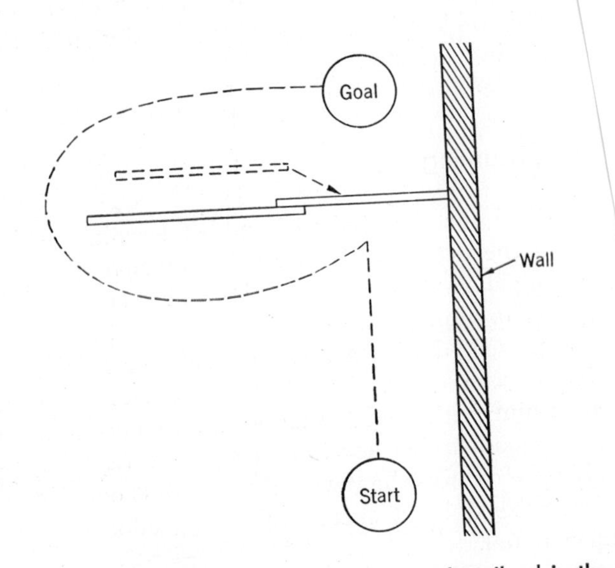

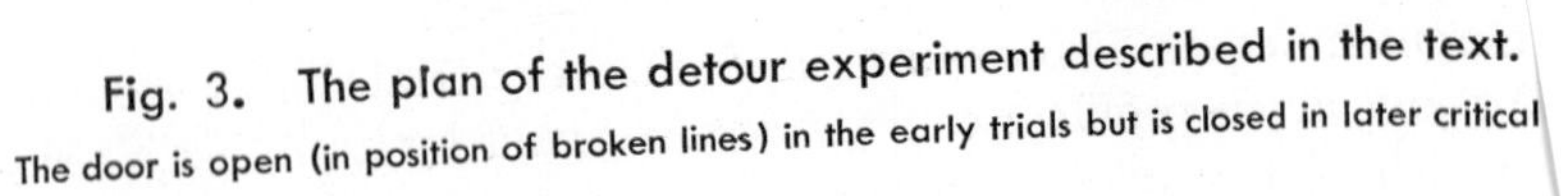
Fig. 3. The plan of the detour experiment described in the text. The door is open (in position of broken lines) in the early trials but is closed in later critical

his roundabout pathway, he may actually have to move in a direct away from the goal. In other words, he goes toward the goal starting to go away from it. This is a difficult sort of response lower organisms to make.

A detour situation which works well with a young baby is illustrat in Fig. 3. The baby is allowed to proceed directly from the startin point to the goal for several trials. He goes in a straight line throug a small passageway which can later be blocked. After he has com pleted several such runs and has been appropriately rewarded, the door to the passageway is suddenly closed. Now the only way to get from the starting point to the goal is by moving sideways from the doorway, around the barrier. If he solves the problem, he will proceed around the detour at once. If unable to solve it, he may stand still

moved toward the subject by the experimenter. The keys which are pushed toward the subject on any trial are the keys he is to use on that trial. If he presses the wrong key, a small electric light will signal that he has made an error; if he presses the right key, a buzzer will sound. His immediate task on each trial is to find the key which will cause the buzzer to sound. He has not solved the problem, however, until he demonstrates that he has learned the principle or relationship which applies to the varying numbers of keys presented on successive trials.

SOME QUESTIONS AND RESULTS

How Does the Organism Learn?

Although it is the province of this chapter to deal more especially with methods than with the results of experiments in motor learning, we should be making a mistake if, before leaving the topic, we did not consider briefly some of the findings and conclusions which have grown out of the actual application of the methods. Perhaps the major objective behind all scientific research in the field of learning is to contribute to the understanding of the process of learning itself. The conditions which retard or accelerate the rate of learning, the factors which are necessary for its successful completion, the order in which certain parts of a task are mastered—these and other similar questions can be answered, at least in part, by the proper use of the experimental methods already examined.

With what parts of the body does the organism actually learn? Does an animal, for example, find his way about a maze or problem box primarily by vision, or is the sense of smell or some other receptor of greater importance? As to the function of the different senses in maze learning, the answer, so far as the white rat is concerned, seems to be that removing any one of them may reduce his efficiency in the early trials. This result holds for the elevated maze [13]. In running the enclosed maze, however, rats which have been blinded perform about as well as normal rats [44]. The organism apparently uses whatever senses will furnish directional cues of aid in discovering the true pathway. If it can learn little or nothing about the problem through vision or from the sense of smell, eliminating these senses produces no detrimental effect on the efficiency of learning.

What parts of the central nervous system are most necessary for motor learning? Studies of animals in which cortical and other brain centers have been experimentally removed and studies of the learning ability of human beings with brain lesions caused by disease or accident leave us with the conclusion that any major mutilation of the brain will reduce the efficiency of learning. In general, the greater the damage, the greater the loss of learning efficiency [27]. In humans and in higher animals the most important cortical centers for the solution of certain kinds of problems appear to be the frontal lobes [20, 24]. Except for the sensory areas essential to the mastery of a particular task, damage to the other lobes of the cerebral cortex produces a less clear-cut effect.

On the response side the student of learning is concerned with the question of just what it is that is learned. Does motor learning, after all, consist in building up a series of specific movements in a certain order? Does the learner improve his method of solution by trying out a variety of responses—eliminating those that are unsuccessful and fixing those that are successful—until he has developed a sequence of reactions which regularly lead him to the goal? Does the perfected method of solution, in other words, always make use of the same movements? Present theory is largely against such an interpretation. In a recent examination of this question by Guthrie and Horton [8], however, the reactions of cats in a puzzle box were automatically photographed at the moment of their escape. Results showed that individual animals tended to move or respond in the same way for many consecutive escapes.

Of special interest in the study of learning is the direct comparison of animals with humans, by some method which is fair to both, for example, the mastery of a spatial maze. When two mazes of exactly the same pattern are employed, one arranged for human subjects and another designed for the laboratory rat, the results show remarkable similarity. The human being is not head and shoulders above the animal, as one might guess without actually investigating the matter. He makes not quite as many blind-alley entrances, and the total time he requires for mastering the problem is shorter, but on the whole he is not as superior as we might like to think [9, 19]. This finding again points to the basic nature of the learning process and shows its similarity in different organisms.

Environmental Factors Affecting Learning

What effect does changing the incentive have upon learning efficiency? Can anything be learned when there is no motivation at all? These are important methodological questions. The answer to the first of these questions is that different sorts of motivation markedly affect the rate of learning. Changing the food used as an incentive stimulus will produce divergent results in the same animals.

Punishment as an incentive may lead to a different response from that elicited by reward. The organism can be too strongly motivated—for example, it can be deprived of food for too long a period or be given too strong an electric shock—to learn with maximum efficiency, just as it can be too weakly motivated. The rate of learning and the degree of motivation are thus seen to be intimately related. For additional relations between motivation and learning, the reader is referred to Chapter 13.

The answer to whether it is possible to learn without any incentive is also affirmative, although one can always raise the question, can any normal organism ever be completely unmotivated? Experiments which show *latent learning* by Blodgett [2], Tolman and Honzik [38], and others prove definitely that the white rat discovers a great deal when placed in new surroundings, even though it is given no definite incentive to go from one place to another in those surroundings. Yet what it learns without a specific incentive does not come to light until the incentive stimulus is introduced at a later time. The efficiency of actually running the maze, in other words, does not improve, because the subject has no reason to improve it. When suddenly given a reason, however, the subject shows that he has actually been learning during the previous non-motivated period.

How do drugs, diet, and similar environmental factors affect learning ability? Will dietary deficiencies severe enough to stunt physical growth retard learning? If a loss in the rate of learning occurs, can it be corrected by subsequently returning the deficient item to the diet? To what degree do known quantities of a depressing drug, like sodium amytal or alcohol, actually reduce mental efficiency? Will stimulating drugs, like caffeine and benzedrine, accelerate the rate of learning, and, if so, to what degree? Not only do the answers to such questions have a practical value in education and in other fields, but they are also of great scientific importance.

It is apparent that the methods of studying motor learning have a wide application, but it is clear also that the understanding of a method is a necessary prerequisite to its proper use. None of these matters could be investigated, nor any of the questions correctly answered, unless the investigator had at his disposal adequate apparatus, a sufficient number of the right sort of subjects, and a complete experimental design already worked out before he attempted to begin.

RECORDING THE PROGRESS IN LEARNING

The standard procedure for recording progress in learning is by means of the learning curve. This is a graphic device for showing the relationship between repetitions (trials) and the performance of the subject. The learning curve is a method of plotting the data of the learning experiment in concrete understandable form. A properly drawn learning curve is therefore a picture or diagram of the results of the learning process itself. The slope of the curve gives the rate or speed at which the learning takes place. The curve for any particular task shows just where the learning is rapid and where it is slow. It serves as a kind of gage which registers the improvement of the learner.

In the typical learning curve, the number of trials (the independent variable) is plotted on the abscissa, and the quantitative measure of performance (the dependent variable) on the ordinate. The measure of performance is the score, or the raw score, for any given trial. It may be in terms of the time consumed per trial, the number of errors per trial, or some other measure which indicates the efficiency of the subject's method of attack upon the problem.

Curves of Decreasing Score

Because of the superfluous or unnecessary responses which the subject makes in the early trials of maze learning or puzzle solving, the time which it takes him to reach the goal of the maze or to complete the solution of the puzzle is relatively long. With temporary exceptions or irregularities, the *time learning curve* obtained in such instances drops rapidly at first and more slowly later, until it levels off in the final trials to remain approximately parallel to the abscissa, as shown in Fig. 4.

A decreasing-score curve can similarly be obtained when the efficiency of the subject is measured in terms of arbitrarily defined errors which can be counted and tabulated. Errors in maze running (blind-alley entrances) and in mirror drawing (allowing the pencil or the stylus to touch either of the parallel lines of the star) yield decreasing scores with practice. In learning to juggle balls, the number of misses made by the subject in a fixed number of attempts can also be treated as errors. When errors of this sort are plotted against trials, the resulting *error learning curve* has a contour similar to that of a time learning curve. There is, however, this important difference: the error score ultimately reduces to zero, whereas the time score cannot go below a certain minimum required to perform the task.

Still a third way of obtaining learning curves of decreasing score is in terms of distance. This method is best illustrated by the animal spatial maze or the human stylus maze. To obtain a *distance learning curve* in these cases, the length of the pathway traversed by the subject (or by the stylus) on each trial must be measured. The distance will be found to decrease with the time per trial and the elimination of blind alleys. It gradually approaches a minimum, which is the length of the true pathway of the maze.

If the problem is of such a nature that learning by insight is possible, and if at the same time the progress in learning can be plotted in the

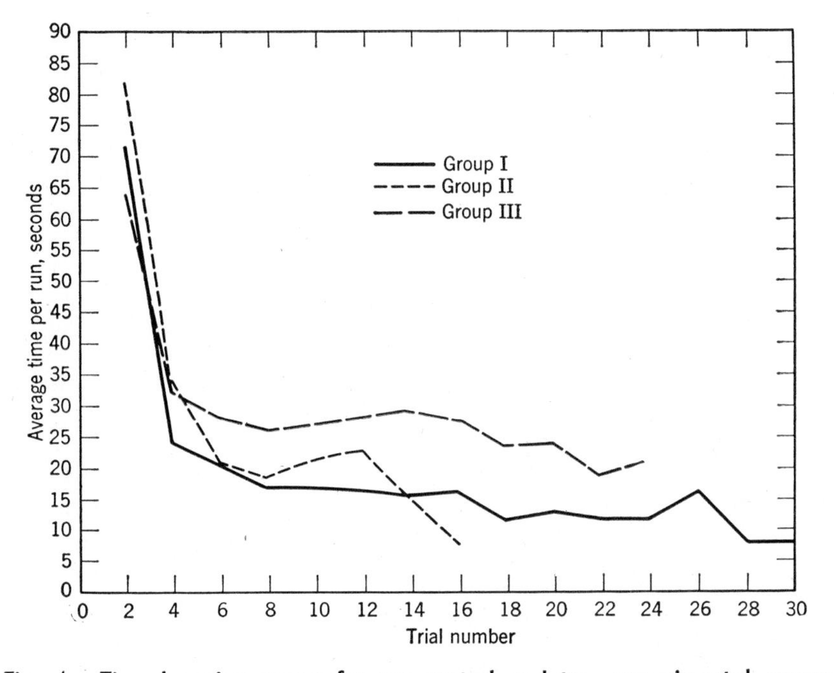

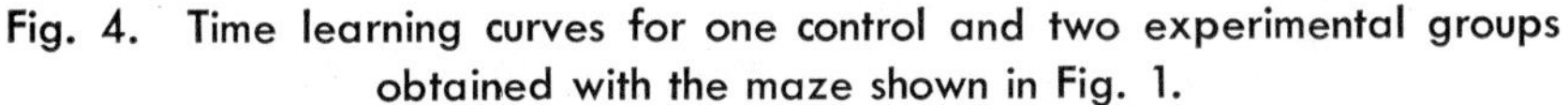
Fig. 4. Time learning curves for one control and two experimental groups obtained with the maze shown in Fig. 1.

Group I is the control group. Groups II and III learned the maze under different experimental conditions. (Reprinted from *J. Comp. Psychol.,* 1935, *19,* 133, by permission of the editor and publishers.)

form of a decreasing-score curve, then the "insight" will appear in the curve as a sudden drop from one level of performance to a much more efficient one [34, 50]. In solving a puzzle, for example, the subject may blunder through to a solution for trial after trial, without ever understanding clearly how he accomplishes it. Should the principle behind the method of solution suddenly dawn upon him, however, he may be able to reduce his time on two consecutive trials from perhaps 10 minutes to less than 1 minute. In such an instance the gradual approach to the base line is replaced by an abrupt and immediate drop to a new level, which is thereafter maintained.

The elimination of any single alley in a maze-learning experiment often occurs in this fashion [28]. Plotting the time spent in that alley alone on each trial, without regard for the other alleys, may show in the early trials that the subject spends considerable time in it. Finally he may "get the point" concerning the alley and recognize it clearly as the wrong way to go on each trial. As a result he avoids it completely, and the time spent in the alleys drops immediately to zero, as shown in Fig. 5.

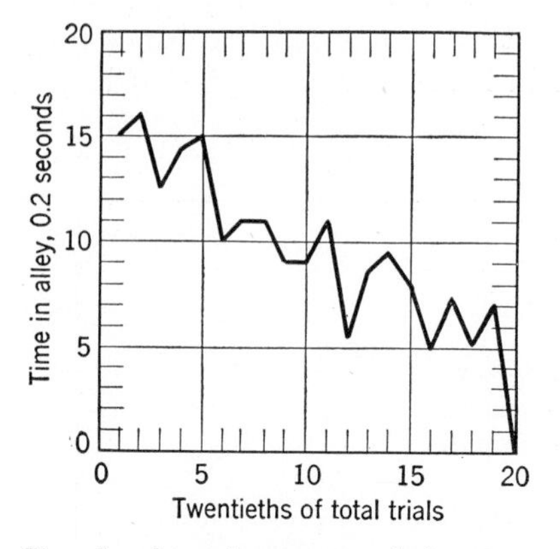

Fig. 5. Learning curve of the time spent in a single alley of a stylus maze, showing sudden drop characteristic of insight.

(From J. A. McGeoch, and H. N. Peters. An all-or-none characteristic in the elimination of errors during the learning of a stylus maze. *J. Exper. Psychol.*, 1933, *16*, 514. Reprinted by permission of the editor and publishers.)

Curves of Increasing Score

In a sense all curves of decreasing score measure the subject's progress in learning *what not to do*. They show how he improves in efficiency through the elimination of surplus or extraneous activity. They record efficiency by a process similar to subtraction, and so they may be said to approach learning from the negative side.

Curves of increasing score, on the other hand, show how the subject learns *what to do*. They record the acquisition of new responses, or an increase in the speed of old responses, which raise the learner's efficiency. In general, they approach the problem from the positive side, and so they may be thought of as measuring learning by a process analogous to addition [3].

When the time per trial is controlled or limited, the subject's improvement consists in completing more and more of the material to be learned within the fixed time limit. Under these conditions the score will increase with practice. Thus, in learning to typewrite, the learning score is usually the number of words or letters which can be correctly typed *per minute*. The better the typist, the faster he can type, and the greater his efficiency will be. A learning curve of increasing score is sometimes called an *amount learning curve*, since the learning is measured in terms of the amount of work turned out by the subject on each trial.

In the decreasing-score situation, on the other hand, it is the task (or amount of work) which is fixed. The puzzle does not change from trial to trial, and the maze remains of the same length and difficulty. The subject has a definite goal to reach in each instance. Here efficiency is measured either in time, or in distance or errors, which are the correlates of time. For decreasing-score curves the task is fixed, and time (or its correlates) is measured. For increasing-score curves, the time is fixed, and the task (or amount of work) is measured.

The Sigmoid Learning Curve

Most non-insight learning curves, whether they are curves of increasing or decreasing score, are *negatively accelerated.* The sub-

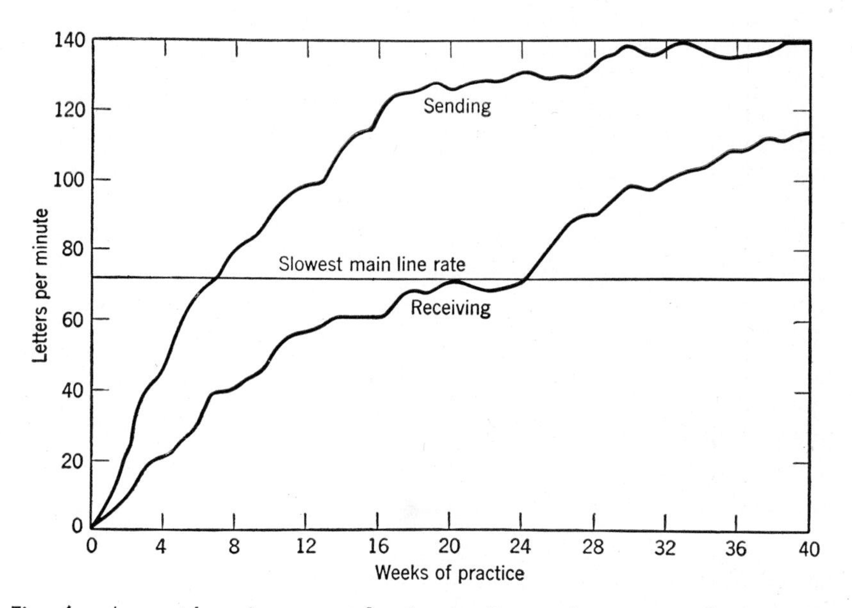

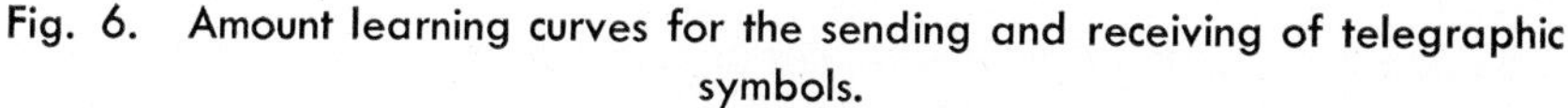
Fig. 6. Amount learning curves for the sending and receiving of telegraphic symbols.

The flat or level places on the curves are plateaus, and the maximum efficiency beyond which the learner does not progress is the physiological limit. (From W. L. Bryan and N. Harter. Studies in the physiology and the psychology of the telegraphic language. *Psychol. Rev.,* 1897, *4,* 49. Reprinted by permission of the editor and publishers.)

ject begins learning at a fast rate, but his *rate* of learning gradually *decreases* (the line levels off horizontally) until finally he improves no further. In more mathematical language, the curve becomes asymptotic to a horizontal line. The asymptote of an increasing-score curve is a horizontal line above it; the asymptote of a decreasing-score curve is the base line.

Some learning curves, however, are not negatively accelerated throughout their entire length but possess a kind of double inflection or S shape. They have positive acceleration early in the learning, zero acceleration next, and negative acceleration later. This would mean that an increasing-score curve would start off nearly parallel to the base line but would increase in steepness or slope as it proceeded. It would subsequently stop turning upward and would proceed for a short distance as an approximately straight line with a constant slope rising from left to right. Finally the slope would reduce as the curve took on a negative acceleration and leveled off horizontally. The curves for the learning of telegraphic symbols in Fig. 6 show a slight tendency to be positively accelerated at the beginning, although this is not a very obvious tendency. Curves of learning obtained by the conditioned-reflex method are quite frequently found to be sigmoid in contour. See Fig. 12.

It has been argued that the double-inflection sigmoid curve is the true curve of learning, and that curves which show negative acceleration alone are incomplete in that they represent only the later stages of the learning process [5]. The experimental subject has not really started at the zero point of learning. The early portion of the learning has already been completed by the subject before he undertakes the experiment. He brings with him previous experience or training relevant to the present problem, which enables him to start well up on the learning curve. As a result the portion of the curve which should show positive acceleration has already passed and cannot appear again. Whether this explanation is correct is not a matter to be decided here, although the final answer is of great importance for the psychology of learning.

Vincent Curves

It is frequently desirable to combine or average learning curves from several subjects so as to obtain a composite curve for the learning of a single task. Because different individuals require different numbers of trials to reach the criterion of mastery, however, this cannot be done directly without introducing distortions into the final curve. For example, if one subject takes 10 trials and another 15 trials to learn, averaging the learning scores trial for trial must either leave out of account the final 5 trials of the subject who took 15 trials or else must include 5 extra trials which were not required by the subject who learned in 10 trials.

The solution of this difficulty is to stretch out the short learning curves and shorten the long ones by dividing each into equal units of its own length. The effect is similar to converting fractions to a common denominator before adding them. The Vincent method for equating the lengths of learning curves divides each curve, usually into tenths of its total length, and then averages these tenths [11, 18, 41]. Assumptions of the method are that every trial is equivalent to every other trial for any given subject, and that the raw score for a trial is evenly distributed throughout that trial.

The Vincent method does not necessarily require that learning curves be converted into *tenths* of their own length. Fifths, twentieths, seventeenths, or any other number of units will do just as well, provided all the curves to be averaged are divided into the same number of units. When many curves are combined, however, the tenth is a convenient unit to use. Aside from its arithmetical advantages, it furnishes a very satisfactory number of points for curve plotting. It is therefore more commonly employed than any other value.

The general method for transmuting raw scores into Vincent scores is first to break up the trials into the proper units and then to divide the raw scores according to those units. Criterion trials are not included in these calculations [11]. The subject is presumed to have learned by the time he has attained the criterion of mastery. The criterion trials themselves are simply the proof that he has actually completed the learning.

If a subject took 5 trials to reach the criterion of mastery, his curve would be converted into Vincent tenths by dividing the raw score for each trial into halves. This would furnish 10 values to plot instead of 5, each value being the raw score for half a trial. If another subject required 15 trials to learn, each Vincent tenth would include the raw score for 1.5 trials. The first Vincent tenth would be the sum of the raw score for trial 1, plus 0.5 of the raw score for trial 2. The second Vincent tenth would be the sum of the remaining 0.5 of the raw score for trial 2, plus the raw score for trial 3, and so on. If a subject learned in eight trials, each Vincent tenth would take in 0.8 of the raw score per trial. If he learned in 31 trials, each Vincent tenth would include the raw scores of 3.1 trials.

In Table I are raw error scores for two subjects who took 13 and 7 trials respectively to master a stylus maze. In Table II the Vincent tenths for each of these subjects have been computed. The 7-trial series is lengthened and the 13-trial series shortened to 10 units, so that the two can be averaged into a single composite curve.

TABLE I

ERRORS PER TRIAL

(Raw Scores)

Trials	1	2	3	4	5	6	7	8	9	10	11	12	13	Total Errors
Subject A	11	12	10	8	6	7	5	3	1	1	0	2	1	67
Subject B	18	10	7	2	1	2	1	—	—	—	—	—	—	41

TABLE II

VINCENT TENTHS

Tenth	1	2	3	4	5	6	7	8	9	10	Total Errors
Subject A	14.6	14.4	11.2	8.2	8.1	4.9	1.7	0.9	1.4	1.6	67.0
Subject B	12.6	9.4	6.7	4.9	2.4	1.2	0.7	1.3	1.1	0.7	41.0
Total	27.2	23.8	17.9	13.1	10.5	6.1	2.4	2.2	2.5	2.3	108.0
Average	13.60	11.90	8.95	6.55	5.25	3.05	1.20	1.10	1.25	1.15	54.0

THE CONDITIONED RESPONSE

Salivary Conditioning

Conditioning as a method for the study of learning was first employed extensively by the Russian physiologist, I. P. Pavlov [30]. The response which he selected for observation was the salivary reflex in dogs. A simple surgical operation moved the opening of the duct of the parotid salivary gland from the inside to the outside of the dog's cheek, so that the flow of saliva could be seen and accurately measured. The original or *unconditioned stimulus* which elicited the flow of saliva was, in most cases, food. By presenting a neutral stimulus (for example, the ringing of a bell) along with the food for a number of trials, the bell or the *conditioned stimulus* eventually came to act as a substitute for the food and would cause the saliva to flow even though no food was given. A connection or association had been established between the conditioned stimulus and the activity of the salivary gland. The flow of saliva now elicited by the bell was an entirely new response for that stimulus. This response was the conditioned salivary response or, more simply, the salivary CR.

Pavlov and his collaborators found in different experiments that many things could be used as conditioned stimuli. Whistles, lights, touching the dog's flank, even mild electric shocks functioned satisfactorily in this capacity. Each of these and many more, when combined with food for a sufficient number of trials, produced conditioned salivation. If the food was permanently removed after a CR had been built up, however, continued presentation of the conditioned stimulus alone caused the CR gradually to die out. The disappearance of a CR under these circumstances was called the *extinction of the conditioned response.* An extinguished response could be rapidly reconditioned by *reinforcing* the conditioned with the unconditioned stimulus for a few trials. Even where no reinforcement with the unconditioned stimulus was given, a conditioned response which had been extinguished could be called out at a later time, provided a sufficiently long rest interval had been allowed to elapse after the extinction. The reappearance of a previously extinguished CR in this way, without subsequent reinforcement, was called by Pavlov *spontaneous recovery.*

In applying the salivary conditioning technique to human subjects, two principal methods have been employed. The first of these requires an especially shaped suction cup or *saliometer,* which fits over the opening of one of the salivary ducts inside the mouth and carries the saliva out of the mouth by means of a small tube [32]. The second method makes use of rolls of dental cotton which are carefully weighed and then placed under the subject's tongue. After a CR has occurred, the cotton is removed and weighed again. The difference between the weights before and after the response indicates the amount of saliva which was secreted [33]. The phenomena of extinction, reconditioning, spontaneous recovery, and so on, originally discovered by Pavlov on dogs, are all demonstrable in human subjects by one or both of these methods.

Conditioning in Other Situations

Although the facts of conditioning were first worked out by means of the salivary reflex, they can also be demonstrated with many other reactions, both muscular and glandular, some of which are not true reflexes in any sense of the word [7, 12]. The idea held by early workers that the basis of conditioning had to be an unlearned reflex has given way to the more general interpretation that practically any response can be conditioned to almost any stimulus. The supplanting in psychological parlance of the narrower term "conditioned reflex" by the more comprehensive term "conditioned response" is a direct expression of this change. Laboratory methods have been developed not only for the application of many kinds of conditioned stimuli, but also for the study of numerous unconditioned stimulus-response combinations as well.

A few of the responses which have been experimentally conditioned to new stimuli in human subjects are winking the eye, opening the mouth, contracting the pupil, the knee jerk or patellar reflex, lifting the finger, a change in the rate of breathing, a change in the pitch of the voice, a change in the pulse rate, the galvanic skin reflex, vasoconstriction, and vasodilation [7, 15]. Moreover, conditioning has been demonstrated in animals as low as the snail and possibly lower [31]. It has also been demonstrated in newborn babies [12, 32]. Considered as a kind of formula for the process of association, conditioning has applications in training of various sorts, in education, and in everyday life [7].

Fundamentals of the Conditioning Process

The methodological requirements for establishing a conditioned response are as follows:

1. There must exist at the start an unconditioned *S-R* combination that works—one that is dependable, permanent, and not subject to extinction. This combination may be a reflex, or it may just as well be a previously well learned *S-R* relationship.

2. There must then be paired with this combination in the proper fashion an extraneous, neutral, or conditioned stimulus which must thereafter be regularly presented with the unconditioned *S* and *R*. The natural response of the conditioned stimulus, if it possesses an observable response, is in many cases ignored by the experimenter in this situation as having no special bearing upon the problem.

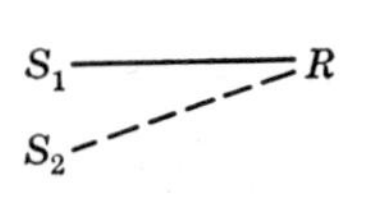

After a sufficient number of trials, i.e., pairings of the conditioned stimulus with the unconditioned *S-R* combination, the conditioned stimulus by itself, without the aid of the unconditioned stimulus, will call forth a new response, the CR, with which it has never previously been associated. The CR may or may not be similar to the unconditioned response.

The simplest scheme for diagramming this arrangement is the substitute-stimulus diagram above, where S_1 = the unconditioned stimulus, S_2 = the conditioned stimulus, and R = the response. It will be noted that such a scheme gives a true picture of conditioned learning only when the CR is identical with the unconditioned response and when the learning consists in transferring the response, which remains unchanged, from S_1 to S_2.

In many instances, however, it is clear that the conditioned response can be distinguished from the unconditioned response in size, in temporal characteristics, and in other important aspects. The two sorts of reacting movements may obviously be of a different nature. Under these circumstances a more complete and accurate diagram of the conditioning situation, which also takes account of the original or natural reaction of the conditioned stimulus itself, is as follows:

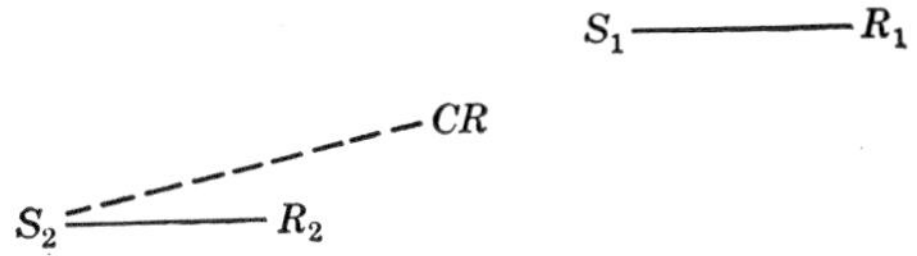

S_1 ———— R_1

- - - - CR

S_2 ———— R_2

In the conditioning of the eyewink, for example, three separate winks may occur on any given trial, each one of which is distinct from the others [10]. The original or unconditional stimulus (S_1)—a puff of air blown upon the cornea of the eye—will produce a full-sized unconditioned blink (R_1). The conditioned stimulus (S_2), which is a beam of light directed into the pupil, will also cause a smaller wink (R_2). If S_2 is presented slightly before S_1 for a sufficient number of trials, still a third wink, the CR, will appear. There are then three responses occurring in order on any given trial: R_2, the CR, and R_1. The CR is the new and original element of the three and is an outgrowth of the conditioning situation alone. It is the learned feature of the entire sequence. The reader is referred to pages 615–621 for the description of an application of the eye-wink conditioning technique.

Additional experiments, in which responses other than the wink reflex have been conditioned, suggest that the exact form of the CR may depend upon the idiosyncrasies of the subject. Although some subjects give a CR which is similar to the unconditioned reaction, others in the same situation respond with a conditioned movement which is different from the unconditioned response [21]. It follows, therefore, that neither the substitute-stimulus diagram by itself nor the more complex diagram by itself can be used to represent all the possibilities of conditioning in a thoroughly adequate manner.

The substitute-stimulus diagram has the advantage of simplicity. It also has the advantage that it sets down in concrete form the methodological essentials with which any experiment on conditioning must begin. Although it does not tell the whole story, it is a convenient tool for the understanding of conditioning procedures. We shall use it, therefore, throughout the remainder of this chapter to illustrate conditioning methods where it seems desirable to employ a diagram.

The Buzz-shock Method

One CR which has been widely studied in the laboratory, both with human and with animal subjects, is the lifting or withdrawal of the finger, hand, or foot. The usual unconditioned stimulus in this procedure is an electric shock; the conditioned stimulus most commonly employed is the sound of a buzzer. When these two stimuli are used together, the method is known as the *buzz-shock method.* If the lifting or flexing of the entire limb is required, as with a dog or some other animal, the method is also called *flexion conditioning* [6, 46]. It is probable that more comprehensive data have been secured in this procedure with the dog as a laboratory subject than with any other organism.

To obtain the best results in buzz-shock flexion conditioning, the animal is placed in a soundproofed room so that he will not be affected by uncontrolled or distracting stimuli. See Figs. 7, 8, 9, 10. He stands inside a wooden stock or framework, which is built upon a large table. To each of his feet is fastened a balanced recording lever. Tambours and air tubes attached to these levers permit the graphic recording of the flexing or stepping movements made by each of the dog's feet. The animal's respiration is similarly recorded by means of a pneumograph, and action potentials may also be obtained from the leg muscles or from other parts of the body. (These techniques of measuring and recording action are described in Chapter 14.) The experimenter manipulates the apparatus and obtains the necessary records from outside the soundproofed room, where he observes the subject through one-way-vision windows [22].

The electric shock, which is of very short duration, is delivered through electrodes which are taped to the foot to be conditioned. The shock causes the animal to make the unconditioned response of flexing or withdrawing the shocked member. The buzz usually starts about 2 seconds before the shock and continues for 2 seconds, so that it ends simultaneously with the occurrence of the shock.

In the procedure of *instrumental conditioning,* the dog can escape the shock by lifting his foot and holding it up at the time when the shock would normally occur. A small mercury switch on the recording lever automatically cuts out the shock when the dog tilts the lever.

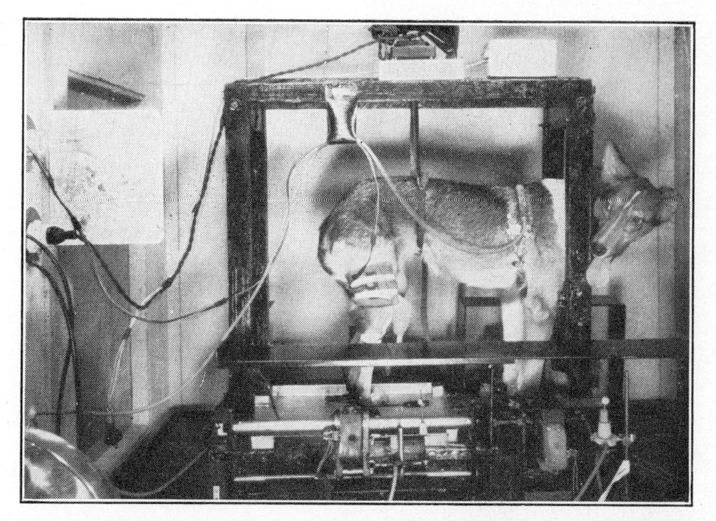

Fig. 7. Dog standing in stock on a table in soundproofed room, for the buzz-shock flexion-conditioning experiment.

The loud-speaker which delivers the (conditioned) buzz is mounted on top of the stock. A pneumograph for recording respiration is around the animal's chest, and electrodes for obtaining action potentials are taped to the right hind limb. Each foot is fastened to a balanced lever for registering the flexion response. (Reprinted from *J. Exper. Psychol.*, 1939, *24*, 323, by permission of the editor and publishers.)

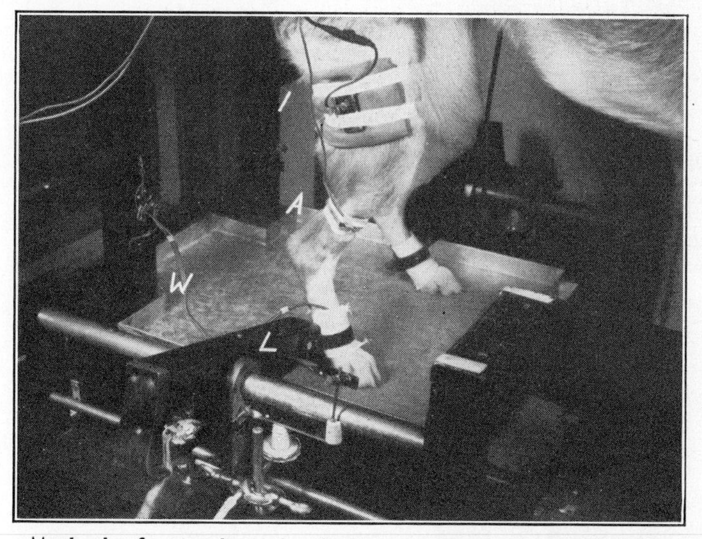

Fig. 8. Method of recording the flexion responses and of delivering the (unconditioned) electric-shock stimuli.

L is the balanced lever, to which a tambour is connected for recording movement or foot-lifts. The wires, *W*, deliver the unconditioned stimuli to the dog's foot beneath the bandage. *I* and *A* are electrodes for recording action potentials. (Reprinted from *J. Exper. Psychol.*, 1939, *24*, 324, by permission of the editor and publishers.)

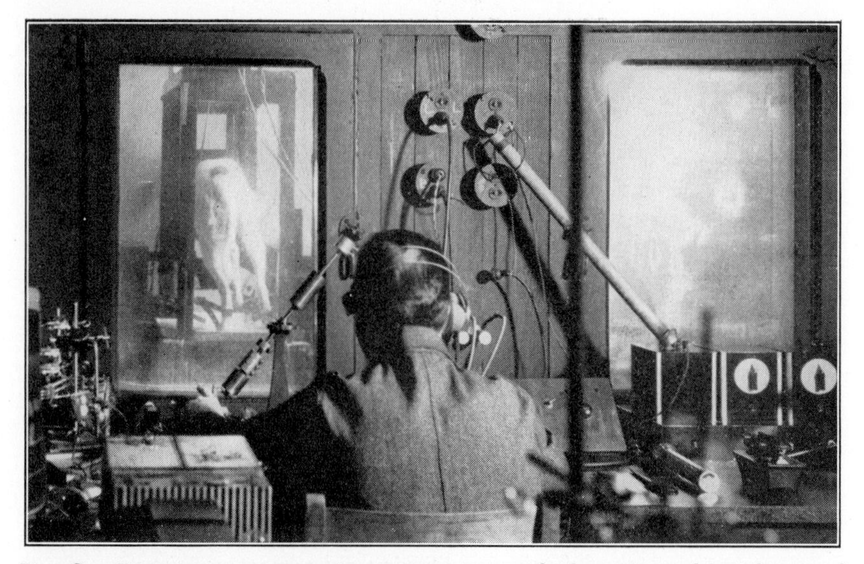

Fig. 9. Experimenter operating apparatus and observing subject in sound-proofed room, through one-way-vision windows.

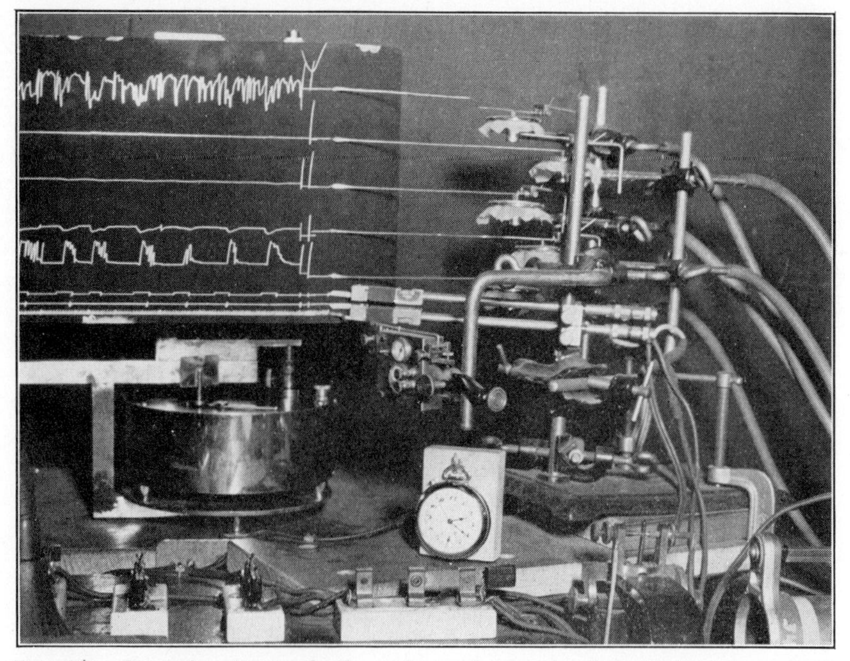

Fig. 10. Records obtained, through tambours, in the conditioning of the right rear foot by the buzz-shock method.

The lines on the kymograph are (*top to bottom*) respiration, response line for left front foot, response line for right front foot, response line for left rear foot, response line for right rear foot (the member to be conditioned), buzz, shock, and time.

In traditional or *classical conditioning,* the animal cannot escape the shock even though he lifts his foot. Control trials in which the buzz alone is presented may occasionally be introduced as a check on the progress of learning. By either the instrumental or the classical procedure, however, the subject will learn to raise his foot to the sound of the buzz. See Fig. 11.

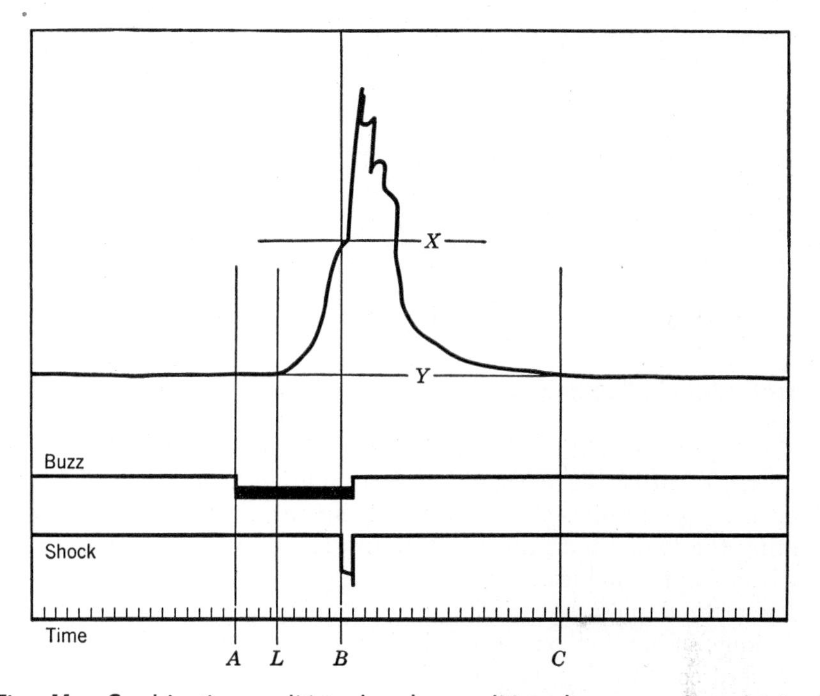

Fig. 11. Combination conditioned and unconditioned response line obtained in buzz-shock flexion conditioning.

The amplitude of the conditioned response is the distance *XY*. The latency of the CR is measured from *A* to *L*, and the duration of the combined conditioned-unconditioned movement is *LC*. *B* indicates the onset of the shock. In the trial diagrammed, the subject did not escape the unconditioned stimulus. That portion of the activity line above the line *X* is therefore the unconditioned flexion reaction to the shock, which is superimposed upon the CR. The duration of the CR alone cannot, as a result, be measured in this instance. (Reprinted from *J. Exper. Psychol.*, 1939, *24*, 326, by permission of the editor and publishers.)

With a method such as this, which records each separate movement or reaction, great precision is possible. The development of the conditioned response can be measured in at least six ways [22].

1. By the amplitude or height of the lift which occurs to the buzz. Amplitude is found to increase gradually as the number of trials

increases. If plotted against trials, the amplitude will give a learning or conditioning curve.

2. By the frequency with which the CR occurs within a fixed number of trials. In the first 20 trials there may be only one CR, which would give a frequency score of 1/20 or 5 per cent. In trials 180–200 there may occur 20 CRs, for a frequency score of 20/20 or 100 per cent. Like the amplitude, the frequency gradually increases with practice and can be plotted as a frequency learning curve.

3. By the latency of the CR. This is the time elapsing between the beginning of the conditioned stimulus and the beginning of the conditioned response. The latency may or may not change with practice.

4. By the contour or form of the CR.

5. By the duration or length of the CR.

6. By the rate of extinction of the CR.

VARIATIONS OF THE CONDITIONING EXPERIMENT

Time Factors in Conditioning

Whether the conditioned stimulus comes before, exactly at the same time as, or after the unconditioned stimulus is a matter which will influence the results. These three temporal arrangements of presenting the two stimuli are the forward, simultaneous, and backward conditioning techniques. There can be no question but that the laboratory method most favorable for developing a CR is the forward technique. Simultaneous conditioning is not as satisfactory, and backward conditioning, although it seems to be possible, produces the poorest result of any of the methods [47, 48].

In Pavlov's laboratory the interval between the presentation of the conditioned stimulus and the presentation of the unconditioned stimulus was extended by two varieties of forward conditioning known as *delayed* and *trace* conditioning. In delayed conditioning the conditioned stimulus is presented continuously for a long time, often for many minutes. At the end of this period, but while the conditioned stimulus is still being presented, the food is given. When the CR is finally established, the salivary response will not occur until just before the time for the food to be presented. The animal, in effect, holds back or delays responding to the conditioned stimulus until the proper time interval has elapsed.

Even more unusual is the trace CR. In this case the conditioned stimulus does not continue until the unconditioned stimulus is presented; it ends before the food is given. The sequence is:

Conditioned stimulus → Time interval → Unconditioned stimulus

Pavlov reported that in some instances of trace conditioning the interval between the occurrence of the two stimuli could be lengthened to half an hour. During early trials false responses were made, i.e., the saliva started flowing too soon. When the trace CR was firmly established, however, there was no saliva until the proper period of waiting had passed.

The Method of Contrasts

By means of the conditioning procedure the limits and accuracy of hearing, vision, and the other senses can be determined. Salivary conditioning and buzz-shock conditioning, as well as other conditioning techniques, have been used for this purpose. If, for example, one wishes to find the upper limit of hearing in the dog, he can first train an animal to flex his leg to a conditioned tone well within the range of hearing—let us say a tone of 1000 cycles per second. After the CR has become established, the conditioned stimulus may be gradually raised in pitch until a point is reached where it no longer produces the lifting of the foot. The conditioned stimulus at that point is at or just above the upper limit of hearing for the subject [30].

For measuring the differential limen, the method of contrasts, otherwise known as differential conditioning, is used. This requires two conditioning situations which are contrasted or differentiated from one another. Suppose that the problem is to find the smallest difference in the pitch of two tones which the organism can just distinguish. The first step, as in finding the upper limen, is to set up a regular CR to a basic or standard tone, which we may assume again to be 1000 cycles per second. This is called a positive CR. The second step is to present the comparative tone repeatedly, but without ever reinforcing it or pairing it with the unconditioned shock. At the start it is well to have the comparative stimulus an octave or more higher than the standard. The first presentations of the comparative tone will elicit conditioned flexion responses, but if these are never reinforced they will soon be extinguished. There will thus be established a negative CR. The reinforcing of one stimulus, but never the other, enables the organism easily to distinguish between the two.

To diagram this method, let S_1 = the shock, S_2 = the standard tone of 1000 cycles per second, S_3 = the higher comparison tone, $(+R)$ = the response of lifting the foot, and $(-R)$ = not lifting the foot. The symbol 0 will indicate the fact that no reinforcement (no S_1) is given in the case of the negative CR. The arrangement for the method of contrasts will then appear as follows:

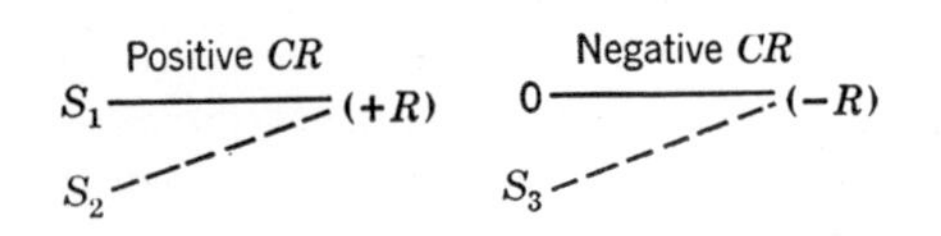

The final step in the procedure is to bring the comparative stimulus down in pitch until it approaches closer and closer to the standard. When the subject begins again to make indiscriminate conditioned lifts to each of the tones, the two stimuli are equivalent for him. The point at which they are just barely distinguishable is the differential limen, or the smallest difference in pitch which the subject can differentiate. A more detailed description of the nature and measurement of sensory thresholds will be found in Chapter 5.

Inhibition and Disinhibition

Pavlov is responsible for the conception that a negative conditioning situation like that employed in the method of contrasts is one in which the organism learns to hold back or inhibit his responses. The extinction of the CR is therefore not to be thought of as a passive process like forgetting, but rather like the building up of restraining tensions. The evidence that the inhibition is an active process lies in the destroying or breaking down of the inhibition by distracting stimuli. After a response has been extinguished, for example, some disturbing noise like the slamming of a door may cause it to return. This has been called disinhibition, or the inhibition of an inhibition. The external stimulus (sound of door slamming) destroys or breaks down the internal inhibition of the subject. Another case of internal inhibition which may be affected by distracting stimuli is the holding back of the CR in delayed and trace conditioning, where a disturbing stimulus will cause the saliva to flow before the proper interval of time has elapsed [12, 15].

Higher-order Conditioning

If conditioning is simply the process of association translated into the more objective laboratory concepts of stimulus and response, it must have universal application. Experiments on higher-order conditioning have indeed attempted to demonstrate the universality of the process by showing how learning can be built upon learning [30, 32]. In higher-order conditioning, a series of conditioning situations follow one another according to the following plan:

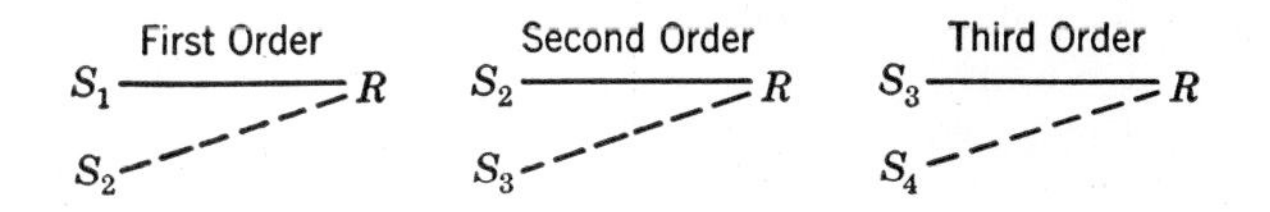

Let the symbols in this scheme have these meanings: S_1 = shock, S_2 = buzz, S_3 = light, S_4 = touch, R = lifting the foot. Then, in first-order conditioning, a CR is established to the buzz. In second-order conditioning the buzz sequence (S_2-R) developed in the first order is used as the unconditioned combination, and a light (S_3) is the conditioned stimulus. When S_3-R has been established as a second-order CR, a touch (S_4) is used as the conditioned stimulus for a third-order CR. It is theoretically possible, by extending this method, to establish CRs to any desired order.

Most experiments on higher-order conditioning have nevertheless broken down because of the phenomenon of extinction. When the shock (S_1) is eliminated from the second and higher orders, the reinforcing or motivating agent is also removed. The pairing of S_2-R with S_3 results in the extinction of the response to S_2 before much progress can be made in associating S_3 with R. From results of this sort it has been argued that conditioning is not, after all, the universal phenomenon it was thought to be.

A serious error in such reasoning has been pointed out in experiments by Finch and Culler [6], in which it appeared that conditioning to any desired order was possible, provided the motivating influence was left in the experiment. This result was accomplished by having dogs shocked on the *flank* if they did not lift the *foot*. To avoid an electric shock in the side they therefore had to raise the foot on every trial. Whenever a subject failed to make a flexion response, the shock automatically prodded him to action. Under these circumstances there was no special difficulty in pairing S_3 with S_2-R, S_4 with S_3-R, and so on.

THE RELATION OF CONDITIONING TO OTHER LEARNING

In view of the established fact that motivation is necessary for efficient learning of all sorts it seems surprising that anyone ever supposed that conditioning could occur without it. The first requirement for establishing a CR, it will be recalled, is an (unconditioned) *S-R* situation *that works*. There must be something to force the response to occur, or, in other words, the response must be motivated. It must be motivated by an electric shock; it must be motivated by giving a hungry dog food; or it must be motivated in some other way. One of the common bonds which ties conditioning to other learning is, in fact, the necessity for motivation in learning of both kinds.

Another similarity between conditioned and non-conditioned learning is that the organism follows the pattern of making unnecessary and useless responses first and of eliminating these as training proceeds. One aspect of this trend which emphasizes the presentation of different stimuli has been described in conditioning experiments as *sensory generalization* or as *stimulus generalization* [7, 12]. This means that, when a CR is built up, it is not at first specific to a single stimulus. The organism can be "tricked" into making the same CR to other similar stimuli. Only after continued reinforcement of the *right* stimulus and non-reinforcement of the *wrong* ones does the response become definitely associated with the conditioned stimulus alone.

Sensory generalization is exactly the phenomenon which appears in the method of contrasts. The response is first generalized to the (higher) comparative stimulus. It becomes specific to the standard stimulus by motivating (reinforcing) it in the one case, but not in the other.

Sensory generalization is the making of the same response to different stimuli; *motor* or *response generalization* is the making of different responses to the same stimulus [46]. During the early trials of buzz-shock flexion conditioning the animal makes many superfluous foot-lifts. Even though the shock is sent to only one of the feet, for example, the right rear, he will lift the other three feet also in response to the buzz. As he becomes better conditioned, however, he flexes more often the member which is shocked and moves the other feet less and less. The generalized behavior which existed at the start of training tends to drop out.

Conditioning and Trial-and-error Learning

The responses of lifting the non-shocked feet are the "errors" of the conditioning experiment. They are just as much errors as entering a blind alley in a maze. In eliminating these responses the subject learns what not to do. In lifting the shocked foot more frequently to the conditioned stimulus he learns what to do.

The relationship between conditioning and trial-and-error learning can be graphically shown by frequency curves plotted from the activity of all four feet in the buzz-shock conditioning situation [46]. See Fig. 12. Error curves which tend to decrease in frequency are obtained from the non-shocked feet. A typical amount-conditioning

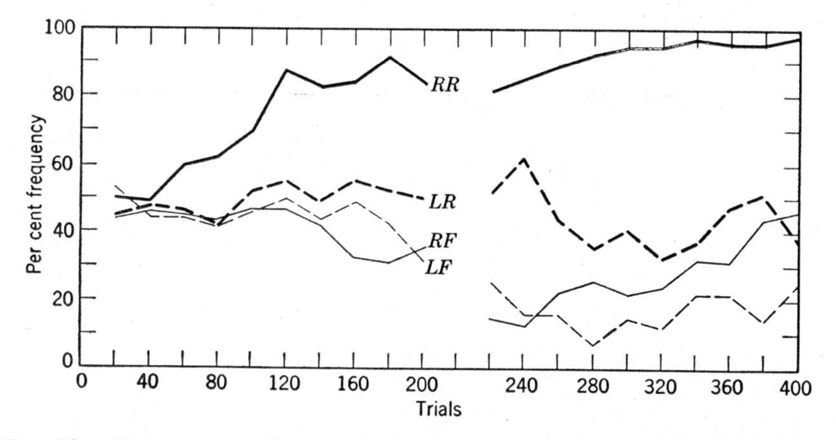

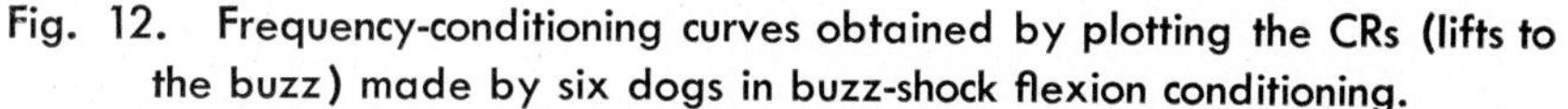

Fig. 12. Frequency-conditioning curves obtained by plotting the CRs (lifts to the buzz) made by six dogs in buzz-shock flexion conditioning.

RR, LR, RF, and *LF* represent the right rear, left rear, right front, and left front feet, respectively. The lifts of the right rear foot are correct responses, and the lifts of the three non-shocked feet are errors. The lifts of the non-shocked feet (especially the front feet) tend to decrease with practice, like errors made in learning a maze. The CRs of the right rear foot increase in a mildly sigmoid manner. The break in the curves at 200 trials represents a rest interval of 2 weeks. (From I. S. Wolf and W. N. Kellogg. Changes in general behavior during flexion conditioning and their importance for the learning process. *Amer. J. Psychol.,* 1940, 53, 390. Reprinted by permission of the editor and publishers.)

curve, with sigmoid characteristics, can be obtained from the same subjects, in the same experiment, at the same time, if only the activity of the shocked member is considered. It would seem as though whether one finds trial-and-error learning or typical conditioning must depend to a large extent upon what he is looking for and upon what part of the activity of the subject he measures.

Conditioning and Learning by Insight

What then is the relationship between conditioning and learning by insight? Are not these two, at least, distinct and irreconcilable varieties of learning? An answer to this question can again be found in the experiment on buzz-shock flexion conditioning [23]. Sometimes the organism eliminates his errors all at once in this experiment. The responses of the non-shocked feet drop immediately to zero (or nearly to zero) within a very few trials. The frequency curve obtained under these circumstances has the same characteristics as curves of learning by insight which are made by human subjects. See Fig. 13. Insight is apparently possible, therefore, even in conditioning the experiments.

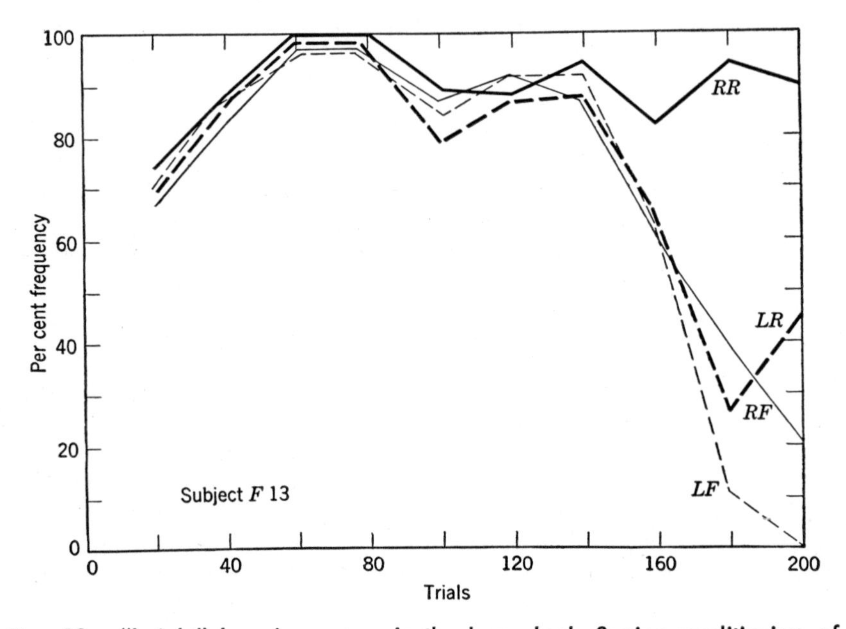

Fig. 13. "Insight" learning curves in the buzz-shock flexion conditioning of dogs.

The lifts of the non-shocked feet (*LR, RF,* and *LF*) drop out suddenly, while the frequency of the shocked foot (*RR*) is maintained. (From W. N. Kellogg and I. S. Wolf. "Hypothesis" and "random activity" during the conditioning of dogs. *J. Exper. Psychol.,* 1940, *26,* 597. Reprinted by permission of the editor and publishers.)

The conclusion of the whole matter appears to be this: Motor learning of all sorts, both simple and complex, is similar. Different "kinds" of learning, as discrete and separate entities, probably do not exist. The "kind" of learning which the experimenter finds depends on the nature of the problem which he sets, on what he is looking for, and on what aspects of the subject's activity he chooses to observe. From the point of view of experimental psychology, conditioning is not so much a kind of learning as it is a basic laboratory technique for the study of the learning process. It is a *method* which specializes in the analysis of small, definable units, like specific movements to specific stimuli, rather than in gross or generalized behavior.

SUMMARY

Since motor learning deals only with non-verbal tasks, it can be studied in animals, in infants, and in other instances where linguistic material cannot be employed. In a way, motor learning is therefore fundamental to the study of rational learning and to other more complex psychological processes. To conduct an experiment in motor learning the experimenter sets the subject some problem or task to master and observes and measures the improvement in the subject's method of performing the task upon successive trials. The dependent variable in such an experiment is the subject's performance. The independent variable is the number of trials or the degree of training.

Undoubtedly the most widely used of all devices for the study of motor learning is the spatial maze, which has a variety of forms, from the elevated maze for animal subjects to the paper-and-pencil maze for humans. Other devices include mirror drawing, tossing balls at a target, and the pursuit-meter. Tasks like these, which require the slow or gradual development of a skill for their mastery, are to be contrasted with tasks in which the learning consists of the discovery of some general principle. In the latter instance the correct method of solution may dawn upon the learner suddenly, like a hunch or bright idea. The *Umweg* or detour experiment, in which the subject must find his way around a barrier, and the mutiple-choice procedure are techniques for the study of insight learning of this sort.

For recording progress in a learning experiment, the standard method is by means of the learning curve, a graphical device for showing the relationship between trials and performance. Curves of decreasing score, like time and error curves, take special account of the subject's early mistakes. They may be thought of as recording the subject's improvement in learning *what not to do.* Curves of increasing score, on the other hand, show more clearly how the subject improves in learning *what to do.* Most learning curves, both increasing and decreasing in score, have been found to be negatively accelerated. The sigmoid curve, which may be the true or absolute curve of learning, however, has both positive and negative acceleration. The Vincent method, a technique for equating curves of varying length, is employed for combining the learning curves of different subjects into a single composite curve.

Although conditioning was first extensively studied by means of the salivary reflex and was called by Pavlov the conditioned reflex, it has since been produced with a variety of responses, many of which are not true reflexes in any sense of the word. It is essentially the process of association expressed in the more objective laboratory concepts of stimulus and response. The fundamentals of the method consist of two steps: (1) there must exist an unconditioned *S-R* situation that works, (2) there must be regularly paired with this in the proper manner a neutral or conditioned stimulus. Forward conditioning, in which the conditioned stimulus precedes the unconditioned stimulus, has been found to be more efficient than simultaneous or backward conditioning.

The conditioning technique can be used to measure both absolute and differential thresholds. In higher-order conditioning, conditioned responses can also be built upon already existing CRs, provided that motivation is maintained. From the point of view of experimental psychology, conditioning is best thought of as a laboratory procedure for the study of learning problems of all sorts, rather than as a "kind" or category of learning to be sharply differentiated from maze learning, insightful learning, or any other learning. It is a method which emphasizes a few specific stimuli and which usually deals with the minute analysis of a single movement or response, rather than with gross or generalized behavior.

REFERENCES

1. Bitterman, M. E., and Elizabeth Bretz. "Centrifugal swing" effects in the human stylus maze. *Amer. J. Psychol.*, 1946, *59*, 267–272.
2. Blodgett, H. C. The effect of the introduction of reward upon the maze performance of rats. *Univ. Calif. Publ. Psychol.*, 1929, *4*, 113–134.
3. Bryan, W. L., and N. Harter. Studies in the physiology and psychology of the telegraphic language. *Psychol. Rev.* 1897, *4*, 27–53.
4. Carr, H. A. Maze studies with the white rat. I. Normal animals. *J. Animal Behav.*, 1917, *7*, 259–275.
5. Culler, E. The nature of the learning curve. *Psychol. Bull.*, 1928, *25*, 143–144.
6. Finch, G., and E. Culler. Higher order conditioning with constant motivation. *Amer. J. Psychol.*, 1934, *46*, 596–602.
7. Guthrie, E. R. *The Psychology of Learning*. New York: Harper, 1935.
8. Guthrie, E. R., and G. P. Horton. *Cats in a Puzzle Box*. New York: Rinehart, 1946.
9. Hicks, V. C., and H. A. Carr. Human reactions in a maze. *J. Animal Behav.*, 1912, *2*, 98–125.
10. Hilgard, E. R. The nature of the conditioned response: I. The case for and against stimulus-substitution. *Psychol. Rev.*, 1936, *43*, 366–385.
11. Hilgard, E. R., and A. A. Campbell. Vincent curves of conditioning. *J. Exper. Psychol.*, 1937, *21*, 310–319.
12. Hilgard, E. R., and D. G. Marquis. *Conditioning and Learning*. New York: Appleton-Century, 1940.

13. Honzik, C. H. The sensory basis of maze learning in rats. *Comp. Psychol. Monog.*, 1936, *13,* No. 64.

14. Hull, C. L. The goal gradient hypothesis and maze learning. *Psychol. Rev.*, 1932, *39,* 25–43.

15. Hull, C. L. The factor of the conditioned reflex. In *Handbook of General Experimental Psychology*. C. Murchison, Ed. Worcester: Clark University Press, 1934 (Chap. 9, pp. 382–455).

16. Hunter, W. S. The temporal maze and kinesthetic sensory processes in the white rat. *Psychobiol.*, 1920, *2,* 1–17.

17. Hunter, W. S. The sensory control of the maze habit in the white rat. *J. Genet. Psychol.*, 1929, *36,* 505–537.

18. Hunter, W. S. Experimental studies of learning. In *Handbook of General Experimental Psychology*. C. Murchison, Ed. Worcester: Clark University Press, 1934 (Chap. 11, pp. 497–570).

19. Husband, R. W. A comparison of human adults and white rats in maze learning. *J. Comp. Psychol.*, 1929, *9,* 361–377.

20. Jacobsen, C. F. Studies of cerebral function in primates. I. The functions of the frontal association areas in monkeys. *Comp. Psychol. Monog.*, 1936, *13,* No. 63.

21. Kellogg, W. N. Evidence for both stimulus-substitution and original anticipatory responses in the conditioning of dogs. *J. Exper. Psychol.*, 1938, *22,* 186–192.

22. Kellogg, W. N., R. C. Davis, and V. B. Scott. Refinements in technique for the conditioning of motor reflexes in dogs. *J. Exper. Psychol.*, 1939, *24,* 318–331.

23. Kellogg, W. N., and I. S. Wolf. "Hypotheses" and "random activity" during the conditioning of dogs. *J. Exper. Psychol.*, 1940, *26,* 588–601.

24. Klebanoff, S. G. Psychological changes in organic brain lesions and ablations. *Psychol. Bull.*, 1945, *42,* 585–623.

25. Koffka, K. *The Growth of the Mind.* New York: Harcourt, Brace, 1925.

26. Köhler, W. *The Mentality of Apes.* New York: Harcourt, Brace, 2nd Ed., 1927.

27. Lashley, K. S. *Brain Mechanisms and Intelligence.* Chicago: University of Chicago Press, 1929.

28. McGeoch, J. A., and H. N. Peters. An all-or-none characteristic in the elimination of errors during the learning of a stylus maze. *J. Exper. Psychol.*, 1933, *16,* 504–523

29. Miles, W. R. The comparative learning of rats on elevated and alley mazes of the same pattern. *J. Comp. Psychol.*, 1930, *10,* 237–261.

30. Pavlov, I. P. *Conditioned Reflexes.* London: Oxford University Press, 1927.

31. Razran, G. H. S. Conditioned responses in animals other than dogs. *Psychol. Bull.*, 1933, *30,* 261–324.

32. Razran, G. H. S. Conditioned responses in children. *Arch. Psychol.*, 1933, No. 148.

33. Razran, G. H. S. Conditioned responses: an experimental study and a theoretical analysis. *Arch Psychol.*, 1935, No. 191.

34. Ruger, H. A. The psychology of efficiency. *Arch. Psychol.*, 1910, No. 15.

35. Skinner, B. F. *The Behavior of Organisms.* New York: Appleton-Century, 1938.

36. Snoddy, G. S. An experimental analysis of a case of trial and error learning in the human subject. *Psychol. Monog.*, 1920, *28,* No. 124.

37. Spence, K. W., and W. C. Shipley. The factors determining the difficulty of blind alleys in maze learning by the white rat. *J. Comp. Psychol.*, 1934, *17*, 423–436.
38. Tolman, E. C., and C. H. Honzik. Introduction and removal of reward, and maze performance in rats. *Univ. Calif. Publ. Psychol.*, 1930, *4*, 257–275.
39. Tolman, E. C., B. F. Ritchie, and D. Kalish. Studies in spatial learning. I. Orientation and the short-cut. *J. Exper. Psychol.*, 1946, *36*, 13–24.
40. Trueblood, C. K. The behavior of white rats in a rotated tunnel maze. *J. Genet. Psychol.*, 1932, *40*, 330–350.
41. Vincent, S. B. The function of the vibrissae in the behavior of the white rat. *Behav. Monog.*, 1912, *1*, No. 5.
42. Warden, C. J. Primacy and recency as factors in cul-de-sac elimination in the stylus maze. *J. Exper. Psychol.*, 1924, *7*, 98–116.
43. Warden, C. J. A standard unit animal maze for general laboratory use. *J. Genet. Psychol.*, 1929, *36*, 174–176.
44. Weaver, H. E., and C. P. Stone. The relative ability of blind and normal rats in maze learning. *J. Genet. Psychol.*, 1928, *35*, 157–177.
45. Witkin, H. A., and T. C. Schneirla. Initial maze behavior as a function of maze design. *J. Comp. Psychol.*, 1937, *23*, 275–304.
46. Wolf, I. S., and W. N. Kellogg. Changes in general behavior during flexion conditioning and their importance for the learning process. *Amer. J. Psychol.*, 1940, *53*, 384–396.
47. Wolfle, H. M. Time factors in conditioning finger-withdrawal. *J. Gen. Psychol.*, 1930, *4*, 372–378.
48. Wolfle, H. M. Conditioning as a function of the interval between the conditioned and the original stimulus. *J. Gen. Psychol.*, 1932, *7*, 80–103.
49. Woodworth, R. S. *Experimental Psychology.* New York: Henry Holt, 1938.
50. Yerkes, R. M. The mental life of monkeys and apes: a study of ideational behavior. *Behav. Monog.*, 1916, *3*, No. 12.
51. Yerkes, R. M. A new method for studying the ideational behavior of mentally defective and deranged as compared with normal individuals. *J. Comp. Psychol.*, 1921, *1*, 369–394.

SUGGESTED READINGS

Crafts, L. W., T. C. Schneirla, E. E. Robinson, and R. W. Gilbert. *Recent Experiments in Psychology.* New York: McGraw-Hill, 1938 (Chaps. 17 and 18).

Garrett, H. E. *Great Experiments in Psychology.* New York: Appleton-Century, 1941 (Chaps. 5, 6, 7, and 8).

Guthrie, E. R. *The Psychology of Learning.* New York: Harper, 1935.

Hilgard, E. R. *Theories of Learning.* New York: Appleton-Century-Crofts, 1948.

Hilgard, E. R., and D. G. Marquis. *Conditioning and Learning.* New York: Appleton-Century, 1940.

Hull, C. L. The factor of the conditioned reflex. In *Handbook of General Experimental Psychology.* C. Murchison, Ed. Worcester: Clark University Press, 1934 (Chap. 9, pp. 383–455).

Hunter, W. S. Experimental studies of learning. In *Handbook of General Experimental Psychology.* C. Murchison, Ed. Worcester: Clark University Press, 1934 (Chap. 11, pp. 497–570).

Köhler, W. *The Mentality of Apes.* New York: Harcourt, Brace, 2nd Ed., 1927.

Morgan, C. T. *Physiological Psychology.* New York: McGraw-Hill, 1943 (Chap. 23).

Pavlov, I. P. *Conditioned Reflexes.* London: Oxford University Press, 1927.

Valentine, W. L. *Experimental Foundations of General Psychology.* New York: Farrar and Rinehart, 2nd Ed., 1941 (Chaps. 16 and 17).

Woodworth, R. S. *Experimental Psychology.* New York: Henry Holt, 1938 (Chaps. 5, 6, and 7).

Chapter 3

Studying Memory and Transfer

Claude E. Buxton[1]

This chapter is concerned with the methods of studying only one kind of learning process, memorizing, and with the means whereby we measure retention and utilization of what is memorized. The distinguishing feature of a memorizing task is that responses are "preset" in their nature or pattern, usually by the environment. That is, certain responses must be mastered, but just which ones and in what order are already more or less arbitrarily defined for the learner. In memorizing the Gettysburg address, certain words must be learned, and no others; they must be learned in a certain preset pattern or order. There is no need to solve a problem or to decide which responses should be made or to discover in what order they should be made.

Perhaps the most significant kind of memorizing is that involving language. More than other species, man is able to represent, and thereby deal with, the present, the past, and the future by means of words or other symbols. Education and socialization are to a large extent processes by which the growing child learns to use language in his thinking and in his momentary relationships with other people. Verbal-learning phenomena, however, are as complex as they are important, and the difficulties of experimental control in this area are great. Such facts justify our placing primary emphasis upon verbal learning in fulfilling our general purpose of surveying the typical methodologies of studies of memorizing, retention, and transfer.

Relationships between Learning and Forgetting

We can never study a learning process without due regard for its converse, forgetting, for the simple reason that they are always con-

[1] Associate Professor of Psychology, Northwestern University.

current processes. Learning, whether haphazard or systematic, occurs as a result of experience, but while this experience occurs, forgetting is also going on. Anyone who has tried to memorize a lengthy poem, the names of people at a party, or the successive route numbers across an automobile road map, has been made aware of the way in which items mastered momentarily can slip away, only to be recovered in memory by further reference to the original material.

There is a similarity and there is also a difference in the way learning and forgetting are studied experimentally. The *similarity* is that both are indexed as a relation between two or more recorded performances by the individual. An initial record is necessary as a reference point, an indicator of how the subject behaved at a certain time or before certain experiences. The later record tells us how much he has changed, whether in the direction we call learning or the direction we call forgetting. The most probable state of affairs is that this later record, if sufficiently detailed, will indicate some changes of each kind.

The *experimental difference* between learning and forgetting is often said to be that measures of performance during, or relative to, practice are measures of learning, whereas measures of forgetting or retention are taken after an intervening time or experience. Such a convention can lead to confusion if followed too literally. This is sometimes true in studying verbal learning, because the subject may study or practice quietly for some fixed period and then write or recite what he knows. It is only when his actions are outwardly observable that *any* index of performance can be recorded, and in this case one could argue equally well that the index is one of either retention or learning. To resolve this difficulty we shall simply ask always: Does the index of performance indicate the acquisition of responses (learning), or the weakening or disappearance of response tendencies (forgetting)? When a certain experiment deals mainly with the period of response acquisition, it is a study of learning; when it deals mainly with the period of response disappearance, it is a study of retention or forgetting.

Interrelationships among Learning, Retention, and Transfer

How we learn *now* is presumably always affected by what we have learned *previously,* and this fact we refer to as transfer of learning. The amount of transfer may be quite small at times, but, in general, growing older and wiser means being able to utilize earlier learning. To reduce this to experimental terms, the study of transfer is the study of how some specified learning experience influences performance on a second specific task. Apart from the possibility of near-zero effects, we can see that transfer may be positive, as when familiarity with the court tactics of tennis facilitates the learning of badminton, or it may be negative, as when learning a friend's new telephone number is hampered by confusion with the old one. Positive transfer, however inefficient, must necessarily occur more often, or it would not be true that maturity brings wisdom.

Just as learning is affected by earlier events, so is retention affected by events occurring during the retention period. Transfer, positive and negative, is therefore a determiner of both learning and forgetting. We shall later work out its relations to each.

BASIC EXPERIMENTAL DESIGNS

Learning

All the factors which are known to influence the learning process can be classified in three general groups: (1) those characterizing the learner: his motivation, ability, fitness, etc.; (2) those characterizing the task to be practiced, e.g., the meaningfulness of the material or the amount of it; (3) those found in the conditions of practice or training—degree of distribution of trials, use of rewards and punishments, amount of self-rehearsal permitted, etc. We can summarize the factors in a learning experiment thus:

Control group: $S_1 \quad T_1 \quad P_0$
Experimental group: $S_1 \quad T_1 \quad P_1$

This notation signifies that two groups are equal in the way the subject variables and the task variables operate, but that they differ in the way some single practice variable operates. (The single difference between the control and experimental conditions obviously could lie in the subject or task variables rather than the practice-condition variables.) Given some such single variation in a factor affecting learning, the basic experiment consists of securing learning curves for the two conditions or groups, or securing measures of time to mastery.

Either the factorial or the functional variety of experimental design may be employed for the basic learning experiment. (See Chapter 1.) To illustrate the application of these types here, we can refer to an experiment in which the major independent variable was the amount of material to be learned and the dependent variable was learning rate or time [6]. Nonsense syllables were memorized. (A typical nonsense syllable is TIV—two consonants with a vowel between, chosen so that no meaningful word is thereby formed. Nonsense syllables are often employed in learning experiments because they give no special advantage to any learner; i.e., they afford control of the variable of familiarity or association value.) In what we shall call a control condition, only eight syllables were to be learned, about as close to zero in amount as can be employed and still have anything more than learning at a single glance. In the experimental conditions progressively larger numbers of syllables were employed.

Suppose that we did not know whether amount of material really has a bearing on the time necessity for memorization. We might then employ only the control and one experimental condition—the factorial treatment. In the experiment under consideration, a table such as the following might have resulted:

	TIME TO MASTERY, Minutes
Control (8 syllables)	0.13
Experimental (16 syllables)	3.67

Clearly, the amount variable makes a difference to the dependent or rate-of-learning variable.

If we now shift to the second form of our basic design, the functional, and add several experimental conditions (differing in amount of material), we learn, not simply that our major independent variable is a significant one, but, in a more complete way, how it relates to the dependent variable. See Fig. 1.

As a final way of stating the difference between the two forms of the basic learning experiment, we can note that the factorial experiment is usually summarized by separate learning curves for the two conditions, rather than by just a single score for each. Each curve *individually* shows the relation between level of mastery and an independent variable which is essential, but of secondary interest in most experiments: amount of practice. We must look at the *difference between* the two curves in order to decide if the independent variable on which they differed is significant—the latter variable enters into the graph only in this *indirect* way, even though it is the main object of study. By contrast, when several experimental conditions (e.g., amounts of material) have been employed, we usually choose a single index to represent the efficiency of learning (e.g., time to mastery) and do not plot curves of learning. We then relate this efficiency-of-learning index *directly* to the independent variable defined by the differences among experimental conditions, as in Fig. 1.

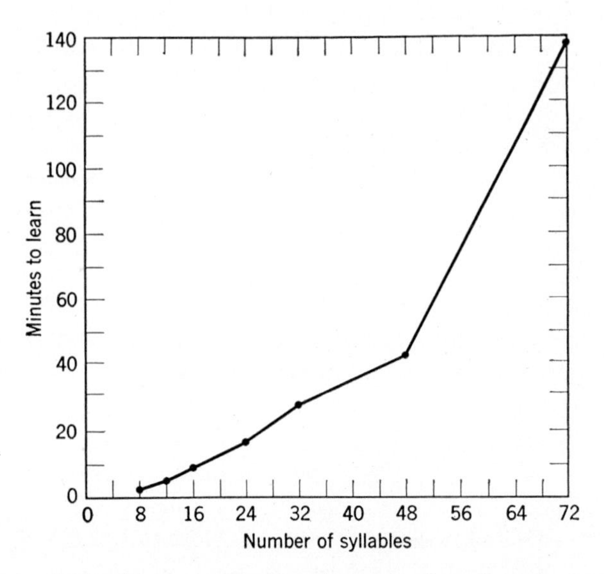

Fig. 1. The relationship between learning rate (time) and amount of material. (After Lyon [6].)

Retention

The basic design of a retention experiment can be schematized thus:

Control group:	L_1	R_0	T_1
Experimental group:	L_1	R_1	T_1

The notation L_1 indicates the original learning; during it, of course, the three classes of variables named in the preceding section are operative but are of equal influence in the control and experimental groups. R indicates the retention period or the activities going on during this time, the subscripts 0 and 1 indicating that in this case a zero "setting" and an appreciably different "setting" on some variable to be identified in the intervening activities are being compared. T_1 indicates the final test of retention, which is identical for the two groups compared, as the scheme is presented above, and which affords the crucial data of the experiment. The major independent variable could, of course, lie in the learner variables or in the situation in which or by which retention is measured, as well as in the intervening period. The implication of this scheme is that in a retention experiment the control and experimental groups must be matched on a larger number of variables than in a learning experiment. That is, in addition to matching in terms of subject, task, and learner variables, there must also be matching, during the retention period, for such factors as the length of retention interval or activities other than those prescribed by the experimental design, as well as at the time of the retention test, for such factors as attitude, fatigue, or physical surroundings.

Needless to say, this experimental design can be employed in a factorial experiment, or in a more complete one.

Transfer

The following is the basic design of a transfer experiment:

Control group.	E_1	—	A_2
Experimental group:	E_1	L_1	A_2

The crucial thing is the comparison of the two groups on A_2, after the experimental group has experienced L_1 and the control group has not. Within L_1 are included the three classes of learning variables. From any one, the major independent variable may be chosen. A_2 may also be a learning task or may be a retention test including variables such as were mentioned in the previous section. The notation E_1 indicates that some preliminary means must be found of *equating* control and experimental groups, and this may be a learning task for which A_2 is a test of retention. Any difference between the two groups on A_2 alone might, without this precaution, be attributable to ability or some other variable, rather than the prior learning of L_1 by the experimental group.

By now the student will expect that this basic design can be varied by the introduction of a series of experimental groups, rather than just one, and by variations in either L_1 or A_2. In all cases, however, learning curves or other data concerning performance on A_2 are the crucial data of the experiment.

VARIABLES ORDINARILY IRRELEVANT TO STUDIES OF LEARNING, RETENTION, AND TRANSFER

Here we shall discuss independent variables which are commonly recognized as playing a role in laboratory experiments on learning and related problems, but which often are not of direct interest and must therefore be kept from contributing to the major result of an experiment. The techniques discussed earlier (see Chapter 1) are used; i.e., some unwanted variables can be *eliminated* altogether, some can only be *held constant,* some can literally be made to operate *identically* for all subjects, and others cannot be held constant in any literal sense, but must be made to *"average out"* the same for each condition or group. We shall show how each technique may be applied to our particular area of investigation.

Individual Differences in Ability

Our main interest is in the principles governing the *processes* of learning and forgetting. It is true that some subjects learn more quickly than others or retain better, and in the absence of other explanations we may attribute such differences to ability. (In this connection a narrow definition of ability, especially one implying hereditary determination, is not intended, because pre-experimental language skills, familiarity with experimental procedures, etc., may all be included within the family of individual-difference variables.) Since we are not directly interested in such variables, the distribution of ability differences should be comparable in the control and all experimental groups, so that ability could not reasonably be thought the factor responsible for differences between their performances. Individual differences cannot be eliminated and therefore must be held constant, as reflected by averages on the irrelevant variables for different groups or conditions.

Motivation

The same statement must be made for individual differences in interest, or cooperativeness. Care must be taken in the experimenter's treatment of the learner, or in the learner's contacts with the assigned task, so that motivation is on the average equally great in all experimental conditions. Preferably, motivation should be maintained at a relatively high level in studies of memorizing, since this aids in reducing the effectiveness of possible distractions or boredom.

Under certain circumstances motivation, especially where it is defined as the *set* the subject has toward his verbal learning task, becomes a variable of direct interest, rather than indirect. By definition it then differs in a planned way from one experimental condition to another and is not to be classed as an irrelevant factor.

Non-experimental Practice

In the realm of verbal learning, control is often made difficult simply because the subject constantly uses language. He needs neither the apparatus nor the conditions of the laboratory in order to rehearse or review or recite. Such additional practice can occur in varying amounts while the learner is in the laboratory or out of it. Special attention must always be given to control of the rehearsal variable, lest it vary along with whatever major independent variable is being studied.

A check on rehearsal should be made by questioning the subjects concerning how much of it they did. Presumably, rehearsal may be reduced by instructions, but not certainly. This immediately brings up the difficult question of what to do about subjects who admit atypical amounts of rehearsal. The most defensible procedure is to compare subgroups of learners who report themselves as affected by the unwanted variable in differing degrees, to see whether their performances on the main dependent variable is thereby affected. Beyond this, there is the possibility of eliminating subjects who admit non-experimental practice. The discarding of subjects, however, is a procedure open to many errors of bias and should be avoided except under the most explicitly defined and rigidly enforced rules. We must conclude that, so long as the conditions of an experiment freely permit the possibility of review or rehearsal, there is no good way to remove this source of ambiguity from the data.

A preferable procedure, to be illustrated later, is to confine the entire study to a period when the subject is under the control of the experimenter and then to design the procedures so that little opportunity is given for uncontrolled practice. For example, if the learner is to be given a rest period, he may well be assigned, during that period, an activity which precludes attention to the main learning activity.

There is another aspect of non-experimental practice which must always be considered. It may be referred to as prior practice or, more specifically, familiarity with the task which is to be practiced. Care must be taken that the learning task is equally familiar or equally unfamiliar to all subjects. Of course, no experimenter would permit a few subjects to have "just a little peek" before the experiment starts, but it is quite difficult to select verbal materials which do not, just on the basis of chance, give special advantage to some learners. One common way of controlling this variable is to employ nonsense materials, i.e., unfamiliar ones, for all subjects (see Lyon's study earlier in this chapter). The familiarity variable is so important that we shall refer to it later in this chapter as though it constituted a special category.

Series or Order Effects

In memory experiments one must guard against the usual series or order effects (see Chapter 1), but the outstanding problem is that a single subject's performance, if he is used more than once in an investigation, may show the effects of familiarization, increased confidence, or some more specific transfer factor, such as practice effects peculiar to his task. Series or order effects, in studies of learning or retention, are ordinarily held constant by *counterbalancing*. We shall illustrate the application of this technique later.

Test-practice Effects

In the field of verbal learning, one must always be alert for the possibility that even a single glimpse or hearing of the materials to be learned will influence the subject. The problem is of special importance in any experiment where it is necessary to give subjects a preliminary trial or a preliminary test of mastery for purposes of equating groups. Where such procedures cannot be avoided, a control group, otherwise identical with the experimental group, must be employed to secure a *measure* of the test-practice or familiarization effects (see Chapter 1).

In concluding this discussion of "unwanted" variables, it should be pointed out that the chance variability in responses among the members of a group is usually greater than the variability in responses of a certain individual under the several conditions of an experiment. We can therefore reduce the influence of a good many random factors by subjecting a single group of people to all the conditions of our experiments, rather than using a new group of subjects in each experimental condition. In the single-group procedure, where the irrelevant and random independent variables are not so significant, there is a greater likelihood of our detecting the influence of the major variable. Such a procedure of course increases the possibility of series or order effects in the data, but since these can be anticipated and taken care of through counterbalancing, they can be controlled quite effectively and do not detract from the success of the experiment. Especially where the preliminaries of an experiment require considerable time or effort for each subject, the single-group procedure may be advantageous.

METHODS OF STUDYING LEARNING

We shall select, from among the large number of variables which can be and have been investigated in learning experiments, only two for discussion here, with mention of a third. It will be recalled that the significant variables fall into three classes: those in the learner, the task, and the practice conditions. Our examples are chosen, one from each class, in the order named, and our emphasis is on methods of investigation, not results.

A Variable in the Learner: Degree of Induced Muscular Tension and Learning Efficiency

It is generally recognized that a moderate degree of alertness is beneficial to learning, or, more obviously, great relaxation or great tension on the part of the learner is not conducive to learning efficiency. To investigate this general relationship adequately, it is necessary to develop a specific measure of bodily tension, a measure of learning efficiency, and an experimental plan to vary the tension (independent variable) while numerous other determiners of learning efficiency are controlled. This has been done by Courts [1].

As did Lyon (see p. 67), Courts required his subjects to memorize syllable lists, with the difference that Courts's lists were 6 items long, and each item was to be *spelled.* The list was presented, one item at a time, by an automatic exposure device, the memory drum. The task of the learner, after the first "reading trial," was to anticipate and spell each syllable by using its predecessor as the cue. In order to be credited as correct responses, the letters had to be pronounced *before* the item actually turned up in the viewing window of the memory drum. The dependent variable thus was the total number of correct anticipations (letters) during the prearranged number of trials given under each experimental condition. On the first and second practice days the subject had 5 trials on each of 4 lists. On the third, or experimental day, the subject learned a total of 12 lists, 2 under each of the prescribed tension conditions, but with other conditions interspersed.

The independent variable, as just implied, was the degree of muscular tension induced in the learner by squeezing a dynamometer continuously as he learned a list. Each subject was asked, on the first day of his service in the experiment, to squeeze the dynamometer as hard as possible and hold that grip for 30 seconds. Whatever his grip strength at the end of the 30-second period, the amounts of effort he later had to exert continuously in different experimental conditions were fractions of it. The control condition of the experiment was of course *no* dynamometer squeeze during learning. In the five experimental conditions, the learner held the dynamometer at $\frac{1}{8}$, $\frac{1}{4}$, $\frac{3}{8}$, $\frac{1}{2}$, and $\frac{3}{4}$ his maximum test grip.

The procedures for controlling several independent variables are implied in what has already been said about this experiment. (1) The factor of meaningfulness or familiarity in the lists was reduced to a low and presumably equal level for all learners by the use of nonsense syllables which had to be spelled. (2) On the other hand, the general strangeness of anticipation learning and memory drums was reduced by practice on two days before the crucial experimental day. (3) Variations in the rate of exposure, legibility, etc., of the lists were eliminated by use of the memory drum. (4) The amount of material, i.e., the length of the list, was a constant for all conditions. (5) The strength of grip possessed by different people varies widely; the use of the fractional grip, where each person set his own standard, assured Courts that the different degrees of tension required in the five experimental conditions would possess the same significance in relation to one another for each learner. (6) The troublesome variable of individual differences in learning ability was held constant by using each subject in all conditions.

We can mention several other controls. (7) The learner was aided in maintaining whatever fractional grip was set for a certain experimental condition by an electrical connection on the dynamometer: so long as his grip was approximately correct, a light in the periphery of his field of vision stayed on; if he changed his grip too much, the light went out. (8) Each learner served under a total of six conditions, each twice, and he of course had to have a different list for each assignment. Three sources of series effect were thus made possible. The first was the order in which the lists were learned; for example, if the same list were always the fourth one, and it by chance was an easy one, the apparent efficiency of learning would be increased but not through the operation of the major independent variable, tension. The second and related effect might occur in the form of transfer; as the learner went from one condition to the next, there might be increasing difficulty in forgetting earlier lists or in keeping them from interfering with the present one. Or, at the opposite extreme, some general practice effects might continue to appear, even after the two preliminary practice days. The third series effect could lie in the fractional grips themselves; if they always increased, or always decreased, as the experiment progressed, systematic fatigue or motivational changes might occur from condition to condition. All three series effects were held constant by using different (random) orders in which the lists occurred *and* different orders in which the fractional grips were employed, for various learners. Any differences among the several experimental conditions therefore could *not* be attributed to a systematic error in the order in which either they or the lists were employed. (9) Fatigue in general was reduced on the experimental day by giving frequent between-condition rests.

Such factors as (10) non-experimental practice were ruled out by using lists which were unknown to the learner until the very moment he was to learn and by giving rest periods only when the trials with a particular list were all completed. (11) Motivation, and perhaps some other factors in the ability category, were in a sense controlled by using only college men. Sixty of them, all interested in psychological work, at least to the extent of being elementary psychology students, served in the experiment.

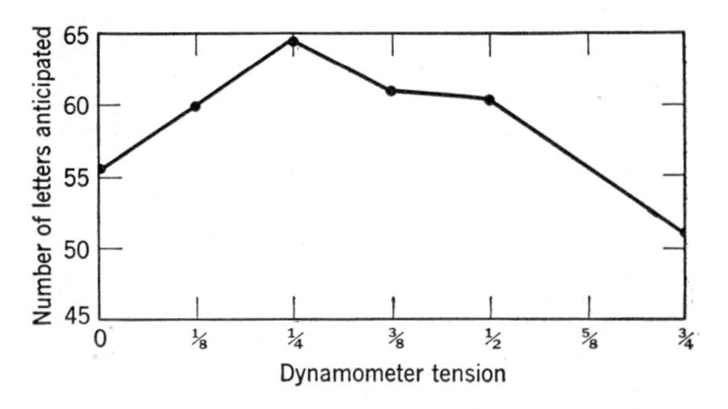

Fig. 2. Number of letters correctly anticipated in five trials, as a function of tension induced by gripping a dynamometer. (After Fig. 2 of Courts [1].)

The major results of Courts's study are summarized in Fig. 2. They speak largely for themselves and will not be treated in detail, since we are primarily concerned here with method. One point, however, deserves mention. If Courts had been content to perform a factorial experiment, i.e., use only the control and one other condition, this is an instance in which either of two exactly opposite conclusions about the relation between muscular tension and learning efficiency might have been drawn. That is, if the one chosen experimental condition had been equivalent to the present ¾-grip condition, the final conclusion would have been different than if any other of the four grip strengths had been used. Thus the more complete form of design employed by Courts turns out to be striking in its advantage for study of this problem. It shows that learning efficiency increases as tension increases, up to some moderate tension level, and thereafter efficiency decreases.

A Variable in the Task: Amount of Material and Learning Efficiency

Since we have already discussed a variable in the task (Lyon's study) we shall not choose a new example here. It will be sufficient to point out that Lyon controlled (1) meaningfulness by using syllables, (2) order effects by randomizing the various lengths of list, (3) non-experimental practice by learning each list at a single and continuous session, (4) ability by doing all the learning himself, and (5) general practice effects by thorough preliminary training. Although the data of Lyon are almost classical now and rarely questioned, we must in honesty point out that (6) he could not be entirely ignorant of the structure of the lists, since he made them up himself (but he made so many, then shuffled them, that memory for each list was probably as good or as bad as for any list of a different length). Nor was there precise control over (7) his technique for learning, (8) transfer effects, (9) daily variations in efficiency. It is a tribute to Lyon's rigorousness as an experimenter that his data are consistent with those obtained on larger numbers of learners by more completely planned and controlled techniques.

A Variable in the Practice Conditions: Distribution of Practice and Learning Efficiency

In the degree to which all independent variables are identified and the irrelevant ones controlled, few studies equal one by Hovland [3]. He himself was interested in the way a certain variable in the learning process affected forgetting, but we can take from his report the procedures by which the desired variable was introduced into the learning process, and the data showing how the learning was thereby affected. This variable was distribution of practice, and the experiment was of the factorial type; i.e., the learner either practiced continuously or had a certain alternation of work and rest periods. In either case he continued practice until he made one perfect recitation.

The task here, as in Courts's study, was the anticipation learning of nonsense syllables by means of a memory drum. The syllable lists were 12 items long and were pronounced, rather than spelled. The dependent variable or score was therefore the number of correct anticipations on each trial. In the control condition each trial was immediately followed by the next, and in the experimental condition each trial was followed by a 2-minute rest interval before the next trial. Thus two "settings" of the major independent variable, distribution of practice, were established within the experimental design.

During the rest periods the learner was given the task of naming bits of colored paper which were mounted on the memory drum and could be exposed at the will of the experimenter in just the same way as were the syllables. Each subject, in the part of the experiment we are concerned with, served four times in the continuous-practice condition and four times in the distributed-practice condition.

(1) Familiarity of task was held constant by the use of carefully selected nonsense syllables. The memory drum ensured that (2) rate of exposure, length of rest periods, and legibility were perfectly constant. (3) The amount-of-material factor was again a constant. (4) The general strangeness of the anticipation-learning and color-naming techniques was reduced and equalized by means of liberal preliminary practice. (5) Rehearsal, an exceedingly important possi-

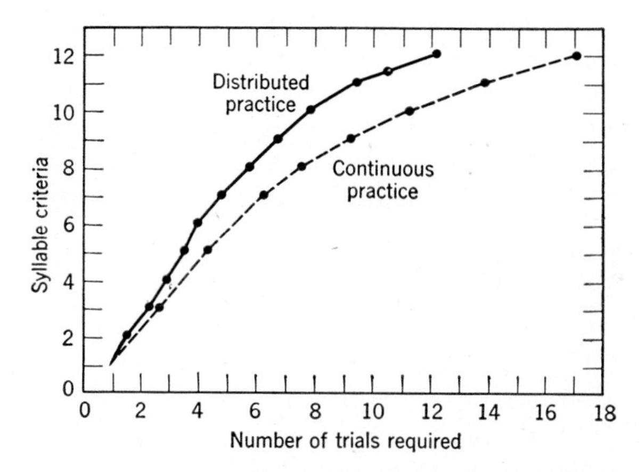

Fig. 3. The average number of repetitions of list required to anticipate the various numbers of syllables correctly. (Adapted from Figs. 2 and 4 of Hovland [3].)

bility in the distributed-practice condition, was precluded or at least greatly reduced by requiring the learner to attend to, or name, the bits of colored paper. Moreover, each list was used only during a single experimental period, so that non-laboratory review was pointless.

(6) In such a long series of experimental periods, there is much opportunity for series or order effects to occur. All these effects were controlled by counterbalancing so that the continuous-practice condition occurred before the distributed practice as often as the reverse was true. (7) Any possible failures of the lists to be equally difficult were spread equally over the two conditions as a part of the same counterbalancing scheme.

(8) The important factor of ability was a constant, since each learner served in both conditions. (9) Distracting influences were minimized by performing the experiment in a soundproof chamber. The experimenter was out of sight behind a screen on the drum table.

(10) The variations in efficiency which go with time of day were held constant by keeping each learner's appointment always at the same hour.

The care which Hovland expended upon the planning and conduct of his experiment was repaid in the clarity of the major finding, which is represented in Fig. 3. One fact must be explained concerning this graph: The learner continued his practice until he could make a perfect series of anticipations, and Hovland later went through the completed record to find the number of trials required to score one correct anticipation, then the number of trials to score two correct anticipations, and so on. For purposes of the graph, this number of syllables correct is placed on the vertical axis, so that you can read Fig. 3 just as though it were a typical plot of a learning curve. The major conclusion, that the distribution of practice is beneficial, is self-evident in the relative heights of the curves above the base line and the number of trials necessary to reach a score of twelve, or one perfect recitation.

Summary

In each of the studies of learning just described, it was the intention of the experimenter to isolate the effects of a single independent variable, i.e., to vary it in a planned fashion and to relate it to a certain dependent variable. It was necessary to keep any other independent variable from contributing to the differences among the experimental conditions which established the major independent variable. This required the experimenter to identify, and then to hold constant or eliminate, a large number of factors irrelevant to the major purpose of the study. Once the problem is stated, all these variables have to be considered.

METHODS OF STUDYING RETENTION

A Variable in the Conditions of Original Learning: Degree of Overlearning

The study by Hovland can be said to follow the classical procedure of relating level of mastery to amount of practice, with the effects of the major independent variable in the study (in Hovland's case, distribution of effort) being apparent only by comparison of the two separate curves. In studying retention there is a similar classical procedure, in which retention (or forgetting) is related to the length of interval since practice, and the major independent variable of the experiment is evaluated by comparing two or more separate forgetting curves. Our first illustration of how retention is studied is an investigation of this type.

Krueger [4] directed his attention to one of the most important factors in retention, namely, how well the material was mastered originally. The general outline of the study was as follows. Subjects memorized twelve-item lists of one-syllable nouns, and after 1, 2, 4, 7, 14, and 28 days returned to the laboratory for a test of retention. The number of nouns correctly recalled was thus the dependent variable. Although time was an independent variable here, as was practice in the Hovland experiment, it is not of direct interest. In Krueger's study the major independent variable was established by having the learner, in one condition, practice until he could make one perfect recitation. This can be thought of as a zero "setting" on the over-learning variable. In the experimental condition he practiced for half again the number of trials necessary to reach one perfect recitation. More specifically, if four trials were necessary in order for a certain person to recite a twelve-noun list without error, he would be given two more immediate (recitation) trials, for a total of six.

The word lists were presented by means of a memory drum; the learner could use any "system" of learning he pleased, but had to be able to use the anticipation procedure on alternate (test) trials. A given learner served in both the control and experimental conditions with a given (constant) retention interval. Six different groups of subjects (twenty in each group, presumably college students) were employed for the six different lengths of interval. Any subject would obviously require a new list for each condition that he served in and would have to come to the laboratory twice, once to learn, once to recall.

In analyzing the variables involved in this study, we for the first time encounter a very common problem. (1) Different groups of subjects had different lengths of retention period, and scores at the ends of the several periods are the crucial data of the study. Confusion would be caused if all the different groups were not equal in their level of original mastery, within the control condition, and again within the experimental condition. For the control condition this possibility was ruled out by Krueger by employing a *criterion* of mastery, one perfect trial. All learners were made alike in level of mastery (by this definition) before the initial practice ceased. For the experimental condition, there is no easy guarantee that all groups were equal. Yet, because of the reasonable procedure of requiring 50 per cent additional practice beyond one perfect trial, and treating all subjects in this condition alike, we can rather safely assume that level of mastery was made a constant within the condition.

The remainder of the controls exercised by Krueger should be routinely expected by now. (2) Rate of exposure of the materials, (3) amount of material, and (4) meaningfulness of the materials were all held constant by the use of the memory drum and the selection of items for the lists. With noun lists, however, there is more leeway for chance operation of the factor of familiarity or meaningfulness than with syllable lists. (5) Series effects were equalized for the two levels of original mastery required, by having different learners go through the control and experimental conditions equally often in the two possible orders. Practice effects were in general reduced by giving each subject preliminary training in the type of learning here required of him. Order effects originating in unequal difficulties of list were ruled out by distributing the necessary number of lists to

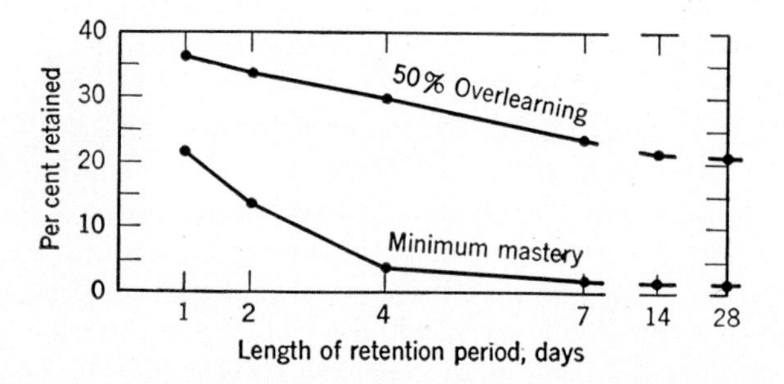

Fig. 4. Average percentage of nouns recalled after varying numbers of days. (After Table II of Krueger [4].)

all the learners in such a way that, for a particular retention interval, twenty *different* lists would be involved at each of the two levels of mastery employed, and the same would be true for each of the other retention intervals.

(6) We do *not* know how constant was the motivation of Krueger's subjects, nor do we know much about their (7) learning abilities. This seventh factor is presumably of minor importance anyway, in view of the steps taken to control level of initial mastery by using a criterion. There is quite a large group of unknown and uncontrolled factors in the retention period through which Krueger's subjects went. For example, (8) did they review at all, or in differing amounts? (9) Did they learn other things which would interfere with retention of materials learned in the laboratory? We do know that final recall was measured in the same way as was the original mastery, so that

(10) variables in the retention test are constant, unless there was variation in time of day, with its implications for fatigue or fitness.

We can only hope, along with Krueger, that such factors did not operate to create a difference between the control and experimental conditions or among the different retention intervals within a condition. That they did not seems probable in view of later research. At any rate the main trend of Krueger's data is very apparent and consistent in Fig. 4. As we have reported this study, 50 per cent overlearning produces a clear superiority in retention. We could have reported additional data from Krueger which at least suggest that further overlearning is not equally beneficial. Data are not available for enough positions along the degree-of-mastery continuum to justify our presenting more than the "presence-absence" portion of the experiment here. That the presence of a moderate degree of overlearning is beneficial to retention, however, is hardly to be doubted.

A Variable in the Conditions of the Retention Test: the Technique of Measurement

Up to this point we have disregarded the fact that there are several different ways of measuring how much a subject remembers. These methods of measurement do not necessarily produce the same appearances of retention, and, indeed, they may not result in the same relative rank for a given person within a group of learners. Variations in the method of measuring retention are included in the general class of variables influencing a person during the retention test. In this same class are such variables as the amount of distraction, the appropriateness of the person's set for what he is to do, and the general similarity of retention-measurement circumstances to the circumstances of the original learning (technically, stimulus *context*).

In another nonsense-syllable, memory-drum experiment, Luh [5] investigated the relationship between the type of retention measure and the amount retained. The learner was required to spell the syllables, using the anticipation procedure, and he continued practice until he had made one perfect recitation. After the criterion was reached, a period of 20 minutes, or 1, 4, 24, or 48 hours ensued before he returned to the laboratory for a retention test. (These intervals establish what for this study is an independent variable of secondary interest.) Each of ten subjects served several times for each of these different retention intervals.

The number of syllables correct was again the dependent variable. The major independent variable was established as follows. In half the tests after a given retention interval, two different measures of retention were secured. One was the person's score on the first trial, for which the anticipation method was employed, as during the original practice. Without pause, he continued this procedure until he had relearned to the criterion of one perfect recitation. The score on the first trial alone was a *recall* score. The difference between the number of trials required for original learning and for relearning to the same criterion was a *savings* index. (It should be clear that the more the subject retains, the more trials or effort he will save in the relearning process.) In the other half of the retention tests, after a certain retention interval, the subject was first tested by being handed pencil and paper and told to make a *written reproduction* of the list he had originally learned. He then was handed a list of twenty-four syllables, among which he had to identify the original twelve. This permitted a *recognition* score. Finally, the subject was given the original twelve syllables, printed on separate cards, and required to place them in the proper order. This yielded a *rearrangement* measure of retention. It will be noted that the independent variable established in these five methods of measurement was a qualitative variable, not a quantitative one; i.e., the "settings" on it differed in kind rather than in degree.

We shall not repeat the listing of variables held constant through by-now-familiar apparatus and learning materials. Certain other controls, however, merit our attention. (1) The use of a criterion of mastery to which all subjects were brought during the original learning was basic to this study. Otherwise, differences in measured retention might be mere reflections of level of original mastery, as Krueger's work would lead us to expect. Using the criterion procedure and (2) using the same subjects for all conditions on the major independent-variable method of measurement, served to reduce the effects of individual differences in learning ability. (3) Since each subject served in several repetitions of each condition of the experiment, there was the usual opportunity for series or order effects to occur. As did the other experimenters whose work we have reported here, Luh gave his subjects several preliminary practice sessions. Then, during the experiment proper, he used the specific conditions and lists in different orders for each subject, so that no particular condition was favored or handicapped by virtue of its position in the series. (4) Each subject used the same hour of the day for his original learning and returned later in the day or on a following day for the retention test. Under such a plan, any retention interval longer than

4 hours, but within the scope of a laboratory day, is almost sure to make the retention test come when the subject is reaching the "fag-end" of his day. Therefore all intervals between 4 and 24 hours were simply not used by Luh, who concentrated his efforts on intervals where relative fatigue was not such a probable differential among the several retention measures.

Again, we must point out that (5) non-experimental practice was not controlled, nor was information sought from the subjects concerning the strength of their tendencies toward review. The factor which probably counteracted such tendencies was the knowledge, on

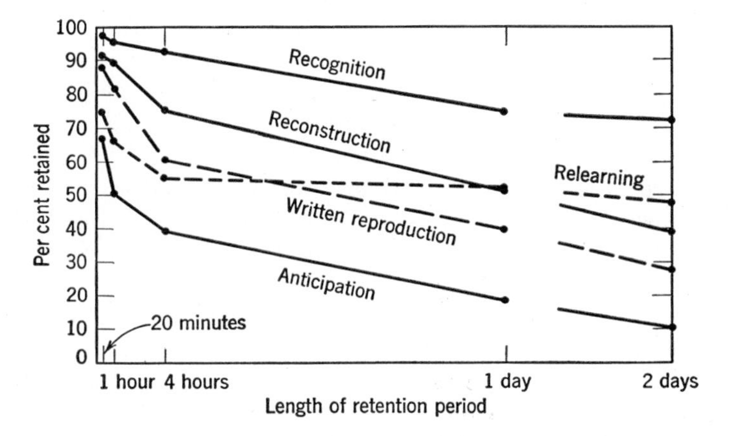

Fig. 5. Percentage of original material retained, as determined by five methods of measurement, and related to length of retention interval. (Adapted from Fig. 2 of Luh [5].)

the part of the graduate students and instructors who served as subjects, that such review would defeat the purposes of a study in which they had a professional interest as well as the usual interest of a cooperative subject. (6) The factor of set, or expectation to use one method rather than another in the retention tests, is not mentioned by Luh, but presumably was kept from being a significant or systematic factor in the results by using an unpredictable order in which the different methods were to be employed for each subject.

Out of this study comes a conclusion significant for all students of retention (see Fig. 5): the percentage of material retained varies according to the type of measurement of retention, and, more than that, the rank order of the several methods is not the same after different lengths of retention period.

A Variable in the Conditions of the Retention Period: Intervening Learning

One classical form of experiment has been that dealing with the phenomenon of *retroactive inhibition.* By this term is indicated the handicap (inhibition) placed on retention of any original learning if there follows, between the original learning and the test for it, any other learning activity. The effects of intervening learning depend, in turn, on several factors, of which one of the most significant is the degree of similarity between the original and interpolated tasks. An experiment on this factor has been performed by Gibson [2], and although it involves perceptual learning rather than purely verbal learning, her report offers the best example for our present purposes.

Since Gibson wished to investigate the relationship between the degree of retroactive inhibition, as we have defined it above, and the degree of similarity between the original and interpolated learning tasks, she had to begin by establishing a degrees-of-similarity variable. This required a preliminary experiment, and we shall describe this first.

Paired-associate learning was employed. Thirteen outline drawings (stimulus forms) were prepared (see the first column of Fig. 6), and with each was paired a monosyllabic word. The task of the learner was to view each successive pair briefly, and to associate the given response word with each form. On the test trial, the stimulus forms alone were shown, and the subject was required to write the response words.

With the assistance of judges, 2 other lists (classes II and III) of forms were prepared; these lists were judged to represent degrees of similarity to each of the forms of the standard list. One additional list (class IV) was judged to have no similarity to the items of the standard list. Then came the experimental determination of the degrees of similarity of stimulus forms in lists II, III, and IV to those in list I. Several different groups of subjects (from 19 to 29 in a group) had 5 presentations of the standard list, each presentation followed by a test trial with the forms only. (This brought all groups almost exactly to the point where they could, on the average, give 12 correct responses out of the possible 13.) Then, after 24 hours, each group was shown *some* of the forms from the standard list intermingled with some forms from classes II, III, and IV, enough to make a list of 13. They were told, at the 24-hour test, that they should write as many responses as possible, and that they might not remember all the stimulus forms exactly. They were *not* told, however, that several of the stimulus forms were merely similar to those originally seen.

Gibson thus could use the percentage of appropriate word responses among her subjects as evidence of *how nearly equivalent* any form in classes II, III, or IV was to its counterpart in class I, i.e., how probable

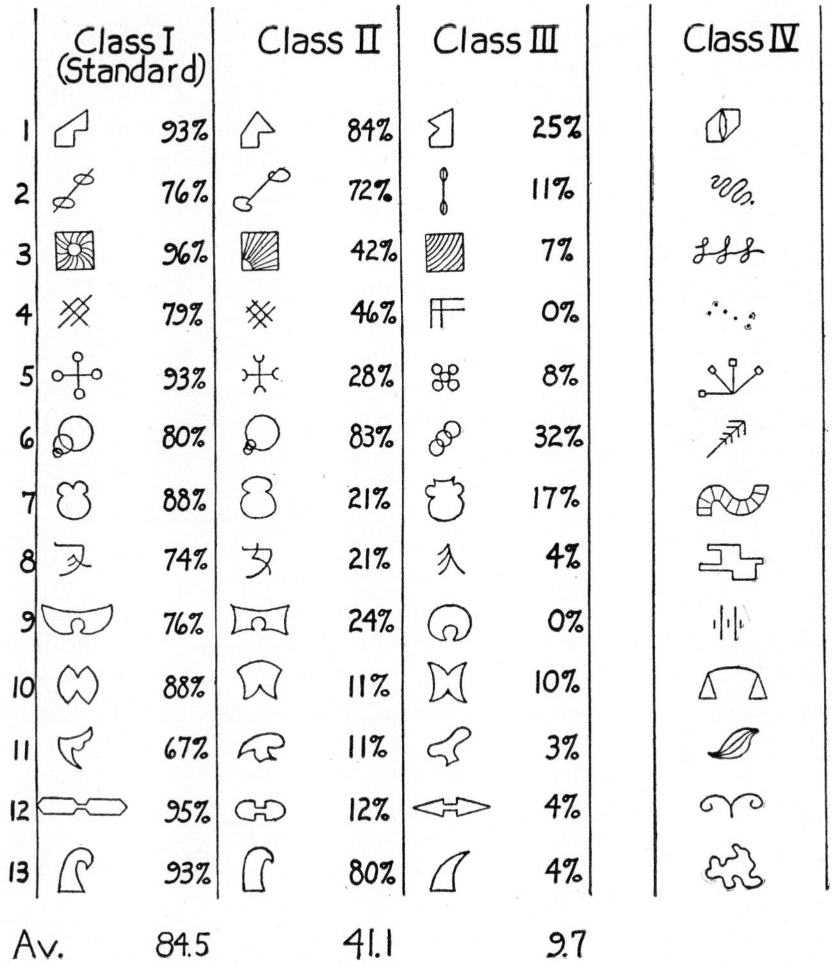

	Class I (Standard)	Class II	Class III	Class IV
1	93%	84%	25%	
2	76%	72%	11%	
3	96%	42%	7%	
4	79%	46%	0%	
5	93%	28%	8%	
6	80%	83%	32%	
7	88%	21%	17%	
8	74%	21%	4%	
9	76%	24%	0%	
10	88%	11%	10%	
11	67%	11%	3%	
12	95%	12%	4%	
13	93%	80%	4%	
Av.	84.5	41.1	9.7	

Fig. 6. The stimulus forms of the four classes, together with percentages of correct responses to each form, and the average percentage correct. (After Fig. 3 of Gibson [22].)

it was that the new stimulus would evoke the same response as the old. Furthermore, the total percentage of appropriate responses, for all forms in each class, was a quantitative indication of the *general* degree of similarity of each list to list I. The percentage of correct responses to forms of class I (standard) was 84.5 on the "retention" test; the percentage for class II, 41.1; for class III, 9.7; and for class IV, zero. These values indicate, then, the relative similarity of each of three lists to a standard list. All this procedure was preliminary to the retroactive-inhibition experiment proper.

In the main experiment the dependent variable was the proportion of correct responses on a final recall trial. This final trial was preceded by the original learning of the standard list of forms paired with *nonsense syllables* and then by interpolated learning. The original and interpolated lists were each given 5 exposure trials which were in every instance followed by test trials as in the preliminary study.

During the interpolated learning period the standard list was used for additional trials by one group of subjects; lists II, III, and IV were used with other groups; and no learning, i.e., rest, was interpolated for a control group. In all but the control group, then, the subject first learned a certain set of syllable responses to the standard list of forms. He then followed the same procedure with a second list of forms, *either identical with or possessing some known degree of similarity to* the original list; paired with the stimulus forms of this second list were *new* syllables. Finally, the subject tried to recall the responses of the original list, when shown only the standard forms. All subjects were college students; in size, the groups ranged from 22 to 39.

The conditions of the retroactive inhibition experiment, as thus far described, indicate the control of several variables. (1) Level of mastery of the original list was not identical for every subject in this experiment, but the *average* test-trial score at the end of original learning was almost exactly 8.0 (out of a possible 13) for every group. (2) It was desirable to rule out variations in the difficulty or familiarity of the response terms, which Gibson did by using nonsense syllables. Also, the responses acquired during the original learning were identical, i.e., of equal familiarity, for all subjects, and the same was true for interpolated learning.

(3) The rate of exposure of the paired-associate lists, the timing on retention-test trials, and the timing of rests were all handled according to a prearranged and exact schedule, so that no group (or condition) had any special advantage. (4) The order in which the pairs was presented was varied from trial to trial to rule out anticipation learning. (5) Once the original learning began, there was little or no opportunity to do any rehearsing. In the control group, which rated cartoons during its rest period, there is at least a possibility that review went on, but probably no subject rehearsed intentionally or systematically.

We must now consider the control group. They merely learned the standard list under the usual conditions, then had no special intervening learning (the time was spent selecting worst and best cartoons from the *New Yorker* magazine), then recalled in the usual way. (6) Any unknown factors correlated with the passage of time in the experimental conditions can be assumed to operate in the same way in this control group. Their recall scores can be called "normal" scores, which are free only of the effects of intervening learning. In the experimental group the retention scores after interpolated learning can be compared to these "normal" scores in the control group by the formula:

$$\text{Per cent } RI = \frac{C - E}{C},$$

where RI is retroactive inhibition, C is the mean recall score of the control group, and E is the mean recall score of the experimental group. We thereby secure a measure of retroactive inhibition in the experimental conditions which is comparable from one condition to the other and which represents the effects of interpolated learning only.

The results of this experiment, as shown in Fig. 7, are quite consistent, but to understand them we must appreciate an important point about the experiment. The subjects of group I learned two different responses to each stimulus form of the standard list. The subjects of, say, group III learned one set of responses to the standard list and a different set of responses to an interpolated list in which the stimulus forms were only slightly similar to those of the original list. The amount of confusion existing at the time of recall (and therefore the number of failures to produce the right response) should be greater in group I. This point underlies the relationship shown in Fig. 7: the greater the similarity of the two sets of stimulus forms, the greater the amount of retroactive inhibition.

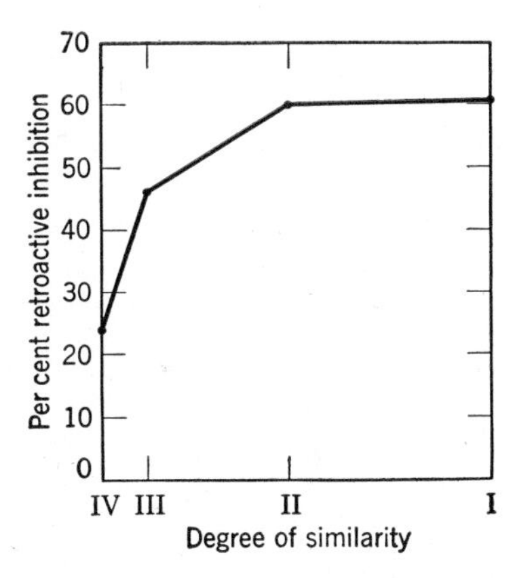

Fig. 7. The relation between degree of similarity between stimulus forms of original and interpolated lists and percentage of retroactive inhibition. (After Fig. 5 of Gibson [2]; abscissa originally labelled "degree of generalization.")

Summary

As was mentioned earlier in this chapter, the design of a retention experiment is inherently more complex than that of a learning experiment; there is simply more possibility for irrelevant factors to operate in the time intervals (or activities) and retention tests which typically follow the original learning. The review in which we have just engaged shows that it is possible, and necessary, to control all these additional variables. Apart from the usual intangible of motivation, the only factor not submitting satisfactorily to control by a careful experimenter is rehearsal in that type of study where non-laboratory intervals are required. It may well be emphasized that, in any study analyzing the effects of factors in retention period or retention test, the original learning *must* be carried either to the same level for all subjects (by use of a criterion) or to the same average level for all groups or conditions (checked after the data have been collected, if necessary).

METHODS OF STUDYING TRANSFER

A Variable in the Task: Interlist Similarity

Gibson's experiment, which has been treated as a study of a factor in retention, also serves as an introduction to the study of transfer. First, and most obviously, the difference between the recall scores of the control group and any experimental group is to be attributed to the interpolated learning. The result is a handicap, i.e., negative transfer.

A second, and as yet unmentioned, illustration of transfer is afforded by Gibson's study; it is found in the learning of the interpolated list. This too is an activity preceded by a learning task. Assuming that the subjects of each experimental group, on the average, were equal in ability, one might possibly expect their learning of the interpolated list to be equal in average rate. Gibson's data show, however, that the similarity of interpolated stimulus forms to the standard (first) list affected the rate at which the second list was learned. More specifically, when the stimulus forms of the interpolated list were identical with those of the original list, we should expect the "old" responses to bob up and hamper the interpolated learning (negative transfer). When the stimulus forms of the interpolated list were not so similar to those of the original list, the transfer of "old" responses was less probable and the learning should have been easier. Evidence that transfer occurred in this manner, i.e., that it was dependent upon the similarity factor, was secured by Gibson: after 5 trials with interpolated stimulus forms identical with the standard list, the average score was 7.7; for interpolated list II, this average was 9.7; for lists III and IV (little and no similarity) the values were 10.0 and 9.8 respectively.

It should be evident that a study of transfer does not literally demand a different method than that employed for retention experiments in general, except that emphasis is placed on the point that the first of any two successive activities must be a learning task. Only then does it make sense to analyze the second activity, whether it be a retention test or further learning, to see what carry-over from the first task there has been.

A Variable in the Conditions of Practice: Amount of Prior Practice

We have had occasion to point out several times that experience with an experimental task may introduce an irrelevant variable, general practice effects. These are in the category of series or order variables; the implication is that positive transfer occurs from one condition of an experiment to another. Although it is true that from an experimental point of view such transfer is often undesirable, outside this setting positive transfer is normally to be desired. After all, as we have indicated, it is the general basis of wisdom or sophistication. The experiment which we now analyze is an example of procedures for investigating these general practice effects, and although the original author was not directly interested in this topic, the design obviously could serve as a framework for many other types of studies.

In one part of a study employing paired-associate learning (see the foregoing account of Gibson's study), Underwood [7] investigated the relation between the ease or difficulty with which a standard list is learned and the number of lists previously learned. Each list contained 10 pairs of two-syllable adjectives, the first or stimulus member of a pair always being the same throughout the several lists learned by a given subject, and the second or response member varying from one list to another. Practice with the last (the standard) list was carried to the point where the subject could make 6 out of 10 responses correctly.

The dependent variable in Underwood's experiment was the total number of trials necessary to reach the criterion of 6 correct. The independent variable was established by using a control group which had zero prior learning (no lists before the standard list), and three experimental groups required to learn 2, 4, or 6 prior lists. If the stimulus and response terms for one pair in the standard list are designated A-B, the corresponding terms in one of the conditions (4 prior lists) would be A-F, A-E, A-D, A-C, A-B. The control group, of course, learned only the list containing the A-B pair. Twenty-four subjects each served in all 4 conditions.

The variables controlled by Underwood and the ways in which they were controlled need only be listed, since his procedures were so nearly those which the student will now recognize as standard in the verbal learning field. (1) Preliminary practice periods, two in number, familiarized the subjects with the learning technique and materials.

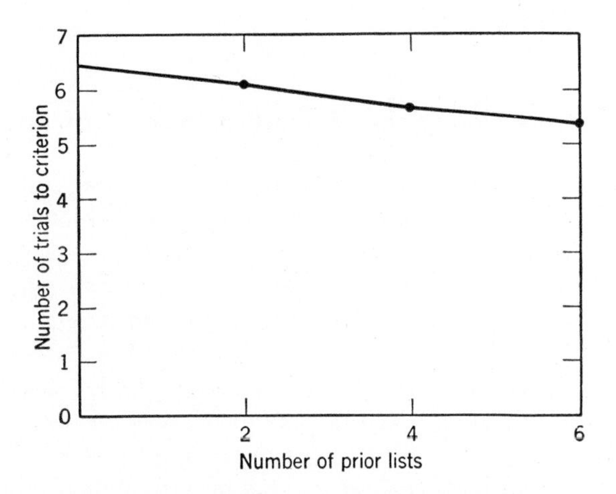

Fig. 8. The relation between number of prior lists and number of trials to learn to a criterion of 6 correct on the standard list. (After Table 13 of Underwood [7].)

(2) Order effects *within* any list were reduced by presenting the paired associates in several different orders, while (3) order effects due to the repeated use of the same subjects were equalized by counterbalancing the order of conditions from one subject to another. (4) Differences among lists were equalized by using each set of lists equally often in all conditions. (5) Individual differences in learning ability were held constant by using the same subjects in all conditions. (6) Level of mastery of each prior list was held approximately constant, on the average, by using a fixed number of presentations, four, for each such list. (7) Rate of exposure was automatically controlled by the use of a memory drum. Such factors as (8) time of day and (9) motivation are not mentioned by Underwood, but the subjects were all volunteers from psychology classes. Presumably they would have been coopera-

tive and would have served at approximately the same time each day.

The results of this study are shown in Fig. 8. They are not quite what might have been expected, for with an increase in the number of prior lists, there is a very slight but gradual reduction in the difficulty of learning the standard list. The way in which the lists were constructed (A-C, A-B, etc.) would, on the basis of Gibson's experiment, lead us to expect negative transfer, or handicap in the learning of the standard list. In Underwood's study, however, the increasing number of lists in the prior learning gave progressively more practice at associating different lists of responses with a stimulus list, and this was the basis of positive transfer to the learning of the standard list. It was a general practice effect *within* an experimental condition. (Literally, for Underwood, this general practice effect was an irrelevant but not fully controlled variable.)

Considered as a design for the study of transfer, Underwood's experiment very nearly avoids one perplexing problem: how to match control and experimental groups for ability before they learn the prior or standard materials of the experiment. In this experiment the same subjects were used in all conditions, so this factor was held constant. We turn now to a study in which this procedure was not feasible.

A Variable in the Learner: Set to Transfer

A study by Woodrow [8] concerns a point of wide interest. For several years before his work, an emphasis had been placed on how little positive transfer there is from one learning situation to another. Woodrow simply shifted the emphasis and asked, Is it possible to train subjects so that the *techniques* of memorizing acquired during the training period *will* be used to advantage on later occasions?

The general plan of the study was as follows. Three groups of subjects were given initial tests of memorizing ability. These were measures of the time necessary to memorize certain materials, or the number of items remembered after a certain study period. A control group (106 college students) had no further laboratory experience until the final (and different) tests were given. One experimental group ($N = 34$) had a total of about 3 hours of *practice* at memorizing with no special training—they were simply told to "learn by heart." Another group ($N = 42$) had special *training*. They too spent about 3 hours, but nearly half of this time was spent in learning seven simple rules and how or when to use them. (A sample rule: use rhythm and grouping to facilitate memorizing; another: learn by wholes, rather than by parts.) Such practice time as they had was spent in consciously applying this knowledge of technique. Both experimental groups had final tests comparable with those of the control group.

The experiment was made somewhat more comprehensive by employing six different types of memory material in the initial and final tests: poetry, prose passages, miscellaneous factual items, Turkish-English vocabulary equivalents, and little-known historical dates. (The last two are, in effect, paired-associate learning.) During the period between the initial and final tests the practice and training groups dealt only with nonsense-syllable paired associates and with poetry. Both groups were told that the practice they had with these materials would be valuable later. Except in the case of poetry, they did not actually have any direct practice with materials like those of the final test.

The dependent variable in this experiment is obviously the score on any given final test material. The major independent variables are really two in number. One, a qualitative variable, is the kind of treatment during the intertest period. For the *training* group and the *practice* group, a secondary variable is the use, on the final test, of materials like those on which the practice had been given (poetry), or materials on which there had been no direct practice.

In analyzing this design we see that first of all, as between the practice and training groups, (1) the amount of practice time was held constant. (2) The over-all length of time between initial and final tests was held constant for all groups. (3) The initial and final tests were the same for all three groups, i.e., their difficulty did not vary from group to group. Most important, for illustrative purposes here, an initial test was used, and on the basis of it we can determine whether (4) ability, on the average, was equal in the three groups. By use of the control group we are able to ascertain whether any changes in test performance occurred which are attributable (5) to factors not already mentioned. For example, were the initial and final tests of equal difficulty? Were there any obvious practice effects from merely taking two tests?

The last-named points must be considered first in the results (see Table I). Comparisons of the initial and final test averages for the control group show that the second poetry test was the more difficult, as was the second list of facts. In two of the three remaining comparisons for the control group, the second test average was better than the first, a finding which could be attributed to either practice effects or the materials themselves. In each case we can reasonably assume that the direction of change in the control group is to be expected in each experimental group, and results for the experimental

TABLE I

Differences Between Initial and Final Memory Test*

Test	Group	Initial Average Score	Final Average Score	Per Cent Change	Net Per Cent Advantage
Poetry	Control	524 secs.	696 secs.	−32.8	
	Practice	571 "	737 "	−29.1	+3.7
	Training	539 "	596 "	−10.6	+22.2
Prose	Control	637 "	454 "	+28.7	
	Practice	654 "	487 "	+25.5	−3.2
	Training	731 "	361 "	+50.7	+22.0
Facts	Control	67.5 cor.	64.2 cor.	−4.9	
	Practice	64.0 "	61.0 "	−4.7	+.2
	Training	64.0 "	72.2 "	+12.8	+17.7
Dates	Control	7.6 "	9.8 "	+29.0	
	Practice	7.2 "	9.9 "	+37.5	+8.5
	Training	6.5 "	12.2 "	+87.7	+58.7
Vocabulary	Control	16.2 "	16.1 "	−.6	
	Practice	14.6 "	15.1 "	+3.4	+4.0
	Training	13.6 "	21.1 "	+55.2	+55.8

* After Table III of Woodrow [8].

groups "adjusted" accordingly to indicate the net per cent advantage gained by the practice program, as distinct from other changes which occurred. This type of computation can be thought of as "control" by statistical means, rather than experimental (see the formula for computing per cent of retroactive inhibition, p. 87).

As indicated by comparisons on the first test, the three groups were approximately equal. The only very large differences were ones indicating that the control group learned the poetry and the prose more quickly than the experimental groups, which at least implied no initial advantage on the part of the latter groups. In the remaining tests the groups were quite well equated, so that comparisons on the final test are defensible, i.e., ability may vary slightly, but in a known way, so that allowances can be made for it.

The last column of Table I gives the clearest summary of the results of the experiment: simple practice, with no special aid or set, produces little or no transfer to the final memory test, whereas knowledge of memory techniques and the intent to use them where possible, as acquired by the training group, definitely transfer to the final test. The major independent variable, then, is a significant one.

The secondary independent variable—whether the final test material is like that used in the training or practice period—is also clearly significant in the training group. Poetry was used in their training period, and on the final test, prose, most nearly like it among the materials used, was memorized with as great an advantage from training as was the final selection of poetry. This appears to be positive transfer to similar material on which there had been no direct practice. Furthermore, while the training period included practice with nonsense-syllable paired associates only, the date and vocabulary lists profited greatly on the final test. They too were, basically, paired-associate material, and although they had been given no direct practice, they showed significant positive transfer.

SUMMARY

1. Learning and forgetting are concurrent changes in behavior and are distinguished in terms of the direction of change (acquisition versus weakening of response tendencies). Transfer can be involved in either type of change and can therefore have a positive or negative effect.

2. In the basic experimental designs for the study of verbal learning, retention, and transfer, it is possible to discern five main groups of variables: three in the learning period proper (learner, task, practice-condition variables), those in the retention interval, and those in the retention-measurement procedures. The key to successful experimental work lies in identifying the relevant variables, isolating one major independent variable, and controlling all irrelevant variables.

3. Experiments may be designed either to ascertain merely whether the presence or absence of the major independent variable is significant or to determine more completely the relation between this variable and the dependent one.

4. In studies of learning, retention, and transfer, we typically must control the effects of individual differences in ability, motivation, non-experimental practice, series or order variables, and test-practice effects.

5. For the purposes of a given experiment, certain variables are known or thought to be insignificant, and they are disregarded. Other specific factors are known or thought to be significant, and each separate experiment must be designed to take account of these factors in a planned way. A few variables cannot be controlled literally, and one can only check on them after the data have been collected (e.g., ability differences, in some studies).

6. Control in a retention experiment, and possibly in a transfer experiment, is inherently more complex than in a learning experiment by virtue of the additional possibilities for operation of relevant variables.

REFERENCES

1. COURTS, F. A. Relations between experimentally induced muscular tension and memorization. *J. Exper. Psychol.*, 1939, *25*, 235–256.
2. GIBSON, ELEANOR J. Retroactive inhibition as a function of degree of generalization between tasks. *J. Exper. Psychol.*, 1941, *28*, 93–115.
3. HOVLAND, C. I. Experimental studies in rote-learning theory. I. Reminiscence following learning by massed and by distributed practice. *J. Exper. Psychol.*, 1938, *22*, 201–224.
4. KRUEGER, W. C. F. The effect of overlearning on retention. *J. Exper. Psychol.*, 1929, *12*, 71–78.
5. LUH, C. W. The conditions of retention. *Psychol. Monog.*, 1922, *31*, No. 3.
6. LYON, D. O. The relation of length of material to time taken for learning, Part II. *J. Educ. Psychol.*, 1914, *5*, 85–91.
7. UNDERWOOD, B. J. The effect of successive interpolations on retroactive and proactive inhibition. *Psychol. Monog.*, 1945, *59*, No. 3.
8. WOODROW, H. The effect of type of training upon transference. *J. Educ. Psychol.*, 1927, *18*, 159–172.

SUGGESTED READINGS

GARRETT, HENRY E. *Great Experiments in Psychology*. New York: Appleton-Century, Rev. Ed., 1941. (Chap. 7, Thorndike's experiments on problem-solving by animals and his "laws" of learning; Chap. 9, Thorndike's and Woodworth's experiments on the transfer of training and their influence upon the doctrine of formal discipline; Chap. 10, Ebbinghaus' studies in memory and forgetting.)

GUTHRIE, EDWIN R. *The Psychology of Learning*. New York: Harper, 1935. (Chap. XII, Skill.)

McGEOCH, JOHN A. *The Psychology of Human Learning*. New York: Longmans, Green, 1942. (Chap. I, Concepts and methods; Chap. II, Curves of learning; pp. 394–405 in Chap. X, Transfer of training.)

THORNDIKE, E. L. *Human Learning*. New York: Century, 1931. (Lecture 9, Ideational learning.)

VALENTINE, WILLARD L. *Experimental Foundations of General Psychology*. New York: Farrar and Rinehart, Rev. Ed., 1941. (Chap. XVII, Learning; Chap. XVIII, Remembering.)

YOUNG, PAUL THOMAS. *Motivation of Behavior*. New York: John Wiley, 1936. (pp. 190–205 and pp. 216–227 in Chap. V, Direction and regulation.)

Chapter 4

Studying Human Thinking

Edna Heidbreder[1]

In most psychological experiments on thinking, the methods employed are adaptations of procedures first used in studying other psychological activities. By introducing complexities and subtleties into modes of investigating animal behavior, by concealing relational patterns in materials presented as in standard experiments on memory, by complicating the classical reaction-time experiment, especially in the already altered form of the association-time experiment—by these and similar devices, psychologists have arranged situations calculated to make their subjects think, and to make their thought amenable to experimental treatment.

This practice implies that thinking may enter into many different kinds of performances and that, through these, it may be made accessible to systematic inquiry. It also implies that thinking enters into a performance when the situation with which an organism is confronted does not merely *elicit* the appropriate response but rather requires the organism to *produce* this response through its own activity—to select it or construct it, to discover it or invent it. Hence arise the subtleties, obscurities, and complexities in the situations presented. Whether a response is elicited from or produced by an organism, however, is not determined by the external situations alone; it is also determined, and importantly determined, by the organism itself. When an adequate stimulus elicits the pupillary reflex, it does so chiefly because the responding organism has the appropriate physiological equipment. Similarly, when a request to recite the alphabet elicits the requested performance, it does so largely because the person who complies has learned to recite the alphabet. Even a performance like solving an algebraic equation may be largely elicited, since the written symbols call out, in a person suitably trained, the interpretations and operations that constitute the adequate response. Clearly a performance

1 Professor of Psychology, Wellesley College.

may be more or less elicited, more or less produced, and the kind of performance which in one person is chiefly elicited may in another be chiefly produced.

The word "problem" may be used to designate a situation which, for a given person, does not merely elicit the appropriate response but rather requires him somehow to produce it through his own activities. Thinking may then be defined as that activity, whatever its nature, by which a person solves a problem, an activity which may be more or less thoughtful as the situation is more or less problematic, and which, like other psychological activities, may be more or less adequate, more or less successful. An experiment on thinking, therefore, involves two major requirements: (1) a problem to be presented, and (2) a method of determining how the subject produces, or fails to produce, the adequate response. It is important to notice that thinking, so defined, and the experimental requirements, so stated, are based on the assumption that thinking, as a psychological activity, is some kind of adjustive activity of a living organism, an activity which may find expression in different kinds of overt performances. Aside from this assumption, however, the specific nature of thinking is an open question. In effect, the definition locates situations where thinking may be found; the business of precisely determining its nature and conditions is left to experimental investigation itself.

ATTEMPTS AT DIRECT INSPECTION

The first attempts to study thinking experimentally were nothing if not direct. Thinking was conceived as a conscious process directly observable by the thinker, and experiments were conducted by the apparently obvious method of confronting subjects with tasks that aroused thought and treating their reported introspections as basic data. The tasks varied widely in the different investigations. They ranged from simple problems, like judging the heavier of two objects apparently exactly alike, to answering recondite questions like, "Can our thought apprehend the nature of thought?" [25].

The results were difficult to interpret and highly controversial, and since agreement could not be secured on what were offered as introspectively observed facts, the whole question of introspection as a method was brought prominently to the fore. The ensuing controversy raised important theoretical issues. These, however, need not be examined at present, since, as a matter of historical fact, the value of introspection as a means of scientific inquiry was determined not primarily by a logical weighing of pros and cons, but by actually trying to use introspection and so discovering its possibilities and limitations. On the whole, the trend has been toward placing less and less reliance on introspection as a method. Many investigators have assigned it a limited role, supplementary rather than central, and some have rejected it altogether as a means of studying thinking and, indeed, of studying psychological processes in general.

ADAPTATIONS OF REACTION-TIME AND ASSOCIATION-TIME EXPERIMENTS

Analysis of Controlled Association

The practical limitations of introspection were most convincingly revealed by some of the introspective studies themselves, especially by those that adhered most closely to the pattern of the classical reaction-time experiment. One of these is Watt's study of controlled association [30], a set of investigations in which objective data on associative reactions were combined with introspective reports on the subjects' consciousness during reaction. The experimental procedure was to assign a task, e.g., naming the whole of which the stimulus word named a part, and then to present visually, one by one, a short series of stimulus words, recording each response, measuring each reaction time by a chronoscope attached to a voice key, and obtaining an introspective report on each reaction. Each subject was used in several series of reactions, the assigned tasks varying from series to series.

One of the most interesting contributions of the introspective reports was that the main period of the reaction—that between the presentation of the stimulus word and the subject's overt response—was often described as relatively bare, and sometimes as entirely bare, of conscious content. This finding, furthermore, was a single instance of what seemed to be the general rule that conscious awareness did *not* keep step, moment by moment, with what the subject was doing. Sometimes, to take a striking case, the clear perception of the stimulus itself rose to maximal awareness only in the afterperiod, the brief period following the overt response. Most significant, however, were the reports on the foreperiod, for here, in the interval between the ready signal and the stimulus word, the subject must somehow have established the set or adjustment which enabled him, often without conscious selection or direction during the main period, to produce the correct response. Introspective evidence for sets and adjustments took a variety of forms; among the reported conscious contents were visual, verbal, and gestural schemata representing the task, and felt muscular tensions and readinesses to react. Even these, however, tended gradually to disappear as the subject became habituated to his task, and at the end of the series the subject was often responding correctly without conscious awareness of the task even in the foreperiod.

Such results give empirical grounds for a radical criticism of introspection as a means adequate in itself to the investigation of thought; for, if crucial functions of thought are effected without consciousness—functions as important as the direction of its course and the selection of relevant reactions—effective determinants must be assumed which are inaccessible to introspection and which must be known, if they are known at all, by some method other than direct observation.

Further Analysis of Controlled Association

An important advance toward meeting this situation is illustrated by the work of May [13], who repeated and modified Watt's experiments, introducing refinements in method, using more subjects, more reactions, and more varied conditions, and placing far more emphasis on objective data. May's inquiry concerned the relation between the foreperiod and the main period. His hypothesis was that the preparatory set is the determining factor in controlled association, and his central problem was to investigate the preparatory set, determining its nature and the kind and amount of its influence on the ensuing associative reaction.

Methodologically one of the interesting features of May's experiment was his practice of systematically analysing introspections and of checking them against objective data when these were available. One very general check was provided by the mere fact that introspections were classifiable—that different subjects, working independently, reported occurrences of the same kinds. A further check consisted in the fact that certain classes of conscious events were reported with consistently greater frequency in some conditions than in others: in the foreperiod, for example, or in the main period, in the early stages of the experiment or after the subject had acquired considerable practice. It was possible, too, through statistical treatment, to establish regularities between reported events in the main period and those in the corresponding afterperiod; for example, reports of absence of conscious content in the main period were most likely to occur when the foreperiod itself was described as automatic or nearly automatic. The most objective check consisted in the correspondence between measured reaction time and the amount of conscious content reported; for foreperiod and main period alike, average times were longer when conscious content was reported than when the subjects found no experience to report. Although the differences in time were not statistically significant, they were consistently in the direction mentioned.

In other words, the experimenter used all possible means of checking reported introspections as *testimony,* evaluated as such, a procedure that involved applying a new standard of scientific acceptability to accounts of introspectively observed experience. In the classical studies characteristic of the first psychological laboratories, trained introspectionists directed their observations upon selected aspects of experience, usually sensory. In those studies introspection was safeguarded, assuming the competence of the observer, chiefly by experimentally controlling the stimulus, i.e., by manipulating it in such a way as to arouse and focus observations upon just the conscious content to be described. The reported observations could then be compared with the experimentally introduced variations in the stimulus. The course of thought, however, cannot be controlled by controlling the stimulus. Therefore, in describing thought, even in short-range reactions like those of May's study, the subject's task is to tell what happens—to report on a course of changing events—not to describe selected aspects of conscious experiences in some sense imposed by the presented stimulus and presumably directly correlated with it. May's standard of scientific validity for such reports was the improbability of obtaining by chance the relationships actually discovered among the reported introspections, and between these and such objective facts as length of reaction time and variations deliberately introduced into the experimental conditions. He treated the data from introspection, not as records of experimentally directed observations on experimentally controlled conscious contents, but essentially as *testimony* to be checked and rechecked as such.

The chief advance in May's method, however, has not yet been mentioned. It consisted in pushing inquiry beyond the limits of the directly observable empirical events. May's hypothesis was that, other things being equal, the more completely the subject was set, the more fully the response was determined, and hence the more automatic and prompt the correct verbal response. On the assumption that a complete set required a certain optimal time, and that the preparation was proportionally less complete as less time was allowed for the set, the relation between the foreperiod and the main period, i.e., between "set time" and "association time," ought to be such that the length of the one period varies inversely with that of the other.

It is especially interesting, from the standpoint of method, that at the time the hypothesis was formulated it was *not* borne out by a statistical analysis of the data then at hand. The variables proved too complexly interrelated to be isolated and ordered by statistical procedures; hence they were incapable of proving or disproving the hypothesis. The experimenter therefore simply set up the hypothesis as worthy of investigation. Guided partly by the introspective reports, but working chiefly from quantitative data, he constructed a rough scale, on which were indicated foreperiods selected as representing four significant lengths: 0.00, 0.15, 0.35, and 0.50 second. He then secured series of reactions corresponding to foreperiods of each of these lengths and found a perfect inverse relationship between length of foreperiod and length of main period. The author strongly emphasized the point that these results were insufficient to constitute proof of his hypothesis, but that they were offered to show that, as far as the data went, they were in agreement with the hypothesis as stated. From the standpoint of method the procedure is important as an illustration of a mode of investigation in which, through construction and inference, knowledge is extended beyond the limits set by direct observation. Specifically the procedure is that of setting up a hypothesis and checking theoretical expectations against factual data.

Introduction of Complex Tasks in Studying Set

The general pattern of the association experiment has proved so adaptable and so widely useful that it is impossible, within a single chapter, to give more than a hint of the part it has actually played in the investigation of thinking. One line of development is marked by the introduction of complex tasks which require the subjects to adopt sets within sets. Jersild [7], for example, studied the compound sets which enable a subject, without breaking his pace, to shift back and forth, within a single series of reactions, between two tasks like subtracting three from each presented number and giving the opposite of each presented adjective. He also demonstrated the effectiveness of the more comprehensive but not more difficult sets which enable a subject, again without breaking his pace, to shift back and forth among four tasks: naming colors, naming forms, naming opposites, and subtracting three.

The Free-association Method

Association experiments have also demonstrated the effective operation of sets so far from the subject's conscious awareness that the term "free association" has been applied to the processes under investigation. The well-known study of Kent and Rosanoff will serve as an illustration [8]. The basic plan of this investigation was to select 100 very familiar stimulus words and to instruct each subject, tested individually, to respond with the first word, other than the stimulus word, that occurred to him. On the basis of the tabulated replies of 1000 normal individuals, it was discovered that the number of different responses to each stimulus word was relatively small, that 1000 people did not respond to a given word with 1000 different replies, but with a relatively small number of common responses, which varied among themselves in degree of commonness, i.e., in frequency within the group. It was further discovered that the failure to give a significantly large number of common responses—a fact subject to quantitative measurement by reference to the tabulated frequencies—was characteristic of people who, according to the usual outside criteria, had failed in making normal psychological adjustments, who presumably had not built up the habitual modes of response which characterize the associative habits of most normal human beings in a given culture. In this way the association technique became a means of demonstrating and even measuring the operation of factors as diffuse, subtle, and obscure as the habitual sets which people acquire casually and incidentally in the course of their adjustments to an environment. It is possible that a person's performance on such a test reflects in some measure his unconscious adjustment to his culture, since the reactions aroused are his immediate "uncontrolled" responses to so important a part of the culture as the most common words in its language.

Such tests themselves have become instruments of research. For example, Woodrow and Lowell [33] employed the free-association technique in studying a group of children. Using 100 stimulus words, 90 of which were taken from the Kent-Rosanoff list, they obtained responses from fourth- and fifth-grade school children, thus securing for children ranging in age from 9 to 12 years inclusive, data comparable to those obtained by Kent and Rosanoff, whose subjects, with a few exceptions, were adults. They found, for example, that there were common responses for children as well as for adults, but that the most common responses for children often differed from the most common responses for adults. They also found that certain types of association, such as giving the opposite of a stimulus word, or one expressing a contrast, were less frequent among children than among adults. In the opinion of the experimenters the method proved the most useful brief device available for studying the mental constitution of children.

ADAPTATIONS OF EXPERIMENTS ON ANIMAL LEARNING AND PROBLEM SOLVING

Association experiments derive very directly from research practiced in the first psychological laboratories. A very different kind of research received its impetus from another quarter. The Darwinian point of view, with its emphasis on comparisons among species, inevitably led to inquiries concerning the mental abilities of animals. From the very nature of the problem introspection could not be used. Instead, an animal was judged to be "intelligent," or to possess a specified ability, e.g., the ability to react to relations, if it could perform tasks or tricks presumably requiring the ability in question. The general direction of the inquiry into animal ability was set by Lloyd Morgan's cautiously interpreted observations of animal behavior under conditions especially arranged to demonstrate intelligence or the lack of it [14]. In Thorndike's hands researches on "animal intelligence" attained the status of laboratory experiments [24], and under the criticisms of Hobhouse [4] and Köhler [9] the methods were extended to include means of detecting in animals signs of insight and of reaction to relations. In all such researches observed overt motor *behavior* constituted the basic data.

Ruger's Exploratory Method of Studying Problem Solving

Obviously such methods of research have advantages when applied to human thinking, and they have, as a matter of fact, been widely used in that field. One such study, conducted by Ruger [20], was, from the standpoint of method, essentially an adaptation of methods used by Thorndike in some of his studies of animal learning. Ruger's subjects were human beings, most of them educated adults. Using mechanical puzzles as his experimental materials, the investigator confronted each subject with a succession of puzzles and secured as complete a record as possible of the reactions in the course of which the problem was mastered. Each subject was of course studied individually, and he worked on a single puzzle not only until he had "solved" it once, i.e., had taken it apart or put the parts together, but until, after repeatedly performing the task, he was executing the actual manual operations with maximal speed as indicated by failure to improve further.

One great advantage of the puzzles as materials was that the solutions were brought about by motor manipulations which were objectively observable throughout. For example, objective measures of time were easily obtained for each of the separate successive occasions, called trials, on which the subject "solved" the puzzle in the sense just indicated. These measures gave learning curves similar to those representing an animal's successive escape from a puzzle box. The experimenter also kept records of the subject's overt behavior from trial to trial, records which gave such information as the part of the puzzle first attacked, the part that seemed to give greatest difficulty, the appearance of a new mode of response, together with the circumstances of its appearance, and also signs of emotional attitudes, such as self-distrust or absorption in the task. Ruger did not limit his data, however, to those obtainable only from animals. He kept records of the subject's spontaneous verbal comments and, in addition, asked him at the end of each trial to report on what he had been doing. Sometimes, too, the subject was interrupted in the middle of a trial and asked to tell what he was thinking at the moment. The subjects' reports were not as a rule descriptions of conscious contents and therefore were not introspections in the technical sense of the term. They were chiefly comments on what the subject was trying to do—on the objects he was trying to manipulate, the course of action he was trying to follow. The references to visible objects and operations were highly useful since they enabled the experimenter to combine the subjects' reports and the objective data in a manner that not only made the whole course of events more intelligible, but also provided a check on the reports as testimony.

It was, in fact, by integrating data of various sorts—quantitative and qualitative, observations of behavior and reports of experience—that the experimenter made some of his most significant contributions. Perhaps the most striking was that "analysis"—something apparently equivalent, in Ruger's terminology, to what the Gestaltists call "insight"—often marked the crucial point in progress toward solution. Many of the learning curves showed, as a conspicuous characteristic, a sudden drop, sometimes preceded by a single unusually long trial, and regularly followed by a consistently rapid rate of performance. In about 80 per cent of the cases, these indications of sudden improvement were accompanied by reports indicating that at just that time the subject had seen or worked out the point of the puzzle, had discovered the essential feature, relation, or operation. Usually, too, the person's general behavior indicated that he had made a discovery. The data also indicated, however, that analysis was not an all-or-none affair; there were degrees of analysis, or cases of partial analysis, ranging from the mere location of the part of the puzzle where a successful reaction had occurred by chance, to the formulation of the general principle on which the puzzle was based.

It is important to notice, too, that these and similar contributions were made, not only by integrating data of several different kinds, but also by taking into account broad molar units both in motor performances and in reports of experience. Without dealing in such units, it would have been impossible to discover, for example, the significant fact that new and better ways of dealing with a puzzle often appeared as variations in motor reactions *before* the subject was aware of changing his procedure. It was also by referring to long stretches of activity from trial to trial that Ruger was able to discover the large amount of typically "animal" trial and error in the behavior of educated human adults, a point that impressed him as the chief outcome of the study. Similarly, it was by taking molar events into account that he was able to note the role of non-rational reactions largely emotional and attitudinal, e.g., reactions indicating confidence or embarrassment or an obstinate determination to work along a given line which had repeatedly proved a failure.

Ruger's work is distinctly exploratory. It serves the function of exploration, not only by providing results rich in factual content, but also—and this is a practice not always followed in exploratory research—by placing them in a quantitative framework in which significant relationships are revealed and significant possibilities suggested. Some of Ruger's results are determined with high probability, and others are merely suggested, but even the latter are presented in a context with reference to which questions for further inquiry can be stated with definiteness.

Experimental Analysis of Achievement in Problem Solving

Experimental research does not stop, however, with exploration. In its most characteristic form it poses a specific question and arranges and controls the conditions of the experiment in such a way that the procedure will bring out just the evidence, positive and negative, that bears on the question about which the experiment has been designed. Investigations of behavioral achievements like those used in studying animal behavior are in fact admirably suited to such inquiry.

One of Maier's investigations [11] will serve as an illustration. It is organized about the question of the role of *direction* in thinking. If a person has at his disposal all the units of reaction necessary for the solution of a problem and also the knowledge that these units are involved in the solution, is this equipment enough in itself to enable him to achieve the solution?

Maier's experiment was performed to test the hypothesis that this is *not* enough—that the solution of a problem involves not merely the selection of the appropriate responses, but also the appropriate general approach, which he calls *direction.* He assigned his subjects the task of erecting a structure consisting of two pendulums which would make chalk marks on the floor at points indicated. The subjects were presented with materials like those pictured in Fig. 1*A*—poles, lead

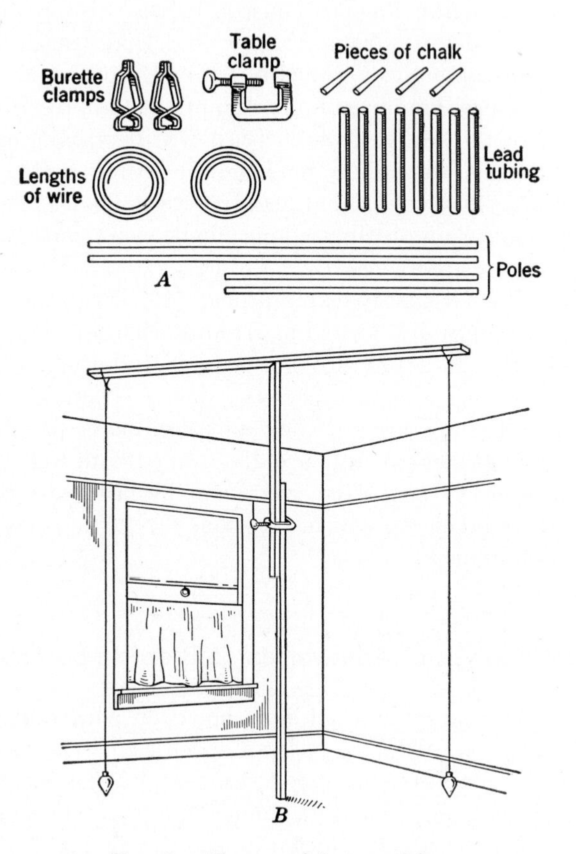

Fig. 1. The pendulum problem.

A. **The materials available to the subject.** ***B.*** **The correct solution. (Courtesy of McGraw-Hill Book Company.)**

T-clamps, pieces of chalk, and lengths of wire. The structure that constitutes the solution of the problem is pictured in Fig. 1*B*.

The essential feature of the experiment consisted in dividing the subjects into five groups approximately equal in tested ability, the subjects in each group being given a different *preparation* for attacking the problem. The subjects were all college students, and each one worked at the problem individually.

In Group A the subjects were instructed in all the part responses and were told that these included everything necessary to the solution of the problem. To each member of this group the experimenter demonstrated the operations of clamping two rods together to make a long rod, of making a plumb line by attaching a clamp or a pencil to a cord, and of making a firm T-structure—a horizontal T, however—by placing a rod against the vertical side of a doorway and then wedging, between its midpoint and the opposite side of the doorway, a horizontal rod of exactly the right length.

In Group B the experimenter gave all the demonstrations given in Group A and, in addition, made the following comment in order to provide the proper approach or *direction:* "I should like to have you appreciate how simple this problem would be if we could just hang the pendulum from a nail in the ceiling. Of course that is not a possible solution, but I just want you to appreciate how simple the problem would be if that were possible."

In Group C the subjects were presented with the same problem, but they received no preliminary demonstrations and no comments on direction.

In Group D the part responses were demonstrated to the subjects, but they were not told that these had anything to do with the problem.

In Group E the subjects were given the direction, but no demonstrations of the part responses.

The results of the experiment were clean-cut. Group B easily surpassed all other groups: of the 22 subjects in this group, 8 solved the problem, whereas it was solved by only 1 of the 62 subjects who made up the other groups. This outcome indicates that both part processes and direction were necessary to the solution of this problem: or, to emphasize the point relevant to the central question, that the appropriate part responses alone were not enough, but that appropriate direction also was required for its solution. It is important to notice that these results apply to direction as defined by the comments actually introduced into the experiment. The interpretation of the factor called direction, whether it consists of additional information or of a more inclusive part-response or of an organizing directive set, is a point that is not answered by the results of this experiment alone. It is, in fact, one of the great advantages of this kind of experimentation that the data and their interpretation are separable from each other—that questions of interpretation stand out as such, pointing to specific assumptions underlying the experimental design. In contrast with exploratory research, experiments like Maier's, which are specifically aimed at particular problems, provide for the more exact location of difficulties of interpretation, as well as the more exact determination of the factors under investigation.

EXPERIMENTS ON INDUCTIVE CONCEPTUAL THOUGHT

Bringing Conceptual Activities under Experimental Control

Thinking, however, does not always engage so directly with overt motor activity. Often the solution of a problem terminates, not in particular motor operations on particular concrete materials, but in abstractions and generalizations expressed by symbols. In an experiment by Hull [5] such thought has been made amenable to experimental control and quantitative measurement. Essentially Hull's method is a means of obtaining quantitative data on the occurrence, under controlled conditions, of verbal responses from which the subject's use of specified concepts can be inferred.

In Hull's experiments the subject's task was ostensibly one of memorizing; each subject was required to learn to name drawings, presented to him singly and successively in twelve consecutive series of twelve drawings each. However, the materials presented for memorization were so arranged that it was possible for the subject to discover, as he encountered series after series of drawings, that although in different series the same name was applied to many drawings, no two of which were exactly alike, all those drawings possessed a common component lacking in drawings not called by that name. (See Fig. 2.) When the subject, without being prompted, correctly named a drawing on its first appearance, he was considered to have responded to a characteristic common to two or more drawings, and in that sense to have used a concept.

The drawings were adaptations of Chinese characters. Some of them are reproduced in Fig. 2, which shows how a single radical, e.g., any of the "free" figures in the first column, may serve as a common component in several drawings which, by virtue of this component, form a class, but which differ among themselves because of the materials in which the radical is embedded. As used in the experiment, the drawings were arranged in an order that varied from series to series in respect to the embedded radicals.

In the first six series each of the twleve drawings contained a different radical. These Hull called the "evolution" series, since they served as the basis on which the subjects were enabled to "evolve" the appropriate concepts. The remaining six series were called the "test" series. In each of these, two or three characters containing the same radical were included, and two or three radicals were necessarily omitted. In the six test series as a whole, however, all the radicals were present with equal frequency. This arrangement in the test series was designed to keep the subjects from making correct responses, merely by a process of elimination, to drawings they could not otherwise have identified.

The subjects were university students, and the general procedure was that known as the method of paired associates in memory experiments. It is not necessary to describe this procedure here. It is sufficient to say that the drawings were presented in an apparatus which exposed them at a mechanically controlled rate, and that each

Fig. 2. Half of the radicals used in Hull's experiment, with their assigned nonsense names and some compounds containing each radical. (Courtesy of Henry Holt and Company.)

series was presented until the subject had responded to all the drawings with neither errors nor promptings on two successive presentations of the entire series. At the beginning of an experiment the subject was told to learn the names of the drawings, which were syllables adapted from Chinese words. Before the presentation of the second series the subject was told that the same names would again be used and that he might be able to guess the names of the drawings without being prompted. Throughout the six evolution series a record was kept of the correct guesses on the first exposure of each series and also of the number of promptings the subject received during the successive exposures of that series. The six test series were then presented in turn. Here the same procedure was used except that no promptings were given and each series was presented three times. The subject thus had three chances to react correctly to each character in each test series. At the end of the experiment the subject defined the concepts by drawing them. The procedure just described was called the standard procedure.

The special feature of the method is that it makes possible the closely organized, directed research which has been contrasted with exploratory investigation. It is possible, by introducing suitable variations and controls, to adapt the standard procedure to specific questions. Hull demonstrated the possibilities of the method by applying it to several questions, including this one: Does the subject arrive at a concept more quickly when the radical is presented outright, or when he encounters it on different occasions embedded in different materials from which he must extricate the common component for himself?

This question was put experimentally by arranging the evolution series so that six of the radicals were presented "free," i.e., without surrounding materials, and the other six embedded in complex characters as in the standard materials. For example, *oo* was represented in all the series by the radical so named in the first column of the illustration; *yer,* by drawings in which that radical was an embedded component. To control possible differences in the inherent difficulty of the materials, the ten subjects used in this experiment were divided into two sets of five each, and the materials were so arranged that the free radicals for one set were the embedded radicals for the other set.

The quantitative results revealed no advantage for either method. For example, the number of failures to respond correctly in the test series showed no significant differences for the two procedures. There were, however, marked differences in the ability to *define* the concepts by presenting their essentials in drawings. For all subjects the drawings for concepts evolved from "free" radicals were distinctly superior as definitions to those for concepts evolved according to the standard procedure—superior not only in the opinion of the experimenter, but according to four judges who independently rated the drawings on a scale representing degrees of excellence.

The problem was pursued by asking a closely related question: May not a combination of methods be more efficient than either one alone? This question was investigated experimentally by arranging the materials so that half the concepts were evolved according to the standard procedure, and the other half according to the following scheme: in the first, third, and fifth series the radicals were presented outright, whereas in the second, fourth, and sixth, they were embedded in accessory materials. Otherwise, the conditions were the same as in the preceding experiment. Ten new subjects performed the task. This set of conditions showed a decided advantage for the combination of methods. The test series, for example, gave a highly reliable difference in number of failures for the two different modes of presentation.

Several other problems were attacked in Hull's study, but those described are sufficient to show that the technique has both the precision and the flexibility necessary for putting specific questions experimentally. It is worth noting especially that the variables are subject both to manipulation and to control. The very excellence of the method as technique, however, calls attention not only to the importance of technique as such, but also, though indirectly, to the fact that technique alone does not produce significant research, that significant research is, at bottom, inquiry into significant problems. In Hull's study, however, the main purpose was precisely that of developing techniques, and the problems, being of secondary importance, were selected merely, or at least chiefly, as convenient means of trying out the techniques. Consequently, the results of the experiment are so many separate facts. For example, it was demonstrated with high reliability that, in the particular conditions of this experiment, a specified combination of methods of presenting the materials for conceptualization was distinctly advantageous. This finding, however, cannot be generalized beyond the limits of the experiment, since both the logical implications of the question and its relevance to existing bodies of knowledge remain unascertained. This point is one which Hull himself not only admits but insists upon with emphasis. It would indeed be grossly misleading not to state in this connection that Hull has devoted a large part of his intellectual career to demonstrating the central importance, in experimental research, of stating the problem for inquiry explicitly and precisely in its context of relevant theory and knowledge. For examples of Hull's approved methods of formulating problems for scientific inquiry, the student is referred to his book, *Principles of Behavior* [6].

Modifications of Hull's Method

The merits of Hull's method have made it something of a standard procedure for investigating conceptual thinking. It has been used with modifications by several investigators. Kuo [10] modified it chiefly by spreading the subject's activities over several days and by asking "detective" questions designed to reveal characteristics of the process at various stages. He, too, used Chinese characters, within which, during the course of memorizing, it was possible for the subject to discover radicals common to various sets of characters. The process was lengthened by permitting the subject only two trials per day on each set of materials, a device which enabled the experimenter to trace the course of events as it developed from day to day. Kuo found that progress was usually gradual, usually far from straightforward, but sometimes marked by sudden discoveries; and that although most of the subjects eventually arrived at the appropriate generalizations and abstractions, some succeeded only partially and with considerable assistance, and that others completely failed to make some of the appropriate generalizations. As Kuo described it, the manner in which his subjects dealt with symbolic materials was remarkably similar to that in which Ruger's subjects dealt with the concrete materials of mechanical puzzles. Like Ruger, Kuo emphasized the large amount of nonrational, trial-and-error behavior his subjects displayed.

Smoke [22] altered Hull's method chiefly by using a different kind of experimental material, discarding Chinese characters because he wished to work, not with "common components" perceptibly the same from instance to instance, but with over-all, non-pictorial, relational patterns. For example, one of the tasks was to discover that a *dax* is always a circle and two dots, one inside and the other outside the circle, regardless of such variations as the size and color of the circles and the particular location of the dots. With this material Smoke too found a large amount of trial-and-error behavior. He emphasized especially the subjects' tendency to disregard, or at least not to use, the negative instances introduced as possible aids to conceptualization.

The Classification Method

A method very different from Hull's, but one which, like his, has become a standard procedure, has been extensively used by Hanfmann and Kasanin [2]. This method, adapted from a procedure invented by Ach, is based on a problem of classification. The subject is presented with twenty-two blocks and is asked to divide them into four groups. The blocks are of five different colors, six different shapes, two heights (tall and flat), and two sizes (large and small) with respect to the area of the top or bottom surface. On the under side of each block, concealed from the subject, is written one of four nonsense syllables: *lag* on all blocks which are both tall and large; *mur* on those which are tall and small; *bik* on those which are flat and large; *cev* on those which are flat and small. The experimental materials are shown in Fig. 3.

It is a highly important feature of the method that the subject, in order to achieve the correct classification, must *construct* the appropriate concept. The blocks cannot be sorted into four groups on the basis of a single perceptual feature like color, form, size, height, or any other characteristic, e.g., volume, that can be named by a single word. Hence the task encourages departure from the concrete and "given" and encourages operation at the level of abstraction and con-

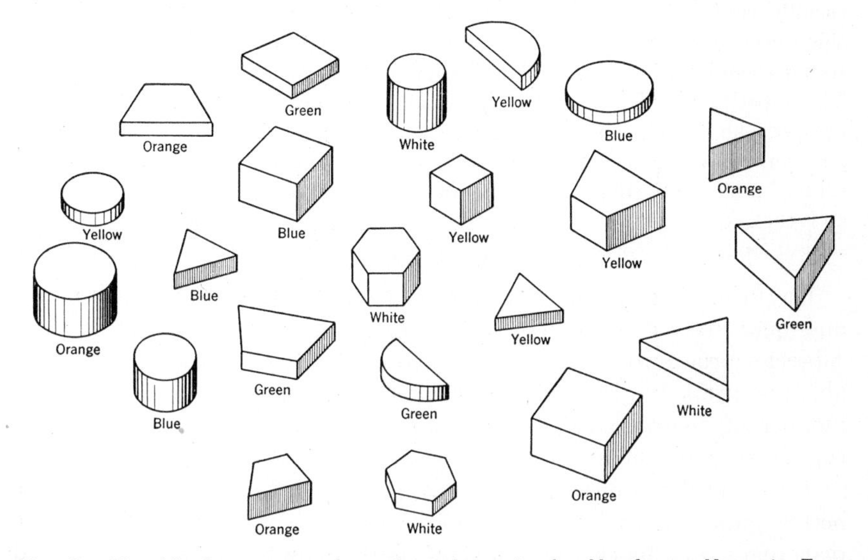

Fig. 3. The blocks presented to the subject in the Hanfmann-Kasanin Test. (From [2], by courtesy of the authors and the publishers.)

struction. It has been widely used as a test in clinical practice and also as a means of investigating Goldstein's theory [1] that concrete and abstract behavior represent two qualitatively different modes of procedure, two distinct levels of activity.

The experiment or test is begun by presenting the subject with a board on which the blocks are placed in random order, as in Fig. 3. The procedure has been described as follows:

> The subject is told that these are four different kinds of blocks, that each kind has a name and that his task is to find the four kinds and to put each of them into a separate corner. The examiner then turns up one of the blocks, shows its name to the subject, and, putting it into one of the corner spaces, suggests that the subject start by picking out and putting in the same corner all blocks which he thinks might belong to the same kind. After he has done so, selecting, for instance, all blocks of the same color or all blocks of the same shape as the sample, the experimenter turns up one of the wrongly selected blocks, showing that this is a block of a different kind, and encourages the

subject to continue trying. This he may do in any way he pleases, either by trying to match the first or the second sample, or by trying to organize the entire material simultaneously into four classes. After each new attempt one of the wrongly placed blocks is turned, and the process continues until the subject discovers the principle of the classification and organizes the blocks accordingly, or until the same result is achieved through all the blocks having been turned by the examiner in the process of correction. In either case the subject is asked to formulate the principle of the classification. After this the blocks are turned over and mixed up again and the subject is asked to put them in order once more, this time without any help from the examiner. This repetition serves as a check as to whether or not the subject has actually grasped the principle of the double dichotomy: *large* or *small,* and *tall* or *flat,* on which the classification is based. Throughout the experiment the subject is encouraged to "think aloud" and a detailed record is made of his and the experimenter's remarks, as well as of all selections made by the subject and of all corrections made by the examiner [2].

The primary concern in this kind of inquiry is not with test scores and quantitative measures; it is with a *qualitative* analysis of the subject's procedure. Although two quantitative measures are available and are actually used—the time of the total performance and the number of "corrections" or blocks turned up—these are regarded as constituting in themselves neither reliable nor significant measures of the subject's proficiency. The quality of the performance is far better indicated by the manner in which the subject arranges and rearranges the blocks and by his accompanying comments. Such reactions are used as evidence of the course of his thinking from moment to moment; in particular, of his interpretation of the instructions, of the kinds of groupings he attempts, of the hypotheses he employs, of the use he makes of the nonsense words and of the "corrections," and above all, of whether he treats the blocks simply as concrete, individual objects or as representatives of the general qualities on the basis of which he makes his classification—in other words whether the level on which he is operating is concrete or abstract, whether he is working with "things" or with "categories." By observing the subject's behavior, the examiner tries to discover whether he realizes that the material affords many possible bases of classification, whether he has insight into the structure of the classification as a whole, and whether, if he has failed to make the classification himself, he is able to grasp the principle when the experimenter demonstrates the correct classification. Thus the subject's reactions are interpreted as indicating degrees of concreteness and degrees of abstractness, i.e., degrees of proficiency within each of the two levels.

Partly because the materials call out modes of attack so varied and covering so wide a range, and partly because the required motor reactions present no difficulty in themselves, the test is suitable for subjects of many kinds. It has been used with normal people, both children and adults, and with patients suffering from mental disorders, organic and functional. There is thus a considerable body of evidence in the light of which its results may be interpreted. In the main, they have been reported as indicating that normal subjects are capable of both the concrete and the abstract attitude, but that in patients suffering from serious brain injuries or from certain kinds of functional disorders, notably schizophrenia, the abstract attitude is impaired in characteristic ways, and the patient tends to be restricted to the concrete level of activity.

The chief limitation of the method is that the results are so largely dependent on the examiner's interpretation. They emerge less clearly as "data," free of the examiner's personal impressions, than do those from experiments in which, once the conditions have been set up and the procedure set going, the results are beyond the experimenter's control and, furthermore, are obtained in units—e.g., reactions of a specified sort or the effects of such reactions—selected in advance and recorded by devices incorporated into the experimental procedure. No experiment, of course, yields absolute "data": "givens" entirely free from the experimenter's interpretation. In the specifically directed, closely organized experiments which have been contrasted with exploratory research, however, data and interpretation are separable in the sense previously indicated. Naturally the contrasting methods must be evaluated in the light of the needs of the particular problem. Those who prefer the less specifically directed research emphasize the need for procedures readily responsive to the changing particulars of the actual behavior under examination. They see in the more precise but less flexible procedures a danger that the subject matter under investigation may be forced into a predetermined pattern, and they believe that this danger is especially acute in investigations of thinking, where much remains to be discovered and where much may be overlooked.

EXPERIMENTS ON SYLLOGISTIC REASONING

The Syllogism as an Instrument of Study

The syllogisms of formal logic have also been used as experimental materials in investigations of thinking. Störring [23] conducted studies of syllogistic reasoning in which the subjects gave full introspective reports on the psychological processes by which they arrived at conclusions from presented premises. Objective tests, too, have been used as a means of studying syllogistic thought—a device interesting in itself from the standpoint of method because it shows how standardized tests, like those commonly used to discover facts about individuals, may be employed as tools for investigating the processes, rather than the individuals, tested. Here the pioneer study is that of Wilkins [32], who used as an instrument of research objective tests of syllogistic reasoning, especially designed to discover to what extent liability to erroneous conclusions is a function of the kinds of materials in which the syllogisms are presented. The problem arose from the experimenter's impression that the use of abstract symbols is in itself a source of considerable difficulty in formal logic, that many people who are willing to infer from "all *a*'s are *b*'s" that "all *b*'s are *a*'s," are in no danger of inferring from "all horses are animals" that "all animals are horses." The tests, when applied to college students, indicated that syllogisms stated in abstract symbols were slightly but significantly more difficult than those stated in terms of concrete materials of various kinds. Much of the actual labor of the research went into the construction and standardization of the tests themselves, procedures which need not be described here, but which must be emphasized as, from the standpoint of method, an extremely important part of the study.

Methods of Analyzing Invalid Conclusions

Objective tests of syllogistic reasoning have also been used in a series of studies by Woodworth and Sells [34]. Their research, because of its carefully planned and executed design, deserves somewhat detailed consideration. Their general problem was: Why do intelligent human beings draw invalid conclusions, and why are they more liable to some errors than to others? What *psychological* factors account for these errors in logic? Their research, however, was centered about a far more specific problem, expressed in a hypothesis which Sells attributes to Woodworth.

Noticing that the false converse of a proposition is very likely to be accepted, Woodworth suggested that the global impression or general atmosphere of an unanalyzed statement might dispose a person to accept a proposition having a similar atmosphere, hence to accept the simple converse, true or false. Thus, the universal affirmative, "all *a*'s are *b*'s" might create an "all-yes" atmosphere, disposing a person to accept the converse, "all *b*'s are *a*'s," which also has an "all-yes" atmosphere.

The outstanding feature of the inquiry into this possibility is the explicitness with which the hypothesis is stated and developed, together with the exactness with which the experimental conditions are designed to bring out the evidence relevant to the problem it poses. Stated in terms of the A, E, I, O propositions of formal logic, the basic hypothesis concerning the atmospheric effect is:

A: universal affirmative (all *a*'s are *b*'s) has an all-yes atmosphere.
E: universal negative (no *a*'s are *b*'s) has an all-no atmosphere.
I: particular affirmative (some *a*'s are *b*'s) has a some-yes atmosphere.
O: particular negative (some *a*'s are not *b*'s) has a some-no atmosphere.

To cover the two premises of the syllogism, the hypotheses must be extended. No problem is present when the two premises are alike—if, for example, the syllogism has the form AA or OO. But when the two premises are different, for example, AI or AE, the mixed atmosphere requires supplementary hypotheses. The following were adopted:

A negative premise creates a negative atmosphere, even when the other premise is positive.

A particular ("some") premise creates a some atmosphere, even when the other premise is universal.

A systematic investigation of the atmospheric effect was conducted by Sells [21]. The hypothesis itself was the most powerful instrument of research, but here, as in Wilkins' study, the construction of a reliable test was an indispensable preliminary to investigating the problem experimentally. In Sells's test all the syllogisms were stated in abstract symbols and were arranged on the page in the following manner, the letters to the left of each syllogism standing for "absolutely true," "partly true," "indeterminate," and "absolutely false," respectively.

1. AT PT I AF — If all *x*'s are *y*'s
And if all *z*'s are *x*'s
Then all *z*'s are *y*'s

2. AT PT I AF — If no *x*'s are *y*'s
And if all *z*'s are *y*'s
Then some *z*'s are *x*'s

The test consisted of 180 items, 128 of which were logically invalid. Only the invalid forms were needed to test the hypothesis, but the 52 valid forms were included to insure sound test procedure. The 128 invalid items provided every possible type of occurrence of atmosphere effect in formal syllogistic reasoning. The test items were arranged in random order, and the test, divided into four equal parts, each part presented in a separate booklet, was given on four successive days. The regular experimental session was an hour long, but by allowing extra time to those who did not finish within the hour, the test was made a "power" rather than a "time" test.

The subjects were all educated adults, thoroughly habituated to testing procedures. No one with training in logic was accepted as a subject, a precaution adopted to protect the results from the reduction or elimination of the atmosphere effect by a subject's application of familiar rules of formal logic. A further precaution was adopted to prevent blurring of the results by a possible ambiguity in the use of the word "some"; the printed instructions included the information that this word is used in logic to mean "at least some and possibly all," not "some but not all." Still another precaution was embodied in the task itself. The subject was required to indicate his judgment by encircling one of four symbols, instead of simply marking a statement true or false. Though the latter is the logically more appropriate procedure, the multiple-choice response was adopted as psychologically more likely to produce careful judgments, to eliminate guessing, and thus to secure maximal reliability. In scoring the tests, however, only two categories were used: AT and T were included in a single category, "True"; I and AF, in a single category, "False." It will be noted that throughout the procedure special precautions were taken to minimize the role of chance, such precautions being especially necessary in investigating so subtle and elusive a factor as atmosphere.

Because the experimental design met the requirements of the hypothesis so closely, the tabulated results reflect the essentials of the method with such fidelity that they serve almost as a diagram of the plan on which the experiment was based. These results are presented in Table I.

In the second column of the table, opposite each syllogistic form indicated in the first column, is stated the form of the conclusion favored by the atmosphere according to the hypothesis; and in the columns headed A, E, I, and O are given the percentages of the *invalid* conclusions belonging to the designated categories. Inspection shows that the empirical findings correspond to the theoretical expectations, that for every form of the syllogism the expected false conclusion occurred with conspicuously high frequency—in fact, with the highest frequency except for the three forms AA, AE, and EA, and even for these with frequencies fairly high. Further statistical analysis indicated that the probability that the obtained results might occur by chance was so slight as to be negligible.

The factor of atmosphere was submitted to further inquiry, but the part of the experiment just described illustrates the distinctive features of the method. Essentially this method consisted in constructing a hypothesis, working out its implications in terms of concrete situations, and discovering whether the theoretical expectations were confirmed by empirical facts obtained under conditions especially designed to test the hypothesis.

TABLE I

PERCENTAGE OF INVALID CONCLUSIONS ACCEPTED IN TESTS OF SYLLOGISTIC REASONING

(Sells's data rearranged for presentation in Woodworth: *Experimental Psychology*, 1938)

Premises Presented	Conclusion Favored by Atmosphere	Invalid Conclusion Presented			
		A	E	I	O
AA	A	58	14	63	17
EE	E	21	38	25	34
II	I	27	9	72	38
OO	C	14	16	38	52
AE	E	11	51	13	63
EA	E	8	64	12	69
AI	I	33	4	70	32
IA	I	36	15	75	36
AO	O	15	26	42	76
OA	O	13	33	28	75
EI	O	8	40	22	62
IE	O	11	42	22	63
EO	O	13	29	29	44
OE	O	15	31	24	48
IO	O	12	19	31	64
OI	O	11	23	33	71

METHODS OF STUDYING THINKING IN ITS CONTEXT

But does not a laboratory experiment impose artificial conditions that inevitably alter the course of thought as it ordinarily occurs? Basically the answer to this question is: Yes, of course. It is the very nature of an experiment to be artificial in the sense that the experimenter does not merely observe a course of events as it comes, but interferes with it in such a way as to make it reveal facts and relationships that would otherwise remain hidden. (See Chapter 1.) This reply, however, fails to reach an important implication of the criticism. How does one know whether the factors discovered in a special set of conditions have any relevance beyond the conditions in which they were obtained? Is there any way of discovering likenesses and differences between laboratory and extra-laboratory thinking?

Analysis of Protocols and Reports

One possibility is to turn to the accounts that some persons, among them such distinguished thinkers as Helmholtz [3] and Poincaré [18], have given of their own modes of thought. Another is to make special inquiries into the habits of work of gifted thinkers, like those made by Toulouse [26, 27] in his studies of Zola and Poincaré. Still another is to question thinkers directly, as Rossman [19] questioned inventors and as Platt and Baker [17] questioned chemists. Sometimes there is an exceptional opportunity for studying an exceptional case. In one of his books Wertheimer [31] discusses, on the basis of a long series of unhurried conversations on the subject, so extraordinary a course of thought as that which led Einstein to his theory of relativity. Patrick [15, 16] attempted a more direct method of comparing laboratory and extra-laboratory thinking, inducing poets and painters to do creative work under conditions in which experimental investigation was approximated. There are obvious weaknesses and dangers in all these procedures, but in spite of different theoretical approaches by different investigators, considerable agreement can be found on certain aspects of the general course of thought, along with striking individual differences among the thinkers studied. Some of these studies have been interpreted as giving evidence for the four stages of creative thought outlined by Wallas [28], namely, preparation, incubation, illumination, and verification.

Importance of Studying Thinking in Its Context

From many points of view psychologists are becoming increasingly aware of the importance of studying the wider context in which thinking is found. They have long recognized the importance of its genetic and phylogenetic history. Indeed, as is apparent from experiments reported elsewhere in this book, some of the most effective work on the psychology of thinking has been done with children and animals as subjects. Psychologists have realized too that thinkers must be studied in the context formed by other psychological processes, among them those that constitute the needs, desires, and urges of the organism. Problems in this field have usually been attacked from the standpoint of motivation, rather than from an interest in thinking itself. Attempts have been made, too, to study thinking in its social and cultural setting. This most recent broadening of this field of inquiry has been strongly influenced by the social sciences, especially cultural anthropology. For example, Malinowski [12], a pioneer in this field, has shown that a language is largely determined by the ways of life in the culture of which it is a part—a fact of great significance in the psychology of thinking because a person's language influences the very way in which he perceives and understands his world, physical and social, and hence some of the unconscious assumptions on which his thinking operates. In the United States studies of the social structure of communities, such as that made by Warner and Lunt [29] of a New England city, and nation-wide surveys by means of public-opinion polls have indicated that certain convictions, biases, and opinions are related in regular ways to such factors as social and economic status and regional residence and are in that sense reflections of the culture in which they occur. These studies suggest possibilities for discovering some of the non-rational factors that may determine the outcome of thinking and, presumably, its course.

POSTSCRIPT

This account, although far from complete, is sufficient to indicate the kinds of methods now available for scientific inquiry into thinking. The evidence is clear that thinking, whatever its nature, is too complexly and obscurely determined to be profitably conceived of as essentially a *conscious* process, sufficiently open to direct inspection to justify introspection as the sole or even the major means of investigation. For this reason the course of research on thinking has been marked by the development of devices for attacking the problem indirectly, i.e., for arranging conditions in which the main experimental data consist of observed *behavior and behavioral achievements,* either symbolic or directly motor. Some of the methods are broadly exploratory, some specifically directed and closely organized. On the whole, the trend has been toward methods whereby behavioral data are secured under conditions in which specified determinants of the behavior under investigation may be *inferred* from specified reactions or specified achievements.

It would be misleading, however, to close this account without stating explicitly that these methods, however effective in specified conditions, have led to little knowledge of thinking that is at once broadly significant, solidly grounded in fact, and unequivocal in meaning. It would be misleading, too, to omit the suggestion that this state of affairs may be due, not so much to a lack of suitable procedures, as to failure to ask effective questions. Effective questions imply effective conceptions of the situations investigated, and at best such conceptions are formulated as definite theories which establish the main lines along which research is directed. Psychology, of course, does not lack theories of thinking, but none of these theories has as yet led to experimental data on the basis of which thinking has been explained in a manner acceptable to all who are competent to judge. Perhaps, in research on thinking, the special need at present is an adequate conception of the problem itself. At any rate these reflections call attention to the fact that in the actual work of science experiment and theory are intimately connected and that scientific research is more than the manipulation of techniques—it is basically an inquiry into significant problems.

REFERENCES

1. Goldstein, Kurt. *After-effects of Brain Injuries in War.* New York: Grune and Stratton, 1942.
2. Hanfmann, E., and J. Kasanin. A method for the study of concept formation. *J. Psychol.,* 1937, *3,* 521–540.
3. Helmholtz, H. *Vorträge und Reden,* 5th Aufl. Braunschweig F. Vieweg. und Sohn, Vol. I, 1896.
4. Hobhouse, L. T. *Mind in Evolution.* London: Macmillan, 1915.
5. Hull, C. L. Quantitative aspects of the evolution of concepts. *Psychol. Monog.,* 1920, *28,* No. 123.
6. Hull, C. L. *Principles of Behavior.* New York: D. Appleton-Century, 1943.
7. Jersild, A. Mental set and shift. *Arch. Psychol.,* 1927, No. 89.
8. Kent, G. H., and A. J. Rosanoff. A study of associations in insanity. *Amer. J. Insanity,* 1910, *67,* 37–96, 317–390.
9. Köhler, W. *The Mentality of Apes.* New York: Harcourt, Brace, 1925.
10. Kuo, Z. Y. A behavioristic experiment on inductive inference. *J. Exper. Psychol.,* 1923, *6,* 247–293.
11. Maier, N. R. F. Reasoning in humans, I. On direction. *J. Comp. Psychol.,* 1930, *10,* 115–144.
12. Malinowski, B. The problems of learning in primitive languages. In C. K. Ogden, and I. A. Richards, *The Meaning of Meaning.* New York: Harcourt, Brace, 1938, pp. 296–336.
13. May, M. A. The mechanisms of controlled association. *Arch. Psychol.,* 1917, No. 39.
14. Morgan, C. Lloyd. *Introduction to Comparative Psychology.* London: W. Scott, 1894.
15. Patrick, C. Creative thought in poets. *Arch. Psychol.,* 1935, 178.
16. Patrick, C. Creative thought in artists. *J. Psychol.,* 1937, *4,* 35–73.
17. Platt, W., and B. A. Baker. The relation of the scientific hunch to research. *J. Chem. Educ.,* 1931, *8,* 1969–2002.
18. Poincaré, Henri. *Science and Hypothesis.* New York: The Science Press, 1913.

19. RUSSMAN, J. *The Psychology of the Inventor.* Washington: Inventor's Publishing Company, 1931.
20. RUGER, H. A. The psychology of efficiency. *Arch. Psychol.,* 1910, No. 15.
21. SELLS, S. B. The atmosphere effect. *Arch. Psychol.,* 1936, No. 200.
22. SMOKE, K. L. An objective study of concept formation. *Psychol. Monog.,* 1932, *42,* No. 191.
23. STÖRRING, G. Experimentelle Untersuchungen über einfoche Schlussprozesse. *Arch. ges. Psychol.,* 1908, *11,* 1–27.
24. THORNDIKE, E. L. Animal intelligence, an experimental study of the associative processes in animals. *Psychol. Monog.,* 1898, *2,* No. 8.
25. TITCHENER, E. B. *Lectures on the Experimental Psychology of the Thought Processes.* New York: Macmillan, 1909.
26. TOULOUSE, E. *Emile Zola.* Societe d'Etiones Scientifiques, 1896.
27. TOULOUSE, E. *Henri Poincaré.* Paris: Flammarion, 1910.
28. WALLAS, GRAHAM. *The Art of Thought.* New York: Harcourt, Brace, 1926.
29. WARNER, W. D., and P. S. LUNT. *The Social Life of a Modern Community.* New Haven: Yale University Press, 1941.
30. WATT, H. J. Experimentelle Beitrage zur einer Theories des Kenkens. *Arch. ges. Psychol.,* 1905, *4,* 289–436.
31. WERTHEIMER, M. *Productive Thinking.* New York: Harper, 1945.
32. WILKINS, M. C. The effect of changed material on ability to do formal syllogistic reasoning. *Arch. Psychol.,* 1928, No. 102.
33. WOODROW, H., and F. LOWELL. Children's association frequency tables. *Psychol. Monog.,* 1916, *22,* No. 97.
34. WOODWORTH, R. S., and S. B. SELLS. An atmosphere effect in formal syllogistic reasoning. *J. Exper. Psychol.,* 1935, *18,* 451–460.

SUGGESTED READINGS

CRAFTS, L. W., T. C. SCHNEIRLA, E. E. ROBINSON, and R. W. GILBERT. *Recent Experiments in Psychology.* New York: McGraw-Hill, 1938. Chaps. XXIII, XXIV, XXV, XXVI.

TITCHENER, E. B. *Lectures on the Experimental Psychology of the Thought Processes.* New York: Macmillan, 1909.

WERTHEIMER, M. *Productive Thinking.* New York: Harper, 1945.

WOODWORTH, R. S. *Experimental Psychology.* New York: Henry Holt, 1938. Chaps. XXIX, XXX.

Chapter 5

Psychophysical Methods

L. L. Thurstone[1]

The Problem of Subjective Measurement

Psychophysics is that branch of psychology which is concerned with subjective measurement. Obviously a subjective unit of measurement is required. Psychophysical theory is concerned with the logic of subjective measurement [8], and psychophysical methods are concerned with experimental procedures.

In order to illustrate the difference between *the psychological continuum* and *the physical stimulus continuum,* let us consider an experiment in the differentiation of lifted weights, which has been investigated by hundreds of experimenters. The experimental subject is presented with a large assortment of small cylinders, all of them equal in size and appearance but different in weight. He is shown two of these cylinders which differ markedly in weight, and they are designated as *standards* for this experiment. Then the subject is asked to select one of the other weights that seems to be midway between the two standards. When the subject has satisfied himself that he has found a cylinder whose weight marks the midpoint between the standards, the three cylinders may be compared as to their "actual" weights. When the intervals are expressed in grams or other physical units, it is found that the lower interval is smaller than the upper one. In other words, the subjective or psychological continuum is not the same as the physical continuum. Measurement on the subjective continuum will be denoted S, and measurement on the physical continuum will be denoted R.[2] The experimental method just described is called the *method of mean gradation.*

Psychophysical problems can be divided into several classes. Per-

[1] Charles F. Grey, Distinguished Service Professor of Psychology, University of Chicago.

[2] R for the German *Reiz* (stimulus).

haps the most fundamental of these is that in which each one of a set of stimuli is allocated to a point in the subjective continuum without reference to physically measurable attributes. In a closely related class is the problem of predicting what people will do in terms of the subjective values of a set of stimuli. If their subjective values for a set of neckties are known, how many of the subjects will select a particular necktie as their first choice in any given assortment of neckties? Another large class of problems is concerned with the relation between the subjective and the physical continua. We shall see that this relation is known as Fechner's law. One of the oldest types of psychophysical problem is that of determining the physical stimulus increment which the subject can just barely perceive. This increment is called the *just noticeable difference.* Since this is the simplest of the psychophysical problems, we shall start with the concepts and the experimental methods that have been used for determining such stimulus increments.

The Limen

The physical stimulus continuum is represented by the vertical line in Fig. 1. If the subject is being examined as to his ability to differentiate fine differences in the lengths of lines, then the stimulus unit might be the centimeter. If he is examined as to his ability to differentiate fine differences in pitch, then the stimulus unit would be cycles per second. The highest stimulus magnitude that the subject can perceive is called his *terminal stimulus* or *terminal threshold.*

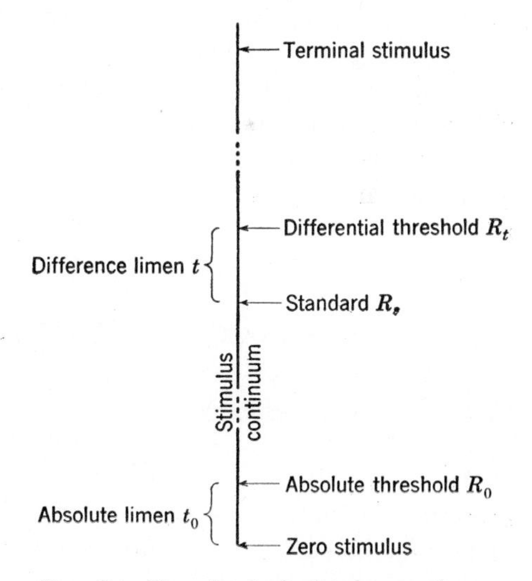

Fig. 1. The physical stimulus continuum.

In one type of experiment, the object is to determine the smallest stimulus difference that the subject can perceive. With a given standard R_s, the experimenter determines that stimulus threshold R_t which the subject can just barely differentiate from the standard. The magnitude of R_t is called the *differential threshold* for the given standard.

The stimulus increment required for discrimination is called the *difference limen t*.

Sometimes the object is to determine the smallest stimulus magnitude that the subject can perceive. Various small intensities are then tried to find the *absolute threshold* R_0, which is the smallest stimulus intensity that the subject can identify. The increment between zero stimulus magnitude and the absolute threshold R_0 is called the *absolute limen* t_0. The absolute threshold R_0 and the absolute limen t_0 are numerically identical.

Another well-known problem in psychophysics is to determine the *two-point threshold.* This is the smallest distance between the two points of a special compass, called an *esthesiometer,* which the subject can just barely differentiate as two distinct points. For smaller separations between the compass points, the subject reports that he feels only one point. For further descriptions of the two-point threshold, see page 260.

We have described the limen here as if it might be a sharply defined stimulus increment, but such is not the case. The subject varies from moment to moment in his sensitivity and attention, so that it usually becomes necessary to define the limen as a statistical measure. We say then that the limen is that stimulus magnitude, or that stimulus difference, which the subject can discriminate in a specified proportion of his attempts. In some experiments this proportion is set at 50 per cent, whereas in others it is set at 75 per cent, or higher. It is customary to define the absolute threshold as that stimulus magnitude which the subject can identify in half of his attempts. The difference limen, however, is usually set at a higher proportion, such as 75 per cent, because otherwise the subject would be right in half of his attempts merely by guessing which of the two stimuli is the higher.

THE MAJOR PSYCHOPHYSICAL METHODS

Method of Reproduction

One of the simplest psychophysical methods is called the *method of reproduction* or the *method of average error.* The essential feature of this method is that the subject tries to reproduce the magnitude of a presented stimulus. For example, he is shown a straight line on a large card, which is placed at a specified distance in front of him, and is given a large sheet of paper with instruction to draw a line of exactly the same length. If he makes, say, one hundred such attempts, then his performance can be analyzed to determine how accurate it is.

In answering the question of how accurately the subject can reproduce the presented stimulus, we encounter in the subject's performance two kinds of error, which are investigated separately in many psychophysical experiments. One of these is the *constant error*, which is also called the *systematic error*. Another type is the *variable error*, which measures the *sensitivity* of the subject.

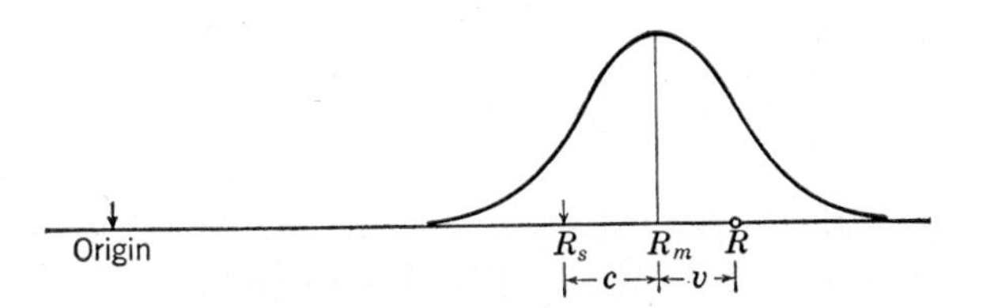

Fig. 2. Distribution of reproductions of a line stimulus.

In Fig. 2 we have a representation of the results obtained by the method of reproduction. The length of the presented standard line is denoted R_s (the distance between the origin and R_s). A distribution curve is obtained from the large number of separate attempts by the subject to reproduce the standard line. The mean of this distribution is denoted R_m. If the length of the standard line R_s and the average length R_m of the lines by the subject are unequal, then the discrepancy is a measure of the amount of *overestimation* or *underestimation*. This discrepancy is also called the *crude constant error c*. In the example of Fig. 2 we infer that the subject overestimated the standard line because his average line is longer than the standard R_s. The crude constant error can be defined by the relation $c = R_m - R_s$.

The consistency of the subject, sometimes also called the sensitivity, is measured by the dispersion of the distribution of his attempts. The standard deviation σ may be used to denote the amount of dispersion. In analyzing psychophysical data it is common to make a formal assumption that the subject's reproduction R is determined by two components: his average amount of overestimation or underestimation c and his variable error v at the moment of drawing a particular line. The formal result is then that his reproduced line $R = R_s + c + v$. Of course, we do not really believe that the degree of overestimation, positive or negative, is truly constant, but the result is treated as if it were the sum of one component that is constant, the constant error c and another component v that is variable from moment to moment.

There is an important limitation in the method of reproduction, namely, that the stimulus magnitude reproduced by the subject is determined in part by his ability to *perceive* the stimulus and in part by his *muscular coordination* in reproducing the standard stimulus, either by drawing a line, as in the present case, or by manipulating some apparatus that controls the stimulus magnitude of his reproductions. In psychophysical studies we are usually interested in the subject's ability to perceive the stimulus, and hence the effect of his muscular coordination is often a distracting and irrelevant element in experiments with this method. In many situations, however, this method is the natural one. An example is the psychophysical analysis of target practice where we are interested in good results, no matter what the perceptual and muscular components may be. Here it is useful to know the constant error, both in direction and in amount, and also the variability of the results over the target.

Weber's Law and Fechner's Law

The two best-known laws of psychophysics are Weber's law and Fechner's law. These two laws are frequently confused, and they are then described in a general way as the Weber-Fechner law, as if they were essentially the same law. The explicit formulation and experimental verification of these two laws will be described here. Their theoretical and experimental separation will be described in a later section in connection with the concept of the discriminal dispersion.

The older law is that of Weber, who stated "in comparing magnitudes, it is not the arithmetical difference, but the ratio of the magnitudes, which we perceive" [27, p. 430]. This law states what is well known in practical observation. In judging two suitcases as to which is the heavier, it is the ratio of the two weights that determines the ease with which we can perceive their difference. If their difference is only a few ounces, then it is unnoticed. If two letters differ by the same number of ounces, however, we easily perceive the difference. In the case of the letters, a few ounces alter their weight ratio very markedly, whereas a few ounces have no significant effect on the ratio of the weights of the suitcases. If a room is lighted by a single candle, then we notice readily the addition of a second candle because the light is then doubled. The addition of a single candle to a well-lighted room is unnoticed, however, because the two brightnesses are practically the same. This principle seems to be general.

Let us attempt to make an explicit scientific statement of Weber's law so that it can serve as a guide to what we actually do in the laboratory in trying to verify this law. We seek, then, an operational statement of Weber's law. Merely to say that it is the ratios of the stimuli that we notice rather than their actual differences does not say just what to look for in the laboratory. The statement will be improved if we say that *the difference limen is a constant fraction of the stimulus.* But the subject compares two stimuli. Which stimulus magnitude shall we take as the denominator? We can resolve this ambiguity by taking the average of the two stimuli as a standard. Then our statement would read: *the difference between two stimuli which can be just barely perceived is a constant fraction of their average magnitude.* When we come to the experiments, we find that this stimulus difference is not stable. Any fixed small difference is perceived by the subject in some trials and unnoticed in other trials. The greater the difference, the more often will the subject notice it. In fact, we are dealing with an experimentally continuous function which has no "jumping-off place" that can be called a limen. The proportion of correct judgments rises continuously with increase in the stimulus difference. Hence we must state Weber's law in terms of the relative frequency of correct judgments that we require in a definition of the limen. This difficulty can be resolved if we state Weber's law in the form, $P_{R<kR} = C$. Here C is any specified proportion of correct judgments except zero and unity. Let us take some arbitrary value, such as $C = 0.75$. If the stimulus value R is 100 grams, we may find that kR is 103 grams, as experimentally determined. The constant k is then 1.03. If we find that the value of k is the same for all values of R, then we have verified Weber's law for the constant $C = 0.75$. If we find that the relation also holds for all permissible values of C, then this formulation of Weber's law is experimentally verified [12].

The constant $(k - 1)$ is called Weber's ratio. This ratio is about 1/100 for brightness, and about 1/30 for lifted weights. The smaller values of Weber's ratio indicate the greater sensitivity. The ratio is much higher for loudness, for which human perception is rather coarse. Weber's law has been found to hold fairly well over the major part of the stimulus range, but it breaks down toward the terminal stimulus values. The law also fails near the absolute threshold.

In considering the method of mean gradation, we noted the distinction between the psychological or perceived continuum and the physical or stimulus continuum. A weight that seems to us to lie midway between two standard stimuli is not ordinarily midway between them in number of grams. The relation between the subjective continuum S and the physical continuum R has been found experimentally to be logarithmic in shape, and hence the relation can be described by the empirical equation $S = k \log R$, where k is a parameter that varies with the nature of the stimuli and the experimental conditions. Although psychophysics is primarily concerned with measurement in the subjective continuum S, it deals also with the interesting relation between the subjective and the physical continua. This relation is expressed in Fechner's law. In the case of limen determinations, we are dealing with the relatively simple problem of expressing a just noticeable subjective difference in the corresponding physical continuum.

Two differences between these laws should be noted. The two laws are expressed as follows:

$$\underset{\text{(Weber)}}{P_{R<kR} = C,} \qquad \text{and} \qquad \underset{\text{(Fechner)}}{S = k \log R.}$$

It can be seen by inspection that Fechner's law deals explicitly with the psychological continuum, whereas Weber's law says nothing explicitly about S. Another conspicuous differentiation is in the stimulus increments with which they deal. A difference that is barely perceptible is called a *liminal difference.* Large stimulus differences which are easily perceived are called *supraliminal differences.* Very small differences about which the subject would nearly always be in doubt are called *subliminal differences.* Now, with regard to the two psychophysical laws, note that Weber's law is always concerned with liminal and subliminal differences, whereas Fechner's law has no limitation in this regard. If the difference between two stimuli is supraliminal, then the subject can always distinguish them, and his proportion of correct discriminations is unity. Weber's law is concerned with stimulus differences that are small enough so that the subject has some difficulty in distinguishing them. Under certain conditions, to be described later, the two laws can be verified in the same set of experimental data, but under other conditions one of these laws can be satisfied when the other one fails [13, 24, p. 383].

The earlier statement of Weber's law—that we perceive the ratios of stimulus magnitudes and not their absolute differences—can be interpretated as implying the logarithmic relation of Fechner's law directly, but experimental work on Weber's law has been universally restricted to the relation between the difference limen t and the stimulus magnitude R. It is thereby restricted to liminal differences. We shall see that there is good reason for separating these two problems, namely, (1) the functional relation between the subjective and the physical continua, and (2) the ease of discrimination between two stimuli. The first is the logarithmic relation that has become known as Fechner's law. The second problem is markedly affected by the stimulus ambiguities to be described later.

The Stimulus Error

In order to understand some problems in psychological measurement, it is essential to be able to observe one's own mental processes. This requires a psychological point of view which differs from that of judging the properties of physical objects. When the subject tries to guess whether a weight actually is midway between two standard weights, we say that he makes an *object judgment.* He tries to describe the physical properties of the object. When he reports whether a weight *seems* to lie midway between two standard weights, as experienced, and without reference to the number of grams or ounces, then we say that he makes a *sensory judgment.* He tries to describe his sensations. When the subject is asked to make a sensory judgment and yet reverts to the more naive object judgment, he is said to commit the *stimulus error.* Then he pays attention to the physical stimulus, although he is asked to report sensory or perceptual intensities [1].

It has been found that the accuracy of object judgments can be improved with practice. For example, a grocery clerk may be so well practiced that he can estimate the weight of a piece of cheese with considerable accuracy. Similarly, a postal clerk may be able to judge the required postage for a letter by merely lifting it. Such individuals would probably find it difficult to serve as subjects in psychophysical experiments if they were required to make sensory judgments in the range of their experience. They have learned to describe perceptual intensities S in terms of the corresponding physical magnitudes R.

Method of Limits

One of the relatively simple methods of determining the limen is the *method of limits,* which is also called the *method of minimal change.* This method will be described separately for the determination of the absolute threshold and for the difference limen.

In the experimental procedure for the absolute threshold the subject is first presented with a single stimulus of very low intensity, so that he cannot identify it. The stimulus is augmented by the experimenter in successive steps until the subject reports that he does perceive it. This is the *ascending series* of judgments. Then the experimenter presents to the subject a stimulus which is definitely supraliminal, and the stimulus is altered by successive decrements until the subject reports that he no longer perceives it. The subject gives a report of presence or absence of the stimulus for each setting. This is the *descending series* of judgments.

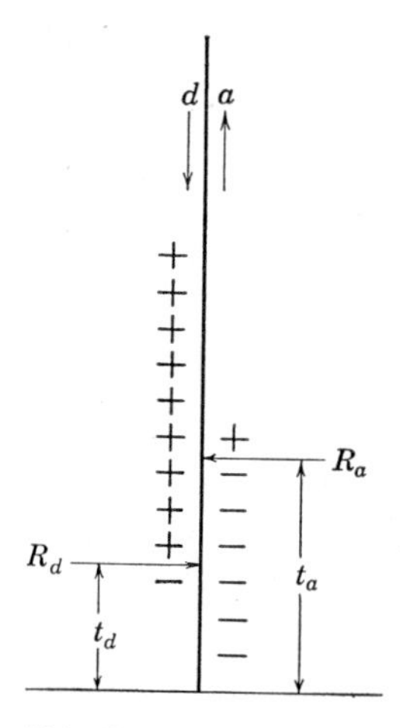

Fig. 3. Judgments of ascending and descending series for absolute thresholds.

In Fig. 3 we have a diagrammatic representation of the ascending and the descending series of judgments. The plus sign represents a positive judgment by the subject, and the minus sign represents failure to identify the stimulus. The ascending series starts with a low stimulus intensity, which the subject fails to identify. It is augmented in steps until the subject reports that he does perceive it. This stimulus is marked plus for the ascending series. Midway between the last two settings we have the *ascending threshold* intensity R_a, which is in this case identical with the *ascending limen* t_a as shown in the diagram.

A supraliminal stimulus which the subject definitely identifies is then presented. It is altered by successive decrements until the subject reports that he fails to perceive it. This last intensity is marked minus. The midpoint between the last two settings is recorded as the *descending threshold* R_d, and this is identical with the *descending limen* t_d. The absolute threshold t_0 is then taken as the average of the ascending and the descending limens. In practice, the experimenter presents a number of ascending and descending series, the average of which is taken as the absolute threshold. Formally, we have:

$$t_0 = \frac{R_a + R_d}{2}, \qquad \text{or} \qquad t_0 = \frac{t_a + t_d}{2}.$$

The difference limen is determined by this method in a similar manner. The subject is presented with two stimuli, which are called the *standard stimulus* and the *variable stimulus* respectively. The subject is told which of the two stimuli is the standard and which is the variable. He is told, further, that the variable stimulus will be altered in magnitude by the experimenter in successive increments, and that he is to judge for each setting of the variable whether it seems to be (1) lower than the standard, (2) equal to the standard, or (3) higher than the standard. These are called three *categories of judgment*. It is also explained to the subject that the initial setting of the variable will be quite low, so that it can be easily differentiated from the standard, and that the variable will then be augmented in successive steps until it exceeds the standard. This is called the ascending series of judgments.

In Fig. 4 we have a diagrammatic representation of the method of limits for the determination of a difference limen. The low initial settings of the variable stimulus are marked minus because the variable is then easily seen to be lower than the standard. After several increments the subject reports that the two stimuli seem equal. The midpoint between these two settings is denoted R_{la} for the lower ascending threshold. After several increments during which the subject reports equality, he finds one stimulus which he reports as greater than the standard. This is marked plus. The midpoint between the last two settings is denoted R_{ua} for the upper ascending threshold. The standard stimulus magnitude is denoted R_s in the figure. The upper and lower difference limens are deviations from the standard and are denoted t_{ua} and t_{la} respectively. A similar diagrammatic representation is shown for the descending series.

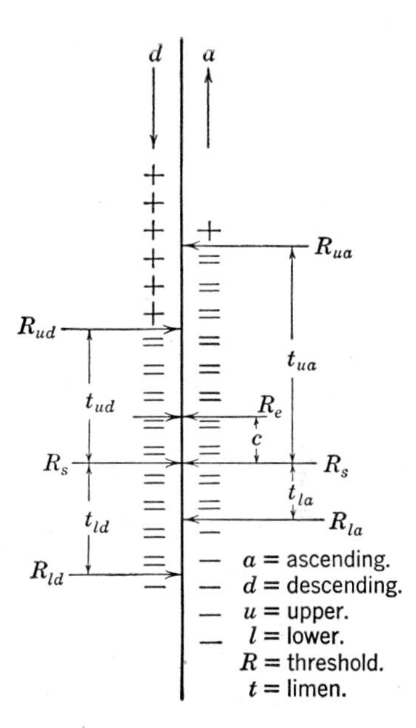

Fig. 4. Judgments of ascending and descending series for differential thresholds.

From data collected in this manner, three determinations are made. The *difference limen* is the average of the four limens, ascending and descending, upper and lower. We have then for the limen t:

$$t = \tfrac{1}{4}(t_{ud} + t_{ua} + t_{ld} + t_{la}),$$

or

$$t = \tfrac{1}{4}(R_{ud} + R_{ua} - R_{ld} - R_{la}).$$

The point of subjective equality R_e is that variable stimulus magnitude which seems, on the average, to be equal to the standard. This is taken as the average of the four thresholds, and we then have

$$R_e = \tfrac{1}{4}(R_{ud} + R_{ua} + R_{ld} + R_{la}).$$

The crude constant error c is the difference between the standard stimulus value and the point of subjective equality. We have then

$$c = R_e - R_s.$$

Both the figures for this method have been drawn so as to represent a usual effect in the method. The ascending thresholds are shown higher than the descending thresholds. The explanation is probably that the subject tends to retain the category of judgment which he has been giving until the conditions have been stretched somewhat beyond the true threshold. This effect is called *habituation.* The opposite effect is sometimes observed when the subject gives the next category of judgment sooner than is expected by his threshold. This effect is called *expectation.* The more common effect is habituation. It seems likely that individual differences in this effect have a temperamental origin. Psychophysical differences might be investigated in the search for objective indices of personality.

The Constant Method

For the purpose of making a limen determination, the experimental procedure should preferably be such that the subject has no knowledge as to which stimulus is being increased or decreased. In most cases he should be unaware of any distinction between the standard and the variable stimulus because this distinction is largely a matter of bookkeeping for the experimenter. As far as the subject is concerned, the two presented stimuli should be coordinate, and his task should be merely to judge which of them has more x-ness, where x is any stimulus attribute that is to be judged. The constant method satisfies these preferred conditions.

The subject is presented with a series of pairs of stimuli and is asked to specify for each pair whether a designated stimulus is the stronger or the weaker. For analytical purposes the two stimuli are called the standard and the variable. The subject may be allowed either two or three categories of judgment. If he has two categories of judgment, then he judges that the stimulus A is greater than B, or that it is less than B. If he has three categories of judgment, then he judges that stimulus A is greater than B, equal to B, or less than B. The stimuli A and B may be defined as right and left, or first and second. These two sets of instructions, for two or three categories of judgment, will be described separately.

When the subject has responded to a large series of comparisons of the standard R_s with different values of the variable R_v, then the results can be represented graphically in what is known as the *psychometric function,* which is illustrated in Fig. 5. Whenever the variable stimulus is much greater than the standard, then the subject returns a large proportion of judgments $R_v > R_s$, and hence the curve "larger" rises with increasing values of the variable stimulus. The curve for judgments "smaller" is the complement of the curve for judgments "larger." The sum of the ordinates for these two curves equals unity for all values of the variable stimulus. The point of subjective equality R_e is that value of the variable stimulus which is defined by the intersection of the two curves at the level $P = 0.50$. The constant error c is the difference between the standard stimulus R_s and the

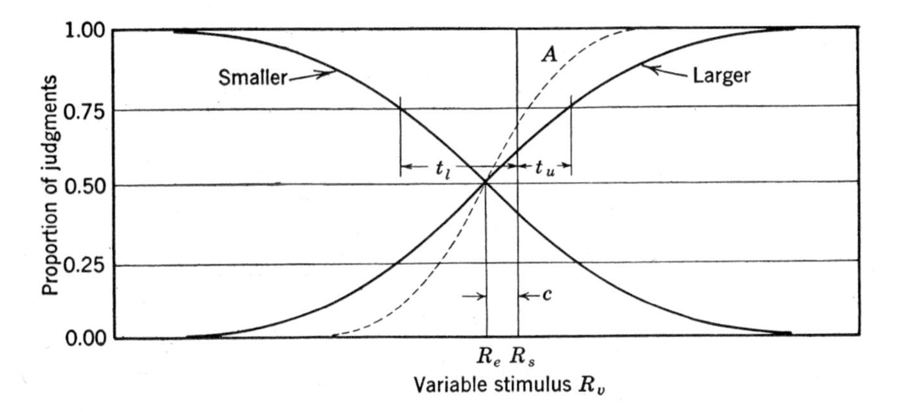

Fig. 5. The psychometric function (two categories of judgment).

value R_e. The *sensitivity* is represented by the slope of the curve, and hence it may be measured by the standard deviation of the distribution of judgments "larger." Because of symmetry, the two curves have the same dispersion. The dotted curve at A is steeper, and hence it would represent a subject with greater sensitivity and lower limen. One common measure of the sensitivity is the distance between the standard stimulus and that variable stimulus for which the psychometric curve has an ordinate of $p = 0.75$. This is the increment which must be added to the standard stimulus in order for the subject to make the correct discrimination in three-fourths of his attempts. This increment is denoted t_u in Fig. 5. In a similar way the lower limen t_l is defined as that decrement below the standard stimulus which the subject differentiates correctly in three-fourths of his attempts. This measure of the lower limen is also shown in the figure. Because of the constant error, the upper and lower limens are not necessarily equal.

If the subject has been allowed three categories of judgment, then the results can be represented graphically by the psychometric curves of Fig. 6. The equality judgments are called the *intermediate category of judgment.* The two psychometric curves then intersect below the median line. The upper threshold R_u is defined by the intersection of the curve for "larger" with the median line, as shown. The lower threshold is defined in a similar way from the psychometric curve for judgments "smaller." The midpoint between these two thresholds is taken as the point of subjective equality R_e, or this value may be

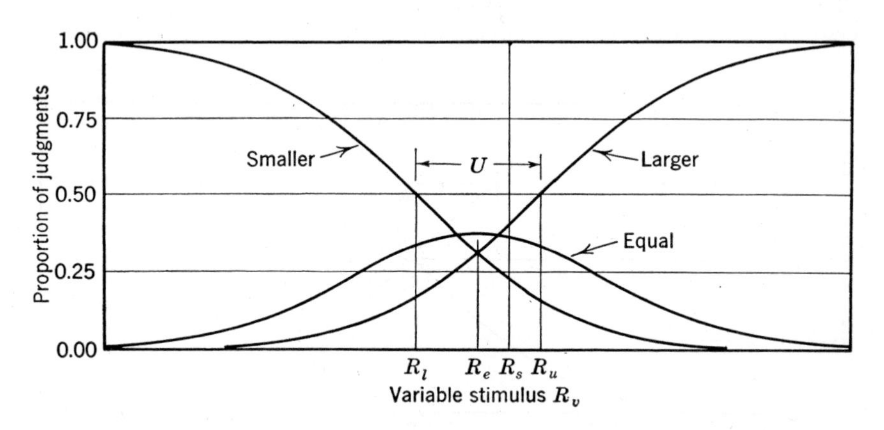

Fig. 6. The psychometric function (three categories of judgment).

defined by the intersection of the two curves. These determinations for R_e are nearly the same. The difference limen can be defined as the standard deviation of either curve, or it may be defined as half of the *interval of uncertainty* U, which is the difference between the upper and lower thresholds. Much has been written about the detailed methods for determining a limen from the psychometric curves, and the question has been the subject of more controversy than it is worth.

The question of whether to use two or three categories has also been much debated [4]. This question is quite easily resolved in terms of the purposes of the experimenter. If he wants to find the limen of a particular subject for a particular kind of sensory discrimination, then he should use only two categories of judgment. If he uses three categories, then the cautious subject will report equality when he is uncertain or when he does not give the necessary effort for a decision. A more confident subject will give decisions with a minimum of equality judgments. Consider what happens to a limen determination if the subject avoids the intermediate category altogether, either by intention or by temperament. The interval of uncertainty U in Fig. 6 then disappears altogether, so that the curves look like those of Fig. 5. The upper and lower limens then vanish, and the interpretation is that the subject has infinite sensitivity, which is absurd. The determination is then markedly affected by temperamental characteristics which are irrelevant for the sensory limen. On the other hand, if the

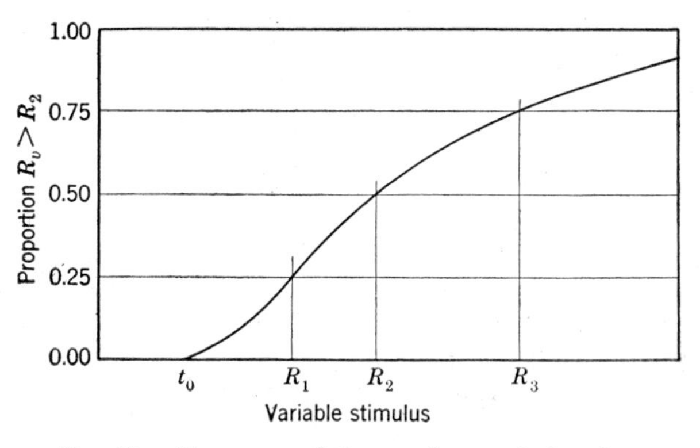

Fig. 7. Skewness of the psychometric function.

purpose of the investigator is to study the experience of equality, then he should use three categories of judgment. The result might give an objective index of some characteristic of temperament, or of the sensory tolerance of the subject, but not of his limen.

Because of the many hundreds of experimental studies with the constant method, there has been considerable interest in the shape of the psychometric curve. It has often been assumed that the curve is symmetric in the sense that the upper and lower limens are essentially equal, but this assumption has been shown to be erroneous on theoretical grounds [20]. The psychometric curve is positively skewed, as shown in Fig. 7. The positive skewness of the psychometric curve varies with Weber's ratio. For keen discrimination where the ratio is, say, 1/100, the skewness is very slight, so that it can be ignored. For coarse discrimination, such as for loudness or smell, the skewness becomes conspicuous [5, 14].

Space and Time Errors

The preferred psychophysical methods usually involve the presentation of two stimuli for the subject to compare. The perception of two stimuli usually requires that they be separated in space over the sensitive surface of the receptor for simultaneous presentation, or that they be separated in time for successive presentation. Because of this circumstance, it is difficult, with two stimuli, to avoid the effects of spatial or temporal separation.

When two stimuli are presented visually with the constant method, they are displaced so that one of them is to the right and the other to the left, or one is above the other. When the comparison is made, it happens not infrequently that the subject tends to overestimate, or underestimate, the stimulus to the right, or to the left. The result is a constant error which is then called a *space error*. Whenever the constant error is of considerable magnitude, one usually looks for an explanation in the experimental situation.

When the two stimuli are presented in succession, there is a frequent tendency for the subject to underestimate the first stimulus. Since the constant error is then due to the temporal displacement, it is called a *time error*. Much experimental work has been done on the nature of the time error [27, pp. 438–449]. When a subject makes a comparison between two successive stimuli, he is in effect comparing the second stimulus with the memory of the first one. There seems to be a tendency of his memory for the first stimulus to *regress toward the mean* of the whole set of stimuli in the experiment, or even toward the mean of the same general class of stimuli in the experience of the subject.

In some experiments the constant errors, either space errors or time errors, are irrelevant for the main purpose. They can be eliminated or ignored in some situations by presenting the same stimulus in some trials to the right and in some trials to the left, or sometimes first and sometimes second. This is called *counterbalanced order* of presentation. In other experiments the constant error is the main object of investigation, as in measuring the magnitude of an illusion. An illusion is an error in perceptual judgment. The cause is usually that the subject tries to judge one thing but is unwittingly affected by other things. If the object is to measure the size of the Müller-Lyer illusion, then the arrow of the figure may be to the right in half of the presentations and to the left in the other half. In analyzing the experimental results, one can determine separately the magnitude of the illusion for the experimental subject and his tendency to overestimate the stimulus on the right or left side. In some experiments a constant error is introduced by differences in movement when the subject tends to make stronger movements toward the right or the left side. Such a constant error is called a *movement error*.

Method of Paired Comparison

In the constant method a single stimulus is chosen as a standard and is compared with all the stimuli in the experimental series. If there are n stimuli in the series, then there are n distinct comparisons to be made, or $(n - 1)$ comparisons if the standard is not compared with itself. In the method of paired comparison every stimulus is compared with every other stimulus, and hence there are n^2 comparisons, or $n(n - 1)$ comparisons if each stimulus is not compared with itself [24, 26]. As regards experimental procedure, the constant method is a special case of the method of paired comparison. The method of paired comparison can be used for the purpose of making limen determinations in which every stimulus serves in turn as a standard, but we shall consider it here for the more fundamental problem of establishing a metric for the psychological continuum.

When the subject has made a large number of comparisons for each pair of stimuli, the results can be arranged in a square table of experimentally observed proportions, like Table I. The entry p_{32}, for example, shows the proportion of the subject's judgments $R_3 > R_2$ in the attribute that was judged. Such a table can be arranged for any attribute x about which the subject can say, "A is x'er than B." The general element in this table may be denoted p_{jk}. It shows the proportion of judgments in which j exceeds k in the specified attribute.

TABLE I

DATA FORM FOR THE METHOD OF PAIRED COMPARISONS

	k				
	1	2	3	—	n
1	0.50	p_{12}	p_{13}	—	p_{1n}
2	p_{21}	0.50	p_{23}	—	p_{2n}
3	p_{31}	p_{32}	0.50	—	p_{3n}
—	—	—	p_{jk}	0.50	—
n	p_{n1}	p_{n2}	p_{n3}	—	0.50

The problem is to allocate each of the n stimuli to a point on the linear subjective continuum which represents the differential experience of the attribute x [6]. Since only two categories of judgment are implied in this table, we have the restriction that $p_{jk} = 1 - p_{kj}$, and, in general, the diagonal elements are 0.50, since we eliminate the constant error by counterbalanced order. Hence, there are

$n(n-1)/2$ experimentally independent values which should be consistent with a set of n subjective scale values, one for each stimulus. For 20 stimuli, the problem is then to account for 190 experimentally independent proportions by 20 scale values.

In solving this problem it has been found necessary to distinguish between two kinds of stimulus series, namely, those in which the stimuli are *homogeneous* in that they differ only in a single attribute, and those in which the stimuli are *heterogeneous* in that they differ necessarily in attributes additional to the one which is being studied. In auditory experiments the attribute that is specified for comparison may be pitch. In a homogeneous stimulus series we should have pure tones that differ only in pitch. If we want to compare noises as to their pitch, however, then we are necessarily dealing with a heterogeneous stimulus series. It has been found that for homogeneous series a single parameter or scale value S_j can be assigned to each stimulus so that the observed proportions are accounted for. A heterogeneous stimulus series requires two parameters for each stimulus, namely, a mean scale value S_j and a measure of subjective dispersion σ_j.

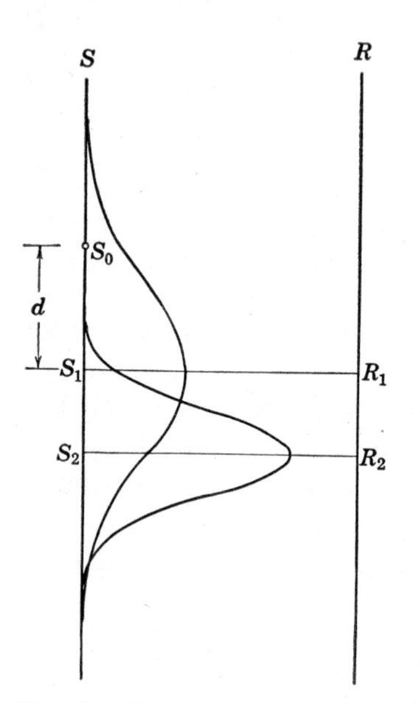

Fig. 8. Discriminal dispersions of two stimuli.

Consider the two continua, R and S, which are represented in Fig. 8. A particular stimulus R_1 is represented by a point on the R scale, determined by its physical magnitude. The apparent or subjective magnitude of this stimulus on a particular occasion is represented at some point S_0 on the S scale. The stimulus R_1 is perceived with different apparent magnitudes S on different occasions. Let S_1 be the median apparent magnitude for the stimulus R_1. This apparent magnitude is mediated by a process of unknown nature which may be considered to be psychical or physiological or both, depending on philosophical preferences. We shall call this process the *modal discriminal process* for the stimulus R_1. The allocation of this discriminal process on the subjective continuum will be denoted S_1. On any particular occasion the stimulus R_1 may be perceived by other processes, such as the *discriminal process* denoted S_0. It will be assumed that each discriminal process is the modal process for some stimulus magnitude. The physical magnitudes and the corresponding average modal processes are covariant, and for every physical magnitude there is a corresponding modal discriminal process.

In order to introduce a subjective metric for the discriminal processes, we make the hypothesis that each stimulus projects a normal frequency distribution on the subjective continuum. By this we mean that the discriminal processes are so separated that the distribution of frequencies with which they are experienced in response to the stimulus R_1 is normal. We are free to define the S scale arbitrarily in this manner for any given stimulus, but it becomes an experimental fact whether the frequency distributions for other stimuli would then also be normal. Since the subjective quality of a single stimulus cannot be communicated, the experimental verification must be indirect.

Having defined the S scale in such a manner that the stimulus R_1 projects a Gaussian distribution, we next define the discriminal deviation d as the linear separation between S and the scale value S_1. This separation is determined by the relative frequency with which S is experienced when R_1 is perceived. The standard deviation of the S values is σ_1.

We now introduce another stimulus magnitude R_2 as shown in the figure. The modal discriminal process for this stimulus is denoted S_2, and it is again assumed that this stimulus projects a normal distribution on the subjective continuum, but not necessarily with the same dispersion. If the second stimulus is of such a nature that it is perceived more consistently as to its apparent magnitude on successive occasions, then it will project a smaller dispersion on the subjective continuum. It will be described as a stimulus of lower *ambiguity* or dispersion. The subjective dispersions are denoted σ_1 and σ_2 respectively. If one of the stimuli is chosen as a standard, its subjective dispersion may be defined as the *subjective unit of measurement* [8, 18].

It is assumed that, if the discriminal process for R_1 is higher on the S scale than the discriminal process for R_2 on the particular occasion when they are compared, then the subject will return the judgment $R_1 > R_2$. When this relation is reversed on the subjective continuum, then the subject returns the opposite judgment, namely, $R_2 > R_1$. If this pair of stimuli is presented, together with other stimulus pairs, for a large number of comparative judgments, then the proportions of judgments, p_{jk}, can be experimentally determined. It can be shown by statistical reasoning that

$$S_j - S_k = x_{jk}\sqrt{\sigma_j^2 + \sigma_k^2 - 2r_{jk}\sigma_j\sigma_k}$$

where S_j and S_k are the scale values of the modal discriminal processes,

x_{jk} is the deviation from the mean of a normal distribution, determined by the proportion p_{jk} of judgments $R_j > R_k$, σ_j and σ_k are the discriminal dispersions of the two stimuli, and r_{jk} is the correlation between the scale values of the discriminal processes.

This equation is the *law of comparative judgment,* by which each stimulus can be allocated to the subjective continuum. The validity of this law is sustained if it is found that a set of consistent scale values S_j and subjective dispersions σ_j can be found by this equation such that they account for the experimentally observed proportions of comparative judgments. The number of stimuli in the experimental series must be long enough so that there is a much larger number of experimentally determined proportions than there are parameters to be determined. In order to make the problem soluble, it is usually assumed that the correlational term vanishes. The correlations can be estimated separately by the method of successive intervals, but most experiments are so arranged that the correlations can be assumed to be negligible.

In the simplest case the discriminal dispersions are also assumed to be equal, so that the law of comparative judgment reduces to the simple form

$$S_j - S_k = x_{jk}\sqrt{2}$$

which is known as Case V of this law [18, 24]. In this case it is assumed that the experimentally observed proportions can be accounted for by a single parameter S_j for each stimulus. This can frequently be done, but it is occasionally necessary to deal with two parameters for each stimulus, namely, the scale value S_j and the subjective dispersion σ_j.

Although the law of comparative judgment is easily applied to the stimuli of classical psychophysics, the more generally interesting applications are those which involve social, moral, and esthetic values, opinion polls, and consumer preferences. One example of the measurement of social distance and racial preferences will be given here. Several hundred students were presented with a schedule in which they were asked to check one of each pair of nationalities or races to indicate with which they would rather associate [19]. The resulting tabulations were analyzed by Case V of the law of comparative judgment. It must be recognized that the preferential values were determined, not only by the nationalities and races involved, but also by the particular groups of subjects, as well as the time at which their preferences were expressed. Students in other countries and at different times would return different subjective values. It is of interest that the average discrepancy between the experimentally obtained proportions and those which are implied by the computed scale values was only 0.03, even with the simplifying assumptions of Case V.[3]

It has been assumed in some earlier psychophysical studies that "equally often noticed differences are equal," but it can be shown that the discriminal dispersion may have a serious effect on this assumption. In Fig. 9 we have represented the discriminal dispersions of three stimuli on the subjective continuum in which $S_A = S_B$. Hence $p_{AB} = 0.50$. Stimulus A has a large dispersion, so that the subject perceives high values in it on some occasions, and low values on other occasions. The proportion of judgments A > C will be high but not unity, because these two subjective distributions overlap. The proportion of judgments B > C will be unity, because stimulus B is never perceived as below C. Here the scale separations (A — C) and (B — C) are equal, but their frequencies of discrimination are not equal. Hence we conclude that equally often noticed differences are not equal if the stimuli have different dispersions. The assumption is valid, however, when the dispersions are uniform.

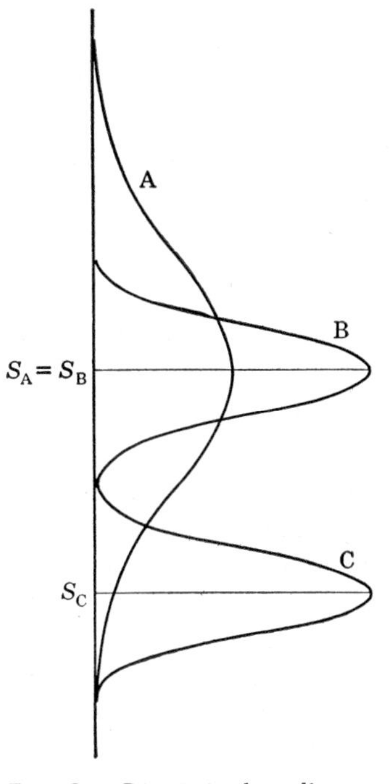

Fig. 9. Discriminal dispersions of three stimuli.

The law of comparative judgment takes no cognizance of the physical stimulus intensity or of any other physical measurement except relative frequency of comparative judgment. Hence it can be used to define the subjective continuum for a stimulus series which has no known physical measure as to the designated attribute. A series of handwriting specimens, for example, can be compared as to their relative degrees of excellence without reference to the fact that this attribute has no known physical measure. One application is in semantic studies of cognitive and affective word meanings. The cognitive content of *famous* and *notorious* is practically the same, but they differ in affective connotation. These differences can be measured with the law of comparative judgment. For each experiment it is necessary, however, to verify the applicability of the law by showing that the scale values S and the discriminal dispersions σ actually do account for the much

[3] For more complete discussion and bibliography, consult [8].

larger number of experimentally observed comparative judgments. This internal consistency must be demonstrated for each kind of application before we can speak of subjective measurement, as distinguished from mere rank order.

Method of Equal Appearing Intervals

In this method the subject deals directly with the psychological continuum, which is represented by a series of successive intervals. He is asked to assign each one of a series of stimuli to one of the intervals. If he does this a number of times, or if a group of subjects do the task with one complete sorting for each subject, then each stimulus will have a frequency distribution in the successive equal intervals. The scale value S_j of each stimulus is the mean of its distribution, and the standard deviation σ_j is called the *ambiguity* of the stimulus as regards the attribute that is being appraised.

A well-known example of this method is the Sanford weight experiment [7, p. 154]. Some envelopes are weighted so as to represent a fairly wide range. The subject is instructed to sort the envelopes into five piles, so that the successive piles seem to be equally spaced. When all the subjects have done this task, the mean scale position S_j can be determined for each envelope. Fechner's law can then be tested by plotting the scale positions S_j against the corresponding weights R_j in grams. The plot is usually logarithmic.

The method of equal appearing intervals has a methodological limitation in that it does not provide a test of internal consistency, as in the method of paired comparison. It has been found that, when the scale values obtained by the method of paired comparison are compared with those of the method of equal appearing intervals, there is a discrepancy, especially toward the ends of the scale, and this has been called the *end effect.* Since the method of paired comparison has a check of internal consistency, and since it agrees well with the method of rank order (to be described), it is assumed that the distortion of the end effect can be attributed to the method of equal appearing intervals [9]. The method is used in experiments where it is sufficient to have approximate estimates of subjective values. The subject easily understands this method, and the task for a long stimulus series can be completed in a relatively short time. The method of mean gradation, which has been described, is a special case of the method of equal appearing intervals because the total subjective interval between two stimuli is there merely bisected.

For the purpose of appraising some types of educational results, there have been constructed a number of *product scales.* Such a scale consists of a graduated sequence of specimens which represent successive degrees of general excellence. Examples are the appraisal of general excellence of handwriting [17], freehand lettering, English compositions [10], and some types of shop work. Although judgments of this kind are frequently made with some confidence and consistency, the judges usually find it difficult to identify the objective components that determine their total appraisal. The construction of a handwriting scale will be used as an example of this type of psychophysical problem.

In the construction of a handwriting scale, one starts with a large collection of handwriting specimens. The subjects who participate in the construction of the scale sort the specimens into a series of, say, ten subjectively equal intervals. On the basis of such experimental data, the mean scale value of each handwriting specimen can be readily determined. Those specimens which have unusually large dispersions are eliminated because they are the ones about which the judges disagree as to general excellence. From the remainder, one can select an evenly graduated sequence of specimens to constitute a descriptive scale for judging general excellence of handwriting [17]. Each specimen that is to be appraised is then described by the number of the standard to which it is equated.

Method of Successive Intervals

In the method of equal appearing intervals, the subject is asked to sort the stimuli into intervals that are subjectively equal. Even though the subject does not realize it, this task is difficult. The intervals toward the ends of the scale tend to become subjectively larger than the intervals in the middle range. This end effect is caused partly by the fact that the total subjective range tends to shift during the sorting procedure. The method of successive intervals is experimentally similar to the method of equal appearing intervals. The subject is asked to make the intervals successive but not necessarily subjectively equal. The successive intervals may be denoted merely by successive numerals, or they may be defined by descriptive terms or phrases whose successive character is readily admitted by the subject at the start of the experiment. By this simple experimental method, the scale values S and the discriminal dispersions σ may be determined for the stimuli. The method is especially useful in studies of consumer preferences which involve judgments of a large number of forms of a product.

Method of Rank Order

When the subject has arranged a set of stimuli in rank order according to any designated attribute, we do not have enough information to transform the rank orders into psychological measurement. When the number of stimuli is quite large, the rank orders are sometimes transmuted into a scale, on the assumption that the group of stimuli represent a normal distribution in the designated attribute. For any given set of numbers, or rank orders, it is always possible to define a scale quite arbitrarily, so that the given set of numbers, or rank orders, represents a normal distribution on that scale. But nothing is proved by doing it.

When a group of subjects has placed a set of stimuli in rank order, we can determine, for each pair of stimuli, the proportion of judges who ranked one higher than the other. If a subject placed four stimuli in the rank order B, D, A, C, then we can extract for him six separate comparative judgments. In each of the six following judgments, the first is ranked higher than the second. We have then BD, BA, BC, DA, DC, AC. If these judgments are tabulated for all subjects, we can determine the proportion of judgments "j higher than k" for every pair of stimuli. With these data we can proceed with the method of paired comparison [21]. The method of paired comparison is theoretically superior to the method of rank order, but rank order is experimentally much easier for the subject and in general less fatiguing. Comparison has been made of these two methods when the same subjects rated handwriting specimens in pairs and also in rank order. The agreement was found by Kate Hevner to be very close [9].

Method of Single Stimuli

In most psychophysical methods there is a preference for the judgment of a stimulus in direct comparison with another stimulus or with a group of stimuli. In the method of single stimuli, however, the subject gives a descriptive rating of each presented stimulus [2, 25]. He is asked to say for each stimulus whether it seems large or small, or he is asked to apply one of several descriptive words to each stimulus. In this method the subject must keep in mind his own standard. It has been found that this standard tends toward the average of the presented stimulus series. The method of single stimuli can be varied, and in one of its forms it becomes similar to the method of successive intervals. The method of single stimuli does not ordinarily imply the calculation of scale values and dispersions, as in the method of successive intervals. The method is sometimes called the *method of absolute judgment.*

Method of Judgment Time

In earlier psychophysical studies it was found that the time for discriminatory judgment was longest for the most difficult comparisons where the physical differences were smallest. If judgment time is plotted against physical stimulus difference, the result is a falling curve that approaches reaction time as an asymptote. It is possible to use this relation inversely, so that the psychological difference is inferred from the average response time [3, 16]. The relation must be calibrated for each type of stimulus.

The negative relation between physical stimulus difference and response time is of some general interest. It is conceivable, for example, that individual differences in this curve may be of significance in judging the temperament of the subject. Some subjects retard conspicuously in judgment time when the physical difference becomes small and hence more difficult. This psychophysical relation may be characteristic of subjects who have difficulty in making up their minds.

In learning experiments it is customary to use the number of correct responses for each trial as a numerical index of learning. Complete learning is then indicated by a perfect score within the time limit allowed for each association. The method of response time can be used for measuring overlearning. If learning continues after perfect scores are obtained, the additional learning can be easily shown in terms of the continued reduction in response time, which becomes then an index of overlearning. It is to be expected that the rate of forgetting will be affected by the amount of overlearning beyond the first perfect response.

The development of psychological test theory has unfortunately been separate from that of psychophysics, in spite of the fact that many of the underlying concepts are similar or identical. This has been due to the fact that the two branches of psychological research have been carried out by different groups of men. In the psychophysical method of response time, we have one of many examples of the close relation between psychophysics and test theory. The ability of a subject to do a certain kind of task is frequently indicated by the speed with which he can do it, and the difficulty of a task is sometimes arbitrarily defined so that the distribution of ability in the population is normal. The power score of an individual as regards a certain kind of task is that degree of difficulty of task which he can do without pressure of time, but all experimental procedures must be finite in time allowances.

APPLICATIONS OF THE PSYCHOPHYSICAL METHODS

Measurement of Affective Attitudes

An attitude represents a restriction of some kind in the manner in which an object is regarded. In dealing with social attitudes we consider primarily the *affective attitudes* toward debatable issues. For the purposes of measuring affective social attitudes, we postulate an affective continuum with a neutral point. Positive affect represents appetition or favorable attitude toward a *psychological object,* which may be any object, person, or idea. Negative affect represents aversion or unfavorable attitude toward the psychological object in question. The purpose of attitude measurement is to assign each individual to this affective continuum, as regards his positive or negative attitude toward a specified psychological object X.

We limit ourselves in the present case to those psychological objects about which a person can express approval or disapproval in various degrees of intensity, which are represented by his position on the affective continuum. If we want to know how strongly a man feels for or against some psychological object X, we can proceed in several ways. We can ask him, and then note the strength of his free expression for or against X. We can watch his overt actions in relation to X, or we can present him with a list of statements of various degrees of intensity of affect for and against X to see which he endorses. Such a list is an attitude scale. The separate statements are called *opinions,* but our interest may be to determine the person's strength of approval or disapproval of X, which we call his attitude, rather than merely to tabulate endorsements and rejections of separate opinions.

The construction of an attitude scale starts with the name, phrase, or symbol which constitutes the psychological object. This object must be something about which people debate quite freely. A rather long list of opinions is then collected so as to include various degrees of both positive and negative affect about X, as well as neutral opinions. A group of readers sorts the opinions by the method of equal appearing intervals or the method of successive intervals. These readers are told merely to consider the question, "How strongly do you think somebody would feel for or against X if you heard him make this statement?" It should be specially noted that the opinions of the readers themselves have nothing to do with the case. They are asked merely to consider where somebody else who made these statements would be on the affective continuum. The main requirement for the readers is therefore that they be able to read English.

With data of this kind one can determine the scale value S_j and the dispersion σ_j for each opinion. The opinions with large dispersion are eliminated because they contain some ambiguity as to affective meaning. From the remaining opinions, an equally graduated sequence is selected to constitute an attitude scale. The score of an individual who records his own responses on such a scale is intended to represent the strength of affective attitude toward the psychological object X. Within the limitations of the psychophysical method used, the intervals of such a scale can be regarded as roughly equal. With a schedule of this kind, it is possible to construct a frequency distribution of affective attitude toward a specified object for a given group of subjects. It is then legitimate to inquire about the shape of this distribution of affect. At the beginning of a political campaign this distribution may be unimodal, but during the course of the campaign it may be expected that the distribution of attitude becomes bimodal, especially if the issues are hotly debated. Psychophysical problems of general interest are involved here.

Many attitude scales have been constructed, and their interpretations have been frequently debated. One of the recurring issues is whether a man's overt behavior is a better guide to his attitude than what he says on an attitude scale. It is sometimes supposed that overt conduct is the criterion against which an attitude scale must be validated, but this is erroneous. If we really want to know how a man feels about some debated question, then the best procedure is probably to learn what he says to his intimate friends when he is not publicly observed or quoted. His overt actions may be guided by administrative, social, or political expediency. What he says on an attitude schedule may, similarly, be determined by the personalities of the examiners and onlookers and those who might quote him. Both these indices are fallible if the issue is at all critical. Even when the verbal and overt indices agree, they may both be wrong. In general, it is probably easier for people to express their likes and dislikes verbally than to commit themselves to the corresponding overt acts. Attitude schedules can be used with confidence only in those situations where there is no strong pressure, explicit or implied, to influence verbal expression. Occasionally a man expresses himself with apparent freedom even when he is in a conspicuous minority, but all studies in this field must be interpreted with due regard to the social pressures that influence both verbal expression and overt conduct.

The question has been raised whether an attitude scale, considered as a psychological measuring device, is itself influenced by the opinions of the readers who determined the scale values of the opinions by sorting them. If this should be the case, then the interpretation of the resulting frequency distributions of attitude scores would be limited by the characteristics of the standardizing group of readers. A collection of opinions about the Negro was sorted independently by three groups of subjects: a group of northern whites, a group of northern Negroes, and a group of southern Negroes. The three resulting attitude scales were linearly related, and they differed only in the allocation of the neutral point. An attitude which was considered by the northern whites to be neutral in affect was considered by the Negroes to be slightly negative. This displacement of the neutral point was predicted. The frequency distributions of attitude obtained from the three scales were the same except for the origin [11].

Measurement of Effects of Propaganda

For many problems in social attitudes it is sufficient merely to count the relative frequencies of endorsement of particular propositions or

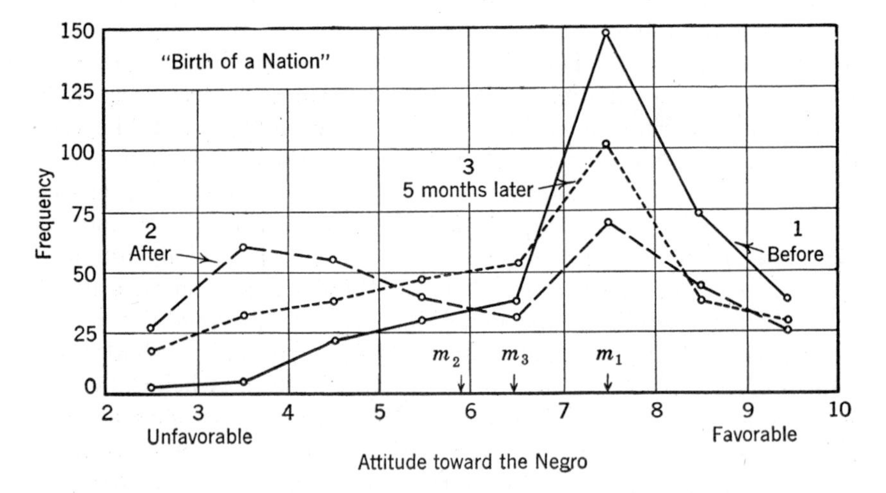

Fig. 10. Frequency distributions of scores on a measure of attitude toward the Negro.

opinions before and after presentation of propaganda material. For such problems the scaling of attitudes is not necessary. On the other hand, if it is desired to describe the shift in a frequency distribution of attitudes which is caused by propaganda, a metric is required, and an attitude schedule is then indicated.[4]

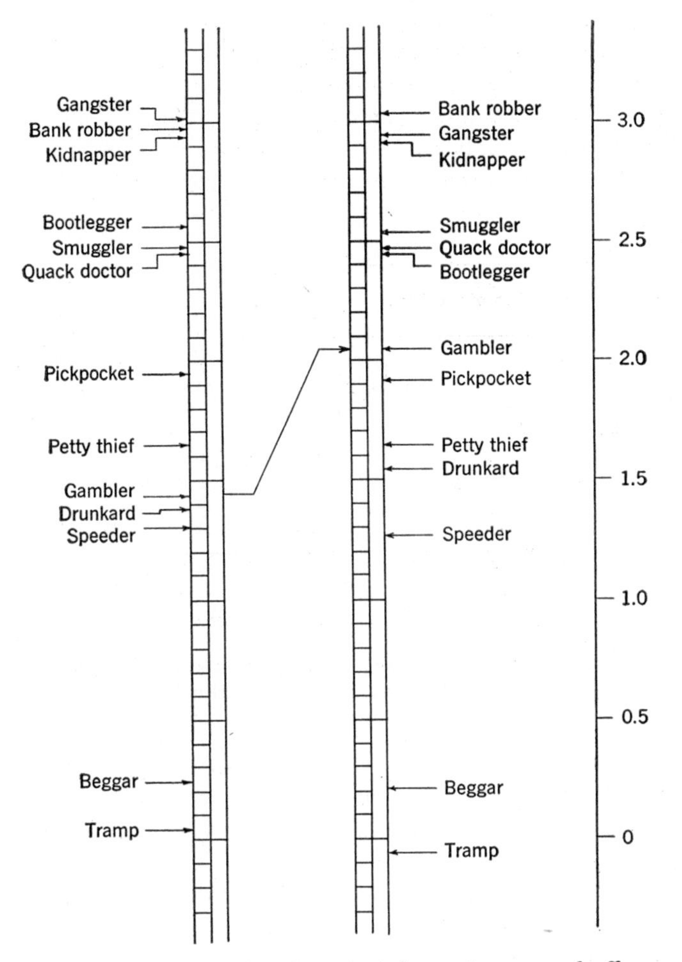

Fig. 11. Two sets of scale values for seriousness of offenses.

Many experiments have been made to study quantitatively the effects of propaganda. One experimental method is to compare the attitude scores on a schedule before and after presentation of propa-

[4] A distinction should be noted between *tests* and *schedules.* A test is a device for appraising an individual in respect to some attribute, and it is implied that the subject does not have voluntary control over the appraisal. An attitude scale is not a test in any sense because the subject is in complete control of the responses. Similarly, personality schedules and interest schedules should not be called tests.

ganda material. Figure 10 shows the frequency distribution of scores on a schedule of attitude toward the Negro. The high school students who participated saw the film "Birth of a Nation" at a local theater. A few days after seeing the film, they were given a parallel form of the same schedule. After 5 months they were given a third schedule on the same issue. The figure shows the striking effect of this film in making the students less friendly toward Negroes. The third distribution shows that only half of the effect had worn off after 5 months. The three m's refer to the means obtained. Experiments have demon-

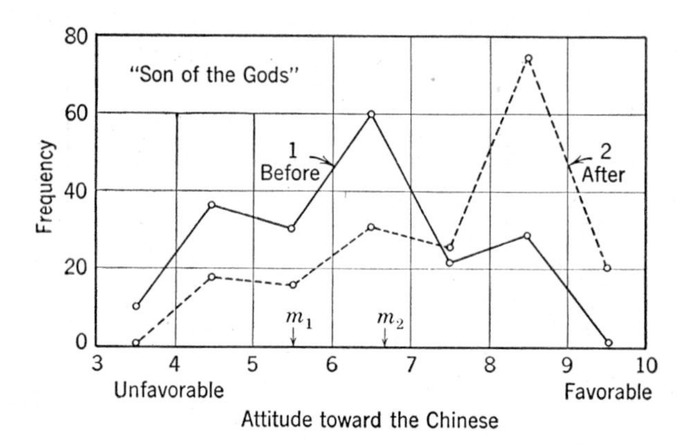

Fig. 12. Distributions of affective judgments toward Chinese, before and after seeing a moving picture.

strated a summation effect with several films. When a single film was inadequate to demonstrate a statistically significant shift in attitude, a sequence of several such films showed a significant summation effect [23].

The paired-comparison method is probably more sensitive in measuring shifts in attitude than the attitude scales. Figure 11 shows two sets of scale values for seriousness of offenses. These offenses were presented in pairs, with instruction to check one of each pair to indicate which was the more serious. Two such schedules were presented, one before and one after the presentation of a film depicting the life of a gambler. The problem was to ascertain the effect of the film on the attitudes of school children toward gamblers. It can be seen in the figure that the only significant shift in scale value was that of "gambler." This experimental audience of school children considered gambling to be more serious after seeing the film. Similar experiments have been made to determine the effect of films on the international attitudes of student audiences. Figure 12 shows the effect of a film in making the student audience more friendly toward the Chinese.

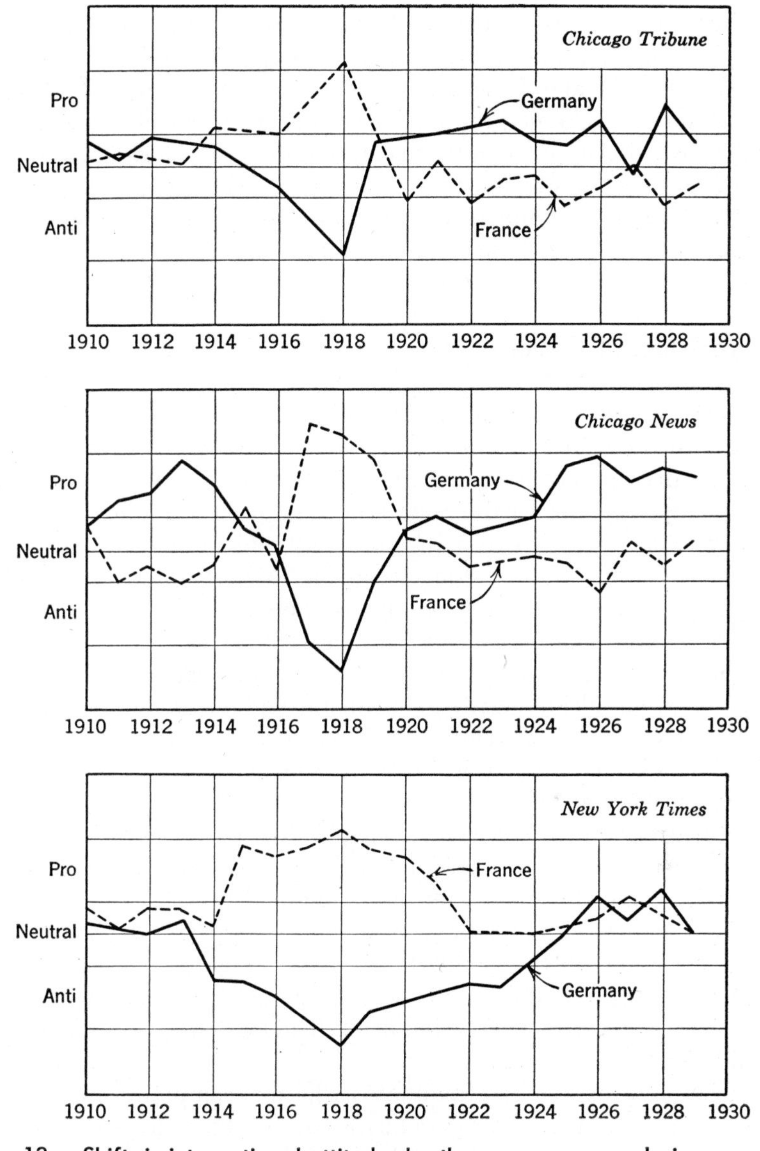

Fig. 13. Shifts in international attitudes by three newspapers during a period covering World War I.

The psychophysical methods can be adapted as a historical method. A tabulation was made of editorial comments about Germany and about France for the period 1910 to 1930. These were sorted by a group of readers, as in the construction of an attitude scale. Mean scale values were then plotted against time in order to ascertain the shift in attitude, as represented editorially, during the 20-year period, which included World War I. Figure 13 shows the shifting attitudes toward Germany and France before and during this war, as well as the gradual recovery of prewar attitudes after its conclusion. It has been suggested that such shifts in international attitudes be used as a sort of barometer of impending crises. A similar psychophysical study was made of Chinese editorial attitudes toward the Japanese, and vice versa, before those countries were at war [15].

The Prediction of Choice

So far we have been concerned with the problem of allocating each stimulus to the subjective continuum with regard to a specified attribute. In the simplest case, such as that of lifted weights, the physical measure of weight is easily ascertained for each stimulus. In more complex situations there is no known physical measure to represent the attribute completely. Such a case is that of handwriting excellence, which can be judged with some confidence but cannot be readily measured in physical terms. In still more complex cases, the attribute to be judged has no available physical measure. An example is affective or preferential judgments about moral and aesthetic values. The law of comparative judgment enables us to allocate a stimulus to the subjective continuum quite independently of whether there exists any physical measure at all.

We turn now to the obverse psychophysical problem. The obverse problem is to predict what people will do in terms of the affective scale values and dispersions of the stimuli. When the scale values and dispersions are known for several competing psychological objects, what proportion of the population will then vote for a particular object as their first choice? This is a new and fascinating field for theoretical and experimental inquiry. The obverse problem will be introduced with an example.

Consider a group of six candidates who are competing for elective office, and assume that their popularities are exactly the same, namely, S_j. Assume, further, that candidate A does or says something for which half of the electors dislike him, and the other half like him, so that his discriminal dispersion becomes much larger than that of the other candidates, who will be assumed, in this hypothetical example, to have negligible dispersions. If all the candidates retain the same average popularity, then a paired comparison schedule of preferences would show proportions of 0.50 for all possible pairs of candidates. From such a table one might infer that the candidates would divide the votes evenly, but such is not the case. At election the more variable candidate would draw half of the votes, and the other candidates would draw only 10 per cent each. Hence the more variable candidate would get the plurality. When a tie threatens between two candidates who are equally popular, it can be shown that the more variable candidate can win the plurality by introducing a third candidate, even if the new candidate is less popular than either of the first two. It seems likely that this principle is known to practical politicians [22].

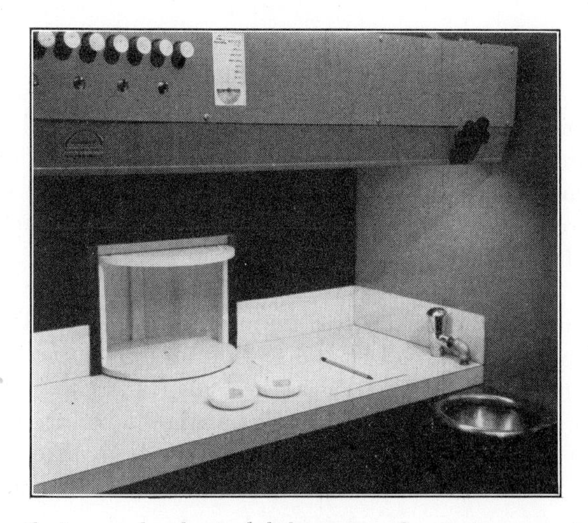

Fig. 14. Booth in psychophysical laboratory for taste experiments in the Quartermaster Food and Container Institute for the Armed Forces in Chicago.

(This photograph was taken by Dr. Franklin W. Dove, Chief, Food Acceptance Research Branch of the Institute.)

In the study of consumer preferences the manufacturer is interested in pleasing every consumer. If a number of commodities or designs are submitted to consumers for rating, the scale value and the dispersion can be determined for each commodity or design. If it is desired to select, say, ten designs for the market, it would be an error to select the designs with the ten highest scale values. To do so might please some people with several designs each, and leave the rest dissatisfied. The designs should be chosen so as to maximize the number of first choices, which are determined partly by the scale values and dispersions and also by the correlations of affective values among the designs. This psychophysical problem can be solved with the method of successive intervals.

In the manufacture of food products, it has been found that human subjects can identify and reject food by criteria that escape chemical and bacteriological tests. It is for this reason that the United States Army has established a food acceptance laboratory for making taste comparisons of food products. Figure 14 shows one of the booths in this psychophysical laboratory. The color of the food specimens can be controlled by color filters. Food products are here studied in formal taste comparisons to determine their relative acceptability for different ingredients, duration and temperature of storage, and various containers.

CONCLUSION

This chapter on psychophysical methods introduces the section of this book which is devoted to the methods of studying perceptual and sensory phenomena. In reading these later chapters the student will find many references to psychophysics, a discipline which is fundamental to the problem of measurement in psychology.

The basic concepts of measuring subjective phenomena have been treated with descriptions of the major and representative methods of classical psychophysics. In the section on *applications* it has been pointed out that the psychophysical methods transcend the older fields to which they have been applied, and that they have become powerful tools in the solution of important problems in political and social behavior, as well as in merchandising and market research.

REFERENCES

1. Boring, E. G. The stimulus error. *Amer. J. Psychol.*, 1921, *32*, 449–471.
2. Bressler, J. Judgments in absolute units as a psychophysical method. *Arch. Psychol.*, 1933, *23*, No. 152.
3. Carlson, W. R., R. C. Driver, and M. G. Preston. Judgment times for the method of constant stimuli. *J. Exper. Psychol.*, 1934, *17*, 113–118.
4. Fernberger, S. W. The use of equality judgments in psychophysical procedures. *Psychol. Rev.*, 1930, *37*, 107–112.
5. Fritz, M. F. Experimental evidence in support of Professor Thurstone's criticism of the phi-gamma hypothesis. *J. Gen. Psychol.*, 1930, *4*, 346–352.
6. Guilford, J. P. The method of paired comparisons as a psychophysical method. *Psychol. Rev.*, 1928, *35*, 494–506.
7. Guilford, J. P. *Psychometric Methods.* New York: McGraw-Hill, 1936.
8. Gulliksen, H. Paired comparisons and the logic of measurement. *Psychol. Rev.*, 1946, *53*, 199–213.
9. Hevner, K. An empirical study of three psychophysical methods. *J. Gen. Psychol.*, 1930, *4*, 191–212.

10. Hillegas, M. B. A scale for the measurement of equality in English composition by young people. *Teach. Coll. Rec.*, 1912, *13,* No. 4.
11. Hinckley, E. D. The influence of individual opinion on construction of an attitude scale. *J. Soc. Psychol.*, 1932, *3,* 283–296.
12. Householder, A. S., and G. Young. Weber laws, the Weber law, and psychophysical analysis. *Psychometrika,* 1940, *5,* 183–193.
13. Luckiesh, M., and F. K. Moss. A restricted extension of Fechner's law from sensation to behavior. *Psychol. Rev.*, 1942, *49,* 135–142.
14. Lufkin, H. M. The best fitting frequency function for Urban's lifted-weight results. *Amer. J. Psychol.*, 1928, *40,* 75–82.
15. Russell, J. T., and Q. Wright. National attitudes on the Far Eastern controversy. *Amer. Polit. Sci. Rev.*, 1933, *27,* 555–576.
16. Steinman, A. R. Reaction time to change compared with other psychophysical methods. *Arch. Psychol.*, 1944, No. 292.
17. Thorndike, E. L. Handwriting. *Teach. Coll. Rec.*, 1910, *11,* No. 2.
18. Thurstone, L. L. A law of comparative judgment. *Psychol. Rev.*, 1927, *34,* 273–286.
19. Thurstone, L. L. An experimental study of nationality preferences. *J. Gen. Psychol.*, 1928, *1,* 405–424.
20. Thurstone, L. L. The phi-gamma hypothesis. *J. Exper. Psychol.*, 1928, *11,* 293–305.
21. Thurstone, L. L. Rank order as a psychophysical method. *J. Exper. Psychol.*, 1931, *14,* 187–201.
22. Thurstone, L. L. The prediction of choice. *Psychometrika,* 1945, *10,* 237–253.
23. Thurstone, L. L., and R. C. Peterson. *The Effect of Motion Pictures on the Social Attitudes of High School Children.* Ann Arbor, Michigan: Edwards Brothers, 1932.
24. Thurstone, L. L. Psychophysical analysis. *Amer. J. Psychol.*, 1927, *38,* 368–389.
25. Volkmann, J. The method of single stimuli. *Amer. J. Psychol.*, 1932, *44,* 808–809.
26. Wherry, R. J. Orders for the presentation of pairs in the method of paired comparisons. *J. Exper. Psychol.*, 1938, *23,* 651–660.
27. Woodworth, R. S. *Experimental Psychology.* New York: Henry Holt, 1938.

SUGGESTED READINGS

Guilford, J. P. *Psychometric Methods.* New York: McGraw-Hill, 1936. (pp. 1–70, 110–262.)

Johannsen, D. E. *The Principles of Psychophysics, with Laboratory Exercises.* Saratoga Springs, New York: the author, 1941.

Chapter 6

Studying Perceptual Phenomena

James J. Gibson[1]

Every student of psychology knows that his awareness of the world is completely dependent on the activity of his sense organs, although sometimes he does not realize that this is a startling fact and not a commonplace one. He tends to take for granted the familiar world which he sees before him, not realizing that in all its aspects and in every detail it is apprehended only because his sense organs are functioning, and that if these functions failed for any reason, so also would his awareness of the world.

The succeeding chapters will describe the study of the sensory mechanisms which make possible this apprehension of the environment. It is obvious, however, that these mechanisms do not fully account for the experience of the concrete world. The world is a good deal more than a matter of colors and sounds, of warms and colds, of tastes and smells and feelings. It is also a matter of surfaces and shapes and distances and objects, not to mention friends and sunsets and symbols and nations. How does the organism come to be aware of these concrete and significant things, as distinguished from the more abstract and unfamiliar ones with which sensory psychology is concerned? Such features of the world are traditionally classified as perceptions rather than sensations, and it is with the investigation of these that the present chapter deals.

SENSATION AND PERCEPTION

A generation ago it was still possible to teach a fairly simple doctrine of the relation between sensation and perception. The experienced world was thought to be built up out of elementary sensations, supplemented by images of past elementary sensations. A perception,

[1] Associate Professor of Psychology, Smith College.

then, was a complex of elementary processes, combined or fused in some way not wholly understood, and logically distinct from the elements which made it up. This distinction has been overthrown in recent years. It has become clear to most psychologists that there is no way of deciding whether a given experience is elementary. The conception of elementary units of mind, therefore, has been abandoned for the more defensible notion of dimensions of variation of experience. In strict accuracy, one should no longer speak of sensations but of modes of discrimination, or variables with respect to which an experience is characterized and specified. These experience variables include perceptions as well as sensations. It thus becomes an arbitrary matter whether a given type of experience is classified as sensory or as perceptual, since the chief logical basis for the earlier meaning of these terms has disappeared. When the variable can be shown to correspond with a stimulus variation of physics, as hue and wave length can be shown to correspond, it is usually considered a sensory variable. When the variable in question corresponds with a complex variation of the physical stimulus, or when the stimulus is not measurable, it is apt to be considered perceptual.

Instead of the doctrine that the phenomenal world is built up out of sensations and images by a process of combination, Gestalt psychologists propose the theory that sensory processes organize themselves spontaneously into higher-order processes at the level of the cerebral cortex and produce physiological events which are fundamentally *like* the perceptions which it is necessary to explain. Perception results from neural organization in the brain. According to this theory also, the distinction between sensation and perception disappears and is replaced by levels of organization. The relation between sensory and perceptual phenomena, we may conclude, is very close, and the difference between them is not in *kind* of function but in *degree.*

Psychophysics and Psychophysiology

The explanation of how we perceive the world must ultimately include a physiological theory of perception, a theory of the correspondence between the experience and the neural process. The effort to find out what goes on in the nervous system has been called psychophysiology. It may be studied in two ways. One mode of approach is by working backward from the properties of experience to the probable properties of the underlying physiology, as the Gestalt psychologists have done. This is a speculative approach. Instead, one may study the neural events directly and experimentally. The techniques for this study are described in Chapter 15.

The study of the correspondence between the experience and the stimulus, without reference to the intermediate physiological stage, is a much older and better established field of research. It is traditionally called psychophysics, and its methods have led to the accumulation of a vast amount of evidence about the sensory capacities of man and the dimensions with respect to which he can discriminate the world. (See Chapter 5.) The predominant methods of studying vision, hearing, and the other special senses are the *psychophysical* methods.

One might suppose that this concentration of sensory research on the correspondence between the experience and the stimulus would also be reflected in the study of perception, but such is not the case. Because of the complexity of the stimuli for perception, because of the difficulty of measuring and controlling them (the stimuli for the perception of distance are an example), and because they are in some cases not even identifiable in our present state of knowledge, experimental research on perception has been diverted from the psychophysical relationship in the direction of other problems. As a result there is a preponderance of experiments on the effect of learning on perception, the effect of attitude on perception, and on the question of whether perception can be accounted for by the theory of sensory organization. Now it will probably be readily admitted that the stimuli for perception, however complex they may be, must be identified before the further problem can be solved of what the organism "contributes to" these excitations. The organism may be imagined to organize the stimulus excitations, to transform them, or, in naïve terminology, to interpret them, but in any event the stimuli should first be discovered and specified. To the extent that a psychophysical correspondence can be established between the perception and some complex order of stimulus variable, it will not be necessary to postulate special processes of interpretation or transformation or special laws of sensory organization. If it is no longer believed that sensations are the elements or the data of experience and that perception is the result merely of combining or interpreting these data, then the first problem in perception is to look for the stimuli.

For these reasons attention will be devoted in this chapter primarily to the study of the psychophysical relationship in perception. Experiments of this type should be understood by the student because, in the judgment of the writer, they promise the greatest immediate advancement of our knowledge of how we perceive the world.

The Major Perceptual Problems

If we assume that the psychophysical relationship is the primary one in the study of perception, the task of the experimenter is straightforward. *He must first describe the perceptions to be studied, then identify their stimulus correlates, and finally set up a relationship between the two.* As we shall see, he may not be able fully to complete this program. What, for example, is the stimulus correlate for the perception of beautiful versus ugly? It would be a bold investigator who would undertake to answer this question. But if he should do so, there are ways in which he can proceed. Even though he cannot identify the stimulus correlate, he can systematically obtain descriptions of the experience, he can vary the objects which carry the stimulus, e.g., drawings or abstract patterns, in as many ways as he can invent, and he may then be able to guess what the stimulus correlate might be, e.g., the ratio of "order" to "complexity" in the drawing. Such a ratio has been proposed by Birkhoff [2] as the essential "stimulus" for esthetic quality.

Some of the principal classes or types of perception which may be experimentally treated in this way are listed below. The list is chosen almost entirely from the field of visual perception, and the classification is tentative. It will, however, exemplify the writer's opinion of what the primary problems of perception are, and will serve as a list of the fields from which experiments will be selected to illustrate the important methods of studying perception.

1. The perception of visual form in two dimensions: lines, contours, and objects.
2. The perception of a three-dimensional world: distance and depth.
3. The perception of objective color, size, and shape in relation to their retinal counterparts, i.e., constancy of object perception.
4. The perception of visual motion and locomotion.
5. The perception of meaning and of symbols.
6. Social perception.

METHODS FOR THE STUDY OF PERCEPTION

The primary method of studying experience, like the method of studying behavior, is systematic observation. In the study of experience, observation is called *introspection*. Although the proposition has sometimes been denied, the observation of experience is not basically different from the observation of objective events, as Boring has shown [3]. Introspection is a necessary preliminary step to the setting up of psychophysical relationships; it defines the perception to be studied and may lead to the identification of its stimulus correlate.

The classical *psychophysical* methods are another fundamental procedure in studying perceptual experience. The experiment is usually more formalized than in simple introspection, and two persons are generally involved, the experimenter and the subject or observer. The experimenter manipulates the stimuli, and the subject makes discriminative judgments or reports. As we shall see, however, the more exact psychophysical methods are not applicable if the perception to be studied, e.g., geometrical shape, cannot be arranged on a scale or dimension. Forms, patterns, or *Gestalten* can be judged in various ways, but the triangularity of a triangle does not vary from more to less in the way that size or brightness does. Consequently, another discriminative method, such as the *method of reproduction* or of *nonserial matching,* must be employed in the study of such perception. The three kinds of method will be discussed in order.

Systematic Observation or Introspection

There is nothing in the least erudite or mysterious in the examination of one's own experiences, despite the popular belief to the contrary, and introspection is as valuable to the contemporary student as it ever was. Like other forms of scientific observation, it may be formalized in an experimental situation or performed in natural or semicontrolled situations. There are at least five different types of observation which may be classified as introspection.

1. Analyzing the Stimulus Situation. Introspection may consist of looking for psychophysical correspondence in the course of ordinary experience. Some of the most acute observations in psychology have been of this type. Leonardo da Vinci, for example, discovered that "aerial perspective" was a cue for the perception of distance by noting that buildings of the same objective color appeared successively bluer as their distance increased, particularly on a hazy day.

2. Listing the Attributes of an Experience. Introspection may involve the sorting and arranging of stimulus objects according to their discriminable features. The intention is to discover the attributes of an experience or its different modes of variation. For example, the colors of the visual world may be serially arranged on the dimensions (scales) of hue, brightness, and saturation. Quality and intensity in the various senses have long since been schematized

in this way, the color cone (page 208) being a familiar example. Perceptual qualities may also be classified and serially arranged, but they seldom fall into quite such neat schemata as these.

3. Observing the Effect of Systematic Variation of the Stimulus. When an experimenter suspects that he can isolate an unfamiliar perceptual property, he may use whatever means are at hand to vary the stimulus object or situation systematically and then observe whether there results a variation in the perception. He may try it on himself or bring in another observer. He may use only the simplest technique of varying the stimulus, or he may build an elaborate apparatus for controlling it experimentally. In any event he is seeking to correlate a property of the perception with some feature of the stimulus. Up to this point his method would be called introspection, but if he observes a relationship, the same procedure can be turned into a psychophysical experiment. An example may be found in studying the property which objects possess of being visually *upright*. More specifically, any elongated object is oriented in the visual field; i.e., it has the quality of being vertical or horizontal or tilted. So far, the introspection is scarcely above the commonsense level. The experimenter may now draw a vertical visual line and rotate it about its midpoint. He observes a perceptual variable which he calls "tilt quality" or, more accurately, two opposed qualities denotable as inclination-to-the-right and inclination-to-the-left. Both qualities vanish into a unique quality when the line is vertical, and both increase with deviation from the vertical. When the line is rotated more than 45 degrees, a new set of qualities emerges, analogous to that described but based on deviations from the *horizontal*. The experimenter now can construct an apparatus and carry out a full-fledged psychophysical experiment to investigate the series of interrelated qualities.

4. Analysis of the Content of Consciousness. Introspection of still another type may consist of the analysis of a single, usually momentary, perception into its discriminable features. The aim is to describe them exhaustively. The familiar example is reporting the experience of tasting lemonade. This experience consists mainly of the qualities of sour, sweet, cold, and touch, with the addition of smell and other minor accompaniments. Such introspection requires the observer to report in terms of accepted sensory variables, which are then likely to be thought of as elements. It aims to describe the content of consciousness, without reference to the stimulus correlate (the "stimulus error"), and is in method unlike a psychophysical experiment. It is no longer in such common use as it was in the laboratory of E. B. Titchener.

5. Description of "Organized" Experiences. The type of introspection favored by Gestalt psychologists is also concerned with the content of consciousness rather than its correspondence to stimuli, but the description is not given in terms of orthodox sensory attributes or qualities. It is sometimes said to be observation on a "phenomenological" level. The important feature of a form or a melody is lost if the perception is analyzed: observation should therefore be directed to the form or organization of a perception rather than its elements or dimensions of variation. This type of introspection has led to the description of a number of types of perception which had been neglected by the older introspectionists and which now constitute some of the chief problems in perceptual psychology. Examples are contour, shape, and surface quality. The fact to be noted about these perceptions is that they are similar to things or entities rather than to variables or dimensions. Experimental variation of their stimulus correlates cannot be a continuous variation, and the judgment of more or less on a scale of quality or intensity is not possible. The experimental methods of studying these phenomena are therefore somewhat different from those by which one studies dimensional perceptions.

The Psychophysical Methods

Introspective observation, as we have seen, may lead directly into a psychophysical experiment. The classical methods of psychophysics, although invented for the study of sensory discriminations, are equally applicable to discriminations called perceptual. One may study the "tilt-quality" of a line or the speed of visual movement or the apparent intelligence of persons as represented by photographs in the same way that he may study the intensity or quality of color. The only requirement for the application of these methods is that the phenomenon to which they are applied must exist in some magnitude, or be such that it can be scaled on a dimension. As we have seen, some of the phenomena of perception do not fulfill this condition, or at least cannot at present be shown to do so. Although it has been said that "everything which exists, exists in some quantity," the triangularity of a triangle has as yet not been quantified.

The psychophysical methods of dealing with sensory or perceptual variables are discussed in Chapter 5. It is therefore necessary in this chapter to emphasize the experimental methods employed when the critical aspect of the stimulus being studied is patterned or configurational. These methods are of course *psychophysical* in the sense that what is investigated is the relation between the stimulus pattern and the perception, but they are not based upon the logic of continuous variables.

Non-quantitative and Semiquantitative Psychophysical Methods

Suppose that an experimenter has isolated and presented some configurational stimulus to an observer. What response can the observer make (other than describing it in words) if we exclude judging it as more or less than its variations? The response must be such as to prove that he can discriminate it. The possibilities seem to be as follows. He can (*a*) report the having or not having of a perception; (*b*) reproduce or construct or represent it (e.g., with a pencil and paper); or finally (*c*) judge it as "same" or "different" in comparison with another stimulus (although he cannot specify what the difference is), i.e., he can match it with another stimulus.

For example, if a visual pattern is shown to the observer under one of a number of conditions which reduce its "visibility," as is done in visual-acuity experiments or experiments with very brief exposures, the observer may report either, "I see only a blur" or "I see a striped figure." If the stimulus object actually was a striped figure, the experimenter has evidence of discrimination. Such reports may consist of any response which will serve to identify to the experimenter the perception by the observer. This simple procedure might be called the *method of identification.* If, however, the visual pattern to be investigated is such that it cannot be readily named, the experimenter may employ other criteria as evidence of discrimination. The observer can draw the pattern, or he can attempt to match it with one of a group (not a series) of two or more patterns. The former is a variant of the *method of reproduction;* the latter is the *method of non-serial matching.* By all three of these methods the experimenter is enabled, first, to distinguish between "correct" perceptions and "errors" and, second, to count or otherwise evaluate the "errors."

Non-dimensional Modification of Patterned Stimuli

The methods described above are the available modes of response of the *observer* to configurational stimuli. What expedients does the *experimenter* have for studying the relation between the stimulus pattern and the perception? When he cannot vary the stimulus in a serial fashion, he can modify the stimulus "situation"—the total complex of stimulation—in a number of ways. The common methods of doing so when the aspect of the situation being studied is patterned are as follows.

1. THE EXPERIMENT OF REDUCING OR "IMPOVERISHING" THE STIMULUS PATTERN. This is probably the method most frequently employed in studying visual perception. It may involve any of several techniques. The pattern may be exposed for only a short time interval; the brightness difference between the figure and its background may be reduced to a barely noticeable one; the figure may be reduced in size; or it may be presented to peripheral vision, where form perception is weak as compared with that produced by direct fixation of the eyes. By all four of these methods a *threshold* is discoverable below which the observer cannot identify the figures. Moreover, it is found that, even when the figure is identifiable, it is seen (or reproduced or matched) more or less incorrectly and is experienced as more or less indefinite or unstable. Experiments on brightness discrimination and on visual acuity are of this type, depending as they do upon the seeing of some kind of a figure in the visual field, although the problems involved are conventionally classified as sensory rather than perceptual. (The student is referred to Chapter 7 for an account of them.) When nonsense figures or meaningful forms are presented to an observer under reduced stimulation, interest is usually centered on the analysis of the errors made by the observer and the trends of these errors. The attempt is generally made to interpret these trends in terms of some special perceptual process of assimilation or organization. More recently, interest in the fundamental problem of visual *contour* has arisen in connection with reduced stimulus experiments, and studies of the problem give promise of linking together the evidence regarding brightness perception, visual acuity, and form perception [15].

By far the most frequently used device in this type of experiment is the tachistoscope, which gets its name from the Greek words for "very rapid" and "view". Its purpose is to present an exposure field for a brief controllable duration; the technique of using it and the requirements of a good apparatus are discussed by Woodworth [17, p. 688]. The difference in brightness between a stimulus pattern and its background may be reduced by various devices for controlling illumination or for projecting an image of the stimulus through a rotating sectored disk. The method of reducing the stimulus pattern in size (or presenting it at a distance) and the method of exposing the stimulus in the periphery of the observer's visual field, although less used, are valuable and have the advantage of presenting fewer difficulties in the construction of apparatus.

2. THE EXPERIMENT OF PRESENTING INDEFINITE OR AMBIGUOUS

Stimulus Patterns. It is possible to devise stimulus fields which, for reasons not thoroughly understood, are only partially patterned or configured. Natural stimuli of this sort occur in cloud patterns and on the inhomogeneous surfaces of plastered walls. The commonest artificial stimuli are ink blots possessing irregular contours and a random distribution of texture. As everyone knows, the onlooker tends to see "pictures" in these objects. Since the stimulus conditions for the perception of pattern or contour are present in such fields but ambiguous and unspecific, the patterns, shapes, objects, and meanings which do appear in perception may take any of a variety of directions. Many different shapes may arise from a single field of stimuli, depending on the observer, or may arise for the same observer on different occasions. The responses which are made in this type of experiment obviously cannot be treated as correct or incorrect, and the experiment itself does not seek to establish a psychophysical correspondence. As applied, the method presupposes a *non-relationship* between the stimulus pattern and the perception; it is used instead to study individual differences among observers, since the attitudes and interests of the individual are assumed to determine what he perceives. This kind of perception is said to be "projective." The use of the Rohrschach ink blots and of other projective methods is described in Chapter 18.

The shapes seen in ink blots are nevertheless not entirely free from the influence of the ink blot itself. It is possible that further study of the indefinite and heterogeneous kind of stimulation which ink blots exemplify may reveal some of the stimulus conditions for the perception of pattern and contour.

3. The Experiment of Devising Reversible or Equivocal Stimulus Patterns. It is possible to construct visual stimulus fields which can be seen in only two ways instead of in many ways. These stimuli are not indefinite; they are clearly patterned, but the patterning yields either one kind of perceived object or a wholly different kind usually incompatible with the first. Three examples are given in Fig. 1. In these illustrations the stimulus conditions, whatever they may be, for the perception of contour and solidity are balanced or pitted against one another. In the first, the "thing quality" may emerge either on one side of a line or on the other; in the third, the solidity may be visible in one part of the figure or in the other. In the second, the contours are such that they can produce either of two quite different shapes: the one being a young face looking away from the observer, and the other being an old face seen in profile.

Are such figures merely psychological curiosities or simply demonstrations that attention may fluctuate or that perception cannot be explained by the stimulus pattern? Although they are often inter-

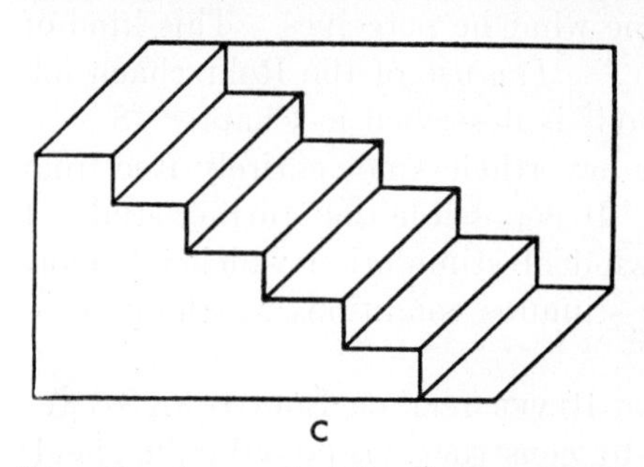

Fig. 1. Equivocal stimulus patterns.

In *A* either a goblet or a pair of faces may be seen. When either object is formed in perception, the remaining area of the picture recedes and becomes background. The latter is "formless," i.e., seems to extend behind the object (Rubin [11].) In *B* the "shaping" function of contour is again brought out; the ear of one face becomes the eye of the other, the jaw and cheek of one become the nose of the other, etc. The artist entitled this picture "my wife and my mother-in-law." (By courtesy of E. G. Boring.) In C the solid surfaces represented in the picture may be shaped in either of two ways; the solid portion of one staircase becomes empty space in the reversed staircase.

preted in this way, they are more properly to be considered perceptual experiments which facilitate introspection, particularly of the "phenomenological" kind. They are also the nearest approximation an experimenter can make to an experimental isolation of such properties as contour, "thing quality," and the other differences between an object and its background. Reversible figure-ground patterns do, in a sense, *isolate* such properties. In the first place the properties become evident to observation, and in the second place the conditions or variables which underlie them, although at first obscure, become susceptible to study by systematically varying the equivocal figure.

More generally, the method of devising artificial constellations of stimuli has proved extremely fruitful for the description of visual pattern phenomena. It has been widely used by the Gestalt psychologists both for that purpose and for the development of a theory of sensory organization considered as a physiological process. Like the method of ambiguous stimulus fields previously described, equivocal stimuli *seem* to imply a *lack* of relationship between stimulus and perception. If they are considered experiments rather than curiosities, however, this conclusion need not follow, and the abstruse conditions which give rise to the perception of form and shape may be clarified by studying them.

4. THE EXPERIMENT OF ROTATING OR DISTORTING THE RETINAL PROJECTION. Physical objects and surfaces are projected as an image on the retina, in accordance with the laws of optics. From the neural processes initiated by this retinal image the organism discriminates the physical object successfully and obtains his visual world of objects and surfaces. This projection on the retina may be changed in several ways by placing optical devices in front of the eyes, whereupon the visual world is changed accordingly. The projection may be inverted, i.e., rotated 180 degrees, by a lens system; it may be tilted, i.e., rotated to a lesser degree, by totally reflecting right-angle prisms; or it may be displaced and differentially distorted by optometrists' trial prisms [13, 7, 4].

Most of these experiments have not proved to be highly illuminating with respect to our phenomenal experience of space, since, as a rule, the phenomenal world simply appears to be modified in the expected fashion and to remain that way. The psychophysical correspondence between the retina and the visual appearance of space does not seem to be affected by the changed projection of objects on the retina. The inverted world, for example, does not shift around in experience and look "right side up," even after many hours of seeing it inverted. With respect to motor adjustments and orientation, however, a learning process occurs, and responses of localization and locomotion become adjusted to the new environment fairly rapidly. Along with this adjustment goes a decrease in the feeling of strangeness and unfamiliarity [13, 7].

There are some indications, however, that if the retinal projection is changed, not by being rotated or translated, but by being *distorted,* as it is to some extent when prisms are worn like glasses in front of the eyes, the psychophysical correspondence between retina and visual space is modified and shifts so as to make the distorted retinal image correspond more nearly to the normal undistorted space. This shift is verified by the fact that there occurs an *opposite* distortion in the appearance of normal space when the prisms are removed—a distortion which itself wears off after a lapse of time [4]. It is possible that other types of optical distortion, e.g., those produced by cylindrical lenses, would yield the same type of effects, but such experiments have not been reported.

5. The Experiment of Maintaining a Stimulus Image on the Same Retinal Area for a Prolonged Interval. The eyes are normally never at rest except for momentary periods of fixation. The retinal image of the environment is constantly changing, the total pattern being shifted on the retina by extremely rapid movements of translation which correspond to the movements of the eyes from one fixation point to another. Pattern stimulation of the retina is therefore of short duration in ordinary perception. It may be prolonged experimentally, however, by requiring the observer to fixate a stimulus field and to maintain fixation for a certain period of time.

The results of this experiment, with respect to color and brightness stimulation in the fixated field, are well known. When illuminated surfaces are used, a colored form on a gray background slowly becomes less saturated; a black form becomes lighter and a white form darker. The relation between stimulus and perception has changed with respect to the color variable. The change is such that in the stimulated area of the retina any new stimulation now evokes a color which is shifted in the direction of the complementary. This shift appears in perception as a negative afterimage.

It is less well known, and only recently established, that in this fixation experiment there may be shifts other than that of color value in the psychophysical correspondence between the retinal pattern of stimulation and the perceived field. Forms do not, it is true, change shape in any noticeable degree, but single lines or contours appear to have the effect of modifying, within the localized area where the retinal image was made to persist, the perception of subsequent lines and contours. The writer discovered that a curved line appeared less curved in the course of continuous prolonged perception and that, when another line was substituted for it, i.e., projected on the same retinal area, the shape of the second line was modified with respect to curvature, a straight line, for example, looking curved in the opposite direction [5]. An analogous effect occurred if the lines of the experiment were, respectively, a tilted line and a vertical line; the negative aftereffect was one of tilt in the opposite direction. Köhler and Wallach [9] subsequently demonstrated certain aftereffects of fixating both line patterns and closed contour figures. The principal aftereffect of a fixated figure seemed to be to displace the contour of *another* figure away from its own (no longer present) contour, when the second figure was not congruent with the first but when its lines were not too far distant. An example is shown in Fig. 2. Both these experiments demonstrate that the relation between retinal shape and seen shape may be modified under the influence of prolonged stimulation. The exploration of this influence, however, has only commenced, and the method needs to be pursued by other investigators.

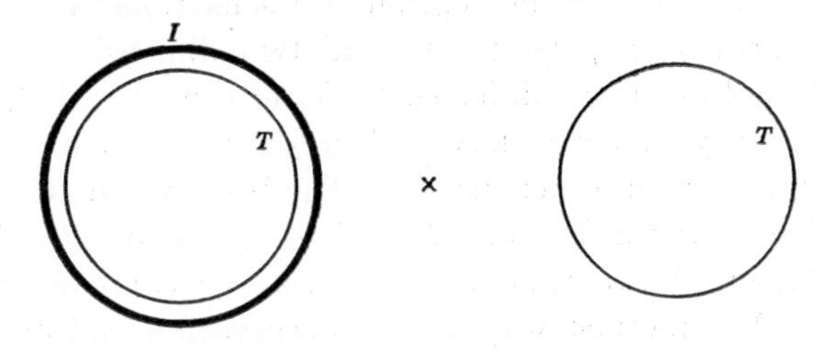

Fig. 2. Displacement of a contour after fixation.

The large circle labelled *I* is the "inspected figure"; the pair of circles labelled *T* is the "test figure." Each is drawn on a separate chart, the two being superimposed in this illustration. The small cross is the fixation mark, which is common to both charts. The *I*-figure is fixated by an observer for several minutes, and then the *T*-figure is substituted for it. The left-hand circle now appears smaller than the right-hand circle, although they are of identical size.

The experiment of fixating printed words for long intervals at one time attracted the interest of experimenters. The reports indicated that the meaning of the word receded from the pattern and also that the word tended to fall apart into letters or letter groups. The study of meaning by this method, using a variety of objects as stimuli, for the most part remains to be carried out.

APPLICATION TO SPECIFIC PROBLEMS IN THE PERCEIVING OF THE VISUAL WORLD

The outstanding problems of perception, already listed tentatively on page 161, may now be taken up. The first three will be discussed from the point of view of the psychophysics of perception. Each of the remaining problems will be exemplified by a single experiment illustrating one of the methods already discussed.

The Perception of Visual Form in Two Dimensions

The environmental world, as perceived, consists in large part of objects or things. How, then, do we perceive them—why do things look as they do? This is a psychological problem of the first importance, although its formulation has been historically delayed by the theory that objects could be explained in experience as bundles of color sensations. Introspection directed toward the perception of objects *as such* reveals a set of properties which they possess independently of their color qualities. Such properties are *line, contour, shape, emergence from the background, solidity, surface quality,* and *distance.* For convenience, perceptions (or sensations) of line, contour, shape, and surface may be treated as two dimensional, the three-dimensional qualities being deferred for later consideration. Actually, as the Gestalt psychologists have emphasized, all these properties of the visual object are interdependent. The best systematic description of them is to be found in Koffka's *Principles of Gestalt Psychology* [8].

The fundamental experiments on *outline* or *contour* are those of Rubin [11]. His method was simply observation and description of the phenomena. A typical experiment consisted of presenting the observer with an ingenious combination of two figures which shared a common contour. An example is the "goblet-faces" pattern already shown in Fig. 1. Rubin could not isolate the role of the contour by *varying it* independently of other properties of objects; what he could do was to isolate it by using the same line for the contours of two alternative figures, the appearance of one figure obliterating the other. He could show that a visual object which is clearly seen at one moment may become non-existent a moment later when its contour is used by or attached to another visual object which was formerly merely the background. The functions of a contour in always possessing an "inside" and an "outside," of acting in only one of these directions (inward) to produce a shape, and of making the shaped figure "stand out" from the unshaped background thus became open to observation. These phenomena may all be observed in Fig. 3. This apparently simple type of experiment, involving the balancing of visual conditions against one another, has been widely used in perceptual research.

Werner [15] has pushed the study of contour formation one step further. His results appear to demonstrate that even a black disk on a white ground can be made invisible, the whole black area being obliterated and the color stimulation being nullified, if its *contour* is not given enough time to develop in perception. The disk was presented tachistoscopically for a brief interval. If, then, a black ring was presented immediately afterward, whose inner contour registered exactly with the contour of the circular disk, nothing was seen but the ring. Presumably the loss of its contour to the ring inhibited the perception of the disk both as a *figure* and as an *area of color stimulation.*

Presumably the stimulus correlate for the perception of an outline or a contour is an abrupt change of stimulation between adjacent retinal areas. A *gradual* change of stimulation along the retinal surface may occur, but such a continuous gradient does not apparently produce a contour. As a hypothesis the suggestion may be made that retinal gradients of this continuous sort have the function of producing three-dimensional perceptions, which are to be discussed in the next section. The *abrupt* change of stimulation may be studied not only by the experiment of equivocal forms and the experiment of brief intervals of exposure but also by the psychophysical method of a just

Fig. 3. Balanced alternatives of figure and ground.

Note how the areas of the circle which constitute the ground seem to extend continuously *behind* the areas which constitute the figure. This is what is meant by saying that the ground is not "shaped," whereas the figure is.

noticeable brightness difference. The study of brightness discrimination and visual acuity employs this experimental method; such studies are described in Chapter 7. All the evidence is consistent with the conclusion that the discrimination of brightness and color, which involves the perception of area and shape, is dependent on the formation of a contour in experience. Since it is also probable that the formation of a contour depends on an abrupt change in areal stimulation on the retina, such a change would seem to be the fundamental stimulus condition.

The visual *line*, which may be produced artificially on man-made surfaces, can be used to represent the kind of contour which makes possible object perception in the natural visual field. If the visual line does not return on itself—is not "closed"—it becomes an isolated stimulus element, separated from its shape-producing function as a contour. Its stimulus is a *double* change in retinal stimulation, the two changes being adjacent to one another, if the line is sufficiently thin, and in opposite directions. The retina is very sensitive to such changes, as the research on visual acuity shows. The visual line, as such, has received some investigation and deserves more. In contradistinction to most of the properties of form and shape, which cannot be arranged on dimensions, the qualities of an isolated line can be scaled and therefore studied by quantitative psychophysical methods. Every student of calculus knows that a line (or a curve) can be analyzed mathematically, i.e., measured. The perceptual qualities of a line, or any chosen segment of it, are its direction (upright, tilted, or horizontal) and its quality of being straight, concave, or convex. The latter property might be called "curvature quality." The mathematician speaks correspondingly of the *slope* and *the rate of change of slope* of the curve. The writer has shown [5] that these two qualitative dimensions are akin to other kinds of sensory dimensions. Not only are they introspectively simple, they also manifest adaptation with negative aftereffect, which is characteristic of supposedly more "elementary" qualities of the world, like temperature and color. It seems possible that further introspective and psychophysical study of simple lines may help to explain how the contour produces the visual shape of objects and things.

Experiments on the perception of surface, or surface quality, have gone no farther than to establish the existence of this property of visual objects and to determine that it probably depends on the sensing of the "microstructure" or texture of the object surface. According to Metzger [10], whenever a surface is seen, it is seen because the area in question is characterized by "grain" or spots or other irregularities of brightness. The terms available to describe this quality are not definite; it needs to be observed and described further. Visual texture, as it will be called here, is nevertheless evident to introspection, and its stimulus correlate is definable as inhomogeneity of retinal stimulation. When an area of perfectly homogeneous light stimulation is presented to the retina, as occurs when one looks at clear sky or certain artificial setups, no surface is seen, and the area appears at an indefinite distance. The area is said to possess film color instead of surface color.

The results of the experiments on line, contour, shape, and surface do not enable us as yet to account for the perception of objects in their two-dimensional aspect. They do suggest, however, the directions which future experiments should take and the methods experimenters should follow to reach this goal. There have been a large number of other experiments dealing with the perception not of objects, i.e., forms with contours, but of visual order and grouping among *constellations* of stimuli. They have received their impetus from the classical experiments of Wertheimer [16]. The stimuli used were abstract dots or lines. These elements, when seen, tend to become organized into groups or units in accordance with certain laws which Wertheimer formulated. Proximity, similarity, or "good continuation" of the elements, for example, all make for unit formation. Wertheimer's method was the balancing of one factor against another or others, with observation of the units which emerged from the constellation; i.e., he studied the factors which made an equivocal constellation less so. These units, however, are not like the objects or forms of the ordinary visual world. Wertheimer's laws are not so relevant to that problem as they are to an even more difficult one—that of the order and interrelations among elements within the visual field, and especially within artificial visual fields. Wertheimer's laws are of special interest to abstract artists and others who are concerned with the problem of visual arrangement, composition, design, and esthetic unity.

A great many studies have also been performed on the perception of *nonsense* forms and patterns, by the method of requiring the observer to draw them (or recognize or match them) immediately after presentation or after an interval of time [17, Chapter 4]. The data available for study are the errors which the observer makes, the discrepancy in each case between the shape of the reproduced or matched figure and that of the original stimulus figure. The former shape is assumed to be indicative of the perception or the memory image. These are qualitative errors and are distinct from the quantitative errors of a regular psychophysical experiment. The discrepancies will be of many different varieties. The experimenter must classify and evaluate them on the basis of his subjective opinion instead of scaling them on a dimension of variation. As a substitute for mathematical averaging of the errors, however, he may utilize the method of composite drawings to obtain a kind of "mean shape" and thereby secure evidence of any general trend among the discrepancies of shape. Trends toward symmetry, toward closure of the contour, and toward resemblance to meaningful shapes have been found. This experiment, as a type, is methodologically appropriate for exploratory studies, but inexact. Future experiments in this field might benefit by first adopting a hypothesis as to the trend of the discrepancies for a given form, then *scaling* a series of forms showing increasing discrepancy from the original (if this is possible), and finally measuring the errors.

This type of experiment may be criticized on other grounds in so far as it purports to study the perception or memory of visual forms. It neglects the main problem and concentrates on a secondary issue. We need to know primarily why there is a *correspondence* between the shape of the stimulus and the shape of the experience, not why there are discrepancies between them. There is small use in studying the errors in form perception when so little is known about the reasons for the psychophysical correlation. Why is the percept (or the memory image) shaped like the stimulus object? To say that it is *organized* is only to say that it is shaped and is not a mosaic of point sensations. To say that it is shaped by memory images of past experience with similar objects is to say even less. The question is, Why is it shaped like the stimulus object? Either a tendency toward precise organization (symmetry, closure of contour) or a tendency toward the standard shape of a meaningful object will account for *errors* in the perception of nonsense forms, but neither will account for the fact of their *correct perception.*

The Perception of a Three-dimensional World: the Problem of Distance and Depth

The properties of visual objects include not only contour, shape, and surface; in addition, things emerge from the background, possess solidity, and appear at a distance. The problem of how these additional characteristics can arise from nothing more than a pair of two-dimensional retinal images is a problem which is older than psychology itself. It is still not adequately solved. If there are three experimental stages to any sensory or perceptual problem, i.e., describing the perception, identifying the stimulus correlate, and setting up a relationship between them, then it may be suggested that the problem of three-dimensional vision exists only in the first stages. Psychologists have not yet succeeded even in identifying the stimulus correlates, presumably complex, for all types of distance perception. Hence they are unable to vary or otherwise modify the stimuli presented to an observer in the effort to establish a psychophysical relationship.

There is, however, one retinal correlate of the depth and solidity of objects which has been identified and experimentally studied. It is the disparity of the images from a single object on the two retinas which is produced by "parallax," i.e., by the fact that the two eyes get their images from slightly different positions in space. Since the two images jointly are the stimulus correlate of a single perceived object, it is easy to suppose that their disparity might be the correlate of a third-dimensional quality of the perceived object. If the disparity can be measured, reproduced, and optically presented to an observer, with systematic variations, the hypothesis can be verified. It was actually verified by Wheatstone over a hundred years ago. He was able to do so because he invented an ingenious instrument, the stereoscope, which enabled him to reproduce and manipulate artificially varying degrees of retinal disparity. As the discrepancy between images increased in certain regular ways, the depth quality of the perception increased correspondingly (Fig. 4).

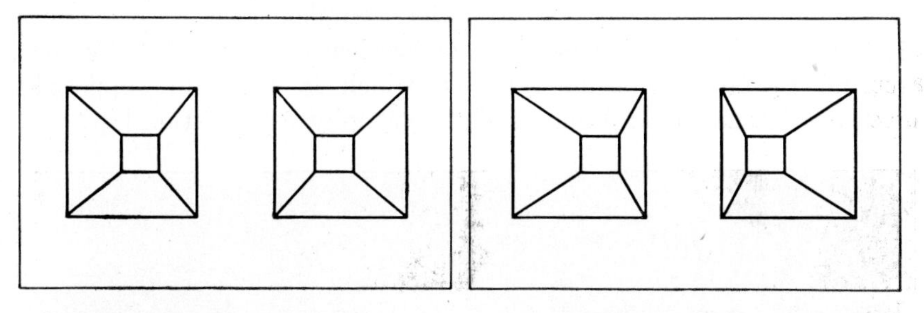

Slight retinal disparity, producing the perception of a low pyramid.

Great retinal disparity, producing the perception of a high, steep pyramid.

Fig. 4. Amount of retinal disparity and degree of perceived depth.

The stereoscope is an example of the way in which the development of apparatus can affect the progress of a branch of perceptual psychology. A major difficulty in studying certain kinds of perception is the constructing of artificial counterparts of the natural physical stimuli. Even though the stimulus correlate may be suspected, it cannot be fully verified, and the correlation cannot be established until it has been "synthesized," as it were, and subjected to experimental control. Synthetic retinal disparity can be produced and modified at will in the stereoscope, but visual texture, for example, has not yet been reproduced in a systematic manner for experimentation. Artists have of course "experimented" with texture in paintings for many centuries, but without use of the method of control and isolation of the "independent variable" which constitutes a scientific experiment. (See Chapter 1.)

The binocular stimulus correlate accounts in part for the phenomena of solidity, emergence from the background, and depth, but it cannot wholly account for them, since it is a fact that one-eyed persons also see depth and distance. There exist monocular cues for these three-dimensional properties, as well as the binocular cue. These monocular cues are, however, only imperfectly identified in our present state of knowledge and have in almost no degree been brought under experimental control. The accepted view is to say that they are "secondary" cues for the perception of space, which have been learned in the course of experience. It does not solve the problem, however, to conclude that these cues are learned. Even if they are, which is probable, the question still remains of exactly what complex stimulus correlate it is to which the experienced observer has learned to react. We come around to face the same question which is asked of supposedly unlearned sensations: What is the psychophysical relationship?

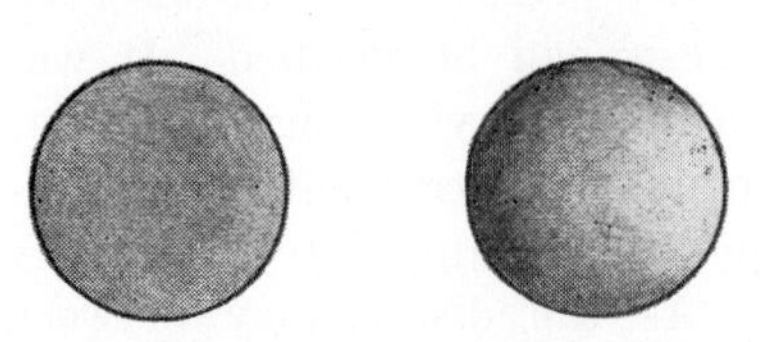

Fig. 5. The perception of solidity in relation to a retinal gradient of brightness.

Fig. 6. The perception of distance in relation to a retinal gradient of texture.

It is a possibility that the monocular cues for distance, depth, and solidity, when considered as stimulus correlates, will be definable as *gradients* of retinal stimulation. A gradient is a continuous, transitional change of stimulation over a retinal area and is to be contrasted with the abrupt change of stimulation between two adjacent retinal areas which is related to a contour. Two examples of retinal gradients will be given, one being a gradient of brightness and the other a gradient of texture. The first (Fig. 5) produces a quality of three dimensionality in a form; i.e., it yields solidity. The second (Fig. 6) produces three dimensionality on the ground and yields the impression of continuous distance.

The "modelling of surfaces by light and shade" implies that there is a psychophysical relationship between specific gradients of bright and dark stimulation on the retina and specific perceptions of the "depth shape" of objects, i.e., their shape in the third dimension as distinguished from their shape in two dimensions. The relation between "depth shape" and gradients (or levels) of brightness could be established if the experimenter proceeded systematically to isolate the variables and devise a method of controlling the stimulus. Figure 6 suggests, likewise, that, since a gradient of coarse to fine retinal texture produces a perception of a receding background, the variable should be synthetically produced and studied.

Gradients of size, linear perspective, aerial perspective, and retinal motion [6, Chapter 9] might also be studied by this procedure. Since they are all capable of being scaled, the ordinary psychophysical methods should be applicable. If a satisfactory experimental analysis can be made of the so-called "cues" for space perception, an age-long puzzle will be on its way to a solution.

The Perception of Objective Color, Size, and Shape in Relation to Their Retinal Counterparts: the Problem of Constancy

Some of the properties of visual objects as perceived do not correlate very well with what we shall call their retinal *counterparts.* They correlate instead with the objects themselves. Since the perception must be mediated by the retinal stimulation, we are faced with a contradiction. How can our perceptions correlate so well with their objects when the retinal counterparts do not apparently correlate with either? This is the problem of perceptual constancy or, as it might better be called, perceptual objectivity.

There is no doubt that the retinal image, considered as a counterpart, is not a reliable indicator of objective shape, for instance. When the face of a flat object is inclined to the line of sight, the shape of the image changes from what it was when the face was perpendicular to the line of sight. As the object is turned, the retinal counterpart changes radically (Fig. 7), but nevertheless we continue to see the same object (not quite the same object, to be precise, for the slant of its surface is part of what we see). The percept, like the object, is said to be "constant," whereas the shape of the retinal counterpart changes. Does this imply that the principle of psychophysical correlation does not hold true for perceptions as it does for "sensations"?

Fig. 7. Perspective drawing of an object in different orientations.

If retinal shape does not correspond with seen shape, neither the basic assumption nor the methods of psychophysics are applicable to the problem. It will have to be studied in terms of mental transformation, interpretation, intuition, or, at best, a process of spontaneous sensory organization.

The difficulty can be resolved if we distinguish between the retinal *counterpart* of objective shape and the retinal *correlate,* which remains to be discovered. We tend to assume, in studying space perception, that the retinal "image" is a counterpart of the object and of the percept. But the retinal image *considered as a complex of stimulation* need not be, and seldom is, such a counterpart. We are misled by the fact that such objects as a circle drawn on paper, viewed head-on, projects a circular retinal image. This is actually a rare situation, except in form-perception experiments in psychological laboratories. In ordinary perception the shape of the retinal image is seldom a counterpart of the object. A genuinely three-dimensional shape could not in the nature of things have a retinal counterpart, since the retina extends only in two dimensions. The phenomenon called depth shape—the "modelling" of a surface—has no retinal counterpart, although it probably has a retinal correlate in the form of gradients or steps of brightness and texture. Objective shape does not need to be copied on the retina to be perceived; it needs only to have specific correlates there for all its objective properties. The contour of the retinal image is only one of these correlates.

If the foregoing argument can be generalized, the objective nature of perception is a subject for psychophysical investigation rather than for theories of epistemology. The so-called constancy of shape, i.e., the fact that a shape is three-dimensional and is located and oriented in space, requires a complex stimulus correlate. The shape is not experienced in isolation; it is always shape in a given orientation. At least two isolated stimulus variables might be tentatively identified within the total correlate: the retinal contour on the one hand, and the cues for slant and orientation on the other. When the object is rotated on a vertical axis, the retinal contours change their horizontal dimensions; at the same time the cues for the slant of the object surface change horizontally. These changes in stimulation are *reciprocal.* It might be supposed therefore that one aspect of the total stimulus correlate remains constant despite rotation of the object—the sum or product of these reciprocal stimulus variables. This would provide a basis *in stimulation* for an unchanging percept.

The perceived size and color of objects are similarly out of correspondence with the retinal stimuli to which they have been found to correspond in the unique situations where distance and illumination are held constant. Retinal size is a poor indicator of perceived size when the distance of the object varies. The brightness of the retinal image is likewise not indicative of the physical nature of the surface of the object when the illumination changes. Nevertheless the size and the color of objects are not much modified by these changes. The object size is seen *at the different distance,* and the colored surface is seen *in the changed illumination.* A summary of the experimental evidence on these types of constancy may be found in Koffka [8] and in Woodworth [17].

Constancy experiments in general consist of demonstrations that the observer perceives the shape, size, or whiteness of an object, with a discrepancy from what would be expected of the retinal counterpart. The procedure is to introduce a variation in orientation, distance, or illumination between the standard and the variable stimulus-objects. Otherwise the procedure is that of a regular psychophysical experiment. The discrepancy between the perceived property and its retinal counterpart is computed and is sometimes called an index of phenomenal regression toward the real object [14]. The chief emphasis is placed on the amount of constancy revealed by the experiment.

The difficulty in these experiments is not in the techniques, but in the preliminary introspection and the definition of the problem. There is dissatisfaction with the term constancy. In the view just presented, it is not so much the shape, size, or color of the object which remains constant under varying circumstances as it is the *object itself.* Its shape and orientation, its size and distance, its color and illumination are all features of the object in its environment. The stimulus correlates of *all* these features are necessary to make the perceived object look like what it is. The interaction between the members of these pairs of stimulus correlates provides the basis for a consistently identifiable, or constant, object in perception. The experimenter, therefore, needs to define a two-variable stimulus complex, e.g., *both* size and distance, when he is setting up a constancy experiment. He can then discover whether the two-variable stimulus is in correspondence with the perceived object.

The Perception of Visual Motion and Locomotion

We turn now to a more specific consideration of the experimental methods of perceptual research. A single experiment only will be described in each field, exemplifying one or another aspect of these methods.

A practical problem in motion perception arises in learning to fly an airplane. How does the pilot sense the exact direction in which he is going, particularly when he is landing? By looking at the ground, obviously, but what does he look for and how can he judge his direction? An airplane cannot be "aimed" like an automobile by pointing its nose toward a distant point; the cue for the guidance of flight has to be looked for in the visual scene ahead. This is a problem requiring the *analysis of a complex stimulus situation*—not an analysis of the content of consciousness but a "phenomenal" analysis—and the *identification of the cues for judgment.* This identification must then be *verified* by an experiment which establishes the correspondence between the stimulus and the judgment. The writer and others [6] undertook a study of this problem, the methods and the results of which may be in part described.

Observation and the facts of optics both suggested that the visual basis of the perception of one's own locomotion is retinal motion, not of an isolated image but over the whole retina. The ground and the objects on the ground are all projected on the retina. When the observer moves, this image is *deformed,* near objects of the visual world corresponding with points which flow rapidly over the retina, farther objects with points which flow more slowly. The only points at which the retinal image is not flowing, during motion of the observer, are those corresponding to extremely distant points in the visual world—the horizon—and the *point toward which one is moving.* If the observer "looks where he is going," his retinal image is expanding radially from a center, and this center corresponds to the point in the physical world toward which he is going. Figure 8 represents the retinal pattern of expansion during an approach glide to an airfield. The arrows are vectors indicating the amount and direction of retinal flow at the given point. Their direction, no matter where one may look, is always *away from* the point toward which the observer is going at the moment. This expansion pattern would appear to be the cue for the pilot's sense of his direction of flight.

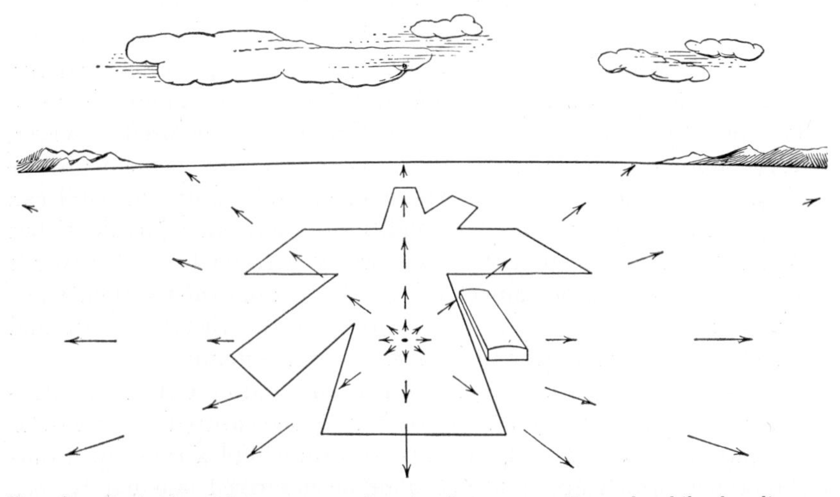

Fig. 8. Retinal motion perspective in the scene viewed while landing an airplane.

The experiment to verify this conclusion was based on a motion-picture sequence of a scene similar to that shown in Fig. 8. The scene was photographed in miniature so as to permit control of the conditions, with the camera moving as the observer would move in that situation. When the film was projected, the velocities and directions of expansion could be plotted on the screen. They proved to be similar to those illustrated. Furthermore, when an observer looked at the screen, he obtained a compelling experience of moving through space in a specific direction. This direction could be judged with some accuracy even in the early portions of the sequence when the expansion was slow, and it could be judged with greater accuracy as the expansion became more rapid.

An experiment of this sort raises many more questions than it answers, but it illustrates a procedure for the study of complex perceptual patterns.

The Perception of Meaning and of Symbols

The problem of meaning and the nature of symbolic perception present a variety of problems for psychology. Most, if not all, meanings are *learned* by the individual. As determiners of behavior, the meanings of objects have been studied in learning experiments. But meanings are also perceptual experiences, and in this aspect they are difficult to study by experimental methods. The meanings of situations, objects, pictures, and words are difficult or impossible to arrange in accordance with their modes of variation, as colors can be arranged, because of their seeming uniqueness and their almost infinite variety.

The method of "impoverishing" the stimulus may be used, however, and the apprehension of printed words exposed in a tachistoscope has been investigated in many experiments. A meaningful word can be apprehended under exposure conditions where an equivalent, but less meaningful, group of letters is scarcely perceived at all. Words and symbols can also be subjected to prolonged optical fixation. The meaning is reported to recede eventually from the visual pattern, and the letters of a word appear to "break up" into subunits.

Symbolic meaning can always be identified and described by introspection, although it cannot be scaled and measured by classical psychophysical methods. There exist certain complex types of meaning, however, which apparently cannot be described adequately, i.e., in such a way as to make other observers of the same phenomenon agree with the one who described it. The study of esthetics and of personality is hampered by this difficulty. Is there, for example, meaning in the handwriting of individual persons? Does the quality of "style," which is almost indescribable, indicate or express the person whose handwriting is examined? Graphologists maintain that such meanings exist, but their claim is doubted. Problems of this sort can be investigated by the method of non-serial matching.

Allport and Vernon [1, Chapter 10] report an experiment on the expressive quality of handwriting, in which this method was used. Ten sketches of personality were written, describing the traits and characteristics of ten individuals. Samples of their handwriting were obtained. The samples and sketches were then submitted to a group of judges, some of whom were professional graphologists. Each judge examined a given sample of handwriting and, from the qualities he saw in it, attempted to select the personality sketch with which it matched. He would be correct by chance only once in ten tries. He then repeated his attempt for the remaining samples. The *perceptual basis* of the selections did not have to be described, nor did it enter into the experiment. The mean number of correct identifications out of ten attempts was approximately two instead of one. The graphologists were somewhat more successful than were those who disclaimed any special ability to interpret handwriting, but both types of judges were more successful than the hypothesis of chance guessing would predict.

Social Perception

A whole realm of perception has scarcely been touched upon in this chapter. The methods and experiments discussed have to do primarily with the perception of the world of objects—the physical world. The methodological problems are difficult enough in that realm, but they become even more complex when we come to deal, as scientists, with the world of values, customs, stereotypes, and fashions. We then have to study the perception of such objects as food, clothing, and articles of daily use; of the actions of other people; of social situations and problems; and of races, classes, and nations. There is one very important difference between space perception, for example, and social perception. It is always possible, subject only to the ingenuity of the experimenter, to establish, in the first case, whether a perception is "correct" or "incorrect." It is a very complex and often controversial matter, however, to establish whether a given social perception is "veridical." Since the realities behind social values and judgments are at best subtle and obscure (some social scientists deny that there *are* any realities), these properties of things are studied by the method used to investigate indefinite or ambiguous stimulus patterns (pages 166–167); that is to say, the experimenter studies the perception not as a function of the stimulus but as a function of variables within the subject—his past experience, his motivations, his prejudices, and his personality.

An experiment of this sort is that of Sherif on the determination of perception by a "social norm" [12]. The stimulus situation he employed was even more ambiguous and "unstructured" than are ink-blots or nonsense patterns; it consisted of a single stationary pinpoint of light in an absolutely dark room. Under these conditions the "autokinetic phenomenon" occurs. Sooner or later in this situation the point of light, being unlocalized on any spatial surface and divorced from any visible frame of reference, begins to drift or change position erratically. This purely illusory impression of movement is variable and indefinite, as one would expect. The judgment which Sherif required of his observers was an estimation of the *amount* of this movement in inches during a certain time interval after the light appeared. The instructions were such as to suggest that the light would *really* move, although it never did.

After a number of repeated judgments, a standard or normal amount of movement began to characterize the estimates of an observer. One individual would report 1 or 2 inches of displacement, while another reported 9 or 10 inches. If at this stage a pair of observers, or a group of three, were given a repetition of the experiment *together*, so that they could hear each other's judgments, the established individual norms of judgment began to be modified, and a *group norm* emerged, to which the individual norms gradually conformed. At the end of three sittings (100 judgments each) all the individuals in a group had standards to guide their estimates, which were very close together. The majority of observers were not aware that their judgments were being influenced by others. The standards were by no means the same in different groups of individuals, one group tending to see 1 inch of movement as the normal amount, whereas another saw as much as 4 inches.

If an individual observer faced the situation *alone*, after first observing as a member of a group, the socially determined norm continued to affect his judgments, although the influence of the group was no longer physically present. Although he did not realize it, the amount of movement which he expected to see was now the result of his interaction with the group. An elementary social custom had been established, both in the group and in the individuals who composed the group.

CONCLUSIONS FOR THE STUDENT OF PERCEPTION

It has been implied throughout this chapter that the first necessity in setting up an experiment on perception is to formulate its aim. Formerly the aim of perceptual experiments was to establish the *differences* between a percept and its presumed stimulus correlate, analyzing the latter in terms of those stimuli which were known to yield "sensations," and then to account for these differences by some hypothesis. Recently, with the breaking down of the logical distinction between sensation and perception, it appears possible in many cases to establish a psychophysical *correspondence* between a percept and its own stimulus correlate. The latter may be a ratio, a gradient, or an integration of stimuli of a more complex order than are the accepted correlates of so-called sensory experience. Whenever such a correspondence is conceivable, the experimenter should first devote his attention to it, on the grounds that, if established, it will reduce the necessity for extra hypotheses. The methodology of such research has been the principal concern of this chapter.

There are, of course, many aspects of human perception for which the corresponding stimulus complexes are unknown. They are presumably based on intricate and subtle discriminations of the physical properties of things, persons, and events, but they are so far from being identifiable by the ordinary procedures of the physical sciences that they can scarcely be guessed at. The meanings, the "dynamic" and "physiognomic" qualities, and the social significances which make up a great part of human experience are all of this type. Although they are perceptions and depend on the functioning of the sense organs for their development, they require hypotheses concerning the organization of experience and the process of learning in order to account for them. They are so much dependent on the concepts, attitudes, and prejudices of the observer that the methods of studying them become indistinguishable from the methods of studying thought processes, which are described in Chapter 4.

The phenomena of object perception, space perception, and perceptual constancy, on the other hand, are probably more nearly akin to sensory processes than they are to concepts. If this is true, they should be studied after the fashion of psychophysical experiments. Evidence is needed on the perceptual resultants of complex stimulation. This evidence can be obtained by introspective analysis, by isolating and controlling the relevant variables in the total stimulus situation or at least by systematically varying the situation, by obtaining discriminative judgments from an observer, and by applying the techniques of psychophysical measurement to the results.

REFERENCES

1. Allport, G. W., and P. E. Vernon. *Studies in Expressive Movement.* New York: Macmillan, 1933.
2. Birkhoff, G. D. *Aesthetic Measure.* Cambridge: Harvard University Press, 1933.
3. Boring, E. G. *The Physical Dimensions of Consciousness.* New York: Century, 1933.
4. Gibson, J. J. Adaptation, after-effect, and contrast in the perception of curved lines. *J. Exper. Psychol.,* 1933, *16,* 1–31.
5. Gibson, J. J. Adaptation with negative after-effect. *Psychol. Rev.,* 1937, *44,* 222–243.
6. Gibson, J. J., Ed. *Motion Picture Testing and Research.* Washington: Government Printing Office, 1947.

7. Gibson, J. J., and O. H. Mowrer. Determinants of the perceived vertical and horizontal. *Psychol. Rev.*, 1938, *4*, 300–323.
8. Koffka, K. *Principles of Gestalt Psychology.* New York: Harcourt, Brace, 1935.
9. Köhler, W., and H. Wallach. Figural after-effects. *Proc. Amer. Philos. Soc.*, 1944, *88*, No. 4, 269–357.
10. Metzger, W. Optische Untersuchungen am Gangzfeld. II. Zur Phänomenologie des homogenen Ganzfelds. *Psychol. Forsch.*, 1930, *13*, 6–29.
11. Rubin, E. *Visuell wahrgenomene Figuren.* Copenhagen: Gyldendalske Boghandel, 1921.
12. Sherif, M. *The Psychology of Social Norms.* New York: Harper, 1936.
13. Stratton, G. M. Vision without inversion of the retinal image. *Psychol. Rev.*, 1897, *4*, 341–360 and 463–481.
14. Thouless, R. H. Phenomenal regression to the real object, I. *Brit. J. Psychol.*, 1931, *21*, 339–359.
15. Werner, H. Studies on contour. I. Qualitative analyses. *Amer. J. Psychol.*, 1935, *47*, 40–64.
16. Wertheimer, M. Untersuchungen zur Lehre von der Gestalt, II. *Psychol. Forsch.*, 1923, *4*, 301–350.
17. Woodworth, R. S. *Experimental Psychology.* New York: Henry Holt, 1938.

SUGGESTED READINGS

Boring, E. G. *Sensation and Perception in the History of Experimental Psychology.* New York: Appleton-Century, 1941.

Carr, H. A. *An Introduction to Space Perception.* New York: Longmans, Green, 1935.

Koffka, K. *Principles of Gestalt Psychology.* New York: Harcourt, Brace, 1935.

Chapter 7

Studying Vision

S. Howard Bartley[1]

The methodology described in Chapter 6 was concerned mainly with visual perception. The present chapter is devoted to the major and most representative methods of studying vision *as such,* independent of the more perceptual qualities related to the field. The student should carry over the material of the previous two chapters and relate it to the methods to be described in the next several pages.

In order to accomplish the most within the boundaries of a single chapter on the complicated methodology in vision, a number of economies are necessary. The first is the reduction of certain of the broader aspects of method to ideas that can be presented in general statements. Accordingly, a number of these statements precede the description of the phenomena of vision and the specific experimental conditions under which they are induced.

FIELDS OF VISUAL INVESTIGATION

One of the major ways in which visual studies differ is in terms of their objectives. These differences are quite marked and are reflected not only in the types of questions for which answers are sought, but also in the procedures involved in the process of experimentation. The different aspects in which attention is directed may be called *areas of investigation,* each of which may be subdivided into several *types of inquiry.* One of the first areas of investigation pertains to the nature of what is perceived. It deals with the problems of how the visual field is organized, what is in it, and similar questions. The study of the most general and basic structure (organization) of the visual field is the first type of inquiry. It so happens that the first differentiable feature of visual-field organization is the separation into

[1] Professor of Psychology, Michigan State College.

figure and ground (see Figs. 1 and 2). Thus figure-ground relations and all similar studies belong in our first type of inquiry.

Studies of the second type of inquiry deal with *objects* as such. Questions of their identification, location, etc., are pertinent here. Size, shape, and similar characteristics are involved only in a secondary way and are of concern only as they distinguish one object from another or help determine object character or position. A third type of inquiry is the investigation of visual properties, such as color.

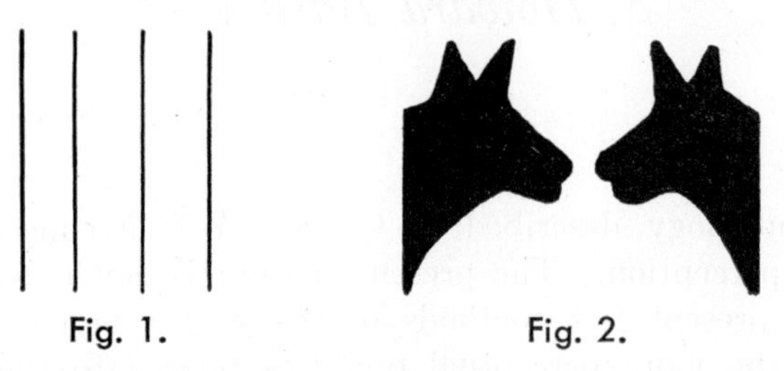

Fig. 1. Fig. 2.

Figs. 1 and 2. These drawings indicate the fact that differentiated visual fields are structured into two parts—the figure and the ground.

In Fig. 1 the lines become figure. Not only are they figures (objects) but also they cluster so as to enclose portions of the field which become part of the figure—representing the surface of posts, boards, etc. Fig. 2 can be seen in two ways—the figure and ground mutually alternate. See also Fig. 1, page 168.

Although color, for example, is often studied as a property of object surfaces, it may be abstracted from the object itself and dealt with under conditions in which it has a minimum of relation to specific objects.

It is obvious from the foregoing that the study of vision necessitates certain amounts of arbitrariness, as do all psychological investigations. As was pointed out in Chapter 1, such arbitrariness is a matter of abstraction which is involved in all our techniques of analysis. We must recognize that the kind of abstraction used plays an important part in our end results. In a certain sense experimental phenomena are products of sensory abstraction.

A second area of visual investigation deals with the functional characteristics of the organism. It is not directed toward descriptions of visual phenomena, but toward understanding visual capacities. For instance, brightness discrimination, adaptation, and visual acuity are terms that refer to a capacity of the organism rather than to its experience. Brightness discrimination and adaptation refer to what the organism does visually. Visual acuity refers to a discriminatory capacity the organism possesses.

A third area of investigation involves study of the organic mechanisms and anatomical relations which underlie the properties just mentioned. These mechanisms may be chemical, motor, or neural. Visual studies in this third area are concerned with inquiry into retinal structure and function, the structure and activities of the remaining stations in the visual pathway of the nervous system, and ultimately the nervous system as a whole. Photochemical activity in the receptor cells and neural interaction in the retina are two very common objects of study in this area of visual investigation.

Still a fourth area of investigation is the study of the role that vision plays in the behavior of organisms. One type of inquiry in this direction seeks to find how vision participates in the general behavior of the individual. A second type is concerned with particularizing the relations of vision and the other senses. Much of what is included in this area is conventionally dealt with in perception and some of these major concepts have been handled in Chapter 6.

In the present chapter we shall limit ourselves to several well-recognized and thus formalized categories in which vision is studied. The categories of adaptation, visual acuity, brightness discrimination, color discrimination, spatial localization, and response to intermittent stimulation (flicker, etc.) have each arisen from observations in everyday human experience. Now, when one speaks of a visual phenomenon, he tends to put it into one of these major categories. Before we take these categories up in detail, we shall survey some of the more important psychophysical relations necessary to an understanding of visual methodology

PSYCHOPHYSICAL RELATIONS IN VISION

Visual experiences are both quantitative and qualitative. To the extent that they are qualitative, they have properties which cannot be directly described in numerical terms. As a series, however, a series of qualitative changes may be related to some numerical order. This order lies outside the qualities themselves and applies to stimulus or internal physiological conditions. The properties of visual experience which appear to be quantitative pertain to time (duration), space (size, direction, etc.), and intensity (brightness, etc.). The stimulus conditions involve time, space, and intensity. Procedures for studying visual processes are those which manipulate these factors precisely to discover new types of phenomena, to make clear the relations between already known phenomena, or to discover the mechanisms underlying the phenomena themselves. This involves relating the visual outcomes to stimulus conditions (psychophysics), although it is recognized that certain conditions lying within the organism are often as crucial in determining the literal outcome in a specific case as are external stimulus conditions (psychophysiology).

One of the most basic and widely employed concepts in the study of biological phenomena is the *threshold* or *limen.* The notion of threshold arises out of the discrepancy between physical conditions which are considered to be potential stimuli and the responses themselves. The smallest amount of stimulation which will produce a given result is spoken of as the threshold amount. The threshold is not absolute, but instead is statistical, because of the unavoidable instability of both the stimulus and the organism. Hence all threshold definitions are couched in statistical terms. Part of what has just been called "a given result" is defined by the numerical probability of detecting a given target or a difference between two of its parts. In vision, for instance, there are amounts of radiant energy which fail to elicit visual experience. A room may be so dark that no objects are visible in it, but if the illumination is increased sufficiently, a point will be reached at which certain objects will just be discernible. The level of illumination will then be just threshold for the objects in question.

If, in a fairly well lighted room, two sheets of paper are put before an observer, he may be able to detect that they are not equally white. The difference may be so slight as just to be perceptible. This means that had the physical difference been any less, the two sheets would have looked alike.

From this description it will be evident that thresholds are of two general types. There are "absolute" thresholds and "relative" ("difference") thresholds, as indicated respectively by the two illustrations.

The subject of thresholds brings us to the consideration of what is new and what is old, what is an enduring object (or experience) somewhat changed, and what is a new (different and discrete) object with some resemblance to an earlier one. When conditions are shifted in such a way as to provide for just barely seeing something in the dark, the something is a new object of experience. With added light it changes in various ways. Were each of these kinds of change to be examined, a series of difference thresholds could be established by simply manipulating conditions step by step, so that notations of the amount of stimulus change necessary to produce each perceivable increment of change could be obtained. In a sense, when an object changes, it is a new object. In another sense, it is not. When the experiential emphasis lies in the continuity between what was and what is, the difference constitutes a change. Without this, the present object is new relative to any other one in the past. Whereas difference thresholds pertain to just perceivable changes, absolute thresholds pertain to situations in which something new emerges. When thresholds pertain to differences, a series of differences are generally obtainable by incremental or decremental changes in physical dimension. Steps from one threshold to the next are called "just noticeable differences" (JND's).

A number of trials (observations) are necessary for determining threshold, for a very weak stimulus will not always evoke a sensory end result. A target seen on one attempt will not necessarily be seen on another. A statistical relation exists between the strengh of the stimulus and the seeing of an object.

It is possible to define threshold in any one of a number of ways. If the target is an object to be seen only in one place and in a single orientation about the axis of regard, the observer has only one of two responses to make. He either reports seeing the target, or he fails to report. If he is apprised of each time the target is presented, he reports either that he does or that he does not see it. Hence, by pure chance, he will be able to be correct half of the time. In such cases threshold is sometimes defined as the stimulus strength which evokes a response in 75 per cent of the trials. In many experiments the number of possible reports is increased by rotating the target into several positions in chance order or by placing it in various predetermined positions eccentric to the fixation point. This reduces the chances of being correct by mere guessing.

In actual experimentation, standardization and short cuts in procedure are necessary. These tend to modify response, making for some predetermination of result. Scoring procedures cannot therefore be constructed on the assumption that only two factors, actual sensitivity and pure chance, operate. They must take into account certain biases of the observer resulting from his ability to predict to some degree from what he has learned of the experimenter's procedure. In what way these biases reduce chance factors has to be determined for the particular method used.

Although a threshold stimulus is one which just succeeds in producing a response, less intense physical conditions are not without their effects. Hence they are called *subthreshold stimuli,* even though such terminology is paradoxical. Literally, that which does not stimulate can hardly be a stimulus. Subthreshold stimuli can be considered effective in bringing about certain chemical conditions, and these effects, when added to more of the same, will end in a response of the same category as that produced by a single threshold or suprathreshold stimulus. There is no such thing, however, as a subthreshold experiential response. The effect produced, if ever to be called a physiological response, is in a category other than the response which was originally meant and which originally determined the definition of the threshold.

Scientific measurement may either be direct, the response itself being measured, or indirect, the measurement being of the stimulus used to obtain a specified response. It is seldom that a visual response can be measured by the first method. Direct measurement is possible only in the case of pupil reflexes and other visuo-motor activity.

The indirect method is necessitated by the fact that the response is something for which there are no physical units, such as length, distance, or volume. This method takes advantage of the fact that response is generally a comparison. Two things are compared: either they are matched and are thus biologically equivalent in some respect, or they are differentiated. In the latter case, the least stimulus difference which enables a differentiation is the threshold or limen which we have just discussed. When, of course, the response in question is not a comparison, the stimulus conditions required to elicit the response are the only measurables. To the extent that a response cannot be predicted by defining stimulus conditions, the experiment moves away from the conventional psychophysical one to a kind in which the organism, rather than the physical surrounds, is the reference point. Methodology for such experimentation is as yet poorly developed, but there is a growing recognition for need of it.

Differentiation is only fully meaningful when conditions are so adjusted as to produce a JND. Discernible differences, when they are larger than JND's, are less definite and are therefore often more poorly measured. For example, one area cannot be as well judged to be twice as bright as another as the two can be judged equally bright or just different in brightness.

FUNDAMENTAL CONSIDERATIONS AND VISUAL PHENOMENA

The Eye

All the precise work on and understanding of vision presupposes a knowledge of the structure of the eye as an energy-receptor system and a translator of this energy into suitable neurophysiological patterns for conduction to the central nervous system. Likewise knowledge of the visual pathway is also becoming more and more necessary in the understanding of visual phenomena.

The outstanding facts regarding the eye are the following. (1) It contains a mosaic of two kinds of sensitive cells, the cones and the rods, each of which is sensitive to radiant energy and capable of transforming it into a series of discrete impulses appropriate to activate in turn the next structural unit in line, the bipolar cell. (2) These receptor cells (the rods and cones) are not alike in their range of sensitivities, and all visual functions on this account are affected by which set of cells participates or in what proportions the two sets participate. (3) These two sets of receptors are unlike in their distribution across the retinal mosaic from center to periphery. The central portion of the retina is populated only with cones, the paracentral (parafoveal) region is populated with both rods and cones. The farther toward the periphery, the greater is the relative number of rods and the smaller the relative number of cones. (4) The neural connections of the rods and cones differ. Each foveal cone has a one-to-one connection with its succeeding unit in the visual pathway. In contrast to this, the fiber processes from several rods converge on a single succeeding neural unit, and cones outside the fovea do not have "private line" connections. (5) Where the bundles of afferent fibers constituting the optic nerve leave the eye, a total absence of receptor cells is assumed. This region is called the optic disk, and the corresponding area in the visual field which is "blind" under some conditions is called the blind spot [1].

Important Units of Measurement

Since the optical system of the human eye involves the focusing of light through a nodal point, the *visual angle* is one of the vehicles of spatial measurement. The visual angle is the angle subtended by the observed object when the nodal point of the eye is the apex. If absolute size of an object (test object or target) is known, the distance of the object from the eye must be known, so as to calculate the area of the retina involved in the image of the object.

A unit of sensitivity which takes into account the light actually reaching the retina should be employed. The *photon* is a unit of retinal illumination which takes into account the size of the pupil and is the conventional unit which most nearly satisfies this demand. Although the reader will have to resort to the proper handbooks [27] to acquaint himself with the various light units and their conversion factors, it is not likely that he will find the definition of the photon among them. When the eye is confronted with a surface intensity ("apparent brightness") of 1 candle per square meter, the illumination on the retina is 1 photon if the pupillary area is 1 square millimeter. Three avenues of procedure are open in applying the photon. One is to use an artificial pupil to limit the effective pupillary aperture to a known area. The second is to measure the natural pupillary area existing at the time, and the third is to calculate pupillary area from graphs or tables providing the standard pupillary aperture for the various intensity levels of target and for given states of retinal adaptation [35].

Adaptation

Adaptation is the adjustment in the visual mechanism underlying improvement in seeing after sudden shifts in stimulus intensity. Adaptation may proceed in either of two directions: progressive improvement in vision after illumination has been suddenly lowered (dark adaptation), and improvement after illumination has been raised (light adaptation). Light adaptation progresses much more rapidly than dark adaptation.

All adjustments toward improved functioning of the visual pathway with reference to the intensity of stimulation might well be called adaptation [1]. The initial tissue process in the receiving of light is chemical and is very influential in setting the quantitative pattern of the processes that follow. That adaptation is confined to the photochemical processes of the receptor cells in the retina has often been taken for granted [4]. Nevertheless it has more recently been shown that all the adjustment phenomena which would naturally be given the label of adaptation are not photochemical [36]. Some of them are neural.

The usual method of studying dark adaptation consists in subjecting the eyes to total darkness and, at regular intervals, testing the ability to see (determining absolute thresholds) [37]. The threshold progressively drops, at first rapidly and then more slowly, till finally no further drop occurs. The series of thresholds are plotted against time in the dark, and the result is called an adaptation curve. One customary target is a figure which can be rotated from trial to trial into any one of a number of fixed positions. For example, a letter *C* (Landolt broken circle) is often employed (see Fig. 3). The open side of the circle may be placed in any one of four or more positions, and the observer is asked to tell in which position the opening is, either by expressing the position in terms of the hour designation on a clock dial, or by pressing the appropriate key on a panel wired to designate the various positions. A plain figure, such as Fig. 4, may also be used. To insure that the observer is looking in the right direction to see the target, a fixation point is customarily provided. This is a very small red light just strong enough to be seen. The target bears a fixed spatial relation to the fixation point, providing the observer does not move his head. If measurement of various precisely known parts of the retina is required, the precaution of a "biting board" or other head-stabilizing device is used. Biting boards are of many degrees of stability, the best being a horizontal plate bearing a wax impression of the observer's teeth. Each time that the observer "bites" into this impression, his head is certain to be placed in the same position with reference to the target as before, if the plate is stable.

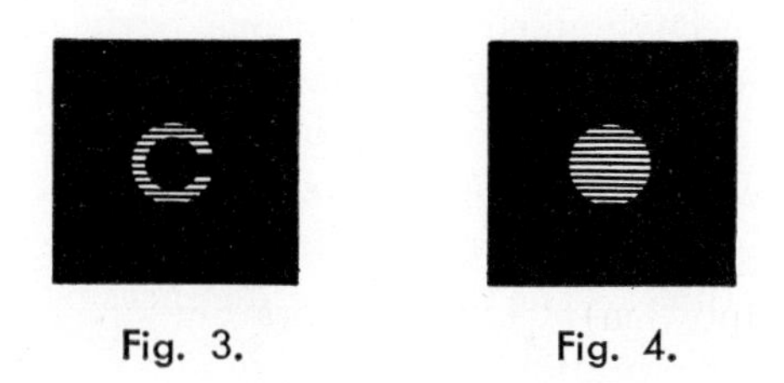

Fig. 3. Fig. 4.

Trials are made at set intervals. Since dark adaptation progresses much more rapidly at first than it does later on, the readings must be closer during this time than later. It is objectionable from the observer's standpoint to make readings quite close together. A number of readings for every desired interval of time elapsing in the dark are necessary to obtain a reliable set of readings for a dark-adaptation curve. Routine clinical examinations, however, follow a shortened procedure [23].

Further to insure the meaningfulness of the results acquired in obtaining a dark-adaptation curve, a preadaptation period of subjection to a known level of illumination is used. Generally a uniformly lighted opal-glass screen large enough to cover most of the angular visual field is employed. The screen may be illuminated at any level of intensity, depending upon the purpose of the investigation, just so the level is known and specified in describing results.

The process of adaptation can be measured for various parts of the retina and for various levels of preadaptation [4]. It has been found that the rods and cones adapt at different levels and at different rates [4]. This is evidenced in the irregular shape of the adaptation curve, it being composed of two parts. The one is an early drop, which reaches virtually its full extent in a very few minutes, and the other is a later and greater drop, which continues for a far longer time.

By the use of dark-adaptation curves it has been shown that vitamin A deficiency affects the process of adaptation [23]. It has also been shown that insulin hypoglycemia and anoxia affect dark adaptation. In vitamin A deficiency, the difficulty has its primary origin in the eye, whereas in hypoglycemia and anoxia, the difficulty is further along in the visual pathway [36].

Brightness Discrimination

Adaptation is the process whereby sensitivity to retinal illumination changes after a more or less abrupt shift in illumination level. Although it has been implied that various parts of the retina can adapt more or less independently, the more usual studies of adaptation have not been limited to localized regions. Brightness discrimination as a process differs from adaptation only in certain arbitrary ways. As the eyes are moved to and fro, the images of dark and light objects move across the retinas. The intensity differences between the various images may be quite great, and therefore it can be said that the areas of the retina just newly stimulated by images differing greatly from their predecessors are not fully adapted to the new levels of intensity. Brightness discrimination is a set of complicated, short, and relatively mild processes of adaptation.

The standard concept of brightness has been reached through use of the photometer, in which the two target areas (standard and test) to be matched are contiguous and appear on an unilluminated field, either lying side by side or the one target surrounding the other. Adjusting for equal brightness involves, as much as anything else, obliterating the boundary between the areas. Under conditions of contiguity the relative size of the two areas is not critical, and the match in brightness is most nearly a physical match in intensity. Hence the standard definition of brightness used by those interested in light from the standpoint of physics follows: *Brightness is the luminous intensity per unit of area.* The term luminous is a recognition of the fact that an observer is involved and that he is not equally sensitive to all wavelengths within the visible spectrum.

Most methods used in studying brightness discrimination differ essentially from the purely photometric in one or more particulars. Whereas the photometric technique, through its simplification, is taken as an absolute one, other setups actually emphasize the fact of relativity in the perception of brightness and must be looked upon from this standpoint. Even when we employ setups apparently similar to those used in photometry, we are investigating brightness discrimination as a biological function, rather than presuming to match two physical quantities.

That brightness depends at times upon total flux (total light emitted or reflected from the target to the eye) rather than flux density (light emitted or reflected by each unit of target surface) is demonstrated in the following illustrations.

Let two surfaces reflecting equal flux per unit area be observed. In the first case let the two surfaces be equal in area and equally distant from the eye. In the second case let their areas be equal, but their distances from the eye be unequal. In the third case let their areas be unequal, but their distances from the eye be equal.

When, in all three cases, the paired surfaces are seen to match in brightness, it may be said that flux per unit area is the crucial factor, for in cases two and three the total flux reaching the eye from each of the surfaces is not equal. But when the paired surfaces in cases two and three are seen as unequal in brightness, total flux may be the crucial factor.

If, for example, the paired surfaces are the sole objects in the field to receive illumination, and one does not focus well upon them but looks beyond them, the surface subtending the greater visual angle of the two will then tend to become the more effective and appear the brighter. In case *two* it will be the surface nearer to the eye; in case *three* it will be the larger surface. In such cases the total flux determines the brightness. Total flux operates in many everyday situations as well.

Methods used to study brightness discrimination are aimed at taking into account (1) the relations between area of total target, or its parts, and threshold, (2) the relation between intensity level of target and surround, and threshold, (3) the relation between time of target exposure and threshold, and (4) the relation of target movement and threshold.

The simplest arrangement of the visual field for the study of brightness discrimination is similar to that for dark adaptation (Figs. 3 and 4). From what we know about retinal anatomy, the angle that the target subtends is an important matter. For central vision the target should be about 1 degree or less (about 1 inch at a distance of 55 inches). The amount by which a target must be either greater or less in intensity than its surrounds so as just to be perceived is a measure of brightness discrimination. This threshold is generally called ΔI, and its relation to the intensity I of the surrounds has often been studied. The ratio $\Delta I/I$, called the Weber fraction, is another measure common in the study of brightness discrimination. This fraction becomes smaller as I increases. The reciprocal of this fraction ($I/\Delta I$) is also a common measure.

It is possible to vary the area of the target and determine the relation of threshold to area. It is also possible to apply the small-area target to various parts of the retina by using a fixation-point whose relation to the target is manipulated systematically.

Another and very definite step is taken when the target is made of two parts of unequal intensity. The particular threshold measured in this case is that of the difference between the two parts of the target. The ratio $\Delta I/I$ in such cases pertains to the difference in intensity between the two parts of the target divided by the intensity of one of the parts.

Under these conditions, as with simple targets, the intensity level of the background or general field cannot be ignored. It has been found to be an important factor in determining the absolute value of the threshold. The level of the background (surrounds) is sometimes

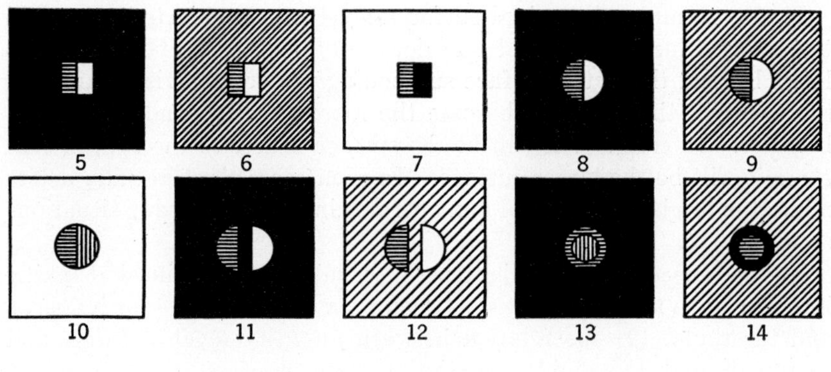

Figs. 5 to 14.

put at an intensity somewhere between levels of the two parts of the target. By a few preliminary trials a point almost halfway between the two parts of the target may be found. The surrounds may also be set definitely below or above the two parts of the target in intensity.

The complex target may be any one of several shapes. In general, there are bisected targets, such as in Figs. 5, 6, 7, 8, 9, 10, 11, and 12, and disk-annulus targets, such as in Figs. 13 and 14. Bisected targets consist of a square, rectangle, or circle divided equally into two parts. At times the two halves are separated, as in Figs. 11 and 12. When separation is employed, the effect of width of separation is studied. The disk-annulus targets do not give thresholds of the same value as the bisected targets. The existence of a difference is a demonstration of a very important matter in visual function, the effect of border-building processes on each other [16]. As another variation in technique, the two halves of the complex target may be held constant in their intensity relation to each other while being varied in relation to the surround.

A totally dark field surrounding a test object (target) could be expected to function one way, and a fairly well illuminated field another way. While black is a sensation, the absence of retinal stimulation is functionally different from the presence of any amount of it. One of the problems that has arisen in connection with surrounds, especially the illuminated ones, is whether a portion of the visual field illuminated at a given level might function as a substitute for the whole field. If so, how many degrees must a surround subtend to be substantially equivalent to having the whole field illuminated at the same level? Some investigators have come to the conclusion that a surround subtending 30 degrees of visual angle is this equivalent, at least for certain purposes. (An ordinary doorway—32 inches—subtends a visual angle of 30 degrees when the eye is about 2 yards from it.)

There is a fundamental phenomenon regarding the behavior of light in the eye that may account for this virtual equivalence. It is the existence of internal stray light, called *entoptic stray light* [10]. The eye as a hollow sphere acts, in principle, like an integrating sphere. In solving certain problems in photometry, a source of light is placed inside a hollow sphere whose walls are coated a matte white. A photometer pointed through a peephole in the sphere measures the "mean spherical candle power" of the light source, because of the fact that light is evenly reflected in all directions from the walls of the sphere. No matter toward which portion of the inside wall the photometer is pointed, the reading will be the same. In the eye the bright image on the retina forms the light source, and although the ocular walls absorb a considerable part of the light, the portions of the retina not involved in the bright image are receiving reflected light. The amount of this depends upon the size and intensity of the image acting as source. As the image increases in size, the differential between its intensity and that of the rest of the eye materially lessens. As the image increases in size, it of course occupies more and more of the total sensitive retina. For these reasons a stimulus covering somewhat less than the whole visual field will substitute for illumination of the whole field.

Certain findings incidental to the study of brightness discrimination have led to the use of figures even more complex than the bisected targets [1]. It appears that the presence of borders in the visual field has an influence on the differential thresholds. For example, if a target such as is found in Fig. 15 is used, the differential brightness threshold decreases as the width of the annulus 2 is increased. Originally this was attributed to a summation process. This hypothesis is tested by use of a pattern, as indicated in Fig. 16. By surrounding the inner disk 1 by an annular field 2, between which and an annular outer area 3 is ring *R*, the combined area of 2 plus 3 can be kept constant while the diameter of the ring is varied to manipulate the distance of the ring from area 1. The inner border of the ring is thus varied in its distance from area 1 without changing total illumination.

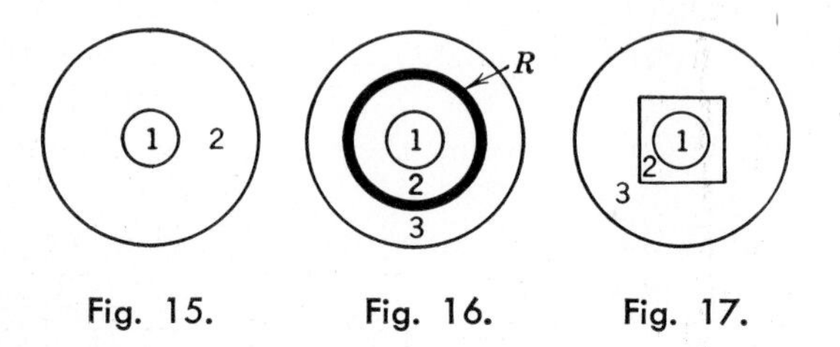

Fig. 15. Fig. 16. Fig. 17.

As the ring is moved farther from area 1, the differential threshold between 1 and 2 decreases. Since the variable is the distance of the inner border of the ring from area 1 and not the total flux, the distance of the border must be the crucial factor.

Figure 17 involves the same kind of border (contour) phenomenon. The effect of varying the intensity of 3 on the differential threshold between 1 and 2 is the object of study. Area 1 is made either brighter or less bright than 2. The lowest thresholds are found when 2 and 3 are equally intense. The threshold becomes greater when 3 is either more intense or less intense than 2. When 3 is either more or less intense than 2, the "contrast" border is thought to interfere with the formation of a border at the outer edge of 1. By this means the differential threshold between 1 and 2 is raised. Additional patterns have also been used to test the assumption that borders in the visual field influence each other, and that it makes a difference whether one border acts on the end of another border or on the side of it.

Whereas the targets just mentioned are those characteristic of academic studies of brightness perception, several other types of targets are dictated by more practical considerations. For instance, the question of detection of targets in actual outdoor situations often involves land and sky divisions of the visual field; i.e., a horizon or boundary between unequally illuminated upper and lower parts of the visual field is involved. Targets may appear fully within the lower part of the field, fully within the upper part of the field, or across the horizon. A target placed *on* the horizon is shown in Fig. 18. Were the square somewhat below the horizon, it would, in this case, be invisible. The target may be of a different intensity from either the upper (sky) or lower (land) parts of the field.

Practical considerations in "detecting" targets introduce the factor of target motion. It would be expected that angular motion could not become very great before an otherwise visible target would become ineffective. The factor of "blurring out" at weak illuminations easily becomes great enough to offset any "attention-getting" advantage a moving target may have.

Fig. 18.

The term *brightness contrast* is often used in the study of brightness discrimination. It is not always kept clear whether the subjective phenomenon, the underlying physiological mechanism for the experience, or the intensity differences in two parts of the stimulus field are being referred to. Simple brightness-discrimination studies become the conventional studies of "contrast" when a number of levels of surround are employed to study the Weber fraction.

Visual experience and the ability to make discriminations are studied sometimes when two eyes are used, and at other times when only one eye is employed. In these two cases certain very decided differences pertaining to adaptation, brightness discrimination, visual acuity, and space perception have been brought out. Targets may be used successively with one and with two eyes, or simultaneous comparisons may be made, part of a target being seen by two eyes and the other part with one. Figure 19 illustrates the latter form of setup [12]. Two disks or other areas form the comparison fields of the target. One eye is allowed to see both comparison fields, and the other eye is prevented from seeing one of them. The obstacle to the one eye may be a solid (opaque) black shield, or it may be a revolving disk (episcotister) with open sectors. This sort of obstruction is only partial; it merely *reduces* the light flux from the one comparison field. By such a method the efficacy of various partial reductions can be tested. By reducing the intensity of the opposite comparison field, which is seen by both eyes, the quantitative effect of the two eyes working together (binocular summation or subtraction) can be studied.

If a setup in which the two eyes can be stimulated independently is employed, the image of a bright disk can be placed on one retina, and the image of a dim disk on the corresponding area of the other retina.

The observer will thus be made to see them as a single disk, since their images fall on corresponding retinal areas. It would be expected that adding to the total stimulation by placing an image on the second retina would brighten the surface of the originally bright disk, but such is not the case. The resulting brightness is less than with a single eye stimulated and lies somewhere between the brightness of the two disks seen individually. This is known as Fechner's paradox. If, however, the two stimuli are equally or nearly equally intense, the resulting disk is brighter than the disk occasioned by only one of the stimuli [9].

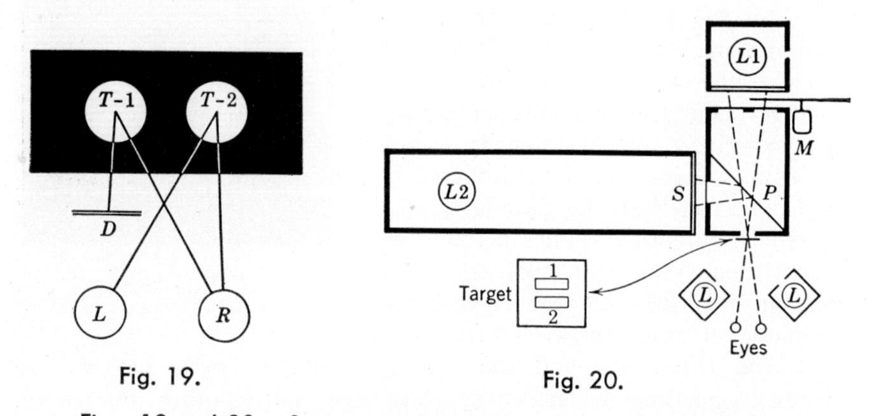

Fig. 19.

Fig. 20.

Figs. 19 and 20. Setups to indicate arrangements for studying binocular vision.

In Fig. 19, *L* and *R* represent the two eyes; *T*-1 and *T*-2 the two test objects, light from both of which reaches the right eye. Light from *T*-1 to the left eye may be partially or totally obstructed by an episcotister wedge (*D*). In Fig. 20, *L*1 and *L*2 are light sources whose effective intensity is determined by their positions in their elongated housings. *L* and *L* provide for the illumination of the surrounds of 1 and 2 in the target. The light from *L*1 to part 2 of the target is obstructed by a blind in the lower half of glass *P*. Light from *L*2 is reflected by the upper half of *P*. *S* and *M* represent any controlling screens or motors to be placed in the apparatus.

Binocular interaction has also been studied with such a setup, as suggested in Fig. 20 [17]. By use of this arrangement not only the two comparison areas but also the field surrounding them can be varied, and by the episcotister *M*, light to one eye can be either partially or totally obstructed. In addition, the factor of Fechner's paradox and that of the effects of one border upon another can be studied.

The effect of the use of two, as compared to one, eye on adaptation has also been studied [14]. It has been found that binocular preadaptation on monocular vision is more prolonged than monocular preadaptation on monocular vision. The time required just to be able to discern an object on its background has been studied under the several possible combinations of preadaptation and test. The longer the time, the slower is the adaptation.

Visual Acuity

Whereas brightness discrimination has to do with the factors of stimulus area, flux per unit area, total flux, duration of exposure to light, etc., in relation to the grosser areal aspects of experience, visual acuity, a form of brightness discrimination, is concerned with the finer spatial aspects of stimulation and resulting experience. Whereas in studies of brightness discrimination *intensity differences* are the primary objects of attention, in visual acuity finer *spatial features* are the central object of study. The aim is usually to discover how small the visual angle between two objects in the visual field may become without the objects still being seen as touching each other. To be able to see close-lying objects or areas as spatially separate is to *resolve* them. The study of visual acuity is the study of the fineness of resolution under various sets of conditions. Resolution depends upon many factors, such as general level of illumination, difference in intensity between the areas involved, pattern of the field, and duration of exposure to stimulation, as well as upon fineness of the retinal mosaic, etc.

Of primary consideration in the usual study of visual acuity is the resolving power of the eye, as dependent upon its relative ability to form a sharp image and upon the fineness of the retinal mosaic. Image formation is by no means a mathematically sharp affair. Such factors as blur circles provide for a tapering illumination, rather than perfectly steep gradients as boundaries between light and dark. Methods for studying visual acuity have had to recognize this fact in more and more ways [1, 18]. The retinal mosaic is the grid formed by the ends (cross-sections) of the receptor cells and intercellular spaces. It is upon this grid that the retinal image is placed; hence "fineness of grain" in the retinal mosaic plays a determining role in visual acuity. Methods in the study of visual acuity pertain to the systematic manipulation of physical conditions to indicate the factors which control visual resolution.

Visual acuity is measured clinically by the use of black letters of standard sizes or of the Landolt broken circle (Fig. 3) in a series of sizes and positions. Letters which subtend 1 minute of arc when viewed at a distance of 20 feet are taken as the normally resolvable size. These letters are placed in rows, successive rows subtending smaller and smaller visual angles. The ability to read the letters of the small rows indicates better than normal vision. The ability to discern only the large letters at a distance of 20 feet indicates less than normal vision. If an individual can read at 20 feet only the letters which should be read at 40 feet, his vision is 20/40 or subnormal according to such crude charts.

In the laboratory the Landolt broken circle is occasionally employed, but the usual target is a pair of bars of different widths, such as Figs. 21 to 23, or gratings, as in Fig. 24. Even very fine single lines, as in Fig. 25, have been used.

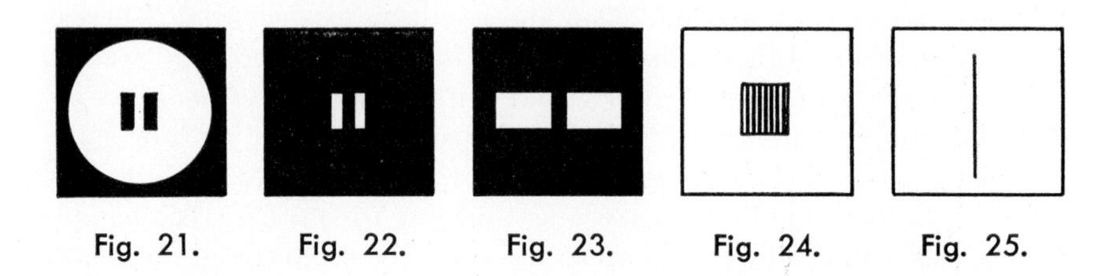

Fig. 21. Fig. 22. Fig. 23. Fig. 24. Fig. 25.

The factors to consider in the formal measurement of visual acuity by bars or lines are: (1) the luminous-intensity relation of bars or lines and field, (2) size of field, and (3) width of bars. The experiment may consist in using light bars on a dark field, or dark bars on a light field. The use of the two procedures has turned out to be more than precautionary, for the results are quite unlike. As in the study of brightness discrimination, the size of the field when it is illuminated is important. It is obvious that these arrangements (Figs. 22 and 23) produce what can be called a glare situation, if the bars are at all intense. For some purposes this is objectionable, but the results of a setup of this sort are nevertheless important to know.

Visual acuity, defined as *the reciprocal of the just resolvable visual angle measured in minutes of arc,* becomes progressively greater as the field illuminated is increased, regardless of whether broken circles or gratings are used. The absolute results, however, are not equivalent. At low illuminations the broken circle provides for a lower visual acuity than the grating. At high illuminations the broken circle provides for a higher visual acuity. Somewhere the curves representing the two functions cross. Light bars on a dark field provide for an increasing visual acuity only until a certain level of intensity is reached (in some experiments, between 0 and +1 log photons), beyond which a reversal sets in [40].

Although it might be thought that resolution depends almost if not exclusively upon the magnitude of the interspace and the related intensity features involved, this is not the case. The width of the bars, as well as their separation, is an effective factor in determining resolution. Broad and narrow bars (Figs. 22 and 23) do not yield the same result [18]. As the intensity of light bars on a dark field is raised, visual acuity first rises rapidly. With wide bars the rise slowly continues after the initial rapid onset, but with narrow bars visual acuity falls again very slowly. This might be explained on the assumption that borders interfere with each other. The highest visual acuity of all has been recorded with the single lines. Resolution of lines which subtended only 0.5 minutes of arc has been recorded.

It is important in methodology to note that the subjective width of bright bars undergoes striking variations during manipulations of intensity. The shift in contours of the bars has been attributed to a form of irradiation. How this irradiation operates has been the subject of study by a number of individuals [40].

Color Discrimination

There are three ways of discriminating color: through its hue, distinguishing red, yellow, green, etc.; through its brightness (brilliance, tint); and through its saturation, the amount of the hue present (deep blue as against a blue-gray). These attributes of color have connections with two aspects of radiant energy, namely, wavelength and flux density. Color may be experienced in several ways in accordance with the conditions under which it appears. There are surface colors, film colors, and volume colors. In looking through a spectroscope, for example, the observed color has a completely different kind of appearance from the same hue on the surface of objects. The former is a film color; the latter is a surface color. Again, the color of some fluids has a certain voluminousness that is absent in the other two cases; the color seen in looking through a clear fluid is a volume color.

The human eye is not equally sensitive to all wavelengths within the visible band. One of the fundamental procedures in the study of vision has been the examination of this differential sensitivity. The findings are represented in a graph called a visibility curve, or a luminosity curve. In obtaining data for this curve, a form of matching is employed. The various wavelengths are adjusted in intensity so as to give equal brightness. The reciprocals of these values are plotted on a scale of 1.0 to 0, the wavelength with the lowest intensity having a value of 1.0. Figure 26 indicates separately the luminosity values for scotopic and photopic vision. The scotopic curve is obtained by using only enough light to activate the rod-receptors, and the photopic by using enough light to activate the cone-receptors. The actual values are not equivalent in the two curves. The curves show only relative values for the different parts of the spectrum, the actual values having been converted to a common scale.

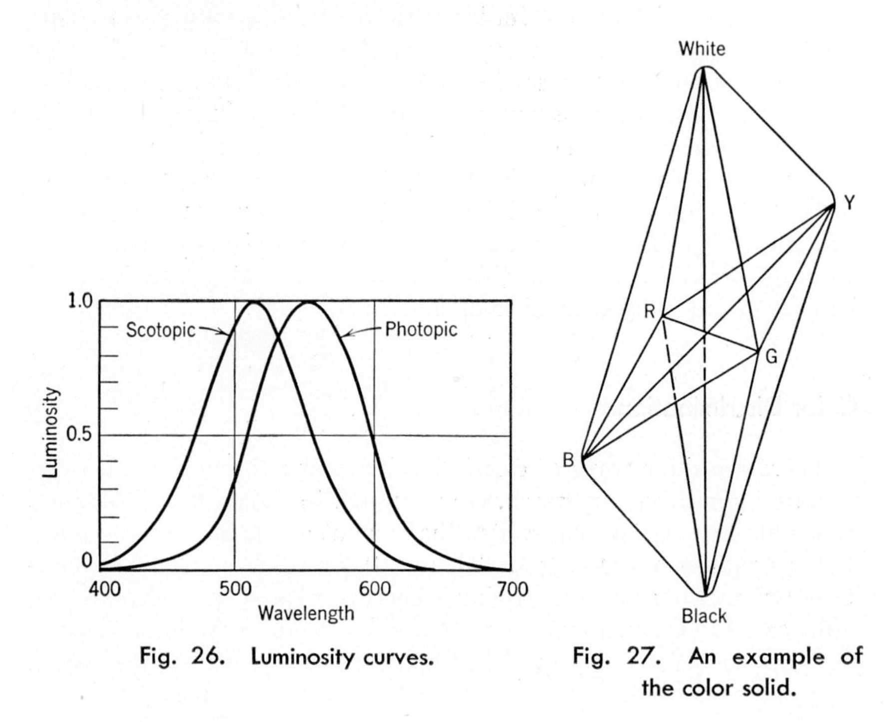

Fig. 26. Luminosity curves.

Fig. 27. An example of the color solid.

The next consideration in understanding color perception is the ascertainment of the total number of colors perceptible. This is done by finding out how many JND's of hue, brightness, and saturation can be discerned.

Since there are three variables to color experience, an orderly representation of colors can be handled by a geometrical solid. Color solids of various sorts have been made. One of the oldest was a double pyramid, base to base (Fig. 27). The axis from apex to apex represented the brightness scale (achromatic axis). The complementaries, red-green and blue-yellow, occupied the opposing corners. Distance from the axis outward to the pyramidal rim represented degrees of color saturation. Such a solid was an oversimplification. Although it represented the most general relationship between the color variables, it by no means approximated quantitative relations.

One of the latest color solids is that of Nickerson and Newhall [33]

(Fig. 28). It consists of nine irregular segments of a "cylinder" placed one on top of the other. Nine segments were chosen so as to make the cylinder compare to the divisions in the brightness (value) dimension of the Munsell system, one of the most used classifications of color. Each of these value segments is different in shape and size. The rims of each represent the hues of the spectrum, and the segments are quite eccentric to the value axis. This eccentricity varies progressively from one segment to the other, as can be seen in the figure.

The two basic facts of color which stand out in the color solid and

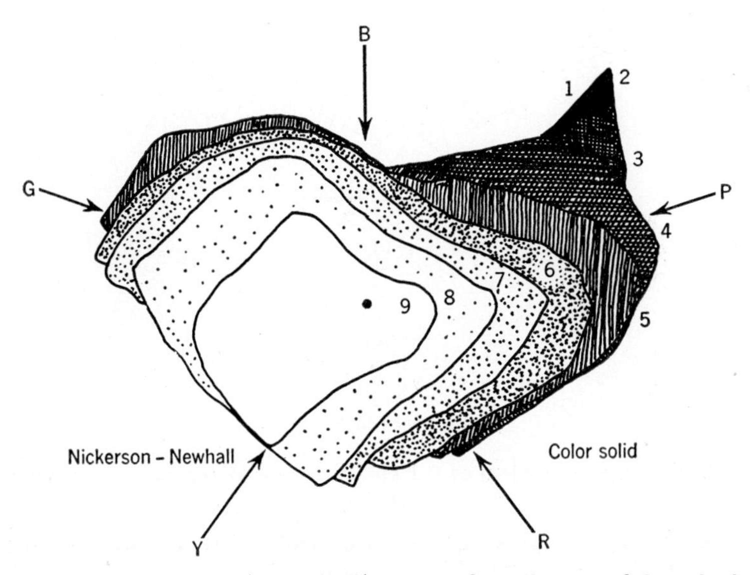

Fig. 28. A color solid ("cylinder") as seen from the top of the cylinder.

The segments from top to bottom are numbered. The letters surrounding the solid indicate the locations of the hues.

in color systems such as the Munsell are that not all hues may reach the same saturation, as measured in JND steps (or multiples thereof) and that the maximum possible degree of saturation varies from one level of brightness to another for almost all colors.

The Munsell color system uses the three dimensions of color in the following way. In it there are forty subjectively equi-spaced hues, and chips (specimens) of them are arranged on twenty charts, each with a hue and its complement. In each chart the chips are arranged on a value (brightness) scale of nine subjectively equally spaced steps. Horizontally the steps are of subjectively equal chroma (saturation). All chips having the same position on the several charts presumably possess the same chroma. Red, for instance, will have more steps in the chroma dimension than will the unsaturated hues, such as yellow.

One of the fundamental procedures in color study has been to determine the experiential (sensory) results from combining selected portions of the spectrum. This has been done by means of the color wheel, on which different colors occupy various radial segments. When the wheel is revolved, the separate fractions "fuse" and become a new color. This procedure has been called color-mixing. Although

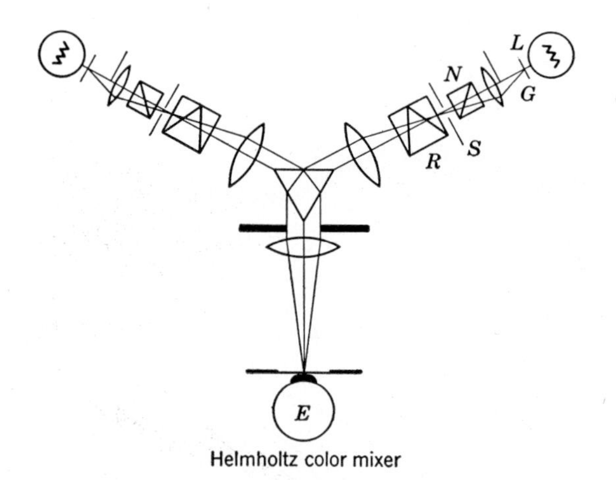

Fig. 29. The optical system of a Helmholtz color mixer, such as was used by Hecht.

G = ground glass, L = light source, N = a Nichol prism, S = slit off a collimator, R = Rochon prism, and E = the eye at the exit pupil of the telescope. Portions of the faces of the prism are visible and are seen as contiguous semicircular fields. The whole field has a visual angle of less than 1.5°, thus stimulating within the rod-free area of the eye. For an explanation of the action of the prisms see [24].

this is simple as a procedure, it involves complexities not under control. The use of surfaces as color sources involves uncontrolled reflectances, uncontrolled qualities of illuminants for the surfaces, etc.

The best analytical way of studying color is with the spectrometer, an instrument by which controlled separation of white light into its spectral components (wavelengths) and recombination of them can be accomplished. One form of the spectrometer is the Helmholtz color mixer, the essentials of which are indicated in Fig. 29 [24].

It has been found that normal color vision is trichromatic. Any part of the spectrum may be matched by a field whose radiation is composed of three properly chosen other parts of the spectrum. By the matching technique, defects in color perception have been found in certain individuals [28]. Some defects are called color weakness; others, color blindness. These defects consist in confusing various parts of the spectrum with each other. The individuals with defective color vision are roughly as follows: (1) persons who confuse parts of the spectrum but who nevertheless require three primary wavelengths to make a spectral match (anomalous trichromats); (2) persons who confuse large portions of the spectrum and can match any part of it with a mixture of only two primaries (dichromats); and (3) persons who are fully color-blind (monochromats).

Dichromats are of three kinds: (*a*) protanopes, who confuse green, yellow, and red and match blue-green with white; (*b*) deuteranopes, who also confuse these colors but have a distribution of brightness perception much like normal persons; and (*c*) tritanopes, who match a point in the yellow with white.

Monochromats are of two kinds: (*a*) the scotopic monochromats, those whose brightness sensitivity follows the visibility curve for rod vision; and (*b*) the photopic monochromats, those whose brightness vision follows the visibility curve for cone vision.

Color weakness consists in a reduction in the number of distinctions (JND's) that can be made when tested with spectral stimulation. Color blindness is the total absence of ability to discriminate on the basis of wavelength. In such cases only intensity discriminations are possible.

Since the eye (the observer) cannot analyze radiation into its spectral components, color experience represents an over-all effect. There are many different stimuli (colored surfaces, etc.) of complex wavelength composition which will elicit the same color sensation. Instrumentally, however, the difference in actual spectral composition can be detected.

A usable connection between color sensation and the spectral reflectance of surfaces has been worked out. The technique of obtaining these relations between the spectral stimulus and color experience is called color specification. Instrumental color analysis by either a spectroradiometer or a spectrophotometer is first necessary. The information obtained from these instruments is transformed by means of standard data from color-matching experiments. The most used system for color specification is based on the supposition that the chromaticity (hue and saturation) of the stimulus can be specified by the quantities representing the proportions of three primary light distributions needed to match the color experience induced by a given stimulus. The primaries stated in terms of their intensities are called the tri-stimulus values.

Intermittent Stimulation

Any portion of the visual field may be illuminated by radiation which fluctuates in intensity. If the one phase of the fluctuation reaches zero, the stimulation is intermittent. The most common experimental setup employs a disk target as the fluctuating field, while the surrounding field is left unilluminated [1]. Among the more complex targets is the disk-annulus pattern, in which the disk alternates in intensity [8]. The intensity level of the annulus may be set at any fixed level or may be systematically varied step by step. The annulus level is often halfway between the high-intensity and the zero-intensity phases of the cycle. The name of the experience of rapidly fluctuating light is flicker.

In general, the objectives involved in the study of fluctuating and intermittent stimulation are the following: (1) to discover the experiences elicited by intermittencies of different rates, when intensities and spatial features are also systematically varied; (2) to relate these experiences to quantitative features of the stimulus situation; and (3) to relate these features to neural events in the visual pathway.

The salient feature of intermittent stimulation is that the series of discrete flashes interrupting darkness gives way to a series of different phenomena as the rate of stimulus intermittency is raised. (1) The flashes cease to be fully discrete; absolutely dark intervals disappear; light begins to fill them in. Finally the experience is one of a continuously lighted field. (2) Superimposed on this is an undulating or flicker component. As the stimulus rate increases, flicker becomes less extreme and more rapid in its undulations; it is said to become "finer." Finally a stimulus rate is reached at which a uniformly bright field is seen; all flicker disappears. The "fusion point" has been reached. The lowest stimulus rate responsible for this is the critical flicker frequency (CFF).

Strangely, little attention has been paid to the experiential phenomena below the fusion point [8]. Most of the work on intermittent light stimulation has been directed toward determining and measuring the various factors involved in the production of fusion, i.e., measurements of CFF. It has been found that area of the intermittent field, intensity of light, and ratio of the stimulus duration to interval between stimuli are the major factors. Various parts of the spectrum do not elicit like responses at all intensities. The intensity level of the surround also plays a part.

It has been possible to study response to intermittent light in subhuman species by the use of certain specific motor reactions of animals while on a stationary floor inside a horizontally revolving drum composed of vertical black and white bands [12].

The study of intermittent stimulation has been instrumental in many ways in disclosing the nature of the photoreceptor process and the nature of the neural processes in the retina and elsewhere along the visual pathway [12]. The fundamental feature of *time* as well as intensity can be studied to best advantage by variously spacing the components in a series of stimuli. Recovery, in addition to excitation, can be examined. With intermittent stimulation the onset and the waxing and waning of brightness sensation in relation to stimulus characteristics can also be studied to advantage.

One of the oldest generalizations which has come out of the use of intermittent light stimulation is Talbot's law,[2] which pertains to the brightness resulting from such stimulation. It states, in effect, that the resulting brightness level is to the brightness level induced by continuous stimulation as the fractional time occupied by the intermittent stimulus is to the continuous stimulation; i.e., if the photic

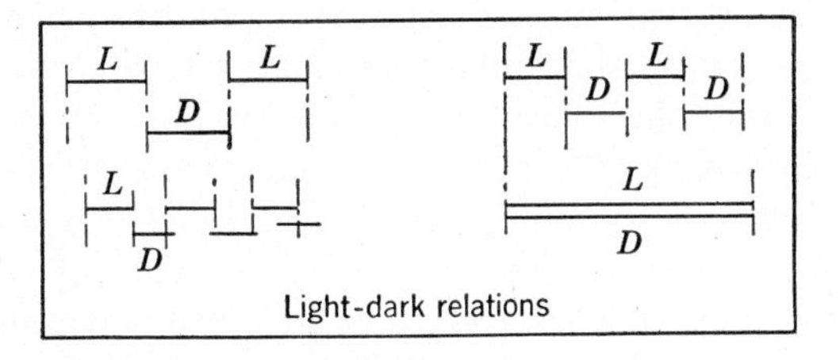

Fig. 30. This figure shows results of varying flash rate with ring annulus target.

Upper left diagram indicates subjective alternation of light and dark phases. Upper right diagram shows the same phenomenon. Lower left diagram shows the beginning of overlapping. Lower right diagram shows the subjective simultaneity of phases, the dark phase seen through the light phase. At still greater flash rates simultaneity is lost and fusion approaches.

pulse and the "dark" period are of equal lengths, brightness is one-half that expected from continuous stimulation. This reduced brightness is often called the Talbot brightness. Thought of as a level, it is often called the Talbot level.

Single pulses of light are seen as brighter than continuous light of the same physical intensity. This greater effect also pertains, within

[2] Talbot's law can be stated mathematically, for example, as follows:

$$I_T = \frac{I_c}{t_i + t_d}$$

where I_T is the Talbot intensity; I_c, the subjective intensity of the same source when continuous rather than intermittent; t_i, the time occupied by the flash; and t_d, the time occupied by the dark interval.

certain rate limits, to repeated pulses and has been called brightness enhancement [1, 21].

Aside from brightness enhancement, one of the outstanding phenomena resulting from subfusion stimulus rates is the existence of the dark and light phases of the cycle simultaneously [1]. This occurs only when the intermittently illuminated surface is surrounded by a steadily illuminated field, e.g., an annulus. With slowly increasing rates of stimulus repetition, the two phases (*L* and *D*) can be seen to shift from alternation to simultaneity (Fig. 30). If the rate is further increased, this phenomenon (*L* and *D* simultaneity) disappears. While the two phases are still seen concurrently, the light phase is a glary translucent film through which the dark phase can be seen lying behind.

The Perception of Motion

Studies on the perception of motion involve various senses and are of many kinds. Those that involve the visual perception of motion may be divided into three kinds: (1) the use of moving stimuli with the observer stationary, (2) the use of successive stationary stimuli to give the impression of motion (apparent movement), and (3) the use of a moving observer (not necessarily in aviation, but in special laboratory experiments) whose relations to well-known objects (earth, horizontality, etc.) are changed. Whereas many investigations of the first two general kinds have been performed, study in the third category (outside of rotation experiments and aviation) is only in its beginning. At the present time the most common procedures in studying visual movement involve two general sets of conditions, those in which the stimuli move and those in which they do not.

It is of fundamental importance to recognize that a necessary requisite in eliciting the visual experience of movement is a certain kind of differential stimulation of receptor mosaic and that this may be accomplished by difference in intensity of stimulation, as well as in time. For example, a homogeneously illuminated field, suddenly increasing or decreasing in intensity, induces the visual experience of movement. When it is remembered that the retina is graded in its sensitivity from fovea to periphery, and when it is assumed from certain neurophysiological facts that conduction to the cerebral centers varies in accordance with strength of peripheral excitation, the necessary temporal factors exist to account for the kinds of visual movement experienced.

Gamma movement, the expansive movement seen as illumination suddenly increases (Fig. 31), can be reversed if the proper target is used (see Fig. 32). If the field is illuminated more intensely at the periphery than in the center, the movement will be centripetal, rather than centrifugal, when illumination is suddenly increased [1].

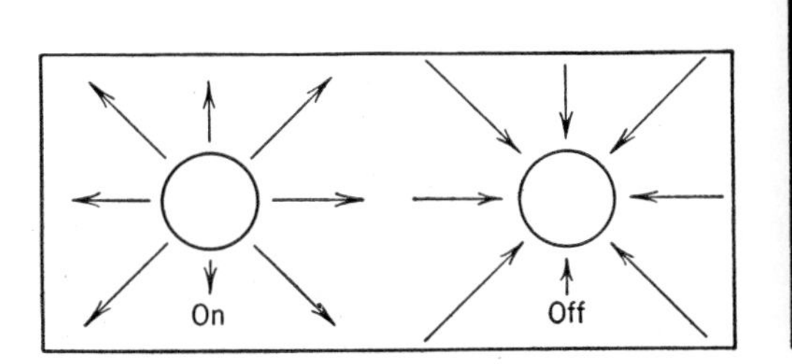

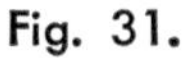

Fig. 31.

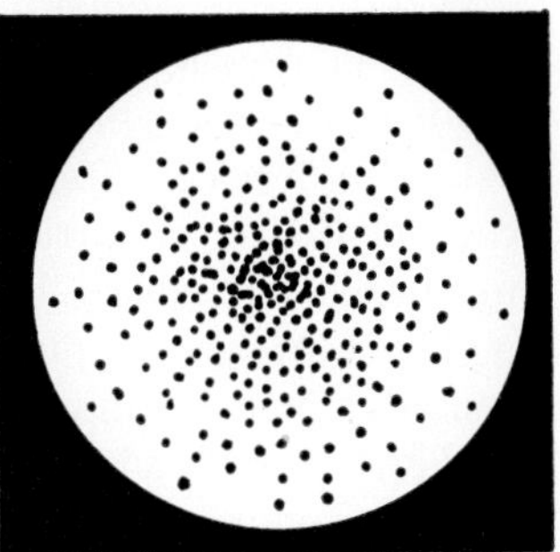

Fig. 32. This diagram indicates a visual field of wide angle and of greater intensity toward the periphery than at the center.

There are many phenomena to be considered in studying the perception of motion, but they, like a number of other visual phenomena, are reserved for Chapter 6 on studying perceptual phenomena.

Motor Aspects of Visual Behavior

Vision as a mode of contact between the organism and its physical surrounds is not fully understood until its motor aspects are considered. These motor aspects include the adjustments of the eyes so as to be optically adequate and the exploratory and "manipulatory"[3] movements of the eyes themselves, as well as body posture and, at times, appropriate bodily movements.

Eye-movement cameras of various sorts have been employed to record the action of the two eyes in reading and in other situations,

[3] A very greatly neglected factor in the study of vision is the roaming behavior of the eyes. Most ideas with regard to vision, i.e., the fineness of visual acuity, etc., tacitly assume the eyes to be motionless. Tactile impressions are generally gained by moving the sensitive part over the object to feel "roughness" or similar properties. The eye does an analogous thing by its own motion. In the hand this activity is called manipulation. It is not too far fetched to speak of the ocular activity as manipulation, if the essence of the word, in both cases, lies in the exploration.

such as observing apparent movement, or the autokinetic movement (Charpentier's illusion, etc.). These situations generally involve the projection of a spot of light onto the eye, from which it is reflected onto a recording film and moves in accordance with eye motion.

By other instrumental setups various measurements of convergence and accommodation and their interrelations have been made. Although most of these measurements have not been made in psychological laboratories, they form an important part of what the experimental psychologist should know about vision. Instruments for this purpose are varied, but characteristically employ lenses and prisms for the purpose of putting either accommodative or convergence demands upon the observer, who is, in effect, instructed to resist either blurring or double vision (diplopia). So-called ergographic procedures have been employed in this connection in the study of convergence and accommodation [26]. By ingenious manipulation of conditions a number of interrelations in function between accommodation and convergence have been worked out.

Pupillary behavior has also been studied. Pupillary diameter has been measured by several devices. One is an optical arrangement which can be adjusted so that, when the second of two points of light can just be seen, a scale is read and the measurement transformed into a known pupil diameter. Other devices include instruments for sighting upon the eye. A final and much better method is photography. This may be either flash photography to determine pupillary diameter at given instants, or ultraviolet or infrared motion-picture photography, which enables one to follow the variations in pupillary diameter from instant to instant [9]. It is only by this method that the most precise knowledge of pupillary behavior can be obtained. One of the problems in pupillary behavior is the question of what parts of the retina are effective, when stimulated by light, in inducing a pupillary reaction (pupillo-motor response, or light reflex).

Another problem, as was implied, consists in determining the speed of pupillary reaction to abrupt changes in illumination level and to transient illumination of various durations. It has been found that the pupil responds by a change in diameter to a transient dark interval and that this response is mediated, at least in part, by nervous paths different from the light reflex to transient light stimulation.

Photographic techniques have indicated that the pupillary light reflex is quite highly differentiated [9]. In many respects it parallels perceptual behavior in quantitative aspects of complexity. For example, it parallels the already described Fechner's paradox in its reactions, as can be demonstrated by using the very same experimental target arrangement already described to demonstrate Fechner's paradox. If the pupils are photographed in infrared radiation, pupillary behavior under the low, as well as the high, level of visual stimulation can be recorded. As the light falling on one retina is increased, the pupils of both eyes constrict. If, after reaching a high level, the light in one retina is held constant, and weak light is cast on the corresponding area of the second retina, the pupils "paradoxically" begin to dilate instead of continuing to constrict. With increasing intensity of light on the second retina, the dilatation becomes still greater. After a certain point in intensity is reached, however, constriction sets in, and

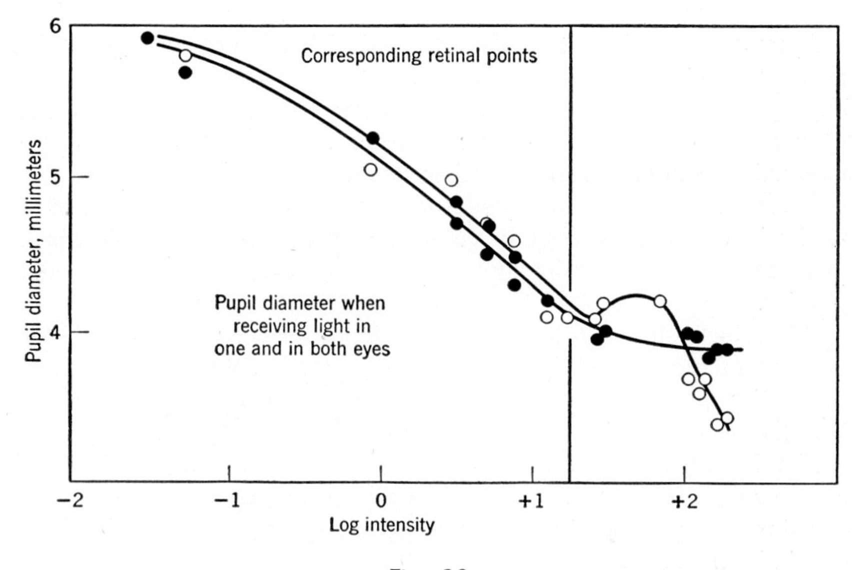

Fig. 33.

by the time that the illumination of the second retina is equal to that of the first, both pupils have constricted to a point beyond that reached before the second retina was stimulated. This constriction is greater than that occurring when all of the same total amount of light is cast on one retina. These results are shown in Fig. 33. The curve with solid circles pictures the results when a given quantity of stimulating light is gradually increased by casting it on one retina. The curve indicated by the open circles pictures the outcome when the same amount of light is used, part being applied to one eye, and part to the other. The vertical line indicates the point at which the second eye became involved.

The parallel to Fechner's paradox consists in the fact that increasing the total stimulation by adding stimulation via the second retina fails to increase constriction, decreasing it instead. Only when the stimulation of the two eyes approaches equality does the brightness of the perceived area or the pupillary constriction become greater. This same pupillary behavior occurs when using non-corresponding retinal areas, and even when using two areas of a single retina. Such a method holds promise for further comparisons between sensations and reflexes.

THE STUDY OF VISUAL MECHANISMS

Among the objectives of the study of vision is accounting for the phenomena that are known to occur. The means involved are generally spoken of as mechanisms. The mechanisms responsible for the phenomena are of interest and significance. For our purposes, these mechanisms lie within the organism itself.

Interest in visual mechanisms leads the investigator to the study of the basis for the phenomena in the several categories already described. It directs him to physiology and anatomy, and to chemistry and physics.

It is evident that, for the most part, adaptation is to be accounted for in terms of the photochemistry of the receptors. Differences between adaptation in binocular and monocular vision have made it evident that the nervous system is also responsible for adaptation.

The knowledge gained from studies of the discharges of single receptor organs [3, 22], as well as studies which disclose how photoreceptor systems operate [4], have helped to account for brightness discrimination.

Processes underlying color vision have possibly received more attention as mechanisms than have those underlying any other aspect of vision [15]. Theorization regarding color vision has been persistent over many decades. Only recently, with neurophysiological techniques which record retinal activity, is new progress beginning to be made in answering some of the fundamental questions upon which any understanding of color vision must rest [20].

It has been shown that the primary ocular mechanisms upon which space perception rests is the differential nature of the images in the two retinas [34]. With every eye movement or change in position between the object and the observer, the relations between the shapes and sizes of the images in the two retinas change and form a basis for the experience of object position. What role the innervation of the extrinsic eye muscles plays is not yet certain, although it is apparent that this role is secondary. As was already pointed out, the perception of motion is dependent upon some sort of temporally differentiated excitation reaching the central nervous system, and this can be induced by either stationary or physically moving objects.

Visual phenomena pose molar as well as molecular problems. This is to say that explanations aimed at accounting for such problems must tell how various parts of the retina, or how the two retinas, or even how other parts of the nervous system work together. Theories developed to solve such problems are often what are called field theories [11]. Field theories are those which describe the system that is known to be involved as a complex unit, the activities of the parts of which are controlled by laws of the system as a whole. There are many phenomena that demonstrate the need for such explanation, but as yet little headway has been made in deriving fundamental field laws.

The phenomena that accrue from casting light on the optic disk or, more inclusively, from casting unequal intensities of light on the optic disk and the rest of the retina, lead quite immediately to questions of underlying mechanisms. It is generally taken for granted that the optic disk contains no receptor elements or photically sensitive tissue, but certain phenomena still pose questions of optic-disk sensitivity in the minds of some investigators. Blind-spot phenomena seem to be dependent on spatial features of stimulation in such a way as to come into the category of field phenomena. Hence, to study blind-spot phenomena is either to study them as examples of field phenomena or to study them for their own sake and to attempt to discover the mechanisms underlying them.

Köhler and Wallach [29] have studied "figural aftereffects" as basic explanatory phenomena or as illustrative of some basic mechanism or mechanisms in the organism. Although they use perceptual phenomena, the ones they select are particularly appropriate for investigating aftereffects which provide for theoretical speculation on physiochemical mechanisms in the central nervous system. (See Fig. 2, p. 171.)

METHODOLOGICAL SUMMARY

In spite of its brevity, the foregoing presentation of methods in vision should lead the reader to develop some such ideas as the following:

1. That visual sensation is capable of measurement when the experimental setup is properly planned.
2. That the measurements pertain to the relations between experience and physical conditions in the individual's surrounds.

3. That such measurements are possible because instructions given the subject rule out, or at least greatly minimize, individual differences in criteria and other contributive features involved in observation.

4. That the phenomena dealt with in the various classes of visual experiments are products of the specific sets of conditions involved. To understand results, the conditions under which the data were obtained must be known.

5. That usable forms of visual observations are comparisons in which two features are matched through manipulation of stimulus conditions, or one is differentiated from the other by manipulating conditions until a just perceivable difference arises.

6. That the measures obtained (thresholds, etc.) are statistical because of the fact that ideal precision is never obtainable. In a series of observations aimed at determining a relationship between stimulus conditions and experiential outcome, both the stimulus and observer change at least enough to provide a series of data differing numerically.

7. That, because of the fact that the observer is a contributor to the experiential end result, not all relations which are important to discover lie solely between stimulus conditions and experience, but lie in part between discoverable features of the individual's organization (alignment, attitude, etc.) and the experiential end results. This leads us to the study of "perception" as such and to the frequent use, in that study, of the organism rather than the physical world as a primary reference.

8. That vision is not fully understood until the mechanisms underlying it are determined and comprehended.

9. Last, but not least in importance, that there is much yet to be discovered about the basic features of the contact between the individual and the physical world.

SUGGESTED READINGS

1. Bartley, S. H. *Vision: A Study of Its Basis.* New York: Van Nostrand, 1941.
2. Duke-Elder, W. S. *Textbook of Ophthalmology,* Vol. I. St. Louis: C. V. Mosby, 1933.
3. Graham, C. H. Vision III: some neural correlations. In *Handbook of Experimental Psychology.* Worcester, Mass.: Clark University Press, 1934, pp. 829–879.
4. Hecht, S. Vision II: the nature of the photoreceptor process. In *Handbook of Experimental Psychology.* Worcester, Mass.: Clark University Press, 1934, pp. 704–828.
5. Luckiesh, M., and F. K. Moss. *The Science of Seeing.* New York: Van Nostrand, 1937.
6. Parsons, J. H. *An Introduction to the Study of Color Vision.* New York: G. P. Putnam, 1935.

7. TROLAND, L. T. Vision I: visual phenomena and their stimulus correlations. In *Handbook of Experimental Psychology.* Worcester, Mass.: Clark University Press, 1934, pp. 653–703.

REFERENCES

8. BARTLEY, S. H. Some effects of intermittent photic stimulation. *J. Exper. Psychol.,* 1939, *25,* 462–480.
9. BARTLEY, S. H. Some parallels between pupillary "reflexes" and brightness discrimination. *J. Exper. Psychol.,* 1943, *32,* 110–122.
10. BARTLEY, S. H. The comparative distribution of the light in the stimulus and on the retina. *J. Comp. Psychol.,* 1935, *19,* 149–154.
11. BROWN, J. F., and A. C. VOTH. The path of seen movement as a function of the vector field. *Amer. J. Psychol.,* 1937, *49,* 543–563.
12. CROZIER, W. J., E. WOLF, and G. ZERRAHN-WOLF. Intensity and critical flicker frequency for visual flicker. *J. Gen. Psychol.,* 1937, *21,* 203–222.
13. DE SILVA, H. R., and S. H. BARTLEY. Summation and subtraction of brightness in binocular perception. *Brit. J. Psychol.,* 1930, *20,* 241–250.
14. ELSBERG, C. A., and H. SPOTNITZ. Some neural components of the visual response. *Amer. J. Physiol.,* 1937, *118,* 792–797.
15. FRY, G. A. A photo-receptor mechanism for the modulation theory of color vision. *J. Opt. Soc. Amer.,* 1945, *35,* 114–135.
16. FRY, G. A., and S. H. BARTLEY. The effect of one border in the visual field upon the threshold of another. *Amer. J. Physiol.,* 1935, *112,* 414–421.
17. FRY, G. A., and S. H. BARTLEY. The brilliance of an object seen binocularly. *Amer. J. Ophthal.,* 1933, *16,* 687–693.
18. FRY, G. A., and P. COBB. A new method for determining the blurredness of the retinal image. *Trans. Acad. Ophthal. Otolaryng.,* 1935.
19. GELDARD, F. A. Measurement of retinal fatigue to achromatic stimulation, I and II. *J. Gen. Psychol.,* 1928, *1,* 123–135, 578–590.
20. GRANIT, R. The color receptors of the mammalian retina. *J. Neurophysiol.,* 1945, *8,* 195–210.
21. HALSTEAD, W. C. A note on the Bartley effect in the estimation of equivalent brightness. *J. Exper. Psychol.,* 1941, *28,* 524–528.
22. HARTLINE, H. K. Nerve messages in the fibres of the visual pathway. *J. Opt. Soc. Amer.,* 1940, *30,* 339–347.
23. HECHT, S., and J. MANDELBAUM. The relation between vitamin A and dark adaptation. *J. Amer. Med. Assoc.,* 1939, *112,* 1910–1916.
24. HECHT, S., and H. SHLAER. Color vision of dichromats. *J. Gen. Physiol.,* 1936, *20,* 57–93.
25. HELSON, H. Some facts and implications of color constancy. *J. Opt. Soc. Amer.,* 1943, *33,* 555–567.
26. HOFSTETTER, H. W. An ergographic analysis of fatigue of accommodation. *Amer. J. Optom.,* 1943, *20,* 115–135.
27. *Illuminating Engineering Nomenclature and Photometric Standards.* Illuminating Engineering Society, 51 Madison Ave., New York.
28. JUDD, D. B. Facts of color-blindness. *J. Opt. Soc. Amer.,* 1943, *33,* 294–307.
29. KÖHLER, W., and H. WALLACH. Figural after-effects. *Proc. Amer. Philos. Soc.,* 1944, *88,* 269–357.
30. KLÜVER, H. The functional significance of the geniculo-striate system. *Biol. Symp., VII,* pp. 253–300. Lancaster, Pa.: Jaques Cattell Press, 1942.

31. Lashley, K. S. The problem of cerebral organization in vision. *Biol. Symp., VII,* pp. 301–322. Lancaster, Pa.: Jaques Cattell Press, 1942.
32. Marshall, W. H., and S. A. Talbot. Recent evidence for neural mechanisms in vision leading to a general theory of sensory activity. *Biol. Symp., VII,* pp. 117–164. Lancaster, Pa.: Jaques Cattell Press, 1942.
33. Nickerson, D., and S. M. Newhall. A psychological color solid. *J. Opt. Soc. Amer.,* 1943, *33,* 419–422.
34. Ogle, K. N. Theory of the space eikonometer. *J. Opt. Soc. Amer.,* 1946, *36,* 20–32.
35. Reeves, P. The response of the average pupil to various intensities of light. *J. Opt. Soc. Amer.,* 1920, *4,* 35–43.
36. Schouten, J. F., and L. S. Ornstein. Measurements on direct and indirect adaptation by means of a binocular method. *J. Opt. Soc. Amer.,* 1939, *29,* 168–182.
37. Sheard, C. Dark adaptation: some physical, physiological, clinical, and aeromedical considerations. *J. Opt. Soc. Amer.,* 1944, *34,* 464–508.
38. Wald, G. Area and visual threshold. *J. Gen. Physiol.,* 1937, *21,* 269–287.
39. Walls, G. Factors in human visual resolution. *J. Opt. Soc. Amer.,* 1943, *33,* 487–505.
40. Wilcox, W. W. The basis of the dependence of visual acuity on illumination. *Proc. Nat. Acad. Sci.,* 1932, *18,* 47–56.

Chapter 8

Studying Hearing

Ernest Glen Wever[1]

In our study of hearing we employ a variety of methods: physical, anatomical, physiological, clinical, and psychological. Most problems must be approached from several directions at once, with all the techniques available. Recent years have seen notable developments of the methodology in this field. Particularly significant is the growth of electronics, which has put in our hands new tools for the production, control, and measurement of tones and thereby has stimulated a re-exploration of auditory phenomena. Also the development of high-gain amplification has given birth to a new physiological approach, the method of electrophysiology, in which acoustic processes are studied in terms of their electrical manifestations. These two types of methodology, the electrophysiological and the phenomenological, are the ones with which we shall be especially concerned.

THE ELECTROPHYSIOLOGICAL METHOD [5]

The electrophysiological method makes use of the fact that all living processes have an electrical aspect, and the activities of tissues are reflected in a change of electrical state. By recording the electrical changes we obtain information on the nature of the organic processes.

In hearing there are a number of levels at which the electrical responses can be studied. They can be observed at the cochlea (see Fig. 1), the auditory nerve, and in any of the nuclei and fiber tracts of the acoustic system of the brain, up to the temporal cortex. At any level we discover the form of the activity, as determined by the initiating stimulus and the various transformations that have taken place up to that point. The study is practically limited to experi-

[1] Professor of Psychology, Princeton University.

mental animals, although in a few instances the effects have been demonstrated in human subjects.

The technical procedure consists of anesthetizing the animal, operating upon it to gain access to the tissues concerned, and then placing

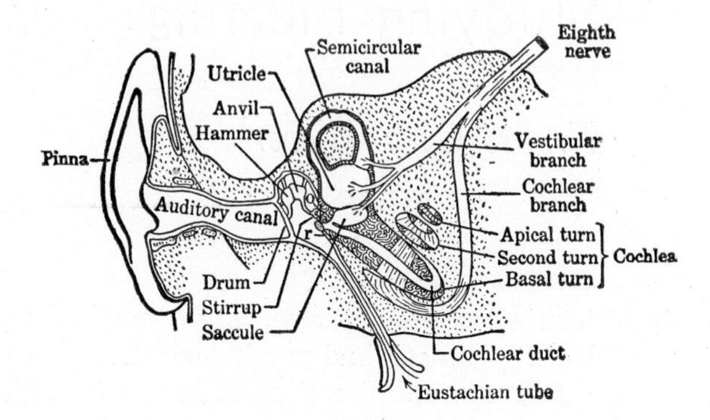

Fig. 1. Diagram of the ear.

The stippled regions represent bone, and the shaded portions indicate cavities filled with perilymph. r = round window, o = oval window. (After Czermak, from E. Boring, H. Langfeld, and H. Weld, *Introduction to Psychology*. Reprinted by permission of the authors and John Wiley and Sons.

an electrode in contact with the active cells or as close to them as possible, with a second electrode near by, usually in inactive tissue. There will generally be a difference of potential between the two regions under the electrodes, and this difference will change when one

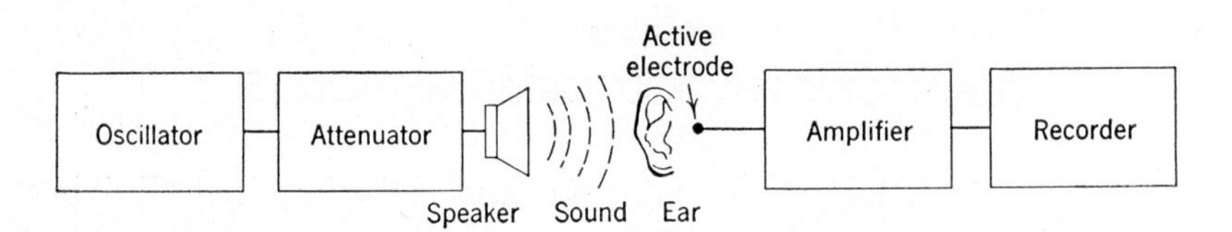

Fig. 2. Apparatus for study of audioelectric responses.

region becomes active. The changes are amplified to whatever degree necessary—usually something of the order of 60 to 120 decibels—in order to operate a chosen recording device. The specific arrangements vary with the problem at hand, especially in the recording of the electrocochlear responses and the various forms of nerve action potentials. See Fig. 2.

The electrocochlear responses are produced by the hair cells of the organ of Corti. We observe them most readily with an electrode on the membrane of the round window, from which there is a good conducting path formed by the cochlear fluids. The electrode is usually a piece of silver foil or some other conductor that is flexible enough to maintain a good contact despite accidental movements and yet imposes no serious restraint on the membrane.

The recording method varies; three instruments are especially useful, and at times all are employed in a single investigation. The amplified signals can be led into a telephone receiver or loudspeaker and then studied by listening. In this method we simply make use of the animal's ear as a microphone. We stimulate his ear with sound and ascertain the character of the responses. It is astonishing on first experience to find that the stimulating sounds are reproduced with great fidelity; indeed, if we select the right kind of ear, e.g., a guinea pig's, we can equal the performance of the finest commercial microphones. This method is best employed for general exploration and qualitative studies, not for precise measurements, because the observer's ear does not discriminate loudness changes very well.

A second method employs the cathode-ray oscillograph, where the electrical changes are presented as a visible wave (see Fig. 6, p. 410). Precise observations of amplitude and wave form are easily carried out. A decided advantage is that the equipment will withstand a sudden overload without damage.

A third method employs a wave analyzer, which is a vacuum tube voltmeter that can be adjusted so as to be sensitive to a single narrow band of frequencies. For a given signal, measurements at a number of frequencies will reveal the composition of the potential wave. A sample analysis is shown in Fig. 3.

The cochlear responses, when studied for various kinds of acoustic stimuli, give information on the nature of the ear's activities up to the hair cells. The method is useful for a vast number of problems. It has been applied in the investigation of the functions of the various parts of the conduction mechanism, the nature and locus of distortion, the roles of the tympanic muscles, the action of drugs on the cochlea, the destructive effects of excessively loud sounds, the comparative efficiency of the ears of different species of animals, and many other problems. In fact, the method can be used to investigate any function of the peripheral mechanism that has to do with the transmission and utilization of sound. A word of caution is necessary, however: these indications are not synonymous with "hearing," for hearing involves processes beyond the cochlea. Thus, for example, the fact that the cat's cochlea gives potentials to tones as high as 30,000 cycles does not thereby signify that this animal hears such tones; the matter must be investigated further by other methods, as described in Chapter 12.

The study of nerve potentials at the auditory nerve or at higher levels requires further attention to special techniques. The active electrode must be placed in intimate contact with the neurons, without damage to them. Because the nerve elements are left *in situ* and remain closely surrounded by fluids and other tissues, a considerable fraction of their potentials is shorted away; consequently the amplification must be greater than that ordinarily required in recording

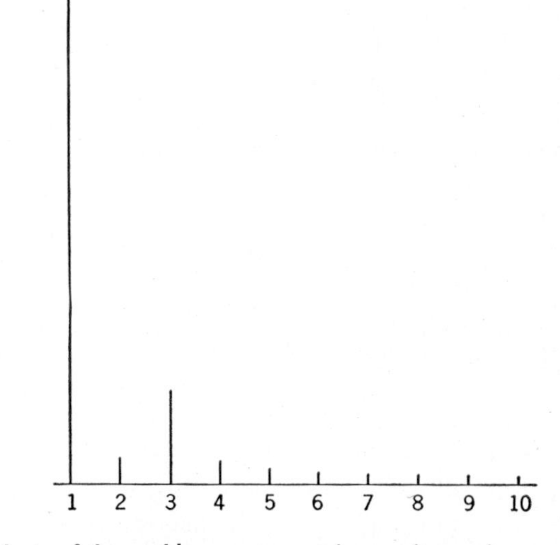

Fig. 3. Analysis of the cochlear response in a guinea-pig ear when stimulated strongly with a 1000-cycle tone.

The heights of the lines represent the magnitudes of the components. The line to the left, marked 1, represents the 1000-cycle component, the next line the 2000-cycle component, and so on.

impulses from isolated nerves. The most suitable recording instrument is the cathode-ray oscillograph. Problems which have made use of the auditory nerve responses include the representation of intensity, the maximum frequency of nerve impulses, the locus of masking, the specificity of the fibers, and others bearing particularly on the theory of hearing.

THE AUDITORY RANGE

The physical vibrations that we call sounds may vary in frequency from zero indefinitely upward, yet tests carried out on any particular ear show sensitivity only within a limited range. A determination of the upper and lower limits of this range is one of the primary problems in the study of hearing.

The Upper Limit of Hearing

If we present to the ear a simple sound whose frequency is gradually raised, we hear a tone that grows higher and higher in pitch until ultimately it can no longer be perceived. For a young person of good hearing the point at which the tone disappears will be somewhere beyond 20,000 cycles, perhaps around 23,000 cycles, provided the stimulus is sufficiently strong. A weaker stimulus will become inaudible at a lower frequency. The upper limit of hearing therefore must be stated, not as a function of frequency alone, but of intensity as well. This situation may seem to mean that, if the intensity were raised sufficiently high, the frequency range would be extended indefinitely; if we attempt to test this possibility, however, we encounter a further condition that imposes a practical and final limitation. The tone becomes painful, and it is a pain that cannot be ignored. Not only does the subject object to it, but if we should persist the ear would be damaged irreparably, as animal experiments have proved. We therefore define the upper limit of hearing as the terminal frequency at which pitch is perceived, for intensities that are below the pain or injury threshold.

Actually we do not have as yet any complete information regarding the upper limit as thus strictly defined, both because investigation in the neighborhood of a pain threshold is disagreeable and somewhat dangerous, and because the production of tones of the necessary frequency and intensity is physically difficult. Our determinations approach the true limit and show the region of frequency beyond which it lies; and for most ordinary purposes we may be content with this approximation.

Early methods of producing high tones made use of small whistles or metal bars. Galton devised a miniature whistle with a variable plunger that could be screwed in or out to change the pitch, and he fitted it to his walking stick so that he could test the reactions of his friends and also of the animals he visited in the zoological gardens. Unfortunately, Galton's whistle—and the same is true of later improvements on it—becomes erratic in performance when screwed down to a very short length and also is subject to variations according to the blowing pressure. Equally serious is the fact that its tone is accompanied by a hiss containing various low frequencies produced by the rushing stream of air, and a subject's ability to disregard this sound in favor of the proper one is often open to question.

A steel bar lightly suspended by strings placed about a quarter-length from the ends will vibrate transversely after being given a smart blow at the midpoint. Such bars are known as Koenig bars, being named for the famous acoustician and instrument-maker. A different bar must be cut for each frequency. So far as accuracy goes, this instrument is decidedly superior to the Galton whistle. The frequency varies slightly with temperature, but this variation can be calculated if desired. The noise made in striking the bar is, however, a drawback.

There are two modern developments of the metal-bar method, each of which avoids the noise of striking by employing an electrical form of excitation. In one, an electromagnet is mounted opposite one end of the bar (which is firmly held at its midpoint), and an oscillating electric current is sent through the electromagnetic coils to produce periodic magnetic attractions. A non-magnetic metal like aluminum may be used for the bar if an iron disk is cemented to the driven end. The periodic stretching of the bar, when carried out at the resonance frequency, quickly builds up an energetic vibration, which in this case is longitudinal rather than transverse.

A second form of excitation, which also gives longitudinal vibrations, employs the principle of magnetostriction. Certain metals and metallic alloys—nickel, cobalt, and especially nickel-iron and nickel-copper alloys—undergo a change of length when exposed to a magnetic field. If a coil is placed about the middle portion of a rod of such metals, and an oscillatory current sent through it, periodic alterations will be produced, and by choice of the proper frequency a resonance can be established, just as in the electromagnetic method. The electrically actuated rod has the further important advantage over the simple Koenig bar that the intensity can be varied at will by control of the electrical input.

Given a suitable source of high-frequency sound, the procedure for determining the upper limit of hearing is simple. The subject, seated comfortably in a soundproof room, is instructed to report at each trial whether he hears a tone. The constant-stimulus mode of psychophysical procedure is the most suitable. (See Chapter 5.)

Because the upper limit generally declines with age and is particularly susceptible to the effects of ear disorders, the experimenter should make careful record of the age of his subjects, their history of ear diseases, and any present condition like head colds, sinus infections, or pressure sensations referred to the eardrum.

The Lower Limit of Hearing

For several reasons, as will be seen, the lower limit of hearing is more difficult to determine than the upper limit. In the first place we need to distinguish between a lower limit of *pitch* perception and a lower limit of frequency at which *stimulation* occurs. These two limits are not the same; the ear is still stimulable by frequencies that are below the lower pitch limit. The lower limit of pitch is the problem on which we have the most information at the present time, but the other, the stimulation limit, also deserves consideration.

The experiences that appear on stimulation with pure tones of very low frequency are complex in nature, and their appreciation and analysis make severe demands on the subject's attention and skill. A good deal of preliminary practice is necessary to acquaint him with his task. If the stimulation frequency is set first around a few hundred cycles per second and then is progressively lowered, several qualitative characteristics emerge. The tone first becomes rough, and as the frequency is further reduced the roughness grows greater. Somewhere in the neighborhood of 30 cycles the roughness grades into intermittence, a quality in which the separateness of the wave pulses is evident. The roughness too becomes greater as the frequency falls, until it passes through a maximum perhaps around 15 cycles. Between 15 and 20 cycles—often around 17 cycles—a new quality arises, called a thrusting effect, which is partly auditory and partly non-auditory; there occurs within each stimulation cycle a burst of high-frequency sound, like a hiss, and at the same time there appear kinesthetic and tactual sensations which are referred to the middle ear. At the very low frequencies, below about 15 cycles, where no low pitch remains, the stimulation is heard as a pumping noise whose pattern is determined by numerous high-frequency components. Although only the lower pitch limit may be the object of investigation in a given experiment, it is obvious that a subject must be aware of these other qualitative characters and must analyze the pitch out of the total complex. These other phenomena might be the objects of investigation also.

Low tones of pure (sinusoidal) form are difficult to produce and to handle. Sinusoidal currents can be generated by electrical means, but not very conveniently, and unless unusual precautions are taken their forms will be distorted by the circuits through which they are passed and especially by the instrument used to convert them into sounds. The most satisfactory apparatus for low-tone production is the pistonphone, a miniature pump driven by a crank mechanism which converts uniform rotary motion into simple harmonic motion.

The frequency is varied by controlling the motor speeds, and here a stroboscope or a tachometer is needed to indicate the speeds. Because the motor used to drive the piston is noisy, good soundproofing is needed to isolate this part of the equipment from the terminal part, where the ear is placed. Also, since some of the motor noise penetrates to the volume of air on which the piston is working, acoustic filters are required to prevent its passage along the line to the ear; these filters are of the "low-pass" type and allow the desired tones to continue unabated. The acoustic pressure set up at the end of the acoustic line is a simple function of the volume displacement of the piston and the total volume of air enclosed in the system, so that a reasonably convenient method of controlling the intensity is to vary this volume. Volume chambers of various sizes may be inserted in the system to give the desired intensity. The changing of volume chambers takes time, however, so that quick modifications of intensity are not easily provided. The system must be airtight, and the terminal end of the line fixed in the external meatus of the ear; with animals a cannula is tied into the ear, but with human subjects a satisfactory junction can be made with a tube having a bulbous ending, like the end of a physician's stethoscope, and a bit of vaseline smeared on the outside to form a seal.

PITCH DISCRIMINATION

The difference limen for pitch is defined as the frequency change in a tone that a subject is able to perceive 50 per cent of the time, under certain specified conditions. If we designate the frequency of the tone by f, then the symbol Δf may be used to represent the statistical value of the difference limen. The ratio of these quantities $\Delta f/f$ is called the *relative* difference limen and is especially useful as an indication of pitch sensitivity, because throughout the middle portion of the range of frequencies it remains reasonably constant.

Any of the standard psychophysical methods may be used to determine the difference limen for pitch. (See Chapter 5.) The method of constant stimuli is generally preferred as the most precise. According to this method, the subject is given two tones in immediate succession and is called upon to judge the pitch of one with respect to that of the other. Several variables in the situation must receive attention. They include the duration of the tones, the time interval between the members of a pair, the intensity level, the number of ears—whether one or two—with which the subject listens, and especially the region of the frequency scale in which the measurements are made. The duration of the tones should be 0.5 second or over, for if it is too brief the discrimination will be impaired. The interval between the tones is a significant condition, and in general should be as short as manipulations of the equipment will allow; the longer this interval, the poorer the discrimination. The intensity level or, more strictly, the level above the subject's threshold, is particularly important for the low-frequency tones, and for these its variations can produce changes as great as two- or threefold in the size of the limen, as Fig. 4 illustrates. As the intensity is raised from bare audibility, the value of the limen diminishes—the discrimination improves—until a level of about 40

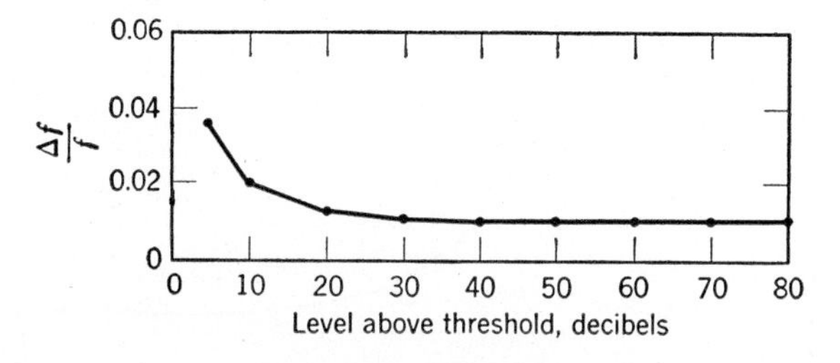

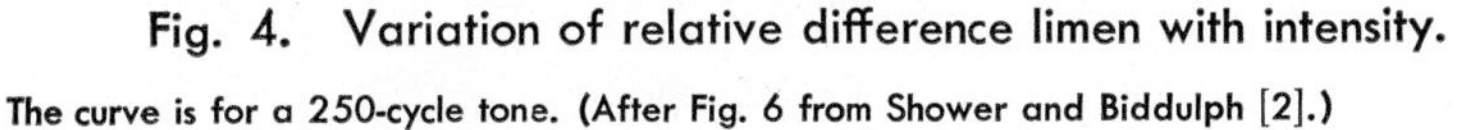
Fig. 4. Variation of relative difference limen with intensity.

The curve is for a 250-cycle tone. (After Fig. 6 from Shower and Biddulph [2].)

decibels above threshold is reached, after which intensity changes have little further effect. Ordinarily a level of about 60 decibels is suitable, but for the very low and very high tones, for which the ear is relatively insensitive, a lower level may be advisable to avoid pain or other extra-auditory sensations. The selection of a suitable level usually requires exploratory tests on each subject. The number of ears used is determined by the interests of the experiment and the experimental arrangements. If the sounds are made by a loudspeaker in the open air, it is more convenient to allow the subject to use both ears; but more often a telephone receiver is used as the source, and but one ear is stimulated. Discrimination is a little better for two ears. As already mentioned, the relative difference limen is fairly constant in the middle of the frequency scale, but it becomes somewhat larger for the high tones, and very much larger for the low tones, as shown in Fig. 5.

A comparatively new method for the study of pitch discrimination is the warble method, which is distinctive not only in the mode of presentation but also in certain of its psychological aspects [2]. Instead of presenting two separate tones of different frequency, this method employs a sustained tone whose pitch is made to vary periodically. The subject is required merely to report whether he hears a steady or a varying pitch. The warble rate, or the rate at which the frequency is changed back and forth, becomes a significant variable, and something like 2 cycles of change per second has been indicated as the optimal rate. Also important is the manner of switching: whether abrupt or gradual. An abrupt change has the disadvantage that it converts some of the acoustic energy into various high frequencies which the subject hears as a series of clicks. A sinusoidal

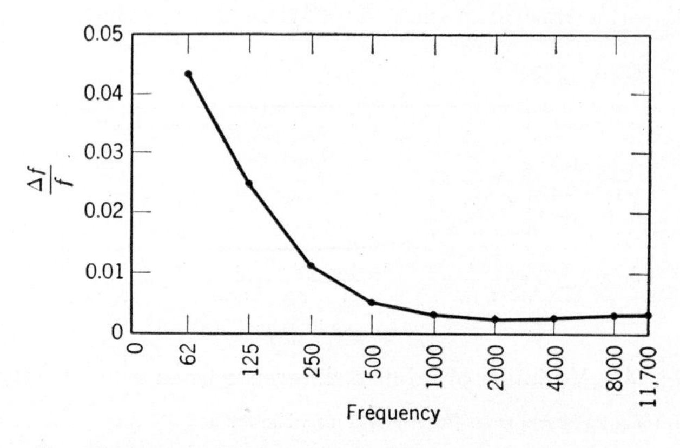

Fig. 5. Variation of relative difference limen with frequency.

All tones were given at an intensity 40 db above threshold. (After Fig. 5 from Shower and Biddulph [2].)

form of transition is theoretically the most suitable, as it gives a minimum of such transient sounds, and in practice has been found satisfactory. With low tones the abrupt changes produce smaller limens, but the subject is probably using the transient patterns to some extent rather than judging merely on the low tones themselves. It is to be expected that the warble method will give smaller limens than the standard methods, because it is easier to judge continuity, as against discontinuity, than to appreciate a difference and correctly indicate its direction. As yet, however, there has been no systematic comparison of these two types of procedure.

For both procedures the electric oscillator is the most convenient source of stimulation, and for the warble method with sinusoidal variations it is indispensable. In the warble method the frequency variation is produced by rotating a small condenser in the tuned circuit of the oscillator.

As is usual, care should be taken that the tones are pure, but it is reported that harmonics in moderate amounts do not greatly affect pitch discrimination. The lower the frequency region, the more serious they would be expected to be.

LOUDNESS

The psychological magnitude of an auditory experience is its loudness, and this dimension varies as a function of several conditions: the physical intensity of the sound, its frequency and composition, the sensitivity of the ear, whether listening is done with both ears or but one, and perhaps others. Let us first consider the physical intensity and the problems presented in its measurement and control.

The intensity of a sound is defined as the rate of flow of wave energy through a given region. It is expressed in power per unit area (ergs per second per square centimeter or watts per square centimeter). In no practical case, however, do we measure this power directly, but rather some other characteristic of the sound from which the power can be calculated. Measurements can be made of the amplitude of movement of the air particles, or the mean velocity of their vibratory motion, or the pressure that they exert when they strike a surface. A simple but very useful instrument for measuring sound pressures is the Rayleigh disk, pictured in Fig. 6. It consists of a thin disk, usually of mica, suspended by a slender thread. When exposed to a sound, the disk tends to turn its surface at right angles to the direction of flow of the sound, and from this torque the pressure can be determined.

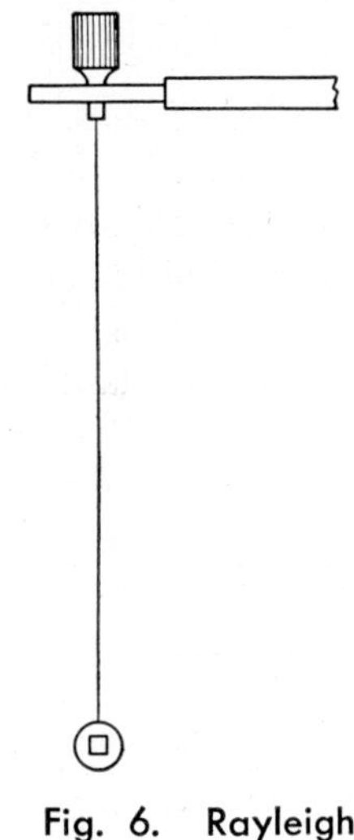

Fig. 6. Rayleigh disk.

Because the ear has an extraordinarily extensive range of sensitivity it is necessary, if we use absolute units, to deal with numbers that are rather cumbersome. Thus the minimum power that will excite the ear is given by Sivian and White [3] as 0.24×10^{-16} watt, whereas the maximum that can safely be withstood is about 0.023 watt. The variation over the intensity range is thus a thousand-million-millionfold! For convenience, therefore, we often employ a logarithmic scale, which compresses this range of numbers into a tolerably simple array. It ought to be mentioned at once that, however convenient it is to use the logarithms of numbers to compress their range, this manipulation carries one important restriction—it does away with any true zero point. The smallest logarithm that we can mention represents some quantity greater than nothing. For this reason it is not altogether proper to refer to a series of logarithmic values as representing a scale; more strictly speaking, they are ratios, and as with any ratio we must know both quantities that are being compared. In other words, a conversion of acoustic intensities into logarithmic terms requires us first to choose a reference level; all our quantities then are so-many logarithmic units above or below that level.

Although any number of logarithmic conversions are possible, the one in current use is the decibel scale. It uses the expression

$$N = 10 \log_{10} \frac{I_1}{I_0}$$

where N is the number of decibels, I_1 is the sound power in question, I_0 is the reference level, and the ordinary decimal or Briggian logarithms are used. A good many reference levels have been employed, so many that it is imperative that in every use of decibels the level be explicitly given. Telephone engineers have sometimes used a "phonic level" of 1 microwatt. Others, in making pressure measurements, have chosen a "zero level" of 1 dyne per square centimeter. Somewhat more useful for auditory work is a level that approximates the human threshold. Unfortunately, though, this threshold is different for different tones. The threshold intensity for 1000 cycles has been used, and also a rather rough average of threshold values through the middle of the range has been taken as 0.001 dyne per square centimeter. Again, many experimenters use as a reference point the threshold intensity for the particular tone in question, which of course is different for each tone and, strictly speaking, varies somewhat for every individual subject; the advantage (though a limited one) of this practice is that it avoids the necessity of any absolute measurements. Finally, in an attempt to reduce this confusion, a standardization committee of the Acoustical Society of America adopted a "reference intensity" of 10^{-16} watts per square centimeter, which is expected ultimately to supplant all the others. Table I shows these various reference levels and their relations to the ASA standard.

TABLE I

REFERENCE LEVELS FOR SOUND-INTENSITY MEASUREMENTS

Designation	Numerical Value	Decibels above ASA standard
Phonic level	10^{-6} watts	100
Zero level	1 dyne-cm^{-2}	73.8
Mean threshold level	0.001 dyne-cm^{-2}	13.8
1000-cycle threshold level	2.4×10^{-16} watts*	3.8
ASA reference intensity	10^{-16} watts	0

* Sivian and White's results for monaural listening [3].

AUDITORY ACUITY MEASUREMENTS

Measurements of auditory acuity are of two types: the precision measurements used generally in experimental investigation, and the more rough-and-ready procedures employed for clinical and other routine testing purposes. In experimental work we desire the most exact indications of the ear's characteristics and can take the pains to control the stimulus thoroughly, train the subjects well, and repeat observations systematically according to standard psychophysical procedures. In clinical and similar testing the exigencies of the situation do not allow so much attention to detail, and a less exacting program must be carried out. Despite the limitations the results of such tests are of great value, not merely for diagnostic use but also in many instances for more fundamental understanding of auditory functions.

The Experimental Methods

In the study of auditory acuity two arrangements are used. In one, which corresponds to the natural method of listening, the source of sound is at a distance, and the ears are open. In the other the source of sound, an earphone, is fitted closely to the head, and the ear therefore is closed. These two methods give results that usually are somewhat at variance, because the ear is mechanically altered by closing it. There are other variables in the measurement situation also. With the open-ear method the observer may use only one ear, the other being plugged. Whether he uses one ear or two, he can face the source or take various other angular positions with respect to it. In the closed-ear situation, if two earphones are provided, both ears may be stimulated simultaneously. For both the open- and closed-ear arrangements it is further necessary to make measurements of the sound intensity that stimulates the ear, and each arrangement presents special problems in this regard.

Once the physical problems are disposed of, the measurement of auditory acuity presents no very serious difficulties. Any of the psychophysical procedures may be followed.

Clinical Testing: Audiometry

The clinical testing methods were developed by otologists for diagnostic purposes. Until recently the procedures and techniques have been seriously limited by the instruments available for sound production. Of the cruder tests, there are the watch test and the whisper or voice test, which use means of sound production that are readily available but subject to little control. Tuning-fork tests represent a notable advance, for they use tones that are reasonably pure and, when handled expertly, give useful quantitative information. After it is struck, a tuning fork dies down rapidly and finally comes to rest, and if it is struck and then held in a standard manner, its curve of decay is fairly constant. The time that a person continues to hear it thus can be used as a measure of his acuity at that frequency.

The most modern methods of clinical testing, with which we shall be chiefly concerned, employ electrical means of generating and varying the tones. The electrical apparatus for this work, when assembled in one unit, is called an audiometer, and the technical procedures in its use constitute the special field of audiometry.

Air-conduction Tests

Audiometers are designed primarily for tests by air conduction. They consist of two main parts, an electric oscillator, which generates oscillating currents, and a resistance network or attenuator, which is used to control the power that is fed to a telephone receiver over the subject's ear. The oscillations cover a considerable frequency range, sometimes almost the whole audible scale. In some instruments there are only fixed steps of frequency, whereas in others a continuous variation is possible. The Council on Physical Therapy of the American Medical Association has specified that, if fixed frequencies are provided, they shall include at least the following seven octave tones: 128, 256, 512, 1024, 2048, 4096, and 8192 cycles per second. Some instruments provide in addition some of the semioctave or sometimes smaller intervals, and it is especially desirable that they be included in the frequency region above 1024 cycles.

The output into the receiver, when in its usual position on a subject's ear, is calibrated for each individual frequency in decibels above a "normal" threshold for that frequency. Each instrument maker has done his own calibrating and has used for the purpose a rather limited number of subjects. Consequently, the calibrations do not represent the "normal" for the population at large, and of course they vary for different makes of audiometer. A good many data are available, however, for the more popular models of audiometers to permit correction of the dial readings; but, on the other hand, the alteration and discontinuance of models make many of these results obsolete.

The receiver is usually provided with a soft rubber cushion, which not only makes it more comfortable against the ear but also gives a more soundtight contact. For ordinary testing the subject holds the receiver in his hand and adjusts it by trial to give an optimum signal. Ordinarily, intensity steps of 5 decibels are provided.

The intensity range usually varies for each frequency, partly on account of variations in the output of the receiver and partly on account of variations in sensitivity of the ear. It is desirable to provide sufficient range to reach the pain threshold at any frequency in order that persons with a grave degree of deafness may be tested, but no present instrument does so. Most fall short of this need at both ends of the frequency scale.

For a test of hearing, a soundproof room is highly desirable but must be dispensed with at times, either because it is not available, or because patients are severely ill and cannot be moved. In these events the examiner must make the best of existing circumstances, perhaps by selecting a time of day when the level of disturbing noise is low. A notation is made on the record to indicate the conditions under which the test was carried out.

In making the test, it is best to have the subject choose his better ear, if he has any preference, and to begin with a tone of medium frequency. This tone is set at an intensity that is expected to be easily audible, and the subject is required to indicate by word or signal whether he hears it. It is then reduced a step at a time until it is no longer audible. Then a setting at an even lower intensity is given, and the intensity raised by steps until the subject reports that he hears the tone. Another descending series, and then an ascending series, will ordinarily complete the test for this tone, unless inattention and inconsistency call for more trials. Here the training and judgment of the examiner weigh heavily, especially with very young and with very ill subjects.

If the subject is properly attentive, the judgments will be so consistent that there is little question of the location of the threshold; the reason is that intensity steps of 5 decibels are large in relation to the difference limen for intensity, and if one step is barely heard, the next lower will commonly be inaudible. The examiner forms a "guessed average" or judgment of the threshold and records that single figure.

This same procedure is then carried out in turn on the remaining frequencies, and the whole performance repeated for the other ear. All the data, when plotted, constitute an audiogram, as illustrated in Fig. 7. In this figure the zero line represents the "normal," according to the instrument's calibration, and distances below the line show the amounts of hearing impairment. One curve, as indicated, is for the right ear, and the other for the left.

When there is a considerable difference in the acuity of the two ears, it is necessary to use masking in the better ear to exclude it from operation. Otherwise, since there is always some leakage of sound through the air from the receiver to the other side of the head, and also some conduction through the skull itself, the sound may reach the better ear in sufficient intensity to give a false perception. This effect is strikingly shown in persons who have suffered a complete loss

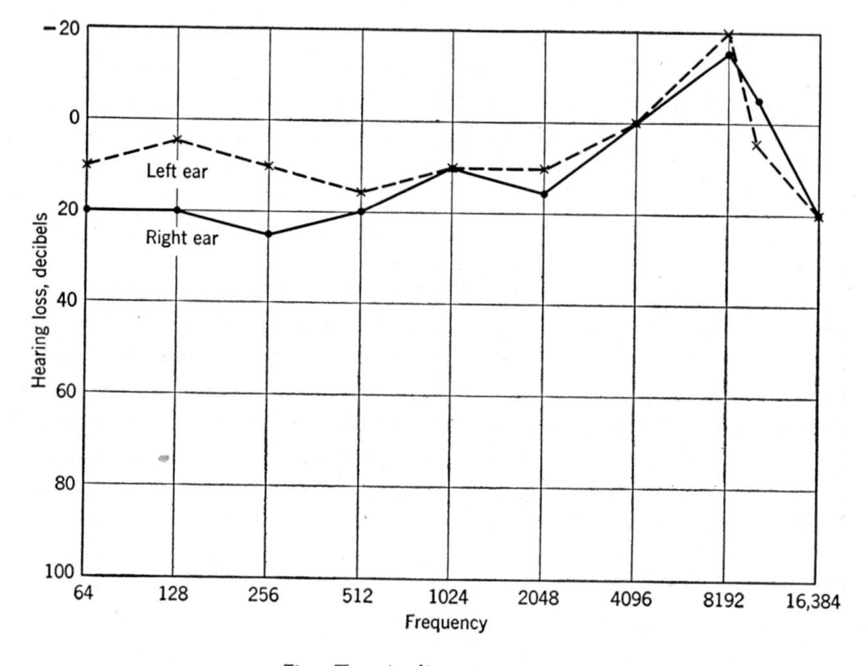

Fig. 7. Audiometer curves.

of hearing in one ear. An audiogram can be secured on the deaf ear, which actually is only a "shadow curve," representing the acuity of the good ear as reduced by the "shadow" of the head. Figure 8 shows such a curve, along with the true acuity curve of the good ear, and it will be noted that the shadow curve follows fairly closely the form of the other but lies about 60 decibels below it. This means that 60 decibels is the amount of attenuation offered by the head under the conditions. Sometimes, when the receiver does not fit well over the ear, or the rubber cushion on the receiver is omitted, the leakage is greater than this, and the curves will be closer together. The necessary amount of masking varies somewhat in every test, for it is a function of the acuity itself. It must be sufficient to prevent hearing of the cross-conducted sounds, yet must not be so great as itself to cross over to the tested ear and impair its performance. The usual course is to test both ears without masking and then to repeat the measurements on the poorer ear, with the better ear masked with a sound that is about 40 decibels above its threshold.

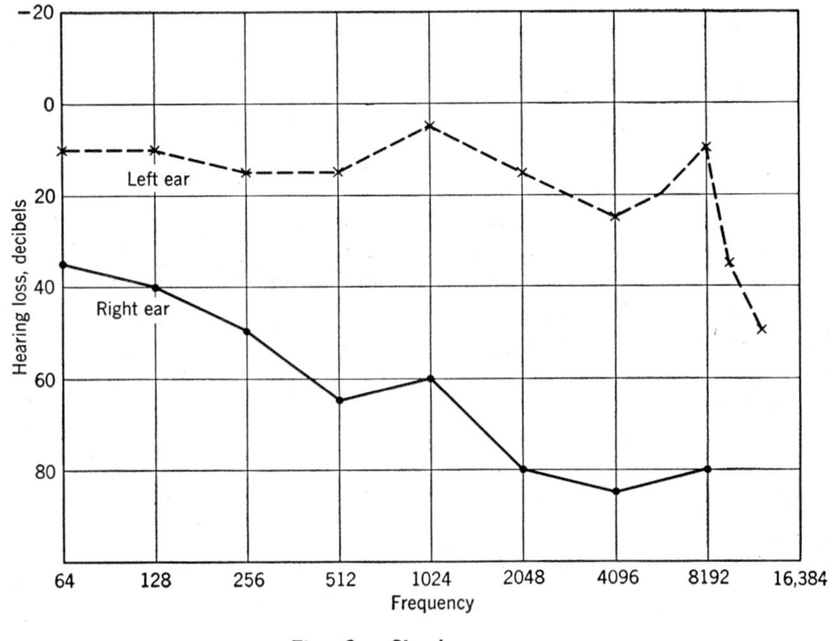

Fig. 8. Shadow curve.

The best type of sound to use for masking is a noise made up of a very broad band of frequencies. Such a noise is effective and at the same time (because it is qualitatively very different from the test tone) occasions the least disturbance to perception in the ear which is being tested.

Bone-conduction Tests

It frequently happens that a test of a person's hearing in the usual manner, by air conduction, reveals an impairment of acuity, yet a test by bone conduction shows that the cochlear endings and nervous elements are functioning normally. A bone-conduction test consists of the application of acoustic vibrations to the skull, through which they are conducted to the inner ear. By this route it is possible to stimulate the ear in spite of obstructions or interruptions in the usual path of transmission through the middle ear.

Most bone-conduction tests have been carried out with tuning forks. The stem of the vibrating fork is held firmly against the mastoid bone, just behind the ear. Most recent models of audiometers are provided with a bone-conduction receiver, which is a mechanical vibrator actuated by the oscillating currents. This receiver has an advantage over the tuning fork in affording good control of both frequency and intensity. Its calibration curve will be quite different from that of the air-conduction receiver.

Both tuning forks and mechanical vibrators suffer from certain limitations. It is difficult with both to secure the amplitude of vibration often needed without so overburdening the instrument that it seriously distorts the sound produced. Also, both radiate a good deal of energy into the air, and the examiner must be alert to the possibility of stimulation by air conduction. This air-conducted sound may not be troublesome if air-conduction acuity is low for both ears, but it is a possible source of error if only one ear is so affected.

Momentarily stopping the meatus will often give a clue as to whether error from this source is present, but the tests ought not to be carried out with the ears closed, as this closure will affect the bone-conduction acuity.

The pressure with which the instrument is applied to the mastoid should be as constant as possible; there is more danger in too light pressure than too heavy, but care must be taken not to use one that will be painful.

A special difficulty appears when bone-conduction tests are attempted with the low frequencies. The stimulus will give tactual sensations as well as sounds, and an inexperienced observer may mistake one for the other. A few trials with the vibrator placed elsewhere on the body, say over a bone on the hand, aids in the desired discrimination.

Masking is even more important in bone-conduction tests than in air-conduction tests. Vibrations applied to one mastoid bone are readily conducted across the head, and they reach the opposite ear at a level little lower than that at the ear it is desired to test. The opposite ear, therefore, must be excluded by masking. This masking is always produced by an aerial sound, and the usual precautions are necessary to prevent its leakage to the ear under test.

In bone-conduction tests it is difficult to ascertain in preliminary trials which is the better ear. Accordingly, it is advisable to make the measurements on each ear while masking the other.

The Upper Limit of Loudness

Acoustic stimuli, when raised in intensity, eventually reach a level at which their effects are not wholly auditory. They excite a variety of other sensations, which vary somewhat with the frequency. At low frequencies excessive stimulation arouses tactual and kinesthetic sensations, which are referred to the middle ear, and also labyrinthine effects, which include dizziness, nausea, vague bodily sensations, and sometimes eye and head nystagmus. Middle frequencies give rise to tactual sensations, which are more of a pressury quality, and also sensations of pain. High tones have similar effects, with perhaps more emphasis on pain.

In the past, attempts have been made to determine one curve as an upper limit of loudness in order to guide the design of hearing aids for the deafened. The foregoing description shows that there is no one curve which forms this boundary, but a family of functions, one for every sensory quality. The determination of these functions remains to be made. The subject will need to be trained to recognize each sensory quality even when it appears in a complex of others. Then a determination, according to the usual psychophysical procedures, can be made for this quality at each frequency at which it appears.

Loudness Discrimination

Methods for the study of loudness discrimination parallel those used in the discrimination of pitch. There are two types. The more usual is one in which two discrete, steady tones are presented, one at greater intensity than the other, and the subject makes a relative judgment. Here, as with pitch, the variables of frequency region, intensity level, duration of the stimuli, and especially the time interval between stimuli must receive attention. The second method is the warble method, in which the intensity is varied at a determined rate, and the subject is asked to report whether he perceives a steady or a wavering sound. The rate of warbling is of course a factor, and, according to Riesz [1], the optimum discrimination appears with a rate around 3 per second. As would be expected, this procedure gives smaller limens than the other, in which the subject must report the direction as well as the presence of a change.

Equal-loudness Curves

The task of comparing the loudness of tones which differ in frequency might be compared, in character and difficulty, to the problem of heterochromatic photometry. The equating as to loudness of sensations of different pitch is one of the most trying exercises that can be given a subject. Certainly intensive practice in this type of judgment is essential, and even then the task will never be carried out with much comfort or confidence. Therefore, to aid the subject and stabilize his judgments it is desirable to modify the usual psychophysical procedures somewhat, and to use a considerably broader range of stimuli than would ordinarily be considered necessary. The relatively easy judgments that will appear from time to time will fortify the subject's confidence and tend to prevent alterations in his criteria of judgment.

In the past, particular interest has centered on the equation of the loudness of various tones with a standard tone of 1000 cycles. The loudness of the 1000-cycle tone is used as a scale by which the loudness of any tone can be designated. The *loudness level* of a tone is then referred to as the equivalent loudness of the 1000-cycle tone; specifically it is the number of decibels above the reference intensity that a 1000-cycle tone must be raised in order to be judged equal to the tone in question. The reference intensity is 10^{-16} watts per square centimeter, or sometimes the 1000-cycle threshold.

INTERACTION PHENOMENA

A number of phenomena result when two or more simple tones act upon the ear simultaneously. Some of these are beats, combination tones, and masking.

Beats

In the observation of beats two oscillators are used, tuned to somewhere near the same frequency. Both may be operated into the same telephone receiver, but it is better to use two receivers in order to avoid any electrical interaction between the oscillators. Both the tones are conducted to one or to both of the subject's ears (not to separate ears, as this arrangement will not produce beats). The intensity of the stimuli will have to be adjusted to somewhat the same level for greatest perceptibility of the beating.

The quality of the experience varies with the beat frequency. It also varies with the frequency region from which these stimuli are taken, and to a lesser extent with the loudness relation. At low rates of beating there is perceived a slow waxing and waning of loudness, at higher rates a pulsing or pounding in which the sound seems to come in sudden thrusts, and at still more rapid rates only a sort of rough whirring in which the individual cycles of variation can no longer be distinguished.

The upper limit of perception of beats naturally depends upon the qualitative criterion selected: if it is the pulsating or intermittent quality described as the intermediate stage, the limit will be lower than if the whirring or roughness characteristic is chosen. In determining the limit, according to any criterion, the general intensity and also the intensity ratio are adjusted so as to provide the most favorable conditions for observation. A fairly high level of intensity is desirable, and a ratio that keeps the loudness of the two components somewhat near equal. The frequency region is an important variable; the higher this region, the higher is the limit of perceptible beats.

At high levels of stimulation two or more beat rates may be present at the same time, and the subject will need to differentiate them. He does so both by the perceived rates and by loudness cues: the more rapid beats are fainter.

It is generally claimed that in the slower beats there is a periodic variation of pitch as well as of loudness, and the observer must be prompted to report this qualitative change along with the others.

Combination Tones

Much the same stimulating conditions as described for beats will give combination tones, when the difference in frequency of the two tones is sufficiently large—perhaps 30 cycles or more. These tones appear in addition to the two primary tones, as products of their interaction in the inner ear. There are a great many of these interaction products, with frequencies indicated by the following expression:

$$\overline{mh \pm nl}$$

where h is the frequency of the higher stimulus tone, l is the frequency of the lower stimulus tone, and m and n are simple whole numbers; the bar above the expression indicates that the absolute value of the quantity is to be used. We distinguish two classes of combination tones, called *difference tones* or *summation tones;* the difference tones are those that arise when we use only the minus sign in the formula, and the summation tones when we use the plus sign. The multipliers m and n take all integral values from 1 on; but as they grow greater, the magnitude of the resulting combination tone falls off rapidly, so that practically only the lower values or *orders* of combination tones need be considered. The *order* [6] of a combination tone is determined by the size of both m and n; it is defined numerically as $m + n - 1$. For example, if $m = 2$ and $n = 3$, the combination tone is either $2h + 3l$ or $2h - 3l$, and since $m + n - 1 = 4$, we have a summation or difference tone of the fourth order.

Three methods have been found useful for the study of combination tones. The first is *simple listening*, in which the subject seeks to perceive and identify some one of the interaction products. This is a difficult matter, comparable to an identification of the several notes comprising a musical chord, and requires special talent and training. The task is aided by a judicious selection of the frequency region for the primaries, in order to throw the combination tone into a part of the auditory range in which the subject's sensitivity is high, and also to get its frequency as far away from the primary frequencies as possible. It is aided also by variation in the intensities of the primaries, the manner of which can be determined only by trial, as it depends in part upon the particular sensitivity function of the subject's ear. For rough guidance it may be said that each primary must be raised in intensity as m or n increases in the expression for the combination tone sought for. Further, it is practically essential that the subject be presented from time to time with a tone corresponding to the frequency of the combination tone he is to listen for.

The second is the *exploring tone method.* It employs a third tone, in addition to the primaries, which is adjusted to a frequency a little different from that of the expected combination tone and therefore gives beats with that tone. It is varied in intensity to make the beats as marked as possible, which, it is assumed, happens for equal loudness of the combination tone and exploring tone. The intensity of the exploring tone then can be used as an indication of the effective magnitude of the combination tone.

A third method employs the electrical response of the cochlea and so far has been practicable only in animals below man. When the stimulus is two pure tones, a vast array of combination tones is found in the potential waves generated in the cochlea. The study is made with a wave analyzer, an instrument by which a component of any desired frequency can be measured in isolation. At high levels of stimulation the greater part of the stimulus energy is transformed into overtone and combination tone frequencies, and scores of components, including some as high as the twentieth order, have been observed. Only by this method has anything approaching the full pattern of combination tones been revealed, and their functional relations to the stimuli worked out.

Masking

When two tones similar in frequency but considerably different in intensity are applied simultaneously to the same ear, only the stronger will be heard; the weaker is said to be *masked.* The study of masking in its simplest form is essentially the determination of thresholds for a given tone in the presence of another that in successive determinations is varied systematically in frequency and intensity. We can study masking also for complexes of tones and for noises.

THE LOCALIZATION OF SOUND

When we perceive a sound under natural conditions, we nearly always localize it in space. This aspect of perception logically may be considered as involving two features, direction and distance. Experimental methods have been developed for the determination of the accuracy of our judgments of these features and also of the cues employed.

Investigation soon shows that most of our cues are secondary, involving the perception of likely sources of the sounds we hear and inferences made from the character of the sounds. When we exclude these secondary or inferential cues and rely upon hearing alone, we find our perceptions considerably reduced. They are even more reduced when the head and the perceived object are kept stationary. We then have left only the ability to judge direction along the right-left dimension, based upon differences in the stimulation of the two ears [8]. Let us consider first this static function.

Two general procedures have been employed for the study of localization as a function of binaural differences. One, the more natural method, consists in listening, with both ears, to some source of sound that is a little distance from the observer and can be moved to various positions. The observer is prevented from using visual or other nonauditory cues and must depend on the binaural stimulation alone to judge the location of the sound.

An instrument called the sound cage is often used in this procedure. The observer, blindfolded, is seated in the center of a metal framework that represents several circles or parts of circles on the surface of an imaginary sphere, and a sound source, usually a telephone receiver, is moved to various positions along these circles. After a sound is produced at any desired point, the observer must indicate the angle from which it seems to come. He may make his judgment known by pointing or by verbal reference to some schema.

This natural method suffers from certain disadvantages. Control of the stimulus is a difficult matter. A sound produced in the manner indicated, in an experimental room, will reach the observer's ear not only by the direct path, but also circuitously after reflection from the walls or near-by objects. These reflected sounds have various, and usually unpredictable, angular positions. The pattern of stimulation is extremely complex, and even if its character were known it would present too difficult a problem for the observer to deal with. Reflections can be reduced by treating all surfaces with sound-absorbing materials, but ordinarily it is not practicable to carry this treatment far enough to eliminate them altogether. What is needed is to suspend the observer in free space and to make the stimulating equipment so unobtrusive as not to disturb the sound field. An approach to this condition is obtained by working on a high, flat roof, preferably with the observer elevated on a pedestal of some kind, and locating the sound source on a slender arm that can be given various positions.

A more serious disadvantage of the natural method is that it presents various binaural cues all at once and does not reveal which ones are operating at any given time or how they may be interacting. With pure tones as stimuli, three kinds of cue are possible: differences of intensity, time of incidence, and phase at the two ears. With complex tones there are also differences of timbre; they arise because the head casts more of a sound shadow for high frequencies, and hence the ear away from the sound will hear it with the high components relatively unfeebled. The method can tell us what our capacity for localization is under usual circumstances but will not provide an analysis or explanation of the process.

In the second method the physical conditions are under better control, and the binaural cues can be studied one at a time. The two ears are stimulated separately by means of telephone receivers or tubes through which the waves are conducted. The experimenter can determine as accurately as he will the character of the binaural pattern. It has been customary to vary one kind of cue at a time and to keep the others constant (or try to), but there is no great difficulty in presenting any sort of combination of cues by this method.

In the early development of this method, sound-conducting tubes were used for separate stimulation of the ears, and by various manipulations a change was made in the stimuli reaching the ears. Partially obstructing one tube, for example, by pinching it, will reduce the intensity on that side. Changing the length of one tube is usually designed to alter the phase relation, but unfortunately this manipulation does other things too. By altering the resonance characteristics of the tube it changes the intensity; and of course, if time is considered apart from phase, it alters the time relation also.

The use of telephone receivers on the ears is much to be preferred. The electrical circuit which actuates the receivers can be adjusted so as to give any desired change of intensity, time, or phase, independently of one another. Intensity is controlled with attenuators, one in a branch of the circuit leading to one ear, another in a second branch to the other ear. Time can be controlled with mechanically operated switches. Phase control involves a special circuit in which resistance, capacitance, and inductance are altered. An electrical method can also be devised for control of the character of a complex sound: a filter network of the low-pass type may be inserted in the circuit to one receiver to reproduce the differential screening action of the head.

One further measure is advisable in the use of this method. Since two telephone receivers may not have identical electrical and mechanical characteristics, it is desirable to pick up the sounds as they actually appear at the two ears and record them on an oscillograph. By this means we may check our manipulations and be certain that the desired differences are present.

Whichever of the foregoing procedures is used, the observer's task is simply defined. Although his ears are stimulated differently, he ordinarily hears but one sound. Subjects often report what is called a "sound image" or "phantom," which may be purely auditory but more often has a visual character also, and they perceive this image at a more or less definite point in space.

In indicating the angular position with respect to the observer, for both the true location of the sound source and the observer's judgment of it, we employ such terms as azimuth, altitude, or angle of elevation. Azimuth refers to position in the horizontal plane. Altitude and angle of elevation refer to position with respect to the vertical axis; they are defined as the vertical angle between any position and the horizon.

When either the object or the head is permitted to move, we add a dynamic factor to localization. We are able to integrate cues over a period of time and thereby increase their significance and reliability. We are able also, by tipping the ears out of their usual horizontal plane, to enlarge the scope of operation of the binaural differences [4].

When the sound is of constant character and familiar to the subject, we can demonstrate certain limited capacities for the judgment of distance. As we know from common experience, sounds grow faint as they become farther away. Under natural conditions, however, this function is interfered with by reflections, which upset the relation of intensity and distance. To study the phenomena exactly requires free-space conditions or as near an approximation to these as possible. If a complex sound is used as the stimulus, attention should be given to the possibility of timbre cues in this situation, for even in free space the different frequencies are not transmitted quite equally, and the presence of obstructing objects may cause significant modifications of the wave composition.

EPILOGUE

The foregoing pages have introduced the techniques and procedures for dealing with the more fundamental problems in the field of hearing. It has been shown that with the refinements of apparatus that recent electronic developments have provided we can produce and handle all kinds of acoustic stimuli and do so with a precision heretofore unknown.

In our enthusiasm over our material equipment, however, we must not lose sight of our other problems—of the more strictly psychological matters of the control of the subject's attitude, his criteria of judgment, and the psychophysical procedures required for systematic measurements. In this area too, by a slow growth over the years, we have at our disposal a wealth of technical knowledge. Finally, through recent physical developments, we have the electrophysiological methods, which have opened up new fields of investigation and already illuminated many problems formerly obscure. We can look to the future for a continuing expansion of our understanding of hearing in all its aspects.

REFERENCES

1. Riesz, R. R. Differential intensity sensitivity of the ear for pure tones. *Phys. Rev.*, 1928, *31*, 867–875.
2. Shower, E. G., and R. Biddulph. Differential pitch sensitivity of the ear. *J. Acoust. Soc. Amer.*, 1931, *3*, 275–287.
3. Sivian, L. J., and S. D. White. On minimum audible sound fields. *J. Acoust. Soc. Amer.*, 1933, *4*, 288–324.
4. Wallach, H. The role of head movements and vestibular and visual cues in sound localization. *J. Exper. Psychol.*, 1940, *27*, 339–368.
5. Wever, E. G. The electrical responses of the ear. *Psychol. Bull.*, 1939, *36*, 143–187.

relatively insensitive regions in between. It has often been assumed that each of these spots corresponds to a single receptor. However, direct microscopic study fails to confirm this simple theory, and indirect evidence suggests that the situation must be much more complex.

As to the actual nature of receptor stimulation, it is evident that mere description of external physical stimuli is insufficient. The critical questions are: What happens in the skin itself when it is stimulated? How is the skin distorted to produce an experience of touch or vibration? What are the significant temperature changes in the tissues which accompany sensations of warmth and cold? We are concerned with such questions as these when we deal with the problem of the actual nature of stimulation.

There are, of course, many additional phases of skin sensitivity which invite study. Some are peculiarly cutaneous problems, e.g., the accuracy with which a stimulated point can be localized, the minimum distance at which two points can be sensed as separate, and the limits in discriminating the size of objects pressed against the skin. Some of these problems involve routine measurements similar to those made for the other senses, such as reaction times, adaptation times, stimulus limens, and difference limens. Still others deal with the perception of form, pattern, and movement by the skin senses, including illusions which are strikingly like those in vision.

In this chapter, methods related to the three basic problems are covered first, and then other problems and methods are briefly discussed. Finally, the various ways in which the skin can be stimulated are summarized.

METHODS OF SEPARATING THE SKIN SENSES

The problem here is essentially to determine the number of skin senses by experimentally *dissociating* them. This can be accomplished in a number of ways: by anesthesia, by cutting or blocking a nerve, by mapping after removing successive slices of skin, and by establishing differential chronaxies.

Disappearance and Recovery under Anesthesia

Under local anesthesia, warm, cold, touch, and pain do not disappear and reappear all at the same time, but straggle out and straggle in again. To anesthetize a section of skin, the most widely used method is electroendosmosis [9]. A pad saturated with novocain or some similar anesthetic is placed on the skin. On top of the pad is fastened the active metal electrode. A large metal plate or a vessel of salt solution is applied to some other part of the body as an inactive electrode. Direct current of low amperage is employed to drive the anesthetic into the skin. Sensitivity to warm, cold, touch, and pain stimulation is tested at intervals during the process of anesthetizing and again during the recovery period.

Although investigators do not wholly agree on the exact order of disappearance and reappearance, some dissociation has been found in every case. In general, warm and cold go out first and come back last.

Regeneration after Nerve Section or Nerve Block

Complete loss of sensitivity followed by long-delayed recovery may be produced by cutting or crushing a nerve or by injecting it with alcohol. Alcohol injection [31] has the double advantage of requiring no surgery and leaving no permanent injury. Figure 1 shows a sample

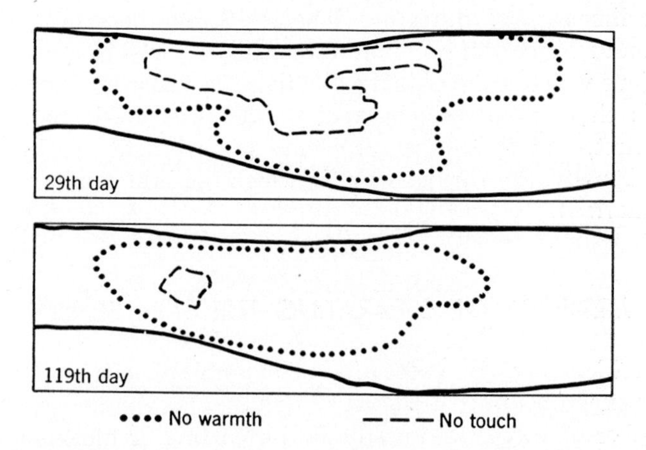

Fig. 1. Dissociation of warmth and touch during recovery from nerve block by alcohol injection. (Adapted from Lanier [31].)

of the dissociation of touch and warmth during recovery after alcohol injection. Effects of shorter duration may be obtained by injecting novocain around a nerve, by blocking a nerve with pressure, or by cutting off the blood supply with an inflated rubber cuff. When novocain is injected around a nerve [6], recovery occurs over a matter of hours. All these methods bring about some measure of dissociation, although the exact order of reappearance varies with the method employed.

Removing Successive Slices of Skin

An interesting if somewhat heroic method was developed by Woollard [51]. He first mapped an area on the thigh, exploring the region systematically with small stimulators to locate the points of maximum sensitivity to cold, touch, and pain. These cold spots, touch spots, and pain spots he marked on a map of the area. He then removed five successive thin slices of skin. After the removal of each slice and after healing had occurred, he retested the area and made comparisons with the original map. Again, some dissociation was evident.

Measurement of Chronaxies

Chronaxy is the minimum time for a current of double the threshold strength to produce a clear sensation of warm, cold, touch, or pain. It is measured with a device which delivers a very brief but accurately timed pulse of electrical stimulation, for example, by the discharge of a condenser. Different chronaxies are found for warm, cold, touch, and pain [28, 29], thus supporting the idea of four separate skin senses.

The general preponderance of evidence seems to favor the existence of four cutaneous senses: warm, cold, pain, and touch, and there appears to be no reason for adding to the number, as proposed by Head [41] or by Katz [30]. On the other hand, the reduction suggested by Nafe [35] leaves too many facts unexplained.

METHODS FOR STUDYING RECEPTORS AND RECEPTOR PROCESSES

Numerous attempts have been made to obtain evidence of the identity of the skin receptors by examining portions of skin under the microscope. In addition, there have been efforts to answer the more limited question of the relative depths of the receptors below the skin surface. There are also a number of studies which are of interest because their results have some bearing on the nature of the receptor processes.

Microscopic Examination

In the direct approach to this problem, portions of the skin are carefully mapped, and the points of maximum sensitivity marked. Then the pieces of flesh are removed surgically, sliced into thin sections, stained, and examined under a microscope [19]. Results that accrue from this technique have been rather consistently negative; i.e., no receptors are seen under the microscope which correspond consistently to warm spots, cold spots, etc. The negative results may be due to inadequate staining methods or simply to the fact that there are no gross receptors which can be identified in this way.

In the indirect approach the warm, cold, touch, and pain spots are separately counted. Then the same area of skin is sectioned, stained, and examined microscopically to determine the number of each type of ending. The counts of spots and endings are compared [4]. For example, if there are fifteen cold spots and the microscope shows fifteen Krause endings, it is assumed that Krause endings are the receptors for cold. Such a correlation of numbers, however, may be quite accidental, even for the special region investigated. Furthermore, in the skin on most parts of the body no Krause endings can be found [17]. Thus the evidence from indirect studies remains inconclusive.

Estimating Receptor Depth

An interesting attempt at a direct approach to the problem of receptor depth is the method of punctiform narcosis [12]. In this scheme warm and cold spots are first mapped and marked. The skin at each spot is then punctured to a measured depth, and a drop of novocain solution placed on the puncture. Warm spots, it is found, must be punctured to a greater depth than cold spots for the novocain to produce loss of sensitivity, suggesting that warm receptors lie deeper below the surface of the skin. Several methods of indirect estimation of depth have been employed, but these are invalid because they depend upon speculative assumptions concerning the nature of the receptors, the process of stimulation, or the rate of heat conduction through the skin—no one of which is adequately established.

Nature of the Receptor Processes

No direct approach has been made to the study of cutaneous receptor processes in human beings. The effects of chemicals upon adaptation in the skin of the frog [23] or of nerve currents from stimulation of the cornea of the cat [45] are suggestive only by analogy. There are, however, a number of methods which are significant because they bear indirectly upon the problem.

The *critical flicker frequency*, or the minimum time interval at which successive stimulations can be sensed as separate, is important in indicating the speed of receptor action. For warmth and cold, this can be determined by using radiant heat or dry ice and a rotating shutter to interrupt the stimulation [15]. Accurate measurement requires the use of not more than two successive stimulations at a time, because repeated exposure changes the skin temperature and thus its differential sensitivity. Warm and cold stimuli separated by approximately 0.2 second can be sensed as separate, indicating a quite rapid recovery in the receptor process. In the case of touch, an extremely rapid receptor process is indicated. At low rates of stimulation the successive touches are sensed as separate. As the rate is increased, the separate touches blend into a smooth vibration, which can be sensed clearly up to several thousand vibrations per second.

Adaptation to warm and cold has been studied with an apparatus in which the stimulator is surrounded by a neutral-temperature field to minimize the effect of spread to surrounding areas [24]. Under these conditions, complete adaptation to warm or cold takes place in a few seconds when a 1-millimeter stimulator is used. With larger sizes, the time for complete adaptation is found to be greater for a narrow rectangular stimulator than for a circular stimulator of the same area, and still greater when the same area is presented in the form of a ring.

Also significant are the effects of *stimulator size and temperature.* Interesting relationships are discovered when the same skin area is mapped repeatedly with different stimulator sizes [26] or with the same size at different temperatures [27]. For such studies a checkerboard pattern of 2- or 3-millimeter squares is stamped on the skin. The squares are stimulated in random order alternately with different sizes or different temperatures. The subject reports 0, 1, 2, or 3 to indicate the experienced intensity from each stimulation. After the mapping has been repeated six or more times, reports from the most consistent subjects are used to determine the relations.

Some unexpected results are encountered. To take a single example, assume that the checkerboard is mapped with temperatures of 38, 41, 44, and 47 degrees. Intensity of warmth experienced from the higher temperatures does not rise uniformly all over the map. Some squares yield consistent reports of 1 at 38 degrees and continue to give 1 at 41, 44, and 47 degrees. Other squares give 0 at 38 degrees, 0 at 41 degrees, and then suddenly become 2 or 3 at 44 degrees. Many other varieties of response are found, indicating that receptor action is not a simple matter of uniformly graded response. Similarly curious relations are found when the same skin area is mapped with different sizes. For example, a larger stimulator covering two squares of differing sensitivity typically yields a report consistently *lower* than the maximum of the two individual squares.

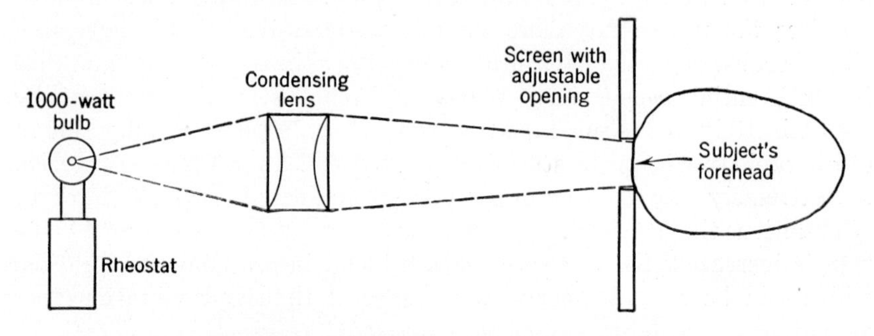

Fig. 2. Radiant heat stimulator. (Adapted from Hardy [37].)

Radiant stimulation produces different results from those obtained with metal stimulators brought in contact with the skin. As the radiated area is enlarged or the radiant intensity increased, the experienced warmth rises quite regularly [22]. In contrast are the irregular changes just described with contact stimulation. Why radiant stimulation and contact stimulation have such different effects has not yet been satisfactorily explained.

An excellent method of using radiant stimulation has been developed by Hardy and his coworkers [21]. Heat from a 1000-watt lamp is condensed by a lens and focused on an aperture of the desired size, as shown in Fig. 2. The length of exposure is controlled by a shutter. The exact strength of radiant stimulation is measured by substituting a radiometer for the subject's skin after each set of stimulations. The same apparatus can be employed to study pain from radiant heat by using much higher intensities.

Warm and cold can be aroused by various forms of *inadequate stimulation,* as well as by the usual increase and decrease of temperature. Perhaps the simplest demonstration is the chemical effect of menthol, which gives a sensation of coolness, and of chloroform (applied under a watch-glass to prevent evaporation), which produces mild warmth. Warm and cold can sometimes be obtained by electrical stimulation, as in chronaxy determinations, or by mechanical stimulation of spots of high sensitivity with a blunted wooden matchstick. Some cold spots will respond with a cold sensation when touched with a small stimulator at 45 degrees centigrade—paradoxical cold. Similarly, some warm spots will respond with a warm sensation to 20 degrees centigrade—paradoxical warmth. Considerable patience is required to find such responsive spots on most subjects.

Changing the skin temperature affects sensitivity to touch, vibration, and pain. The temperature in a limited area may be raised by exposing it to a radiant heater or lowered by holding a block of dry ice near the surface. Sensitivity to touch, vibration, and pain can then be tested while the skin surface is at various temperatures. Lowering the skin temperature merely reduces sensitivity. Raising the skin temperature at first makes the skin more sensitive to touch, vibration, and painful stimulation, but with still further increase the sensitivity rapidly falls off [49].

Although these various phenomena do not give a clear and consistent picture of the nature of the skin receptor processes, they do warn against the ready acceptance of any oversimplified theory of their operation.

METHODS OF STUDYING THE ACTUAL NATURE OF STIMULATION

Attempts have been made to measure what actually happens in the skin when mechanical and thermal stimuli are applied, and some illuminating if only partial answers have been obtained.

Mechanical Distortion

To produce an experience of touch, the critical factor is the bending or distortion of the skin and not pressure as such. In small areas, careful pulling on a stimulator glued to the skin produces sensations which are indistinguishable from those obtained by pressing down gently on the same stimulator [8].

No way has been found to estimate the total amount of skin distortion in any meaningful fashion, but the depth of its depression can be measured. Perhaps the most precise determinations were made by von Bagh [47], who used two different types of apparatus. In one, weights were applied to a balanced arm bearing a stimulator which rested on the skin, as shown in Fig. 3. In the other, the stimulator was forced into the skin to a measured depth. With both methods, measurements were made of the minimum depression necessary to arouse a sensation of touch, and the minimum difference in depression which could be detected. Effects of different stimulator areas were also compared. Apparently no similar measurements have been made of stimulation by pulling up instead of pressing down on the skin. The *rate* at which the stimulus is applied is found to be an important factor [20], since the experienced intensity is greater with a faster rate.

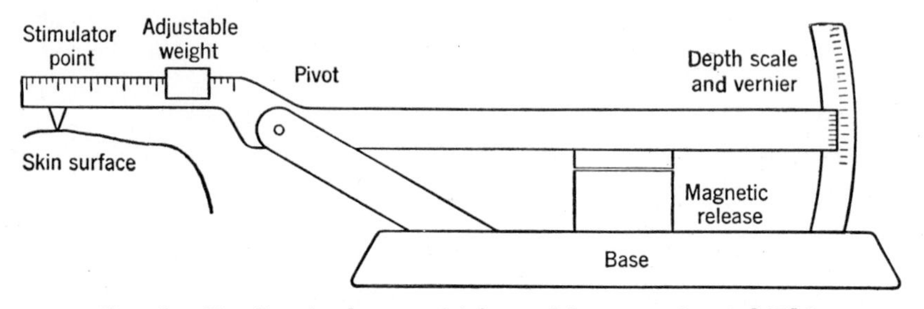

Fig. 3. Tactile stimulator. (Adapted from von Bagh [47].)

Skin Vibration and Spread

In vibratory stimulation, measurement is more difficult because the skin is in constant motion. A neat solution involves the use of a neon light interrupted at the same frequency as the vibrating stimulator. Proper adjustment of the light frequency causes the skin to appear to stand still or to move very slowly up and down. The extent of the swing can then be measured on a microscope scale by focusing first at the upper and then at the lower limit of the movement [16]. The amount of spread of vibration to surrounding areas can be determined by using a lightweight phonograph pick-up suspended so as just to make contact with the skin, and then amplifying the result so that it can be measured in a cathode-ray oscilloscope. Vibration applied to the skin at a single point is typically found to spread over a considerable area.

Thermal Changes

Accurate measurements of the heat absorbed by the skin from radiant stimulation can be made by substituting a Hardy radiometer for the subject's skin and repeating the stimulation [37]. Estimates of the actual skin temperature at the instant of stimulation have been attempted by making radiometric measurements 15, 30, and 60 seconds after radiant stimulation [38], but extending this curve of cooling backward to the time of stimulation gives results that are too unreliable to have much meaning. The technique might work better if measurements could be begun immediately after stimulation.

Measurement of temperature changes below the surface of the skin has been attempted with fine wires drawn through the skin to form thermocouple loops [3]. When an ordinary metal stimulator is brought against the skin above the thermocouple junction, the temperature at even a slight depth never fully reaches that of the stimulator. This discrepancy is probably due to the stabilizing action of blood circulation. However, the relatively slow-moving string galvanometer used in this method probably does not reveal the true rate at which the temperature changes occur.

OTHER PROBLEMS AND METHODS

What is actually the greatest bulk of experimental investigations of the skin senses may be grouped under this more miscellaneous heading. Though numerous, these experiments have relatively little to contribute in the way of interesting methods. Problems of localization, two-point threshold, and tactile extent and linearity are peculiar to the skin senses but involve rather simple techniques. Measurements of stimulus thresholds, differential thresholds, reaction times, and adaptation times mainly parallel those in other sensory fields. Perception of the form and motion of objects pressed against the skin follows much the same rules as in visual perception.

Measurements Peculiar to the Skin Senses

Localization, two-point threshold, and other problems of spatial discrimination have been studied mainly in relation to touch, although similar questions arise in connection with warm, cold, and pain, where the use of "pure" stimuli uncomplicated by touch is an essential difficulty to be overcome.

If the skin is touched while the subject has his eyes closed, how accurately can he locate the stimulated point? Results vary according to the method of designating the locus, whether by exploring the skin with another stimulator, by pointing to the spot, or by describing its location in relation to coordinates stamped on the skin [34]. Among the factors which have been studied are the influence of age and of training, the effect of moving the stimulated part, comparison of blind and sighted subjects, and the ability to localize two simultaneous stimulations [42]. Localization of painful and thermal stimuli has been less extensively studied.

If the skin is stimulated at two points simultaneously, how far apart must the points be in order to be clearly sensed as separate? This is not a simple matter to determine. Introspectively the change from one to two points is not clean cut but involves a series of transition figures, such as ovals and dumbbells [7]. Consequently, the subject's self-instruction is important. If he reports "two points" as soon as the stimulation is no longer clearly sensed as a single point, the obtained limen is much smaller than if he waits until he clearly perceives two separate points. Partial control of suggestion in this instance might be achieved by actually using oval- and dumbbell-shaped stimulators, as well as two separate points. Among the variables studied in the tactile two-point limen are the relative accuracy across the midline of the body, as compared with two stimulations on the same side, the influence of the strength of the stimuli, and the effect of moving the stimuli. Measurement of the successive two-point limen, in which the subject judges whether two successive stimulations are at the same or different places, seems to be simply a special phase of the problem of localization.

How well can a subject discriminate the difference in length of two cardboard edges pressed against the skin [13]? If three points in a line are pressed against the skin, how far must one be displaced to become noticeably out of line? In such experiments it should be noted that pure tactile sensitivity is involved only when the stimulators are pressed against the skin. When the fingers are run along a stimulator, kinesthetic as well as tactile sensitivity comes into play.

Routine Psychophysical Measurements

Determinations of cutaneous stimulus limens, difference limens, reaction times, and adaptation times are basically similar to the analogous measurements in other sensory fields.

The *stimulus limens* for pain, warm, cold, and touch have been measured on various parts of the body, with different sizes of stimulators and under different conditions of adaptation. The more important types of apparatus, such as the Hardy radiant stimulator for warm, cold, and pain, and the von Bagh apparatus for tactile determinations, have already been described. Of special interest in connection with pain is the influence of various drugs, such as aspirin, upon the pain threshold. With vibratory stimulation, thresholds are found to vary at different frequencies, much as is found in hearing. A number of studies have dealt with "threshold lability" [46], i.e., the tendency for threshold values to rise rapidly under the influence of intermittent stimulation, a condition found most strikingly in certain nervous disorders.

Difference limens, or the smallest detectable difference in pain, warm, cold, and touch, can be measured by applying successive stimulations of different intensity or by changing the intensity of an applied stimulus. The *rate* of stimulus change is an important factor which has frequently been neglected. For example, the difference limen for detecting a change of pressure on the skin is much smaller if the change is made suddenly than if it is introduced gradually.

Reaction times to cutaneous stimulation are measured by the usual chronoscope and reaction-key methods. Reactions to touch involve no complications, but contact stimulation of pain, warm, and cold are complicated by the presence of simultaneous touch, which has a shorter reaction time. Instructing the subject to neglect the touch is scarcely a satisfactory solution. Efforts must be made to eliminate the touch element completely. In radiant stimulation this difficulty does not appear [14].

The measurement of *adaptation time,* or the time for a cutaneous sensation to disappear under continued stimulation, is greatly affected by the standard used by the subject in deciding that a sensation is completely gone. A subject can be trained to give consistent results, but there is no way of telling whether his standard of complete disappearance is the same as that of another subject. Consequently, comparisons from subject to subject are apt to be meaningless. With thermal stimulation the spread of the stimulus can be minimized by surrounding the stimulated area with a metal ring maintained at skin neutral by circulating water. With mechanical stimulation the skin must be fixed in position to prevent movements which would accidentally arouse adjacent regions.

An interesting effect in connection with adaptation is the tendency for a sensation to wax and wane, sometimes disappearing completely and then spontaneously reappearing [43]. Another topic which has not been thoroughly investigated is long-term adaptation in the sense of "getting used" to painful or thermal stimulation as the result of repeated exposure.

Cutaneous Perception

There is a striking similarity between visual perception and cutaneous perception of forms, movement, and apparent movement. Tactile perception of forms and illusions of form have been studied by pressing wooden squares, triangles, etc., against the skin [40]. Tactile perception of actual movement has been studied by moving an air jet across the skin [11]. Tactile apparent movement can be obtained by touching a series of points in rapid succession, giving the illusion of an object being drawn across the skin surface [36]. Thermal perception of form and pattern is rather poor. It has been investigated with warm and cold metal stimulators of various shapes and also by radiant stimulation without contact [44].

Analyses have been made of the experiences of tickle, itch, and burn, but mainly at the level of introspective description. Also attempts have been made to synthesize the experiences of roughness and smoothness [1], moisture [32], and heat [25] by combining various cutaneous stimuli. For example, an illusion of "wetness" can usually be produced by a stimulator that is both cold and slippery, although entirely dry. Some subjects report "heat" when stimulated with a grid of alternate warm and cold tubes, although the effect is difficult to obtain in most naïve individuals. An interesting finding is the dependence of the *Anziehungseffekt* (tendency of a weak touch to seem displaced toward a stronger touch) upon the *perceived* separation of the two points, rather than upon their actual physical separation [33]. This suggests that conditions as perceived might be more important than conditions as they are in our other psychophysical measurements.

SUMMARY OF METHODS OF CUTANEOUS STIMULATION

Although a variety of methods of stimulating the skin have been mentioned in connection with specific problems, it seems well to summarize the chief methods, with some comments on their limitations.

For Touch

The traditional stimulators for mapping touch spots are hairs of differing stiffness, which bend at known pressures. An esthesiometer or a stiff wire operating against a spring acts in a similar fashion. These hand-operated stimulators give control of the maximum pressure applied, but not of the rate of application. For any precise measurements, some sort of mechanically or electrically controlled stimulator is desirable, so that the *rate* of application can be controlled and the depth of the skin distortion measured. The von Bagh apparatus

(Fig. 3) represents a type of device that is useful in a number of different kinds of experimental work. Little has been done toward developing methods of stimulating the skin by traction (pulling up instead of pressing down), although the same sort of apparatus could be readily adapted for this purpose. Another neglected field is the controlled stimulation of individual hairs on the skin, which, like the cat's whiskers, are extremely sensitive indicators.

For Vibration

Practically all experimenters now use an oscillator to generate the desired frequencies and the analog of a dynamic speaker to transform the electrical oscillations into mechanical vibrations. The use of an interrupted neon light and a microscope to measure the amplitude of skin movement has already been mentioned. Alternating currents applied directly to the skin produce effects similar to those obtained with mechanical vibration [18], although the actual nature of the stimulation is different. An interrupted air jet has also been used for vibratory stimulation, but is a poor method because of the inertia of the individual air puffs.

Vibratory stimulation readily spreads to other parts of the skin, even when the stimulator is a fine needle point. Anesthetizing the skin under the stimulator does not prevent such spreading and may in fact aggravate it, since the anesthetized area tends to vibrate as a whole [48]. The actual extent of spread can be checked by using a lightweight pick-up suspended so as just to make contact with the skin. In addition to spread, another source of confusion is the presence of deep sensitivity, which continues to respond to vibratory stimulation after the skin itself has been completely anesthetized.

For Pain

The chief ways of arousing pain experimentally are by pricking and burning. Any of the devices used for tactile stimulation may be employed to prick the skin by substituting a fine needlepoint for the tactile stimulator. A very fine needle will sometimes penetrate the skin so smoothly as to give pure pain without any accompanying sensation of touch. Heavy pressure with larger stimulators may arouse deep pain, causing some confusion.

Radiant heat has no touch element, and the burning pain can be subjectively discriminated from painless warmth and heat. The

Hardy apparatus (Fig. 2) is excellent for this purpose. There is some evidence, however, that deep pain can be aroused by strong radiant heat, even when the skin has been anesthetized [39]. Electrical stimulation with high-voltage, low-amperage current gives a painless prick which becomes painful with stronger stimulation [5].

For Warm and Cold

Warm and cold spots are usually mapped with a water-circulated stimulator having a circular tip approximately 1 millimeter in diameter [10]. For repeated mapping of a checkerboard pattern, square and oblong stimulators which exactly fit the checkerboard squares may be used [26]. The subjects must be trained to neglect the simultaneous touch sensation and report only experiences of warm and cold.

In the measurement of adaptation times, difference limens, and stimulus limens, the stimulator at neutral temperature can be allowed to rest on the skin until tactile sensation has disappeared. Then the desired temperature can be applied by suddenly changing the temperature of the circulating water. With a very small stimulator, touch can be virtually eliminated by applying the stimulator through a small opening in a neutral field to such a level that the skin is not distorted.

For radiant stimulation the Hardy type of apparatus is admirably adapted. A block of dry ice can be substituted for the heating element to obtain "radiant cold." The heat absorbed or lost by the skin during stimulation can be accurately measured by radiometer. Since results obtained from radiant stimulation appear to differ markedly from those secured with contact stimulation, parallel investigations using the two forms are desirable. Diathermy has also been used for thermal stimulation [50], and thermal sensations are aroused when blood circulation is cut off and then suddenly released [2].

Especially in studies of adaptation, false results may arise from the spread of the stimulus beyond the desired area. Spread can be minimized by surrounding the stimulator with a metal ring maintained at skin temperature or by anesthetizing the surrounding region by electroendosmosis [9]. Constriction or dilating of the blood vessels usually accompanies thermal stimulation, but these vascular changes must be considered part of the normal stimulus situation.

REFERENCES

1. Basler, A., and H. Schuster. Über das Erkennen von "rauh" und "glatt." *Z. Sinnesphysiol.*, 1935, *66*, 33–44.

2. Bazett, H. C., and B. McGlone. Studies in sensation. III. Chemical factor in the stimulation of end-organ giving temperature sensation. *Arch. Neur. Psychiat.*, 1932, *28*, 71–91.
3. Bazett, H. C., B. McGlone, and R. J. Brocklehurst. The temperatures in the tissues which accompany temperature sensations. *J. Physiol.*, 1930, *69*, 88–112.
4. Bazett, H. C., B. McGlone, R. G. Williams, and H. M. Lufkin. Sensation. I. Depth, distribution, and probable identification in the prepuce of sensory end-organs concerned in sensations of temperature and touch; thermometric conductivity. *Arch. Neur. Psychiat.*, 1932, *27*, 489–517.
5. Bishop, G. H. Responses to electrical stimulation of single sensory units of skin. *J. Neurophysiol.*, 1943, *6*, 361–382.
6. Bishop, G. H. The peripheral unit for pain. *J. Neurophysiol.*, 1944, *7*, 71–80.
7. Boring, E. G. The stimulus error. *Amer. J. Psychol.*, 1921, *32*, 449–471.
8. Clark, G. P. On certain characteristics of the pressure sensations of the human skin. *Amer. J. Physiol.*, 1898, *1*, 346–358.
9. Cummings, S. B. The effect of local anesthesia on tactile and vibratory thresholds. *J. Exper. Psychol.*, 1938, *23*, 321–338.
10. Dallenbach, K. M. The temperature spots and end-organs. *Amer. J. Psychol.*, 1927, *39*, 402–427.
11. DeCillis, O. E. Absolute thresholds for the perception of tactual movements. *Arch. Psychol.*, No. 294. New York: 1944.
12. Endres, G. Punktions-narkose von Rezeptoren. *Z. Biol.*, 1930, *89*, 536–540.
13. Gatti, A. The perception of space by means of pure sensations of touch. *Amer. J. Psychol.*, 1937, *50*, 289–296.
14. Geblewicz, E. La relation entre l'intensité du stimulus et le temps de réaction pour les excitations thermiques en durée indefinie et en durée brève. *Compte rend. soc. biol.*, 1933, *119*, 1362–1364.
15. Geblewicz, E. L'influence de l'intensité sur la persistance apparente des excitations thermiques pour deux stimulations successives. *Compte rend. soc. biol.*, 1938, *127*, 173–175.
16. Geldard, F. A. The perception of mechanical vibration. II. The response of pressure receptors. *J. Gen. Psychol.*, 1940, *22*, 271–280.
17. Gilbert, R. W. Dermal sensitivity and the differentiated nerve terminations of the human skin. *J. Gen. Psychol.*, 1929, *2*, 445–461.
18. Gilmer, B. von H. The sensitivity of the fingers to alternating electrical currents. *Amer. J. Psychol.*, 1937, *49*, 444–449.
19. Gilmer, B. von H. The glomus body as a receptor of cutaneous pressure and vibration. *Psychol. Bull.*, 1942, *39*, 73–93.
20. Grindley, G. C. The variation of sensory thresholds with the rate of application of the stimulus. II. Touch and pain. *Brit. J. Psychol.*, 1936, *27*, 189–195.
21. Hardy, J. D., and T. W. Oppel. Studies in temperature sensation. III. The sensitivity of the body to heat and the spatial summation of the end-organ responses. *J. Clin. Investig.*, 1937, *16*, 533–540.
22. Herget, C. M., L. P. Granath, and J. D. Hardy. Warmth sense in relation to skin area stimulated. *Amer. J. Physiol.*, 1941, *135*, 20–26.
23. Hoagland, H. Adaptation of cutaneous tactile receptors. VI. Inhibitory effects and potassium and calcium. *J. Gen. Physiol.*, 1936, *19*, 943–951.
24. Jenkins, W. L. Studies in thermal sensitivity. 3. Adaptation with a series of small annular stimulators. *J. Exper. Psychol.*, 1938, *22*, 164–177.

25. Jenkins, W. L. Studies in thermal sensitivity. 5. The reactions of untrained subjects to simultaneous warm + cold stimulation. *J. Exper. Psychol.*, 1938, *22*, 451–461.

26. Jenkins, W. L. Studies in thermal sensitivity. 12. Part-whole relations in seriatim cold-mapping. *J. Exper. Psychol.*, 1939, *25*, 373–388.

27. Jenkins, W. L. Studies in thermal sensitivity. 16. Further evidence on the effects of stimulus temperature. *J. Exper. Psychol.*, 1941, *29*, 413–419.

28. Jones, F. N. The chronaxy of cold and warmth. *Amer. J. Psychol.*, 1940, *53*, 216–228.

29. Jones, F. N., and M. H. Jones. The chronaxy of pain. *Amer. J. Psychol.*, 1941, *54*, 240–242.

30. Katz, D. The vibratory sense and other lectures. *Univ. Maine Bull.*, 1930, *32*, 90–104.

31. Lanier, L. H. An experimental study of cutaneous innervation. *Proc. Assoc. Res. Nerv. Ment. Disease*, 1935, *15*, 437–456.

32. Lauterbach, C. E., and R. E. Crouser. Sensation cues to moisture. *J. Exper. Psychol.*, 1933, *16*, 328–338.

33. Madlung, K. Über anschauliche und funktionelle Nachbarschaft von Tasteindrücken. *Psychol. Forsch.*, 1935, *19*, 193–236.

34. Munn, N. L. Tactual localization without overt localizing movements and its relation to the concept of local signs as orientation tendencies. *J. Exper. Psychol.*, 1937, *20*, 581–588.

35. Nafe, J. P. Toward the quantification of psychology. *Psychol. Rev.*, 1942, *49*, 1–18.

36. Neuhaus, W. Taktile Scheinbewegung. *Arch. ges. Psychol.*, 1932, *83*, 519–562.

37. Oppel, T. W., and J. D. Hardy. Studies in temperature sensation. I. A comparison of the sensation produced by infra-red and visible radiation. *J. Clin. Investig.*, 1937, *16*, 517–524.

38. Oppel, T. W., and J. D. Hardy. Studies in temperature sensation. II. The temperature changes responsible for the stimulation of heat end organs. *J. Clin. Investig.*, 1937, *16*, 525–531.

39. Rein, H. Beiträge zur Lehre von der Temperaturempfindung der menschlichen Haut. *Z. Biol.*, 1924, *82*, 189–212.

40. Revesz, G. System der optischen und haptischen Raumtäuschungen. *Z. Psychol.*, 1934, *131*, 296–375.

41. Rivers, W. H. R., and H. Head. A human experiment in nerve division. *Brain*, 1908, *31*, 323.

42. Schöbel, R. Über die absolute Erkennung zweier Druckreizorte. *Z. Sinnesphysiol.*, 1934, *64*, 310–324.

43. Sjöstrand, T. Über die Enstehung von wiederholten Stichempfindungen, Hyperalgesie, Rötung und Oedem bei kontinuerlicher mechanischer Reizung der Haut mit dem Algesimeter. *Skand. Arch. Physiol.*, 1938, *78*, 17–39.

44. Stone, L. J. An experimental study of form perception in the thermal senses. *Psychol. Rec.*, 1937, *1*, 234–338.

45. Tower, S. S. Unit for sensory reception in cornea. *J. Neurophysiol.*, 1940, *3*, 486–500.

46. Tschlenoff, L. Sensibilitätstudien an Nervenkranken. II. Über die Schwellenlabilität der Hautsinne. *Deut. Z. Nervenheilk.*, 1931, *122*, 89–113.

47. von Bagh, K. Weitere Versuche über die Summation von gleichzeitigen Berührungs. bzw. Druckreizen. *Deut. Z. Nervenheilk.*, 1936, *140*, 95–101.

48. WEITZ, J. Vibratory sensitivity as affected by local anesthesia. *J. Exper. Psychol.*, 1939, *25,* 48–64.

49. WEITZ, J. A further study of the relation between skin temperature and cutaneous sensitivity. *J. Exper. Psychol.*, 1942, *30,* 426–431.

50. WINDISCH, E. Untersuchungen über den adequäten Reize für Warmerezeptoren. *Z. Biol.*, 1931, *91,* 126–136.

51. WOOLLARD, H. H. Observations on the terminations of cutaneous nerves. *Brain,* 1935, *58,* 352–367.

SUGGESTED READINGS

GELDARD, F. A. The perception of mechanical vibration. *J. Gen. Psychol.*, 1940, *22,* 243–308.

JENKINS, W. L., and L. J. STONE. Recent research in cutaneous sensitivity. II. Touch and the neural basis of the skin senses. *Psychol. Bull.*, 1941, *38,* 69–91.

STONE, L. J., and W. L. JENKINS. Recent research in cutaneous sensitivity. I. Pain and temperature. *Psychol. Bull.*, 1940, *37,* 285–311.

WOODWORTH, R. S. *Experimental Psychology.* New York: Henry Holt 1938 (Chap. XIX, The skin senses).

Chapter 10

Studying the Senses of Taste and Smell

Carl Pfaffmann[1]

The flavor of food, which we often uncritically call taste, is usually a complex experience or perception depending not only on the sense of taste but also on the sense of smell and the common sensitivity of

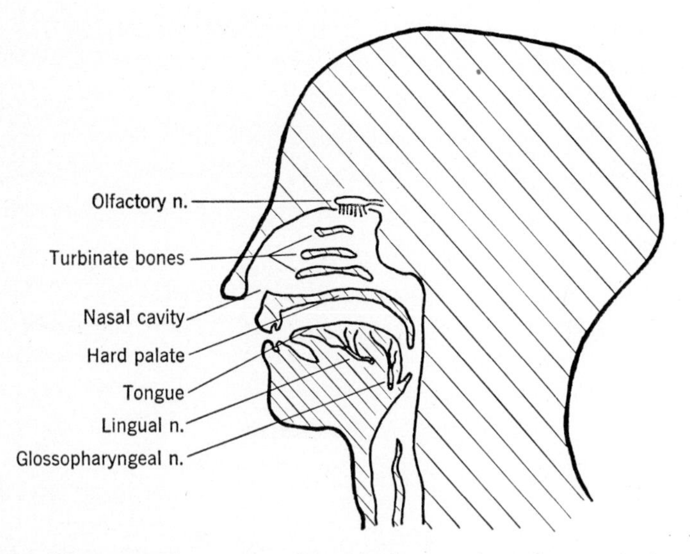

Fig. 1. Diagram of a section through the mouth and one nasal cavity.

the mucous membrane of the nose and mouth. Kinesthetic sensations from the muscles of mastication and even sight and hearing may contribute important components. Imagine if you can, the flavor of celery without the cool, crisp feel and crunchy sound as you chew

[1] Assistant Professor of Psychology, Brown University.

the fresh, firm stalk. Coolness, feel, and sound are not true taste qualities. It is with true taste that you appreciate the flavor of salt, citric acid, sugar, or quinine; it is largely by odor that you know the flavor of fruit, coffee, or butter.

Anatomical studies have shown that the olfactory sense organ consists of a small patch of nervous tissue located in the upper recesses of the nasal passages. The sense organs of taste consist of small goblet-shaped sense cells primarily in the fungiform and circumvallate papillae of the tongue, although some taste buds may be found on adjacent structures, such as the epiglottis and soft palate. The sense organs of the common sensitivity are nerve endings throughout the mucosa of the nose and mouth. The relative position of these sensory areas is shown in Fig. 1.

This chapter will discuss methods of investigating taste and smell. For the present purposes the sensitivity of the mucous membrane to mildly irritating chemicals, called by some the common chemical sense, will be included under the term common sensitivity, which includes sensitivity to warmth, cold, pressure, and pain.

METHODS OF STUDYING TASTE

Distinguishing Taste from Smell and the Common Sensitivity

In some cases taste can be distinguished from its neighboring senses quite readily. By plugging the nostrils, the sense of smell can be eliminated almost entirely. Something of this sort occurs naturally during the common head cold, when food seems to lose much of its aroma. More specifically, the elimination of olfaction eliminates such qualities as fruity, foul, spicy, or burnt. The touch and temperature sensations which often accompany taste can be minimized by applying the stimulus as a solution warmed to body temperature.

With olfaction, temperature, and touch eliminated, there remain only such qualities as sour, sweet, bitter, and salty. These are the true taste qualities, for they can be elicited only from areas known to possess taste buds. Very weak acid solutions, for example, will arouse no sensation from the gums, cheeks, or undersurface of the tongue, but will call out a definite sour taste on the tip and sides of the tongue, where taste buds are found in great abundance. Stronger acids may call out the additional quality of pain or sharpness. This, however, occurs everywhere in the mouth and must therefore be an added component from the common sensitivity of the mucosa.

Methods of Studying Taste Qualities and Their Sensory Basis

The relation of taste quality to stimulus composition is most commonly investigated in man by one of the integrative stimulation methods, in which the solution spreads over a large part of the tongue surface to stimulate as many receptors as possible. In general such methods are standardized versions of normal sipping or tasting. In other cases small amounts of fluid are dropped on the partially extended tongue by means of a pipette or medicine dropper (drop method). Appropriate intervals (½ to 5 minutes) between stimuli avoid adaptation or contrast effects, and a delay of 2 or more hours after eating minimizes taste aftereffects from the food.

In certain experiments the subject is asked merely to describe the taste experience as accurately as possible. In other instances he may compare the test sample with standard solutions possessing pure salty, sweet, sour, or bitter tastes. Both methods show that many different substances have pure sweet, sour, or bitter tastes, whereas the pure salty taste is elicited only by sodium chloride. All other salts give rise to complex tastes which can be matched by mixtures of solutions, as specified by the following mixture equation [40, p. 455]:

$$N = xA + yB + zC + vD$$

where N is the concentration of substance giving the compound taste, matched by a mixture of x, y, z, and v concentrations of the bitter, salty, sour, and sweet standard solutions, respectively. It is important to specify the concentration at which such qualitative comparisons are made, for taste quality often changes as the concentration increases. Saccharine in dilute solutions tastes sweet; in stronger solutions the taste is bitter.

In general it may be said that acids have a sour taste, a large number of alkaloids a bitter taste, many carbohydrates a sweet taste, and many salts a complex salty taste. It should be pointed out, however, that there are many exceptions to this simple rule. Certain substances radically different from the sugars in chemical composition, such as saccharine, lead acetate, and various alcohols, have sweet tastes that are indistinguishable from each other.

In the method of punctate stimulation the stimulus is restricted to a single point or small area on the tongue. It was by a gross form of this method, as mentioned above, that the end organs for taste were identified. The qualities of salty, sour, bitter, and sweet could be elicited only from areas known to contain taste buds.

"Inadequate" stimulation by electric currents is well suited to the punctate method. Since stimulation takes place through metal wire or wick type of electrodes, these can be placed on a particular tongue region with great accuracy. There is no danger of the stimulus diffusing away from the point of application, as might occur with solutions. Monopolar stimulation occurs when one terminal of a battery is connected to a single electrode on the tongue, and the other terminal to a large indifferent electrode on some other part of the body. If the tongue electrode is attached to the positive pole of the battery, a sour taste will result; if the tongue electrode is negative, the taste is alkaline [29]. With bipolar electrodes, i.e., both leads on the tongue, or faradic or alternating currents, the taste may be complex. The

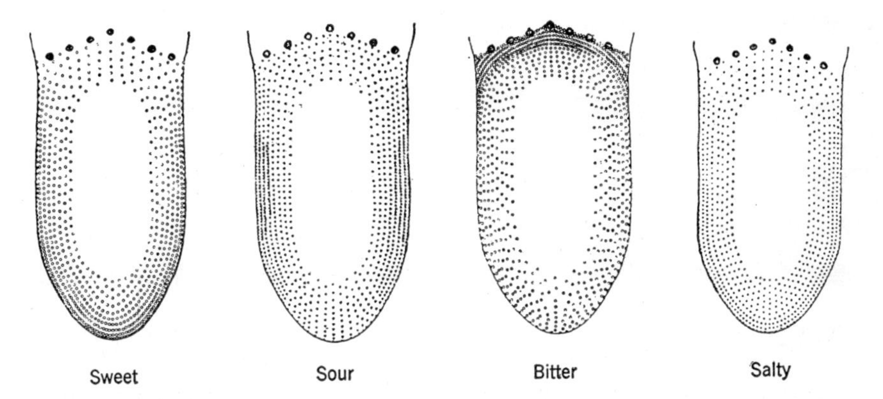

Fig. 2. Diagram showing the relative sensitivity of the tongue for the different tastes.

The regions of greatest sensitivity, i.e., with the lowest thresholds, are indicated by the greatest density of dots. (After Hänig [19].)

essential point for our purpose is that no "electric taste" is elicited from those regions devoid of taste buds.

To use the punctate method with liquid stimuli, small brushes saturated with taste solutions are most commonly employed. By this means the sensitivity of the tongue to each of the four basic tastes has been mapped. The tip of the tongue is most sensitive to sweet, the sides to sour, the back to bitter, and the tip and sides to salty, as shown in Fig. 2 [19]. This distribution suggests that the four qualities of taste are mediated by four types of receptor organ. If all tastes depended on the same receptor organ, every region of the tongue should be equally sensitive.

If very small brushes are used, so that individual papillae can be stimulated, the majority of papillae will be sensitive to all taste stimuli. A small number, however, will respond exclusively to salt, sweet, or sour stimuli [26]. This suggests that certain papillae may contain only one type of taste receptor.

The four taste qualities can be further dissociated by the suppressor action of certain drugs. In weak concentrations cocaine primarily reduces bitter sensitivity; another substance, gymnenic acid, depresses sweet sensitivity [39].

It will be noted that the methods so far described are indirect, in that they depend on correlations between the stimulus and response of the intact organism. Changes in threshold or in the quality of the

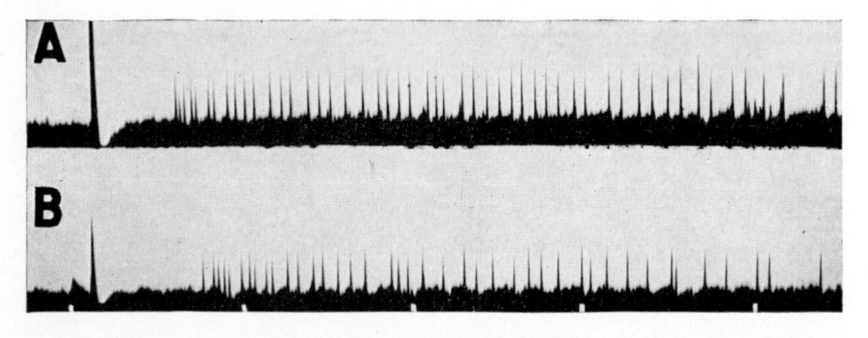

Fig. 3. Record of a single nerve fiber preparation responding to acid on the tongue.

The large initial upward deflection signals the time of applying the stimulus. This is followed by the train of nerve impulse spikes. (A) stimulus 0.5 N acetic acid. (B) stimulus 0.01 N hydrochloric acid. Each white time mark at base of record (B) indicates 1/10 second.

sensation are believed to reflect changes in the sense organ, providing, of course, that such factors as fatigue, inattention, and practice have been adequately controlled. The development of electrophysiological methods in recent years permits a more direct attack on the analysis of sensory function. It is now possible to record with an electronic amplifier and oscillograph the nerve impulses in a sensory nerve fiber following stimulation of its associated sense organ. (See Chapters 14 and 15.) In one study single afferent nerve fibers in the nerves from the tongue of the cat were dissected under a binocular microscope and placed upon the recording electrodes.[2] The discharge in a typical single nerve-fiber preparation from the chorda tympani nerve is illustrated in Fig. 3. Instead of four types of single nerve fiber, each responding only to acid, salt, sugar, or quinine, as might have been

[2] It will be appreciated by the student that this is essentially a unitary or punctate method of analysis, in which the restriction to a single unit is introduced at the recording rather than the stimulating phase.

expected from the evidence presented so far, only three types of single nerve fiber were found. One was activated only by acids, a second by both acids and sodium chloride, and a third by acids and quinine. No single fiber preparations responsive to sugar were found. These results confirm the view that there are different types of taste receptor but suggest further that these receptor types do not necessarily correspond to the four fundamental taste qualities [34].

Methods of Studying Taste Sensitivity

Most techniques in this category are primarily concerned with taste sensitivity as a whole. Differences in sensitivity from one part of the tongue to another are averaged by applying the stimulus to a large area of the tongue. In man the stimuli may be applied by any of the integrative methods already described, such as the drop method or sipping method. Of these, the sipping method will give lower and less variable values of the absolute threshold [38]. In certain cases where precise control of such factors as the area, pressure, temperature, and duration[3] of stimulation is required, some form of applicator may be

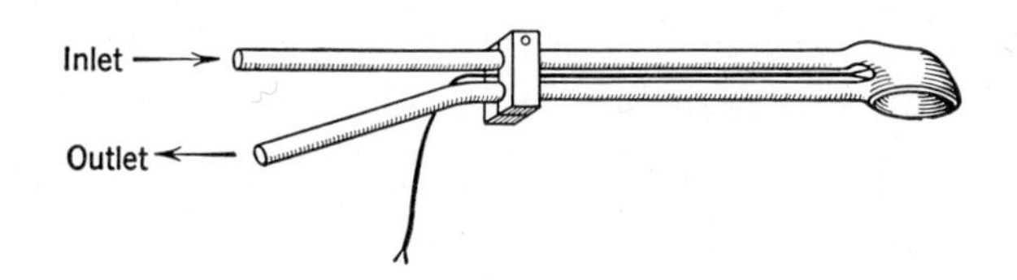

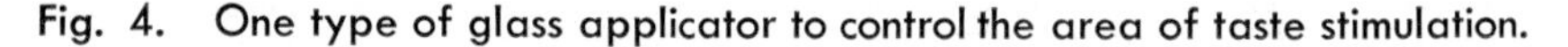
Fig. 4. One type of glass applicator to control the area of taste stimulation.

The applicator aperture is placed on the subject's tongue. The inlet is connected to a system of tubes so that various solutions can be directed through apparatus.

employed [17, 23, 32]. One such device is shown in Fig. 4. The most frequently employed psychophysical procedures are the methods of constant stimuli, single stimuli, and limits. (See Chapter 5.) In the method of limits the descending series is often omitted, because the aftertastes of the suprathreshold stimuli in the early part of the descending series tend to mask the weaker stimuli in the later part of the series.

Studies indicate that marked differences in taste sensitivity may exist even in a relatively small group of individuals. In a group of forty-seven subjects the thresholds for different taste stimuli distribute

[3] Especially important in studies of adaptation [1, 18].

over the ranges shown in Fig. 5. Note that one substance, phenyl thiocarbamide (PTC), has an unusually wide range of thresholds [7]. This substance has been employed in tests of "taste blindness." Persons unable to taste PTC crystals are known as "non-tasters." Actually such individuals are not taste blind. They are only relatively insensitive, for with sufficiently strong stimuli their thresholds can be reached. In Fig. 5 their values would lie in the upper part of the distribution curve for PTC. The notion of taste blindness as an all-or-none attribute gained credence largely as a result of early tests with the commercial crystals. In this form the stimulus cannot be graded in intensity so that the subject either tastes or does not taste. This dichotomy is quite arbitrary [7]. If the commercial crystals are purified, a more effective stimulus can be obtained, and some of the "non-tasters" will become "tasters." This is an important point of methodology, for it shows how experimental results may be influenced by the method of measurement.

It is of particular interest that taste sensitivity in the same person may change from day to day and even during the same day. Such variations probably reflect changes in the physiological state of the individual. The direct action of chemical agents in the blood has been demonstrated in a number of cases. For example, decholin (a bitter-tasting substance) gives rise to a bitter taste shortly after injection directly into the blood stream [20]. Stimulation sufficient to elicit a sensation in this way probably occurs only if the change in the blood takes place suddenly. Normally, the taste receptors are in a state of equilibrium with the chemicals in the blood. As these blood factors change slowly, there may be corresponding changes in the sensitivity of the receptor. With high concentrations of sodium chloride in the blood, for example, it would be expected that the threshold for the same substance applied to the tongue would be high. With a lower concentration the threshold might be lower.

Methods which depend upon unlearned feeding preferences or aversions have been employed primarily in animal studies. (See Chapters 12 and 13.) To determine sodium chloride preference thresholds, for example, the animals, placed in individual living cages, are provided with two graduated drinking bottles. After they have become adjusted to the situation and are drinking about equal amounts of water from each bottle, sodium chloride is added to the water in one of the bottles. On successive days the concentration of salt is increased gradually until the animal consistently takes more salt than water. The concentration at which the animal first shows a preference for salt is the preference threshold concentration. See Fig. 6. This preference is abolished when the taste nerves to the tongue are cut.

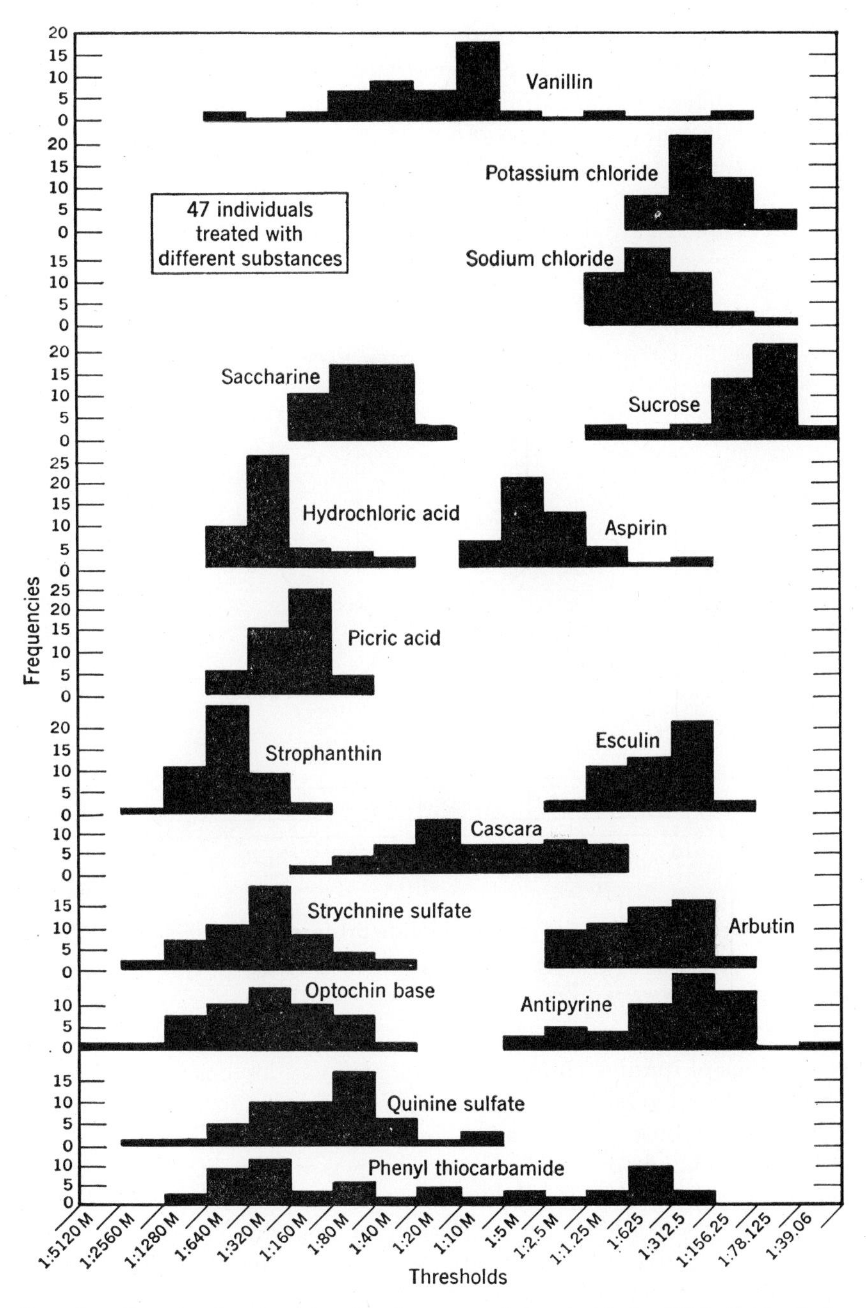

Fig. 5. Graphs showing the distributions of thresholds in 47 individuals for different substances.

Values indicated at the base line range from a dilution of 1 part in 5,120,000 (1:5120M where M = 1000) to 1 part in 39.06 parts of water (1:39.06). (From Blakeslee and Salmon [7].)

The preference threshold for sodium chloride and the aversion threshold for quinine in the white rat agree with the threshold concentrations for these substances found in man by other means [37, 42]. There is a methodological question, however, whether the preference or aversion threshold is a true index of sensitivity. Studies to be discussed later show that in man, the same taste substance may be pleasant, indifferent, or unpleasant, depending upon the concentration. Weak con-

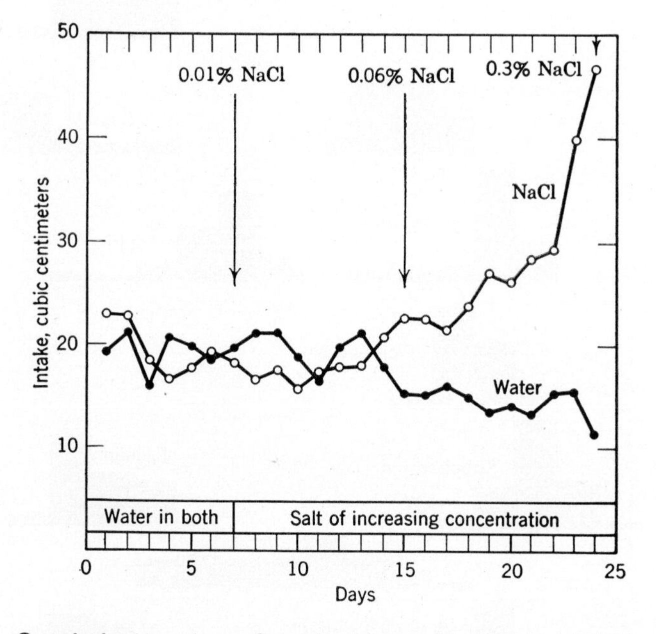

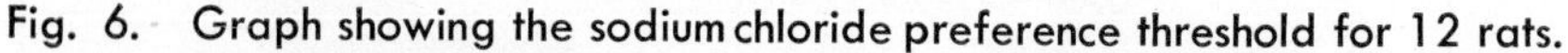
Fig. 6. Graph showing the sodium chloride preference threshold for 12 rats. At 0.06% the animals begin to show a definite preference for salt solution, which becomes greater as the concentration increases. (From unpublished results of J. K. Bare.)

centrations of quinine sulfate, for example, may have a pleasant taste. Preference or aversion may be related to that factor in man known as the pleasantness or unpleasantness of taste.

Closely related to the above procedure is the method of observing reflexes or the modifications of reflex activities after taste stimulation. The sucking response is particularly suited to studies of taste in infants and young mammals. Although the early workers simply observed the sucking movements when taste stimuli were introduced into the mouth, later investigators graphically recorded the sucking reflex by utilizing the pressure and volume changes in the nursing bottle as the fluid was sucked out [24, 33]. A modified nursing bottle was connected by a system of tubes to the recording bellows of a polygraph or kymograph. Figure 7 shows the response to 0.9 per cent sodium chloride, a concentration above threshold for the particular child

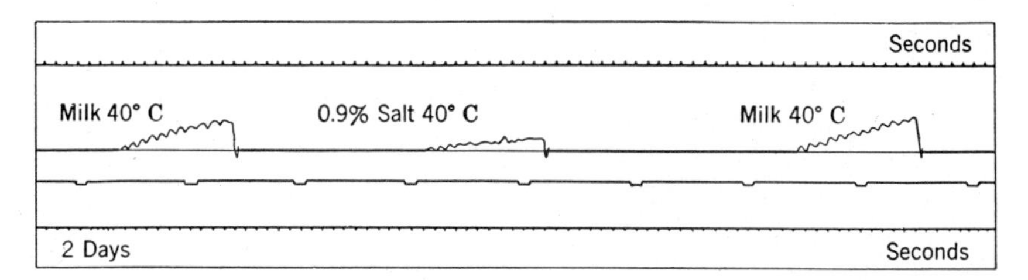

Fig. 7. Polygraph record showing a differential response to 0.9% sodium chloride compared to the normal sucking response to milk. (After Jensen [24].)

studied. Thresholds defined as the concentration that caused a just noticeable distortion of the sucking response were found to range between 0.2 and 0.9 per cent for one group of infants.

Methods for Studying Suprathreshold Stimuli

The designation or specification of taste intensity for concentrations above the threshold is of practical as well as theoretical interest [8]. One common method for designating the strength of a sweetening agent is in terms of a standard substance, such as cane sugar. The sweetness grade is given by the number of grams of cane sugar required to match 1 gram of test substance in sweetness when both are dissolved in equal volumes of water. By this measure, fructose was found to have a value of 1.05. Since 1.05 grams of sucrose were required to match 1 gram of fructose, fructose is the sweeter of the two substances. Glucose and lactose have values of 0.53 and 0.27 respectively and are therefore less sweet. This method holds only for the particular concentration at which the comparisons are made. As concentration increases, some substances become relatively less sweet [40].

This latter effect presumably depends on the fundamental relation between subjective intensity and objective stimulus intensity. The study of intensity discrimination in taste shows a relation similar to that for other senses [22]. As the concentration increases, the value of $\Delta I/I$ for the taste of sodium chloride decreases as shown in Fig. 8. At higher intensities, a relatively smaller increase in the stimulus is required in order to produce a just noticeable increment in taste.

In addition to these effects, changes in the intensity of taste stimu-

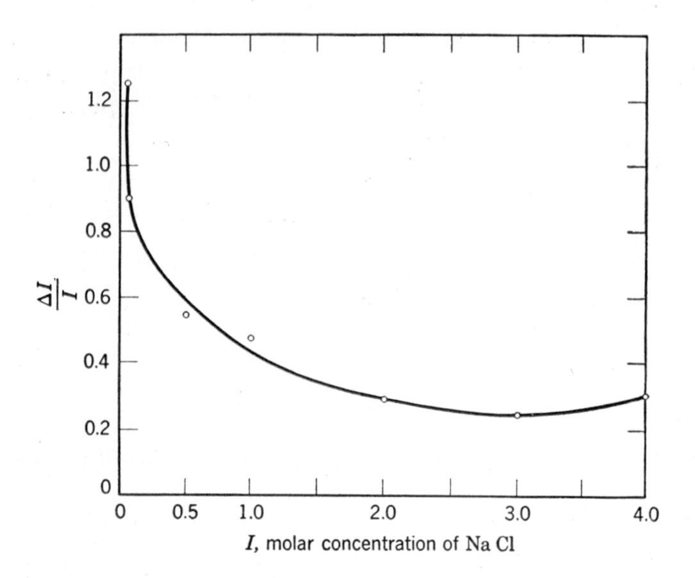

Fig. 8. The change in the value of the Weber fraction $\Delta I/I$ as a function of intensity I. (From A. H. Holway and L. M. Hurvich [22].)

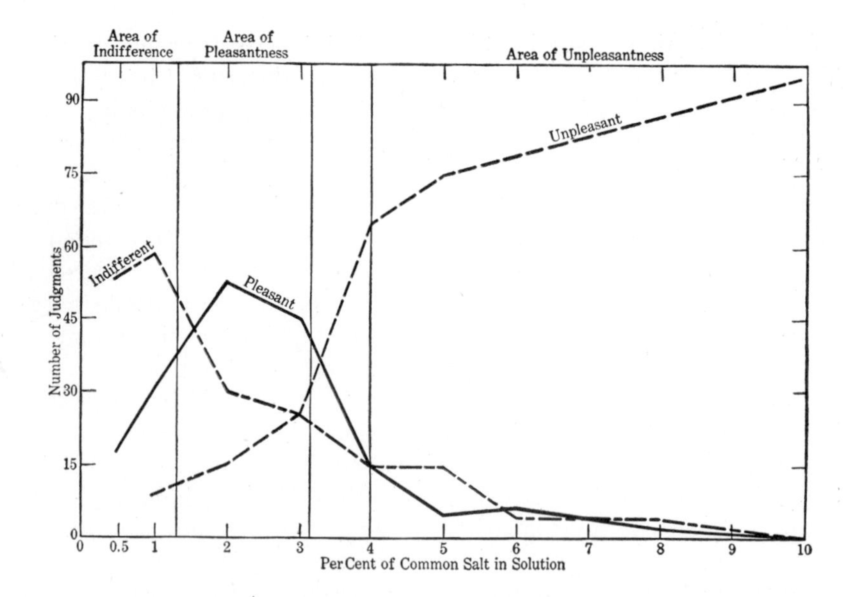

Fig. 9. Graph showing the number of indifferent, pleasant, and unpleasant judgments made by 7 observers for different concentrations of sodium chloride. (After Engel [14].)

lation are usually associated with changes in the pleasantness or unpleasantness of taste. When we use salt, pepper, vinegar, or other condiments to improve the palatability of food, our recipe usually calls for just enough to give a good taste, but not so much as to be too strong and unpleasant. The relation of hedonic tone, i.e., pleasantness or unpleasantness, to the intensity of stimulation can perhaps be demonstrated better in taste than in any other sense field. In Fig. 9 the degree of pleasantness or unpleasantness of salt solutions of different concentration is shown [14]. The method of single stimuli was employed. The subject reported whether the taste was pleasant, unpleasant, or indifferent. For weak concentrations around 0.5 per cent the judgments of indifferent predominate. At 2 per cent the pleasant judgments predominate; for concentrations of 4 per cent and up the taste is mostly unpleasant. Acid solutions show the same progressive changes as intensity is increased. Certain other substances, like sugar, are pleasant for nearly all concentrations, whereas others, like quinine, are unpleasant in nearly all but the weakest concentrations.

Such findings are representative of most individuals. Nevertheless, there are certain persons whose judgments of pleasantness and unpleasantness may diverge from that described. Whereas most people dislike strong salt, a few may like it. Although most people find sugar pleasant in all concentrations, some may dislike it. In one experiment two subjects were found who had such a dislike for sugar. Their judgments for concentrations above 9 per cent, which most people like, were predominantly unpleasant. Both subjects reported excessive indulgence of sweets in their youth. Just how such past experiences or current daily variations in physiological state in response to nutritional needs may influence the hedonic tone of taste stimuli is not yet understood and is a fertile field for further investigation.

METHODS OF STUDYING OLFACTION

As we have seen, independent stimulation of smell or taste is possible only under certain conditions. In olfaction, it is particularly difficult to eliminate those extraneous effects due to the common sensitivity of the nasal mucosa. Such double action occurs with ammonia, which has, in addition to its characteristic odor, a strong, irritating effect leading to such obvious reflex acts as crying and sneezing. The methods by which these effects have been shown to depend on the nerve endings of the nasal mucous membrane as well as on the sense of smell will be discussed in the following section.

In all investigations of olfactory sensitivity, several general precautions must be observed. Wherever possible, pure chemicals are employed to avoid contamination by small amounts of impurity, which are capable of severely altering the odor. The experimental rooms for olfactory investigation are well ventilated, and precautions against the clinging of odorous substances to rubber tubing, stoppers, glassware, etc., are taken. Stimulation in most cases is achieved by introducing the odorous vapor into the nostrils, either through a system of tubes inserted into the nostrils or by active sniffing on the part of the subject when a flask is brought close to the nostrils. The odor may be applied to both nostrils (dirhinic) or to one nostril (monorhinic), or a different odor may be presented to each nostril separately (dichorhinic).

Methods of Distinguishing Olfaction from the Common Sensitivity and Taste

The difference between true smell and the common sensitivity can be demonstrated rather simply by means of a menthol nasal inhalator sold commercially for the relief of head colds. When the inhalator is inserted in the nostrils in the usual way, the cool sharp menthol odor is perceived. If the subject now places the inhalator to the lips while holding the nostrils closed, the sharpness and coolness will be felt in the mouth. The aromatic true smell of menthol will not be experienced, however, until the nostrils are opened and the air currents of normal respiration can carry the odor into the nasal passage by way of the posterior nares. The contribution of taste to other odors can be investigated similarly with inhalators containing other substances.

Surgical dissociation of olfaction and the common sensitivity has been employed in animal experiments [3]. It is possible to remove the nerve supply to the mucous membrane of the nose by cutting certain branches of the Vth cranial nerve (trigeminal), so that only the sense of smell remains. This preparation is known as an olfactory animal. In other animals the sense of smell can be removed by cutting the Ist cranial nerve (olfactory), leaving only the common sensitivity in a so-called trigeminal animal. The insufflation of ammonia or other irritants leads to marked changes in respiration and blood pressure in both types, as well as in the normal animal. Both olfaction and the common sensitivity therefore are stimulated by such irritants. Animals so prepared have been employed in other experiments on olfaction.

The method of localization, an indirect method for use in man, assumes that only those stimuli which activate the common sensitivity can be localized in the right or left nostril when monorhinal stimulation is employed. Pure olfactory stimulants cannot be so localized [40]. Another indirect method, that of stream injection [13], defines pure olfactory stimulants as those which do not lead to pain or crying when a stream of the odorous vapor is continuously injected into the nostrils at a known rate of flow. During such tests the subject breathes through the mouth. Very few odors have been found that do not lead to pain. Even many of the stimuli classed as pure olfactory stimulants by the method of localization have been found to produce pain under these conditions. Clinical experience with this test suggests that certain brain tumors may impair true olfaction with little effect on the common sensitivity.

Methods of Studying Olfactory Qualities and Their Discrimination

Early classifications of odors were based in part on the literature of the perfume industry and to some extent on apparent resemblances and relations among groups of odors as experienced by casual observers. The work of Henning [21] is noteworthy as an attempt to derive a classification based on the description of odors by both trained and untrained observers and on the serial arrangements of odors when a number of scents were presented to the subject for such arrangement. Over 400 scents were employed in these experiments. They were contained in wide-mouthed, stoppered bottles which could be held under the subject's nostrils for dirhinic stimulation.

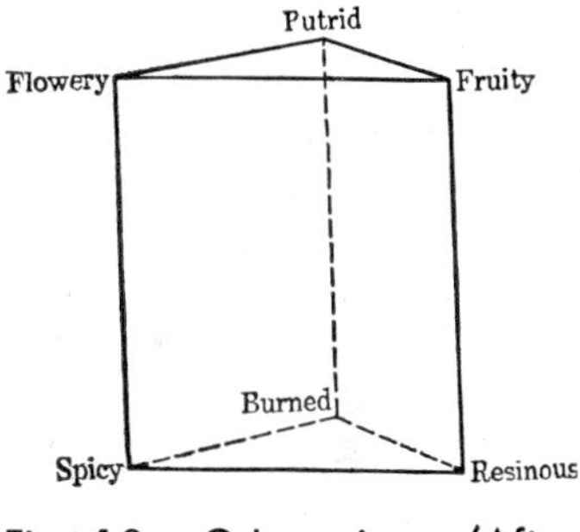

Fig. 10. Odor prism. (After Henning [21].)

The schema shown in Fig. 10 was devised to show the interrelations among the various odor qualities as indicated by these experiments. This is the odor prism, of which only the surfaces represent the psychological dimensions. No odor qualities are represented in the interior. Odors along an edge resemble the corners bounding that edge; the odors on the surface resemble all corners in proportion to the distance from the point to each of the corners. Other workers attempting to validate this schema have obtained variable results [11, 16, 30]. All agree that the precision of representation on this figure does not compare with that for the color double pyramid. See Fig. 27, page 208. On the other hand, the odor prism more or less represents the relations existing in the manifold of odor sensations. More recently, other workers [9] have reduced these six salient qualities to four—fragrant, acid, burnt, and caprylic or goaty—in developing a nomenclature for practical work.

The method of differential exhaustion should be mentioned for completeness, although it has not yet been successfully applied to the analysis of the fundamental olfactory qualities [29]. This method depends on the fact that olfactory fatigue is often selective. Fatiguing the sense of smell by ammonium sulfide reduces the sensitivity to hydrogen sulfide, hydrochloric acid, and bromine, whereas the sensitivity to etherial oils is unaffected. The conclusion seems warranted that all of the first group of substances act on the same sense organs, whereas the etherial oils stimulate a different group of receptors. Such groupings might serve as the basis for a classification of odors.

The correlation between the stimulus for smell and the quality of the odor is difficult to establish, largely because the exact nature of the adequate stimulus is unknown. In many cases the aromatic fraction of naturally occurring odorous objects has been isolated and identified. The odor of roses, for example, is due in great measure to geroniol, yet the odor of the natural plant extract can be matched only if a small amount of the genuine extract is added to synthetic geroniol [35]. Of the chemical elements, only the halogens—bromine, iodine, fluorine, and chlorine—appear to be odorous. The great majority of odorous substances are organic compounds, i.e., compounds containing carbon.

The electrophysiological technique has proved less effective for investigations of olfaction than for taste. So far, the electrical activity in the olfactory bulb, olfactory tract, and other parts of the brain has been recorded [2, 5]. All these structures are one or more synapses removed from the primary sense cells. The latter are virtually inaccessible, since the fine nerve filaments leading from the olfactory epithelium pass through perforations in the floor of the cranium to enter the olfactory bulb of the brain directly.

The earliest studies on the olfactory sensitivity of animals were based simply on observations of their general behavior when confronted with olfactory stimuli. Numerous incidental observations on olfaction have been made in connection with studies of maze learning, food selection, and mating behavior. For the white rat the standard discrimination box of the Watson-Yerkes type, modified to permit olfactory stimulation, has not proved very successful [27]. More success has been obtained with a technique in which the animal can reach a food box by digging through one of two tunnels filled with scented wood shavings. One of the scents is the cue for the open tunnel. On successive trials the odor stimuli are alternated from one side to the other in chance order. Discrimination between butyric acid and a disinfectant, trail scent[4] and gasoline, anise and a disinfectant, and male and female odors was established [41]. Another method was employed recently, in which the stimulus containers were fashioned from three small blocks of wood, each containing a smaller well provided with glass container at the bottom and covered with a perforated sliding metal cover, which the rats could pull open [28]. The blocks were impregnated with paraffin so that they could be washed and recoated to remove odors. One block was placed in each of the three corners of a square cage, and the rat was admitted at the fourth corner. Milk-soaked bread was placed in one well, and cotton with a few drops of oil of wintergreen was placed in the others. The position of the blocks was varied in random order during the trials. Any attempt by the rat to open the cover of a well not containing food was counted as an error. The discrimination between milk-soaked bread and oil of wintergreen established in this situation was lost when the olfactory bulbs were removed.

Conditioned reflex methods were early applied to the determination of the olfactory sensitivity of the dog [36]. In a recent study leg withdrawal to electric shock was conditioned to the presentation of an odorous vapor 7 seconds before the shock [4]. Stimuli were presented in wide-mouthed bottles held before the animal's nostrils. Bottles containing no odor were presented periodically as a control. In some cases the stimuli were delivered by means of a system of tubes opening close to the animal's snout. This proved less convenient because of the time between trials required to free the room of the odor. Normal, olfactory, and trigeminal dogs could be conditioned in 15 to 25 trials. Certain substances, such as cloves, lavender, anise, and asafetida, gave rise to conditioned reflexes only in the olfactory animal. Camphor, butyric acid, ether, and chloroform could be conditioned in both olfactory and trigeminal animals.

Methods of Studying Sensitivity

Absolute threshold values in man are frequently stated in terms of the minimal concentration, i.e., milligrams per liter of air, that can be detected. Starting with a given weight of odorous material evaporated in a container of known volume, the subject sniffs at the mouth of a series of flasks of increasing dilution until he is no longer able to detect the odor. For ethyl alcohol the threshold figure is 200 milligrams per

[4] A commercial paste supposed to attract animals to a trap.

liter; for musk vanillan or skatol the figure may be as low as 0.001 milligram per liter. The actual quantity acting as the stimulus will be some fraction of this figure, since only a portion of the inspired air reaches the olfactory receptor [10].

Other more elaborate ways of controlling the strength of odor have been employed. In one apparatus [6] a series of flow meters indicated the rate at which pure air bubbled through a chamber containing the odorous material. From the weight lost by the material after known volumes of air had passed over it, the concentration could be calculated. This concentration could be diluted by mixture with air in varying proportions, as indicated by another system of flow meters. The stimulus mixture was led to a funnel placed over the subject's nostrils. Artificial musk could be detected with this apparatus in concentrations as low as 0.00004 milligram per liter of air.

Threshold values stated in relative terms have proved useful for measures of the lower threshold in different individuals, for measures of differential sensitivity, for measures of changes in sensitivity in the same individuals as a result of adaptation or other factors, for studies of the interaction or neutralization of odors, and for studies of the relative stimulating efficiency of different substances. One simple procedure is to determine the greatest distance from the blindfolded subject at which the odor of an opened odor bottle can be detected. The more sensitive subject will detect the odor at a greater distance

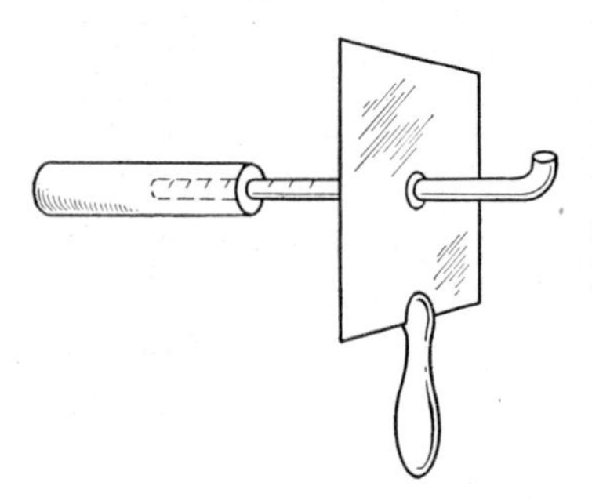

Fig. 11. Olfactometer. (After Zwaardemaker [43].)

A more quantitative procedure makes use of the olfactometer devised by Zwaardemaker [43]. The essential feature of this instrument is an odor tube of glass which can be slipped inside a larger rubber tube or hollow kaolin cylinder impregnated with odor-bearing material, as in Fig. 11. The outer kaolin cylinder is encased with glass or otherwise sealed from the atmosphere of the room. When the glass tube is pushed all the way through the odor tube, no odorous material is imparted to the air stream being drawn through the tube. As the glass tube is pulled out to expose more and more odor-bearing surface, the concentration of the odorous material in the air stream is said to increase proportionately to the extent of the surface exposed.[5] One end of the glass tube is curved upward, so that

[5] The accuracy of this assumption has been questioned by certain experimenters.

it can be inserted into the nostrils. The flow of air through the olfactometer is controlled by the subject's inspiration. All parts of the apparatus except the nasal tip are concealed by a screen. Sensitivity is measured in terms of the *olfactie,* the length of the odor-bearing surface exposed to the current of air as measured in centimeters. Stimulation may be monorhinic, dirhinic, or, with the double olfactometer, consisting of two odorous cylinders leading separately to each nostril, dichorhinic. It is by the use of the double olfactometer that the interaction and neutralization of odors have been most extensively studied. Various modifications of this or similar principles have been developed for practical purposes [15].

In most of the procedures so far discussed, the subject draws the odorous vapor into the nostrils by inspiration. Variations in the force and rate of inspiration might influence the values obtained. These factors have been controlled in a recently developed procedure, the blast injection method, in which the odor is forcefully injected into the subject's nostrils [12]. The odorous material is contained in a 500-cubic-centimeter bottle closed by a stopper except for an inlet and outlet tube. The inlet is connected to a hypodermic syringe; the outlet, to a double or single nasal tip by means of a rubber tube that is normally closed by a strong pinch clip (see Fig. 12). The pressure in the bottle is raised by injecting a few cubic centimeters of air into the bottle with the syringe. If the nosepiece is then inserted into the nostrils and the pinch clip suddenly released, a volume of odorous gas equal to that introduced into the bottle is injected into the nostrils. Thresholds are stated in terms of the number of cubic centimeters that must be injected before the olfactory sensation occurs or the substance is correctly identified. From an analysis of the pressure-volume relations it appears that the pressure of the injection, and not the amount of vapor injected, is directly related to stimulation [25]. Approximately the same injection pressure is required over a wide range of volumes when bottles of different volumes are employed as the odor container. The exact significance of this fact in terms of the process of stimulation is not clear. Further investigation of this point is needed.

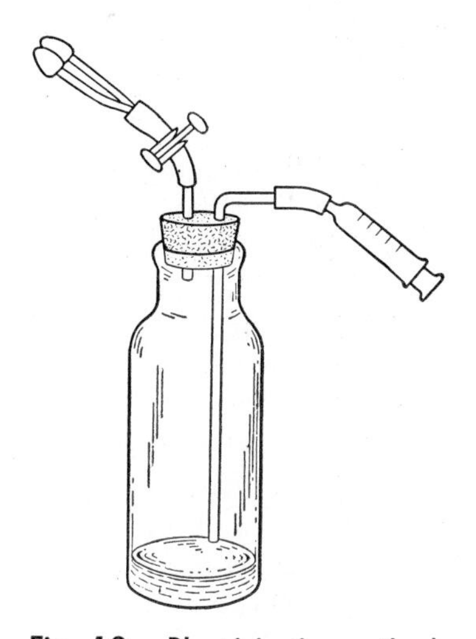

Fig. 12. Blast injection method. (After Elsberg [12].)

CONCLUSION

The student will have noted that the analytical and quantitative approach to the study of taste and smell has been emphasized. To be sure, our daily experiences with these senses is rarely analytical in character. Our selection and enjoyment of food is based on flavor, the composite of taste, smell, and the common sensitivity. Yet the contribution of each to the composites must be known if we are to understand how the complex experience comes about. The professional tea or wine taster distinguishes between the nose and the tongue in making his tests. He first smells and then tastes the sample under investigation according to a schedule that will avoid adaptation and fatigue effects. A recent volume on flavor written for the food industry says, "Sensation analysis . . . , considered first from a theoretical and then a practical standpoint, provides a unifying basis for a mass of otherwise heterogeneous matter" [9].

We have seen that there are at least two major difficulties in the study of taste and smell. The first is largely instrumental, resulting from the difficulty of presenting the chemical stimulus in a convenient and highly controlled way. Although various applicators and injectors have been developed, these do not approach the accuracy of control which is attainable with visual and auditory stimulation.

Even more fundamental is our lack of knowledge of the true stimulus for taste and for smell. The stimulus property that makes sugar and all other sweet-tasting substances sweet has not yet been determined. There is no logical unification of the many relations between chemical constitution and taste and smell. It is for this reason, perhaps, as much as any other, that the experimental study of taste and smell has been retarded.

REFERENCES

1. Abrahams, H., D. Krakauer, and K. M. Dallenbach. Gustatory adaptation to salt. *Amer. J. Psychol.*, 1937, *49*, 462–469.
2. Adrian, E. D. Olfactory reactions in the brain of the hedgehog. *J. Physiol.*, 1942, *100*, 459–473.
3. Allen, W. F. Effect on respiration, blood pressure, and carotid pulse of various inhaled and insufflated vapors when stimulating one cranial nerve and various combinations of cranial nerves. *Amer. J. Physiol.*, 1929, *88*, 117–129.
4. Allen, W. F. Olfactory and trigeminal conditioned reflexes in dogs. *Amer. J. Physiol.*, 1937, *118*, 532–539.
5. Allen, W. F. Distribution of cortical potentials from insufflation of vapors into the nostrils and from stimulation of olfactory bulbs and pyriform lobe. *Amer. J. Physiol.*, 1943, *139*, 553–555.

6. Allison, V. C., and S. H. Katz. An investigation of stenches and odors for industrial purposes. *J. Indus. Eng. Chem.*, 1919, *11*, 336–338.
7. Blakeslee, A. F., and T. H. Salmon. Genetics of sensory thresholds: individual taste reactions for different substances. *Proc. Nat. Acad. Sci.*, 1935, *21*, 84–90.
8. Cameron, A. T. The relative sweetness of sucrose, glucose, and fructose. *Trans. Roy. Soc. Can.*, 1943, *37*, 11–27.
9. Crocker, E. C. *Flavor.* New York: McGraw-Hill, 1945.
10. Crozier, W. J. Chemoreception. In *Handbook of General Experimental Psychology.* C. Murchison, Ed. Worcester, Mass.: Clark University Press, 1934, pp. 987–1036.
11. Dimmick, F. L. The investigation of the olfactory qualities. *Psychol. Rev.*, 1927, *34*, 321–335.
12. Elsberg, C. A., and I. Levy. The sense of smell. I. A new and simple method of quantitative olfactometry. *Bull. Neurol. Inst.*, 1935, *4*, 5–19.
13. Elsberg, C. A., I. Levy, and E. D. Brewer. The trigeminal effects of odorous substances. *Bull. Neurol. Inst.*, 1935, *4*, 270–285
14. Engel, R. Experimentelle Untersuchungen über die Abhängigkeit der Lust und Unlust von der Reizstarke beim Geschmackssinn. *Arch. ges. Psychol.*, 1928, *64*, 1.
15. Fair, G. M., and W. F. Wells. The air-dilution method of odor determination in water analysis. *J. Amer. Water Works Assoc.*, 1934, *26*, 1670–1677.
16. Findley, A. E. Further studies of Henning's system of olfactory qualities. *Amer. J. Psychol.*, 1924, *35*, 436–445.
17. Hahn, H., and H. Gunther. Über die Reize und die Reizbedingungen des Geschmackssinnes. *Pflug. Arch.*, 1932, *231*, 48–67.
18. Hahn, H. Die adaptation des Geschmackssinnes. *Z. Sinnesphysiol.*, 1934, *65*, 8–145.
19. Hänig, D. P. Zur Psychophysik des Geschmackssinnes. *Phil. Studien,* 1901, *17*, 576–623.
20. Hartridge, H. Importance of taste and smell in nutrition. *J. Physiol.*, 1945, *103*, 34P–35P.
21. Henning, H. *Der Geruch.* Leipzig: Barth, 1924.
22. Holway, A. H., and L. Hurvich. Differential gustatory sensitivity to salt. *Amer. J. Psychol.*, 1937, *49*, 37–48.
23. Holway, A. H., and L. Hurvich. On the psychophysics of taste. I. Pressure and area as variants. *J. Exper. Psychol.*, 1938, *23*, 191–198.
24. Jensen, K. Differential reactions to taste and temperature stimuli in newborn infants. *Genet. Psychol. Monog.*, 1932, *12*, 361–479.
25. Jerome, E. A. Olfactory thresholds measured in terms of stimulus pressure and volume. *Arch. Psychol.*, 1942, No. 274.
26. Kiesow, F. Schmeckversuche an einzelnen papillen. *Phil. Studien,* 1898, *14*, 591–615.
27 Liggett, J. R. An experimental study of the olfactory sensitivity of the white rat. *Genet. Psychol. Monog.*, 1928, *3*, 1–64.
28. Lashley, K. S., and R. W. Sperry. Olfactory discrimination after destruction of the anterior thalamic nuclei. *Amer. J. Physiol.*, 1943, *139*, 446–450.
29. Luciani, L. *Human Physiology.* Vol. 4, *Sense Organs.* New York: Macmillan, 1917.
30. MacDonald, M. K. An experimental study of Henning's system of olfactory qualities. *Amer. J. Psychol.*, 1922, *33*, 535–553.

31. Moncrieff, R. W. *The Chemical Senses.* New York: John Wiley, 1946.

32. Pfaffmann, C. Apparatus and technique for gustatory experimentation. *J. Gen. Psychol.*, 1935, *12*, 446–447.

33. Pfaffmann, C. Differential responses of the new-born cat to gustatory stimuli. *J. Genet. Psychol.*, 1936, *49*, 61–67.

34. Pfaffmann, C. Gustatory afferent impulses. *J. Cell. Comp. Physiol.*, 1941, *17*, 243–252.

35. Poucher, W. A. *Perfumes and Cosmetics.* New York: Van Nostrand, 1923.

36. Razran, H. S., and C. J. Warden. The sensory capacity of the dog as studied by the conditioned reflex method (Russian schools). *Psychol. Bull.*, 1929, *26*, 202–222.

37. Richter, C. P. Self-regulatory functions. *The Harvey Lectures*, 1942, Series *38*, 63–103.

38. Richter, C. P., and A. MacLean. Salt-taste thresholds of humans. *Amer. J. Physiol.*, 1939, *126*, 1–6.

39. Shore, L. E. A contribution to our knowledge of taste sensations. *J. Physiol.*, 1892, *13*, 191–217.

40. Skramlik, E. V. Die Physiologie des Geruchs und Geschmackssinnes. *Handbuch der Physiologie der niederen Sinne,* Bd. 1. Leipzig: Thieme, 1926.

41. Swann, H. G. The function of the brain in olfaction. I. Olfactory discrimination and an apparatus for its test. *J. Comp. Psychol.*, 1934, *15*, 229–241.

42. Wedell, C. H. Taste sensitivity of the white rat. *J. Comp. Psychol.*, 1936, *21*, 233–244.

43. Zwaardemaker, H. Prüfung des Geruchssinnes und der Geruche. In *Handbuch der biologisches Arbeitsmethoden.* R. Abderhalden, Ed. Abt. V, Teil 7, Heft 3, 1920.

Chapter 11

Studying Proprioception

W. D. Neff[1]

We maintain an upright posture, we alter this posture and move about in a coordinated manner, and we are aware of our postural attitudes and of our movements. Our ability to make these postural and locomotor adjustments and our awareness of what we do are dependent upon the activity of several of our sensory systems, principally, vision, touch, and *proprioception.* Of these three, proprioception is of primary importance.

The proprioceptive system is made up of two major parts: (*a*) the *kinesthetic division,* which includes end organs or *proprioceptors* in the muscles and tendons, the peripheral nerves which connect the proprioceptors with the central nervous system, and the related nerve tracts and centers in the central nervous system; and (*b*) the *vestibular division,* which includes the proprioceptors in the non-auditory part of the inner ear and the associated neural structures.

In reviewing methods of studying proprioception it is important to bear in mind that activity of the proprioceptive system, unlike that of the other sensory systems, is characterized by a lack of conscious experience. Postural and locomotor adjustments are carried out to a large extent on a reflex level. We shall find, therefore, that methods involving discriminatory responses, e.g., psychophysical methods, will not be of such fundamental importance as they are in studying vision, hearing, or any of the other senses. Instead, we shall see that most of our present knowledge about proprioception has come from experiments in which the activity of end organs or connecting nervous structures was examined directly or from experiments in which the reflex responses of individual muscles or muscle groups were carefully recorded and analyzed.

[1] Assistant Professor of Psychology, University of Chicago.

METHODS USED IN STUDYING KINESTHESIS

Anatomical Methods

The proprioceptors, which are stimulated by the activity of the muscles of the body, were discovered by the anatomists of the eighteenth and nineteenth centuries through histological techniques. Three main kinds of receptors were isolated and described: (1) encapsulated nerve endings (Pacinian corpuscles), located in the sheaths of muscles and tendons; (2) muscle spindles, which lie within voluntary muscles and end upon individual muscle fibers;[2] and (3) Golgi tendon organs, which are found at the juncture of muscle fibers and tendons. See Fig. 1. Free nerve endings may also be stimulated by muscular movement and thus serve a kinesthetic function. It is usually suggested, however, that these endings mediate pain.

Discovery of histological structures which, because of their location in or near muscles or tendons and their connection with nerve endings, appeared to be the sensory end organs stimulated by movement of the muscles was suggestive, but additional evidence was needed to establish the true nature of these receptor-like structures.

Sherrington [29] showed that the muscle spindles were supplied by sensory nerve fibers. By cutting the motor roots of peripheral spinal nerves of experimental animals, he caused all motor fibers to a given muscle of the lower limb to degenerate. He then examined the muscle spindles and their nervous connections under the microscope and found that every spindle still was supplied by sound, undegenerated nerve fibers. These fibers could have come only from the dorsal spinal roots, which are the paths for sensory fibers entering the cord. Similar techniques were used to show that the Golgi tendon organs and Pacinian corpuscles are innervated by sensory nerve fibers.

The anatomical studies which have been described provided no direct evidence of the *function* of the proprioceptive system; however, they did provide evidence upon which shrewd inferences could be based, and they paved the way for studies using methods by which the function of the kinesthetic system could be directly examined.

Selective Ablation

In any dynamic system where many parts act together, information concerning the function of a part or of the whole minus that part can

[2] Two types of muscle spindle endings have been described, "annulospiral" and "flower spray" [14, p. 8].

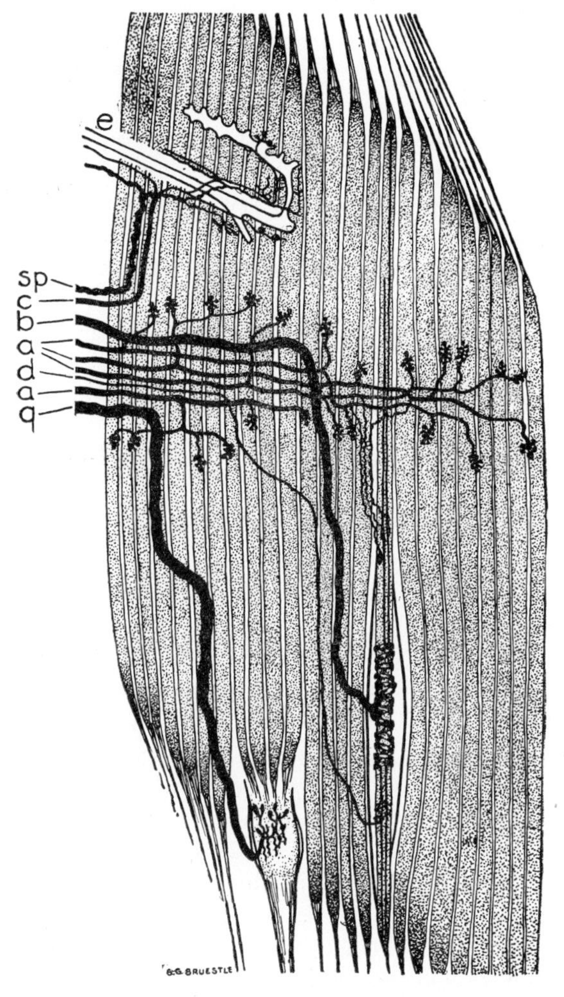

Fig. 1. Denny-Brown's diagram illustrating the sensory and motor innervation of a group of 23 mammalian muscle fibers.

The motor innervation comes from 4 fibers: *a, a, a, a*; the muscle spindle is made up of 3 intrafusal fibers, each one innervated by branches of motor nerve fibers *a, a, a, a*. The spindle has one large annulospiral ending, *b*, and a single flower spray ending connected with the nervous system by a fiber of relatively small diameter, *d*. There is a single Golgi tendon organ, *g*, and a sympathetic plexus, *sp*, accompanied by a small myelinated pain fiber, *c*, from the blood vessel, *e*. (From Fulton [14], by courtesy of the Oxford University Press.)

be obtained by destroying the part and studying the activity of the remainder. Classic examples of the use of selective ablation may be found in experiments of Sherrington, Magnus, Fulton, and their coworkers.[3] Their investigations, although concerned chiefly with analysis of the postural and locomotor reflexes, produced a major portion of the knowledge which we now possess of the kinesthetic system.

To illustrate how the selective-ablation technique is used, we may describe briefly an experiment by Pi-Suñer and Fulton [25]. These investigators were interested in the reflex coordination of the movements of the front and hind limbs in quadripedal locomotion. In order to study one aspect of the problem, i.e., how impulses set up in the proprioceptors of hind-limb muscles affect the posture of the fore limbs, they limited the functional parts of the system under examination as follows:

1. Voluntary control of limb movement was eliminated by decerebrating[4] the experimental animals (cats).

2. Reflexes initiated by cutaneous stimulation were ruled out by cutting the appropriate sensory nerves.

3. The exact manner of stimulation of individual muscles or muscle groups in the hind limbs was brought under control by destroying the nerve supply to the other muscles and by dissecting out those to be stimulated. Some muscles were detached from their tendons, and stimulation was applied artificially.

It was found that, when certain proprioceptors in the quadriceps muscles of one hind limb were stimulated in a manner similar to that which occurs during flexion of the knee joint, reflex responses occur in the other three limbs, so that the fore limb of the opposite side is flexed and the fore limb of the same side and the opposite hind limb are extended. This reflex pattern is at once suggestive of movements which occur during locomotion in the quadriped. By a number of experiments such as this one it has been shown that the series of progressive movements which constitute locomotion are in large part dependent upon reflex responses set off by stimulation of muscle proprioceptors.

Electrical Stimulation and Recording

Kinesthetic receptors and their nervous connections were discovered by anatomical methods; individual reflex arcs and integrated patterns

[3] Summaries of these experiments may be found in 14, pp. 51–179, and 10.

[4] A decerebrate animal is one in which the brain stem has been transected, usually at a level between the vestibular nuclei and the superior colliculi.

of reflexes were found and carefully examined by means of selective ablation. Exact analysis of the function of individual parts of the system, e.g., isolated receptor units, had to await the invention of suitable methods of stimulating and recording action. Development of such methods has closely paralleled the development of electronic instruments.

An outstanding example of the application of the electrical recording method in the study of proprioception is the experiment in which Matthews [22] distinguished four kinds of receptors corresponding to the four kinds of endings which had formerly been described by the anatomists. Matthews isolated a muscle and its sensory nerve in the limb of a cat and then, under the dissecting microscope, used sharpened needles to divide the nerve into separate bundles of fibers and to destroy these bundles one by one. After each bundle had been cut, electrodes were placed on the nerve central to the lesion, so that the point at which the fibers were cut was between the electrodes and the muscle; the muscle was then stretched, and the electrical response of the intact nerve fibers recorded. This procedure, namely, redividing the nerve and sectioning successive bundles, was repeated until stretching of the muscle gave rise to a single rhythmic discharge in the fibers remaining uncut. The response thus finally obtained was from a single kinesthetic receptor in the muscle. By varying the nature of the stimulating conditions and carefully analyzing the electrically recorded responses, Matthews was able to show that different kinds of proprioceptors in the muscles and tendons may be distinguished, not only on anatomical but also on functional grounds.

Clinical Methods

Results of histological, ablation, and electrical studies on experimental animals have been corroborated by clinical studies of man. The disturbances of movement in locomotor ataxia were described as early as 1851 [26] and were later shown to be due to degeneration of dorsal spinal roots and nerve tracts in the dorsal part of the spinal cord. Later clinicians, on the basis of postmortem examination of the central nervous system and peripheral nerve endings in the muscles of tabes dorsalis patients, reported atrophy of the kinesthetic end organs and the sensory fibers innervating them.

Innumerable studies of the symptoms resulting from lesions of the spinal cord in man have been made. The classical syndrome resulting from lateral hemisection of the spinal cord at the cervical level was first described by Brown-Séquard on the basis of his observations of patients with spinal lesions. The Brown-Séquard syndrome consists of homolateral loss of voluntary movement and *kinesthesis* and contralateral loss of thermal, pressure, and pain sensibility caudal to the lesion. The clinical studies have been of value both in tracing the central kinesthetic pathways and in clarifying the role of kinesthesis in reflex activity.

Psychophysical Methods

Since the time of Fechner there have been countless experiments on the discrimination of lifted weights. Although the judgments required are based principally upon kinesthetic cues, these weight-discrimination studies have contributed far more to the development of psychophysical methodology than to an understanding of the kinesthetic system. The exception to this generalization is a series of investigations conducted recently in which the effect of cortical lesions on discrimination of lifted weights was studied [27, 28]. To summarize the results of these studies briefly, it was found that partial destruction of the parietal lobes produces only transient defect in ability to discriminate lifted weights; total destruction, a permanent defect. Comparison of monkey, chimpanzee, and man indicates an increase in corticalization of the function in question as the phylogenetic scale is ascended.

METHODS USED IN STUDYING VESTIBULAR FUNCTIONS

For many thousands of years man must have known that experiences such as loss of equilibrium, dizziness, and nausea are aroused when the body is subjected to certain kinds of motion, such as the pendulum-like movements of a swing, the undulations of a boat, or the gyrations of the dance. Nevertheless, he did not discover until 1824 that the inner ear contains specialized receptors which are stimulated by the position or movement of the head. At that time Fluorens showed, in a series of experiments on birds and rabbits, that destruction of the semicircular canals produces severe defects in the ability of the experimental animal to maintain equilibrium and to make coordinated movements. Later experimenters corroborated Fluorens' results, and during the next 100 years more than 1500 reports of studies on the vestibular system were published [16].

It is obviously impossible to give even a brief description of all the methods employed in these studies. We shall, therefore, group the

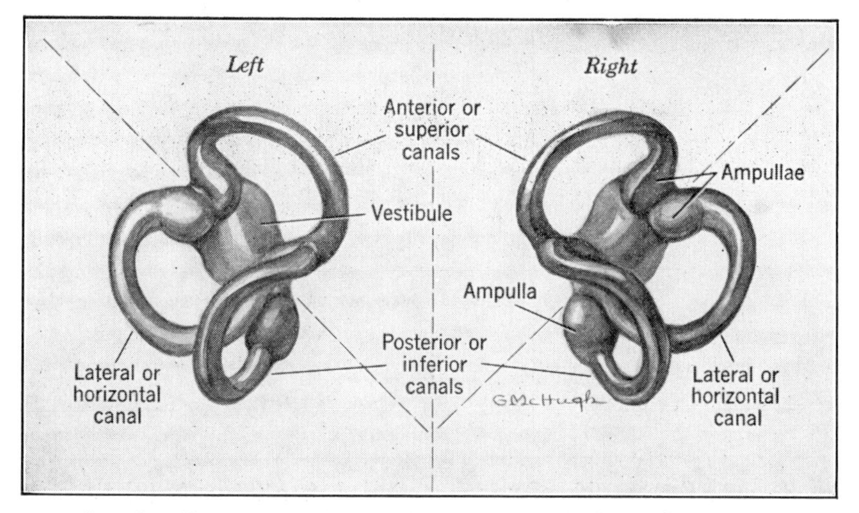

Fig. 2. The semicircular canals as seen from behind and above.

The distance between the two sets of canals is not to scale. Note that the three canals on one side lie in planes at approximately right angles to one another and that the following pairs of canals lie in approximately the same planes: (*a*) the lateral canals, (*b*) the right anterior and the left posterior, and (*c*) the left anterior and the right posterior.

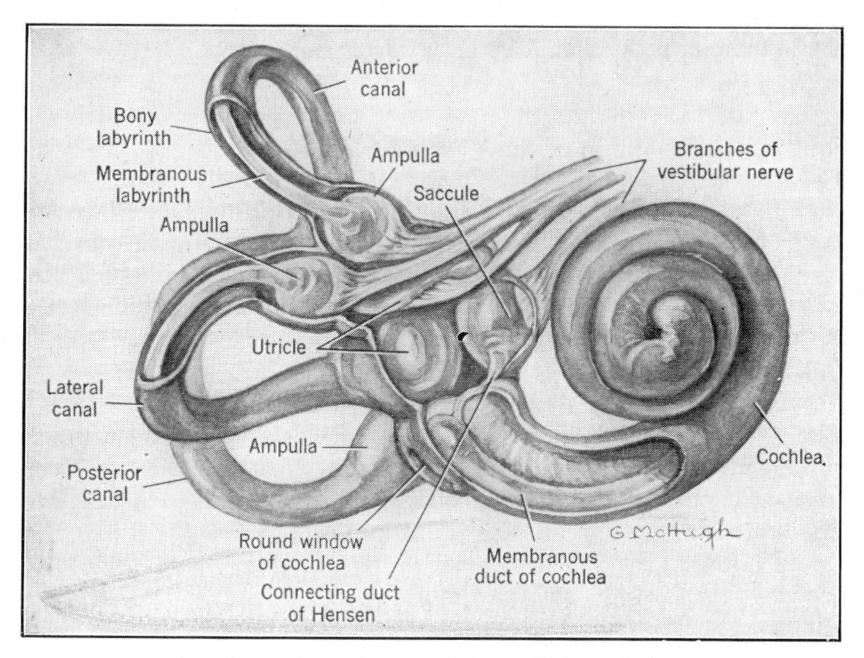

Fig. 3. A lateral view of the right labyrinth.

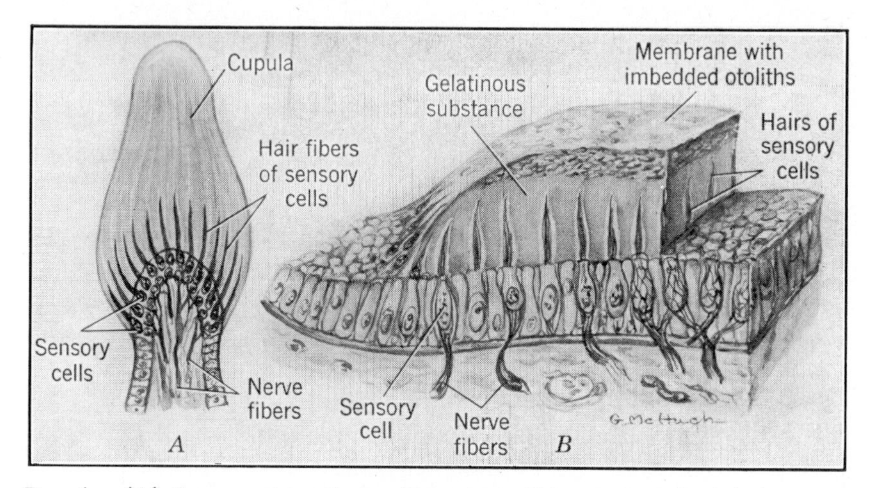

Fig. 4. (A) Cross-section of ampullar crista. (After Kolmer.) (B) Macula in three-dimensional cross-section. (After Kolmer.)

methods under three main headings—*methods of stimulation, methods of recording and analyzing responses,* and *ablation methods*—and we shall give representative examples of each class. First, however, the structure of the vestibular receptors and the probable functions of the individual parts should be briefly mentioned.

Structure and Function of the Vestibular Receptors

The vestibular[5] portion of the inner ear labyrinth includes the semicircular canals, the utricle, and the saccule; the remaining part, the cochlea, contains the receptors for hearing. The vestibular receptor cells are found in the ampullar cristae of the canals and in the maculae or otolith organs of the utricle and saccule. See Figs. 2, 3, and 4.

The most generally accepted view at the present time is that the cristae of the semicircular canals are the chief receptors for rotary movement, the effective stimulus being angular acceleration or deceleration. Continued rotation at constant velocity ceases to be effective. The utricular maculae are the primary receptors for position of the

[5] The vestibule of the labyrinth is the cavity containing the utricle and saccule. By common usage, however, the vestibular part of the inner ear has come to mean not only the utricle and saccule, but also the semicircular canals which open directly into the vestibule. Likewise the vestibular part of the 8th cranial nerve includes the fibers innervating the saccule, utricle, and semicircular canals, i.e., the non-auditory fibers.

head and may also be the most important receptors for rectilinear acceleration and deceleration, although the relative roles of the semicircular canals and the utricle in rectilinear motion have yet to be definitely established. Furthermore, there is evidence that the semicircular canals may play a secondary role in static stimulation and that the utricle may be stimulated by marked angular acceleration.[6] The function of the saccular maculae is uncertain. If they serve as proprioceptors, their part is apparently a minor one, since no obvious defect occurs as a result of their destruction. They have been suggested as receptors for vibration and for sounds (especially low frequencies), but experimental evidence in support of these suggestions is lacking.

Methods of Stimulation

POSITION. The problem of stimulating the receptors for position of the head is simple; the head is merely held fixed in various positions. Avoidance of stimulation of other receptors is not so simple. Time must elapse after any change in position in order that stimulation due to motion will have ceased. Care must also be taken to eliminate stimulation of muscle proprioceptors, because the reflex responses aroused by labyrinth position are also affected by the other proprioceptors, especially those in the neck, which give rise to reflex responses of limb and trunk muscles. Visual and cutaneous stimulation must likewise be avoided. Several techniques have been devised to eliminate stimulation of these other receptors. Plaster casts enclosing the shoulders, neck, and head are sometimes used to keep the relative position of head, neck, and body constant. Tilt boards and other mechanical devices make possible accurate control of the subject's position and minimize the stimulation of receptors other than those being investigated. Visual stimulation can be eliminated by blindfolding or, in experimental animals, by destroying the eyes. In some

[6] One of the tasks which early experimenters set for themselves was to discover the function of each separate part of the vestibular end organ. Looking back, we are better able to appreciate the difficulty of their problem and to understand the controversies which often resulted. It seems clear, when we sum up all the evidence, that one part of the system may be the primary receptor for a particular kind of stimulation (e.g., the horizontal canals for rotation in their plane), but the same receptor or set of receptors may also supplement the function of other parts for other kinds of stimuli and may be supplemented by other parts in turn (e.g., the horizontal canals may be stimulated by rotation in other planes or by linear acceleration, and the utricles may be stimulated by rapid rotation in the horizontal plane).

experiments nerve impulses arising in proprioceptors other than those of the labyrinth have been excluded by appropriate lesions in the nervous system.

ROTATION. The methods of rotation which have been devised vary in complexity from simply instructing the human subject to whirl around rapidly a number of times to elaborate apparatus designed to regulate accurately rate of angular acceleration, velocity, and plane of rotation. For most experimental purposes the rotator must possess several additional features. Smoothness in starting and stopping is often a requisite. In experiments where the subject is required to make discriminatory responses to vestibular cues, all other cues—visual, auditory, tactual, and kinesthetic—must be eliminated. The noise of the motor or other driving mechanism is usually kept constant under all conditions of operation through the use of suitable clutch and brake devices. Control of other extraneous cues is obtained both by design of the rotator and arrangement of the experimental situation.

The Bárány chair, which has been widely used for clinical testing, is simply a straight-back chair mounted on a rotating platform in somewhat the same manner as a barber's chair. A headrest is provided to keep the head position fixed. The typical procedure is to rotate the subject 10 times in 20 seconds. Because the chair is usually rotated by hand, control of acceleration and rate of rotation is only approximate.

For more accurate experimental work many elaborate devices have been constructed for rotating both experimental animals and human subjects. Dunlap [9] designed a rotator with which smooth, constant acceleration and deceleration and a constant maximum speed may be obtained. See Fig. 5. The rate of acceleration and deceleration and the speed of rotation are measured on a kymograph record.

Dodge carried on a series of careful experiments on thresholds of rotation, habituation to rotation, and the effect of rotation on eye movements [4, 5, 6]. In the course of these experiments he developed a rotator with which he was able to control and measure angular displacement (i.e., number of degrees of rotation), angular acceleration, and angular velocity. See Fig. 6.

For the purpose of testing the susceptibility of military personnel to motion sickness, several investigators have recently designed modified versions of the Bárány chair. Modification has been in the direction of simulating the forms of motion encountered in flying or on ships. A chair designed by Travis [38] is operated from a multiple harmonic cam, which is driven at a constant rate by an electric motor. The cam pattern is such that during one revolution of the chair seven different rates of acceleration and one period of rest are produced.

A somewhat different apparatus used in experiments by Spiegel [33] is constructed so that during each rotation the head is tilted either forward or to the side, thus producing continuous stimulation of the vestibular receptors even when rate of rotation is constant.

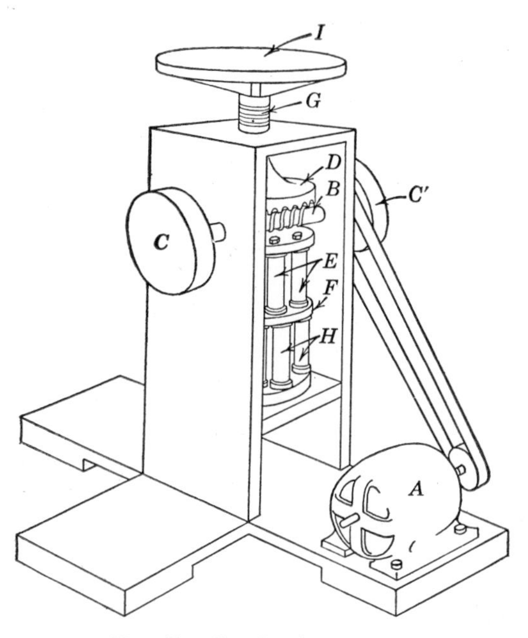

Fig. 5. The Dunlap rotator.

The motor (*A*) drives the horizontal shaft (*B*), which carries the flywheels (C) and (C'). Rotation of the shaft (*B*) drives the worm-wheel (*D*), which is attached to the gang of magnets (*E*). When electric current is applied to the magnets (*E*), they act as a clutch and "pick up" the iron disk armature (*F*), which is attached to the vertical shaft (G). The vertical shaft is thereby set into motion. The amount of "slip" of the clutch is determined by the load and by the amperage of current applied to the magnets. Acceleration may thus be controlled. To stop the rotation of the vertical shaft, the current to the clutch magnets (*E*) is interrupted, and current is applied to the set of magnets (*H*) which are firmly fastened to the framework of the apparatus. Magnets (*H*), therefore, act as a brake, the rate of deceleration depending upon the current applied. A chair or platform may be bolted to the platform (*I*). (After Dunlap [9].)

Linear motion, like angular, may be readily obtained through the subject's own movements, e.g., walking, running, falling, or rising. For experimental purposes, however, apparatus is required which makes possible control of velocity, acceleration, and the direction of movement with relation to the axes of the head. Elimination of non-vestibular cues is, of course, a factor in many experiments.

One of the simplest methods of obtaining approximately linear acceleration which can be accurately measured is by use of a swing, because a swing behaves according to the principles of motion governing a simple pendulum. The swing technique was widely used during World War II in experiments on motion sickness. A typical arrangement consists of a carriage suspended so that the distance from the overhead bar to the swing seat is about 14 feet. To insure stimulation of the same receptors in all subjects, an exact position of the head

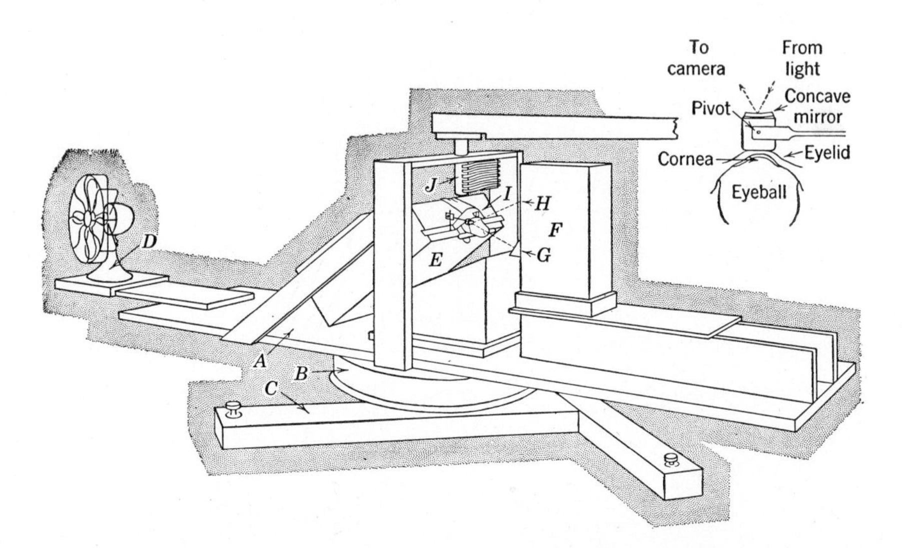

Fig. 6. Dodge-Wendt rotator and eye-movement recording apparatus.

The platform (*A*) and the equipment which it carries are mounted on an automobile wheel (*B*) and rotate on the bearing of the wheel. The platform may be levelled by means of the adjustable base (*C*). The rotator is driven by the electric fan (*D*). A brake applied to the rim of the wheel (*B*) controls starting and stopping. When the apparatus is used for animal experiments, the animal is restrained in the box (*E*) and its head held fixed by a head-holder. A photokymograph (*F*) may be mounted on the platform and the animal's eye movements recorded by directing a beam of light from (*G*) onto the concave mirror which rests on the closed eyelid, as shown in the insert at the upper right. The light reflects back to a vertical slit at (*H*) and produces a line upon the moving film of the photokymograph. Head movements may also be recorded by means of a light beam directed upon a concave mirror attached to the head at (*I*). Electrical circuits are led to the platform through the slip-ring contacts at (*J*). (See reference [39].)

is obtained through the use of a headrest. In experiments using this apparatus subjects were swung through an arc of 150 degrees for a period of 20 minutes or until vomiting occurred [17].

A "wave-machine," so named because it was designed to simulate the wave-like linear motion of boats and planes, has also been used in experiments on motion sickness [1]. This machine consists of a closed cab set in a vertical shaft so that it may be raised and lowered by hydraulic pressure. Linear motion in the vertical direction is produced by this elevator-like apparatus. Acceleration, velocity, and amplitude of movement can be exactly controlled and measured.

In still other war researches experimenters have produced vestibular stimulation by movements of a Link trainer,[7] by maneuvers of a real plane in flight, and by rotation on a human centrifuge [20, 3, 15]. The motion to which subjects were subjected in these experiments often possessed both angular and linear acceleratory components.

CALORIC STIMULATION. The vestibular receptors may be stimulated by the injection of hot or cold water into the external auditory canal. Apparently temperature changes set up convection currents in the endolymph, the fluid which fills the membranous labyrinth, and these currents stimulate the receptor cells. By means of the caloric-stimulation technique the labyrinth of each ear can be separately stimulated. With the head in the normal upright position, the vertical canals are affected by caloric stimulation. The horizontal canals may be stimulated by tilting the head backward through 60 degrees. Injection of cold water (about 68 degrees Fahrenheit) produces eye nystagmus with the quick phase toward the side opposite that stimulated. Injection of hot water (about 112 degrees Fahrenheit) produces nystagmus with the quick phase toward the stimulated side.

Several methods of producing caloric stimulation have been used. Early investigators syringed the ear or allowed water to flow into it through a tube connected with a container suspended above the subject's head. Large doses of water (100 to 1000 cubic centimeters) at either very high or very low temperatures were used. It has since been found that a few cubic centimeters of water at temperatures only slightly above or below body temperature provide effective stimulation. When these very small quantities are used, more care must be taken to insure proper injection. A syringe with a blunt needle is usually used, and the stream of water is directed against the posterior superior wall of the external auditory canal.

The caloric method of stimulation has been used mainly for diagnostic purposes by clinicians. Most experimental studies utilizing this method have been concerned with the mechanism whereby the injection of hot or cold water into the external auditory meatus excites the vestibular receptors.

MECHANICAL STIMULATION. One aim of the many methods that have been invented to stimulate the proprioceptors of the inner ear has been to control conditions so that different receptors can be stimulated individually; e.g., it is desirable to be able to stimulate the crista of one

[7] A device modeled after the cockpit of a plane and mounted so that it can be rotated about its vertical axis and tilted about both the horizontal and longitudinal axes.

horizontal canal or the otolith organ of one utricle. Ewald [12] accomplished this by devising a technique to produce pressure changes in the endolymph of the labyrinths of experimental animals. He drilled a small hole in the wall of one of the semicircular canals and over this sealed a metal cylinder 1.4 millimeters in diameter and 9 millimeters in length. The cylinder contained a tapered piston by means of which pressure could be applied to the membranous labyrinth and the intralabyrinthine fluid. Using this "pneumatic-hammer," Ewald was able to stimulate each of the canals individually and to study the response made by the animal to both compression and decompression. It was assumed that compression produced movement of the endolymph toward the ampulla (ampullopetal flow), and decompression, movement away from the ampulla (ampullofugal flow). When the right horizontal canal was stimulated, it was found that compression caused turning of the head and eyes to the left, i.e., away from the side stimulated; decompression caused turning to the right or toward the stimulated side. The intensity of stimulation produced by Ewald's technique was probably greater than any resulting from natural stimulation, such as rotation under ordinary conditions.

In human patients suffering from otosclerosis, an otological disorder accompanied by ankylosis of the stapes[8] in the oval window and a consequent reduction of hearing, an artificial window (fenestrum) is sometimes made surgically in the wall of the horizontal semicircular canal. The success of the fenestration operation depends upon the artificial window remaining open, i.e., covered only by a membranous flap. In many cases it is closed by regrowth of bone. One test to discover whether the window has remained open is to apply pressure to it by pressing with the index finger at the appropriate point in the external auditory canal. If the fenestrum is still open, nystagmic eye movements can be produced.

Electrical stimulation. Both direct and alternating currents have been used to stimulate the vestibular receptors of human subjects and experimental animals. When direct current is employed, a typical arrangement in the intact subject is to place the stimulating electrode on the mastoid bone and the neutral electrode on some other part of the body, such as the muscles of the neck. If only one ear is stimu-

[8] The stapes is one of the three small bones (ossicles) which conduct sound from the ear drum to the cochlea. The footplate of the stapes is sealed into the oval window of the cochlea by cartilaginous tissue, which allows the stapes to rock back and forth about its heel and thus transmit vibrations to the fluids within the cochlea. In otosclerosis the normally elastic tissue around the footplate of the stapes becomes stiff and hard and so anchors the stapes firmly to the edges of the round window. It can then no longer transmit effectively to the cochlear fluids the vibrations produced by sound waves striking the ear drum.

lated in this manner, nystagmic eye movements are produced, with the fast phase toward the side of stimulation when the cathode is applied to the mastoid and away from the side of stimulation when the anode is applied. Alternating-current stimulation does not produce nystagmus but does give rise to rotation of the head away from the side stimulated.

What part of the vestibular system is stimulated by electric current has been a point of controversy. Some experimenters have suggested that the electric current induces movement of the endolymph; others, that it acts upon the sensory cells in the cristae or maculae; and still others, that it acts directly upon the fibers of the vestibular nerve. This uncertainty concerning the locus of stimulation has limited the usefulness of the method; nevertheless some experimenters have attempted to analyze the effects of stimulation of individual ampullae or maculae by applying electrodes to them and noting the resulting reflex responses. Most of the experimental evidence to date supports the view that electrical current applied to the walls of the labyrinth acts directly upon nerve fibers in the vestibular nerve.

Methods of Recording and Analyzing Responses

There are a number of different levels at which we may examine the response to stimulation of a sensory system. We may study:

1. The activity of the end organ or receptor.
2. The activity of the afferent nerve fibers, tracts, or centers.
3. The reflex responses of effectors.
4. The discriminatory responses, which in the human subject will usually be verbal reports and in lower animals will be overt learned responses, e.g., conditioned responses.

In experiments on vision, hearing, smell, taste, and the cutaneous senses, we depend heavily upon responses of the fourth type: the verbal reports of human subjects and the discriminatory responses of lower animals. In studying proprioception we usually make use of responses which fall in one of the first three classes. This, as we have already seen, was true in experiments on the kinesthetic system, and it is equally true in the case of the vestibular proprioceptive processes. The human subject can report an awareness of position or of movement of the head, but to what extent this awareness is the direct result of sensory impulses initiated in the vestibular receptors and to what extent it is the result of sensory impulses aroused in receptors of the muscles, viscera, and skin by the reflex responses brought about by vestibular stimulation is not clearly understood. Although the bulk of the experimental data points toward the importance of the sensory impulses reflexly aroused, there is some evidence for direct sensory connections from the vestibular receptors to higher nervous centers. The existence of such connections suggests, of course, the likelihood that part of our awareness of head position or movement results from the passage of impulses directly from the vestibular receptors to the brain.

ACTIVITY OF THE END ORGAN. Fluorens' discovery that the inner ear contains a sense organ which is stimulated by the position or movement of the head immediately led to speculation as to what parts of the inner ear are concerned and as to the manner in which the movement or position is translated into sensory nerve impulses. The anatomy of the inner ear was already known, and it is not surprising, in view of their triplane structure, that the semicircular canals were immediately seized upon as the principal receptors. The utricle and saccule were also suggested by some as additional end organs, the cochlea being excepted as a rule because of its known auditory function. Experiments in which ablation techniques were used or in which stimuli were applied directly to different parts of the labyrinth soon showed that the inferences based upon knowledge of structure were approximately correct—the proprioceptors of the inner ear were to be found in the ampullae of the canals and in the utricular maculae. As already noted, the function of the saccular maculae has not been established.

It was not so easy, however, to determine by experiment the nature of the intralabyrinthine events whereby head movement or position causes impulses to be set up in the eighth cranial nerve. Because of the microscopic size of the structures involved and the fact that in most animals they are completely encased in bone, direct observation or recording of activity within the labyrinth is almost impossible. For that reason, methods which have been developed to overcome these obstacles are of special interest.

Ewald, who is noted for the precise surgical techniques he employed in his studies of the vestibular labyrinth, introduced the "bridge method" in which he exposed a limited portion of the membranous canal of the pigeon by removing a short length of the surrounding bony canal [2, p. 43]. By introducing a minute amount of lampblack or other coloring matter into the endolymph of the canals, Ewald and other investigators using similar surgical procedures were able to observe, under the microscope, movements of the endolymph in the exposed part of the membranous labyrinth.

More recently Steinhausen [34, 35, 36] has developed a technique whereby not only endolymph movement but also, more important, movement of the cupula of the ampullar crista can be observed. Using the pike, which has rather large semicircular canals the outer walls of which are of cartilage rather than bone, he exposed an ampulla and part of the adjoining canal and injected a minute amount of Chinese ink into the endolymph. He was then able to observe and photograph movements of the cupula during rotary, caloric, and mechanical stimulation. Steinhausen's studies show that, when the canals are stimulated, the endolymph exerts pressure upon the cupula

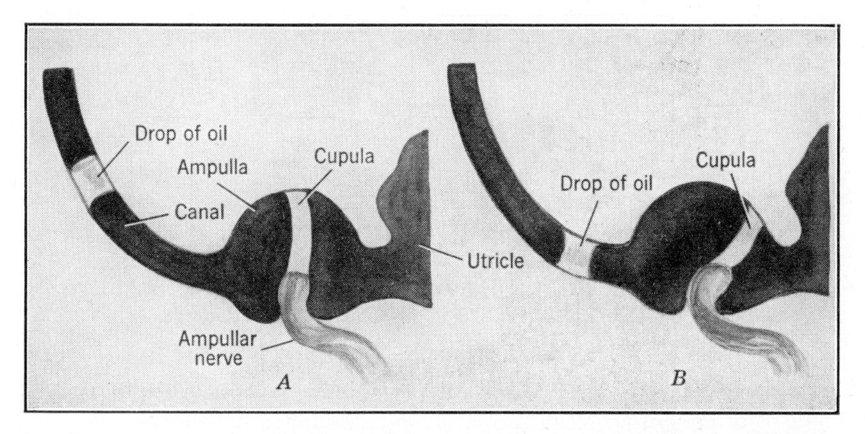

Fig. 7. Movement of cupula and endolymph during angular acceleration.

A. Position of cupula with the canal at rest. A drop of oil has been injected into the canal in order to obtain a record of fluid movement. *B.* Position of cupula during angular acceleration. The fluid in the canal has moved toward the ampulla, as indicated by the change in position of the drop of oil, and the cupula has been displaced toward the utricle by the fluid movement. (After Dohlman [8].)

and displaces it to one side or the other of the ampulla. See Fig. 7. It is apparently through this movement of the cupula and the resulting distortion of the sensory hair cells that the hydrodynamic changes produced in the endolymph are transformed into nerve impulses. The mechanism by which deformation of sensory hair cells stimulates the nerve endings is not known. In his experiments Steinhausen was also able to show that the movement of the cupula is that of a heavily damped elastic system having a natural period of about 20 seconds. This finding fits well with observations by many experimenters that nystagmus ceases after approximately 20 seconds of rotation at constant speed and that the period of postrotary nystagmus is of similar duration.

Neural activity. Connections of the vestibular labyrinth with the central nervous system were first traced by anatomical methods. More complete mapping of these connections and analysis of the activity going on in the nervous paths and centers under various conditions of stimulation have been made possible by electrical recording techniques.

One of the earliest studies of the electrical response of the vestibular nervous system was made by Mowrer [23]. With electrodes placed on the eighth nerve of the *painted terrapin,* he recorded action potentials during and after rotation of the animal on a turntable. He

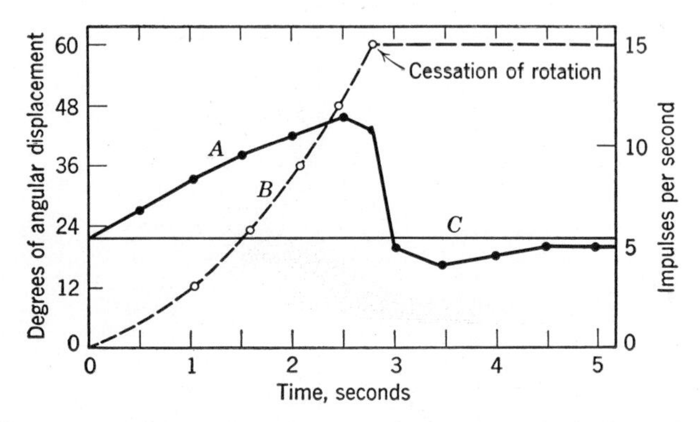

Fig. 8. Frequency of nerve impulses in a single nerve fiber from the ampulla of the left horizontal canal during stimulation by rotation.

The rate of angular acceleration was approximately 15 degrees per second per second. Curve A shows the frequency of discharge in impulses per second (read from scale at right). Curve B gives the degree of angular displacement from the resting positon (read from scale at left). The horizontal line C indicates the frequency of discharge with the labyrinth at rest. Direction of rotation was toward the side from which the recording was made. (From Löwenstein and Sand [21].)

reported that the action potentials lasted only a fraction of a second after rotation had ceased.

In later experiments Löwenstein and Sand used more refined techniques to record the impulses in a single nerve fiber from the ampulla of the horizontal canal of the *ray* [21]. They found a steady flow of impulses even when the labyrinth was at rest. The frequency of impulses increased during angular acceleration when the direction of rotation was toward the side being examined and decreased when the direction of rotation was toward the opposite side. Cessation of rotation was also reflected in the rate of discharge; and during rotation at a constant speed a steady state was reached within 20 to 30 seconds, after which the frequency remained at the same rate as that during rest. See Fig. 8.

Although anatomical methods have so far failed to reveal completely the paths followed by vestibular fibers between the end organs and the cortex, functional evidence indicates that direct connections do exist. Spiegel [30] found that convulsions can be produced in cats and dogs by stimulation of vestibular receptors if strychnine is applied to certain areas of the temporal lobes. No convulsions occur when strychnine is applied to other parts of the cortex. In other experiments Spiegel [31] recorded changes in the electrical activity of the cortex of the

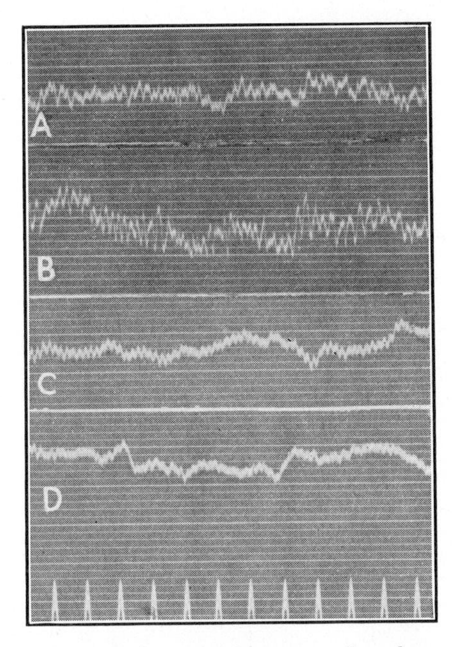

Fig. 9. The effect of vestibular stimulation on the electroencephalogram of the cat.

All records were taken during bulbocapnine catalepsy. The recording electrode was placed on the suprasylvian sulcus of the temporal lobe. Record *A* was taken with the head at rest, both labyrinths intact. The animal was then rotated 15 times; the change in the electroencephalogram after rotating is clearly shown in record *B*. Record C was taken with the animal at rest after destruction of both labyrinths. That no change in the electroencephalogram now occurs is shown by record *D*, taken after 20 rotations. (From original records of E. A. Spiegel.)

cat and monkey during stimulation of the labyrinth by rotation. See Fig. 9. That these changes are due to the flow of impulses directly from the labyrinth to the cortex by way of centers lower in the central nervous system, e.g., cerebellum and medulla, and not from stimulation of the eyes or of receptors in the muscles or viscera was demonstrated by a series of control experiments. Visually aroused activity was eliminated by covering the eyes and placing the animal in the dark. Reflex and voluntary activity of the muscles was excluded by the injection of curare and bulbocapnine.[9] Sensory impulses from the skeletal muscles and viscera were blocked by transecting the spinal cord in the upper cervical region and by cutting the vagus nerves. None of these control measures eliminated the changes in electrical response of the "vestibular area" of the cortex during rotation. On the other hand, no changes in electrical activity occurred during deep ether anesthesia, after bilateral labyrinthectomy, or after undercutting of the responsive cortical area.

Evidence such as that brought forth by Spiegel's experiments lends weight to the supposition that our awareness of head position and movement is in part, at least, due to nerve impulses flowing directly from the vestibular receptors to the brain.

REFLEX RESPONSES. Since there are a great many reflex responses resulting from stimulation of vestibular receptors, it is convenient to classify them in some systematic fashion. The following scheme represents a modification of one proposed by Dusser de Barenne [10]:

I. Positional reflexes: reflexes for which the adequate stimulus is the position of the head, not the movement occurring during attainment of that position.
   - A. Tonic reflexes: reflexes which maintain certain patterns of tonus in the musculature:
     1. Of eye muscles.
     2. Of neck muscles.
     3. Of limb and trunk muscles.
   - B. Righting reflexes: reflexes of neck muscles which restore normal position of head when it has been displaced.

II. Acceleratory reflexes: reflexes for which the adequate stimulus is angular or linear acceleration.
   - A. Reflexes resulting from angular acceleration (rotation):
     1. Of eye muscles.
     2. Of neck muscles.
     3. Of limb and trunk muscles.
     4. Of visceral muscles.
   - B. Reflexes resulting from linear acceleration:
     1. Of neck muscles.
     2. Of limb and trunk muscles.
     3. Of visceral muscles.

III. Artificially induced reflexes:
   - A. Reflexes resulting from caloric stimulation.
   - B. Reflexes resulting from mechanical stimulation.
   - C. Reflexes resulting from electrical stimulation.

Any of the three artificial stimuli may produce reflex responses of eye, neck, limb, trunk, and visceral muscles.

In many investigations experimenters have been satisfied to observe carefully the reflex responses produced by vestibular stimulation and

[9] Curare and bulbocapnine produce paralysis of the skeletal muscles, curare by blocking impulses to the muscles at the motor end plate, bulbocapnine by affecting motor centers in the central nervous system.

have not tried to make quantitative measurements. This was particularly true in the first exploratory experiments and even in most of the later studies of reflex responses of the neck, limb, and trunk muscles. In some instances, as in the experiments of Tait and McNally [37], measures of the extent and duration of movement have been desired, and techniques have therefore been developed to make these measurements. These two investigators used decerebrate frogs in which one or both hind legs were divided from the remainder of the body and head except for a connecting link, the sciatic nerve. The hind leg was then mounted so that the contractions of individual muscles could be recorded by means of a muscle lever. The head-body part of the preparation was placed on a tiltboard whose movement subjected the labyrinth to the stimulation of angular acceleration.

Direct observation of visceral muscle responses is impossible unless surgery is performed. The contractions of the stomach or of other parts of the gastrointestinal tract have been recorded by inserting a rubber balloon attached to a rubber tube, the other end of which is connected to a tambour recorder. The balloon is inflated after insertion so that it fills the cavity in which it rests. Contraction of the walls of the cavity will then exert pressure on the balloon, and the pressure on the enclosed air of the balloon-tube-tambour system will produce movement of the tambour diaphragm and of a recording lever attached to it. See Figs. 2 and 3, p. 396.

It is in the study of reflex responses of eye muscles to vestibular stimulation that the most elaborate recording and measuring techniques have been developed. To measure the tonic reflex movement of the eyes in human subjects, Benjamins designed a special pair of spectacle frames with cylindrical eyepieces [2, p. 221]. One of a pair of fine cross-wires is set so that it crosses two points marked by white paste on the anesthetized cornea. After a change in head position the angle through which the eye rotates is measured by adjusting the second cross-wire to include the new positions of the two points on the cornea.

Many different techniques—mechanical, photographic, and electrical—have been employed to record the nystagmic eye movements which occur during rotation. Dusser de Barenne and de Kleyn [11] recorded the movements of individual eye muscles of the rabbit. The apparatus which they used was so arranged that threads attached to each of the eye muscles operated separate levers, which recorded on the smoked paper of the kymograph. The animal was rotated about its longitudinal axis, and the reflex responses of each eye muscle were registered. By careful fixation of the head and proper design of the thread and lever system, all changes in tension on the threads as the result of rotation, except changes due to muscle contraction, were eliminated. The experimenters were able to demonstrate the reciprocal innervation of certain pairs of eye muscles.

The total movement of the intact eye during and after rotation is more often recorded than are the responses of the separate eye muscles. In some of the earliest attempts at such recording mechanical methods were used, but these were anything but satisfactory because they lacked sensitivity, annoyed the subject, and could easily have a distorting effect upon the response itself. These difficulties were overcome by the use of photographic methods. Among the first to devise a satisfactory technique of recording eye movements photographically were Dodge and Cline [7]. They took advantage of the facts that (*a*) the cornea of the eye readily reflects a light beam directed upon it and (*b*) the surface of the cornea bulges out from the spherical surface of the rest of the eyeball. Movement of the eyeball, therefore, results in changes in the angle of reflection of a beam directed upon the cornea. See Figs. 4 and 5, p. 407, and the accompanying description on p. 408. Although this technique was first used to study eye movements during reading, it was readily adapted to the study of the eye movements which result from stimulation of the labyrinth by rotation. For the latter purpose, however, it is usually desirable to photograph eye movements with the eyes closed and during rotation as well as afterward, and it is necessary to be able to distinguish between changes in the record which are caused by head movements and those caused by eye movements. These added requirements may be met by modifying the setup shown in Fig. 5, page 407, as follows. The eyelids are held shut by a clamp or by narrow strips of adhesive tape. A small, freely-pivoting wooden block on which is mounted a concave mirror is allowed to rest lightly against the eyelid directly over the cornea. See Fig. 6 insert. Movement of the cornea causes the block to rotate about its axis, the direction of rotation being opposite to that of cornea movement. A light beam is now directed on the mirror and reflected by it instead of the cornea. A similar concave mirror may also be mounted in fixed position on the head so as to reflect the beam from a second light onto the photographic record. With this double record deflections of the recorded eye-movement line which are produced by head movements may be detected. To record eye movements during rotation it is necessary to mount the light source, camera, and associated apparatus on the same rotating platform with the experimental subject. See Fig. 6.

Another photographic technique which has proved useful in the study of eye movements is to take pictures of the eye with a moving-picture camera. The successive frames of the film may then be examined, and, the rate at which the frames were exposed being known, a plot of movements per unit time can be made. In making such plots it is desirable to have a fixed reference point on the eyeball. This may be accomplished by fixing a small piece of reflecting material to the eyeball. Judd, who was one of the first to use this method, placed a small particle of China white, coated with paraffin to prevent irritation, on the eyeball in the region of the iris [19]. In order to have a record of all eye movements, even during the time between successive frames of a moving picture, some experimenters have used a dual camera recording system, in which a frame in one camera is being exposed at the time the film in the other is moving in preparation for exposure of the next frame.

Changes in electrical potential during eye movements have been recorded from electrodes placed near the eye, e.g., one on each temple for horizontal movements or one above and one below for vertical movements [18, 24]. These electrical records show a close correspondence to the eye-movement records obtained by photographic techniques.

Discriminatory responses. Although we do not yet know the relative importance of sensory impulses flowing directly from the vestibular receptors to higher centers and sensory impulses from kinesthetic receptors stimulated by the positional and acceleratory reflexes, we can nevertheless in our experimental investigations make use of sensory experiences accompanying vestibular stimulation. Several early investigators, such as Wells (1792), Erasmus Darwin (1801), and Purkinje (1820), described the sensory phenomena which could be noted introspectively during and after rotation. It remained, however, for Griffith (1920) and Dodge (1923) to furnish accurate introspective reports under carefully controlled conditions.

Griffith, aroused by the mistaken notion persisting in studies on the selection of aviation candidates during World War I that lack of sensitivity to rotation was an undesirable trait in such candidates, conducted careful laboratory studies in which he was able to demonstrate that *dizziness* is subject to habituation [16]. Experienced pilots or others who had been exposed repeatedly to rotatory motion were likely to show decreased responses during the typical test situation. Of less practical importance, perhaps, but of greater theoretical interest were his conclusions that the sensory experience which we call dizziness is the combination "of a large number of processes the most prominent of which are (1) kinesthesis from the eyes and neck and in the arms, (2) pressure from the region of the abdominal viscera, the chest, and head, and (3) certain vascular processes which supply an obscure background and which give to the whole experience a characteristic shading."

Dodge measured thresholds of rotation by having his experimental subjects report any change noticed in their position [6]. With rapid onset of rotation, he found the threshold to be about 2 degrees per second. In several studies Dodge obtained both introspective reports and records of eye movements under different conditions of stimulation by rotation. Although in some instances reports of awareness of onset or cessation of rotation coincided with appearance or disappearance of eye movements, this was not true under all stimulating conditions.

In addition to reports of awareness of movement and of dizziness, subjects have been asked to report feelings of discomfort and nausea and to make judgments about apparent movement of surrounding objects. Examples of experiments involving both these kinds of reports may be found in the work of aviation research groups during World War II. In a summary of experiments by several investigators Bard has listed the symptoms of motion sickness as occurring usually in the following sequence: "drowsiness, pallor, cold-sweating, nausea (usually ushered in by some degree of epigastric awareness), and vomiting (which may not occur)." He adds that "headache and dizziness are vague symptoms occurring only irregularly" and that true vertigo[10] and nystagmus are evoked only when there is angular acceleration.[11]

Graybiel, Clark, and associates, working at the Naval School of Aviation Medicine, Pensacola, Florida, have described two visual illusions reported by human subjects in whom vestibular stimulation was brought about by maneuvering a plane or Link trainer or by rotation on a human centrifuge. One, which they call the *oculogyral illusion,* occurs during angular acceleration and is therefore thought to result from stimulation of receptors in the semicircular canals. The second, named the *oculogravic illusion,* occurs when centrifugal force is acting and is thought to result from stimulation of the otolith organs. The oculogyral illusion consists of the apparent movement of a fixed object; the oculogravic illusion, of the apparent displacement of the object [3, 15].

It has been stated earlier that discriminatory responses of animals have seldom been used in the study of the vestibular system. Note should be taken, however, of experiments by Spiegel and Oppenheimer, in which they report obtaining a conditioned response in dogs to changes in position and to angular acceleration [32]. The animals were carefully fastened in position on a tilt-table or rotating platform.

[10] The sensation that the external world is revolving about oneself or that one's own body is revolving in space, when actually neither movement is taking place.

[11] Personal communication.

One leg was free to flex upon application of the unconditioned stimulus, shock. Conditioned responses to slow changes in position about the horizontal axis were established not only in the intact animal but also in animals in which the following surgical ablations were carried out: (*a*) section of the posterior columns and dorsal spinocerebellar tracts at the first or second cervical level, (*b*) destruction of both labyrinths, (*c*) combination of *a* and *b*. In animals in which operation *c* was performed, the experimenter concludes that the conditioned responses must have been based upon non-vestibular sensory impulses carried by the remaining ascending tracts of the spinal cord.

The conditioned responses to angular acceleration were established readily after section of the posterior and dorsal spinocerebellar tracts and paralysis of the eye, facial, and mastication muscles by local anesthetic. After bilateral labyrinthectomy, on the other hand, conditioned responses could not be obtained for a period of ½ to 2 months. Repeated training trials finally resulted in conditioned responses, first to rapid and eventually to slow rates of acceleration. Discriminatory reactions to direction, which were obtained in normal animals, could not be established in the labyrinthectomized dogs.

Because of their experimental findings, Spiegel and Oppenheimer question the adequacy of theories which account for the awareness of rotation entirely on the basis of sensory impulses from muscles whose contractions are reflexly produced upon vestibular stimulation. These results, in addition to those obtained by Spiegel in other experiments (see p. 307), suggest the need of further investigation of the direct connections of the vestibular receptors with higher nervous centers.

Ablation Methods

As in the study of kinesthesis, selective ablation has been of fundamental importance in the study of the vestibular system. It was the method employed by Fluorens in the classical experiments in which he firmly established the role of the semicircular canals in postural adjustment and coordinated movement [13]. Fluorens not only destroyed the whole of the vestibular system on one or both sides; in some experiments he sectioned individual canals and pairs of corresponding canals, e.g., both lateral canals or the anterior canal on one side and the posterior on the other.

Following the work of Fluorens ablation was the method most often used to analyze further the functions of the vestibular system. Surgical procedures differed widely, and the results often reflected the exactness or crudeness of the procedure. Knowledge of the vestibular system was nevertheless rapidly advanced by the experiments in which careful, refined techniques were employed.

Not only were the experimenter's surgical skill and carefulness important in the ablation experiments but also of significance was the type of animal used. In birds and fishes the canals, utricle, and saccule can be exposed easily, and individual parts separately destroyed or damaged. In the frog, the amphibian usually studied, the small size of the labyrinth makes destruction of separate parts extremely difficult. Nevertheless, several investigators, by using a dissecting microscope, have been able to render separate parts of the labyrinth non-functional by crushing or cauterizing them or by sectioning the nerve supply.

In mammals the labyrinth lies imbedded in the very hard portion of the temporal bone. Exposure and destruction of any part of the vestibular mechanism without damage to other parts are all but impossible. Furthermore, the position of the labyrinth is such that injury may be done to the cerebellum or to neck muscles, both of which are important in postural control. If unintentional damage is done to either vestibular or non-vestibular structures without the experimenter's knowledge, the results of ablation will be misinterpreted. Disagreement among many early experimenters using ablation techniques was often the result of differences in exactness of surgical procedure.

The ablation method has also been applied in studying the central nervous connections of the vestibular system. For example, in experiments on motion sickness, Bard has obtained results which throw new light upon the role of the cerebellum in controlling responses aroused by vestibular stimulation.[12] Tests were made of the vomiting responses of dogs subjected to swing stimulation before and after ablation of parts of the cerebellum. A typical animal vomited within 8 to 25 minutes in each of 11 test periods given at weekly intervals. After destruction of all the cerebellar cortex no vomiting occurred in 14 separate test periods, in each of which swinging was continued for 60 minutes, nor in one additional period of 2 hours. Similar results were obtained in other experiments in which only limited portions of the cerebellum were ablated.

SUMMARY

The proprioceptive system consists of a kinesthetic division and a vestibular division. Kinesthetic receptors, i.e., proprioceptors in the muscles and tendons, were first discovered through anatomical methods.

[12] Personal communication.

Selective ablation methods were then used to establish the functions of the different kinds of receptors and to investigate the role of kinesthesis in the control of posture and locomotion. With the development of electrical stimulation and recording methods it has been possible to make a more exact analysis of the functions of the receptors and nervous elements of the kinesthetic system.

Evidence from experimental studies on lower animals has been corroborated and supplemented by clinical studies of man. In a few instances psychophysical methods used in animal experiments or clinical investigations have added to our knowledge of kinesthesis. For the most part, however, methods requiring discriminatory responses have not been used.

The structures in the inner ear which make up the vestibular end organ had been described in detail by anatomists long before anyone suspected that they served as the receptors which are stimulated by position and movement of the head. Their function was first discovered by ablation methods. After this discovery progress in understanding the vestibular mechanisms depended mainly upon the development of methods of stimulation, methods of recording and analyzing responses, and improved ablation techniques.

The natural forms of stimulation of the vestibular receptors are position of the head, angular acceleration (rotation), and linear acceleration. In addition, these receptors may be stimulated artificially by caloric, mechanical, and electrical stimuli.

There are several levels at which we may record and analyze the response to vestibular stimulation. We may examine: (1) the activity of the receptor; (2) the activity of afferent nerve fibers, tracts, or centers; (3) the reflex responses of effectors; (4) the discriminatory responses of human subjects or of experimental animals. In most instances, experimenters have been interested in responses of the first three classes. A wide variety of mechanical, electrical, and photographic recording techniques has been developed. In some experiments, however, subjects have been instructed to report the least noticeable motion or to make judgments about the position and motion of objects in space or to describe such experiences as dizziness, vertigo, and nausea. In animals conditioned responses have been established to angular acceleration and to slow changes in position.

REFERENCES

1. Alexander, S. J., M. Cotzin, C. J. Hill, Jr., E. A. Ricciuti, and G. R. Wendt. Wesleyan University studies of motion sickness. I. The effects of variation of time intervals between accelerations upon sickness rates. *J. Psychol.*, 1945, *19*, 49–62.

2. Camis, M. *The Physiology of the Vestibular Apparatus.* (Translated from the Italian and annotated by R. S. Creed.) London: Oxford University Press, 1930.
3. Clark, B., and A Graybiel. Visually perceived movement caused by angular acceleration and by centrifugal force during flight (abstract). *Amer. Psychol.,* 1946, *1,* 238.
4. Dodge, R. The latent time of compensatory eye-movements. *J. Exper. Psychol.,* 1921, *4,* 247–269.
5. Dodge, R. Habituation to rotation. *J. Exper. Psychol.,* 1923, *6,* 1–35.
6. Dodge, R. Thresholds of rotation. *J. Exper. Psychol.,* 1923, *6,* 107–137.
7. Dodge, R., and T. S. Cline. The angle velocity of eye movements. *J. Exper. Rev.,* 1901, *8,* 145–157.
8. Dohlman, G. Some practical and theoretical points in labyrinthology. *Proc. Roy. Soc. Med.,* 1935, *28,* 1371–1380.
9. Dunlap, K. A rotator for vestibular and organic stimulation. *J. Comp. Psychol.,* 1921, *1,* 365–367.
10. Dusser de Barenne, J. G. The labyrinthine and postural mechanisms. In *A Handbook of General Experimental Psychology.* C. Murchison, Ed. Worcester, Mass.: Clark University Press, 1934.
11. Dusser de Barenne, J. G., and A. de Kleyn. On reciprocal innervation of the eye muscles in the tonic labyrinthine reflexes. *Acta Oto-Laryng.,* 1931, *16,* 97–116.
12. Ewald, J. R. *Physiologische Untersuchungen über das Endorgan des Nervus Octavus.* Wiesbaden: Bergmann, 1892.
13. Fluorens, M. P. J. *Recherches expérimentales sur les propriétés et les fonctions du système nerveux dans les animaux vertébrés.* 2nd Ed. Paris: Baillière, 1842.
14. Fulton, J. F. *Physiology of the Nervous System.* New York: Oxford University Press, 1943.
15. Graybiel, A., B. Clark, K. MacCorquodale, and D. Hupp. Role of vestibular nystagmus in the visual perception of a moving target in the dark. *Amer. J. Psychol.,* 1946, *59,* 259–266.
16. Griffith, C. R. *An Historical Survey of Vestibular Equilibration.* Urbana, Illinois: University of Illinois Press, 1922.
17. Hemmingway, A. Cardiovascular changes in motion sickness. *J. Aviat. Med.,* 1945, *16,* 409.
18. Jacobsen, E. Electrical measurements of neuromuscular states during mental activities. *Amer. J. Physiol.,* 1930, *95,* 694–702.
19. Judd, C H., C. N. McAllister, and W. M. Steele. General introduction to a series of studies of eye movements by means of kinetoscopic photographs. *Psychol. Rev., Monog. Supp.,* 1905, *7,* 1–16.
20. Kerr, W. A., and A. Graybiel. Thresholds of stimulation of the horizontal semicircular canals in man (abstract). *Amer. Psychol.,* 1946, *1,* 237.
21. Löwenstein, O., and A. Sand. The mechanism of the semicircular canal. A study of the responses of single-fibre preparations to angular accelerations and to rotation at constant speed. *Proc. Roy. Soc. London,* Series B, 1940, *129,* 256–275.
22. Matthews, B. H. C. Nerve endings in mammalian muscle. *J. Physiol.,* 1933, *78,* 1–53.
23. Mowrer, O. H. The electrical response of the vestibular nerve during adequate stimulation. *Science,* 1935, *81,* 180–181.

24. Mowrer, O. H., T. C. Ruch, and N. E. Miller. The corneo-retinal potential difference as the basis of the galvanometric method of recording eye movements. *Amer. J. Physiol.,* 1936, *114,* 423–428.
25. Pi-Suñer, J., and J. F. Fulton. The influence of the proprioceptive nerves of the hind limbs upon the posture of the fore limbs in decerebrate cats. *Amer. J. Physiol.,* 1928, *83,* 548–553.
26. Romberg, M. H. *Lehrbuch der Nerven-Krankheiten des Menschen.* 2te Aufl. Berlin: Duncker, 1851.
27. Ruch, T. C. Cortical localization of somatic sensibility. The effect of precentral, postcentral, and posterior parietal lesions upon the performance of monkeys trained to discriminate weights. *Res. Publ. Assoc. Nerv. Ment. Disease,* 1935, *15,* 289–330.
28. Ruch, T. C., J. F. Fulton, and W. J. German. Sensory discrimination in monkey, chimpanzee, and man after lesions of the parietal lobe. *Arch. Neurol. Psychiat.,* Chicago, 1938, *39,* 919–937.
29. Sherrington, C. S. On the anatomical constitution of nerves of skeletal muscles; with remarks on recurrent fibres in the ventral spinal nerve-root. *J. Physiol.,* 1894, *17,* 211–258.
30. Spiegel, E. A. The cortical centers of the labyrinth. *J. Nerv. Ment. Disease,* 1932, *75,* 504–512.
31. Spiegel, E. A. Labyrinth and cortex: the electrencephalogram of the cortex in stimulation of the labyrinth. *Arch. Neurol. Psychiat.,* 1934, *31,* 469–482.
32. Spiegel, E. A., and M. J. Oppenheimer. Conditioned reactions to position and angular acceleration. *Amer. J. Physiol.,* 1939, *125,* 265–275.
33. Spiegel, E. A., M. J. Oppenheimer, G. C. Henny, and H. T. Wycis. Experimental production of motion sickness. *War Medicine,* 1944, *6,* 283–290.
34. Steinhausen, W. Über den Nachweis der Bewegung der Cupula in der intakten Bogengangsampulle des Labyrinths bei der natürlichen rotatorischen und calorischen Reizung. *Arch. ges. Physiol.* (*Pflügers*), 1931, *228,* 322–328.
35. Steinhausen, W. Über den experimentellen Nachweis der Ablenkung der Cupula terminalis in der intakten Bogengangsampulle des Labyrinths bei der thermischen und adäquaten rotatorischen Reizung. *Z. Hals-Nas.-u. Ohrenheilk.,* 1931, *29,* 211–216.
36. Steinhausen, W. Das Bogengangssystem des inneren Ohres als Wahrnehmungsorgan für Drehungen. Berlin: *Reichstelle für den Unterrichtsfilm zu den Hochschulfilm,* 1939, No. 323.
37. Tait, J., and W. J. McNally. A method of recording the responses of individual muscles to appropriate stimulation of the semicircular canals. *Amer. J. Physiol.,* 1929, *90,* 536–537.
38. Travis, R. C. Perception and bodily adjustment under changing rotary acceleration: a new technique. *Amer. J. Psychol.,* 1944, *57,* 468–481.
39. Wendt, G. R., and R. Dodge. Practical directions for stimulating and for photographically recording eye-movements of animals. *J. Comp. Psychol.,* 1938, *25,* 9–39.

SUGGESTED READINGS

Boring, E. G. *Sensation and Perception in the History of Experimental Psychology.* New York: Appleton-Century, 1942, pp. 523–544.

Camis, M. *The Physiology of the Vestibular Apparatus.* (Translated from the Italian and annotated by R. S. Creed.) London: Oxford University Press, 1930.

Dusser de Barenne, J. G. The labyrinthine and postural mechanisms. In *A Handbook of General Experimental Psychology.* C. Murchison, Ed. Worcester, Mass.: Clark University Press, 1934, pp. 204–246.

Fulton, J. F. *Physiology of the Nervous System,* Rev. Ed. New York: Oxford University Press, 1943, pp. 1–179.

Fulton, J. F., Ed. *Howell's Textbook of Physiology.* Philadelphia: W. B. Saunders, 1946, pp. 202–217.

Griffith, C. R. *An Historical Survey of Vestibular Equilibration.* Urbana, Illinois: University of Illinois Press, 1922. (Includes a bibliography of 1701 titles.)

Morgan, C. T. *Physiological Psychology.* New York: McGraw-Hill, 1943, pp. 283–293.

McNally, W. J., and E. A. Stuart. Physiology of the labyrinth reviewed in relation to seasickness and other forms of motion sickness. *War Medicine,* 1942, *2,* 683–771.

Spiegel, E. A., and I. Sommer. Vestibular mechanisms. In *Medical Physics.* O. Glasser, Ed. Chicago: The Yearbook Publishers, 1944, pp. 1638–1653.

Chapter 12

Studying Animal Behavior

Harry F. Harlow[1]

Psychologists have studied the behavior of animals other than man out of sheer curiosity—a desire to know how and why all animals respond as they do. In addition, psychologists have made comparative studies of the behavior of different animals to determine whether comparable response patterns show progressively increasing complexity as we ascend the phyletic scale. Such a finding would be in keeping with general evolutionary theory.

The primary reason, however, for the use of subhuman animals in psychological experiments lies in the fact that more precise methods and more adequate controls can be exercised over animals other than man in the laboratory. Indeed, many psychological problems can be tested only on subhuman animal subjects.

Thus the essential reason for the study of comparative psychology is a methodological reason, a desire on the part of the psychologist to study as completely as possible all the factors which underlie behavior and to test and determine under controlled experimental conditions all the variables intervening between the presentation of stimuli and the measurement of responses.

Advantages of Subhuman Subjects

The general methodological advantages found in the use of subhuman animals as experimental subjects are as follows:

1. *It is possible to control the external environment to a greater degree with lower animals than with man.* Psychologists have long been interested in the nature of visual organization in animals before these functions have been modified by experience. No practical and precise method of testing vision in any newborn animal has ever been

1 Professor of Psychology, University of Wisconsin.

devised. The logical solution of the problem is to deprive the subject of any opportunity for visual experience until he has reached such an age that adequate experiments can be made. Such procedures are impracticable with children but were actually employed by Hebb [16] in determining the innate organization of visual functions in rats.

Analysis of the roles of heredity and environment in sex behavior demands that drastic control be maintained over the external environment. Such controls have been carried out, using guinea pigs and rats as subjects. The animals were raised in isolation from early infancy until maturity, and the nature of the sexual response patterns then tested.

These examples illustrate the general principle that greater control can commonly be exercised over the environment of any laboratory animal than over man. For most experiments such control is desirable, and for many experiments it is essential.

2. *The life span of most subhuman animals is shorter than that of man.* As the science of psychology develops, greater emphasis may be expected to be given to long-term, as opposed to short-term, experiments. The effect of various external and internal environmental conditions over considerable portions of the life span and the nature of inheritance come to command greater attention.

An example of long-term study is that of the influence of feeding frustration during late infancy (15 days of age) upon the behavior of adult rats. This specific investigation was carried out by Hunt [18], who found that an experimental group hoarded more than twice as many pellets as their *litter mate controls* in the postfrustration tests. These tests began at 150 days of age, approximately 11 years in terms of man's life span. Hunt specifically states, "The rat was chosen because it is a convenient laboratory animal, with a brief life cycle."

Tryon's [31] comprehensive investigation of inheritance of maze-running ability in the rat was carried out for 20 generations (600 years had human subjects been used!). Progressive differentiation between maze-bright and maze-dull rats took place for 7 generations (210 "human years"). Similar studies have been carried out at Minnesota on the inheritance of maze-running ability and on the inheritance of general activity.

The use of animals in inheritance studies is facilitated not only by the abbreviated life span of the subhuman animal but also by the ability of the experimenter to maintain control over the environment. Human inheritance studies give results obscured by the fact that men have enough control over their environment to mate frequently by the dictates of whimsy and transient preferences—conditions not permitted rats at the California and Minnesota laboratories.

3. *A greater degree of control can be exercised over the physiological state and organic structure of animals other than man.* Many important psychological problems cannot be investigated unless the physiological state of the organism can be drastically altered. Also, other basic psychological problems can be solved only by operative procedures which leave the organism suffering permanent deficit.

Some basic problems of motivation can be solved only by experiments in which the animal undergoes serious physiological deprivation. This is illustrated by Warden's [32] investigations on strength of drives, in which restrictions on food and water were carried to critical limits with some experimental groups.

The alteration of organic structure through operative intervention is one of the important methods of animal psychology. This method cannot be used in any deliberate and radical manner on man. The importance and extent of this technique are attested by the fact that such procedures are described in Chapters 6, 7, 9, and 15 of this book.

The use of operative methods in the analysis of complex behavior patterns is illustrated by Beach's [3] studies. Elicitation of such basic reaction patterns as the copulatory responses in the male rat is affected by inactivation or partial inactivation of the visual, olfactory, and cutaneous receptor systems after enucleation of the eyes and transection of the olfactory bulb and trigeminal nerve. Likewise, cortical lesions above a minimal size seriously affect the arousal of the male copulatory responses.

Lashley's [22] classical study of the effect of cortical lesions showed clearly the use and importance of such methods in the field of learning. In the analysis of factors operating in complex learning problems these techniques have been used to test delayed response in rat, monkey, and chimpanzee, reasoning in rats, and hypothesis formation by rats and monkeys.

General Methods of Comparative Psychology

Historically the broad general methods of comparative psychology have been described as (1) the anecdotal, (2) the observational, and (3) the experimental.

The anecdotal method implies the acceptance of the undocumented and often casual accounts of *untrained* individuals. The limitations of the anecdotal method, so defined, have already been explicitly formulated [33].

The observational method has been described as observation of the animal without attempt to control or alter the conditions of the natural environment. Defined in this manner, the "observational" method has become associated with studies of the behavior of the wild animal in the field or with studies of the development of domesticated animals under circumstances in which no special or unusual controls were exerted. The observational method has been contrasted to the experimental method, in which precise, multiple controls are exerted over both the external and internal environment of the animal.

Field studies illustrate the observation method, and the studies by Carpenter on the behavior of the howler monkey, spider monkey, rhesus monkey, and gibbon are examples of unparalleled excellence of the efficiency of the observational method when carried out by the skillful and patient investigator. In his research on the howler monkey, for example, Carpenter was able to make a highly adequate census of the howler population of each of the twenty-eight clans inhabiting Barro Colorado Island in the canal zone. He was able to differentiate the animals into age and sex groups, to plot and time the typical daily activities of the monkey, to determine the essential group integrations, social relations, and intragroup behavior, and to determine basic reaction patterns of feeding, language coordination and control, play, mating, nesting, and arboreal movement and progession.

Carpenter's study [4] is of particular importance, since he emphasized the number of different procedures which were used or could be used in the field study, and it should be noted that *these are by no means limited to techniques of uncontrolled observation.* These procedures are given below:

1. Direct observation with complete concealment of the observer.
2. Direct observation from ambush.
3. Direct observation after neutral conditioning of the animals to the observer.
4. Indirect observation: the study of spoor.
5. Experimentation.
6. Photography.
7. Collections.

The observational method should be thought of as a technique in which the responses measured are recorded by the experimenter by graphic or oral means. Experimental techniques involving control over the environmental and organismic variables may be used when the responses are observationally recorded.

Observational recording methods, as opposed to mechanical recording methods, are commonly used in or out of the laboratory when the response to be measured is so complex or delicate that it is impossible or impracticable to utilize the more strictly objective methods of mechanical recording.

The shortcomings of common mechanical recording methods are indicated by Guthrie's [10] descriptive study of the behavior of cats in the solution of puzzle-box problems. Guthrie has emphasized the fact that psychologists have usually measured the results of the animal's responses—movements of levers, opening of doors, choice of alleys—and have failed to measure the actual responses, the movement patterns of the animal. Guthrie stressed the importance of measuring these movement patterns. To do this, he made extensive use of photographs and motion pictures, but the pictorial record merely amplifies and objectifies the more essential and more complete observational records presented in written language form.

Many psychologists have used both observational and instrumental techniques to obtain independent measures of the same psychological trait. In his study of the inheritance of temperament, Stone [29] made observational ratings of wildness in terms of eleven items and also measured wildness in terms of an instrumental measure, the percentage of animals failing to run a labyrinth and enter a food box in a limited temporal interval. The results of this study and many other studies in which both observational and instrumental measures have been used show that observational records may be as reliable and as valid measures of the trait investigated as are the instrumental records.

Although historically the experimental method has been contrasted to the observational method in comparative psychology, a better dichotomy is to oppose the observational recording method and the instrumental recording method.

Comparative psychologists have quite properly emphasized methodology and have made great efforts to obtain objectively recorded measures of their data. This has commonly been done either by having the responses recorded completely automatically or by having the responses, which are actually recorded by observational means, so simple that there is little or no chance for error.

There can be no question of the desirability of the use of recording devices as long as the instruments effectively measure the responses essential for problem testing. It must be remembered, however, that recording instruments can seriously interfere with efficient response by the animal. Furthermore, it may be impossible to measure by existing instrumental means responses and response systems of great psychological importance.

In their urge to attain complete objectivity, comparative psychologists have not infrequently become victims of the *Procrustean method;* i.e., they have "adapted" the animal to the apparatus rather than devise apparatus adapted to the animal. Negative results have been obtained, and the responsibility for these results has been erroneously laid on the subhuman member of the research team.

Effective apparatus for testing subhuman animals can be devised only by trying out many forms and types and selecting those which prove to be most efficient. Likewise techniques for taming and adapting animals to apparatus and effective testing methods can be discovered only by trying out different procedures and retaining those which prove to be efficient.

Failure to recognize these basic facts has led highly competent comparative psychologists into gross errors—the "discovery" that animals did not have some capacity or could not solve some problem that actually lay well within their range of capabilities. The failure of subhuman animals to solve problems has often demonstrated nothing other than the faulty design of the apparatus or the inadequacies of the test procedures.

TECHNIQUES OF MEASURING MOTIVATION

The investigation of the motivational forces which initiate, activate, maintain, and direct the behavior of the animal is basic to all psychological investigation. The distinctive techniques which comparative psychology has devised have contributed much to our knowledge of motivation.

The problems of motivation may be divided into two broad categories: (1) the drive mechanisms—the internal stimuli and organic sets initiating activity and predisposing the animal toward making differential responses; and (2) the incentives or goal objects—the external stimuli toward which or away from which the responses of the animal are directed.

It should be emphasized that these two motivational categories are never separate but are constantly interacting, so that techniques and apparatus primarily designed for investigating the properties of one may also be useful for investigating the properties of the other. For purposes of classification, however, they may be treated separately.

Methods of Studying the Drive Mechanisms

The simplest function of the various drive mechanisms is the liberation of energy which results in "spontaneous" or general activity on the part of the animal. This *general activity* can be measured by recording the movement of the subject's housing unit or by direct observation of the overt behavior of the organism.

The most commonly used apparatus for recording general activity is the revolving drum (see Fig. 1) and its adaptations, which measure activity in terms of revolutions or partial revolutions of the metal cylinder. The activity score may be quantitatively recorded by a cyclometer, or it may be recorded on a kymographic drum if a continuous record showing the temporal distribution is desired.

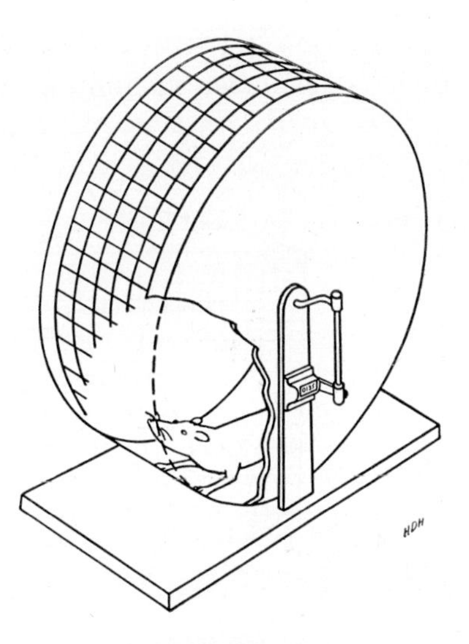

Fig. 1. **Revolving cage and automatic counter.**

The revolving-cage method gives reliable results if adequate tests are made of the physical characteristics of the individual cage units. Large numbers of animals can be tested, and scoring is simple and unequivocal. The limitation of the method lies in the difficulty of adequately measuring the role played by any individual drive (or incentive) in determining the total score.

A continuous measure of general activity may be obtained using Richter's tambour cage [25], which is illustrated in Fig. 2. The tambour cage has been used less frequently than the revolving cage because of greater mechanical difficulties and because a kymographic record gives a score less quantitatively recorded and less efficiently handled than the record from a cyclometer.

The tambour cage has been used to measure direction, as well as mere amount, of activity. For example, the apparatus can be so arranged that incentive chambers for food and water open directly into the tambour cage, and the exact response made to either incentive can be recorded.

Spontaneous activity in sheep and man has been measured by the pedometer, which, like the revolving drum, gives a measure of total activity per unit time.

Various simple cage devices have been used to measure activity recorded by direct observation; the number of units of floor space touched, entered, or passed over is the common criterion of responsiveness. The disadvantage of such techniques lies in the fact that, since the experimenter is the measuring instrument, the technique becomes extremely time-consuming. Such difficulties might be alleviated in part by standardized time sample procedures.

The drive mechanisms, particularly the strength of a particular drive, may be effectively studied by obtaining a measure of the presence or absence of response, or the frequency of response in a given period of time, to a stimulus of constant intensity. *Stimulus satiation* has frequently been measured by the direct observation of the experimenter with the use of simple apparatus, often nothing more than a chamber delimiting or directing the subject's behavior.

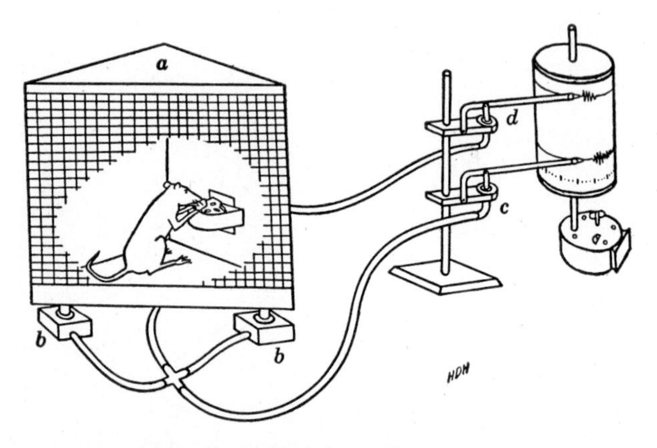

Fig. 2. Richter's tambour cage.

a = tambour cage, b = tambours supporting cage corners, c = recording tambour from cage, d = recording tambour from food box.

Strength of the sex drive has been studied in the male rat by observing the frequency of copulation in a limited time interval when the male was presented with a female in estrus. With such techniques the effects of previous experience, inanition, castration, hormonal injection, sense-organ destruction, and cortical injury have been investigated.

Maternal behavior has been similarly tested by recording the number of infants which a mother rat will return to the nest in a given time interval [2]. This technique is unquestionably applicable to other species. The strength of both maternal and temperature-regulating drives has been measured by determining the satiation point for the collection of paper strips and their incorporation into a nest.

The Skinner box [27] (see Fig. 3), is an apparatus designed to determine automatically a quantitative measure of satiation. The strength of drive is measured in terms of the *rate* of manipulation (frequency of response per unit time) of a lever which releases a food pellet each time it is depressed. This scoring technique makes it possible to measure not only satiation but also any progressive tendency toward satiation. The Skinner box, it may be noted, has been used successfully in measuring certain simple aspects of the conditioning or learning process and, when modified by using two levers instead of one, may be used to measure discrimination.

The great merits of the Skinner box are the control of environmental stimuli, the automatic recording, and the accurate quantitative

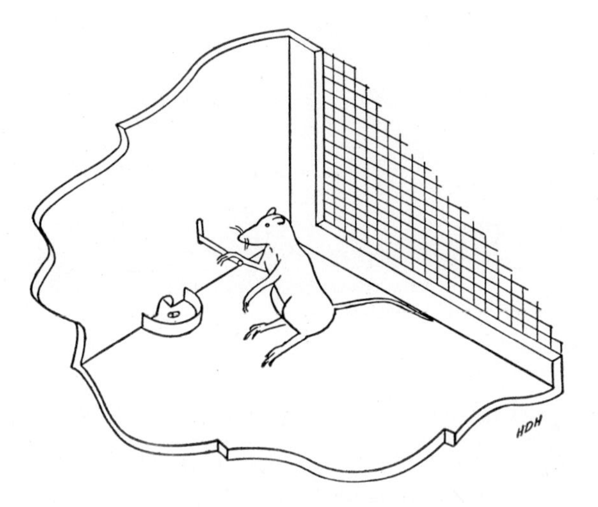

Fig. 3. Skinner box.

A pellet of food is automatically released in the food pan each time the lever is depressed.

measures obtained. The limitation of the box lies in the fact that it cannot be easily adapted for use in measuring drives other than hunger and thirst.

The Columbia obstruction box (see Fig. 4) measures the strength of a drive in terms of its ability to overcome or counterbalance the constant negative stimulus of an electrically charged grill. The strength of any particular drive is given in terms of the approaches, contacts, or crossings of the grill in a 20-minute period. Test-retest methods indicate that the measures are reliable, and the results correlate well with other more direct methods of measuring specific drive strengths.

The value of the Columbia obstruction method lies in the fact that quantitative measures of the strength of a particular drive can be made under varying conditions of physiological need. A direct comparison of the strength of different drives is practicable with this technique [32]. Although this method has proved to be one of the outstandingly effective techniques for measuring animal motivation, certain limitations should be noted. No animal other than the rat has been successfully tested by means of the obstruction method, even though a serious attempt was made to adapt the technique to monkeys, an animal family emotionally allergic to electric current. Furthermore, there is the possibility that electric shock, even in the rat, may disturb, in varying degrees, the normal relationships between each and every drive and its natural goal objects.

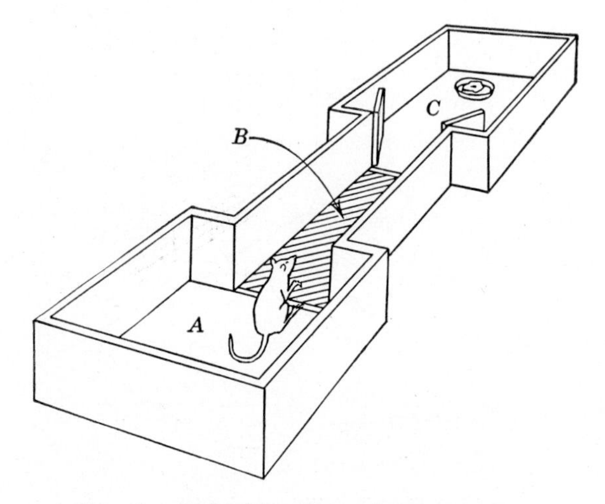

Fig. 4. Columbia obstruction apparatus.
A = entrance compartment, B = electric grid, C = incentive compartment.

Methods of Studying Incentives or Goal Objects

The drive mechanisms are characteristically investigated by holding the incentives constant (or relatively constant) and studying the effect of the systematic introduction of variable experimental conditions upon the strength or frequency of response. Similarly, the role of incentives as motivational forces has been studied by holding drives constant and measuring the strength or frequency of response to various incentive conditions or other related environmental factors.

When drive conditions are held constant, various incentives have differing motivational values. The detailed studies of food preferences are good examples of *incentive preference* investigations. Young [37] has shown that food incentive preferences in the rat form a transitive series and become more consistent with practice. He also found that the form of the apparatus has an effect upon incentive preferences. Thus, when the stimuli to be discriminated were close together and their position constantly interchanged, the choice was made on the basis of head receptors—those of taste, smell, and vision. If, on the other hand, the foods were widely separated and kept in fixed positions, the preferential choices were based to a large extent on bodily needs and metabolic state. Figure 5 illustrates an apparatus now being used in preference studies.

There is a wealth of investigations demonstrating preferential food incentives for many animals—rat, pig, cow, monkey, chimpanzee, and man. The role played by preferential incentives, the appropriate goal objects, to the primary drives other than hunger, has not been investigated as widely, as accurately, or in such detail. There are, however, many researches showing that preferential incentives appropriate to the thirst, sex, maternal, and temperature drives do exist and play an important role in directing behavior.

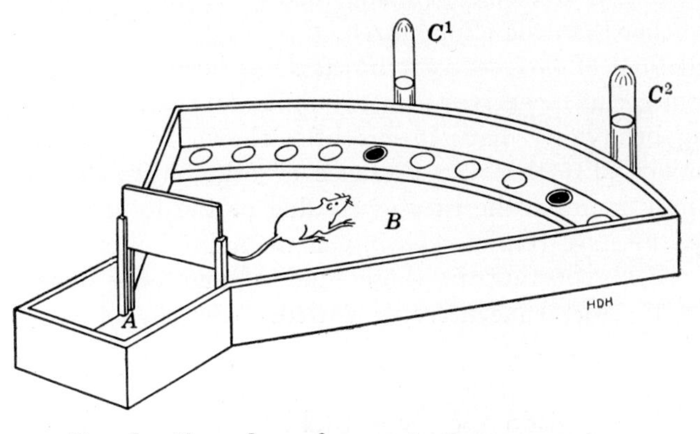

Fig. 5. Young's preference-testing apparatus.

A = entrance chamber, B = test chamber, C¹, C² = food choices.

Incentives are effective motivational agents only if they are appropriate to some particular drive. Thus water is an effective incentive only if the animal is thirsty. This basic relationship between incentive and drive was clearly demonstrated in studies carried out by Tolman and coworkers [30] on maze learning. Hungry animals were found to perform efficiently on mazes only if they had been rewarded with food on the previous trial, and thirsty animals, only if they had been rewarded with water on the previous trial.

The role of *incentive appropriateness* has been indirectly recognized in many motivational studies. In studying the hunger, thirst, maternal, or exploratory drive by means of the Columbia obstruction method, an appropriate incentive is always offered in the incentive chamber.

The appropriateness of particular incentives to particular drives rests upon a biological basis—the incentives are especially efficient agents for reducing physiological tensions underlying the drive mechanisms. By association or conditioning, however, previously indifferent incentives may become goal objects for particular drives. Such second-order incentives have been demonstrated by using conditioning and maze-learning techniques and the Skinner box apparatus.

Chimpanzees will work to obtain chips from a vending machine and will utilize these tokens appropriately to obtain food and activity rewards [34]. Some animals will collect as many as thirty tokens before exchanging them for food. Simple habits have been established using "poker"-chip token incentives instead of food [5]. The general method has been used with limited success on rats and dogs and would be of the greatest potential value in the analysis of complex motivational factors if it could be made readily adaptable to the study of animals other than the chimpanzee.

The method of *incentive facilitation* has been used in investigating the role of social incentives in many animals, particularly with regard to eating behavior. Thus it has been shown in hen [1], rat [12], and monkey [13] that the presence of other members of the same species may increase the rate of feeding or the total amount of food consumed or may reinduce eating in an animal previously satiated. Drive is held constant in these studies, and only the facilitating incentive, the social incentive, is varied.

TECHNIQUES OF MEASURING DISCRIMINATION

The investigation of the ability of animals to discriminate between different stimuli is important, since receptive capacities are basic factors influencing all behavioral adjustments, innate and acquired.

Stimulus receptivity is measured in subhuman animals by consistency of response to a particular stimulus-cue when all other conditions are constant or controlled. Consistency of response is statistically defined and must be sufficiently rigid to exclude explanation in terms of chance factors. The response itself may be a visceral response, such as salivation, a skeletal response, such as limb flexion, or the *end result* of some complex pattern of response, such as always choosing the blue stimulus and always avoiding the yellow. Discrimination can be tested only if the animal perceives the stimulus and can be induced to respond to it. Since neither of these conditions can be proved beyond question, negative results, failure to demonstrate discriminative abilities, are always open to question, as many competent psychologists have found to their regret.

The upper and lower limens or limits of receptivity are commonly measured by demonstrating consistent response to one stimulus and consistent failure of response to another. Stimulus differentiation, including difference limens (the minimal stimulus differences to which consistent differential response is made), is frequently measured by consistent selection of one stimulus and avoidance of the other.

Discrimination in subhuman animals has commonly been measured by four different types of response; the first two types may measure unlearned responses, but the last two always involve training. These four types are as follows: (1) consistent unlearned responses, changing in a predictable manner, following changes in a stimulus; (2) consistent preferential responses to multiple stimuli; (3) learned differentiation of successively presented stimuli; (4) learned differentiation of simultaneously presented stimuli.

Representative techniques employed in the measurement of discriminations in subhuman animals, and the associated problems, limitations, and particular merits of the various representative techniques may be adequately discussed in terms of these four types of measures.

Consistent Unlearned Responses, Changing in a Predictable Manner, Following Changes in a Stimulus

When an animal climbs a slope, the pull of gravity stimulates cutaneous and kinesthetic receptors. As the steepness of the slope increases, the effects of the pull of gravity on the climbing animal become greater, and the receptors are presumably subjected to greater intensity of stimulation. The ability of rats to respond to such stimulation and to make differential responses to differential stimulus intensity was demonstrated by Crozier and Pincus [6]. Inexperienced and immature rats, whose eyes had not yet opened, were used as subjects, and tests were made under low red-light illumination. Typical results are illustrated in Fig. 6. The *consistent unlearned* responses are the rats' climbing angles (θ) across the wire mesh grid, and these change in a predictable manner when *changes occur in the stimulus*, which is the angle (α) of inclination of the wire mesh grid to the horizontal plane.

Thus Fig. 6 shows climbing angle θ to be 45 degrees when the angle of inclination α of the grid is 20 degrees, and θ increases to 88 degrees when α is increased to 70 degrees.

If an animal is restrained in a box, as illustrated in Fig. 7, and its head is held relatively immobile, automatic optokinetic or optically induced nystagmic reactions will take place when a series of lines is rotated across the visual field. As the stimulus of line width is reduced, the unlearned nystagmic responses change in a consistent, predictable manner until finally no measurable nystagmic responses

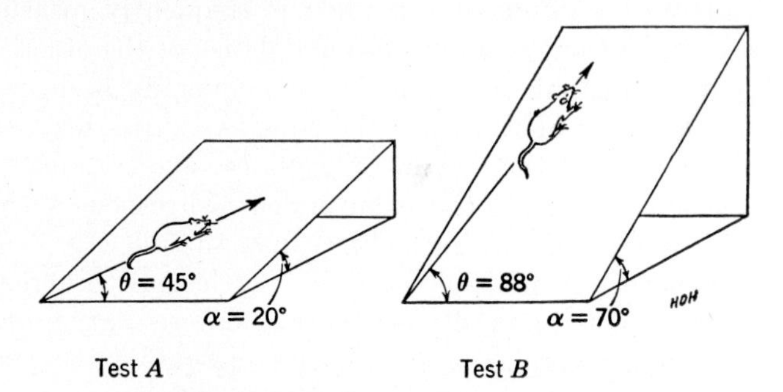

Fig. 6. Crozier's geotropism test.

Test *A*: Angle α = grid inclination = 20°, Angle θ = climbing angle = 45°.
Test *B*: Angle α = grid inclination = 70°, Angle θ = climbing angle = 88°.

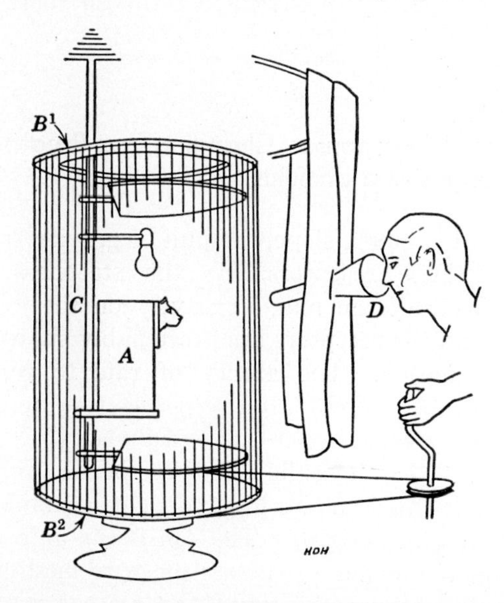

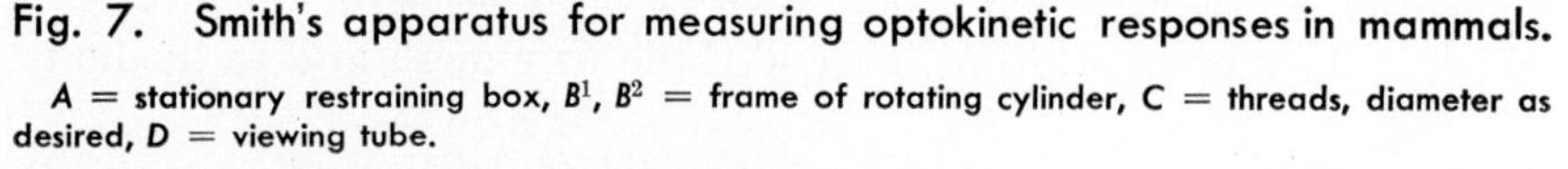

Fig. 7. Smith's apparatus for measuring optokinetic responses in mammals.

A = stationary restraining box, B^1, B^2 = frame of rotating cylinder, *C* = threads, diameter as desired, *D* = viewing tube.

occur. At this point a reasonably accurate measure of minimum separable visual acuity is obtained.

This technique, extensively used by Smith [28] and associates to study visual discrimination in both normal and brain-injured animals, is known to be applicable to many mammals. Smith's technique enabled him to test many subjects *rapidly* and efficiently. In this regard, use of the method gives an admirable illustration of the fact that consistent unlearned responses can often be measured more rapidly than learned responses, an important practical conclusion if large groups of animals are to be tested. Furthermore, unlearned responses can be used to measure receptive capacities in animals, even though the ability to learn has been impaired or abolished by extensive cortical damage. Indeed, the only justification for the use of training methods as techniques for the measurement of sensory capacities lies in the fact that greater precision has been obtained with learning procedures.

Consistent Preferential Responses to Multiple Stimuli

Preferential discriminatory responses based on gustatory-olfactory cues were demonstrated in the rat by Richter [26], using an apparatus such as that in Fig. 8. The small tubes were filled with various foods in aqueous solution, and the subjects showed an amazing ability to

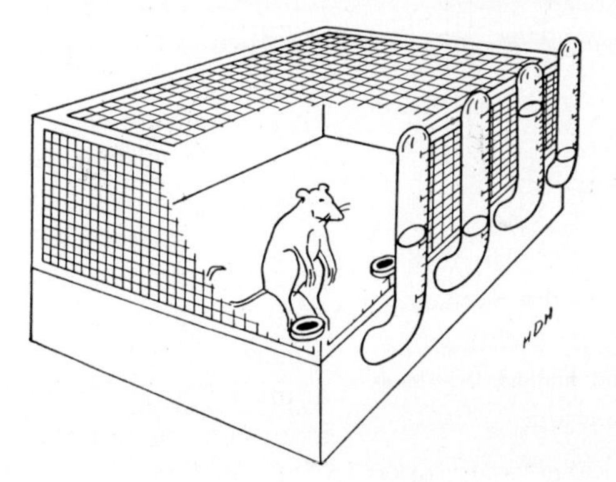

Fig. 8. Richter's self-selection feeding cage and food receptacles.

discriminate between the contents and select solutions conducive to the maintenance of appropriate bodily economy.

Unfortunately preferential discriminatory responses are comparatively inaccurate for receptor systems other than the gustatory-olfactory. Yoshioka [36] demonstrated that rats will eat a greater number of large sunflower seeds than small ones and that this response is dependent upon visual cues. The preferential responses demonstrated, however, are comparatively gross. Preferential discriminatory responses have been indirectly demonstrated by showing that chicks, rats, monkeys, and chimpanzees learn better when either larger amounts or more highly preferred kinds of food are used as incentives.

Learned Differentiation of Successively Presented Stimuli

Sensory discrimination in animals may be tested by training the subject to respond consistently whenever a particular stimulus is presented and not to respond whenever either (*a*) no stimulus is presented, or (*b*) a different stimulus is presented. This technique is commonly used when sensory abilities are tested by conditioning methods, which were described in detail in Chapter **2**.

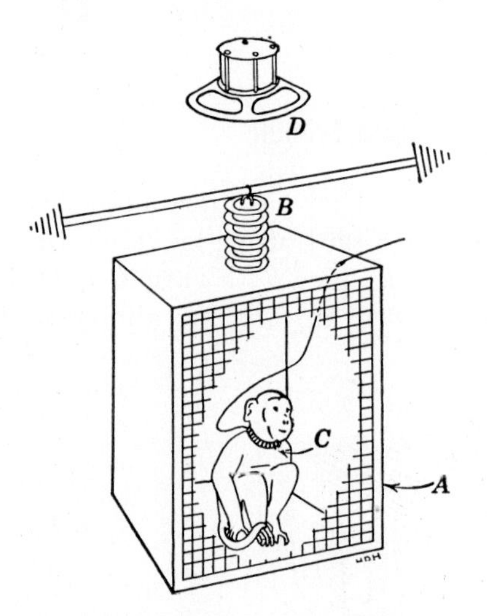

Fig. 9. Stabilimeter for testing auditory acuity in the monkey.

A **= restraining cage,** ***B*** **= metal bellows, C = wire-wound harness,** ***D*** **= loudspeaker.**

This general method was used by Harris [15] to test auditory acuity in monkeys by means of the stabilimeter shown in Fig. 9. The stabilimeter is essentially a cage suspended from a sensitive metal bellows. Responses by the subject produce cage movements which can be observed easily or recorded mechanically. Training is carried out by presenting the conditioned stimulus, a tone, and then presenting the unconditioned stimulus, a shock, administered by applying current from the floor of the cage to a wire-wound leather harness strapped to the monkey.

The stabilimeter is an adaptation of a rotating-drum apparatus [7] used in testing absolute intensity thresholds in guinea-pigs and cats. The animal was placed in the movable drum, and the conditioned stimulus, a tone, was presented. If the subject made no movement of the drum when the tone was sounded, it received a shock; if it did move the drum, it was not shocked. By this method the number of electric shocks, which can easily disrupt learning, was kept at a minimum.

The general technique described in this section—the learned differentiation of stimuli successively presented—has proved particularly valuable to comparative psychology in measuring auditory capacities and especially in the determination of lower limens. The general technique can, of course, be used in measuring other receptive capacities and in the determination of difference limens as well as lower limens. Any assumption, however, that discriminations, other than auditory discriminations, are measured better by methods in which the stimuli are presented *successively* instead of *simultaneously* is not substantiated by the most precise studies on either subhuman or human subjects.

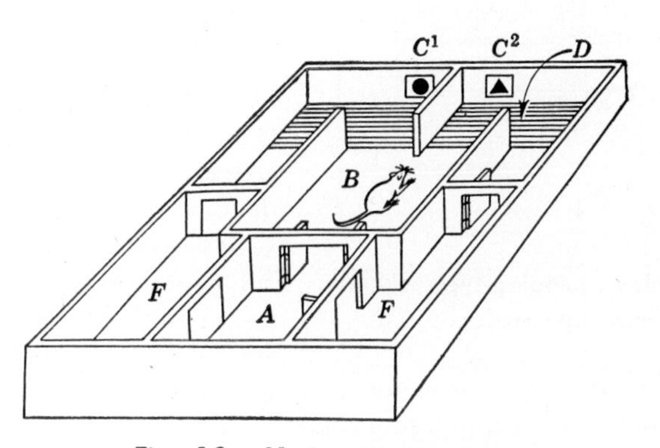

Fig. 10. Yerkes-Watson box.

A = entrance box, *B* = reaction compartment, C^1, C^2 = stimuli, *D* = electric grid, *F* = food compartments.

Learned Differentiation of Simultaneously Presented Stimuli

Most of the investigations on sensory discrimination by subhuman animals have used techniques which involve simultaneous presentation of the stimuli. This general technique is highly efficient if the apparatus used is designed in accordance with basic laws of learning and is adapted to the animal subject.

The Yerkes-Watson discrimination box [9], illustrated in Fig. 10, afforded admirable control over the physical characteristics of the stimuli but suffered from certain limitations: (1) the stimuli were so arranged that the animal would not be assured of attending to and perceiving the stimuli when responding; (2) the incentive for correct response was not in close *spatial contiguity* with the stimuli—the subject actually had to *run away from* the stimulus to get the reward; (3) the incentive for a response to the correct stimulus was *temporally distant* from the correct stimulus, thereby delaying reinforcement.

These limitations were overcome in the Lashley [23] jumping-type discrimination apparatus (Fig. 11), in which the rat subjects were immediately rewarded for a correct response to a stimulus easily perceived during the process of responding. The rat jumps from a heart-shaped platform having one crest pointing to the correct stimulus and the other crest to the incorrect stimulus, across a gap to a stimulus. If the choice is correct, the card on which the stimulus is inscribed falls, and the animal reaches the food platform and can immediately obtain food; if the choice is incorrect, the card remains in place, and the rat falls into, and is retrieved from, a net below.

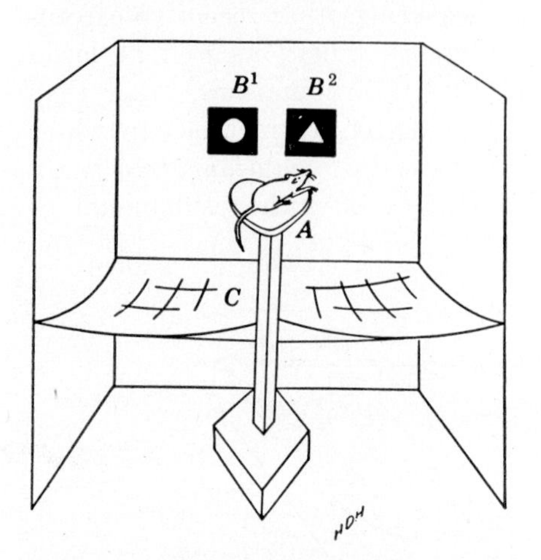

Fig. 11. Lashley's jumping-type discrimination apparatus.

A = jumping stand, B^1, B^2 = stimuli, C = net.

The importance of apparatus design is illustrated by the discovery that rats learn simple brightness discriminations much more rapidly in the jumping box than in the Yerkes-Watson apparatus, and by the fact that form discriminations which cannot be solved with the Yerkes-Watson apparatus are mastered without undue difficulty in the Lashley jumping box.

The success of the Lashley apparatus does not depend upon the jumping response, since efficiency has been achieved with other apparatus which present the stimuli in such a manner that they are readily perceived, and the reward is in close temporal and spatial relationship to the correct response. Fields [9] successfully used discrimination apparatus in which rats and raccoons *ran under* the correct stimulus and were immediately rewarded. Rats will also learn discriminations with ease if they run through freely swinging cards placed at the end of a forked elevated runway.

An entirely different type of discrimination apparatus was designed by Klüver [19] and called the "pull-in" technique, a technique used with success in studies of rats, monkeys, and chimpanzees. As seen in Fig. 12, strings are attached to the stimuli, and the ends of the strings placed within reach of the animal. During the time the subject pulls on the string he can scarcely avoid perception of the stimulus. If the correct stimulus is drawn in, the animal *immediately* finds food *just behind* the stimulus. A possible limitation of the method lies in the fact that the animal must engage in fairly extensive manipulations before being rewarded (or not rewarded) for response to the correct (or incorrect) stimulus.

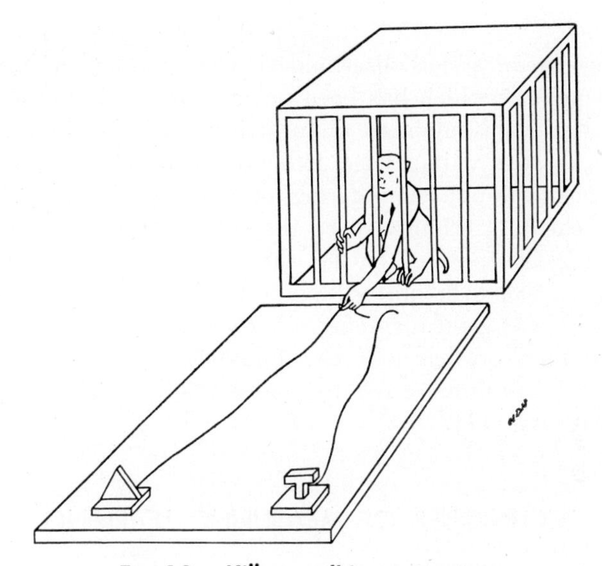

Fig 12. Klüver pull-in apparatus.

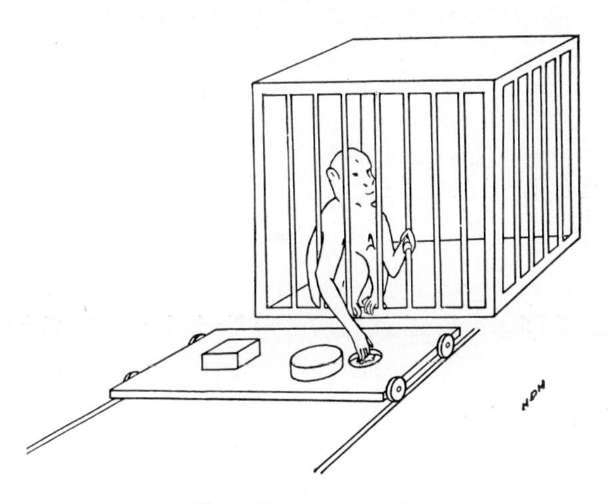

Fig. 13. Klüver "form board" apparatus.

Klüver's [20] "form-board" technique (see Fig. 13) has received little attention, although data obtained by Klüver and by others [14] has indicated that it attains unparalleled efficiency in discrimination tests on monkeys. The Klüver "form board" meets all criteria of a good discrimination apparatus and has in addition the merit of complete simplicity. Its primary limitations lie in lack of control of the physical properties of the stimuli used and in the fact that its adaptability to testing subprimate animals *has not yet been demonstrated.*

No discussion of *visual* discrimination is complete without noting the great emphasis which has been placed on utilizing efficient apparatus and the little emphasis on utilizing efficient stimuli. Kohts's [21] work on the chimpanzee indicated that stereometric objects (three-dimensional objects differing in over-all size and form) are much more easily discriminated by the chimpanzee than are the types of stimuli (designs painted on flat surfaces) commonly used in comparative psychology laboratories, and it is not unlikely that this finding would hold good for many other species. Harlow has demonstrated that monkeys learn to discriminate stimulus objects differing in color or total form more readily than stimuli differing only in their inscribed patterns [14].

TECHNIQUES OF MEASURING LEARNING

Comparative psychologists have given more attention to problems of learning than to any other single field. In spite of this fact, the number of new and distinctive techniques devised for the study and analysis of learning phenomena is surprisingly limited.

Many studies on the analysis of learning and the factors influencing learning have used the same techniques that have been developed for studying discrimination and motivation, or slight modifications of these techniques.

Adaptation of Discrimination Learning Techniques to Other Learning Problems

As has already been described in Chapter 2, the *conditioned reflex methods and techniques* have been used in the analysis of the basic phenomena theoretically underlying the learning process and in the attempted analysis of more complex forms of learning, the so-called higher-order conditioned responses.

Recently a series of conditioning studies [17] was made, using the Skinner box (see Fig. 3) for analysis of some of the more basic conditioning phenomena, such as reinforcement, extinction, generalization, and relation of drive to learning.

Conditioning techniques have proved successful in detailed and quantitative analysis of the phenomena underlying conditioning. There is no reason, however, to assume that these results or these phenomena have wide generalization to all learning situations. Conditioning techniques have not been successfully adapted to the study of more complicated kinds of learning.

The typical *discrimination techniques,* in which two or more stimuli are simultaneously presented, have been frequently used in their original or modified form in the study of the phenomena of learning.

Both the Lashley jumping box and the Klüver "form board" (see Figs. 12 and 13) have been used to test the ability of various animals to respond to some generalized form, such as "triangularity," and to avoid all other forms.

The nature of the results may be indicated by noting that Fields [8], in a comprehensive study, was able to train rats to respond to the triangle without regard to size, rotation, color, or number. Furthermore, the rats were able to distinguish the triangles from a host of different negative figures. After Fields' original study, investigators have used discrimination techniques to measure similar abilities in cats, dogs, raccoons, monkeys, chimpanzees, and children. Although the exact theoretical import of these studies has occasioned dispute, the tests show how effectively discrimination techniques may be used in the investigation of more complicated learning problems.

A host of learning problems of widely varying complexity has been studied with slight adaptations of accepted standardized discrimination techniques: discrimination box, jumping box, and "form board" (see Figs. 10, 11, and 13). Thus "hypotheses" in rats have been investigated, delayed responses in rats, monkeys, and chimpanzees tested, and the ability of rats, monkeys, and chimpanzees to comprehend differences (oddity) and similarities (matching) has been measured.

In comparative psychology the *maze* has been the most widely used apparatus for investigations of learning. It has been applied to the study of learning in the earthworm, cockroach, fish, turtle, rat, monkey, chimpanzee, and man and has proved useful in testing a wide variety of conditions that influence learning, including spaced practice, delayed incentives, strength of drives, and factors of age, sex, heredity, inanition, sensory control, and neural injury.

Two kinds of mazes have been used: alley mazes and elevated mazes, as illustrated by Figs. 14 and 15. Alley mazes are passageways of wood or metal, usually covered by hardware cloth. Elevated mazes are narrow wooden runways, an inch wide or less, raised 1 to 3 feet above the ground. Direct comparison of homologous patterns indicates that rats learn more readily on the elevated than on the alley form.

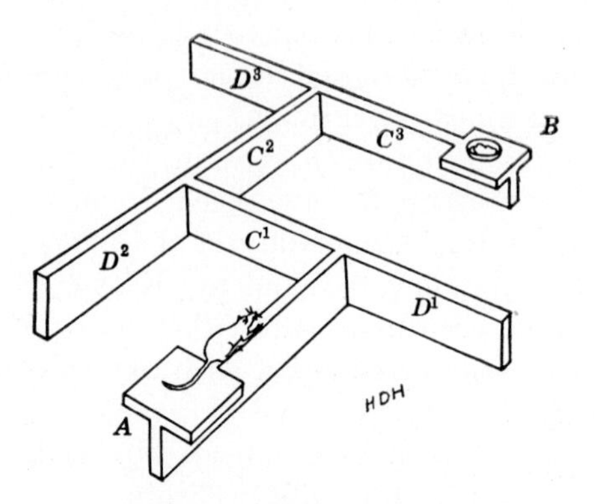

Fig. 14. Elevated maze.

A = starting point, B = food point, C^1, C^2, C^3 = correct pathways, D^1, D^2, D^3 = incorrect pathways or culs-de-sac.

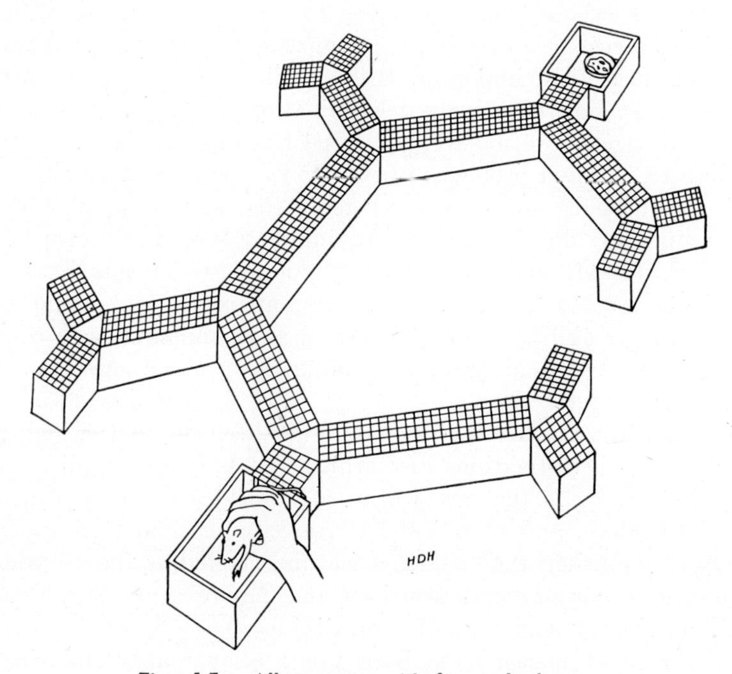

Fig. 15. Alley maze with four culs-de-sac.

Intensive research has been done on the nature of the pattern in mazes, i.e., the nature and arrangement of the correct pathway units and the culs-de-sac, or incorrect pathway units. In the early mazes the individual units, both true pathways and culs-de-sac, differed greatly in form and in length. The more recently developed mazes attempt to equate the physical properties of all individual units, with the result that multiple T- or U-shaped units are commonly used. Such mazes have proved far more reliable than those in which the form of the choice points or the lengths of the individual units differ.

The limitations of the maze lie in the fact that different species adapt to it with varying success (a superior rat will do better than the average college student; the inferior college student may be surpassed by the cockroach), and that it apparently tests a limited form of

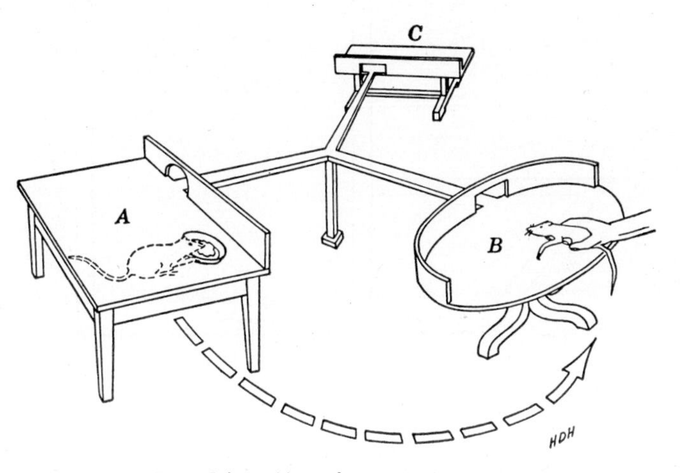

Fig. 16. Maier's reasoning test.

See text for explanation.

learning, a kind of serial learning. In this regard it should be noted that rats selectively bred to be maze geniuses show no unusual abilities on other learning apparatus [31].

The maze, particularly the elevated maze, may be adapted for use in other problems, possibly measuring more complicated learning functions.

Maier's reasoning test [24], as shown in Fig. 16, is a case in point. The rat is first allowed to explore the entire situation (experience I), and then is placed on one of the tables (*A* in Fig. 16) and given food (experience II). The rat is then placed on a different table (*B* in Fig. 16) from the one on which he received food, and the problem is to combine experiences I and II and immediately go to the food-rewarded table.

Adaptations of the elevated maze apparatus have also been extensively used by Tolman and his associates [30] in the demonstration of insightful and ideational behavior in the rat. These investigators demonstrated rapid and appropriate selection between alternate pathways after established habits had been altered by changed motivation or by mechanical obstruction of preferred pathways.

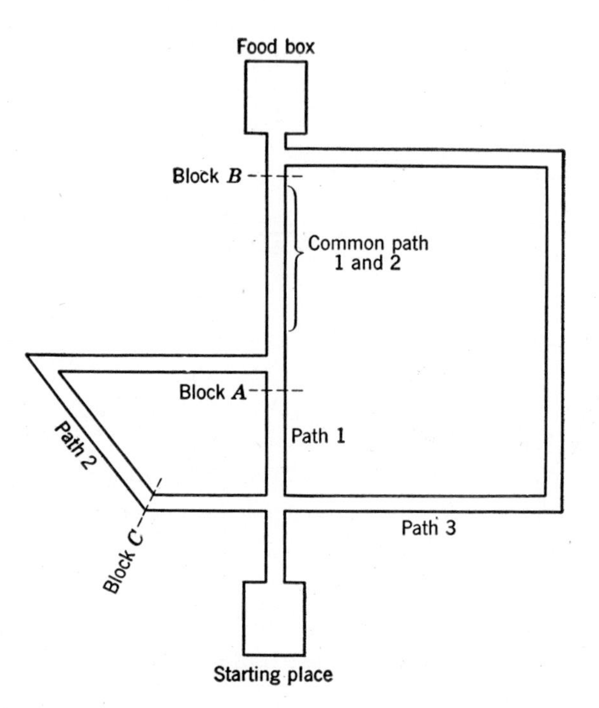

Fig. 17. Maze used to demonstrate inferential expectation based on perception.

See text for explanation.

In Fig. 17 is shown a maze used by Tolman and Honzik to demonstrate inferential expectation based on perception. In this maze a rat may go from starting place to food box by path 1, which is the shortest, path 2, the next shortest, or path 3, the longest. Paths 1 and 2, it should be noted, have a section which is common to both and *not common* to path 3. During preliminary training path 1 was blocked at *A*, and the rats learned to back out of path 1 and take path 2. Only when path 2 was blocked at *C* did they choose path 3. In the final tests the block was placed at *B* across the common section of paths 1 and 2. Almost all the rats then backed out of path 1 and chose path 3 rather than path 2. Since path 2 had previously been preferred to path 3, it may be assumed that they had perceived the relationship of the common path and "inferred" that block *B* obstructed it.

In behalf of the maze it should be said that many different kinds of learning problems may be investigated with it, that tests can be run rapidly and efficiently, that the maze may be made automatic if the experimenter so desires, and that the generalized maze structure may be adapted for special learning problems.

The Problem Box

Next to the maze, the problem box has been used in more studies in comparative psychology than any other apparatus. One essential difference between these two instruments is that the maze has commonly given more satisfactory and more reliable data.

The problem box is usually a box with a door, which is restrained by some instrument: a bar, hook, string, latch, lever, plunger, chain, or ring. Another form of problem box opens automatically when a pole, plate, or series of plates is touched or moved. A single restraining device or multiple restraining devices may be used; in the latter case, these devices may be opened in any order, or they may be opened only in some fixed order. The animal may be placed in the problem box and the incentive outside, or the animal may be placed outside and the incentive inside.

The results with most problem boxes have been far from satisfactory. Difficulty has been encountered in maintaining motivation; efficient control of the stimulus conditions has not been described; and the data usually have low reliability. In spite of all these difficulties, however, the problem box has been used in detailed analysis of the learning mechanisms in cats, in investigations of cortical lesions in monkeys and chimpanzees, in studies of age factors in rat learning, and in the comparison of learning capacities in various species of mammals.

Multiple-choice Apparatus

A number of different kinds of apparatus devised for the investigation of complex learning problems require that the animal select from multiple stimuli. One of the earliest was the quadruple-choice apparatus devised by Hamilton [11]. The animal was faced with four different doors, and the only principle of correctness was that the same door was never correct for two successive trials. Success was measured in terms of total doors opened per one hundred trials or in terms of kinds of errors made. Tests were made on gophers, rats, a horse, cats, dogs, monkeys, and men, and success was related to position in the phyletic series.

The Yerkes multiple-choice apparatus [35] (see Fig. 18), presented the subject with nine or more compartments, of which only some, such as three, five, or seven, were commonly used in any single experiment or experimental setting. The animal was required to respond consistently to such arrangements as "first on the right," "second on the left," "alternate right and left," and "middle."

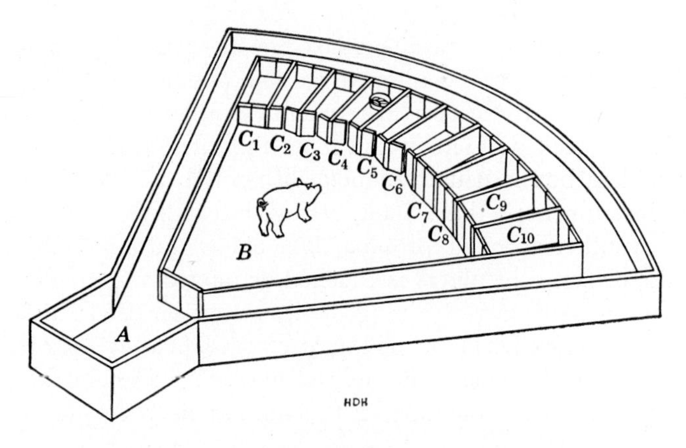

Fig. 18. Yerkes multiple-choice apparatus.

A = entrance compartment, B = reaction compartment, C_1–C_{10} = test compartments. Test is for middleness," with compartments 2–6 used on the illustrated trial.

The multiple-choice apparatus, as originally designed, was a large enclosed cage, and the stimuli were doors leading to compartments. More recently tests were made on primates with multiple-choice apparatus in which the stimuli were boxes with lids. The improved scores made by primates on the second as opposed to the first type of apparatus, attest to the fact that apparatus must be suitable to the animal tested and that apparatus of a particular form is seldom if ever equally adapted to all animal species.

Any discrimination technique which permits choice of stimuli simultaneously presented can be adapted as a multiple-choice apparatus. Multiple-choice techniques may be used to test a variety of problems, limited only by the ingenuity of the experimenter. In terms of range of problems which may be tested and ready adaptability to a wide

Motives are internal determinants of behavior and include organic states of hunger, thirst, fatigue, bladder tension, and sexual tension, as well as determining sets or intentions to act in some specific manner. *Incentives* are of two main kinds: goal objects, such as food or mate, and the various spurs and checks to behavior. A word of praise, a gold star placed after one's name, a recognition of merit, the presence of a rival—these are incentives to action. The distinction will be illustrated in the methods described below.

The Method of Equivalent Groups in the Study of Incentives

In most experimental work a major requirement is to keep conditions constant except for one factor, which is systematically varied. In studies of incentives it is customary to start with several groups of subjects which have been equated in initial ability, the amount of previous practice, and other factors which may affect the quality of performance. One of these groups serves as a control, and its members carry out the imposed task under standard conditions of motivation.

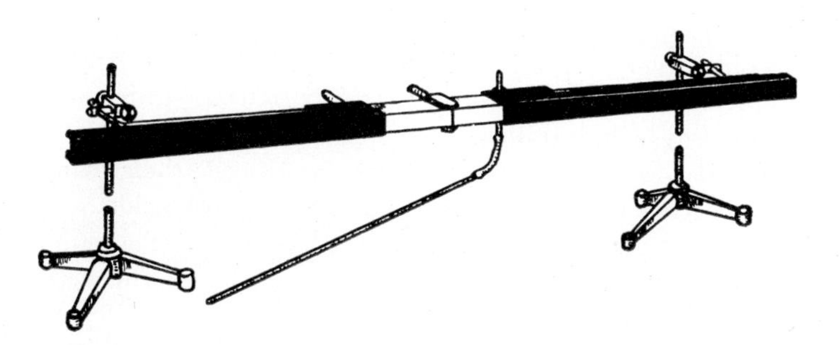

Fig. 1. Galton bar for studying incentives in relation to visual space discrimination.

By rotating the rod clockwise or counterclockwise, the subject can move the shield at the right of the hair line until the visible extent at the right appears *equal* to that on the left or, as in the present experiment, *twice* that on the left.

The other groups carry out the same imposed task with different incentives and so compose what are called experimental groups. To illustrate the method of equivalent groups an experiment by Hamilton [13] will be cited.

The problem of Hamilton's study was to compare the relative effectiveness of different incentives: punishment, reward, punishment combined with active guessing, punishment combined with passive information, knowledge of results.

The apparatus employed was a modified form of the Galton bar, Fig. 1. This instrument, invented by Francis Galton, has been extensively used in experiments upon visual space perception. It consists of a bar of pure white divided in the middle by a hair line. To the right and left of the hair line are adjustable shields. One of these shields is fixed by the experimenter in a standard position. The subject can move the other by rotating a light rod clockwise or counterclockwise.

In the experiment under consideration a standard visual extent to the left of the hair line was employed. In an actual trial the shield at the right was placed at the hair line, and the subject moved it in an outward direction until he was satisfied that the variable extent was twice the standard. After completing the adjustment he pressed a button to signal that the task had been completed.

On the reverse side of the bar (not shown in the illustration) were adjustable electric contacts. These contacts could be so adjusted that a bell would ring when the subject's setting of the apparatus was within a certain range of error or when his setting was greater than a specified range of error.

On the first day of the experiment sixty subjects made a series of settings of the Galton bar. For each subject the average deviation from the objectively correct setting was computed. On the basis of the average errors Hamilton formed six groups (ten subjects in each) of approximately equal ability.

On following days all the subjects continued their work with the Galton bar but under different conditions of motivation.

1. A *control* group received no special incentive. The subjects in this group were instructed, as on the first day, to set the instrument so that the variable extent appeared to be twice as long as the standard.

2. The subjects in a *punishment* group were told that a bell would ring upon pressing the button if the adjustment of the apparatus was wrong.

3. The subjects in a *reward* group were told that a bell would ring upon pressing the button if the adjustment of the apparatus was right.

4. The subjects in a *guess-with-punishment* group were given the same instructions as those in the punishment group, but in addition they were required to guess the direction of their errors, i.e., whether a given setting was too short or too long. They were not told, however, whether they had guessed correctly or incorrectly.

5. The subjects in a *told-with-punishment* group were given the same instructions as those in the punishment group, but in addition every subject was consistently told the direction of his error.

6. The subjects in a *knowledge* group were told by the experimenter,

in a matter-of-fact voice, whether each setting was right or wrong. If wrong, they were told whether the setting was too short or too long. No bell was used.

In defining a right and a wrong adjustment of the apparatus the average error was employed. Since an average error was computed for each subject separately, individual differences in the acuity of perception did not matter. For each subject right and wrong settings were about equally probable. Moreover, as the experiment progressed, the subjects improved in accuracy. To counteract the effect of practice a new average error was computed at the close of each series. Thus throughout the experiment right and wrong settings occurred with about the same frequency.

In comparing the performance of the groups Hamilton used the average errors on the first day as a basis. For each group he computed the percentage of gain or loss through practice. The following figures summarize the findings:

Group	Percentage of Initial Error
1. Control	127
2. Punishment	24
3. Reward	26
4. Guess-with-punishment	15
5. Told-with-punishment	20
6. Knowledge	45

As will be seen from the figures, the control group deteriorated; in the absence of any special incentive their final score was 127 per cent of the initial score.

Punishment and reward were not significantly different as incentives. In this experiment punishment and reward had the same physical characteristics, since ringing of the same bell served for both. The difference between reward and punishment was in the attitude of the subject. In the punishment group the subjects tried to prevent the ringing of the bell; when it rang, they showed disappointment, made a wry face, or occasionally swore at the bell. In the reward group the subjects tried to make the bell ring; when it rang, some of them showed satisfaction; they said, "What a relief," or "That's better."

From the standpoint of objective gain through practice the guess-with-punishment and the told-with-punishment groups were the best of all. Guessing requires an active attitude toward the task which is highly effective when combined with punishment for errors.

The subjects with knowledge of results made a marked gain through practice in a comparison with the control group, but knowledge alone was not as effective as the motivations which contained a factor of reward or punishment.

Among the general conclusions Hamilton makes the arresting statement that the special incentives yielded a greater accuracy of spatial discrimination than heretofore obtained in the well-known laboratory experiment upon visual extent. The conclusion is important because it shows that in psychological experiments generally the experimenter must control the motivation of the subject. Other experiments might be cited to show that reaction time, the strength of pull on a dynamometer, the score in an intelligence test, the amount of type set per hour, and other measured variables of performance depend upon the subject's motivation.

Approaches to the Analysis of Determining Set

The concept of a determining set arises in almost every field of experimental psychology. It is important in studies of reaction, learning and recall, perceiving, thinking, and other processes. In laboratory situations the task (*Aufgabe*) given to a subject by the instruction produces a set (*Einstellung*) which is a highly significant determinant of performance.

Even if the subject has forgotten the instruction, there is a determining tendency (*determinierende Tendenz*) which acts as a selective and patterning agent. For example, if the subject has been instructed to add, the numbers 6 and 4 evoke the response 10. If he has been instructed to subtract, these same numbers elicit the response 2.

Gibson [11] has pointed out that in contemporary psychology the term *set* has several different meanings. Some of these are illustrated below.

Two examples of experimental method in the analysis of determining set have been selected: first, the conditioned-response method combined with control of instructions; second, the method of controlling the subject's set by presenting spatial patterns, point by point, and requiring the subject to reproduce the patterns immediately.

The first illustration is taken from the work of Hilgard and his collaborators [14, 15]. They systematically varied the instructions to the subjects in an experiment dealing with conditioned discrimination. Their work is important in that it demonstrates a difference between two kinds of set—expectancy and intention—in the acquisition of a conditioned discrimination.

In the investigation the eyelid reflex was used as the unconditioned response. A puff of air delivered to the cornea of the left eye produced reflex closure of the lid. This reflex was conditioned to the illumination of a small window in front of the subject.

There were, in fact, two small windows, each 10 centimeters square, at a distance of 40 centimeters in front of the eyes. Illumination of the window at the left was the *positive* stimulus; the illumination was invariably followed, after an interval of 0.6 second, by a puff of air to the left eye. Illumination of the window at the right was the *negative* stimulus; this illumination was never followed by an air puff.

On the first day of the experiment only positive stimuli were presented. On the second and third days both positive and negative stimuli were employed with equal frequency in a haphazard order.

Sixty subjects participated in the investigation. These were divided into five groups of twelve each. Only three of the groups are here considered, and only the results for the first 2 days.

On the first day each subject was given sixty paired presentations of light followed by air puff. The presentations were spaced at approximately 30 seconds, and there was a 2-minute rest period between successive groups of twelve presentations. No special instructions were presented. In this respect the work was similar to animal experiments upon the conditioned reflex.

On the second and third days the groups were treated differently. The subjects in Group A served as a *control*. They were given no special instruction and no information; they were treated in the same manner throughout the experiment. The subjects in Group B had *knowledge* of conditions. They were told that the illumination of the window at the left would be followed by a puff of air on the cornea of the left eye and that the illumination of the window at the right would not be followed by an air puff. In Group C the subjects also had knowledge of conditions, but in addition they were instructed to react as promptly as possible to the positive stimulus and to refrain from reacting to the negative stimulus. The subjects in this group had *knowledge plus an intention* to behave in a specific manner.

Some of the results of the experiment are presented graphically in Fig. 2. The three curves on the left show that for all subjects the frequency of CR increased with practice on the first day. The three curves on the right are of special interest in that they show differences dependent upon the instruction of the subject.

The subjects of Group A, without special instruction, responded at first to the negative stimulus. In other words, the CR was generalized. With repetition of positive and negative stimuli, however, a conditioned discrimination was built up.

Group B, with knowledge of stimulus conditions, differed from Group A at the start. At the close of the day, however, Groups A and B were

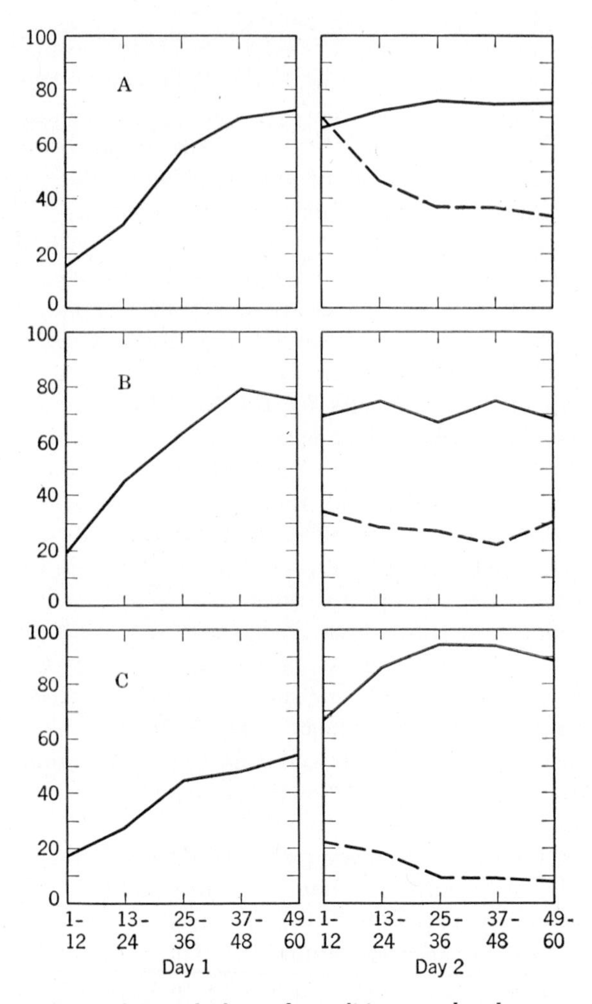

Fig. 2. The effect of knowledge of conditions and voluntary set upon the course of conditioned discrimination.

Each point on the curves represents the percentage of conditioned eyelid responses aroused by illumination of a small window. Each percentage is based upon the responses for a group of 10 subjects with 12 trials per subject. Successive trials are represented on the base line from left to right.

The three graphs at the left show the gradual increase in the frequency of CR with practice. The three graphs at the right show changes in the frequency of CR on the second day of the experiment. Conditioned responses to a positive stimulus are shown by a solid line and those to a negative stimulus by a broken line.

The differences in instruction among the three groups of subjects are described in the text. (After Hilgard and collaborators [14].)

similar. We assume that the information given to Group B built up in these subjects an expectancy which gave them an initial advantage over Group A. With repetition Group A in some manner learned to discriminate between positive and negative stimuli, and so in the end the two groups were not unlike.

Group C, with knowledge plus an intention, made a marked discrimination between positive and negative stimuli at the start. With practice the frequency of discrimination increased. It is assumed that the set to react to the positive stimulus and not to the negative stimulus is an important factor underlying the results.

A comparison of the results for Groups B and C supports a distinction between determining set in the sense of *expectancy* and determining set in the sense of *intention.*

Incidentally, all eyelid reactions were recorded with the Dodge pendulum-photochronograph (see page 616). The photographic records showed the magnitude of the response as well as the latency of both conditioned and unconditioned reactions.

The second illustration presents a very different experimental method for the study of determining set. In the investigations of Compton and Young [8] and Thomas and Young [33] the general plan was to control determining set directly by presenting spatial patterns, point after point, and instructing the subject to reproduce these patterns immediately. In the vicinity of the subject lights were flashed, buzzers sounded, contacts made with the skin. After a series of such point stimulations the subject attempted to indicate the positions and sequence of the stimulations.

Under the general instruction the successive stimulations from different points in space built up a determining set. The subject acted immediately upon the basis of his set, reproducing or attempting to reproduce the pattern. The investigation as a whole was concerned with the relation between set and the sensory mode of presenting patterns and the motor mode of reproducing them. To what extent do central and peripheral processes enter into the bodily mechanism of determining set?

In the first experiment patterns were presented to the eye, the ear, and the skin, singly and in combination. Each pattern consisted of six point stimulations given successively from five positions. The subject was instructed to reproduce the patterns immediately by pressing keys which corresponded in position to the sources of stimulation. The plan of the experiment will be made clear by reference to Fig. 3.

Patterns were presented visually by the successive flashing of lights located at the points marked *A, B, C, D, E*. In other trials the same patterns were presented to the ear by successive sounding of electric buzzers located at *Q, R, S, T, U*. The buzzers were separated so widely that there was no error of sound localization. The same patterns were also presented to the sense of touch by a series of sharp contacts. The subject was instructed to rest his forearms on the felt pad upon the table. There were five holes through this pad at points

Fig. 3. Apparatus for presenting spatial patterns, point by point, to the different senses. (After Compton and Young [8].)

designated *I, J, K, L, M*. Through each hole a sharp point (actuated by a silent electromagnet) made contact with the skin. The same patterns, moreover, were presented in mixed modes: to the eyes and ears alternately, to the eyes and skin alternately, to the ears and skin alternately, and to all three senses in rotation (eye-ear-skin).

The subject reproduced or attempted to reproduce all patterns immediately after their presentation by pressing five signal keys located at 1, 2, 3, 4, 5. From the point of view of the subject the signal keys had the same angular separation as the lights, the buzzers, and the contact points.

Before considering results let us turn to the second experiment. In the first experiment there were seven modes of presenting spatial patterns and only one mode of reproducing them. In the second experiment there was only one mode of presenting patterns. All patterns were presented to the eye by the successive flashing of six lights located at 1, 2, 3, 4, 5, 6 (Fig. 4). There were, however, seven modes of reproducing the patterns through three motor systems employed singly and in combination.

On a given trial, for example, the subject was instructed to reproduce a pattern by hand. Throughout the trial the word *hand* was exposed at point *X*, Fig. 4, to indicate that the hand alone was to be used in reproducing the pattern. With this instruction the subject pressed the keys located at *G, H, I, J, K, L*. If the instruction was *foot,* the subject reproduced the pattern by pressing the pedals *M, N, O, P, Q, R*. If the instruction read *head,* the subject reproduced the pattern by pressing head keys conveniently located upon an arc at

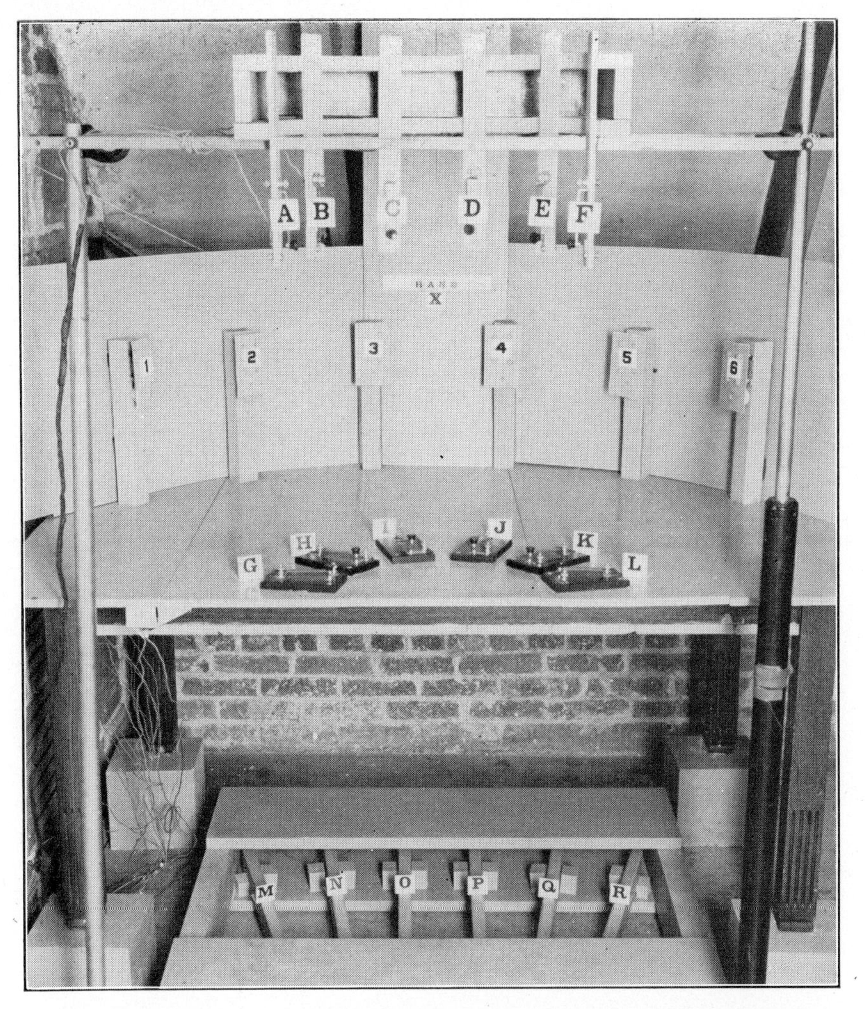

Fig. 4. Apparatus to control the motor mode of reproduction of patterns presented visually, point by point. (After Thomas and Young [33].)

A, B, C, D, E, F. There were, moreover, mixed modes of reproduction in which the subject used alternately the hands and head, hands and feet, head and feet, or all three motor systems in rotation (head-hand-foot).

In both experiments a buzzer served as a foresignal, commencing 2 seconds before the first stimulation. The point stimulations followed each other without pause, each lasting for 0.7 second.

In both experiments the patterns were controlled by a telephone switchboard remote from the subject. On this switchboard the flashing of lights indicated to the experimenter that a pattern had been correctly reproduced or that there were omissions or transpositions in the attempt of the subject to reproduce a given pattern.

Some of the more general results of these two experiments are as follows: A correlational analysis of the scores for correct reproduction of patterns showed that the relative difficulty of reproducing different patterns depends to a high degree upon the space-time relationships of the point stimulations. If a pattern is difficult when presented to the eye, the same pattern is difficult when presented to the ear or to the skin. If a pattern is difficult when reproduced manually, the same pattern is difficult when reproduced with the pedals or with the head keys. In other words, difficulty lies in the sequence of point stimulations.

It was also found that, if a subject makes a relatively high score in reproducing visual patterns, he tends to make a relatively high score in reproducing auditory or tactual patterns. If he makes a relatively high score when reproducing patterns with his hands, he tends to make a relatively high score when reproducing them with his feet or his head. In other words, there is a factor of central ability in accepting a set and acting immediately upon it.

There is, however, good evidence for the importance of peripheral factors in determining set. In general, the single modes of presentation (one sense) and reproduction (one motor system) give higher reproduction scores than the mixed modes (two or three senses or two or three motor systems). Also there are differences among the senses and the motor systems which may depend upon familiarity or some other condition.

The investigation as a whole demonstrates that both central and peripheral processes enter into the bodily mechanisms involved in accepting a determining set and acting immediately upon it.

The Technique of Goal-setting in Experiments upon the Level of Aspiration

The experiences of success and failure are relative to some norm. If a high jumper places the cross-bar at 1 foot, he will not experience success, because the jump is too easy. If he places the bar at 8 feet, he will not experience failure, because for him the jump is impossible. If he places the bar at 5 feet, he can sometimes clear it but more commonly he misses. The experiences of success and failure are clearly relative to the goal which has been set. If a performance is better than the goal which has been set, the individual experiences success; if poorer, he experiences failure. The experiences of success and failure are also relative to the performance of a group, success being a relatively good performance and failure a relatively poor one.

In their early experiments upon the setting of goals Lewin and his students were concerned largely with the *experiences* of success and failure. More recent work in America has led to objective formulations.

In experiments upon the *level of aspiration* (translation of the German *Anspruchsniveau*) the subject is required to make a public declaration of what he aims to achieve. A second requirement is that the information be put in quantitative terms. A variety of experimental tasks which meet these requirements has been used: throwing darts at a target, running a maze of given complexity, sorting cards, writing letters in code, adding.

The level of aspiration can thus be expressed in terms of a unidimensional quantitative scale of difficulty. The actual level of performance is measured on the same scale. The difference between the level of aspiration and the level of performance is known as the *difference score*.

In addition to the difference score other measurements have been employed in experiments upon the level of aspiration. The *height*, expressed directly in units of the scale of achievement, is a useful measure in comparing individuals and in studying the successive goals set by an individual. The *rigidity* of an individual (or conversely his *mobility*) is a measure of the frequency of changes in the level of aspiration or the total magnitude of such changes. The *responsiveness* of a subject is measured by the number of times he lowers his goal if the preceding performance was poor and the number of times he raises his goal if the preceding performance was good.

In a critical review of methodology in experiments upon the level of aspiration, Rotter [29] pointed out that there is ambiguity in the instruction: What score will you get next time? Some subjects respond to this question in terms of a hope or wish. Others respond to it by indicating an objective judgment or expectation based upon experience. Still others respond in terms of a compromise between wish and objective judgment.

If it were possible to remove this ambiguity, two forms of goal setting would remain: first, a wishful, autistic expression based upon a desire to appear well in public; second, an objective, realistic judgment of future performance based upon previous experience. Some psychologists have thought that the existence of this ambiguity makes the technique of goal-setting useful in studies of personality. Some persons are realistic in the setting of goals; others resort to wishful thinking. Experiments upon the level of aspiration throw light upon this difference in personality.

From the point of view of methodology, the essential feature in experiments upon the level of aspiration is the requirement that the subject set for himself a quantitative goal in a social situation. He is required to exhibit his skill or lack of skill. He risks failure and occasionally wins success. In some studies the experimenter resorts to some justifiable trickery in order to make the subject succeed or fail. Inevitably the setting of a goal involves the attitudes of self-evaluation and the question: How good am I in this kind of thing?

Because the attitudes of self-evaluation are involved, the experiments on goal-setting are theoretically and practically important. For further details and bibliography the student is referred to the reviews by Frank [10] and Lewin *et al.* [22].

METHODS FOR THE STUDY OF FEELING AND EVALUATION

The experimental methods considered in the foregoing division of this chapter have been employed in the analysis of human motivation. The group of methods next to be examined are directed toward the study of related psychological processes: feeling and evaluation.

Evaluation is a process of judgment which depends upon attitudes and motives (wishes) as well as upon habits. To explain human conduct we must know about the likes and dislikes, the wishes, and the habits of individuals. In the development of attitudes, motives, and habits the affective processes play a dominant role, and for this reason they must be considered in any psychological discussion of human motivation.

Broadly considered, the affective processes include emotions, moods, sentiments, and interests, as well as the simple feelings characterized as pleasant and unpleasant. More narrowly, the affective processes are pleasantness and unpleasantness themselves. The latter are conscious experiences which can be reported and studied from the subjective point of view.

The Introspective Description of Felt Experience

Feeling is a conscious experience, and to study it one must employ the introspective method. This method will be illustrated by reference to an investigation by Nafe [27].

Before the work of Nafe it was commonly assumed that pleasantness and unpleasantness are non-sensory processes. They differ in quality, in intensity, and in temporal course, but they lack attensity (attentive clearness). If one attempts to attend to a feeling of pleasantness or unpleasantness, he finds only sensory processes, especially organic and kinesthetic patterns. These patterns are attentively clear, but they are sensory in nature, not affective.

Nafe argued that earlier experimenters upon affective experience had been too much concerned with arousing feeling. They had made *feelers* of their subjects, rather than *observers of feeling.* To correct this state of affairs, feelings of only moderate intensity were aroused. The subjects were given a variety of stimulus objects in the visual, auditory, olfactory, gustatory, and tactual fields and were trained to observe feeling. Nafe started from the assumption that pleasantness (P) and unpleasantness (U) are *palpable* experiences, i.e., that these experiences in some way or other are observable and reportable.

In an actual experiment Nafe presented a stimulus object intended to arouse a moderately pleasant or a moderately unpleasant sensory experience. He instructed his subjects to attend as exclusively as possible to the affective side of experience and to describe the feeling itself as accurately as possible.

At first the observers had some difficulty in carrying out the instruction, but as the experiment continued they came increasingly to describe P as a bright pressure or pressure-like experience and U as a dull pressure or pressure-like experience. These affective pressures were described as varying in intensity, duration, and voluminousness. They were not precisely localized; usually they were not localized at all. Sometimes they were vaguely localized in some region of the body, and occasionally they were projected out from the body.

In a further experiment upon affective experience, however, Hoisington [16] reported some observations upon the localization of P and U. The dull pressures of U were localized in the general region of the abdomen, well inside the body. The bright pressures of P were localized in the upper part of the body in the region of the shoulders and neck. The pressures of P were described as bright, light, expansive feelings in the chest; the pressures of U as dull, contracted feelings in the abdomen.

The interpretation of Nafe's result is a different problem. One may ask: Are these bright and dull pressures true sensory processes? If so, what and where are the receptors? Or are the pressure-like experiences merely the sensory concomitants of non-sensory affective processes? Further research will answer these questions.

The Direct Report of Affective Reaction

In a good many psychological experiments the subject is instructed to indicate whether he *likes* or *dislikes* some object or activity. There is no attempt at descriptive analysis, as in the foregoing investigation.

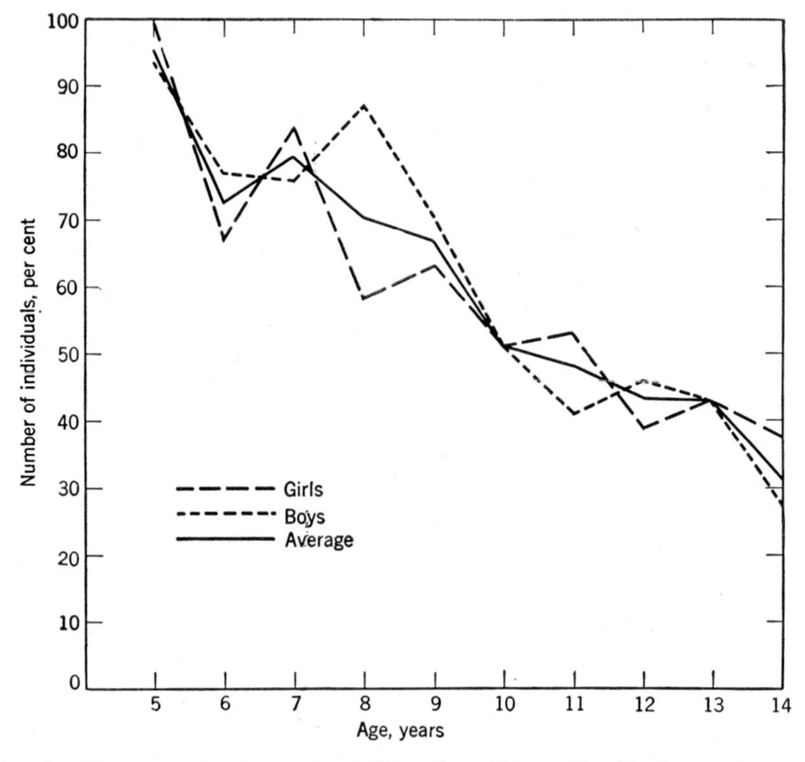

Fig. 5. Decrease in the palatability of cod-liver oil with increasing age of individual.

The curves are based upon a group of 328 Baltimore school children, age 5 to 14. The percentage of individuals liking the taste of cod-liver oil is shown by the vertical scale. (After Richter [28].)

The verbal report of the subject is commonly supplemented by observations of gross behavior. This method will be illustrated by reference to a study by Richter.

Richter [28] tested over a thousand children, ages five to fourteen, by letting each child taste a small spoonful of unadulterated cod-liver oil and asking him whether he liked or disliked it. The response of each child, verbal and non-verbal, was observed and recorded.

The results were changed into percentages of individuals *liking* cod-liver oil at each age level. These results are summarized graphically in Fig. 5, which shows the results for 328 children tested in one school near the Johns Hopkins Hospital.

In the 5-year group 100 per cent of the girls and 92 per cent of the boys liked the cod-liver oil. Progressively with increasing age, more and more children manifested a dislike for the substance. In the 14-year group only 36 per cent of the girls and 28 per cent of the boys liked it. Incidentally, Richter comments that some children at 14 years had an almost insatiable appetite for cod-liver oil. When allowed to satisfy their craving, they took as much as 16 tablespoonsful in 1 day and continued to take high amounts for 5 to 10 days. After this they took small amounts and finally stated that they no longer liked it. See also Chapter 10, pages 276–279.

The psychological procedure in an experiment of this kind is relatively simple. No special training is required of the subject. It is necessary to determine through the words of the subject and by observing his gross behavior whether the affective reaction is one of acceptance or rejection, liking or disliking, yes or no.

Objective Observation in Affective Psychology

When the problems of affective psychology are approached with a strictly objective point of view, they are found to center around the processes of acceptance and rejection and especially around preferential discrimination. The objective approach to affective psychology is illustrated by the studies of Young [38] upon food preferences of the rat.

On a given trial the animal is offered a choice between two kinds of food presented simultaneously. As soon as he accepts one of the pair, both are removed from his reach. The foods are presented side by side, and their relative positions are interchanged from trial to trial so that, if a rat forms the habit of accepting the food in a given position, this fact can be readily detected. If he develops a preference between the foods, this is clearly apparent in a series of trials.

The foods are placed in glass food tubes, which are shown at *F* in Fig. 6. At the start of a test the rat is locked into a box (*B*). When a sliding door (*D*) is raised, the animal is permitted to enter the compartment containing the foods. The unpracticed animal explores the apparatus and discovers the foods in the process. The trained animal runs directly from the box to the foods and takes a bite or sip of one of them. His behavior is observed by the experimenter through a window (*W*).

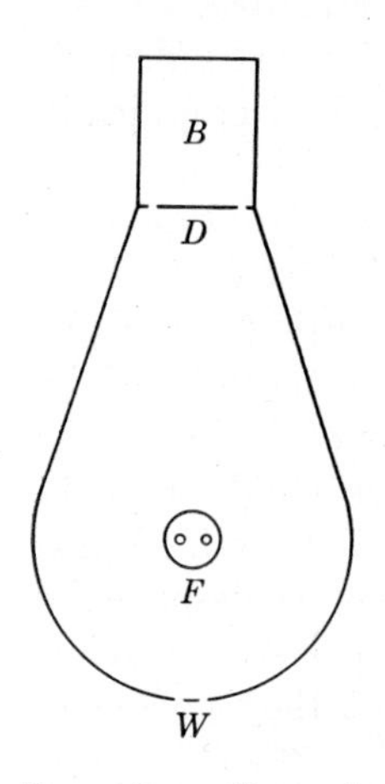

Fig. 6. Ground plan of apparatus for testing food preferences.

After the rat has made a choice or nibbled one of the foods, both are lowered, and the opening in the floor is closed. The experimenter then waits until the rat returns to the box and the sliding door is closed. The time required for a rat to return to the box varies with the amount of training he has had and with the relative palatability of the foods.

The photograph in Fig. 7 gives further details of the technique. The food tubes (*F*) are held in a turntable (*T*), which can be rotated 180 degrees, clockwise or counterclockwise, by pulling upon strings (*S*). The foods can be raised or lowered by an elevator (*E*), so balanced that it remains indefinitely in the upper or lower position. The door to the box is attached to a lever arm (*A*), which the experimenter can control by means of a cord (*C*). Throughout a test a signal lamp (*L*) flashes once a minute. (In more recent work a buzzer, sounding once a minute, has been substituted for the lamp as a means of time control.) The observation window is seen at *W*.

A single trial reveals no preference, for behavior may be determined by spatial factors without true preferential discrimination. It requires at least two successive trials, with the relative positions of the foods interchanged, to indicate any preference. A pair of successive runs is thus the true unit of the test. In recent work ten pairs (twenty runs) have been arbitrarily used as a complete test of preference.

Among various results which have been obtained with the method of preference, several are as follows: (1) The foods in a group, when tested in all possible pairs, arrange themselves in a transitive series from high to low palatability. (2) When dietary conditions are held constant, the rats of a group show remarkable uniformity and stability in the food preferences they reveal. (3) A given food preference can be reversed by permitting a rat to approach satiation upon the preferred food before a test and by then running repeated tests of preference. (4) Food preferences depend upon the diet. By permanently adding an element to the diet, the relative palatability of this dietary component can be permanently lowered. (5) Rats tend to form dietary habits. Not only do they learn to run back and forth on the apparatus to obtain nibbles of food (shuttle habit), but also they some-

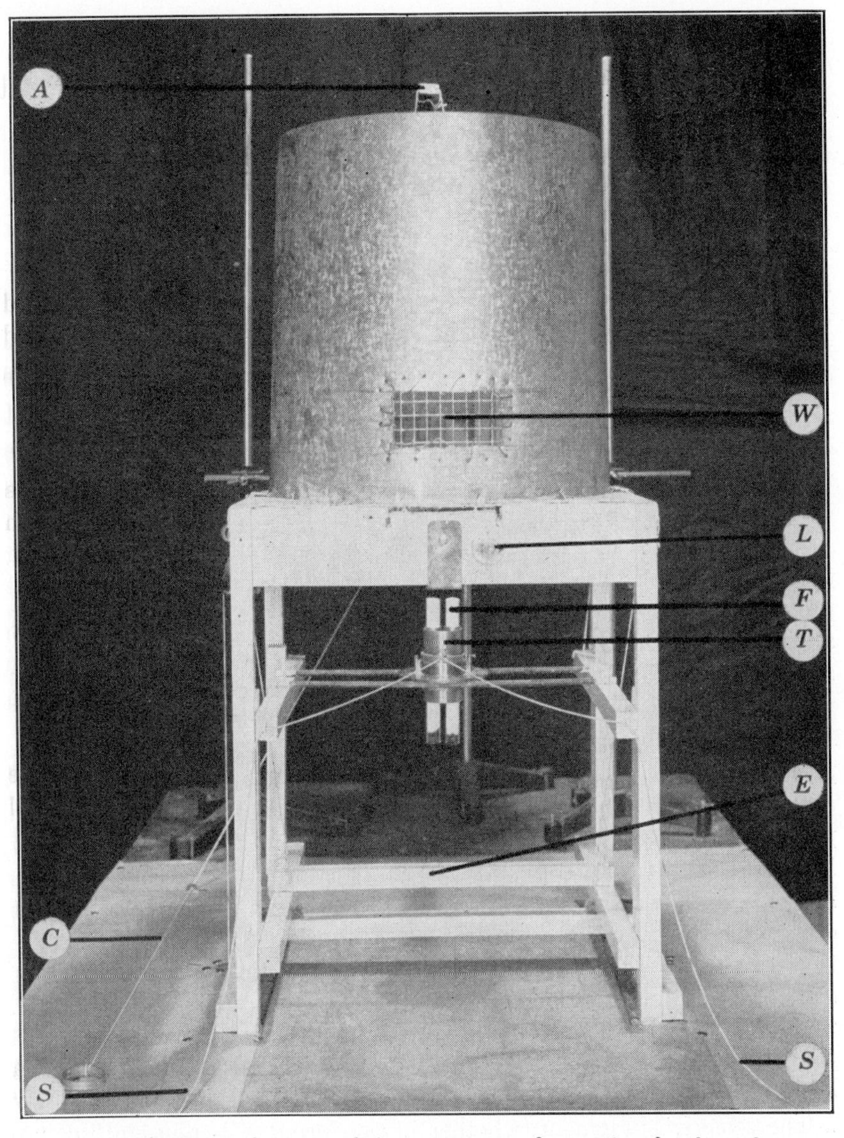

Fig. 7. Experimenter's view of the apparatus for testing food preferences. See explanation in the text.

times learn to accept the food in a given position (position habit) and sometimes the food of a given quality (food habit). (6) Preferential food habits tend to form in agreement with bodily needs. Once a food habit has been formed, however, it may persist as an independent factor in behavior regardless of whether it meets a bodily need.

A Comment upon the Basis of Affective Judgment

Carr [6] has proposed a theory that reports of pleasantness and unpleasantness are actually judgments based not upon any unique and characteristic conscious content but rather upon our normal reactions to the stimulating situation. We are so organized, he points out, that we normally react to enhance, maintain, or repeat certain situations and to minimize or avoid others. A situation which normally arouses the positive kind of response is judged to be pleasant, and one which normally arouses the negative response is judged to be unpleasant. Carr adds that motivating factors complicate the problem. For considerations of health we swallow disagreeable medicine, stop smoking, or refrain from foods which we enjoy. Even though we swallow the medicine, we still judge it to be unpleasant because, if freed from considerations of health, we would reject it.

From the point of view of methodology, it is important to indicate that there is a difference between a judgment and the psychological processes upon which that judgment is based. Carr states that affective judgments are based upon the normal reactions of acceptance and rejection. He adds, however, that other factors than the normal reaction may determine the actual acceptance or rejection.

From the subjective point of view the affective judgment "*X* is pleasant" is not equivalent to the direct psychological report, "Pleasantness was felt." For example, the common statement, "This is a pleasant day" conveys a definite meaning, but it does not necessarily indicate the existence of pleasant feeling at the time the statement was made. As a matter of fact, a person may say, "This is a pleasant day," even though in a grouchy mood of unpleasant depression at the time of the judgment. The present writer has repeatedly found that subjects can describe the quality and intensity of their felt experience. They can trace out its temporal course—the beginning, the waxing and waning, the qualitative shifts, the ending. This is psychological report of existential experience, however, and not affective judgment.

The affective judgment, whether in the form "*X* is pleasant" or "*X* is more pleasant than *Y*," is ambiguous. It tells nothing directly about the affective processes within the subject.

This comment is made to point out that, if an experimenter accepts an affective judgment at face value, he is still ignorant of the psychological basis of that judgment. The experimenter must ask: Upon what is the affective judgment based? He must distinguish between the cognitive process of judging and the affective process of feeling.

Methods of Impression and Expression

It has been traditional in affective psychology to classify the available methods as those of *impression* and those of *expression.* This classification implies that the study of consciousness is the central problem of psychology. The methods of impression are concerned with the relation between stimulus object and the conscious feeling it arouses. The methods of expression are concerned with the relation between conscious feeling and its bodily manifestations.

Historically considered, the methods of impression stem from the pioneer work of Fechner upon experimental esthetics. Of the several methods described by Fechner, the one which he designated as the *method of choice* has been developed into several contemporary forms. The forms differ in the number of stimulus objects presented simultaneously for affective judgment.

In the *order-of-merit method* the subject is presented simultaneously with a series of stimulus objects. (See Chapter 5.) These may be colored papers, spatial forms, works of art, photographic proofs, or other kinds of material. The subject is instructed to arrange the materials in order from the most to the least agreeable. The statistical analysis of results starts with the obtained orders of merit.

In the *method of paired comparison* the subject is presented with two stimulus objects at a time and is instructed to indicate which he prefers. A series of paired presentations is so planned that in the total series the subject compares each stimulus object with every other one. A record is kept of the choice. From the series of choices it is easy to determine the rank order of the stimulus objects in the group. See Chapter 5.

The method of paired comparison has also been used with the *successive* presentations of materials such as tones, musical chords, melodies, rhythms. With successive presentations both time orders are used to balance out a possible time error, just as both spatial arrangements are employed with *simultaneous* presentations to balance out possible space errors.

The number of comparisons with a single spatial arrangement or a single time order is equal to $N\ (N - 1)\ /2$. If N (the number of stimulus objects) is relatively large, the method is not feasible because of the large number of required judgments.

In the *method of single exposure* the subject is presented with only one stimulus object at a time. This stimulus object is then judged or rated by means of a verbal scale of values, a graphic rating scale, or in some other manner. For example, the subject is given two whiffs of a perfume and asked to rate it in terms of the following scale:

+3 Very pleasant
+2 Moderately pleasant
+1 Weakly pleasant
0 Indifferent
−1 Weakly unpleasant
−2 Moderately unpleasant
−3 Very unpleasant

Instead, he may be given a graphic rating scale consisting of a horizontal line of fixed length, marked at one end as *maximally pleasant* and at the other as *maximally unpleasant*. He is instructed to indicate by a mark upon the line his affective rating of the stimulus object.

A technique combining the scale of values and the graphic rating scale has been described by Singer and Young [31]. Another modification, designated as the *percentage-of-pleasantness method,* has been described by Beebe-Center [3].

In the percentage-of-pleasantness method the subject is instructed to respond in terms of three categories: pleasant (P), indifferent (I), unpleasant (U). Repeated ratings are made of the stimulus objects by the same subject or by a group. On the basis of the ratings a percentage of pleasantness is computed by this formula:

$$\text{Percentage of } P = \frac{P + I/2}{P + I + U} \times 100$$

The formula implies that indifference is statistically equivalent to one-half pleasant and one-half unpleasant. It might be argued that judgments of indifference should be disregarded on the ground that they indicate no affective arousal. We would then be left with the two affective categories: pleasant and unpleasant. These two affective ratings could be handled statistically in a very simple manner, as indicated by the data of Richter upon liking and disliking cod-liver oil.

A discussion of the statistical procedures employed in the analysis of results obtained with the methods of impression is beyond the scope of this chapter. The interested reader is referred to the discussion of psychological scaling methods by Guilford [12] and to Chapter 5 of this book.

Next let us examine the methods of expression. At the turn of the century and in the first decade of the present century a good many experiments were carried out by the methods of expression. The general aim of these experiments was to study the relation between conscious processes, especially feeling and attention, and peripheral bodily changes, such as those in respiration, pulse, blood pressure, and glandular secretion. It was hoped to find some physiological *sine qua non* of pleasantness and unpleasantness, but this hope was not realized. Significant correlations were obtained, but no bodily process was invariably present when the subject reported *pleasant* or when he reported *unpleasant*.

The reasons for this failure are a matter of opinion. Several possible explanations occur to the writer. First, it is likely that the introspections of the subjects were ambiguous. At that time a clear distinction was not drawn between affective judgment (purely cognitive statement of meaning) and true affective report of existential pleasantness and unpleasantness. Second, the experimental techniques were directed exclusively to peripheral changes. In view of the results obtained, it seems likely that the physiological *sine qua non* of felt pleasantness and felt unpleasantness lies hidden within the dynamic interrelationships of central neural processes. Peripheral manifestations do not go to the heart of the problem. Third, it is a historical fact that at about this time American psychologists turned toward objective methods in psychology. Watson's behaviorism relegated the study of consciousness to the ash can. Since the methods of expression imply an interest in conscious feeling, these methods fell into disrepute.

This failure, however, does not imply that the problem is closed. Some day, with sharper definitions of terms and with more adequate physiological techniques, the central physiology of pleasantness and unpleasantness will be discovered.

The instruments employed in the study of bodily changes were for the most part borrowed from physiology. A partial list, with a few modern additions, follows:

PLETHYSMOGRAPH. An instrument for studying changes in the volume of the arm, hand, finger, or other part of the body. Volume changes are due to constriction or dilation of the blood vessels.

SPHYGMOGRAPH. An instrument for recording the pulse, showing changes in the rate, amplitude, or pattern of the beat.

SPHYGMOMANOMETER. An instrument for measuring blood pressure. Absolute blood pressure can be measured at a given moment. Continuous variations in blood pressure can be measured by setting the instrument at a pressure level between maximal (systolic) and minimal (diastolic) pressure.

PNEUMOGRAPH. An instrument for measuring changes in the rate, depth, and pattern of respiration. (A pneumograph for registering abdominal respiration may be seen in Fig. 9.)

Dynamometer. An instrument for measuring the strength of pull of a group of muscles.

Ergograph. An apparatus for recording the work done by a group of muscles. An ergograph requires the subject to lift a weight rhythmically by arm or leg muscles.

Tremograph. An instrument for measuring involuntary muscular tremor in the skeletal muscles. In using the tremograph, the subject is instructed to hold steady his finger or a stylus.

Automatograph. An apparatus for recording involuntary movement. The subject is required to rest his arm on a suspended board or to place his fingers lightly on a glass plate which rests upon steel balls. Involuntary movements are recorded graphically or photographically.

Ataximeter. An instrument for recording body sway.

Galvanometer. An instrument used in studies of the skin galvanic reflex for measuring changes in the electrical potential of the body.

Voice keys and microphones. Instruments employed for recording vocal reactions.

Electroencephalograph. An instrument for recording changes in electrical brain waves during psychological processes, emotional and non-emotional. See Chapters 14 and 15.

These instruments are commonly employed to investigate bodily changes for their own sake and without reference to conscious experience. Some of the methods used in the objective study of the bodily changes of emotion will be described in the next main section of this chapter. For further discussion of the classical methods of impression and expression see Chapter 2 of Beebe-Center [3]. For a discussion of the apparatus and methods used in recording bodily changes see Chapters 14 and 15 as well as pages 374–384 of the present chapter.

Psychological Tests

Two kinds of psychological tests are especially pertinent to the present topic. First, there are tests of attitude, interest, and value. Second, there are tests which reveal emotional and motivational traits of personality.

Tests of attitude, interest, and value reveal some specific readiness of the individual to react positively or negatively. An *attitude* has been defined as a neural or mental readiness to respond toward or against some psychological object. A persistent prejudice against the Japanese or a bias favoring the Catholic Church is an attitude. An *interest* is an activity which one carries on, with enjoyment, for its own sake, such as playing golf or singing. Activities which are unpleasant are called *aversions*. A *value* is that which a person regards as worth while.

In testing values, for example, the subject is required to make a discrimination between possible alternatives. Let the reader answer this hypothetical question: Would it be justifiable to remove all the water from Niagara Falls, thus destroying its beauty, to generate electric power? If the answer is yes, economic value is placed ahead of esthetic. If the answer is no, esthetic value is placed first. There is no right or wrong answer. It is a question of what one regards as more worth while.

The Allport-Vernon [2] test of value requires the subject to make a series of such discriminations. From the scores a profile is constructed to show the relative balance for that individual among six forms of value: theoretical, economic, esthetic, social, political, religious.

The extensive literature upon tests of social attitude has been reviewed by Allport [1]. See also Chapter 22 of this volume.

After a program of testing and factor analysis, Cattell [7] described twelve primary factors in personality. Several of these factors are described as emotional or motivational traits. The *C* factor is described in these terms:

realistic, facing life	vs.	demoralized, autistic
stable, integrated character	vs.	changeable, characterless, unrealistic
calm, self-effacing, patient	vs.	restless, sthenic, hypomanic
emotionally mature, adjusting	vs.	infantile, demanding, self-centered

The *E* factor, designated dominance (hypomania) vs. submissiveness, is described in these contrasting terms:

self-assertive	vs.	self-submissive
willful, egoistic, predatory	vs.	mild, self-effacing, tolerant
smart, assertive	vs.	simple-hearted, meek
tough, solid, talkative	vs.	introspective, sensitive, scared
rigid, tyrannical, vindictive	vs.	adaptable, friendly
surly, hard	vs.	good-natured, easy-going

In the *E* factor the emphasis is upon self-assertiveness and submissiveness in social situations. Hence this factor has motivational implications.

The Method of Sociometry in the Analysis of Interpersonal Relations

When the study of the affective processes is carried on in the field of social psychology, there arises at once a host of problems relating to social attitudes and values, interests, and the social expressions of emotions and motives. Instead of delving into this field of psychology, we will here be content with a single illustration of methodology in the area of interpersonal relations.

Moreno [26] required the individual to express attitudes of liking or disliking toward his associates. These attitudes were tested by instructing the subject to choose among his associates at home, at work, at school. To discover the choices of the persons in a group Moreno called them together and made a little speech. For example, to the children in a classroom a statement something like this was made:

"You are seated according to directions your teacher has given you. You did not choose the neighbor who sits beside you. Now you are given an opportunity to choose the boy or girl whom you would like to have sit on either side of you. Write down your first choice; then your second choice. Look around the room and make up your mind. Remember that next term the persons you choose now may sit beside you."

After the speech 1 minute was allowed for making the choices. From the data a sociogram was constructed which revealed the social position of each individual in the group.

Again, in studying a group of girls living in an institution, Moreno called together the total population and addressed them about as follows:

"You now live in certain houses with other persons according to directions from the administration. The persons who live in the same house with you were not chosen by you, nor were you chosen by them. You are now given the opportunity to choose the persons whom you would like to have live with you in the same house. You can choose any individuals of this community, whether or not they happen to live in your house. Write down your first choice; then your second, third, fourth, and fifth choices, in order. Look around and make up your mind. Remember that the ones you choose now will probably be assigned to live with you in the same house."

In Moreno's procedure three points of methodological significance should be noted. First, every individual is included as a center of affective response. Second, the choice of the subject is motivated by some wish or practical consideration. Third, the choice of the subject is always relative to some criterion, such as *sitting beside* or *living in the same house with.* In work with infants other criteria were employed, such as observing whether one infant noticed another or whether he entered into playful relations with another.

In studying the development of psychological group structure, Moreno placed a group of babies in close proximity and observed their interactions. During the first year of their life they were repeatedly placed together in a room within which they had been living from birth. In making the observations upon interpersonal relations of the infants, Moreno had in mind important questions such as these: Do groups develop like individuals? If so, how do they grow? Some of the results are presented in the sociograms of Fig. 8.

View *A* shows the stage of *organic isolation.* Nine babies of the same age level were placed in the same room in close proximity. This was done repeatedly throughout the first year of life. The problem was not concerned with the development of patterns of response, such

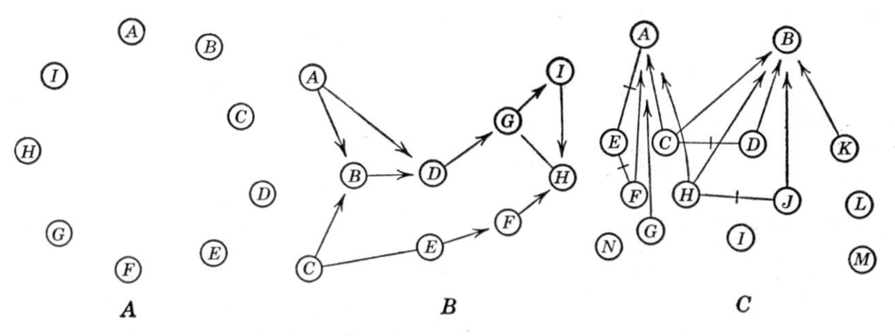

Fig. 8. Development of psychological group structure.

(*A*) Stage of organic isolation. (*B*) Stage of horizontal differentiation. (*C*) Stage of vertical differentiation. (After Moreno [26].)

as crying or sucking, but rather with the development of interpersonal relations and the formation of a group. During the first 26 weeks no group formation could be observed in the infant-to-infant relationships. Each baby lived in isolation from the others; each was self-absorbed. Within the period of isolation, however, the voice of a crying baby sometimes aroused the attention of a neighbor. This was the beginning of recognition of others.

View *B* shows the stage of *horizontal differentiation.* The sociogram illustrates the true beginning of group development. One baby, *C,* recognizes its neighbor, *E,* who recognizes it in return. (This mutual recognition is represented by a line connecting the two individuals, with a short cross-line in the center.) One baby, *D,* is recognized by two neighbors, *A* and *B,* but does not recognize them in return; *D,* however, recognizes neighbor *G.* *B* is attracted to *D, C* is attracted to *B;* by indirection through *C* baby *B* is influenced by *E.*

At this stage of group development, at 20 to 28 weeks and older, physical proximity produces psychological proximity. Infants attend to those near by. Moreno calls this horizontal differentiation.

View *C* shows the stage of *vertical differentiation.* As soon as the babies are able to move around freely and to walk, the differences in physical strength and mental alertness begin to affect group organization. The group begins to develop a top. From 40 or 42 weeks on, one or more infants begin to command a disproportionate share of attention. The structure of the group becomes more complex. *A* and *B* are leaders. *C, D, E, F, G, H, J,* and *K* are dependents. *N, I, L,* and *M* are isolated individuals.

Just as the higher animals have evolved from the simplest forms of life, so the more complex forms of group organization evolve from the simple ones. The analysis of dynamic interpersonal and intergroup relations lies at the heart of social psychology. As a matter of fact, the study of interpersonal (or interbehavioral) relations distinguishes social psychology from individual psychology. For this reason Moreno's methods are important. For further discussion of the methods of studying social behavior see Chapters 21 and 22 of this book.

The experimental methods which have been described are very different from one another. Some are directed toward the analysis of conscious experience. Some are oriented toward the bodily correlates of conscious experience. Some are aimed toward the analysis of behavior—acceptance, rejection, or preferential discrimination. Some are pointed toward the solution of social problems—dynamic interpersonal relations, social attitudes and values, traits of personality. The only thing that ties these methods together into some kind of unity is that they all relate, directly or indirectly, to the psychological processes of feeling and evaluation.

We turn now to the next major division of the chapter, dealing with emotion.

METHODS FOR INVESTIGATING BODILY CHANGES OF EMOTION

An emotion is a natural event. It is something that happens, as does a thunderstorm or a sunrise. It is a complex occurrence, so complex that it must be analyzed piecemeal and from different points of view.

In the older writings of Wundt, James, Titchener, McDougall, and others, an emotion was regarded as a conscious event, and the fundamental problems centered around the relation between the conscious emotion and its bodily expressions. Today psychologists are more interested in the objective aspects of emotion. When viewed objectively, however, the emotion is still exceedingly complex. One must distinguish between the situation which arouses an emotion and the reaction thereto. The emotional reaction itself has both inner and outer aspects. The following example illustrates the different objective aspects.

Cannon [4] has pointed out that during emotional excitement there is an increase in the number of red blood corpuscles (erythrocytes per cubic millimeter) circulating in the blood stream. This increase can be attributed directly to the action of the spleen. The spleen, a muscular organ, contracts and expands; it is a reservoir for erythrocytes. It renders the organism the service of quickly increasing and later of storing away the red corpuscles in the blood. Contraction of the spleen occurs in carbon monoxide poisoning, in hemorrhage, in the lessening of the oxygen content of the blood, as during asphyxia and muscular exercise, and after injections of adrenalin and pituitrin, as well as during emotional excitement.

Cannon has interpreted this fact. The erythrocytes carry oxygen from lungs to heart, brain, and active muscles. In a biological emergency which might involve a struggle for one's life, this reaction of increase is serviceable in that it facilitates the release of energy within the body. The increase in the number of erythrocytes in the blood is a small part of the pattern of bodily changes aroused by an external situation.

If a dog barks at a cat, the cat's hair bristles, his back arches, he spits and growls, his claws protrude, and there are widespread internal bodily changes, including the increase of erythrocytes in the blood stream. Just what is the emotion?

Some psychologists and physiologists use the term *emotion* to designate certain reflex patterns of response—the rage pattern, crying, laughing, etc.—which are coordinated by neural centers in the region of the hypothalamus and below. Others prefer a broader definition: An emotion is an acute disturbance of the individual, arising from the psychological situation, revealed in conscious experience, in behavior, and through marked changes in the vegetative organs.

The emphasis in this definition upon the psychological situation serves to distinguish emotions from organic appetites, which arise from internal bodily conditions. In the above example the barking of a dog is an environmental event. It arouses internal bodily changes which have environmental significance. The bodily changes of emotion arise from a psychological situation—meeting an enemy or a mate or being socially ostracized.

Simultaneous Recording of Bodily Changes in Emotion

For practical purposes it is usually necessary to record only one or two kinds of bodily change in emotion. In lie detecting, for example, a continuous record of respiration or blood pressure or both is sufficient to indicate emotional upset in the prevaricator. Lie detecting, from the point of view of experimental psychology, is really emotion detect-

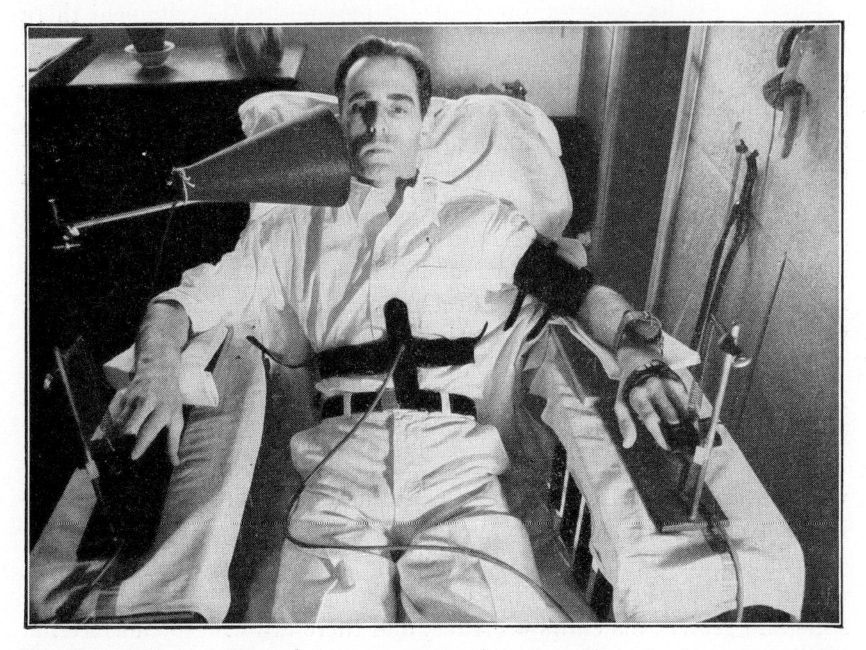

Fig. 9. Subject adjusted to apparatus for recording simultaneous bodily changes in emotion.

The subject shown in Fig. 9 is a normal individual employed by the U. S. Public Health Service when the picture was taken. (Photograph, courtesy of Dr. Ralph R. Brown.)

ing. It rests upon the fact that the involuntary bodily changes of emotion can be observed with the proper apparatus and recorded. Whether the involuntary bodily changes of emotion are due to the telling of a lie cannot be determined from the record, but only from the relation of these bodily changes to the questions asked by the examiner and the total situation. Lie detecting is an art, not an exact science.

In scientific investigations of emotion it is often necessary to record several kinds of bodily change simultaneously in order to see how they are interrelated. To show the simultaneous recording of bodily changes in emotion several illustrations will be given.

Figure 9 shows the subject comfortably seated in an easy chair. A pneumograph attached to the abdomen records the cycle of respiration. The middle finger of both hands is placed in a tremograph to record involuntary muscular changes. A cuff is attached to the left arm of the subject for obtaining a continuous record of changes in blood pressure. Electrodes in the wrist and palm are for obtaining galvanic skin changes. The head of the subject is near a voice key.

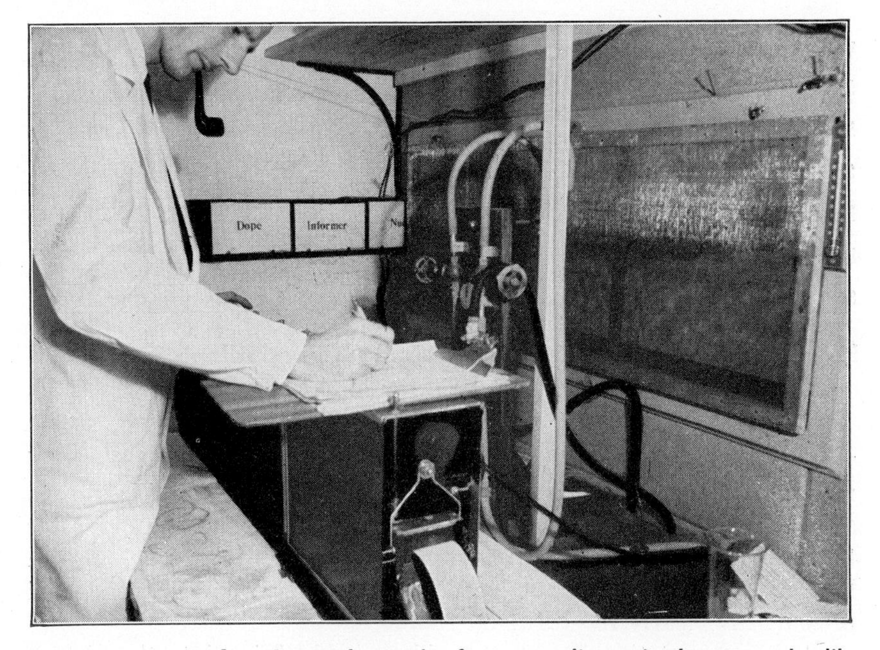

Fig. 10. Darrow's photopolygraph for recording simultaneous bodily changes in emotion. (Photograph, courtesy of Dr. Ralph R. Brown.)

Figure 10 shows the experimenter's apparatus, which is located in an adjoining room. Through a one-way-vision screen the experimenter can observe the subject seated in the easy chair and can, if necessary, communicate with him. Any pertinent observations upon the gross behavior of the subject, as well as a record of the experiment itself, can be written down on the spot. All bodily changes, whether mechanical or electrochemical, are converted into movements, which can be photographically recorded within the instrument shown in this picture.

Figure 11 is a sample strip of photographic record. In the actual trial the word "dopey" was visually exposed, and the subject responded with "junkie." (Dopey is commonly used to mean one who uses narcotic drugs. Junkie means drug addict. Morphine or heroin is frequently called junk in the argot of the addict, and one who uses such drugs may be called a junkie or junker or old dopey.) The break in the voice-response line indicates the moment that the vocal response occurred.

Involuntary hand movements are registered at the top and bottom of the record. The curve of respiration is clearly shown. From the

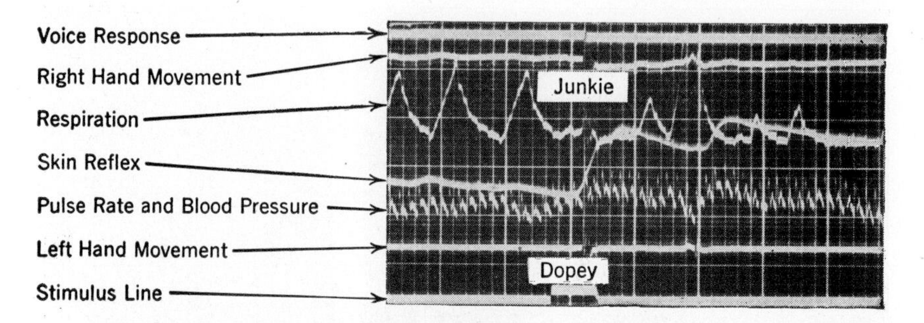

Fig. 11. A sample strip of record obtained from Darrow's photopolygraph. (Photograph, courtesy of Dr. Ralph R. Brown.)

vertical time lines it is possible to determine the fraction of the total respiratory cycle given to inspiration, or the rate of breathing, or to study changes in the pattern or depth of respiration. The curve for the galvanic skin response crosses the respiratory curve, but both can be readily measured and analyzed. Changes in pulse rate and blood pressure are clearly recorded.

At the present time Darrow would probably bring into the picture the more modern electroencephalograph. See Chapters 14 and 15.

Analysis of Patterns of Response, Illustrated by the Startle Response

Everyone has experienced the general muscular contraction which occurs reflexly when there is an unexpected and intense noise, such as the bang of a gun. The startle response is often followed by the emotion of fear, but the reflex itself is typically over before a true emotion can arise.

Landis and Hunt [21] analyzed the startle pattern in both man and animals. To produce startle, they fired a gun near the subject. Since the gun was of known caliber (0.22 and 0.32 were used), there was at least a rough standardization of the stimulus.

To record the response Landis and Hunt made use of high-speed motion-picture cameras. Startle was photographed with cameras taking 64 exposures per second. In some parts of their work, cameras making as many as 300 to 3000 exposures per second were employed. Later the pictures were projected at the usual rate of 16 per second.

To obtain a photographic record of certain bodily movements, levers were employed. The levers were attached to the back of the trunk and to the knees, so that forward movement of these parts was con-

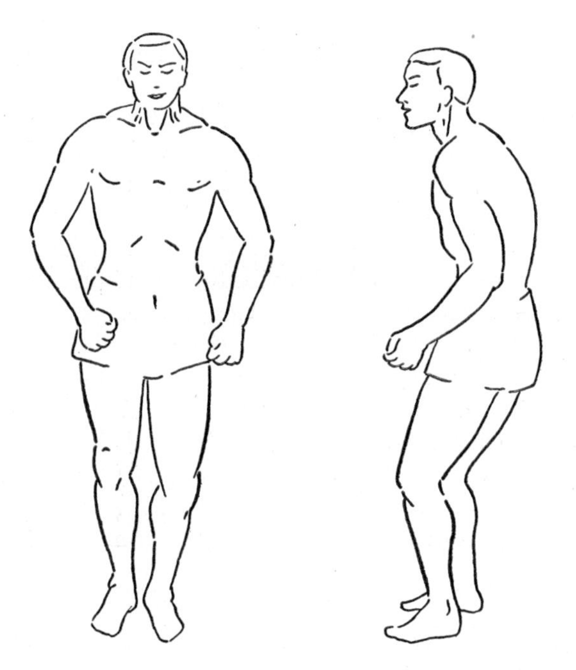

Fig. 12. Schematic representation of the startle pattern, showing front and lateral aspects of the response to a revolver shot. (After Landis and Hunt [21].)

verted into vertical movement of the levers. Abdominal contraction was recorded by a pneumograph attached to a tambour, which moved a lever in the field of the camera.

From the motion-picture records it was possible to reconstruct the spread of the startle response throughout the body. The startle response usually comes and goes in less than half a second, although the range for the total response varies from 0.3 to 1.5 seconds. Startle begins with closing of the eyelids, both eyes reacting simultaneously. Next there is a widening of the mouth, as though in a grin, but only occasionally does this lead to the baring of the teeth. Then the head and neck are brought forward and down, but the chin is tilted up, so that the features are still directed straight ahead. The muscles of the neck stand out prominently. Then the response sweeps downward. There is raising and drawing forward of the shoulders, abduction and pronation of the upper arms, flexion of the fingers, forward movement of the trunk, contraction of the abdomen, and bending of the knees. A schematic representation of the startle response is shown in Fig. 12.

Observations of startle were made with animals at the Bronx Zoological Park. Although startle was not observed in reptiles and amphibia, the pattern was clearly present in mammals. With animals the most notable addition to the human pattern is the flexion of the ears. Frequently the ears are laid back close to the skull. Sometimes there is a crouching posture with legs braced as if to spring; this suggests biological utility of the response in self-defense. With monkeys and chimpanzees the response is more widespread and complete than with man.

The methodological significance of the work of Landis and Hunt lies in the fact that they have described a technique for the objective investigation of at least one pattern of response. The motion-picture technique can probably be applied to the analysis of other patterns of response which appear as components of emotional behavior, such as the rage pattern, the pattern of disgust, crying, smiling, laughing, and possibly the sexual patterns. Certain physiological psychologists, in fact, have defined an emotion as a *pattern of response.* Although this definition is somewhat narrow, all would agree that the experimental study of patterns of response is a task of major importance.

Surgical Methods in the Investigation of Emotional Behavior

Although the possibilities of applying surgical methods to the investigation of emotion are numerous, only two illustrations are here considered: first, the operation of decortication; second, the technique of implanting electrodes in the hypothalamus for purposes of direct stimulation.

If the cerebral cortex is surgically removed, the preparation can, with care, be kept alive for experimental study and observation. Culler decorticated dogs for experiments upon conditioning, but the animals were also used for observation of emotion. Culler prepared a motion-picture film showing the machine-like behavior of the decorticate dog. In a quiescent environment the dog may walk monotonously around a circular path. If an obstacle is placed in his path, he simply comes to rest. If the skin of such a preparation is rubbed, even lightly, however, there is a display of vicious rage. The pattern of rage includes baring of the teeth, snapping, and biting. There is also snarling or growling, along with diffuse struggling of the entire body. The biting of the animal is localized at the point of stimulation and is so vicious that the experimenter is in real danger when handling the animal. The pattern at the height of its intensity is illustrated in Fig. 13, which is the enlargement of a frame in Culler's film. Incidentally, this pattern of rage is similar to that of a normal dog, as pictured years ago by Darwin.

Fig. 13. Pattern of rage in a decorticate dog. (Printed by Dr. John T. Cowles from Professor E. A. Culler's film on behavior of the decorticate dog.)

Other investigators have performed the operation of decortication upon cats. The decorticate cat gives a remarkable exhibition of rage, which includes lashing the tail, arching the trunk, protrusion of the claws and clawing movements, snarling or growling, spitting, turning the head from side to side with attempts to bite, rapid panting with the mouth open, movements of the tongue. Along with these bodily changes are others due to excitation of the sympathetic nervous system: erection of the hairs on the tail and back, sweating at the toe pads, dilation of the pupils, increased rate of heart beat, increased arterial pressure, increased blood sugar, abundant secretion of adrenalin.

Fig. 14. Surgical techniques for studying the role of the hypothalamus in emotion.

See explanation in text. (After Masserman [24].)

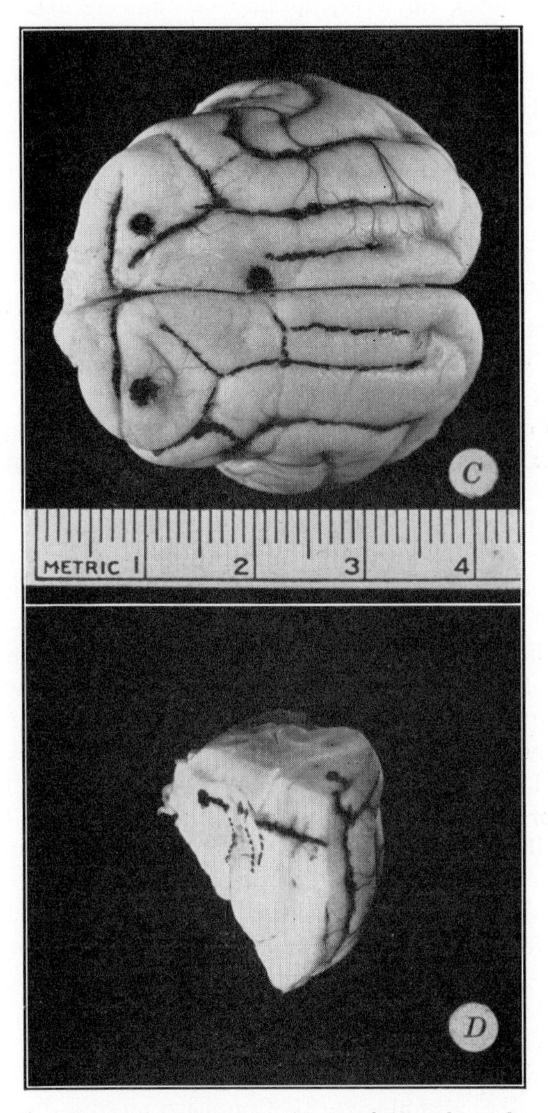

Fig. 14 (cont'd). Surgical techniques for studying the role of the hypothalamus in emotion. (After Masserman.)

The pattern of rage in a decorticate or decerebrate animal has been designated *sham-rage* on the assumption that, since the cerebral cortex has been removed, the animal cannot consciously experience an emotion. There is, however, no way of knowing about the possible consciousness of a decorticate cat or dog.

The second illustration of surgical methods in the investigation of emotional behavior is taken from the work of Masserman [24, 25] upon the role of the hypothalamus. His method has been to implant electrodes, so that a given center can be stimulated directly by electrical or chemical means. Figure 14 illustrates Masserman's method.

View *A* shows the frame of the Horsley-Clarke apparatus for orienting and fixing the head of an anesthetized cat. Control bars slide into two curved earplugs (*seen in the foreground*). The upright carrier of the apparatus can be moved to direct electrodes stereotactically into the brain. The electrodes are used to produce electrolytic lesions of nerve tracts and nuclei. Further, one or more needle electrodes (*foreground center*) may be inserted and held *in situ* by means of skull screws (*seen behind the earplugs*). The electrodes make it possible to stimulate a selected neural center with accuracy after the animal has recovered from the operation.

View *B* is a close-up of the apparatus in use. The head of an anesthetized cat is shown in position. Above is a hypodermic needle for pharmacologic stimulation of the hypothalamus.

View *C* shows the brain of a cat used in an experiment upon the differential effects of alcohol upon the hypothalamus and the cerebral cortex. The sulci have been outlined on the photograph to show clearly the points of insertion of the separate electrodes.

View *D* shows a section of the right hemisphere of the brain of a cat. The brain has been marked to show the paths (actually less than 0.5 millimeter in diameter) of the electrodes through the cortex and into the hypothalamus. The fornix is outlined in dots to aid in orientation. The exact location of the electrodes and lesions was determined for each brain by study of histological sections.

It is not possible to consider in detail the significance of work such as that of Masserman. In general, his research has demonstrated the following: (1) The emotion-like patterns of behavior produced by direct stimulation of the hypothalamus ended abruptly with the cessation of the stimulus. (2) Conditioning did not occur when sensory signals were associated with hypothalamic stimulation as frequently as 480 times. (3) Animals which recovered from the severe metabolic disturbances caused by lesions in the hypothalamus regained their normal emotional reactions.

These and other findings have led Masserman to infer that, although the hypothalamus is undoubtedly a coordinating center for the sympathetic and motor pathways of emotional *expression,* it is not the source or the seat of affective experience.

Emotional Expressions and Social Expressions

When Darwin wrote his great book, *The Expression of the Emotions in Man and Animal* [9], he was concerned in a thoroughly objective manner with the outward manifestations of emotion. He did not consider what it is, whether conscious feeling or neural process or organization of personality, that these outward manifestations express. One result of Darwin's objectivity is that his careful observations are valuable today, even though psychology has made great advancement in the methodology and factual knowledge of emotion.

Today the phrase *emotional expression* is commonly used. It contains, however, a certain ambiguity. The phrase may refer to innate patterns of response, such as crying, smiling, laughing, rage, and disgust, which are common to mankind through the world. The phrase may also refer to individually acquired patterns of response. For example, it is customary in our society to smile in salutation. The smile is learned and enacted as truly as the words that go with it. Superficially, the social expression of smiling may be very similar to the truly reflex pattern. A line of distinction between the innate reflexive pattern and the acquired social expression is not always easy to draw. The distinction was drawn, however, by Landis in interpreting the results of an experiment upon emotion.

Landis [20] brought real-life situations into the laboratory to arouse genuine emotion. He required his subjects to listen to music, read the Bible, smell ammonia, view pictures of skin diseases, examine pornographic material, read sex case histories, handle live frogs, decapitate a rat, receive electric shocks, etc. The facial responses were photographed. The extent of involvement of the different groups of facial muscles was determined by measuring the distance between dark marks placed on the subject's face before photographing. Measurements of the distances between these marks revealed the groups of muscles involved in a given expression and the extent of the muscular contraction.

For a group of twenty-five subjects Landis failed to discover any fixed pattern of facial expression common to any one of his situations. Each subject tended to use some particular group of facial muscles habitually to the exclusion of others. Landis concluded that emotion, as shown in the face, is commonly not a true pattern of reflex response.

He suggested a distinction between innate reflexive patterns and acquired social expressions of emotion.

The same distinction was drawn by the social psychologist Klineberg [19] on the basis of very different evidence and methodology. Klineberg examined the conventional expressions of emotion in the Chinese novel and upon the Chinese stage.

These conventional expressions differ so widely from those in our own country that some of them would not be understood by a man from our Western civilization. For example, "They stretched out their tongues" is an expression of surprise. "Her eyes grew round and opened wide" usually means anger to the Chinese, and the sentence, "He made his two eyes round and stared at him," can mean only anger. To us this description suggests fear. "He scratched his ears and cheeks" might to us suggest embarrassment, but in the Chinese novel the phrase means happiness. "He clapped his hands" is likely to indicate worry or disappointment.

On the other hand, Klineberg discovered certain expressions in the Chinese novel and on the stage which beyond a question describe the truly reflexive bodily changes of emotion. To illustrate, the emotion of fear is described by the Chinese in such sentences as: "Everyone trembled with a face the color of clay," "Every one of his hairs stood on end, and the pimples came out on the skin all over his body," "A cold sweat broke forth on his whole body, and he trembled without ceasing," "They were so frightened that their waters and wastes burst out of them."

It is obvious, therefore, that a distinction must be drawn between the innate bodily changes of emotion and the acquired social expressions. In designing any experiments in this field the distinction must be kept in mind. The distinction was not clearly drawn in a group of early experiments upon the expression of "emotion" in the face, in the voice, by gesture and in gross behavior. A good many experiments have been concerned with the agreement among groups of judges in rating photographs. In evaluating these experiments one should ask: To what extent are the bodily changes innate reflexive patterns? To what extent are they acquired conventional expressions? And, in any event, just what is meant by the *expressions* of an emotion?

CONCLUSION

The present chapter is concerned with a representative group of methods used in the experimental study of motivation, feeling, evaluation, and emotion. Although diverse methods are considered, the list is far from complete. On the one hand, a good many other methods are employed in comparative and physiological psychology. These methods are used in the study of animal drives, emotionality and temperament of animals, and conflict and neurosis, and for the analysis of internal bodily processes which release the energy of behavior and regulate its pattern. On the other hand, there are further methods in social psychology, clinical psychology, psychiatry, child development, the psychology of counseling, and other areas of applied psychology. In the applied psychologies at least the following methods are used: the psychoanalytical methods of aided recall, the word-association method, hypnosis, the projective techniques, a variety of tests and psychological measurements not considered in this chapter, the life-history method, and the social case method, as well as the study of individual conflicts, frustrations, and sources of satisfaction. The variety and diversity of methods would be even greater if the scope of the chapter were extended.

In conclusion it is well to ask: Why is there such a diversity of method?

One answer is that the processes under consideration are exceedingly complex. They are so complex, in fact, that they must be examined piecemeal and from different points of view. There is a diversity of point of view, a diversity of interest, a diversity of aim among investigators, a diversity of problem. And along with these diversities there is, as we might expect, a diversity of experimental method in dealing with such complexity. As stated at the start of this chapter, unity lies not in the methods themselves, for they are many, but in the fact that the methods are all oriented toward the solution of a group of interrelated problems.

The real explanation of the diversity of experimental methods probably lies in the fundamental importance of the processes and problems under consideration. In any theory of personality the dynamics of behavior is a topic of major concern. One cannot understand frustration, conflict, satisfaction, adjustment and non-adjustment, tics, impulsions, traits, habits, and other characteristics of the individual without a sound understanding of motivation, affectivity, and emotion. These processes are basic in importance. And, practically considered, the processes considered in this chapter are of major importance in clinical psychology, psychiatry and psychosomatic medicine, educational psychology, the psychology of counseling, the analysis of social problems, and the other fields of applied psychology.

It is because the problems of motivation, affectivity, and emotion are so important and so central, theoretically and practically, that there have been varied attacks upon them. When complex problems of central importance are studied by men with different aims and points of view, it is to be expected that a diversity of method will develop in the attack upon them.

REFERENCES

1. Allport, G. W. Attitudes. In *Handbook of Social Psychology*. C. Murchison, Ed. Worcester, Mass.: Clark University Press, 1935. (Chap. 17.)
2. Allport, G. W., and P. E. Vernon. *A Study of Values* (Tests). New York: Houghton Mifflin, 1931.
3. Beebe-Center, J. G. *The Psychology of Pleasantness and Unpleasantness*. New York: Van Nostrand, 1932.
4. Cannon, W. B. *Bodily Changes in Pain, Hunger, Fear and Rage; An Account of Recent Researches into the Function of Emotional Excitement*. New York: Appleton-Century, 1929.
5. Cannon, W. B. *The Wisdom of the Body*. New York: Norton, 1932.
6. Carr, H. A. *Psychology, a Study of Mental Activity*. New York: Longmans, Green, 1925. (Chap. 13.)
7. Cattell, R. B. Interpretation of the twelve primary personality factors. *Char. Personal.*, 1944, *13*, 55–91.
8. Compton, R. K., and P. T. Young. A study of organic set: immediate reproduction of spatial patterns presented by successive points to different senses. *J. Exper. Psychol.*, 1933, *16*, 775–797.
9. Darwin, C. *The Expression of the Emotions in Man and Animal*. London: Murray, 1872.
10. Frank, J. D. Recent studies of the level of aspiration. *Psychol. Bull.*, 1941, *38*, 218–226.
11. Gibson, J. J. A critical review of the concept of set in contemporary experimental psychology. *Psychol. Rev.*, 1941, *38*, 781–817.
12. Guilford, J. P. *Psychometric Methods*. New York: McGraw-Hill, 1936. (Part II.)
13. Hamilton, H. C. The effect of incentives on accuracy of discrimination measured on the Galton bar. *Arch. Psychol.*, 1929, *16*, No. 103.
14. Hilgard, E. R., R. K. Campbell, and W. N. Sears. Conditioned discrimination: the effect of knowledge of stimulus-relationships. *Amer. J. Psychol.*, 1938, *51*, 498–506.
15. Hilgard, E. R., and L. G. Humphreys. The effect of supporting and antagonistic voluntary instructions on conditioned discrimination. *J. Exper. Psychol.*, 1938, *22*, 291–304.
16. Hoisington, L. B. Pleasantness and unpleasantness as modes of bodily experience. In *Feelings and Emotions, the Wittenberg Symposium*. M. L. Reymert, Ed. Worcester, Mass.: Clark University Press, 1928. (Chap. 20.)
17. Hunt, W. A. A critical review of current approaches to affectivity. *Psychol. Bull.*, 1939, *36*, 807–828.
18. Hunt, W. A. Recent developments in the field of emotion. *Psychol. Bull.*, 1941, *38*, 249–276.
19. Klineberg, O. Emotional expression in Chinese literature. *J. Abn. Soc. Psychol.*, 1938, *33*, 517–520.
20. Landis, C. Studies of emotional reactions. II. General behavior and facial expression. *J. Comp. Psychol.*, 1924, *4*, 447–501.

21. Landis, C., and W. A. Hunt. *The Startle Pattern.* New York: Farrar and Rinehart, 1939.
22. Lewin, K., T. Dembo, L. Festinger, and P. S. Sears. Level of aspiration. In *Personality and the Behavior Disorders.* J. McV. Hunt, Ed. New York: Ronald Press, 1944. (Chap. 10.)
23. Lund, F. H. *Emotions: Their Psychological, Physiological and Educative Implications.* New York: Ronald Press, 1939.
24. Masserman, J. H. *Behavior and Neurosis, an Experimental Psychoanalytical Approach to Psychobiologic Principles.* Chicago: University of Chicago Press, 1943.
25. Masserman, J. H. *Principles of Dynamic Psychiatry, Including an Integrative Approach to Abnormal and Clinical Psychology.* Philadelphia: Saunders, 1946.
26. Moreno, J. L. *Who Shall Survive? A New Approach to the Problem of Human Interrelations.* Washington, D. C.: Nervous and Mental Disease Publishing Company, 1934.
27. Nafe, J. P. An experimental study of the affective qualities. *Amer. J. Psychol.,* 1924, *35,* 507–544.
28. Richter, C. P. Total self-regulatory functions in animals and human beings. *The Harvey Lectures,* Series 1942–3, *38,* 63–103.
29. Rotter, J. B. Level of aspiration as a method of studying personality. I. A critical review of methodology. *Psychol. Rev.,* 1942, *49,* 463–474.
30. Ruckmick, C. A. *The Psychology of Feeling and Emotion.* New York: McGraw-Hill, 1936.
31. Singer, W. B., and P. T. Young. Studies in affective reaction. I. A new affective rating scale. *J. Gen. Psychol.,* 1941, *24,* 281–301.
32. Stone, C. P. Motivation, drives and incentives. In *Comparative Psychology.* F. A. Moss, Ed. New York: Prentice-Hall, 1934. (Chap. 4.)
33. Thomas, W. F., and P. T. Young. A study of organic set: immediate reproduction, by different muscle groups, of patterns presented by successive visual flashes. *J. Exper. Psychol.,* 1942, *30,* 347–367.
34. Tolman, E. C. *Purposive Behavior in Animals and Men.* New York: Century, 1932.
35. Warden, C. J. *Animal Motivation, Experimental Studies on the Albino Rat.* New York: Columbia University Press, 1931.
36. Woodworth, R. S. *Experimental Psychology.* New York: Henry Holt, 1938. (Chaps. 10–13.)
37. Young, P. T. *Motivation of Behavior: the Fundamental Determinants of Human and Animal Activity.* New York: John Wiley, 1936.
38. Young, P. T. *Emotion in Man and Animal: Its Nature and Relation to Attitude and Motive.* New York: John Wiley, 1943. (Chap. 3 for studies of food preference.)

READING SUGGESTIONS

For a survey of the broad field of motivation see the book by Young [37]. For experimental methods and results in the field of animal behavior and the internal bodily processes which regulate behavior, see the works of Cannon [5], Richter [28], Stone [32], Tolman [34], and Warden [35]. See also Chapter 12 of this book.

For general reading on feeling and emotion see especially Chapters 9 to 13 in Ruckmick [30], Chapters 10 to 13 in Woodworth [36], and Young [38]. On pleasantness and unpleasantness, see the book by Beebe-Center [3]. On the bodily changes of emotion and the techniques for studying them, Lund [23] is recommended, especially Chapters 4 to 6.

For advanced study of current work upon affectivity and emotion excellent reviews are available by Hunt [17, 18].

Chapter 14

Methods of Measuring and Recording Action

R. C. Davis[1]

In the two chapters immediately following this one the student will read about the important psychological problems which involve measuring and recording responses. These studies in methodology involve a rather complex series of laboratory arrangements and principles of physical measurement. This chapter is designed to acquaint the student with some of the more important principles of psychological recording techniques and the relative values of certain more commonly used measuring systems. Because experimental results are so dependent on technique, a knowledge of the principles and practices of recording seems basic to the understanding and evaluation of the experimental studies that form such an important part of modern psychology.

THE PURPOSES AND PRINCIPLES OF MEASUREMENT

Whenever an experimenter speaks of recording a response, he is not speaking literally but is referring to some particular feature of the response which he judges to be important for the problem at hand. The feature of the response recorded may be the dependent variable in a particular experiment, and the investigator naturally desires to preserve the records for future study and analysis. In examining modern psychological literature, the student is quickly impressed by the diversity of instruments and techniques of measurement with which the experimentalist deals.

One general class of measurements consists of measures of accomplishment: measures which supply information about the adjustment

[1] Professor of Psychology, Indiana University.

of the individual to the situation confronting him. The most obvious feature of most actions is their effect on the relationship between the individual and his environment. Does the action bring him closer to a designated goal, does it solve any problems for him, or, in general, does it leave him in a milieu different from the original one? To answer such questions it is necessary to use a measure which is based on some object in the environment rather than on the individual, so that one may ascertain the individual's initial and final standing with respect to that object. Consequently there are measurements of number of questions correctly answered (as in arithmetic performance), number of choices of a certain food (as in studies of food preferences), and the time required to effect an escape (as in a puzzle box or maze). In measurements such as these the scales are necessarily constructed with units appropriate to each environmental situation, because the point of interest is the effect of the action in changing that situation.

The present chapter, however, is chiefly concerned with measurements of a second class, which may be taken as more nearly "absolute" measurements of action. These measures have to do with some aspect of a response other than its consequences for the organism-environment relations. For example, this second class of measurements is more concerned with the strength or the duration of the response as such. To measure these phenomena the investigator conceives of the subject as being, at the outset, at the center or zero point of a scale which is arranged to measure in terms of such variables as distance, force, energy, or velocity. The investigator then uses appropriate apparatus to register how far along such a scale the response goes. In this second class of measurements, there is some literal truth in the saying, "The experimenter makes the record." He not only selects the characteristics to be recorded but also he may employ very abstract measuring scales. This type of measurement is necessarily used in the study of tendon reflexes, changes in the autonomic nervous system, and brain potentials, to mention a few examples.

Some Rules of Procedure for Measurement

In all measurement the experimenter must insure that his apparatus follows certain standard rules of procedure which he has settled on beforehand. For measurements of the second class, as described above, the rules involved and the scales used follow those of physiology and classical physics, which have no serious competitors as far as techniques of measurement are concerned.

The first procedural rule for any scheme of measurement is that a single record should bear a constant relation to the particular dimension chosen. Otherwise the resulting record is distorted and lacks validity. For a system of physical measurements this principle means that readings should preferably be linear and should be proportional to such physical variables as time, motion, energy, or a specified function of one or more of these. The measurement will be misleading and allow for false interpretations if a change of three units in the physical variable produces a record of three units, two units, or one unit, depending on the part of the scale being used. This situation sometimes exists in a recording system, but usually the experimenter is aware of it and can convert the records made into a real scale.

A second procedural rule for recording is to keep the apparatus itself from changing the action under study. Such a change is known as *back action,* and to allow it of course is to change the rules of the game by substituting something else for the original goal of the investigation. The existence of back action is a troublesome problem in the theory of experimentation in all sciences; it is almost as though the experimenter is turning on a light to see what the darkness looks like. It must be the experimenter's goal to disturb the response as little as possible with his paraphernalia of measurement.

In psychological work there are two sorts of back action possible, the general type and a type called local. The general type of back action appears when the subject is disturbed by the formidable appearance of the equipment or the presence of the experimenter. In planning an experiment the investigator usually does his best to reduce these factors and arrange for the process of adaptation and familiarity to reduce them further. Local back action would be illustrated by an absurd apparatus for counting eyeblinks, which attached such a heavy weight to the eyelid that it could move very little if at all. No one, of course, would use an instrument as bad as that, but so long as any weight is attached there is some interference with movement. This local back action, whether produced by weight or something else, must be eliminated or reduced to trivial proportions.

A third procedural rule for measurement is a rather simple-sounding one: an experimenter should know that his apparatus has a sensitivity and range sufficient to pick up and record the changes he wishes to measure. With apparatus which is not sensitive enough—which does not show a readable change when the action changes—an experimenter may of course simply miss what he is looking for. If a response makes the recording pointer hit its ceiling or its floor, the experimenter has not measured the change but only an unknown part of it. Such a

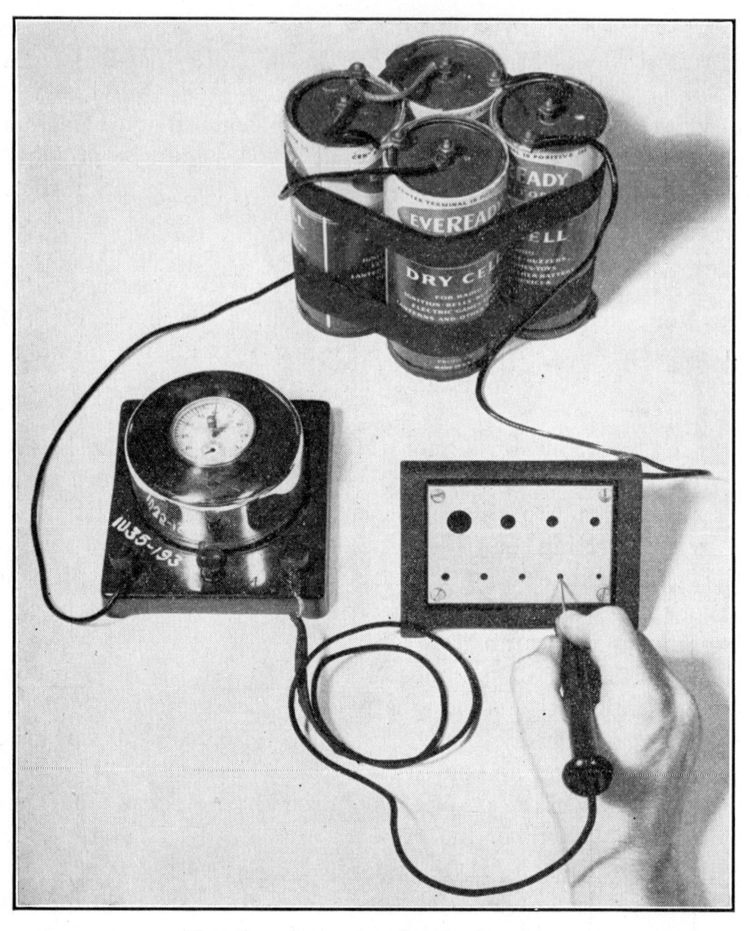

Fig. 1. A simple electrical system.

An electromagnetic counter is used as an indicator for number of occurrences. In the steadiness tester shown at the right the subject holds the stylus in one of the holes so as to avoid touching the edges as far as possible. When he does touch the edge, a contact is made and the counter is activated. The tester serves therefore as a coupling device.

result is due to overloading, which may be a fault in any part of the recording system.

The General System of Apparatus

As a means of performing the operations of measurement according to the above rules, the experimenter selects what may be called a system of apparatus. A recording or registering system must do these things: (1) connect the subject to the system, so that it will be affected by some desired type of variation in him; (2) transmit the changes from the subject; (3) record or indicate the changes somewhere. In most systems a separate piece of equipment: the coupling, the transmitter, and the indicator, respectively, is used for each purpose. Very frequently the coupling device and the indicator serve another purpose as well, by converting one form of energy into another so as to make the change more convenient to transmit or record. Figure 1 illustrates a simple apparatus for counting movements. All the features mentioned are present in this system. The simple coupling is the steadiness tester, with which the subject makes and breaks the circuit; the transmission is accomplished by the wires of an electric circuit which runs from the subject to the indicator; and the electromagnetic counter with its dial and pointer is an indicator. The steadiness tester and the counter are also converters; the former converts stylus movements into electric impulses, and the latter converts these into pointer movements.

The same essentials can be seen in the pneumatic systems shown in Figs. 2 and 3. In Fig. 2 the pneumograph and the finger tambour are for coupling and converting; the rubber tube transmits the change; and the writing tambours are converters and indicators.

When he plans his recording, an experimenter has a choice of four principal kinds of apparatus systems, classified according to the kind of transmission used. There is the *mechanical system,* in which the response is transmitted by such things as rods, levers, or pulleys; the *pneumatic system,* such as is shown in Figs. 2 and 3, in which the transmission is accomplished by a change in air pressure; the *optical system,* such as is shown in Figs. 4 and 5, in which light rays transmit the effect of the response; and the *electrical system,* as shown in Figs. 6, 7, and 9, in which the transmission depends on changes in electric current or voltage.[2]

CHARACTERISTICS OF RECORDING SYSTEMS

The major operational characteristics of a system are its *range* and *sensitivity or amplification,* the amount of its *distortion,* and its *back action.* These characteristics can be discovered either by analyzing its structure or by observing how it works when some known action is applied to it. To illustrate, the minimal sensitivity of a lever can be found by producing very small variations at the input end and noting whether

[2] For more detailed accounts of the first three classes, the student is referred to the articles by Wendt [27], Dittler [9], Broemser [3], and Straub [24]. A fifth class, *thermodynamic,* is little used except in some measurements of metabolism.

Fig. 2. Pneumatic systems working on a continuous feed polygraph.

The recording tambours shown in the top of the figure are operating capillary pens which carry ink from the trough to the paper. One is connected to a pneumograph shown in the foreground; the other, to the receiving tambour just above it. This latter tambour is arranged for picking up finger movements. The third recording pen is operated by a small electromagnet to give records of such things as stimulus presentations. The polygraph is driven by a constant-speed motor, and knobs at the side of the polygraph set the speed of the drive. (See the discussion of polygraphs later in the chapter.)

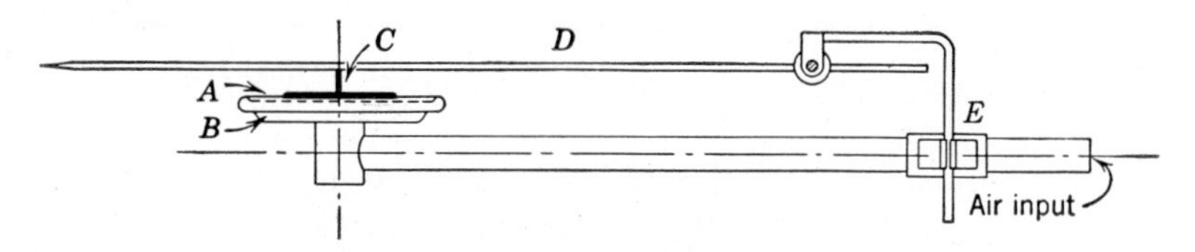

Fig. 3. A tambour with writing lever.

The air-input end is continuous with the closed pneumatic system of a pneumograph or some other such instrument. *B* is a metal case at the end of the closed air system, and *A* is a drum surface of thin rubber pulled tightly across the top of the metal case. C is a small plate of metal fixed to the rubber surface and having a projection on which the freely moving stylus, *D*, rests. Variations in air pressure within the pneumatic system will produce movements of the rubber membrane *A*, which in turn moves the stylus *D*. Note that the position of coupling between C and *D* can be made to vary by adjusting the position of *E* on the hollow rod, and thus variations of degree of amplification are produced.

these are reproduced at the output end. To test amplification the experimenter may take the ratio of the lengths of the two arms around the fulcrum of the lever, or he may move the input end a certain distance and compare the resulting movement of the output end with that distance. Such means, however, will serve only for a very preliminary estimate of such characteristics, but if the experimenter is building or revising a system he usually needs to know something about the effects of the structural elements on the characteristics.

Range and Sensitivity

The experimenter usually pays considerable attention to the range of his measuring instruments. He is concerned with the smallest change and the largest change which his apparatus system will register. The general nature of a particular investigation determines the points of these limiting factors. For example, the *lower limit* of a pneumograph could theoretically be set in such a way that the instrument would pick up heart beats as well as breathing curves of inspiration and expiration. So low a limit would of course be undesirable in a purely pneumographic investigation. The usual procedure is to determine the range, i.e., the largest and smallest values, desired for a particular study and insure by test that the system registers in this specified range.

For an illustration of the *upper limit* we may return to the pneumograph. Careful inspection of Figs. 2 and 3 will indicate that inspiration stretches the rubber pneumograph and so diminishes the air pressure in the system, resulting in a drop or downstroke of the tambour stylus shown in Fig. 3. If the tambour were so arranged that a full drop could be obtained with less than full inhalation, a certain part of the response would be cut out of the record, and only a flat place, rather than the full curve, would show.

A large range is, of course, a desirable characteristic for a system. The experimenter, however, will usually have to accept a compromise on this point, for, other things being equal, a system with a wide range will have a low *sensitivity* (gain, or amplification). This is defined as the ratio of the output reading to magnitude of input—more precisely, the ratio of the change in output to the change in input. In general, these two values will not represent the same physical dimension, for the output will be measured as the distance moved by a point, whereas the input may be movement, pressure, temperature, voltage, or whatever else the experimenter is measuring. Sensitivity, of course, needs to be measured with inputs of different sizes in order to find the operating range of the system and to determine whether its action is proportional to input throughout its ranges. It is likewise checked under various external conditions to verify its constancy.

In a pulley and lever system the only general structural features which will affect the gain are the ratio of the arms of the lever and the mechanical advantage in the pulley system. A change in any one of the structural elements of a pneumatic system will affect its amplification characteristics. Direct photography of the individual's response is the simplest kind of optical recording system, and the amplification (enlargement) of the record depends on the curvature of the lens used and its nearness to the object being photographed. With extremely great enlargement, of course, the upper limit of the range is fixed by the graininess of the film used. Purely optical amplification is determined by the length of the beam of light after it is reflected and by the angular position of the source and recording surface with respect to the mirror. These features are described later in this chapter.

The problem of sensitivity in electrical systems becomes somewhat more complex. In the simplest electrical system, a source of electric potential in the body, e.g., brain potentials, muscle potentials, sweat-gland potentials, is connected directly to a recording instrument, which will also serve as a converter. To this basic circuit a number of supplementary devices may be added for one purpose or another. The system may include such converting coupling devices as a microphone, vibration pick-up, or photoelectric cell between the subject and the electrical circuit; and additional and more complex indicators, such as oscilloscopes and magnetic pens, may be added.

In electrical recording systems much greater control over sensitivity is obtained by the introduction of vacuum tubes into the circuit. The general arrangement of such a system is as follows: There is a source, called a *signal source,* which the experimenter is attempting to amplify and measure or record. In addition to this signal source there is a power source, which supplies the vacuum tubes directly. The faint signal is led to the first tube, where its characteristics are impressed on the comparatively large flow of current through the tube. Variations in current flowing through the tube now have the same form or pattern as that of the signal, but the magnitude of the variations is greatly increased. A simplified analogy may be described in terms of a large water dam (a great power source) at which a small valve is manipulated in certain patterns of movement (the signal). The resulting powerful flow of water from the dam will be modified by variations in the small control so that their pattern of variations will be the same. Thus a small force exerted on a valve greatly varies the flow of water from the dam. In both cases variations in a small force produce magnified variations in a large force. In the electrical system described above, a single tube is involved, giving a single stage of amplification. If the process is repeated, i.e., the amplified signal is allowed to vary the current flow of a second tube, we get further amplification. This process may be continued through three or four tubes, with the output perhaps reaching ten million times the original signal input.[3]

The gain of an amplifier may be easily controlled by adjusting voltages. Quite frequently arrangements are made so that the gain is set at a desired value by turning a knob or throwing a selector switch. Once set, the sensitivity or amplification is a rather stable value.

Amount of Distortion

The sensitivity of a recording system is what is known as a "static" characteristic; it appears when the input moves from one steady state to another which lasts indefinitely. In measuring responses, however, the experimenter is seldom confronted with so simple a problem. Responses are generally of very limited duration, and the experimenter cannot wait for the appearance of a new steady state before he takes a reading. It is necessary to have a system that will keep up with its input changes without distorting the record; hence one is forced to think of the "dynamic" characteristics of measuring systems.

In any mechanical system there are three forces acting in addition to the one to be recorded: the *inertia* (perhaps determined by mass moved), a *restoring force* (e.g., elasticity), and a *damping force* (e.g., friction). A non-mechanical recording system is also likely to have some or all of these forces operating within it and so, if they are improperly combined, to distort the record when the input is changing—and distort it more the faster the change. Greater inertia makes a system slower in action; greater restoring force makes it faster but tends to make it oscillate; greater damping makes it less sensitive to transient changes but makes it come to rest sooner.

Some recording systems are free from inertia; pure optical systems and several electrical systems which are used with cathode-ray oscilloscopes as indicators have none. See Fig. 7. Systems of another group have inertia but lack restoring force, e.g., a horizontal piston. A great many systems—lever, pneumatic, and certain electrical—have all three factors. In these types of apparatus there is, therefore, a

[3] For details of amplifier construction the reader is referred to [17] and [20].

limitation on the speed of change that can be accurately recorded, and the hope of a true record lies in keeping the speed of the apparatus well above that of the responses to be recorded. The most direct way of finding the speed limitations of a system is to introduce into it changes of a standard size but of varying speed and to observe how well the system follows these changes.

If the possible speed of the apparatus is not high enough, it is sometimes said to "lag," although this term is not quite descriptive. What happens is that the indicator does not reach its full reading before the input changes again, whereupon the indicator reverses its direction and never reaches a true reading of the first change. Any system which has both inertia and restoring force will have a "resonant point" or natural frequency of vibration. If this is below the frequency of the responses to be recorded, the indicator may show oscillation or "bounce" before coming to rest. The bounce may be eliminated by more damping, e.g., by friction, but is better cared for by adjustment of inertia and restoring force, e.g., by increasing elasticity. The three factors of inertia, restoring force, and damping force may be determined by the size and material of the parts or by the way they are connected (their "coupling").

Local Back Action

The third operational characteristic mentioned is local back action, which arises from the fact that whenever the organism does "work" on a system, the system also does "work" on the organism. In this way the recording system may tend to destroy the very thing it is supposed to measure. To illustrate, an experimenter might try to measure the temperature changes of an area of the skin by passing a stream of air over it and measuring the temperature of samples of the air. It is clear that his results would bear no simple relation to skin temperature, because while the body is heating the air, the air is cooling the body. Of course, the experimenter must decide what aspects he wants to measure before he can decide whether his system has much or little back action. For our purposes of measurement we may consider the organism as a generator on which we may measure several physical variables. Some of these measurements we may call *potential,* others *displacement.* Readings of muscular force, pressure (as in blood pressure), temperature, and electromotive force are examples of potential measurement; readings of movements, flow of electric current, and heat dissipation are examples of displacement measurement. From displacement measurements values for energy or work may be derived.[4]

To avoid local back action, one essential is that in measuring potential no part of the potential be lost in producing displacement, and in recording displacement that no part of the potential motion be kept as mere potential because of some opposing force. As simple examples of this problem we may desire to measure strength of hand grip (potential) and the extent of the knee-jerk reflex (displacement). We would need to prevent the hand from moving while measuring tension, and we would need to prevent the string or bar coupling from holding back on the leg so that it could not produce a full excursion.

Evidently apparatus which will prevent back action in one kind of measurement may produce it in the other, and in any sort of mechanical system it is impossible to attain the ideal. The relationship of the three basic features—inertia, restoring force, and damping—determines the back action of a system, as it does the distortion. In measuring force or pressure, movement is usually kept at a minimum by giving the recording system a high elasticity to oppose the movement. In a pneumatic system the rubber membrane provides some of this elasticity, and a spring is often added to produce more. For purposes of recording pure movement those features which will impede movement, namely, mass, elasticity, and friction, are minimized. A pure optical system is ideal for recording movement because it has none of these features. If the optical system is used to record pressure or force (potential), it needs a mechanical or electrical supplement.

Summary of Characteristics

From the requirements for recording systems and their capabilities we may make a general summary of the assets and liabilities of the four principal types. The most familiar in the psychological laboratory is probably the pneumatic system, which with the lever and pulley system has been the basis of most recording apparatus in the past. An experimenter soon feels "at home" with these systems because so much of their action is visible and because they resemble so many appliances found outside the laboratory. On the other hand,

[4] A few measurements used in psychological work are of a third type; in these the organism is considered the recipient rather than the generator of force, and its resistance or reaction to the force is measured. The measurement of galvanic skin response is the commonest example (pages 377–378 and 413–414). Ultimately these are force measurements, for by comparing applied force with the resultant, one discovers the characteristics of the organism.

the mechanical systems, which look rather simple, are dynamically very complicated, because their operational characteristics depend on so many structural features. Their back action can be only reduced, not completely eliminated. For recording unimpeded movement an optical system has the great advantage of lacking inertia. Even when it is necessary to mount a mirror or some other coupling or converting device onto the subject, the mass moved can be kept negligible. On the other hand, optical systems, including direct photography, have the disadvantage of forcing the experimenter to wait until the film has been developed before analyses of the records can be made. Electrical systems can also operate without inertia if they use cathode ray tubes as indicators. See Fig. 7. If permanent records are desired with such a system, there is, of course, the necessity of adding photographic equipment and waiting for the development of the films.

All these methods have been used to good advantage in psychological experiments by investigators who were careful that their instruments should meet the requirements of the situation. In recording the knee-jerk reflex, for example, Wendt [26] used a pulley and lever system which was very fast and had little back action. He took advantage of the thickening of the quadriceps muscle during the response by attaching a light lever to it, so that the lever would move when the muscle thickened. This lever then pulled a thread attached at the other end to a writing lever, which traced an accurate record of the response.

Pneumatic recording was developed to a high point by European workers a generation or more ago. In modern times an important example of pneumatic recording is found in a series of studies by Luria [19], who used a system for recording finger movement or pressure very much like the one pictured in Fig. 2. With it he recorded the involuntary and voluntary finger responses which subjects produced in a serious conflict situation.

An interesting case of direct optical recording is found in the studies made by Landis and Hunt on the startle response [16]. These studies are described in Chapter 12, pages 378–380.

There are many good examples of electrical recording techniques used to great advantage in the psychological laboratory. The recording of electric potentials from the brain (electroencephalography), for instance, is usually carried out with a great deal of attention to instrumentation, and there has been built up a large body of information about brain actions in relation to psychological states and processes, which would have been impossible without this technique. Descriptions of this important work are given in Chapter 15.

SOME COMMON RECORDING SYSTEMS

In order to make one of the general types of recording systems serve a particular purpose, the experimenter usually employs an appropriate coupling device as the first element and then makes sure that the remainder of the system is adequate to indicate the changes picked up by the coupling unit. It is the coupling unit that determines what is to be measured.

Temporal Measurement

Probably the simplest response characteristic to record is the time or frequency of occurrences. In this type of measurement the experimenter first decides what constitutes an occurrence for his purpose: will he count a slight muscle twitch, for example, or any actual limb movement, or only those of sufficient energy to move a telegraph key against the opposition of its spring? The system most often used for temporal recording is electrical, and the commonest coupling device is the closing or opening of the gap (or switch) between two contact points in a circuit. The gap is closed by a specified movement, and with each closure the counter is activated by the electrical circuit so formed. This is the setup for the measurement of reaction time (see pages 461–463), the tapping board, the steadiness tester (see Fig. 1), and the devices for counting departure from a prescribed path in a star or maze tracing with a stylus.

If the response is a sound, the air vibrations operate a simple switch, as in the plan of the original "voice key." Electronic devices are now available which are more sensitive and reliable [8, 18]. In these the sound is converted into electrical impulses, which activate a circuit through a special tube. Electronic devices are also advantageous for timing movement; the movement may interrupt a beam of light which activates a photoelectric cell. In addition to being more sensitive and reliable, such a device also avoids putting any load on the subject.

For counting or timing the indicating device is usually quite simple; it needs only to indicate the presence or absence of a response at a specified time. In a counter such as that shown in Fig. 1, an ordinary electromagnet moves the pointer one scale division each time the circuit is closed by the key.

The *chronoscope* has long been a very important instrument in the psychological laboratory because of the many problems which demand measurement of the time between stimulus and response—reaction time. The student is referred to Chapter 16 for descriptions of the psychological applications of reaction-time measurements. Although chronoscopes have been constructed on many plans, the usual mechanism now is a synchronous motor driven at a constant speed by the regular pulsations in the 60-cycle electric power line. The driving mechanism is not connected to the pointer hands at all times, but the connection is made when an electromagnet moves a wheel to engage it with the driving mechanism. When the current through the magnet is turned off by the subject's breaking his coupling switch, the hands are disengaged again by a spring. Therefore, the hands on the dial will run only so long as current flows in the magnet and will register the length of time it has been flowing. Such chronoscopes usually measure in hundredths or thousandths of a second, the latter unit sometimes being called millisecond or sigma (σ).

Another type of chronoscope has been introduced which works on an electronic principle [13]. As long as the circuit of this instrument is closed, a condenser will build up a higher and higher voltage. Thus the voltage on the condenser is a function of the time the circuit has been closed, and a voltmeter connected to the condenser by a vacuum tube is used to measure this resulting voltage, which can be converted into milliseconds. This kind of chronoscope is absolutely noiseless and avoids the mechanical inaccuracies that are likely to afflict an instrument with moving parts.

Graphic Recording with Time

In many experiments more than the time or frequency of a given change needs to be recorded; it may be necessary to determine the progress of changes in some other dimension as they take place in time. For this two-dimensional recording a graphic record is most convenient. A paper or film surface may be arranged to move steadily, while an indicator marks on it changes in some other variable in a perpendicular direction to its time motion. Such a device is generally termed a *kymograph* or, if several records are being made, a *polygraph*. Tracing on the paper is made by a lever, often delivering ink through a capillary tube. See Fig. 2. A very common plan, however, is to cover a glossy surface of paper with a light coating of soot, which the writing lever then removes as it moves along. Such a record is preserved by coating it with shellac. Sometimes a wax-covered surface is passed by a heated stylus or lever, which removes a thin line of the wax and uncovers the darker paper underneath, thus producing a graphic record of the lever's movement. For optical recording, a photopolygraph is constructed in such a way that an enclosed roll of film is passed by a slit at a constant speed, and the light beam is led in through the slit. Illustrations of polygraph records will be found on pages 378, 412, and 617.

Whatever general plan of graphic recording is used, several variables may be measured simultaneously by using more than one pen, stylus, or light beam. The investigator also needs an additional writing source to indicate equal time intervals, and this is of course essential when the kymograph is not driven by a synchronous motor. For recording time intervals the usual device is a small electromagnetic marker activated by contacts regularly made by a small synchronous motor. The same sort of marker is generally used for indicating on the record whenever a stimulus is given or some other event takes place. In optical recording a small argon glow lamp is flashed with the closing of a circuit, and this may take the place of the electromagnetic marker for purposes of timing or stimulus recording. See Fig. 8.

Coupling for Measuring Movement

It is frequently desirable to record the variations in movement or force (pressure) with time. Movement is recorded, for example, in studies of breathing, blood distribution and pulse, and eye movements. Any of the four kinds of recording systems may be used for the registration of movement, although the electrical is not often used for this purpose at the present time. Of course, the feature that makes a system suitable for recording a certain movement is the nature of the coupling or conversion unit which connects it to the organism.

Reflexes or voluntary movements are often recorded with a lever and pulley system, with a direct attachment of a lever or thread to the moving member, if the position of the body as a whole is fixed in some way. Sometimes the "dimensionality" of the movement is ignored, and the hand and arm are allowed to move about freely on a horizontal plate while the complicated pattern of movement is being recorded. Such is the case with the *automatograph*. Similar movements of total body sway are measured by attaching a horizontal plate to the head of the subject and allowing a fixed vertical marker to record on this plate as the body produces involuntary swaying motions. This instrument is called an *ataxiameter*.

More often, however, the problem is to record limb movements in one dimension, as for patellar reflex, finger tremor, or voluntary movement in a particular direction. In such responses the part of the body which is going to move, e.g., the limb, is often attached to a writing lever directly or by means of a thread running over pulleys, so that the writing lever deflects and marks on a moving kymograph whenever the part moves. Usually a weight is added to the lever to bring it back into position as the response comes to an end. Or a pneumatic transmission system like that shown in Fig. 2 is used. In this system as the part (the finger) moves, the membrane on the capsule is depressed or released and produces through the pneumatic system a movement of the writing lever. An optical system has the advantage of avoiding inertia in the registration of movement. The optical system is arranged so that the moving part casts a shadow, of which a camera with a moving film takes a picture. Instead, a tiny mirror may be fixed to the moving part, and a small source of light made to reflect a beam from it into a moving film camera (a *photopolygraph*).

With a suitable coupling device, an electrical transmission system is sometimes used. A photoelectric cell serves this purpose, or a small plate is attached to the subject, so that, as it is brought closer to a fixed plate during the process, it acts as a variable condenser, the changes in which operate the electrical transmission system [22].

There are some objections to using the limb itself as a lever in recording movement because it is so heavy. Another plan is to record the thickening of the muscle which moves the limb. Coupling then may be accomplished by surrounding the limb with an elastic band and letting the variations in the band activate the system, according to one of the above schemes. A more useful plan, however, is to attach the coupling device to just one point on the surface over the muscle without a surrounding band. This was the plan used in the Wendt experiment described previously.

The movements of breathing are most often recorded pneumatically with an elastic-band arrangement. A device called a *pneumograph,* consisting of a hollow rubber tube arranged like a bellows, is stretched and tied around the chest, and the amount of air in and out of the tube or chamber is communicated to the rest of the pneumatic system. Several plans for using electrical rather than pneumatic recording for breathing movements have been suggested [14, 15, 22]. These require, of course, some coupling device which will convert movements into electric waves. One plan is to have the movement vary the distance between two plates, which act as a condenser, the same plan as mentioned above for recording limb movements.

Registering Ocular Movements

Recording the movements of the iris, eyeball, or eyelid is a rather special problem because the attachment of any mechanical device tends to introduce too much back action in addition to being annoying to the subject. Optical or electrical devices are used for this purpose

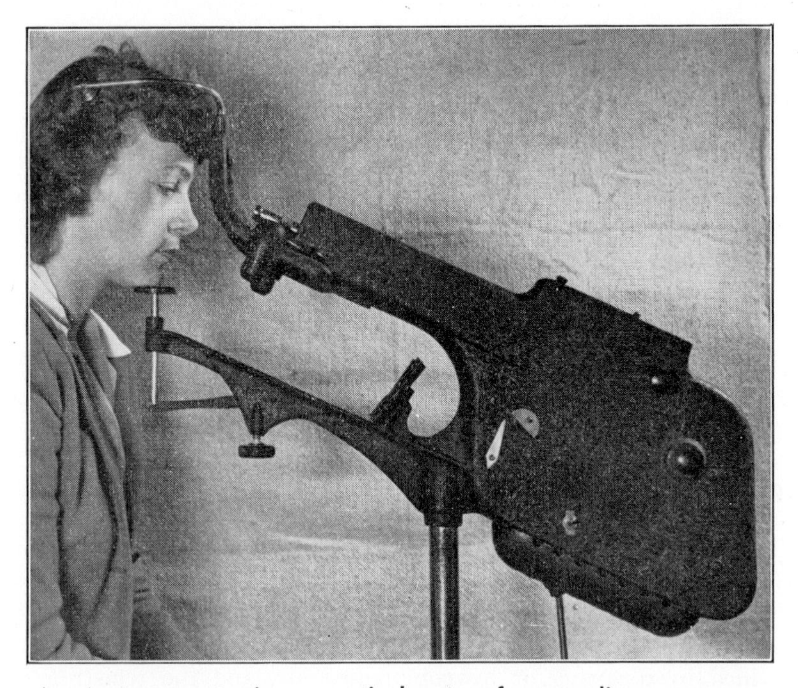

Fig. 4. An instrument using an optical system for recording eye movements. The cornea of each eye reflects a light beam onto the photographic paper which is continuously moving in the back part of the instrument. See also Fig. 5 below.

[2]. Changes in pupillary size (iris movement) may be photographed, although the presence of a bright light is a handicap because it will itself affect pupil size. The *pupilometer* is a telescope with cross hairs or circles, which may be manually adjusted until they are tangent to the size of the pupil. The manual settings are sometimes recorded graphically [1].

Light source
Adjustable lens tube
Surface of cornea
Moving photographic paper

Fig. 5. Diagram of the optical system in Fig. 4 above.

Movement of the eyelid is sometimes recorded by attaching a sliver of paper to the lid ("artificial eyelash") and providing a beam of light so that the shadow of the artificial eyelash will fall onto photopolygraph. See page 616.

The instrument most often used for recording eye movements, chiefly horizontal movements, is of the type shown in Figs. 4 and 5. In this instrument small light sources are housed in the knob-like projections opposite the subject's mouth in the picture, and these throw beams of light, one on each cornea, where they do not affect the subject's vision. The glossy surface of the cornea reflects the light beam, which is then transmitted through the tubes just above the light sources and focused onto the moving film or paper. This recording scheme depends on the fact that the eyeball is not perfectly spherical, for if it were, the angle of reflection would not of course be changed by rotation of the eyeball. Because the recording film or paper moves at a steady rate, the record of the ordinary jumpy or saccadic movements used in reading looks like an irregular staircase. The instrument is of course calibrated when the experimenter wishes to measure the size of the movements.

Registering Force or Pressure

To measure force or pressure, a potential measurement, a system of apparatus must offer enough opposition to prevent any great amount of movement; otherwise, measurement will be falsified by back action. For the measurement of mechanical force the opposition is most often provided by a spring or by compressed air, and the registration is accomplished by a mechanical or pneumatic system.

A simple force-measuring instrument is the *dynamometer,* ordinarily used without any time recording. The object of this instrument is to indicate the maximum force of a muscular contraction (voluntary), and arrangements are made so that the muscular force works against a very stiff spring, whereupon a pointer registers the compression (or extension) of the spring.

One of the commonest and, at the same time, most difficult of pressure measurements is the measurement of blood pressure. The chief difficulties of the problem are that the pressure of the blood in the arteries changes so rapidly and that it must be measured rather indirectly. The pressure goes through a cyclic change with every pulsation of the heart, reaching a maximum with the systolic stage and a minimum with the diastolic. There are, therefore, three kinds of blood-pressure values: the systolic, the diastolic, and the pulse pressure, which is the difference between the two. Clearly if a measurement is to be at all definite, it must represent some particular point in the cycle, such as the maximum or the minimum.

If the experimenter could sever an artery and connect the pulsating end directly to a pressure-recording system, a *manometer,* the flow of blood would be stopped, and the manometer would indicate pressure variations. Since this direct method is usually impossible, the experimenter obtains a reading by applying enough pressure to the sides of the unsevered artery to cut off blood flow. This pressure is applied by means of a cuff, which is inflated by the experimenter. For systolic measurement the cuff is inflated until only the pulse is heard below it by means of a stethoscope. For diastolic measurement, there is less cuff pressure; it is deflated until the experimenter can hear a dull thud instead of the snapping sound of the pulse. The pressure of the cuff is, in general, just equal to that of the blood stream, which it balances; thus the blood pressure is determined by reading the cuff pressure on a manometer when the balance has been reached.

Such a method as the foregoing gives a reasonably good indication of the general level of the blood pressure, but the general level is of more interest in medical practice than in psychological studies. The experimenter usually wishes to obtain a series of rapidly successive measures, and this is much more difficult, although some apparatus systems have been devised to obtain rapid and automatic readings of blood-pressure changes [4, 23].

To record the pressure of the pulse presents a similar problem, because it is often measured by a comparison of systolic and diastolic pressures. Most frequently a less accurate record is made by having a small knob press against an artery by a spring, by weight, or by air pressure; and the movements of this knob are then recorded by an appropriate system [9, 21]. The pulse wave with its complex harmonics is so rapid that accurate recording is almost beyond the limits of mechanical devices [28].

Recording Vocal Responses

For the recording of vocal responses electrical systems have almost wholly supplanted all other kinds. In this case air-pressure variations (sounds) are converted into electrical waves by a microphone, and these waves are enlarged by an amplifier. Because of the relatively high frequencies (short wavelengths) involved, the best indicating instrument is the cathode-ray oscilloscope. The resulting wave forms may be viewed directly on the oscilloscope, as in Fig. 6, or they can be photographed on a fast-moving paper for later analysis.

Fig. 6. Oscilloscope used with a microphone for registering vocal sound.
The subject is uttering the sound oo.

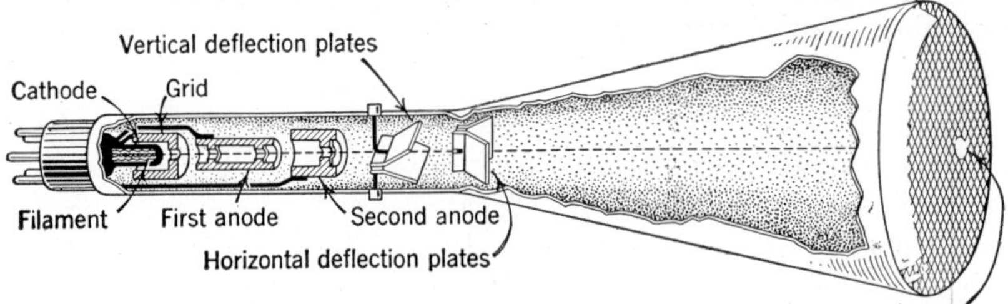

Fig. 7. A typical cathode ray tube, as used in the oscilloscope represented in Fig. 6 above.

The horizontal deflection plates cause the stream of electrons to move back and forth across the screen. The vertical deflection plates are connected with the microphone and produce the vertical movements in accordance with the sound.

Measuring Work

As different from movement and pressure, investigators usually employ the terms *work* and *energy* in rather specialized senses. Work refers to the work done by an organism on an external object, and energy refers to the heat energy generated in the whole organism (metabolism).

Because work implies movement of an object, the recording is therefore a recording of movement under special conditions. As different from the studies in which displacement is measured, the subject's movement is opposed by some force for purposes of studying work, because it is the movement of a load that constitutes work. The load which the subject moves is usually a weight or a spring, although the spring has the disadvantage of offering more and more counterpull as it is stretched. The load may be attached, of course, to any part of the body capable of doing work. Because it has been found that there is a tendency for the subject to shift to another set of muscles when one set becomes fatigued, it is necessary to restrict undesired movements which might serve as substitutes by restraining adjacent parts of the body.

Work is performed, of course, when the subject is lifting a weight or stretching a spring. In the strict sense, no work is done on the "down" stroke when the subject eases the load back to the resting position, yet the subject will tend to exert a retarding force which might otherwise be used to do more work. To avoid this waste, a catch mechanism is sometimes provided on the ergograph to take the load off the subject each time he reaches the top of his pull. For a description of the psychological measurements and factors involved in work study, the student is referred to Chapter 16.

Measuring Energy

For the measurement of energy production in the whole organism (general metabolism), there are two chief methods: the physical, which depends on measurement of heat produced over a period of time; and the chemical, which depends on measurement of oxygen consumption or carbon dioxide production [10]. In order to obtain a measure over a shorter period of time, variables which correlate with general metabolism are sometimes used as indices. One plan measures what is called "insensible perspiration" by keeping a very accurate record of the subject's weight loss from moment to moment with an elaborate automatic balance [5]. The theory behind this procedure is that water is produced as one of the results of metabolism, and that weight will be lost as the water vapor is given off.

Measuring Electrical Changes

Because every bodily response generates electrical changes, the recording of these changes is often the most convenient means of studying the response, and sometimes it is the only one. Electrical changes are commonly recorded in four types of measurement: of heart action (electrocardiography), of skeletal-muscle action (electromyography), of brain waves (electroencephalography), and of sweat-gland action (galvanic skin response). The first three are electric potential measurements and may be accomplished with the same

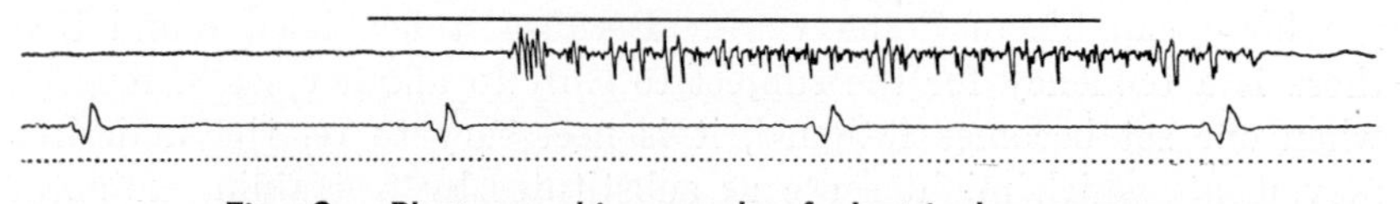
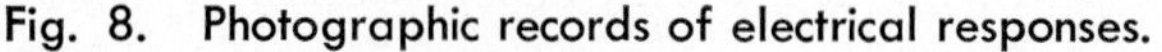

Fig. 8. Photographic records of electrical responses.

The lower record is an electrocardiogram, the upper an electromyogram taken simultaneously. The dots are produced by the flashing of an argon lamp and represent intervals of 1/60 of a second. The solid horizontal line, produced in a similar manner, represents the delivery of a signal to the subject indicating that he should lift his forefinger.

apparatus; the fourth may be either potential or resistance measurement. The coupling device for picking up any of these changes is very simple in principle, consisting merely of a pair of electrodes.

The placement of the electrodes may be "bipolar" or "monopolar." When both electrodes are placed close to the site of the change, the arrangement is called bipolar. For monopolar recording, one electrode is placed near the site of the change, and the other on some distant and inactive tissue. With bipolar recording the responses of two areas will be picked up by the electrodes; with monopolar recording the responses of only one area are picked up. Hence monopolar recording is easier to interpret [6].

The *electrocardiogram* represents a large potential wave, or rather a series of waves, arising as a result of the action of the heart muscles, but permeating the body so that it can be picked up by electrodes located almost anywhere on the body, provided they are far enough apart. A conventional arrangement is to put one electrode on each hand or one on a hand and one on an ankle. The electrocardiogram in Fig. 8 was recorded in this way. The *electromyogram* needs to have at least one electrode quite near the muscle which is active. The recording shown in Fig. 8 was made with one electrode on the back of the forearm about 2 inches below the elbow, and the other on a large thick pad on the upper arm, which had the effect of making the recording monopolar. Because the *electroencephalogram* represents a potential arising in certain parts of the brain, one or both of the

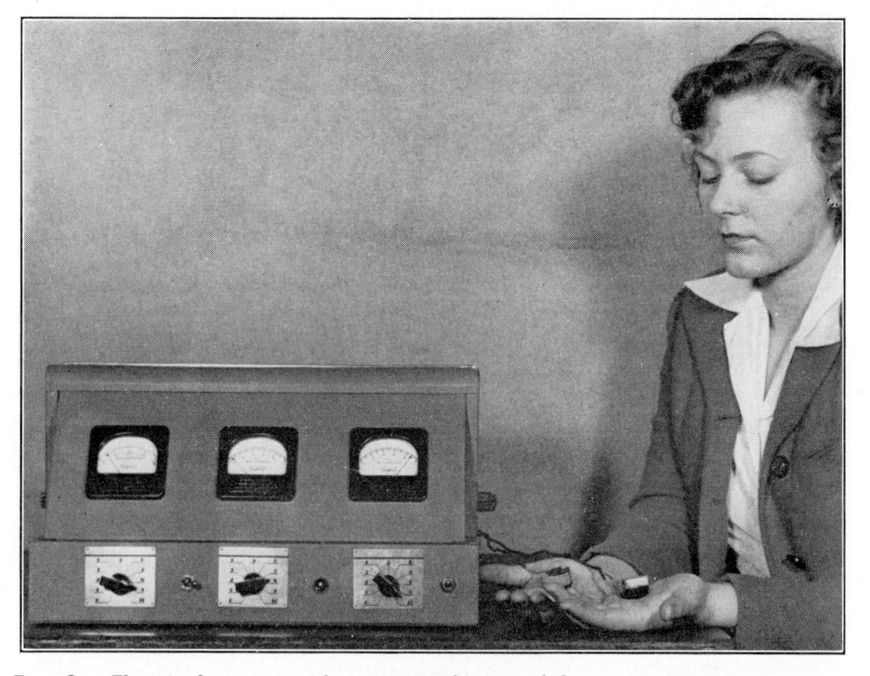

Fig. 9. Electrical system with vacuum tubes used for measuring the galvanic skin response.

The electrodes here are cups with zinc plates covered with MnO_2 soaked in 0.9% salt solution, that in turn being covered with a pad soaked in saline. The meter at the right registers changes in the subject's resistance, GSR. The meter at the left shows the constant current through the subject. The reading of the meter in the center is used to compute the subject's total resistance. The operator keeps the third needle on the scale by turning the center knob.

electrodes must be attached to the scalp [17]. For monopolar recording, the second is usually attached to the lobe of the ear.

For recording any of these phenomena the waves picked up by the electrodes are fed into an amplifier and sent to the recording instrument, which is usually either a cathode-ray oscillograph (Figs. 6 and 7) or a magnetic ink writer. The latter is a light capillary pen moved across a recording paper by the pull of an electromagnet, which is energized by the waves coming from the amplifier. See also pages

448–452. Special devices are sometimes added to electroencephalographs and myographs to help in the interpretation of the resulting records. An integrating circuit may be arranged to add all the waves coming through the amplifier in a specified period of time and to indicate their sum [11, 12]. For electroencephalography there has been much interest in the frequencies of the waves generated, and one device has been perfected to perform a harmonic analysis on the waves as they come through the amplifier. It then adds together all the waves of each frequency and records their sums [25].

Apparatus for the measurement of the *galvanic skin response* (*GSR*) may be arranged to record either potential or apparent resistance, for the skin connected at two points to an electric circuit will show either a certain potential or a certain apparent resistance to a current made artificially to flow through it. Most frequently the experimenter desires to measure changes in apparent resistance produced by certain stimuli. Current is passed through the skin of the subject, and enough resistance added to the circuit to adjust it to a predetermined value. From this the initial resistance of the subject can be computed. The deviations from this initial value form the galvanic skin response, which the experimenter records. The current will naturally change somewhat while the subject is responding. Because of this factor it has been found desirable to make the current adjustments automatic by means of a vacuum-tube circuit [7]. An instrument operating on this plan is shown in Fig. 9. The changes may, of course, be amplified and recorded with a magnetic ink writer, rather than being measured by a simple meter.

SUMMARY

This survey of the recording apparatus of the psychological laboratory might be described as a discourse on the theory of recording. A distinction was made between adjustments that are environment directed and those that are more nearly absolute. In attaining the more abstract types of experimental measurements the experimenter is cautioned that his readings must refer to real measurement scales, and that the apparatus must not markedly change the thing to be measured and must have sufficient sensitivity to record adequately the changes that are arbitrarily chosen for the dependent variable in any investigation.

Apparatus units have been analyzed in terms of their coupling, transmission, indicator, and conversion parts. The major types of recording systems have been discussed, and their relative advantages indicated for different types of investigations.

This brief treatment of laboratory techniques of recording action should make the student feel more at home in reading the literature of experimental psychology, in which process it is usual for him continually to be asking how the apparatus was used and what assumptions were involved in the recording of each particular response.

REFERENCES

1. Baker, L. E. The pupillary response conditioned to subliminal auditory stimuli. *Psychol. Monog.*, 1938, *50,* 32.
2. Bitterman, M. E. Electromyographic recording of eyelid movements. *Amer. J. Psychol.*, 1945, *58,* 112–113.
3. Broemser, P. Anwendung mathematischer Methoden auf dem Gebiet der physiologischen Mechanik (Theorie der Registriermethoden, Methoden der Kurvenkorrectur, harmonische Analyse). In *Handbuch der biologisches Arbeitsmethoden.* R. Abderhalden, Ed. Abt. 15, Teil 1, 81–106, 1930.
4. Darrow, C. W. Continuous records of systolic and diastolic blood pressure. *Arch. Neurol. Psychiat.*, 1937, *38,* 365–370.
5. Darrow, C. W., and G. L. Freeman. Insensible perspiration and the galvanic skin reflex. *Amer. J. Physiol.*, 1935, *111,* 55–63.
6. Davis, R. C. Properties of electrodes used in recording action potentials from the intact organism. *Amer. J. Psychol.*, 1935, *47,* 693–695.
7. Davis, R. C., and J. M. Porter. A measuring device for the galvanic reflex. *J. Gen. Psychol.*, 1931, *5,* 115–120.
8. DeSilva, H. R., and L. Jacobson. An electronic voice reaction timer. *Amer. J. Psychol.*, 1936, *48,* 43–145.
9. Dittler, R. Allgemeine Registriertechnik. In *Handbuch der biologisches Arbeitsmethoden.* R. Abderhalden, Ed. Abt. 5, Teil 1, 1 Hälfter, 1–80, 1930.
10. DuBois, E. F. *Basal Metabolism in Health and Disease.* 3rd Ed. Philadelphia: Lea and Febiger, 1936.
11. Freeman, G. L., and E. L. Hoffman. An electrical integrator for "action currents." *Rev. Sci. Instrum.*, 1941, *11,* 283–284.
12. Jacobsen, E. Recording action potentials without photography. *Amer. J. Psychol.*, 1941, *54,* 266–269.
13. Jasper, H. H., and H. L. Andrews. A multi-range vacuum tube chronometer. *J. Gen. Psychol.*, 1936, *14,* 248–256.
14. Judson, L. S., and P. E. Griffith. A variable resistance pneumograph and an electromagnetic tambour. *Science,* 1930, *72,* 369–370.
15. Krasno, L., E. Hoffman, and G. L. Freeman. An electropneumatic method of recording respiration in small animals. *J. Comp. Psychol.*, 1940, *29,* 135–138.
16. Landis, C., and W. A. Hunt. *The Startle Pattern.* New York: Farrar and Rinehart, 1939.
17. Lindsley, D. B. Electroencephalography. In *Personality and the Behavior Disorders.* J. McV. Hunt, Ed. New York: Ronald Press, 1944, pp. 1033–1103.
18. Loucks, R. B. Simplified photoelectric recorder, timer and stimulus control devices. *J. Exper. Psychol.*, 1941, *28,* 443–453.
19. Luria, A. R. *The Nature of Human Conflicts.* New York: Liveright, 1932

20. Müller, R. H., R. L. Garman, and M. E. Droz. *Experimental Electronics.* New York: Prentice-Hall, 1943.
21. Nixon, H. K. A sphygmograph with an electrical attachment for recording pulse rate at a distance. *J. Exper. Psychol.,* 1924, *7,* 358–370.
22. Sheer, C., and J. G. Lynn. Electronics in the study of head injuries. *Electronics,* 1944, *17,* beginning p. 112.
23. Stovkis, B. A new method of registering blood pressure as a psychophysiological research technique for the study of psychic stimuli in blood pressure. *J. Exper. Psychol.,* 1938, *22,* 365–376.
24. Straub, H. Bestimmung des Blutdruckes (direkte und indirekte Methoden). In *Handbuch der biologisches Arbeitsmethoden.* R. Abderhalden, Ed. Abt. 5, Teil 1, 1 Hälfter, 135–366, 1923.
25. Walter, W. G. Appendix on a new method of electroencephalographic analysis. *J. Ment. Sci.,* 1943, *89,* 222–223.
26. Wendt, G. R. An analytical study of the conditioned knee-jerk. *Arch. Psychol.,* 1930, *19.*
27. Wendt, G. R. Methods of recording action. *Arch. Psychol.,* 1938, *32,* 1–82.
28. Willemse, W. T. A new type of sphygmograph. *Brit. J. Psychol.,* 1930, *21,* 68–72.

Chapter 15

Studying Neuropsychology and Bodily Functions

Donald B. Lindsley[1]

Neuropsychology is not a field by itself. It is simply an area of investigation which cuts across the disciplines of psychology and neurology and, to some extent, other related fields, such as physiology, anatomy, biochemistry, and biophysics. Primarily it attempts to study behavior in relation to some aspect of nervous processes. This may be done in the course of development of the nervous system, on occasions when the nervous system is delimited by pathology or special operative techniques, by stimulation of selected parts of the nervous system, and by electrical recording techniques which serve as "listening posts" along nervous pathways.

The objectives of neuropsychology, like those of psychology, are a better understanding of behavioral processes, so that ultimately the prediction and control of behavior may be advanced. Psychological experiment is concerned with responses or behavioral changes which may be correlated with specific stimulus variables or stimulus situations. With certain variables eliminated, held constant, or otherwise controlled, the reactions of the organism may be said to be a function of the independent or experimental variable. Neuropsychology is concerned with certain *intervening variables,* as well as with the external stimulus variables, i.e., with the part played by the nervous system in mediating and influencing the responses of the organism to its environment.

There are certain properties of the nervous system which are essentially intrinsic to it, and the extent to which they may be modified by the environment, either external or internal, is not fully known. It is known that the internal milieu may temporarily change some of

[1] Professor of Psychology, Northwestern University.

the properties. What are these properties? Irritability, excitability, conductivity, summation, facilitation, inhibition are some, and there are others. These, together with the effects of the internal environment upon them, constitute what has here been called *intervening variables*.

One might ask how the nervous system can be modified or dealt with in order to observe its effects upon response. One way is to observe the effects of stimulation on response before the nervous system has developed completely and assumed its full integrative functions. This may be done during the prenatal or embryonic period. Another way is to delimit the nervous system by removing, or otherwise reducing the action of, selected parts of it. This may be done by operative removal, the use of drugs, and by other means. Still another method is to stimulate parts of the nervous system electrically or chemically, or to "tune in on" or record electrically from parts of it while its total function is unimpaired. Finally, generalized or specific stress may be imposed on the nervous system or parts of it by varying its metabolic functions or by interfering with homeostatic mechanisms which tend to maintain its environment in stable equilibrium.

In the subsequent sections of this chapter the methods of studying behavior in relation to the nervous system will be discussed. The three areas which have been selected, from among others, as samples include the *embryology of behavior:* changes in behavior with development of the nervous system; the *internal environment:* stresses imposed upon the nervous system by modifications in the internal milieu; and *cortical functions:* stimulation of, delimitation of, and selective recording from, parts of the central nervous system.

Other important areas of investigation whose methods might have been described in this chapter are concerned with the electrical recording of sensory- and motor-nerve discharges. Recently, for example, successful techniques for recording electrical potentials from single nerve fibers in auditory [25] and optic [31] tracts have been described. These and similar techniques developed for cutaneous nerves permit analysis of receptor response in terms of the smallest functional unit of the sensory system; single motor unit responses or the electrical responses from single motor-nerve fibers permit a similar analysis on the motor or effector side of the reflex arc. Many of the techniques and the results of such studies are to be found in books by Adrian [1], Erlanger and Gasser [22], Stevens and Davis [63], and Bartley [4], as well as in other sections of this book (see Chapters 8, 10, and 11).

The purpose of studying the beginnings of behavior might be considered to be three-fold: (1) To determine the manner in which sensory and motor functions develop and are combined in integrated behavior. This aim is concerned with the time of onset, the conditions of onset, and the nature of the earliest patterns of behavior. (2) To determine the relationships between development and differentiation of body structures and the progressive elaboration of the higher nervous centers. These relationships bear on the organizing influences within the organism and the levels of integration effected by the nervous system. (3) To obtain a better understanding of the nature of the earliest and simplest modifications of behavior in terms of environmental factors, including external and internal stimulation and the influence of physiological regulating mechanisms. This third kind of information should throw light upon inherited tendencies, maturational influences, and learning processes.

Just as we seek an understanding of the behavioral mechanisms of the human adult through genetic probing of simpler processes in the infant and child, it is reasonable to expect that prenatal stages of development may reveal basic facts concerning the manner in which form and function are differentiated from an initially homogeneous mass of protoplasm, the way in which primary needs of the organism develop, and the conditions of modifiability and adjustment to an ever-changing environment. Are not these the kinds of information we need for understanding and controlling the growth and development of the organism and for gaining insight into the progressive complexities of behavior, including the processes of perception, emotion, motivation, learning, thinking, and the like?

Four methods of securing information on fetal activity and reaction to stimulation will be described. The first is a *direct, extrauterine approach* and includes premature and Caesarean births in humans and experimental hysterotomies (incision of abdominal wall and uterus) in animals. The other three may be labelled *intrauterine techniques,* since they do not interfere in any way with the fetal-maternal relationship, do not involve harmful operative procedures, and leave the fetus intact throughout the period of gestation.

Extrauterine Methods of Direct Stimulation and Observation of the Human Fetus

If birth of a human fetus is spontaneous but premature, or if a pregnancy must be terminated by abortion or Caesarean section, the chances are that pathological abnormality exists in the fetus, the mother, or both, and that the physiological environment and hormonal influences have had a detrimental influence upon the fetus. In any event the fetus is not a reliable subject for experimental test of normal developmental functions. Furthermore, the human fetus born more than 4 months prematurely is ill-prepared to cope with the external environment and usually succumbs. Thus, even though a fetus may be removed with the placental membrane and is immediately placed in a suitable bath of physiological saline kept at an appropriate temperature, any observations of behavior or reactions to stimulation must be qualified as being subject to the influence of asphyxia, accumulation of carbon dioxide, and other metabolites. These factors, depending upon their nature, may operate to diminish or increase muscle and nerve excitability, as well as general reactivity.

Consequently the extrauterine observation of human fetuses cannot be considered a reliable index of sensory-motor functions and integration of behavior according to a time schedule. Positive reactions, at least so far as reflexes are concerned, are better indicators than are negative ones, since it may be inferred that a reflex response would not occur consistently in the absence of the necessary receptors, nerve pathways, and effectors. Also from such fetuses much can be learned about the structure and differentiation of body parts, the direct responses of muscle to stimulation before innervation, the response to stimulation of receptors through reflex channels, and spontaneous activity. For much of our information about human fetal activity and responsiveness we are indebted to Minkowski (see Carmichael [13] and Windle [65]), whose observations of specimens removed by Caesarean section extend from the embryonic period at about 5 weeks to the end of the gestation period.

Minkowski's technique consisted of removing the fetuses by Caesarean section, often under local anesthesia, in order to prevent the transmission of effects of a general anesthesia from the mother to the fetus. The fetus was removed with the placental membranes and amniotic sac intact and was immediately placed in a solution of physiological saline at body temperature. Observations of "spontaneous" activity, response to sensory stimulation with blunt and sharp probes over various body areas, and electrical stimulation of muscles by direct (galvanic) and alternating (faradic) current constituted the usual procedures. In some of the younger fetuses, when it was obvious that they would not survive, transections of the central nervous system at different levels were made. The results of studies on human fetuses by Minkowski and others have been carefully described in chronological and growth sequence by Carmichael [10].

One might ask why, in Caesarean births, it is not possible to leave the fetus attached to maternal membranes and its source of metabolic exchange and to make observations through the incised uterus and the amniotic sac, or to remove the fetus still attached to the umbilical cord. In either case the necessity of closure of the uterine and abdominal incisions in order to forestall hemorrhage and otherwise protect the mother is imperative. Furthermore, the conditions would undoubtedly demand general anesthesia for the mother, which in itself would invalidate fetal observations.

Extrauterine Studies of the Animal Fetus

Whereas one cannot gamble with human life by taking undue chances with the mother at time of Caesarean operation, greater risks may be taken with animals at time of hysterotomy. As a consequence much of our knowledge of fetal reactivity has come from this source. According to Windle [65], even with the greater liberties allowed in animal experimentation, there are several factors which must be considered in selecting an animal for embryologic study of behavioral development, especially if the results are to be related to behavior in the human species at a corresponding age.

First, there is the matter of the normal physiology of the uterus and placenta, i.e., the degree of intimacy between fetal and maternal tissues. The number of tissues separating fetal blood from maternal blood and the efficiency of transmission of metabolites through these membranes vary widely among mammals. Whereas there are several intervening tissue layers in marsupials (opossum), with relative inefficiency of transmission, there is a single endothelial layer in rodents, e.g., rat, guinea pig, and rabbit, with the greatest intimacy of fetal-maternal relationship and with efficiency of transmission apparently higher than that in man. Histologically and physiologically the increasing order of simplicity or intimacy of relationship and efficiency of transmission is horse and swine, cattle and sheep, cat and dog, man and monkey, and rabbit, guinea pig, and rat.

A second qualification in the selection of the species for experimentation is that the rate of embryonic growth and development must not be so rapid as to obscure stages of functional development. Duration of gestation ranges from 13 days in the opossum to 21 days in the rat, 63 days in the dog, 68 days in the guinea pig, 24 weeks in the monkey, 38 weeks in man, and 48 weeks in the horse. Thirdly, differences in fetal structure do not always permit complete comparison of all functional possibilities; e.g., hoofed animals do not present hand

and foot reflexes. Fourth, the size of the fetus may be an important factor; the very small fetus of the rat in the early stages does not permit readily the stimulation and observation of response. Finally, if one's interest is in growth and development of the fetus in relation to endocrine and hormonal influences transmitted through the mother, or in dietary factors, the permeability of the placental membranes must be considered. With these cautions in mind the experimental animal may be chosen to suit the particular problem or condition to be investigated.

Windle [65] also emphasizes that in the selection of the experimental method care should be taken to interfere as little as possible with the maternal-fetal relationship. Thus, in immobilizing and rendering the mother free of pain during hysterotomy, one has to choose among a general anesthesia, local anesthesia, spinal transection, and anemic decerebration. All things considered, the anemic-decerebration procedure is to be preferred. This involves tying off the carotid and basilar arteries which supply the brain, thus immobilizing and desensitizing the mother, but necessitating artificial respiration through a cannula inserted in the trachea. One final caution pertains to operative procedures: opening the uterus may so modify pressure relationships that normal placental interchange may be disrupted, and the effects of operative shock in the mother may be transmitted to the fetus.

In view of this somewhat forbidding list of precautions the techniques employed in embryologic studies of living fetuses should be scrutinized most carefully before accepting results and interpretations. No amount of care in the making of observations will correct for artifacts or spurious behavioral manifestations induced through faulty techniques or oversight in setting the stage for the observations.

Carmichael [11] developed a technique which seems to satisfy many of the foregoing requirements and also provides refinement in observation through the medium of continuous motion pictures. The animal selected was the guinea pig. The age of the fetuses was carefully determined with reference to the time of insemination, which is known as copulation age. Spinal transection was used to immobilize and desensitize, after hysterotomy had been performed under deep ether anesthesia. After sufficient time for the anesthesia to wear off, the animal was placed in a bath of physiological saline at 37.5 degrees centigrade, and the fetuses were shelled out of the uterus into an illuminated bath. With the aid of magnification, motion pictures were taken of the spontaneous and stimulus-induced behavior of the fetuses. Carmichael and his collaborators have published a series of studies which provide a complete repertory of the behavior and responsiveness to a variety of stimuli for the fetal guinea pig from its earliest mobility (25 days copulation age) to the end of the normal gestation period. These investigations, as well as those of other workers, have been summarized by Carmichael [10, 12, 13]. Other important sources of information on studies of fetal behavior in mammals may be found in publications by Barcroft [3], Hooker [35, 36], and Windle [65] and in the numerous research reports by these men and their associates. The work of Coghill [16] on amphibian embryos, especially in *Amblystoma,* was a tremendous impetus to studies of embryologic behavior, and both he and Carmichael [12] have stressed the importance to psychology of such studies for a better understanding of behavioral development.

Intrauterine Recording of Electrical Activity in the Fetus

There has long been a need for objective indicators of human fetal activity which can be applied in normal pregnancies without harmful effects to the mother or fetus and without disturbing the fetal-maternal relationship. Two such measures of physiologic activity in the fetus *in utero* have been described by Lindsley [46]. These measures are the *fetal electrocardiogram* (EKG), providing a measure of heart rate, and the *fetal electroencephalogram* (EEG), which furnishes a measure of cortical activity.

It has long been known that the fetal heart begins to beat as early as the third week of pregnancy, before it has received its nerve supply, so that the rhythmic beat is presumed to be myogenic rather than neurogenic in the early stages. By the fourth or fifth month the heart beat can be detected by means of a stethoscope applied to the abdominal wall of the mother. One of the first to attempt to record the fetal EKG *in utero* was Sachs [55], a German investigator, who thought he was successful, but whose records strongly suggest that he was misled by muscle action potentials from the abdominal wall. Later Maekawa and Toyoshima [49] and Geiger *et al.* [27] were successful in their attempts. The technique employed by Lindsley [46] not only provided very clear records of the fetal EKG but allowed for differential recording of maternal and fetal EKG's or simultaneous records of both.

FETAL ELECTROCARDIOGRAM. The magnitude of the fetal heart potential recorded through the abdominal wall of the mother is of the order of 50 to 100 microvolts (millionths of a volt), so that high amplification is necessary. Lindsley used a sensitive amplifier arrangement and both a mirror-type oscillograph for photographic records and a four-pen inkwriting oscillograph, which traced the records on paper tape. Figure 1 shows a typical record obtained by means of the mirror-type oscillograph, with electrodes attached to the abdominal wall of the mother. Both the maternal (m) and fetal (f) heart potentials appear in the record; the maternal heart rate averages about 72 beats per minute, whereas the fetal heart rate is about 150 beats per minute. For this particular record the electrodes were about

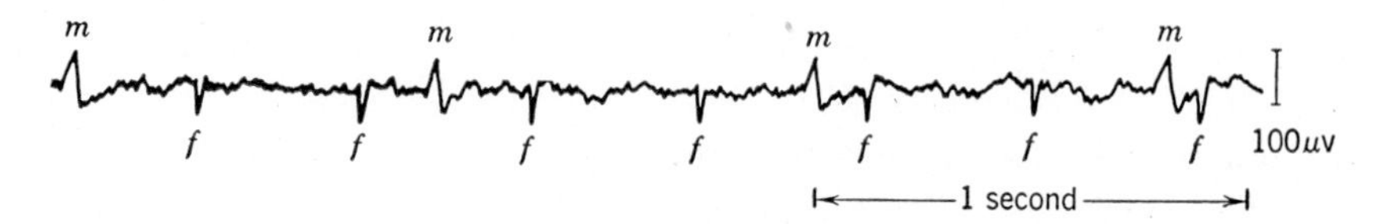

Fig. 1. Maternal (*m*) and fetal (*f*) electrocardiogram records obtained from the wall of the abdomen of the mother during the fifth month of pregnancy.

7 centimeters apart and just below the umbilicus or navel. The record was obtained during the fifth month of pregnancy, or 125 days before full-term delivery.

Electrodes, consisting of small silver disks, were attached by means of collodion or adhesive tape to various points on the maternal abdomen. An electrode paste served as the electrolyte between the electrode and the skin. Some of the electrode positions are shown in Fig. 2 on the diagram of the maternal abdomen. Usually some preliminary experimentation in the placing of the electrodes is required in order to find the most favorable spot for recording potentials created by the fetal heart beat. The optimal location varies, depending upon the position of the fetus at any given moment. Although it may be desirable to have the maternal heart potential appear in the same record as the fetal EKG, the greater frequency of the fetal heart beat, together with the greater size of the maternal EKG, may result in interference of patterns at times. In order to avoid this, electrodes may be placed fairly close together, preferably only 2 or 3 inches apart. If the further precaution is taken to orient the electrodes along the midline below the umbilicus, the maternal EKG may be eliminated entirely or be greatly reduced in size. Various tests have demonstrated that a superior method of recording consists of placing one electrode just below the umbilicus (point y in diagram) and the other at point x on the right thigh. This procedure frequently provides a good fetal EKG without the often troublesome maternal EKG accompaniment.

For experimental purposes, if one wishes to study the effect of drugs, fatigue, and so forth upon the maternal heart rate and also the fetal heart rate, through possible placental transmission of the effects, simultaneous tracings of both the maternal and fetal EKG's should be obtained on the same record, or if multiple recording channels are available, single simultaneous records of each should be made. The effect of exercise, fatigue, emotion, and a variety of other conditions which might affect the mother and/or the fetus can thus be studied in terms of the maternal and fetal heart rate. In addition, the heart-rate response recorded in this objective fashion can also be used as an index of conditioned response. The principal types of stimuli which

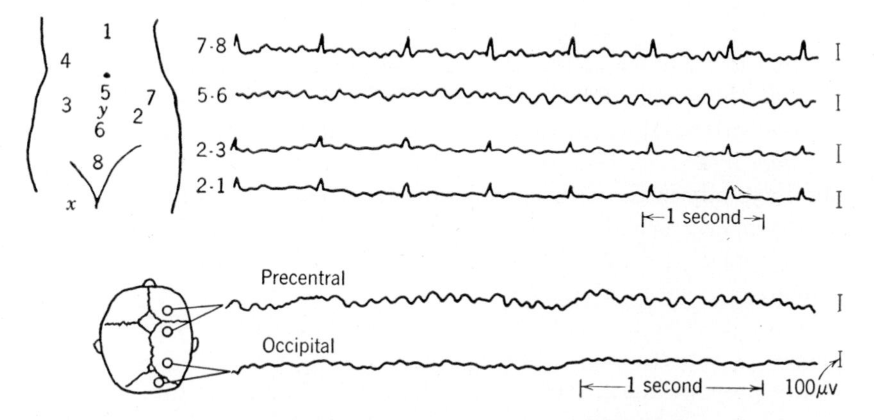

Fig. 2. Fetal and infant electroencephalograms.

The diagram at left shows numbered electrode placement; in the four tracings on the right the EEG or brain waves appear, principally from electrodes 5-6. The maternal EKG appears in all tracings except 5-6. The bottom tracings from occipital and motor regions of the same infant 3 weeks after birth show the presence of brain waves in the motor region which resemble closely those from electrodes 5-6 prenatally. The occipital region of the newborn has no characteristic rhythm until about 3 months postnatally.

may be used in connection with this effort are auditory, vestibular, vibratory, pressure, and tactual. Care should be taken, however, to insure that heart-rate change in the fetus is not secondary to actual movement of the fetus after stimulation, or to possible contraction of the abdominal wall and uterus after emotional stimulation or excitement in the mother, thus furnishing a tactual stimulus to the fetus, rather than a response to the auditory "startle" stimulus assumed to elicit the heart-rate change. Moreover, after emotional stimuli in response to which the mother may be aroused, the possibility of transmission of adrenin through the placental membranes should be considered; this occurrence would undoubtedly show a longer latency for a change in fetal heart rate than would a direct response to sensory stimulation.

FETAL ELECTROENCEPHALOGRAM. While recording the fetal EKG during the seventh and eighth months of pregnancy, Lindsley [46] found that rhythmic activity resembling brain waves in newborn infants appeared over certain regions of the abdominal wall of the mother. When a careful check of the location was made, it was found that these rhythmic potential variations were coming principally from pairs of electrodes over a region where the fetal head could be palpated by finger pressure on the maternal abdomen. When the position of the fetal head shifted, the rhythmic brain waves shifted with it to the new position. As further proof that the rhythmic potentials were fetal brain waves, records were taken on the same infant shortly after birth, when it was found (bottom tracings in Fig. 2) that the same pattern of waves could be obtained over the motor (precentral) region of the newborn infant's brain. The first four tracings in Fig. 2 show that the rhythmic waves from the brain were obtained only in those tracings involving electrodes 5–6 and 7–8, which were properly oriented with respect to the fetal head. The maternal EKG appears in all records, except that coming from electrodes 5–6, which were placed along the midline below the umbilicus.

What can be accomplished with the fetal EEG? It furnishes a means of determining when the cerebral rhythms first appear and makes possible the tracing of development of such rhythms from the time they first appear prenatally and on through postnatal life. The curve of growth of cerebral rhythms postnatally has been described by Smith [60] and Lindsley [45]. Correlation of the onset of cerebral rhythms prenatally with histological studies of cortical development of fetuses of a corresponding age might be made. It is known that the motor region of the cortex in newborn infants is more completely developed histologically than are the sensory areas of the cortex. The earlier onset of brain rhythms over the motor region thus is in agreement with this anatomical finding. Furthermore, persistent brain rhythms first appear 2 or 3 months after birth in the occipital region [60, 45] and appear to be correlated with developing visuo-motor behavior.

It is doubtful that the fetal EEG can be used as a routine measure because of the difficulty of picking up the brain waves unless the head of the fetus is favorably placed and the electrodes are immediately over it. For certain experimental studies, however, careful exploration with different electrode positions and possibly the manipulation of the fetus into an appropriate position would make recording of the fetal EEG possible.

Intrauterine Observations of Fetal Activity

Another method of studying at least the gross behavior of the fetus is to observe the actual movements. This can be done in several ways. The movements can be observed *fluoroscopically,* but this can be done only for short periods of time because of the danger of harming the fetus or the mother by X-rays. Movements can be detected by *listening with a stethoscope,* but it is uncertain that all movements can be observed, and furthermore this procedure would not be very practical for prolonged periods of observation. *Palpation or visual observation* of the maternal abdomen can be resorted to but is subject to the same criticisms as the immediately preceding technique. Recording by means of *tambours and mechanical levers* has been tried by Sontag and Wallace [61] and Spelt [62]. The tambours were arranged over different areas of the abdomen. It is doubtful whether movements of the fetus directed toward the sides and back of the mother are detected by such an arrangement. Finally, a method which has been used successfully is the *maternal report.* This method, described by Richards *et al.* [54], requires that the mother report when she feels a movement of the fetus.

The method of maternal report, as employed by these investigators, required that the mothers, in various stages of pregnancy, come to the laboratory at regular intervals, daily or weekly as the experiment necessitated. For a period of 5 or 6 hours they remained in bed resting, except for visits to the bathroom, and were served lunch and were permitted to read, sew, or talk as they desired. The mother was made comfortable and was able to relax during the observation period. Two push-buttons were arranged, so that by means of one the mother could signal any movements or changes of position she made, according to a prearranged coded system for different types of activity; with the other she signalled all fetal movements that could be perceived. Each button activated a signal marker, which recorded on a polygraph. A third signal marker recorded time signals in minutes.

Some fetal movements are discrete or abrupt, whereas some are slow and more persistent, but no attempt was made to discriminate between them. The mother simply pressed the button when each new movement was felt. The records were then analyzed in terms of the number of minutes during which, as the mother's signals indicated, the fetus was active. The "minutes active" criterion was found to be a good index of the absolute number of movements (correlation .93). The correlation between readings of the polygraph records by two separate analyzers was found to be .99, indicating high reliability in the scoring of the records.

Richards and collaborators utilized this method to study individual differences in fetal activity, the peak point of fetal activity during the prenatal period, and the relationship between the amount of fetal activity at its peak and the performance on infant developmental schedules at six months postnatally [53].

Method of Conditioned Response in Intrauterine Study

Forbes and Forbes [24] reported some observations suggestive of fetal conditioning during the ninth month of pregnancy, when repeated sounds at first producing reactivity in the fetus gradually gave evidence of cessation of response or "negative adaptation." Later, a few days after birth, the infant again responded with a slight body jerk. These observations were poorly controlled, and it was uncertain whether the sound or a vibratory stimulus produced the response. Attempts at prenatal conditioning by Ray [52] and Sontag and Wallace [61] were not very successful. However, Spelt [62], working with fetuses of 7 or 8 months, found that noise stimuli produced responses consistently, whereas vibratory stimuli did not. After pairing the two types of stimuli, the vibratory stimulus being started against the mother's abdomen 5 seconds before the noise stimulus, response to the vibratory stimulus alone was observed within 100 paired presentations. Spelt recorded the response of the fetus by means of tambours attached to the mother's abdomen. Apparently no detailed report of this study has ever been made. Since even neonatal conditioning in infants less than 2 weeks old is difficult and unstable, according to Wenger [64], it is still doubtful whether fetal conditioning can be established.

One of the most profitable methods to pursue in this kind of study would seem to be to utilize the fetal heart rate (EKG) as a measure of response, and paired auditory and vibratory stimuli. Preliminary observations (unpublished) indicate that auditory stimuli produce a heart-rate change in the fetus independent of that in the mother, whereas vibratory stimuli do not produce a response. Thus we have the possibility of pairing a positive with a negative stimulus and objectively recording the fetal heart-rate change, if any, to the vibratory stimulus alone after a number of pairings of the two stimuli.

THE INTERNAL ENVIRONMENT AND BEHAVIOR

The importance of the internal environment or the fluid matrix in which our life processes take place is not newly recognized. Cannon

[7] states that Claude Bernard, more than 85 years ago, observed, "We do not live in the atmosphere that surrounds us—we are separated from that atmosphere by a layer of dead cells or by a film of mucus or a salt solution. All that is alive within these lifeless surfaces is immersed in the fluids of the body, the blood, and the lymph, which form an internal environment." When the fluid matrix is markedly altered, severe dangers may arise, says Cannon, and he stresses the need for constancy and stability of the internal milieu.

The human organism especially is provided with an elaborate set of checks and balances which regulate the internal environment. Were it not for these finely balanced and compensating mechanisms, life itself would cease. For example, an elevation of body temperature by 6 to 8 degrees, a reduction in blood sugar to a little less than half its normal value, a shift in the acid-base balance of the blood up or down from its slightly alkaline state, a change in the blood-calcium level are only a few of the departures from a condition of relative constancy which may result in disaster. It should be emphasized further that smaller changes in these and other physicochemical conditions of the fluid matrix, changes which may be well within the tolerance range compatible with life, may nevertheless modify the receptivity and reactivity of the organism and thus affect its behavior. It is also recognized that psychological factors, especially emotion and anxiety or worry, may affect the constancy of the internal environment and in turn be affected by it.

Homeostatic Mechanisms

The condition of constancy or stability of the internal environment has been called *homeostasis* by Cannon. He points out that the equilibrium of the fluid matrix may be altered by both external and internal conditions, but, except in extremes, a balance or homeostasis tends to be restored. Sometimes this is accomplished quickly, as in the restoration of the blood-sugar level after exercise by calling upon glycogen reserves stored in the liver; in other cases, as in acclimatization to the reduced oxygen supply on a high mountain range, a much longer period of adjustment is necessary before a new equilibrium is established.

There are a variety of ways in which homeostasis may be preserved, but the complexity of these mechanisms does not permit discussion of them here. It is sufficient to say that general metabolic processes are concerned, including the intake of food and oxygen and the elimination of waste products after chemical reactions have taken place. Among the myriad factors upon which homeostasis depends are the amount and concentration of various chemical elements in the blood stream, the presence of hormones secreted into the blood by the ductless glands, the release of stored reserves, the permeability of tissue membranes and the diffusibility of certain substances in the body fluids, and finally the adequacy and flexibility of the two main transporting and communicating systems, the circulatory and the nervous.

Cannon [8] believes that the *autonomic nervous system* is one of the prime agencies for maintaining uniformity or homeostasis in the body fluids. The cranial and sacral divisions, known as the *parasympathetic system,* he believes operate only indirectly and somewhat remotely to assure constancy, whereas the thoracolumbar division, known as the *sympathetic system,* acts promptly and directly to prevent serious changes in the internal environment. There is considerable evidence that these two counteracting systems, the sympathetic and parasympathetic, play a major role in preserving physiological balance or homeostasis. Recent evidence of the importance of the autonomic nervous system and its associated endocrine glands in the regulation of the internal environment and bodily functions has been presented by Cannon and Rosenblueth [9] and by Gellhorn [28].

The purpose of this section is to discuss some of the methods which have been used to produce changes in the internal environment in order to investigate the effects of such changes upon behavior and various psychological functions, including memory, association, learning, reaction time, and visual acuity. The results of these studies cannot be reported here, except in so far as they have a bearing on the method of investigation employed. Reviews of many recent psychophysiological studies have been presented by Shock [57, 58].

Changes in Blood Gases: Oxygen and Carbon Dioxide

Both oxygen and carbon dioxide are essential in the blood in certain minimal amounts if a person is to live. Body cells require oxygen in order to carry on normal metabolic processes involved in growth and in the utilization of food substances as energy. One of the waste products of metabolism is carbon dioxide, which must be constantly removed from the blood stream. The process by which carbon dioxide is thus removed and by which oxygen is obtained is respiration. As one breathes oxygen in the atmosphere, it enters minute air sacs or alveoli in the lungs, where it comes in contact with blood vessels, is taken up by the blood, and is transported throughout the organism by the arterial system. As the waste products of metabolism are formed, the carbon dioxide is transported in the blood to the lungs, where it is released and blown off in expiration. The center controlling respiration is in the medulla at the base of the brain. Lack of oxygen affects this center and stimulates it to activity, but the presence of excess carbon dioxide in the blood is even more important in increasing respiration. With increased respiration, i.e., increased rate and depth of breathing, more oxygen is made available to the blood, and more carbon dioxide is removed.

Anoxia refers to lack of oxygen in the body from any cause. Anoxemia is a more limited term referring to lack of oxygen in the blood; this condition may be due to factors internal as well as external. Here we shall be concerned primarily with *anoxemia* or *anoxic anoxia,* i.e., lack of oxygen in the blood due to external factors. Anoxemia may be produced by (1) interference with the passage of air containing oxygen into the lungs and thence into the blood, (2) reducing the partial pressure of oxygen in the inspired air, and (3) breathing air under reduced barometric pressure. The first of these possibilities is not particularly adapted to experimental work; interference with air passage into the lungs comes about principally through accident, as in drowning, or in diseases which cause congestion of the lungs or blocking of the trachea or bronchial tubes.

The second procedure, involving reduction in the partial pressure of oxygen in the inspired air, is the one most frequently employed in experimental work. Normally atmospheric air at sea level contains 20.9 per cent oxygen, 79 per cent nitrogen, and a few hundredths of a per cent of carbon dioxide and slight traces of a few other rare gases. Commercial gas mixtures may be obtained with 10 per cent oxygen and 90 per cent nitrogen, or in any combination of reduced oxygen pressure desired. A 10 per cent oxygen mixture is about equivalent, in terms of oxygen available, to an altitude of 18,000 feet; 8 per cent is approximately equivalent to an altitude of 22,000 feet. Thus, by varying the amount of oxygen in the respired air, one can simulate at ground level the effects of reduced barometric pressure at altitude.

There are several ways of controlling the amount of oxygen a subject receives. One method is the usual *basal metabolic rate* (BMR) *technique,* using the BMR machine. This apparatus usually consists (see Fig. 3) of two cylindrical tanks, each open at one end; the bottom and stationary tank has a double wall which is filled with water, the top and movable tank is inverted and fits into the double wall of the bottom tank. The water thus forms a seal but allows the top tank to move freely up and down. When the combined tank system is filled with room air, the subject may breathe the air through a tube connected with the tank. The subject wears a mouthpiece and a nose clip or a snugly fitting mask which encloses both the nose and the mouth; this insures that all respired air comes from the tank rather than from the surrounding atmosphere. Two tubes from the tank are connected to the mouthpiece; each tube has a one-way valve, permitting the passage of air in opposite directions. When the subject

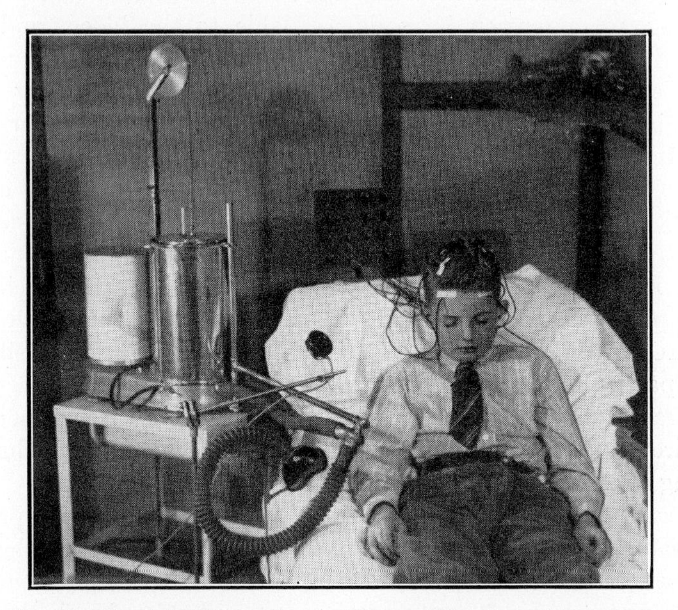

Fig. 3. Standard BMR machine for determining basal metabolic rate.

Tracing on drum shows normal respiration (low) and deep respiration or hyperventilation (high). Tube and mask are visible. When the inner can of the BMR machine is down as shown, the air supply is exhausted. The chain running over the pulley attaches to the pen, which writes on drum chart as the inner can moves up and down with respiration. The boy in this picture has electrodes attached to his head for recording brain waves.

inspires, air passes from the tank through the first tube; when he exhales, the expired air passes through the other tube and into the tank, but usually it first passes through a container of soda lime, which extracts the carbon dioxide. As the subject breathes, the inverted tank moves up and down, and a pen attached to it makes a tracing on a revolving drum, around which is placed a special chart or graph.[2]

[2] When basal metabolic rate (BMR) is to be determined, the subject must be in a so-called "basal" state; i.e., he must go without breakfast and must rest for one-half hour before the test is made. He then breathes pure oxygen from the tank, usually for two 8-minute periods. The rate of oxygen consumption is determined from the graph and converted to a percentage-of-normal value.

In the course of the inspiration-expiration process the contents of the tank are gradually exhausted; i.e., the oxygen is utilized, whereas the nitrogen, which is an inert gas, is returned. Thus, if one starts with an oxygen level of 20.9 per cent, continued rebreathing of the mixture gradually reduces the oxygen to 10 per cent or lower. At various stages during the process samples of the air mixture may be withdrawn by means of a hypodermic needle inserted through the rubber tube. These samples may be submitted to one of the methods of gas analysis in order to determine the exact oxygen composition. While in the course of this process of reducing the oxygen in the tank, the subject may be presented with various tasks or problems. One of the commonly employed procedures is to have the subject write his name. When the oxygen has been reduced sufficiently to produce confusion bordering on unconsciousness, the handwriting usually becomes illegible. Before that stage coordination is lost in varying degrees.

Another procedure for reducing the oxygen tension is to start with a fixed gas mixture, say 10 per cent oxygen and 90 per cent nitrogen. Such a mixture may be breathed from a BMR machine as described above, although the usual procedure is to employ a larger container. A commonly employed container is the large rubber Douglas bag, which may be filled with enough gas mixture to last for a longer period of time. The subject is attached to the bag by means of a single tube, which permits intake of the gas mixture through the mask. The expired air is blown off into the atmosphere through a valve attached to the mask. With this type of procedure, using a fixed percentage of oxygen, an experiment may be continued for a longer period of time and with a constant level of reduced oxygen supply.

The third method mentioned above, namely, reduction of barometric pressure, may be accomplished in three ways: (1) by ascending in an airplane to a high altitude, where the barometric pressure is low, (2) by climbing to the top of a high mountain or living at a high elevation, and (3) by placing the subject in a decompression chamber, where the pressure may be reduced to correspond to any reasonable altitude. Although low-pressure chambers were used before World War II, they were expensive and rather complicated and consequently were not used extensively. The many problems associated with high-altitude flying and with sudden shifts in altitude and barometric pressure, as in dive-bombing, created a great demand for low-pressure chambers where one or more men could be enclosed during simulated ascent or descent. Because of the roominess of some of the larger chambers, various kinds of motor-performance tests, as well as other psychological and physiological tests, could be administered. These decompression chambers usually employ a double pump arrangement whereby, in simulating ascent, air is pumped out faster than it is pumped in; for simulating descent, the reverse procedure is followed. In the chamber both the pressure of the air and the oxygen concentration can be altered so as to simulate exactly the effects of high-altitude flying.

Briefly, the results of oxygen-deprivation experiments indicate that the higher mental processes, such as memory, attention, association, and problem solving, are the first to be affected and show a deterioration with relatively little reduction in oxygen concentration. Sensory and motor functions of a simple type are not greatly affected until the subject is near the point of collapse from lack of oxygen. One of the first functions to show a loss, even under minimal reductions in oxygen, is night vision. This fact led to the use of oxygen on most night missions at all altitudes, especially when the pilot or observer was depending heavily upon his night vision to identify enemy planes or special "blacked-out" targets. Another observation made by the military services is that pilots or others in a plane at an altitude corresponding to perhaps only 14 per cent oxygen frequently show signs of poor judgment or failure to take heed of signs or warnings which otherwise might be respected. This has frequently been the cause of air accidents.

Although compensatory mechanisms begin to operate as soon as oxygen deficit occurs, with increasing loss of oxygen these homeostatic mechanisms soon fail to meet requirements. After unconsciousness, if the condition of low oxygen persists, death may ensue. Even if recovery occurs in time, serious damage may still have been inflicted upon the nervous system, which is one of the most vulnerable parts of the organism. With the beginning of anoxia, deeper and faster breathing occurs. This is called hyperpnea, or labored breathing, and leads to overventilation of the lungs. It is a compensatory attempt to supply more oxygen to the blood. Unfortunately, overventilation also blows off more carbon dioxide, which tends to produce acapnia, or a reduction of carbon dioxide tension in the blood, with attending symptoms of dizziness, blurring of vision, and tingling sensations in fingers and toes.

Carbon dioxide tension. The principal method of studying the effect of increasing the carbon dioxide tension in the blood is to increase the carbon dioxide content of the inspired air. This can be done by one of the methods described above for oxygen; i.e., a commercial mixture of 5 per cent carbon dioxide, or some lower fraction, mixed with the normal atmospheric content of oxygen and a lower than normal percentage of nitrogen, may be used, either in a BMR machine or in a Douglas bag. In order to reduce the carbon dioxide content of the blood one may have a subject overbreathe or hyperventilate, i.e., breathe deeply and at a rate faster than normal for a period of 3 to 5 minutes. With good, deep breathing the average person is apt to feel a little light-headed and possibly have some tingling in the fingers and toes at the end of 3 minutes. Depending upon the amount of overventilation of the lungs, with consequent greater loss of carbon dioxide, some persons may lose consciousness after 5 minutes or more of deep breathing. Patients susceptible to convulsive seizures, particularly of the petit mal type, frequently have a seizure after less than a minute of deep breathing. Consequently it is evident that a change in the acid-base balance has occurred, and this can be confirmed by taking samples of blood from arteries and veins. With loss of carbon dioxide through overventilation the *p*H or hydrogen-ion concentration of the blood shifts further toward the alkaline side.

A study that illustrates a special compensatory or homeostatic mechanism serving to protect the brain from undue shifts in carbon dioxide and oxygen content of the blood has been reported by Gibbs *et al.* [30]. Before, during, and after overventilation they took samples of blood from the arterial system and the internal jugular vein as it leaves the brain. The arterial blood in these human subjects showed a marked decrease in carbon dioxide content during hyperventilation, as was expected, but the internal jugular blood coming from the brain maintained relative constancy. The investigators interpret this to mean that with loss of carbon dioxide in the arterial system the cerebral blood vessels constrict in an effort to preserve carbon dioxide and oxygen content in the brain. When this mechanism fails, in the face of persistent loss of carbon dioxide, abnormalities in the brain waves or electrical potentials from the brain tend to occur, and convulsions, especially in susceptible individuals, may supervene. This suggests that, when homeostatic control in the brain is lost, abnormal function may occur.

Blood Chemistry: Sugar, Calcium, etc.

The brain derives its energy from carbohydrate metabolism, i.e., the oxidation of blood sugars. Consequently the amount of sugar in the blood is critical for normal brain function. Normally the blood-sugar level ranges from 70 to 120 milligrams per 100 cubic centimeters of blood. If it falls below the lower limit, the condition is called *hypoglycemia;* if it rises above the upper limit, the condition is called *hypergly-*

cemia. With excessive increases or decreases beyond the limits given, serious symptoms develop. It is well known that a diabetic patient, without insulin, will suffer intensely after a meal heavy in carbohydrates, will become confused and incoordinated and, in some instances, comatose. Similarly after prolonged fasting or in diseases which lower the blood-sugar level, thus producing a condition of hypoglycemia, a series of symptoms occur. Cortical functions are affected first, with loss of association, memory, and ability to perform problems; later sensation and perception may be affected, and speech disturbances may occur. Finally, in marked reduction of sugar-level, convulsions, stupor, and even death may ensue. Normally, during the course of the day, there are fluctuations in the sugar level, the highest levels occurring after a meal, the lowest before a meal. Unlike oxygen, of which there are no reserves in the blood, there are sources of energy reserves in the body, the liver being the principal one.

There is comparatively little evidence on the effects of variations in blood-sugar level on mental performance or other psychological processes. This should be a profitable area of investigation, since there are undoubtedly diurnal variations within the normal sugar-tolerance level, which may well be related to fluctuations in efficiency during the day. In addition, there may be individuals whose sugar level is consistently on the low side or high side of the normal range, with consequent variations in psychological efficiency.

The principal methods or times of studying hypoglycemia, or low blood sugar, are three: (1) after a period of fasting or during the course of a diet low in carbohydrates, (2) after insulin injections, as in an insulin-tolerance test, and (3) in chronically hypoglycemic individuals. Because of the possible danger involved in such studies they should be conducted only under competent medical supervision. In any of the procedures, samples of blood may be taken at suitable intervals for the analysis of blood sugar by one or more of several methods available. In the first procedure mentioned above, the sugar level may be increased by feeding carbohydrates; or, if an immediate increase in sugar level is desired, glucose may be injected intravenously. Psychological tests and measures may be administered during control periods, when sugar level is within normal limits, and during experimental periods, when the level is reduced. Hyperglycemia, or excess sugar in the blood, may be produced by injections of glucose or by a diet high in carbohydrates.

A study which may reveal significant information of this type was conducted at the University of Minnesota. During World War II a sizable group of conscientious objectors volunteered for the experiments, which involved prolonged periods of semistarvation during which psychological, physiological, biochemical, and clinical observations were made [6].

Very little is known about the possible effects of varying the inorganic constituents of the blood stream, such as calcium, potassium, and phosphorus, except from clinical observations which in general have not included objective psychological evaluations. Studies of this type should be made in a controlled medical environment where complete blood analyses are available for correlation with psychological test results. Experimental variation of these constituents of the blood stream may be accomplished through diet and injections, as described above for blood-sugar level.

Other factors associated with the internal environment which might be studied profitably with reference to behavioral changes and special psychological functions are basal metabolism, water balance, body temperature, vitamin deficiency, and the extensive and complicated ramifications of hormonal secretion by the endocrine glands. Experiments of this type would seem best to be undertaken in collaboration with physicians in a general hospital, where there is constant medical supervision and adequate dietary and biochemical control.

CORTICAL FUNCTIONS AND BEHAVIOR

The central nervous system consists of the spinal cord and the brain; the brain is enclosed within the skull cavity, and the spinal cord within the spinal column. All incoming and outgoing impulses, except those in the cranial nerves, are transmitted to and from the brain via the spinal cord. The spinal cord becomes continuous with the brain at the base of the skull, where it expands into the medulla, pons, midbrain, and other portions of the "brain stem," including the thalamus, hypothalamus, and subcortical motor centers. If a skull is split fore and aft and the two halves opened like the shell of an English walnut, one can see two large, convoluted hemispheres; connecting the cerebral hemispheres is a broad band of fibers known as the corpus callosum. On the bottom surface of the cerebral hemispheres and almost surrounded by them is the "brain stem." Under the posterior portion of the hemispheres lies the cerebellum. See Fig. 4.

We are here concerned, not with the brain as a whole, but rather with the so-called gray mantle which completely envelops each hemisphere. This is called the *cerebral cortex.* Although the cortex is only a few millimeters thick, it has a greater surface area than is generally supposed because of its infolding grooves or sulci and outfolding gyri, and it contains thousands of brain cells and their ramifications. Immediately beneath the cortex are numerous nerve pathways interconnecting different parts of it, and many descending and ascending pathways connecting lower centers and the periphery

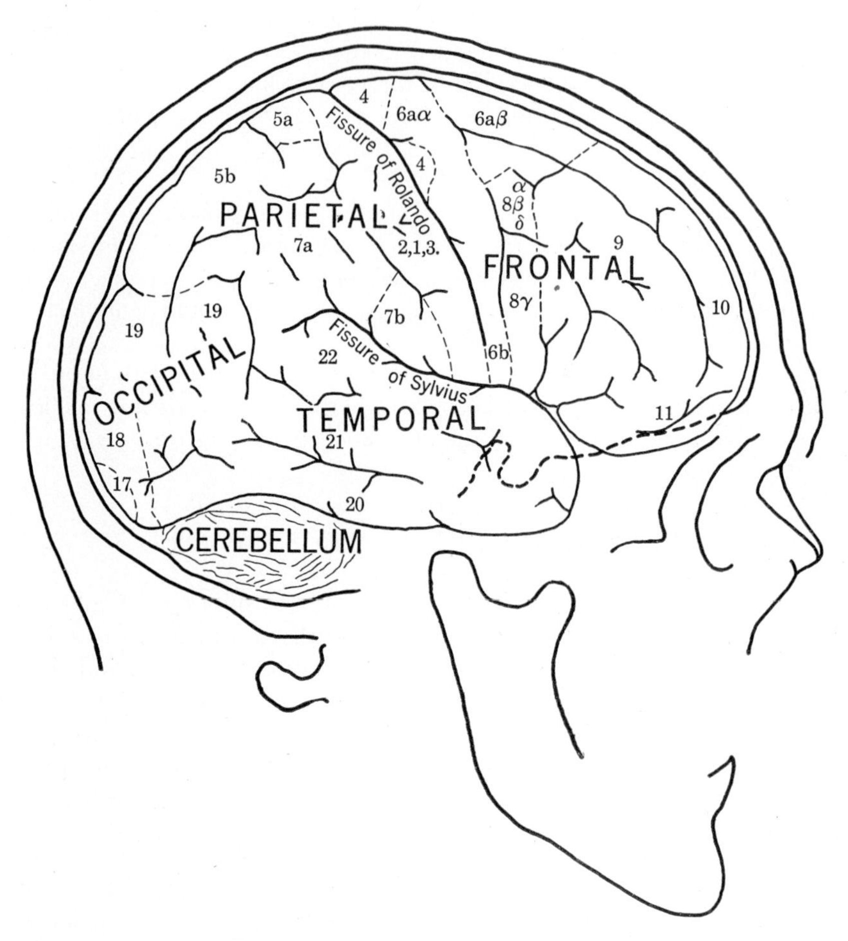

Fig. 4. Brain map fitted to tracing of X-ray photo of scalp and skull.

The principal lobes are indicated, and the numbers refer to architectonic areas of Brodmann and the Vogts.

of the organism with the cortex. These intercommunicating pathways appear white and are called white matter, whereas the aggregations of cell bodies in the cortex and in subcortical centers have a slightly grayish cast and are known as gray matter. Histologically, six or more layers in the cortex of man may be differentiated by cell type and structure; even in the rat, whose cortex is smooth rather than convoluted and is of course much simpler, there are six distinguishable layers. Phylogenetically, the cerebral cortex is the most recently developed portion of the nervous system, and in man it has attained its highest development. Likewise, in man it seems to be most vulnerable, and injury to it results in the greatest and most pervasive deficit.

The importance of the cerebral cortex lies in the fact that it is an integrating center which manifests some degree of control over all lower centers of the nervous system and hence enters into the control of all behavior. Practically all incoming impulses reach the cortex, and apparently most outgoing impulses originate there. The cortex has both excitatory and inhibitory effects upon lower centers, as well as similar intracortical effects. Experimental study of the cortex has demonstrated that some portions are specialized for the reception of certain kinds of sensory impulses and therefore are designated as sensory regions. Among these are the occipital lobes for vision, the temporal lobes for audition, the parietal lobes for general bodily sensation, including tactile, pressure, temperature, pain, and vibratory sensitivity; olfaction is served by the somewhat vestigial olfactory lobes at the base of the brain and the inferior surface of the temporal lobes; the cortical areas for taste are not well established but are probably represented in the hippocampal region of the temporal lobes.

The frontal lobes comprise almost half the total area of the cerebral cortex. The posterior half of the frontal lobes is concerned with the initiation and integration of motor activities, whereas the anterior half consists of association or higher integrating centers. The frontal portion is often referred to as the *prefrontal area* and is believed to be associated with higher intellectual functions, especially abstract thinking, memory, initiative, social inhibition, and so forth. Figure 4 shows schematically how the lateral surface of the brain would appear with the right half of the skull removed. In this drawing the lobes and the two major fissures have been labelled; the numbers refer to some of the principal architectonic areas which have been differentiated histologically by Brodmann, the Vogts, and others, but should be considered mainly as general landmarks rather than rigidly defined areas.

Although much remains to be learned about the brain, especially about the cortex, considerable serviceable information is available to the clinical neurologist, who is able, from his knowledge of neuroanatomy and physiology of the brain, to determine from a series of symptoms presented by a patient the probable location of gross lesions in the brain. This is especially true of behavioral abnormalities resulting from expanding lesions, such as brain tumors, abscesses, hematomas, and atrophy, but less true of small and relatively fixed areas of destruction. Much of the neurologist's ability to localize depends upon his knowledge of how a particular lesion will affect the reflexes and the sensory and motor capacities of his patient. Recent studies suggest that a fuller knowledge of the effects of lesions on psychological capacities, when measured objectively, will help to refine diagnosis of brain injury and defect. In addition, it should provide a sounder basis for understanding behavior. Many psychological phenomena exhibited by man are apparently dependent upon the cerebral cortex; about them we have relatively little understanding. Among these may be mentioned perception of various types, memory, learning, motor coordination and rhythm, sleep and dreams, and hypnosis.

Scarcely more than one hundred years ago the pseudo-science of phrenology was in full popularity, and it was not until the latter half of the nineteenth century that anatomical and histological studies, together with the beginning of experiments involving removal of brain tissue and electrical stimulation of different parts of the brain, began to provide some reasonably valid concepts of brain function. Our present knowledge of brain function still rests in part upon neuroanatomical and neurophysiological experiments performed at the end of the last century. Much of the work has been repeated and extended with new and better techniques, but at least some of the basic concepts still persist. With advances in microscopy, operative techniques, tissue-staining techniques and others, finer and finer structural analysis has become possible. Refinements in procedures for studying physiological phenomena have gone hand in hand with anatomical developments, although not until relatively recently have neuroanatomists become somewhat functional-minded. Since the 1920's, when greater sensitivity of amplifying and recording equipment became available with the development of radio, there has been great progress in the investigation of the functional activity of the cortex and other nervous structures in terms of the electrical phenomena which accompany such activity. Thus, in the following section an attempt will be made to describe some of the techniques which have provided the most recent information on brain function and which bid well to open new vistas of knowledge of man's most highly developed and yet most elusive activity—cortical function.

Cortical-stimulation Techniques

In 1870 Fritsch and Hitzig discovered that it was possible to produce movements of the hind leg of a dog by stimulating an area in the frontal lobe on the opposite side with a weak electrical current. Later Hitzig quite accurately outlined what we now recognize as the excitable area of the motor cortex by stimulating a series of points on the exposed cortex of the dog and monkey. Although Bartholow first reported similar electrical excitability in the cortex of man, our most detailed information on the motor areas (principally areas 4 and 6; see Fig. 4) in man have come from electrical stimulation studies by Foerster [23], Penfield and Boldrey [51], and Scarff [56].

Electrical stimulation. The usual procedure for stimulating electrically the motor cortex in animals or man is to incise the scalp and turn down a bone flap, exposing the cortical areas it is desired to stimulate. The transparent membranous coverings of the cortex, the *dura, arachnoid,* and *pia,* are then incised, exposing the very surface of the cortex; although in many instances electrical stimulation may be applied directly to the outer membranous covering, the dura. This procedure, however, is apt to lead to diffusion of the current and lack of discreteness of the stimulus and the resulting response. The stimulating current is delivered by means of wires attached to two electrodes. One electrode is usually attached to skin or muscle on some part of the incised scalp and serves only to complete the circuit through the animal. The "active" or "stigmatic" electrode is usually a small metal rod, insulated except at its tip, which may be applied directly to the region to be stimulated. Frequently the tip of such an electrode is covered with a small bead of cotton or has a cotton wick or thread attached to it which is saturated with physiological saline solution. This is done to provide better contact with the surface of the cortex as well as to prevent injury to it.

The source of the current may be a battery or other direct-current supply for a *galvanic current shock,* or an alternating-current supply for a *faradic current shock.* The voltage and current must be properly controlled. A common laboratory device for electrical-stimulation experiments is the *inductorium.* This consists of two simple coils of wire which telescope one another, the inner coil being wound on an iron core. A current led into the primary coil will induce, on opening and closing the primary circuit, single "make" and "break" shocks. If it is desired to produce a series of rapidly alternating (faradic) shocks, the inductorium is connected in such a manner that a spring switch in the primary circuit is alternately drawn to and released from the magnetic attraction of the iron core. This interrupts the primary circuit at a frequency determined by the tension applied to the spring mechanism and induces a series of "make-break" shocks in the secondary circuit, which is attached to the electrodes. Ordinarily a stronger current must be applied in a single "make" or "break" shock than when a series of rapidly repeated shocks is given, for in the latter case a type of summation or build-up occurs at the stimulated point. The current strength is usually set initially at a low value and gradually increased until a response is just produced; i.e., a threshold-stimulus level is determined. Then the current may be increased slightly above threshold value to insure stimulation every time the electrode is applied to an excitable point. Thereafter various points over the entire cortical field under investigation may be touched gently with the stimulating electrode, and the response, if any, is observed. Care must be exercised not to stimulate different points on the cortex too quickly, since the effect of stimulation in one area may "inhibit" or "facilitate" response in an adjacent area on a subsequent trial unless 20 or 30 seconds are allowed to intervene between stimuli.

If the stimulating electrode is applied to the left motor region (area 4) for the foreleg in the dog, for example, one may look for movement of some part of the foreleg on the opposite side of the body. If the stimulus is applied over the right motor region for the trunk, movement of the trunk musculature on the left side may be expected.

Penfield and Boldrey [51] electrically stimulated the exposed cortex of human patients under local anesthesia, so that the patients could report their sensory experience. With both direct- and alternating-current shocks, the region along the posterior edge of the Rolandic fissure was found to produce sensory experience on the opposite side of the body, corresponding to the cortical region stimulated. In both the motor area of the frontal lobe, just anterior to the Rolandic fissure, and the sensory area of the parietal lobe, just posterior to the Rolandic fissure, the organization of the excitable points began with the feet and legs at the top of the fissure, near the midline separating the two hemispheres. As the stimulating electrode was applied farther and farther down on the lateral surface of the cortex, the region of response or sensibility moved up the trunk to the neck and head. Thus the order of representation in the cortex is just reversed from that in the peripheral sense fields of the body, with excitable points on the cortex at the bottom of the fissure representing the head, eyes, and neck, and the points at the top representing the lower extremities. Some points were found in the parietal region which elicited motor responses, and some points in the frontal motor region which produced sensory experience, but in general the sensory area was chiefly along the posterior margin of the Rolandic fissure and the most excitable motor regions were along the anterior margin of the fissure. Stimulation of area 17, the primary visual center in the occipital lobe, sometimes produced flashes of light, according to the patient's reports;

stimulation in area 22 of the temporal lobe produced "buzzing" sounds or "ringing" in the ears and sometimes dizziness and dream-like states.

Within very recent years improvements have been made in electrical stimulating devices. These new stimulators make use of electronic circuits for generating controlled electric shocks. Wave form, current strength, and frequency of electric shocks are carefully calibrated and can be controlled and varied readily. These characteristics are important, since the effectiveness of an electric stimulus depends upon its intensity, form, and duration.

A unique method of presenting continuous electrical stimulation to a particular brain area in animals, without wires fastened to the animal, was developed by Loucks [48] and Chaffee and Light [14]. Two fine wires, insulated except at the tips, were planted in a particular region of the brain which it was desired to stimulate. These wires led to a small secondary coil of wire which was insulated and implanted under the surface of the scalp of a monkey. A large, primary coil was so placed in a diagonal position across the cage of the animal that, wherever the monkey moved within the cage, it was in the electromagnetic field of this primary coil; thus a current was set up in the secondary coil and produced a continuous source of electrical stimulation at the electrodes in the brain. The animal was free to move about and was not subject to the possibility of infection, as might well have occurred with wires extending from an open wound.

One of the difficulties with electrical stimulation of the cortex is that we know comparatively little about the manner in which the electrical current excites cortical cells, how much it spreads around the point of application, and how deeply it extends. Despite these facts electrical stimulation is of great service to the neurosurgeon in locating regions on the surface of the cortex and has provided much information about the organization of the cortex, especially with respect to sensory and motor representation.

STIMULATION BY LOCAL STRYCHNINIZATION. Nerve tissue is highly sensitive to strychnine, and a weak solution of strychnine sulfate applied to the cortex markedly increases its excitability. Dusser de Barenne [17] first used the method of local strychninization to map the sensory cortex of the cat in 1916. Later he delimited the sensory cortex of the monkey by the same technique [18]. When a few square millimeters of filter paper soaked in a weak solution of strychnine sulfate is applied to the sensory area of the cortex of the cat or monkey, it produces marked symptoms of sensory stimulation in various parts of the body. For example, if it is applied to the region of the sensory cortex in the right hemisphere, just behind the fissure of Rolando and near the midline, it will produce during the next 30 minutes or so a marked hypersensitivity to tactual stimulation on some portion of the left hind leg or foot. Frequently, without any external stimulation, the animal will start to scratch or bite the area of skin corresponding to the region of the cortex from which the sensory experience originates. In other words, the sensory experience produced by stimulating a local region of the sensory cortex is "projected" to the appropriate part of the body from which the experience would normally arise. By means of this procedure, then, it is possible to explore the surface of the cortex and note the regions of the body showing hypersensitivity to tactual and pain stimuli. When the strychnine is applied to a region outside the sensory field of the cortex, hyperesthesia and hyperalgesia are not detectable in any region of the body. Thus the technique enables the investigator to differentiate between somatic sensory areas of the cortex and non-sensory areas.

The local strychninization procedure has been used in conjunction with the electrocorticogram, which will be described subsequently, to determine the interrelationship of different parts of the sensory cortex [21, 2]. The essence of these combined procedures is that strychnine applied to one region of the cortex produces electrical potentials in other regions. The records or tracings show spike-like waves, called strychnine "spikes" because of their sharp appearance. If region A, to which strychnine has been applied, produces strychnine "spikes" in region B, but not in regions C or D, functional connections between regions A and B are indicated. At least, excitation in region A "fires" or produces "spike" potentials in region B, and the assumption is that nerve cell bodies in A send impulses into region B and excite it. By cutting the cortex between regions A and B, it can be demonstrated that this functional relationship is blocked. Since excitation in region A does not excite activity in regions C or D, it is assumed that there are no functional relationships, at least none conducting impulses from A to C or D. On the other hand, if strychnine is applied to C or D, it may turn out that activity is induced in A. This would mean that the conducting pathways between A and C or D run in only one direction. It thus becomes evident that by utilizing such a technique one can map some of the multitude of interconnections between different parts of the cortex, and the same may be done for relationships between cortical and subcortical centers [20].

Cortical Deactivation Techniques

One of the earliest techniques employed in studying the brain and its functions was used by Flourens in 1823. It is the method of ablation.

Ablation. The removal of cortical tissue by surgical means is called ablation. After exposing the brain under deep anesthesia, ablation is usually accomplished by incising the margins of the cortical area to be removed with a scalpel and then gently scooping out the circumscribed brain tissue with a surgical spoon or spatula. If only cortical tissue is to be removed, care must be exercised not to cut too deeply, for the cortex in some animals may be only a millimeter or two in thickness. A further complication, apart from the surgical care with which the scalp and skull must be opened under a deep anesthesia, is the possibility of cutting cerebral blood vessels. Large vessels should be avoided, and care must be taken that all bleeding is stopped before the incision is closed. If blood seepage or hemorrhage occurs after the wound is closed, pressure and hematoma (blood cysts, etc.) may develop and the animal may not survive, or if it does its behavior may reflect the changes caused by increased pressure within the skull, rather than the effects of removal of cortical tissue. In some ablation experiments an *electrical cutting knife,* utilizing high-frequency current, is employed, which cauterizes blood vessels as it cuts, thus reducing the amount of bleeding. Another device which may be used to destroy cortical substance is an *electrocautery.* This consists of a metal tip or junction offering high resistance to an electrical current and thus becoming almost "white hot" when the current flows through the two wires connected to the cautery. Usually such a device has a voltage control so that the heat may be adjusted. The cautery tips are made in convenient shapes for approaching the surface of the cortex. In all ablation techniques there is likelihood of the formation of "scar tissue" along the margins of the excision. In some instances it has been suspected that this scar tissue serves as an irritant and thus may excite or inhibit cortical activity and behavior which otherwise might not have been affected by the ablation.

Many psychologists have employed ablation techniques in their studies of animal behavior in relation to brain function. These studies range in subject from the effect of certain lesions on sensory and motor capacities to problem solving, habit formation, memory, emotionality, and handedness. Lashley's work with the rat is especially well known [44]. He established two principles with regard to the relationship between brain tissue destroyed and habit formation and retention in the rat. These are known as the principle of *mass action* and the principle of *equipotentiality.* The former holds that the rat's learned habits, especially maze-learning habits, are reduced in proportion to the amount of cortical tissue destroyed; the latter, that the foregoing principle is true regardless of the areas involved. Thus, in the rat, maze learning is related to cortical tissue in a non-specific way;

i.e., it is dependent upon mass or amount of tissue rather than upon a specific area, and in general one area may serve as well as another. Jacobsen [38, 39] did not find this to be true in the monkey and chimpanzee when tests of problem solving and memory were made after frontal-lobe lesions. Here apparently, with the progressive encephalization or corticalization of function as the phylogenetic scale is ascended, there is, on the one hand, a greater specialization of function and, on the other, a greater complexity and more highly integrated pattern of function so far as the whole cortex is concerned.

LAMINAR THERMOCOAGULATION. The method of laminar thermocoagulation, which was developed by Dusser de Barenne [19], is a means of selectively destroying successive layers of cortical tissue from the surface inward. The cortex has been shown by neuroanatomists to consist of an exceptionally complicated network of nerve cell bodies and their processes. As was stated earlier, the cortex of mammals from rat to man is generally conceded to be composed of six histologically differentiated layers or laminae. This differentiation is based on the concentration, size, and structure of nerve cells. Apart from the histological evidence, which in itself is by no means yet complete, comparatively little is known about the significance of the different layers. In order to investigate their functional characteristics, Dusser de Barenne developed the laminar thermocoagulation method.

Briefly, this method consists of applying heat to local regions of the cortex in such a way that various layers of the cortex from the surface inward may be selectively destroyed. The device is composed of a small heating coil or element containing a metal rod with a base plate which fits against the surface of the cortex. By regulating the resistance in the circuit to the heating element, the temperature of the metal plate can be controlled. According to Dusser de Barenne, heating the cortex over a few square millimeters of surface to a temperature of 65 degrees centigrade for 2 seconds destroys the nerve cells of the two outer layers; 70 degrees for 3 or 4 seconds destroys four layers, and 80 degrees for 5 seconds destroys all the layers. With such a method it is possible to destroy one or two layers and then stimulate the immediately subjacent layer electrically or by application of strychnine. In this way the effects of stimulating different layers can be determined. Furthermore, this method of controlling depth of destruction should be useful for any of the types of experiments in which ablation techniques have been used.

LOCAL FREEZING. The reverse of the method just described for deactivating cortical tissue is local freezing of the cortex, described by Nims *et al.* [50]. They used two procedures: the first involved only a small trephine opening in the skull, through which the freezing was done without interfering with the dural membrane; the second involved exposing a larger area of the cortex and the removal of the dura before the cortex was treated with cold. The freezing was done locally by applying a very small metal bucket containing carbon dioxide snow and ether, or in the more extensive areas by spraying with ethyl chloride.

When brain tissue exposed to local freezing was examined microscopically, it was found that all cells and fibers were destroyed in the center of the exposed area, but that around the periphery of the area various degrees of degeneration were noted. It does not appear, therefore, that this method permits discretely placed or sharply localized lesions. In the dog these investigators found that local freezing tends to produce convulsions and abnormal electrical potentials in surrounding areas. The mechanism of the disturbance is as yet unknown, but it is suspected that certain chemical changes in the brain tissue result from the freezing.

UNDERCUTTING AND TRANSECTION. A method which has long been employed to demonstrate the hierarchical arrangement of levels of organization and integration in the nervous system is *transection.* Cutting across the spinal cord in the cervical or thoracic region in a *spinal transection* produces a paralysis and eliminates sensory impulses for all regions of the body supplied by nerve fibers originating in segments below the cut. This method has been used by Shurrager and Culler [59] and by Kellogg [42] in experiments on conditioning in the spinal dog. Transections of the nervous system may be made at higher levels in the brain stem, and by this means the integration of lower reflex levels by the higher centers has been studied. A common procedure in many physiological experiments, either for studying reflex action at that level of integration or for immobilizing and desensitizing the animal to pain, is *decerebration,* which usually means transection of the neuraxis at the level of the midbrain. With artificial respiration such a preparation will persist for hours, making prolonged physiological investigations possible. Decerebration produces extensor rigidity in antigravity muscles. When *decortication* is performed, the cerebral hemispheres, except for the brain stem and subcortical nuclei, are removed; this amounts to stripping off all cortical tissue.

In some studies, notably one by Bartley and Bishop [5], cortical tissue has been isolated by *undercutting* and thus severing the connections of the cortex with the subcortical areas. Sometimes cortical lesions are made by cuts almost encircling an area and then undercutting it. This leaves a tab of cortical tissue connected to the rest of the cortex at only one isolated point. Such procedures are sometimes useful in attempting to determine how a particular area of the cortex is influenced by other areas or by lower centers.

Electrical Recording Techniques

In 1929 Hans Berger, a German neuropsychiatrist, first reported that electrical potentials of rhythmical nature could be recorded from the surface of the scalp of human subjects. The tracings or records of electrical variations from the brain are called *electroencephalograms*. The potentials have been shown to arise in the cortex and are believed to be associated with metabolic processes. The potentials recorded from two electrodes attached to the scalp range from a few microvolts (millionths of a volt) to about 100 microvolts, depending upon the area and the individual. In some abnormal conditions, such as

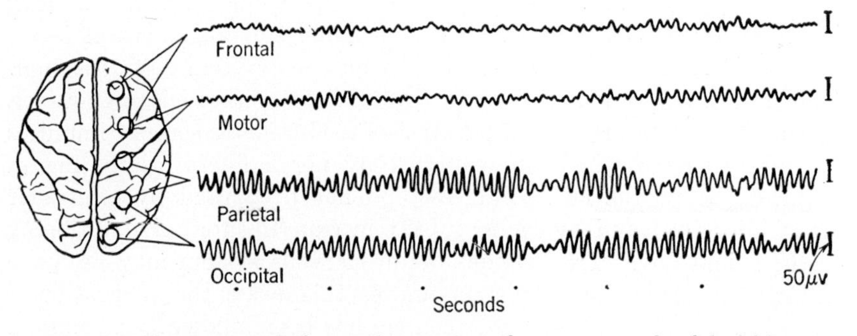

Fig. 5. Electroencephalographic tracings from a normal adult subject.

Alpha waves predominate in all brain regions, but motor and frontal regions show a mixture of alpha and the smaller beta waves. The strong alpha rhythm of the occipital and parietal areas has a frequency of about 10 per second. All tracings are normal. The brain map shows the relative positions of the electrodes on the scalp.

epilepsy, the potentials during a seizure or convulsion may be several times the size of those in normal persons. Typically, in the normal individual there is a predominant rhythmic electrical activity, known as *alpha waves* or the *alpha rhythm.* These rhythmic waves in the normal adult occur at a frequency of about 10 per second, with a range from 8 to 12 or 13 per second in different individuals, but with a range of variation of only 1 or 2 cycles per second in the same individual. The alpha waves are most prominent over the occipital and parietal regions, but also occur over the temporal and frontal regions. Smaller and faster *beta waves* are found in all areas, but are usually most prominent in records from the frontal lobes, especially over the motor areas. Figure 5 shows simultaneous tracings from four pairs of electrodes covering different areas of the brain. This is the record of a normal adult subject and shows the alpha rhythm at about 10 per second.

The alpha waves occur when the subject has his eyes closed or is in a dark room. When he opens his eyes or when a light is turned on, there is a blocking of the alpha rhythm; i.e., the waves are either greatly reduced in size or obliterated (see Fig. 6). Auditory stimuli will also block the alpha rhythm, although usually not as effectively and as persistently as a visual stimulus.

Fig. 6. Alpha rhythm at about 10 per second from the occipital lobe is blocked by the onset of light at the arrow for the brief duration of 0.010 second.

The waves remain blocked for about 1 second and then return to their normal rhythm.

The *electroencephalograph,* briefly referred to as the EEG, is now used extensively in hospitals and clinics, especially as an aid in the diagnosis of neurological disorders, such as epilepsy, and in the location of brain tumors, injuries, and so forth. Furthermore, it is a useful measuring instrument for detecting changes in cortical activity induced by drugs and other forms of therapy. The instrument has also been applied in the study of psychological disorders and as an indicator of cortical response in a variety of psychological studies. Details of the technique and results in these studies may be found in articles by Jasper [40, 41], Gibbs [29], and Lindsley [47].

Procedure for electroencephalogram. In recording the electroencephalogram or brain waves, as the records are sometimes called, small metal electrodes about 5 millimeters in diameter are fastened by means of collodion to the surface of the scalp over different regions of the head, depending upon the areas of the brain one wishes to study. The electrodes are usually spaced 2 or 3 inches apart. Wires lead from the electrodes to a switching arrangement, where any two electrodes may be made to connect with each of the amplifiers and recording instruments available. One pair of electrodes is connected to each amplifier and recording system. Since the potentials coming through the skull and scalp are very small, they must be amplified nearly a million times. This requires sensitive amplifiers. The recording unit may be a cathode-ray oscillograph, a mirror oscillograph, or an inkwriting oscillograph. The inkwriting type is most frequently used, since it writes directly in ink on paper tape moving at a uniform rate and provides an immediate record. Usually the standard electroencephalographic machines, like that shown in Fig. 7, include from

Fig. 7. Equipment for recording the electroencephalogram.

The subject with electrodes attached to her scalp normally sits in the electrically shielded room, which may be darkened and is semisoundproof. The experimenter is leaning over the box containing pre-amplifiers and switching arrangements for interconnecting different electrodes. He is adjusting the inkwriting oscillograph, which writes on the paper tape. On either side of the experimenter are two black boxes which contain voltage and power amplifiers. On the far right the white circle is the face of the cathode-ray oscillograph, which may be used to record brain waves.

two to six amplifying and recording units, so that records may be obtained simultaneously from as many different areas of the brain.

In addition to having high sensitivity, the amplifiers must have special characteristics suitable for recording without distortion the waveform and low frequencies encountered. Because of the high sensitivity of the amplifiers, they tend to pick up magnetic interference radiating from alternating-current lines, and static interference from motors, elevators, electric fans, and so forth. In order to reduce the interference the subject is placed in an electrically shielded room. Such a room must be completely enclosed in a conducting material, e.g., copper or galvanized screening. All parts of the screened surface are soldered together and connected to ground, so that interference effects are conducted away. It is desirable, although not necessary, to have a room which may be darkened. The subject may sit in a chair or relax on a cot. During the taking of the record the subject closes his eyes and attempts to relax physically and mentally.

The brain-wave records may be analyzed by counting the frequency or number of each different type of wave per second, measuring the amplitude of the waves, and determining the percentage of time that certain rhythms are present in the record. In addition to these measurable aspects of the record, there are often significant qualitative differences from subject to subject. There may be unusual wave forms, variations in the patterns of the waves, and sudden surges, which are characteristic of abnormal records. Swallowing, blinking, frowning, tension of scalp muscles, and bodily movements often produce artifacts, and one must learn by experience how these non-cortical sources of potential variation affect the record. Usually such disturbances can be quickly detected and identified by their wave form, sequence, and pattern, although sometimes they are not so readily identified.

ELECTROCORTICOGRAM. Brain waves may be recorded from the surface of the scalp of animals by the same general technique that has been described above for humans. With animals, however, it is frequently desirable and possible to make localized recordings from specific brain areas. After the cortex is exposed by operative procedures, electrodes may be placed directly on it. When electrical potentials are recorded in this way, the records are called *electrocorticograms.* The electrodes may consist of rounded metal tips gently applied to the cortex and held in place by a special holder, or of cotton wicks soaked in salt solution, which serves as an electrolyte or conducting medium. In some instances needle electrodes, insulated except at the very tip, may be inserted in the cortical tissue. The method of recording the potentials is the same as that described above.

Some experimenters employ an electrode holder, which is specially constructed to fit the contour of the skull of a particular animal. This device, known as a *Horsley-Clarke stereotaxic instrument,* is so constructed that the electrode may be manipulated in three dimensions. Each dimension of movement has a scale, so that the exact coordinates of a point may be determined; in this way electrodes may be accurately placed, and a record kept of the points from which potentials were recorded.

The electrocorticogram traces not only the "spontaneous" potentials, as in the electroencephalogram, but also *evoked potentials.* Evoked potentials are those variations induced by sensory stimulation; i.e., stimulation not only blocks or reduces "spontaneous" electrical activity of the cortex but also produces discrete potential waves limited to the specific region concerned in the sensory process. This method has been used by Woolsey *et al.* [66] in mapping the sensory area of the cortex of the monkey. By means of a mechanical vibrator they stimulated cutaneous tactile sensory endings of the skin over various regions of the body. While stimulating a particular region, they moved the cortical electrodes to different regions within the sensory area in the parietal lobe and recorded the "evoked" potentials. The region of maximal electrical response on the cortex was taken to be the primary region of representation of the peripherally stimulated area on the skin surface. In this way they were able to map the sensory cortex for tactile sensibility.

Electrocorticograms may also be obtained from the exposed cortex of human patients at the time of operation [41]. The magnitude of the potentials recorded directly from the cortex is ten or more times greater than those recorded from the surface of the scalp; otherwise the pattern of activity is very similar. According to Jasper, records obtained in this way are primarily useful for research purposes.

Neuropathology and Neurosurgery

Two types of disruption of cortical function will be briefly described: (1) behavioral disturbances arising from neuropathology in the cortex, as a result of brain injuries, disease, circulatory failure, or brain tumors and other growths; (2) neurosurgical intervention where operative removal of brain tissue is necessary, and in the recently developed field of psychosurgery, in which lesions of intracortical pathways are deliberately made in order to restore a measure of "normality" to mentally disturbed patients.

NEUROPATHOLOGY. The clinical neurologist sees many patients with lesions affecting the different cortical areas. They arise from the various causes noted above. Unfortunately it is not always possible to delimit accurately, by the usual clinical neurological procedures, the exact site and extent of the lesion. This inability may be due in part to lack of sufficiently detailed and definitive tests of physiological and psychological functions, but it is also due to the lack of time available to study each patient intensively and over a prolonged period of time.

A further requirement is that eventually the brain of a patient, studied carefully with respect to deficit in psychological and physiological adjustive functions, must also be studied postmortem by neurohistological techniques in order to confirm the location and extent of the lesion. This presents a difficulty, in that a considerable lapse of time may intervene between the first behavioral observations and the autopsy, thus preventing correlation of early symptoms with later objectively determined pathology.

Despite the difficulties involved in research in this area it appears to be extremely important to build up a battery of psychological tests and measures, especially in the areas of sensation, perception, action, learning, memory, and similar categories, which might be routinely applied at regular intervals to patients suspected of having different types of cortical lesions. Tests of this kind should be based as far as possible upon techniques developed in experimental psychology. In addition, many of the standard tests employed in clinical psychology should be utilized.

The work of Head, Goldstein and Gelb, Poppelreuter, Rylander, Weigl, and others in this field has been outstanding. More recently Halstead, Hebb, Harrower-Erickson, Babcock, Shipley, Wechsler, Beck, Piotrowski, and others have made considerable progress in extending the realm of psychological measurement in neuropathological cases. The work of Halstead [32, 33, 34], utilizing procedures adapted from experimental psychology and psychophysiology, appears to be especially promising. A review of psychological studies which have reported changes of psychological functions associated with brain lesions and ablations in human patients has been presented by Klebanoff [43].

PSYCHOSURGERY. Frontal lobotomy is the name applied to an operation first undertaken by Moniz in Portugal. In recent years many operations of this type have been performed by Freeman and Watts [26], who refined the operative procedure and who have reported considerable detail concerning the behavioral changes which follow the operation. In general, the operation is performed as a last resort in patients who are suffering from severe mental symptoms and maladjustment. The operation consists in the cutting of the conducting pathways from the anterior portion of the frontal lobes to other cortical and subcortical centers. An opening in the skull is made on either side of the head in the region of the frontal lobes. A blunt-edged knife is then inserted through the cortex and is made to describe an arc-like cut, up and down in each hemisphere. This severs the white matter connecting various centers of the brain with the frontal poles. As a result of the operation many apparently "hopeless" sufferers of mental ills have shown remarkable recoveries. The operation is by no means always successful, and although some patients are improved a great deal, few are entirely "normal." The transition in behavior after the operation is, however, often striking and offers a challenging field of investigation to the psychologist.

The frontal lobotomy should be distinguished from the frontal lobectomy, in which the anterior portion of the frontal lobes is actually removed. Lobectomy is usually performed for the removal of frontal-lobe tumors or abscesses but may be undertaken also in psychiatric cases. These operations, together with the neuropathological conditions discussed above and the various types of shock treatment (insulin, metrazol, and electroshock), all afford unusual opportunity for the clinical and experimental psychologist to apply old and to develop new methods of measuring behavioral changes.

The personality and behavior changes associated with brain lesions and operative procedures in the brain have been surveyed by Cobb [15], and the methods and results of psychological investigations in organic and functional disorders have been critically reviewed by Hunt and Cofer [37].

SUMMARY

One phase of neuropsychology is concerned with the *embryology of behavior;* i.e., the earliest responsiveness of the fetus to sensory stimulation, the earliest motor responses, and the beginnings of patterned behavior are part of the embryology of behavior. The behavior and development of the neonate and infant have important forerunners in the prenatal life of the fetus, and these in turn may be correlated with studies of the developing nervous system. In addition, some of the techniques for studying human fetal activity provide a means of measuring the possible effects of maternal health, activity, and environment upon fetal reactivity and development.

Extrauterine studies of human fetuses removed prematurely must be interpreted with caution because of asphyxia and lack of normal metabolic exchange. Similar cautions are necessary in animal experimentation, but reasonably valid results should be possible if care is taken in selecting the animal and the type of experimental procedure. For studies of human fetuses *in utero* the fetal electrocardiogram, the fetal electroencephalogram, and the maternal report of fetal activity appear to be the most promising methods of approach.

Normal behavior and even life itself depend upon the proper regulation of the *internal environment.* The chemical constitution of the blood and lymph, which must be maintained in a relative state of equilibrium or homeostasis, is dependent upon the autonomic nervous system and the endocrine glands. When the internal environment fluctuates widely with respect to the amount of oxygen, carbon dioxide, sugar, calcium, and other constituents of the blood stream, serious behavioral aberrations, disintegration of mental processes, and other dire symptoms may result. Even the minimal fluctuations within the tolerance level may reduce the efficiency of the individual and modify receptivity, reactivity, and higher integrative processes.

Some of the methods of studying behavior in relation to *cortical function* have been discussed. These include *cortical stimulation, cortical deactivation, electrocortical recording,* and *neuropathology* and *neurosurgery.* It is emphasized that there is a great need for the application of principles and methods of experimental psychology in the investigation of behavioral changes associated with modifications in cortical function. There should be concerted effort on the part of the neuroanatomist, neurophysiologist, and neuropsychologist to work together and maintain a continuous correlation of their results.

REFERENCES

1. Adrian, E. D. *The Mechanism of Nervous Action.* Philadelphia: University of Pennsylvania Press, 1932.
2. Bailey, P., J. G. Dusser de Barenne, H. W. Garol, and W. S. McCulloch. Sensory cortex of chimpanzee. *J. Neurophysiol.,* 1940, *3,* 469–485.
3. Barcroft, J. *The Brain and Its Environment.* New Haven: Yale University Press, 1938.
4. Bartley, S. H. *Vision.* New York: Van Nostrand, 1941.
5. Bartley, S. H., and G. H. Bishop. Factors determining the form of the electrical response from the optic cortex of the rabbit. *Amer. J. Physiol.,* 1933, *103,* 173–184.
6. Brozek, J., J. C. Franklin, H. Guetzkow, and A. Keys. Human behavior in prolonged experimental semi-starvation. *Amer. Psychologist,* 1946, *1,* 269–270.
7. Cannon, W. B. The Linacre lecture on the autonomic nervous system: an interpretation. *Lancet,* 1930, Part 1, 1109–1115.
8. Cannon, W. B. The significance of the emotional level. *J. Missouri State Med. Assoc.,* May, 1934, 177–184.
9. Cannon, W. B., and A. Rosenblueth. *Autonomic Neuro-Effector Systems.* New York: Macmillan, 1937.
10. Carmichael, L. Origin and prenatal growth of behavior. In *Handbook of Child Psychology.* C. Murchison, Ed. Worcester, Mass.: Clark University Press, 1933 (Chap. 2).
11. Carmichael, L. An experimental study in the prenatal guinea-pig of the origin and development of reflexes and patterns of behavior in relation to the stimulation of specific receptor areas during the period of active fetal life. *Genet. Psychol. Monog.,* 1934, *16,* 337–491.
12. Carmichael, L. The experimental embryology of mind. *Psychol. Bull.,* 1941, *38,* 1–28.

13. CARMICHAEL, L. The onset and early development of behavior. In *Manual of Child Psychology.* L. Carmichael, Ed. New York: John Wiley, 1946.

14. CHAFFEE, E. L., and R. U. LIGHT. A method for the remote control of electrical stimulation of the nervous system. *Yale J. Biol. Med.,* 1934, *7,* 83–128.

15. COBB, S. Personality as affected by lesions of the brain. In *Personality and the Behavior Disorders,* Vol. I. J. McV. Hunt, Ed. New York: Ronald Press, 1944 (Chap. 18).

16. COGHILL, G. E. *Anatomy and the Problem of Behavior.* New York: Macmillan, 1929.

17. DUSSER DE BARENNE, J. G. Experimental researches on sensory localizations in the cerebral cortex. *Quart. J. Exper. Physiol.,* 1916, *9,* 355–390.

18. DUSSER DE BARENNE, J. G. Experimental researches on sensory localization in the cerebral cortex of the monkey (Macacus). *Proc. Roy. Soc.,* 1924, B96, 271–291.

19. DUSSER DE BARENNE, J. G. The method of laminar thermocoagulation of the cerebral cortex. *Yale J. Biol. Med.,* 1938, *10,* 573–576.

20. DUSSER DE BARENNE, J. G., H. W. GAROL, and W. S. MCCULLOCH. Physiological neuronography of the cortico-striatal connections. *Res. Publ. Assoc. Res. Nerv. Ment. Disease,* 1941, *21,* 246–266.

21. DUSSER DE BARENNE, J. G., and W. S. MCCULLOCH. Functional organization in the sensory cortex of the monkey (*Macaca mulatta*). *J. Neurophysiol.,* 1938, *1,* 69–85.

22. ERLANGER, J., and H. S. GASSER. *Electrical Signs of Nervous Activity.* Philadelphia: University of Pennsylvania Press, 1937.

23. FOERSTER, O. The motor cortex of man in the light of Hughlings Jackson's doctrines. *Brain,* 1936, *59,* 135–159.

24. FORBES, H. S., and H. B. FORBES. Fetal sense reactions: hearing. *J. Comp. Psychol.,* 1927, *7,* 353–355.

25. GALAMBOS, R., and H. DAVIS. The response of single auditory-nerve fibers to acoustic stimulation. *J. Neurophysiol.,* 1943, *6,* 39–57.

26. FREEMAN, W., and J. W. WATTS. *Psychosurgery.* Springfield, Ill.: Thomas, 1942.

27. GEIGER, A. J., W. M. MONROE, and A. V. N. GOODYER. Clinical fetal electrocardiography: its practical accomplishment. *Proc. Soc. Exper. Biol. Med.,* 1941, *48,* 646–648.

28. GELLHORN, E. *Autonomic Regulations.* New York: Interscience Publishers, 1942.

29. GIBBS, F. A., and E. L. GIBBS. *Atlas of Electroencephalography.* Boston: F. A. Gibbs, Boston City Hospital, 1941.

30. GIBBS, F. A., D. WILLIAMS, and E. L. GIBBS. Modification of the cortical frequency spectrum by changes in CO_2, blood sugar and O_2. *J. Neurophysiol.,* 1940, *3,* 49–58.

31. GRANIT, R. Color receptors of the mammalian retina. *J. Neurophysiol.,* 1945, *8,* 195–210.

32. HALSTEAD, W. C. Preliminary analysis of grouping behavior in patients with cerebral injury by the method of equivalent and non-equivalent stimuli. *Amer. J. Psychiat.,* 1940, *96,* 1263–1291.

33. HALSTEAD, W. C. Brain injuries and the higher levels of consciousness. *Res. Publ. Assoc. Res. Nerv. Ment. Disease,* 1945, *24,* 480–506.

34. HALSTEAD, W. C. A power factor (*P*) in general intelligence: the effect of brain injuries. *J. Psychol.,* 1945, *20,* 57–64.

35. HOOKER, D. *Atlas of Early Human Fetal Activity.* Privately printed, 1939.
36. HOOKER, D. Reflex activities in the human fetus. In *Child Behavior and Development.* R. G. Barker, J. S. Kounin, and H. F. Wright, Eds. New York: McGraw-Hill, 1943 (Chap. II).
37. HUNT, J. McV., and C. N. COFER. Psychological deficit. In *Personality and the Behavior Disorders,* Vol. II. J. McV. Hunt, Ed. New York: Ronald Press, 1944 (Chap. 32).
38. JACOBSEN, C. F. Functions of frontal association areas in primates. *Arch. Neurol. Psychiat.,* Chicago, 1935, *33,* 558–569.
39. JACOBSEN, C. F. Studies of cerebral function in primates. I. The function of the frontal association areas in monkeys. *Comp. Psychol. Monog.,* 1936, *13,* 3–60.
40. JASPER, H. H. Electrical signs of cortical activity. *Psychol. Bull.,* 1937, *34,* 411–481.
41. JASPER, H. H. Electroencephalography. In *Epilepsy and Cerebral Localization.* W. Penfield and T. C. Erickson, Eds. Springfield, Ill.: Thomas, 1941 (Chap. XIV).
42. KELLOGG, W. N. A method for the maintenance of chronic spinal animals. *J. Exper. Psychol.,* 1946, *36,* 366–370.
43. KLEBANOFF, S. G. Psychological changes in organic brain lesions and ablations. *Psychol. Bull.,* 1945, *42,* 585–623.
44. LASHLEY, K. S. *Brain Mechanisms and Intelligence: A Quantitative Study of Injuries to the Brain.* Chicago: University of Chicago Press, 1929.
45. LINDSLEY, D. B. Electrical potentials of the brain in children and adults. *J. Gen. Psychol.,* 1938, *19,* 285–306.
46. LINDSLEY, D. B. Heart and brain potentials in human fetuses *in utero. Amer. J. Psychol.,* 1942, *55,* 412–416.
47. LINDSLEY, D. B. Electroencephalography. In *Personality and the Behavior Disorders,* Vol. II. J. McV. Hunt, Ed. New York: Ronald Press, 1944 (Chap. 33).
48. LOUCKS, R. B. A technique for faradic stimulation of tissues beneath the integument in the absence of conductors penetrating the skin. *J. Comp. Psychol.,* 1934, *18,* 305–313.
49. MAEKAWA, M., and J. TOYOSHIMA. The fetal electro-cardiogram of the human subject. *Acta Scholae Med. Univ. Imp. Kioto,* 1930, *12,* 519–520.
50. NIMS, L. F., C. MARSHALL, and A. NIELSEN. Effect of local freezing on the electrical activity of the cerebral cortex. *Yale J. Biol. Med.,* 1941, *13,* 477–484.
51. PENFIELD, W., and E. BOLDREY. Somatic motor and sensory representation in the cerebral cortex of man as studied by electrical stimulation. *Brain,* 1937, *60,* 389–443.
52. RAY, W. S. A preliminary report on a study of fetal conditioning. *Child Develop.,* 1932, *3,* 175–177.
53. RICHARDS, T. W., and HELEN NEWBERRY. Studies in fetal behavior. III. Can performance on test items at six months postnatally be predicted on the basis of fetal activity? *Child Develop.,* 1938, *9,* 79–86.
54. RICHARDS, T. W., HELEN NEWBERRY, and RUTH FALLGATTER. Studies in fetal behavior. II. Activity of the human fetus *in utero* and its relation to other prenatal conditions, particularly the mother's basal metabolic rate. *Child Develop.,* 1938, *9,* 69–78.
55. SACHS, H. Elektrokardiogrammstudien am Foetus in Utero. *Arch. ges. Physiol.,* 1922, *197,* 536–542.

56. Scarff, J. E. Primary cortical centers for movements of upper and lower limbs in man. *Arch. Neurol. Psychiat.*, 1940, *44*, 243–299.
57. Shock, N. W. Some psychophysiological relations. *Psychol. Bull.*, 1939, *36*, 447–476.
58. Shock, N. W. Physiological factors in behavior. In *Personality and the Behavior Disorders*, Vol. I. J. McV. Hunt, Ed. New York: Ronald Press, 1944 (Chap. 19).
59. Shurrager, P. S., and E. Culler. Conditioning in the spinal dog. *J. Exper. Psychol.*, 1940, *26*, 133–159.
60. Smith, J. R. The electroencephalogram during normal infancy and childhood. I. Rhythmic activities present in the neonate and their subsequent development. *J. Genet. Psychol.*, 1938, *53*, 431–453. II. The nature of the growth of the alpha waves. *J. Genet. Psychol.*, 1938, *53*, 455–469.
61. Sontag, L. F., and R. F. Wallace. A study of fetal activity. *Amer. J. Diseases Child.*, 1934, *48*, 1050–1057.
62. Spelt, D. K. Conditioned responses in the human fetus *in utero*. *Psychol. Bull.*, 1938, *35*, 712–713.
63. Stevens, S. S., and H. Davis. *Hearing, Its Psychology and Physiology.* New York: John Wiley, 1938.
64. Wenger, M. A. Conditioned responses in human infants In *Child Behavior and Development*. R. G. Barker, J. S. Kounin, and H. F. Wright, Eds. New York: McGraw-Hill, 1943 (Chap. V).
65. Windle, W. F. *Physiology of the Fetus*. Philadelphia: Saunders, 1940.
66. Woolsey, C. N., W. H. Marshall, and P. Bard. Representation of cutaneous tactile sensibility in the cerebral cortex of the monkey as indicated by evoked potentials. *Bull. Johns Hopkins Hosp.*, 1942, *70*, 399–441.

SUGGESTED READINGS

Cobb, S. *A Preface to Nervous Disease.* Baltimore: William Wood, 1936.
Fulton, J. F. *Physiology of the Nervous System.* New York: Oxford University Press, 1943.
Goldstein, K. *The Organism.* New York: American Book Company, 1939.
McFarland, R. A. The psychological effects of oxygen deprivation (Anoxemia) on human behavior. *Arch. Psychol.*, 1932, No. 145, 1–135.
Morgan, C. T. *Physiological Psychology.* New York: McGraw-Hill, 1943.

Chapter 16

Studying Motor Functions and Efficiency

Arthur G. Bills[1]

The traditional approach to an understanding of complex behavior patterns, such as are involved in mental and physical work, is to break them down into simpler components. For example, the act of typing a letter can be considered a series of unique key-pressing responses or stimulus-response units. There is a certain amount of truth in assuming that, if we can discover the explanatory laws which apply to a single stimulus-response unit, we can explain the whole act of typing a letter. Two points, however, must not be overlooked: one, that a stimulus-response unit is not itself as simple a thing as it appears, in anything but a logical sense; and the other, that complex processes are more than mere aggregates of the *S-R* units which compose them. Therefore, in adopting the analytical approach for studying motor functions, we must recognize that it is preliminary only, and needs to be supplemented by methods which interpret acts as integrated wholes. Let us first examine some of the typical laboratory methods of studying simple *S-R* units.

ELEMENTARY MOTOR PATTERNS

If the term *elementary* is interpreted in a developmental or genetic sense, then the physiologist's reflex is the model of an elementary reaction. It is also assumed to be relatively simple in nervous pattern, involving a single sensory-motor arc, although this is probably never strictly true in practice. Even if it could be assumed that a single primary arc is involved, there would still be the possibility of modi-

[1] Head of the Psychology Department, University of Cincinnati.

fication of the primary impulse by simultaneous impulses in other related arcs, which might weaken or reinforce the reflex. The reflex has the advantage, however, of being relatively free from voluntary control and relatively unaffected by learning. This makes it ideal for studying such factors as reinforcement and inhibition. The most accessible and easily controlled reflex for laboratory study is the knee-jerk or patellar-tendon reflex. It has been a standard laboratory method of demonstrating the quantitative influence of such factors as muscular set, adaptation, fatigue, emotional excitement, voluntary effort, and distraction ever since the classical studies of Lombard in 1888 and Bowditch and Warren in 1890.

The Knee-jerk Experiment

If the subject is seated on top of a laboratory table, so that the knee projects over the edge, and the lower leg is allowed to swing freely from the knee, a quick blow delivered to the patellar tendon just below the knee cap causes the lower leg to jerk forward. Since the vigor of the jerk varies with the strength of the blow, as well as with the exact point of contact, the apparatus used to deliver the blow must be automatic. The usual equipment includes a rubber hammer, suspended from an adjustable pivot above the subject's knee, which can be released by a lever so as to fall with a constant force against a constant point on the tendon.

The extent of the knee jerk can be measured in various ways. A common method is to attach a spur to the side of the subject's foot, which pushes a lever equipped with a recording marker on the end. The marker indicates on a millimeter scale the extent of the jerk.

To measure the reflex reaction time, it is necessary to record the time between delivery of the blow and the beginning of the knee jerk. This is accomplished by having the fall of the hammer operate an electric switch which starts a chronoscope; the kick of the foot operates a second switch, thereby stopping the chronoscope. A simple automatic device for recording the time is described by Schlosberg [27].

Both the extent and speed of the knee jerk vary with many factors. Reaction times have been found to vary from 10 milliseconds to 90 milliseconds, indicating that the slowest knee jerk is faster than the fastest voluntary reaction. Fatigue, sleep, and drugs retard the reflex, whereas general or specific tension, hunger, mental activity, and emotional excitement accelerate it. Extraneous stimuli occurring near the time of the blow may reinforce or inhibit the reflex, depending on the time relations. For example, Bowditch and Warren [6] found that, if the subject's fist is clenched just before the blow is delivered, the effect on the extent of the jerk is (*a*) to increase it if the blow follows the clench by less than 0.4 second; (*b*) to decrease it if the blow follows more than 0.4 second but less than 2 seconds later; (*c*) neutral, if the blow follows more than 2 seconds later.

The chief objection to the physiologist's reflex as the elementary unit of behavior is that it is involuntary, whereas most of the behavior in which we are interested is voluntary. We need a unit which represents the simplest voluntary response. The so-called simple reaction is of this sort. For example, if a subject is instructed to press a key with his finger the instant a light is flashed on as a signal, the behavior can be assumed to involve the operation of a simple *S-R* connection between the visual stimulus and the finger response. The objection could be raised that the simple reaction is not strictly voluntary, at least at the time it occurs, but is, instead, a prepared reflex, in which the subject gets set beforehand to react automatically when the signal is given [34, p. 305]. This distinction, however, is not very important.

The Simple Reaction-time Experiment

How rapidly can the average person make a specific voluntary reaction to a specific stimulus? On what factors does the speed of such a reaction depend? How widely do persons differ in their reaction-time speed? To answer these questions it is necessary to measure with a high degree of accuracy the time between delivery of the stimulus and the beginning of the response movement. The unit of measurement used is the millisecond, or thousandth part of a second. The apparatus required is (*a*) a stimulus key, to be operated by the experimenter, which both controls the presentation of the stimulus and starts the chronoscope or other timing device, so that these are exactly synchronized; (*b*) a response key, to be operated by the subject, which stops the chronoscope instantly; and (*c*) the chronoscope itself, which registers in milliseconds the time between its starting and stopping.

Electric controls are best, because it is essential that no time lag of the apparatus invalidate the human reaction-time measurement. The response-movement time should not be included; therefore the response key should be so arranged that the subject, by lifting his finger, can break the electric circuit. A downward movement against the tension of a telegraph key requires muscular effort and introduces an undetermined time error into the measurements. Another source of error is the lag in the stimulus device. Light-bulb filaments which are slow to warm up or sound-producing devices with a mechanical lag must be avoided. Of course, a constant known time lag can be corrected for, by subtracting from all reaction-time measurements, but frequent recalibration of chronoscopes against a reliable criterion is necessary. The essential features of the chronoscope are a graduated arc or dial, over which moves a clock hand or pointer driven by a mechanical or electrical clock mechanism at a rapid rate, so that

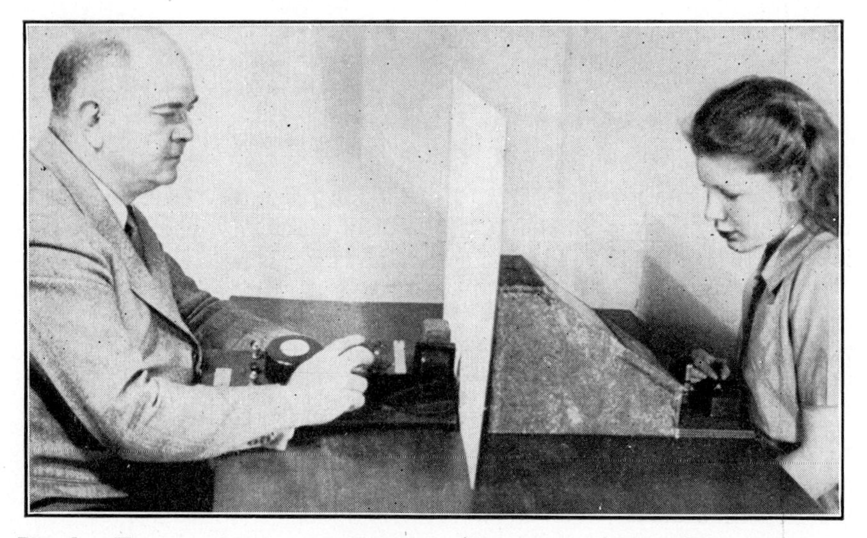

Fig. 1. The reaction-time experiment. (Apparatus designed by J. Vaughn for Cincinnati Psychology Laboratory.)

a single scale unit indicates a millisecond. The pointer must be capable of instantaneous starting and stopping, in order that a reaction time can be calculated from the difference between the two scale readings.

Frequently a chronograph is used instead of a chronoscope. According to this method, the stimulus and response switches operate a signal marker, which marks reactions on a kymograph drum. Since the recording paper moves at a constant rate, the distance between the marks can be interpreted in terms of reaction-time units. For very accurate work, a time line is simultaneously inscribed on the kymograph record by a stylus controlled by a vibrating tuning fork.

The subject sits at one side of the table, as shown in Fig. 1, with his index finger resting on the reaction key. In front of him is the apparatus for presenting the stimulus, e.g., a light, a buzzer sound, or a tactual stimulator. The experimenter sits behind a screen at the opposite side of the table and operates the switches controlling the stimulus apparatus and chronoscope. Reaction times depend on the readiness or alertness of the subject at the instant the stimulus is given; therefore it is customary to give a preparatory signal a short time before the stimulus. This is done by saying "Now!" or flashing a small pilot light. It was discovered by experiment that the optimal time between stimulus and signal is 2 seconds, with a range of 1 to 4 seconds [33]. During this interval the subject tenses his muscles, particularly those of the reacting hand, and attends closely to the stimulus. A slight difference in the speed of the reaction results, depending on whether the subject directs his attention mainly to the stimulus or mainly to the responding hand. The former is called the "sensorial" type; the latter, the "muscular" type [34, pp. 306–308]. Some subjects give quicker reactions of the sensorial type, some of the muscular type; but a combination of the two, called the "natural" type, is most satisfactory for general laboratory studies. Practice in any particular type of reaction tends to shorten the reaction time, whereas fatigue lengthens it. The following are typical reaction times for different modalities:

Sense Modality	Reaction Time, Milliseconds
Vision	150–225
Audition	120–182
Touch	117–182
Warmth	180–240
Cold	150–230
Pain	400–1000

When verbal reactions are called for, a special type of reaction key, called a voice key, is used. The subject speaks into a special type of microphone, and vibration of its diaphragm breaks an electric circuit and stops the chronoscope.

Discriminatory and Choice Reactions

If the subject is told that the stimulus may be a *red* light or a *green* light and that he is to react only if it is red, his reaction time is lengthened considerably. If the problem is still further complicated by instructing the subject to react with the *right* hand if the light is *red,* and with the *left* hand if it is *green,* still longer reaction times result. Increasing the number of alternative stimuli and responses still further slows the reaction. A particular type of complex reaction is the "associative" reaction, in which the subject is instructed to respond with the first word which occurs to him when a stimulus word is presented. Since the choices are infinite, his reaction is very slow, from 1 to 3 or more seconds in length. Any limitation of the choices, such as directing the subject to respond with the opposite of the stimulus word, shortens his reaction time.

Serial Reaction Time

In actual behavior the single isolated reaction is the exception rather than the rule. Much more common is the serial reaction, in which a whole series of responses follow one another in temporal sequence. Often each response in the series acts as a stimulus to set off the next response in order. This is true of walking, typewriting, playing a piano, and many other everyday activities. Is reaction time longer or shorter when reactions occur in such a sequence with no pause between, and how is this time affected by factors inherent in the serial form of response? To answer these questions, a different type of reaction time experiment is used. Either the stimuli are presented at some arbitrary rate, or else the subject determines the rate himself by his speed of responding. Usually he performs under instructions to work as fast as possible without making errors.

Two typical serial tasks used in the experimental laboratory are tapping and color naming. Tapping is performed, with a metal stylus held in the right hand, on a tapping board with metal contact surface, which is in electrical circuit with the stylus, so that each tap can be recorded kymographically or counted by an electric counter. A commonly used type is the Dunlap tapping board, which has two contact surfaces, one at each end, requiring the subject to tap alternately at opposite ends. The average reaction time can be computed from the number of taps delivered in a stated period of time.

Color naming is typically performed as follows: A large card, 8 × 10 inches, contains 10 horizontal rows of small colored squares, 10 to a row. The colors red, green, blue, yellow, and black are arranged in random sequence. The subject is instructed to name the colors in order, following the rows, as rapidly as he can. When the card is completed, it is rotated 90 degrees and read again. Two more rotations of the card are possible before the identical order of colors is repeated, making 400 stimuli in all, so that the subject cannot memorize the order. The time from starting to finishing is recorded, and divided by 400 to obtain the average single reaction time.

The principles involved in the two serial reaction tasks described above differ in several ways from those governing discrete single reactions. In the tapping performance, we can assume that the stimulus which initiates each tap, except the very first, is the kinaesthetic-tactual sensory cue furnished by the preceding tap. In this respect we are dealing with a simple reaction. Instead of being given a warning signal and an adequate preparatory interval, however, the subject must execute the response before he has recovered from the preceding reaction. Attention cannot be maintained at a high pitch very long. Also there is a cumulative muscular fatigue from successive taps, not to mention pain sensations, all of which affect the later reactions in the series. In the color-naming performance, we are dealing with the "choice" type of reaction, since the subject must react to one of five possible colors by one of five possible verbal responses. However, he has a chance to glance ahead and anticipate whole groups of colors. His response is therefore to groups or patterns rather than to discrete stimuli. Scarcely any muscle fatigue is involved, but there are other cumulative factors within the central nervous system, and their effects may be appreciable.

Improved Methods of Studying Serial Reactions

An ideal apparatus for studying such a performance as color naming should permit the presentation of only one color at a time, so that grouping is minimized, while at the same time letting the subject control the rate of presentation to conform to his maximum speed. Time between each successive stimulus and response should be automatically registered, so that progressive changes in reaction time and other significant tendencies can be studied. For comparative purposes manual as well as verbal reactions should be provided for. The order of appearance of the colors should be as near chance as possible, with infrequent recurrence of any particular sequence. A large amount of trial-and-error experimentation resulted in the development of the apparatus shown in Fig. 2 [32]. The kind of record obtained from the apparatus is shown underneath the photograph. The distances between the short vertical marks represent reaction times. It can be seen that, in addition to the irregularity in reaction times displayed throughout, there are recurrent blocks or prolonged reactions at intervals which are peculiar to the serial reaction type of performance and which indicate some cumulative effect of repeated stimulation. A block can be defined arbitrarily as a reaction time which is twice the length of the modal reaction time prevailing during the minute in which the block occurs. Experimental evidence shows that the frequency and length of these blocks tend to increase with prolonged work and with any agents which have a depressant action on performance, such as drugs or anoxia. On the other hand, prac-

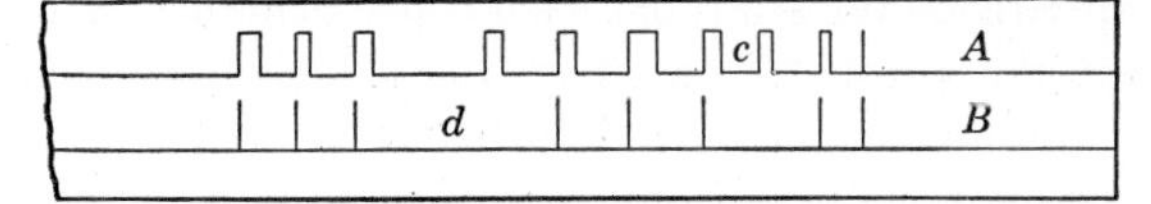

Fig. 2. Color discriminator and kymogaph record.

tice decreases their frequency and length [1]. Individuals differ widely in the blocking tendency, from the person who shows practically none to the one who blocks after every five or six responses.

Facilitative and Inhibitive Sets

One important discovery which has come out of the work on reaction time is that the character of the response depends very much upon the state of preparation of the subject at the time the stimulus is delivered. It has even been suggested that the response is not a voluntary response so much as it is a "prepared reflex," since the voluntary element is entirely a matter of assuming a preparatory set, and that the reaction itself occurs reflexly to the stimulus. Certainly the difference found between the reaction time with and without a ready signal upholds this opinion; and the difference between the reaction times obtained with the "sensorial" versus the "muscular" set suggests that the preparatory state of the musculature is all-important. Not only is there evidence that the muscles directly used in the reaction become tense during the foreperiod, but also other muscles of the body quite remote from the reacting member show increase of tension [10]. When the subject is instructed to assume a tense attitude, reaction times are shortened.

When voluntarily induced tension has been used with serial reaction times of the controlled-association type, there has been found an optimal degree of muscular tension which gives the quickest performance, and any increase or decrease from this optimum affects the rate of performance detrimentally [29].

There are a number of methods of studying quantitatively the amount of tension in muscles. Tension in the reacting hand itself can be determined by the pressure exerted upon the response key, provided this key is equipped with a device for registering it [19]. When the response consists of writing with pencil or stylus, a rough estimate of the degree of pressure can be obtained by placing several layers of carbon sheets and copy paper under the writing surface, or by having the subject write on a surface underneath which are sensitive springs and a kymographic device for recording pressure variations. Still another method is to use one of the various types of pressure stylus equipped with a pneumatic chamber or electrical device for transferring a record of the pressures, exerted at the stylus point, to a kymograph [30]. Finally, the action current method, mentioned in the following paragraph, is often employed.

When the tension in muscles other than those used in responding is being studied, somewhat different techniques for measuring tonus are desirable. For example, it has long been recognized that the amplitude of the knee jerk is a good indication of the general tension in body muscles, not merely that of the patellar tendon and quadriceps or thigh muscle. The more selective kinds of muscular set, however, may be local and actually involve reductions in tonus of remote muscles. To study them, it is necessary to measure directly the changes in the muscle itself. Three methods for this purpose are: (*a*) the *resiliency* method, (*b*) the *deformation* method, and (*c*) the *action current* method. The resiliency method is based on the fact that a muscle becomes more resilient to external pressure when it is tense. For example, if a rubber hammer is suspended in such a way as to swing through an arc against the muscle when released, the distance through which the hammer rebounds is roughly proportional to the tension in the muscle. The deformation method consists essentially in recording the movement of a lever held against the muscle so as to deform it. The thickening of the muscle with increased tension moves the lever and can be recorded kymographically by a marker attached to the other end of the lever. Or a small mirror arranged to tip with the movement of the lever can be made to reflect a beam of light whose amplified excursions can be photographed on moving film. The action current method has been described at length in Chapter 14, pages 412–414.

The application of these tension-measuring methods to human behavior patterns has made clear the intimate relation between subjective states of attention and volitional effort and those changes in muscular tension which underlie them.

Studying Decrement in Working Muscles

In all overt responses there is a muscular element involved, even though the amount of this element varies widely with the kind of response. In the simple reaction it is purposely reduced to a minimum, and in such serial reactions as color naming it is relatively insignificant. An understanding of the role played by muscular fatigue in determining efficiency in continuous serial reactions is, however, essential. Therefore psychologists devised a method of studying this element in as simple and uncomplicated a situation as possible: the *ergographic experiment.* The most widely used type of ergograph is that invented by Mosso, which bears his name [20]. Its purpose is to force an isolated muscle group (the middle finger muscles) to work against strong resistance repeatedly until a point of apparent exhaustion is reached. A weight, suspended by a wire from a pulley projecting from the edge of a table, forms the resistance against which the middle finger of the subject's hand pulls. The finger is equipped with a small sleeve, to which the wire is attached. The subject is instructed to flex his finger repeatedly to its full extent at intervals of 1 second until he can no longer flex it. The hand and arm and unused fingers are tightly bound and all backward movement of the elbow is blocked, so that all the strain is placed upon the finger itself. As the weight rises and falls, a lever attached to the wire moves a marker, which records kymographically the extent of each excursion of the finger. The resistance can be increased or decreased by adding more units of known kilogram weight to the wire's end or by removing some of them.

The resulting record is called an ergogram. It presents certain common characteristics, even though every subject's ergogram is unique in form. An initial period of high efficiency is followed, within a few minutes, by a complete stop. That this stop does not represent total or permanent exhaustion is shown by the fact that a brief rest enables the subject to begin working again. If the weight is reduced, the subject can begin again immediately. Of course, the amount of work accomplished in such a second attempt is less than that done in the first, but with short rests after each exhaustion point the work can be kept up almost indefinitely.

The pattern of the ergogram, which was long considered typical for the fatigue of all isolated muscle groups, is one in which the excursions gradually decline in extent from the initial high level until they finally cease. Perhaps if the fatigue of the *muscle* were the only factor involved, such a curve would really be typical. It is, however, a false assumption that the ergogram reflects only muscular decrement; it reflects also the decline in volitional effort and control exerted by the central nervous system. This is demonstrated by the fact that an electric current applied directly to the "exhausted" muscle will elicit vigorous flexions. It is because of the importance of the central factor that such wide individual differences occur in ergograms and that, as was demonstrated by Yochelson [35] for arm flexion, each individual seems to possess an ergogram which is characteristic of him. Some persons show an early decline followed by a period of virtual equilibrium before the final sudden drop occurs; others maintain a relatively high level almost to the end. A third type exhibits an initial rise followed by a gradually accelerated decline.

WORK OF THE INTEGRATED ORGANISM

Now that we have surveyed the methods used in analysing elementary motor patterns, we are ready to consider the methods of studying the course of efficiency in the integrated activities of the entire organism, the individual at work. Earlier attempts to distinguish between physical or muscular work, on the one hand, and mental work, on the other, have been given up because of ample demonstration that no such clear dichotomy exists. For, on the one hand, there is no purely muscular work which is free from the control of the central nervous system with its conscious voluntary component; and, on the other hand, there is no purely mental work carried on in complete independence of motor sets, reinforcing tensions, or small muscle activities. Equally fruitless have been attempts to distinguish between the energy expenditure involved in the "mental" versus the "physical" component in such activities as taking a written examination. What we really wish to study is the course of efficiency in work and the factors which influence it. This calls for a definition of the terms *work* and *efficiency*.

Work is sometimes defined in terms of the product and sometimes in terms of the process. The physical definition of work is expressed in terms of the movement of a given weight (M), through a given distance (D), in a given time (T), but this fails to take account of the directing and controlling work involved even in such simple activities as packing chocolates. Moreover, an activity like solving arithmetical problems cannot be expressed in weight-moving terms at all. If we substitute *difficulty* of the task in place of weight, *amount done* in place of distance, and retain the term *time,* we can then state that work equals difficulty times amount divided by time. This still fails, however, to include the factor of control, so important in human work, unless we add a fourth term, *quality*. This gives us the formula:

$$\text{Work} = \frac{\text{Difficulty} \times \text{Amount} \times \text{Quality}}{\text{Time}}$$

In measuring performance, three of these values are standardized, and the variations of the fourth are measured. The hardest terms to which to assign objective values are difficulty and quality, because what is difficult for one person is easy for another, and vice versa; and quality is frequently a matter of individual opinion. Fortunately, however, absolute scaling methods are available by which difficulty and quality can be quantified for any given task.

Efficiency must be thought of in terms of the economy of effort with which the work is performed and is therefore a "process" concept. Four factors must be considered: speed, accuracy (or quality), effort, and satisfyingness. The first two factors, speed and accuracy, have sometimes been combined into a single speed-accuracy score by imposing a fixed time penalty for errors. Effort is measured in terms of the physiological energy expended, either directly or indirectly. Satisfyingness is the only subjective factor to be dealt with, but it is nonetheless important because of the effect it eventually has on the other factors. It refers to the worker's degree of satisfaction or distress in the performance of the task and must be determined by some standardized introspective report.

Studying the Course of Efficiency in Continuous Work

Most investigations of efficiency in work have been concerned with four main problems:

1. *The effect of work on its own efficiency.* This is the study of the changes that occur in the level of performance and efficiency in a particular task because of continuous work at that task. These changes are graphically shown in the curve of work, to be described presently. In all prolonged work periods a decrement eventually appears which is attributed to fatigue, but this is by no means the only effect of work upon itself.

2. *The effect of work on efficiency in other subsequent activities.* The working organism is an integrated whole, and the effects of work at a given task are not confined to that task, but transfer to other activities in varying degree. It is important to discover the principles governing such transfer.

3. *The course of recovery from the effects of continuous work.* What influence do rest periods have in bringing about recuperation from the effects of continuous work?

4. *The effect on the efficiency of work exerted by extraneous factors.* How do distractions and environmental influences, physiological agents, suggestions, and motivational factors influence the course of efficiency in work?

Each of these four problems will be taken up in succession. Each presents its own peculiar difficulties in eliminating uncontrolled variables.

The Curve of Work

A typical work curve is shown in Fig. 3. The abscissa scale is divided into equal parts of the total work period. These may be time units, as hours, or amount units, as pages of material to be typed. The ordinate is divided into accomplishment units, which may express quantities of material completed per hour or minutes taken to complete a given amount of work. When an ordinate value has been plotted for each successive abscissa step in the graph, it is possible to trace the course of efficiency throughout the work period. Just as in learning curves, a drop in the curve indicates a decline in efficiency, provided the ordinate scale represents amount units, but it indicates a rise in efficiency when the ordinate scale stands for time or effort. Conversely, a rise in the curve indicates an improvement in efficiency in the former case, but a loss in the latter. It is well to remember that the points on a work curve represent relative rather than absolute values, because there is neither a known zero nor a known 100 per cent efficiency. Some experimenters arbitrarily call the first point 100 per cent, in which case all points falling below it represent less than 100 per cent and all points above it indicate more than 100 per cent. Some such method is necessary if work curves are to be compared with one another.

When efficiency is measured in terms of performance in the major task itself, the method is known as the *continuous work method.* When it is desired to obtain a gage of the individual's *general activity level* resulting from work at the major task, however, it is customary

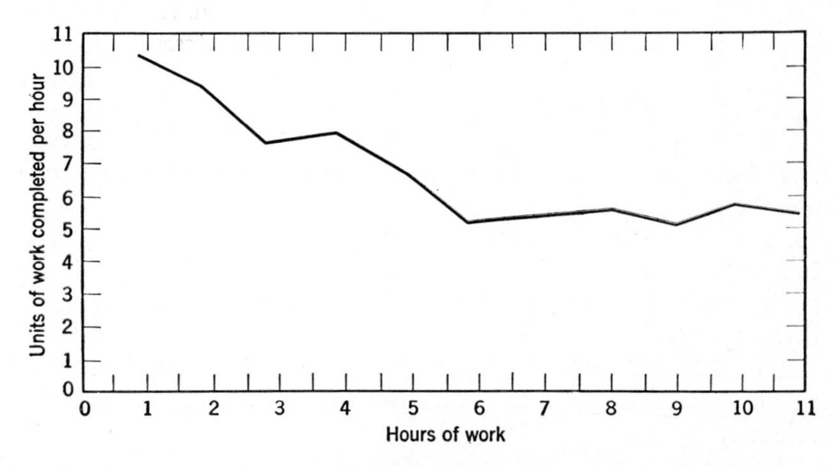

Fig. 3. Work curve for mental multiplication. (Drawn from E. S. Robinson's graph in *Practical Psychology,* The Macmillan Co., 1926.)

to introduce test activities at stated intervals and plot a curve showing the variations in performance level in these test activities. For example, if the major task is working problems in addition, the test activity might be measuring the subject's strength of grip. A test of his dynamometer grip might be interpolated every 15 minutes during the addition work. There is a falacious assumption involved in this method, i.e., that the effects of work are general for the whole organism and can therefore be measured just as well in activities extraneous to the major task as in the major task itself. The experimental evidence shows that such effects as fatigue are more specific. Nevertheless, this method, which is known as the *interpolated task method,* is widely used. Some of the test activities used are described below:

1. Strength of grip, measured by a hand dynamometer graduated in kilograms or pounds.
2. Physical endurance, measured by obtaining an ergogram.
3. Motor speed, indicated by the rate of tapping on a tapping board.

4. Muscular precision and steadiness, measured by an instrument such as is depicted in Fig. 1 on page 394. In this method a pointed metal stylus is thrust repeatedly into each of the holes in the upright plate. If the subject touches the sides of the hole, the contact operates an electric counter, recording an error against him. His score is the number of errors.

5. Reaction time; simple, choice, or associative.

6. Tests of specific mental functions, as immediate memory, attention, perceptual speed, judgment, reasoning, and control of imagery.

Measures of Organic State

If the criterion of efficiency used is the amount of effort required to do a given amount of work, there must be some measure, in physiological terms, of effort expended. We mentioned previously that some investigators have considered the tension in body muscles to be an index of effort and have used one of the tension-measuring methods described on page 467 to estimate the degree. The safest index of the amount of energy used by the organism, however, is the metabolic rate. This is studied in one of two ways: (1) by measuring changes in the physiological processes, such as breathing, heart or pulse rate, blood pressure, blood volume, temperature, or the psychogalvanic reflex; or (2) by analysing the products of metabolism, as carbon dioxide in the expired air or oxygen consumed or the ratio between the two, called the respiratory quotient, or by analysing the blood and urine for changes in carbon dioxide content, sugar level, alkali reserve, etc.

The techniques for measuring the physiological processes are simple and can be used in any laboratory. Continuous kymographic records can be obtained through the use of tambour-controlled markers. An apparatus called the Darrow behavior-research photopolygraph combines most of these measures in a continuous photographic record.

Analysis of the products of metabolism, on the contrary, requires chemical techniques for which special skills are necessary. The method most commonly employed is respiratory calorimetry. The oxygen intake, rate of oxygen consumption, and carbon dioxide elimination are determined through chemical analysis of the expired air. Probably the best single index is the oxygen-consumption rate, since carbon dioxide elimination varies with the strength of breathing and may not indicate the rate of carbon dioxide production at the time. When respiratory calorimetry is being studied, the subject must wear a face mask or helmet for controlling the oxygen intake, and expired air must be collected in bags and chemically analysed. The effect of the work is shown in the percentage increase over the resting metabolic rate. Experimental results obtained from applying this method to the study of work efficiency indicate that, when the muscular component of the work is large, there is a rather close relation between energy consumption and objective output; but in predominantly intellectual work the energy requirement is small, and the relation to work output is less close. In neither case does the metabolic rate continue to rise cumulatively in proportion to the length of time the work goes on. Instead, an oxygen debt is incurred, which is paid back gradually after work ceases [26].

Measures of Satisfyingness or Feeling-tone

The fourth criterion of the efficiency of work is its satisfyingness to the worker. This can be determined only by an introspective report from the subject as to his feeling-tone from time to time. Unstandardized introspections, however, are notoriously untrustworthy, and many of the problems dealt with make it necessary to state the subject's feeling-tone in terms of degrees on a quantitative scale, so that a curve can be plotted showing improvement or decline with continuous work. For example, we wish to answer such questions as the following:

How is feeling-tone correlated with organic state and with output?

Can there be alterations in feeling-tone with no corresponding changes in bodily state or objective efficiency, and vice versa?

A serious obstacle in the way of getting reliable reports of feeling-tone is the fact that verbal reports tend to be vague and to vary in meaning from person to person. When one subject reports feeling "very tired," his actual state may be the same as that of another subject who reports "average feelings." This makes it difficult to compare the feeling-tone curves of different persons or even of the same person at different times, but experience with other rating-scale construction problems indicates that such difficulties can be overcome. The scale should have between five and seven steps, because a smaller number makes it too insensitive and any larger number requires too fine distinctions for the worker to make significantly. Should the scale points be represented by single words or phrases like "very tired," or are long phrases or sentences better, as "the greatest eagerness for work I ever experienced"? Certainly the less ambiguity, the better. How can the scale be anchored as to zero point and limits? If a subject's feeling-tone curves from different days are to be combined or compared, the upper and lower limits should be fixed. For example, the lower limit might be described as "the greatest aversion I ever experienced toward beginning or continuing work," and the upper limit by the phrase quoted above. The middle of the scale would be "average feeling-tone." If, however, a *relative* scale is required, then the subject's initial feeling-tone, at the beginning of the particular work period, can be used as a zero, and any rise or fall can be given plus or minus values. How often should reports of feeling-tone be obtained during a work session? The subjects must not be interrupted too often or the continuity of work will be destroyed. A test can be given each 20 minutes, by having the worker make a check, on a scaled chart, opposite his feeling-tone level at that time.

In general, it has been found that satisfyingness of the work, or feeling-tone, drops off almost from the start and declines much more rapidly than does output level. However, persons who show the greatest decline in feeling-tone also show the most loss in objective performance. It is possible for a rise in output to be accompanied by a drop in feeling-tone [22].

Studying the Features of the Work Curve

Students of the objective work curve have described a number of characteristics which seem to indicate fairly constant trends. To the extent that these trends are universal, they probably have underlying causes. Among the major trends noted are (*a*) the general decrement, (*b*) warming up, (*c*) practice effect, (*d*) spurts and rhythms of specific sorts, and (*e*) blocks. Special methods have been devised for analysing these various trends, which will be discussed presently.

The most constant of the above trends is the *general decrement,* which is the tendency for efficiency to fall off in the later stages of a prolonged work session. Although commonly associated with the concept of "fatigue," it is not necessarily identical with it, since fatigue has come to imply an organic breakdown. If fatigue is defined as Thorndike [31] suggested, i.e., as that loss of efficiency resulting from continuous work which can be eliminated by rest, then fatigue and general decrement can be considered identical. But decrement is not always reflected in an objective drop in the work curve. There are other trends which may obscure it, such as *practice effect.* Let us examine the methods by which investigators have estimated the decrement in work curves.

One method is to subtract the final level of the curve from the initial level, but this procedure has the disadvantage that both these points are subject to wide fluctuations and are not significant of the trend of the curve as a whole. Similarly inadequate is the method of subtracting the lowest from the highest point in the curve, for a curve whose general trend is downward may show its highest point in the second half because of a sudden spurt. A more satisfactory method is to subtract the average level of performance during the second half of the work period from the average level in the first half. If decrements in different curves are to be compared, the above score can be converted into a ratio by dividing by the average level in the first half, thus:

$$\text{Decrement} = \frac{\text{Average level in second half} - \text{Average level in first half}}{\text{Average level in first half}}$$

This method is satisfactory in work curves in which practice effect is negligible. Ideally, of course, since work of an organism is supposed to involve the operation of perfected habits, there should be no practice effect to complicate the curve. Practically, however, it is impossible to bring habits to a point where no further improvement from practice occurs, before obtaining a work curve. As a result the improvement due to practice obscures the decrement due to work, and the objective curve may appear flat or may even rise. That this fact does not mean that no decrement has occurred can be demonstrated in the following way: We know that decrement disappears with rest, but practice effect is retained. Therefore the level of performance after a sufficient rest will indicate what the level would have been at the end of the work period if no decrement had been present. The difference between this level after rest and the level at the end of the previous work period gives a measure of the decrement which would have appeared in the objective work curve, if no practice effect had been present to obscure it. Hence the formula for decrement by this method, in the form of a ratio, is:

$$\text{Decrement} = \frac{\text{Level at rest} - \text{Level at end of work}}{\text{Level at beginning of work}}$$

This indicates the proportion of the initial efficiency which the subject has lost during the work period.

Studying the principles of the decrement. Experimental studies using the above method of computing decrement show that it is almost always present in some degree, but the amount varies greatly. If we could say that the amount is a simple function of the length and difficulty of the task, as we ordinarily define difficulty, our problem would be solved easily. Actually, however, such a supposedly difficult task as multiplying three-place numbers by three-place numbers "in one's head" produces a very gradual decline in the work curve, whereas an ostensibly simple task like reading off *pqpqpq* or other typed rows of letters from a card produces a steep decline in a short time [2]. Evidently a more analytical approach is needed to determine the causes of the work decrement. Tasks must be broken up into their stimulus-response elements, and these elements systematically varied. Such an analysis reveals that tasks differ in the following significant ways: (*a*) their *continuity,* the degree to which the units follow one another without a break; (*b*) their *homogeneity,* the degree to which identical units are repeated over and over without introducing variations; (*c*) the degree of *conflict* between units, whether they arouse antagonistic reactions; (*d*) the degree of *familiarity* with the task, whether the habit systems utilized have been thoroughly practiced; and (*e*) the degree of *meaningfulness* of the task, its interest value. Three of these principles, *a, b,* and *e,* characterize what is popularly known as monotony and account for the subjective state called boredom. The other two, *c* and *d,* explain what is known as the complexity or difficulty feature of certain tasks [23].

In addition to the improvement in level of performance in work curves due to the practice effect, a distinctly different factor causes an initial rise in efficiency in many curves. It is easy to distinguish this effect from practice effect because it disappears with rest, whereas practice effect persists and shows up after rest. The name given to the second factor is *warming up.* It is possible to measure warming up quantitatively by the following method: First determine "raw warming up" by finding the high point of efficiency reached at the peak of the early rise in the curve; then find the level of efficiency after a rest at the end of the work period. This latter value represents permanent improvement. Subtract this from the raw warming up to obtain "net warming up." The formula is

Net warming up = Raw warming up — Level after rest

The defect in this procedure is that practice has taken place during the work period subsequent to the high point at which raw warming up is measured. This additional practice is, of course, included in the level after rest. The result is an underestimation of the amount of net warming up. This, however, is not too serious, considering that the bulk of the practice effect takes place early in the work period.

There are certain major deviations in the work curve which, although not always present, occur often enough to warrant experimental study. These are known as "spurts," or rather sudden and temporary peaks of efficiency. The most important are *initial spurt* and *end spurt*.

The first of these is found especially in curves obtained from homogeneous work in which speed is an important factor. It occurs during the first few minutes of work and consists in an initial high point of efficiency followed by a steep drop, with a subsequent leveling off after 5 or 10 minutes. Investigators who have failed to obtain this deviation have questioned its reality, but their failure is accounted for by two errors in their method of computing the curve. Since initial spurt is so brief, it is concealed by using tasks in which either the units of work are too large or the increments along the base line too long. How could one expect to discover a spurt which lasted only 5 minutes, in a work curve plotted in 10-minute intervals? Yet the extreme importance of this initial peak and drop is shown by the fact that it accounts for 25–40 per cent of the total decrement in many curves. The explanation for the phenomenon lies in the fact that the worker begins the task with a reserve of energy which is rapidly dissipated until a stabilization point or point of equilibrium is found which can be maintained indefinitely. Part of this is a conscious readjustment by the worker to the realization that he has overestimated his ability at the start. Initial spurt can be computed by the formula

$$\text{Initial spurt} = \frac{\text{Initial level} - \text{Lowest level in first 10 minutes}}{\text{Initial level}}$$

The second phenomenon, end spurt, occurs only in work curves in which the worker has some way of knowing when the end of the task period is coming, so that he can anticipate it and be stimulated by it. This knowledge can be gained in a variety of ways other than being told by the experimenter. For example, it can be learned from past experience with the same task situation. Thus animals sometimes show end spurts in their performance on a learning task in which a certain number of runs occurs each day. Conscious realization or intention need not be involved. The method of computing end spurt is to subtract the lowest performance level during the final 10 minutes of work from the final level.

Rhythms and blocks. In addition to the spurts just described, other variations in efficiency occur throughout the work curve. Some of these are doubtless due to chance factors; but some show a tendency toward periodicity. Early attempts to relate them to some common underlying central energy fluctuation, such as an "attention wave," were abandoned because their periodicities failed to agree with each other. Thus, in attending continuously to minimal sensory stimuli, experimenters have found periodic fluctuations in clearness, but the periods vary with the sense organ involved and must therefore depend on processes in the particular peripheral organs or corresponding brain centers [11]. Again, in continuous work in which the work units are small enough, it is possible to demonstrate a number of different rhythms of efficiency, varying from those with very high periods of a few seconds to much longer cycles of several hours' duration. Perhaps even the cycles of several days' or weeks' duration recently described by Hersey [12], and attributed to physiological rhythms belong in this group. The same difficulty, however, confronts the experimenter in studying all of them, namely, proving that they are true rhythms and not artifacts or chance variations. Phillpots [21] attempted to rationalize these rhythms by seeking a mathematical formula which would describe them. He concluded that they follow a law of "damping," since there is a progressive increase in their length with time. Thus he considered short and long rhythms to be a part of the same fundamental process. Be that as it may, the mathematical analysis involved is beyond the average student.

Another phenomenon which occurs in continuous work of a homogeneous type may be related to the rhythms just described. It is the tendency for *blocks,* or pauses, i.e., prolonged reaction times, to recur at frequent intervals. These were mentioned on page 465, in the discussion of serial reaction time. The mental state accompanying them is one of temporary confusion, inability to respond correctly, or in some cases lapse of attention. If a response is attempted, it is likely to be an error. Frequently the block is accompanied by emotional tension because of the frustration involved. In order to have a standard by which to identify it, a block is arbitrarily defined as a reaction time which is twice the length of the modal reaction time prevailing during the minute of work in which the block occurs. The mode is used in preference to the arithmetical mean, because it excludes the atypical block reaction times from the computation of the average reaction time, whereas the arithmetic mean, if computed before the blocks are identified, includes them. By defining the block in terms of the typical reaction time for the particular task in which it occurs, we permit it to vary in length from task to task, and from the early part of the work curve to the later part. For example, in tasks like color naming, in which the modal reaction time does not exceed a second, the block may last less than 2 seconds, but in such tasks as solving figure analogies, in which the modal reaction time is several seconds, a block will be a half minute or more in length.

Two major questions about blocks are these: (1) Can they be

shown to be real (i.e., not just extreme variations within the normal dispersion range of reaction times) and rhythmic or periodic in occur-

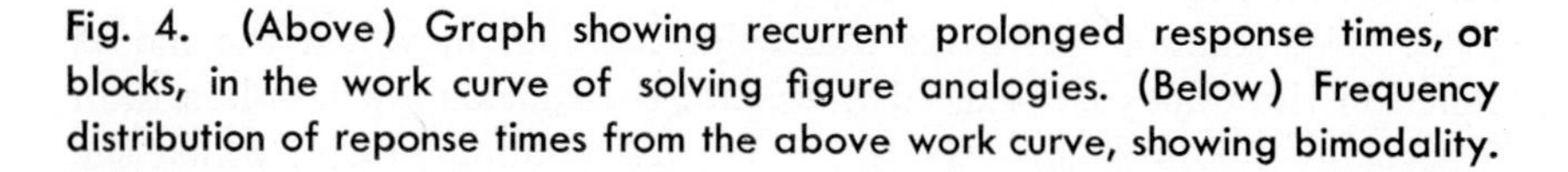

Fig. 4. (Above) Graph showing recurrent prolonged response times, or blocks, in the work curve of solving figure analogies. (Below) Frequency distribution of reponse times from the above work curve, showing bimodality.

rence? (2) What causes them? The first question can be answered statistically by plotting a frequency distribution of reaction-time lengths for an entire work period. When this is done, as in Fig. 4, it is evident that the blocks do not fall into place as extreme measures in a normal unimodal distribution, but sometimes emerge as a second modal hump lying at the periphery of a J-shaped curve. To demonstrate periodicity, it is necessary to measure all the interblock distances and plot a frequency curve of them. If no periodicity exists, the frequency curve of interblock distances should show a normal or chance dispersion. If, on the other hand, a definite periodicity exists,

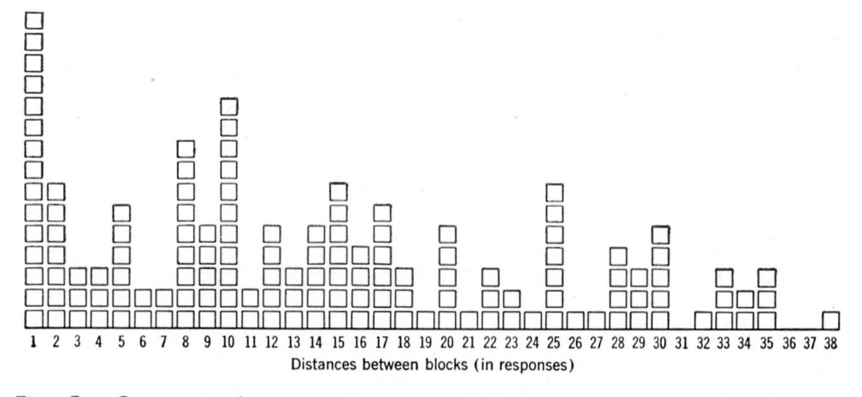

Fig. 5. Composite frequency diagram for color-naming, vocal and manual, showing multimodal distribution of interblock intervals. (From Bills [3].)

it should emerge as a mode at some definite point along the base line, with a narrow range of dispersion of the measures from it. If more than one periodicity exists, there should be a multimodal distribution of the interblock distances, with a separate mode for each periodicity. Figure 5 indicates that not one, but two or possibly three, distinct rhythms exist which are multiples of the shortest rhythm [3].

The second question, What causes blocks? has been partially answered in terms of the hypothesis of cumulative refractory phase. Just as the sensory-neuro-motor elements involved in responding to a stimulus require a short recuperative period (refractory phase) after each response, so, in homogeneous work in which the same elements occur repeatedly, if each response in series is forced to occur before complete recovery from the preceding one, a debt accumulates which must be paid by a prolonged refractory period, or block, at frequent intervals. The frequency of the blocks should be directly related to the continuity and homogeneity of the work. That this is true has been demonstrated by systematically varying the homogeneity and continuity of the tasks used and noting the variations in frequency of blocks resulting. Table I presents the data for a task of writing letter sequences of two-letter and six-letter combinations [24].

TABLE I

HOMOGENEITY AND BLOCKING

Condition	Average Blocks per Minute	Total Average Length
1. Most homogeneous	2.1	74.4
2. Least homogeneous	1.4	52.7

Before leaving the discussion of blocks, it should be pointed out that, since they usually increase in length and frequency with fatigue and decrease with rest, they offer a sensitive index to the state of efficiency of the worker.

Studying Transfer of Decrement Between Tasks

To what extent do decrements in efficiency which were developed in the performance of one task transfer to other tasks engaged in immediately afterward? What principles govern such transfer? Special methods developed for answering these questions experimentally must be based on recognition of the complex character of the decrement from work. There are at least three different kinds of decrement: (*a*) the specific decrement that develops in the operations directly involved in the task; (*b*) the decrement in functions related to, but not directly involved in, the task operations; (*c*) the decrement in those broad work attitudes, attentive sets, and volitional controls which carry over to almost any subsequent task because they are so general. The analytical *S-R* approach has proved most enlightening in studying the first two types of transfer of decrement, and the Gestalt approach has yielded the most fruitful concepts for understanding the last. The present discussion will be limited to the first two.

The conventional method of studying transfer of decrement—having subjects engage in some such task as addition, and then immediately afterward working at cancellation, multiplication, or memorizing words, to determine whether they accomplish less in the second task under these conditions than they would if no addition work had preceded—is of little value. It merely answers the question whether there is *any* transfer of decrement, leaving unanswered the questions of *what, how much,* and *in what way.*

The analytical method consists in selecting tasks which can be broken up into simple S-R components and finding out whether the amount of decrement transferred between tasks is a function of the number of such S-R components present in both tasks in common. For example, in one study [5] the work consisted in writing letter sequences. One task always involved writing *ABC* continuously. This was the standard. The other tasks differed in the number of letters which were identical with those in the standard task: *ABD* has two such letters, *AEF* one, and *EFG* none. Five conditions were used. The standard task was always worked on first, then a second task immediately afterward, in which either all elements were the same as those in the first task, or two were the same, or one was, or none. Standard and comparison tasks were worked on in alternate minutes for a total work period of 16 minutes. A fifth condition involved *resting* in the alternate minutes.

Table II shows the average results, under each of the five conditions, in terms of number of *ABC* units written. It can be seen that the number of units done is inversely proportional to the number of elements common to the two tasks. The greatest transfer of decrement occurs when the standard and comparison tasks are identical; the least, when they have no elements in common. Rest, of course, involves no transfer of decrement and hence gives us a control in terms of which to estimate the relative amounts of transfer in the other conditions.

TABLE II

TRANSFER OF DECREMENT

Total *ABC* Units Written in Each Condition

Conditions	All Elements in Common	Two Elements in Common	One Element in Common	None Common	Rest
	7911	8252	8403	8609	8756

A striking fact is that, as compared with the rest condition, the condition in which the two tasks have no elements in common produces very little decrement transfer.

Transfer of Set

The common element in two tasks may be a particular set or work attitude, such as an accuracy set, a speed set, or a rhythm set. For example, if a subject is first given a task requiring a high degree of accuracy, this accuracy set will carry over to a subsequent task and will result in a higher degree of accuracy in the performance of the second task than would have occurred otherwise. If the first task emphasizes speed, the tempo of the second task will be accelerated correspondingly. Cathcart and Dawson [7] demonstrated this in the following way: Their subjects were allowed to perform a wide variety of tasks, from simple tapping to playing musical selections on the piano, at their natural or self-selected rate. They were then asked to perform at a different rate, either faster or slower than the first. Finally they were again allowed to revert to the rate which seemed natural to them. Table III shows that the final rate of work tended to be deflected in the direction of the intervening rate.

TABLE III

NUMBER OF TAPS IN 5 SECONDS

Initial Rate	Intervening Rate	Final Rate
11	23 (faster)	15
12	7 (slower)	10

Sharp [28] demonstrated that such sets as the foregoing have a physiological basis in residual tensions in the muscles which persist into the later performance.

REST AND RECOVERY FROM WORK

In studying memory, we have a curve of learning and a curve of forgetting. The second begins where the first leaves off and may be considered the reverse process. Analogously, in studying fatigue, we have the curve of work and the curve of recovery after cessation of work. It is only recently that the curve of recovery has been investigated quantitatively. Two typical experimental procedures will be described: one for studying the curve of recovery from muscular work, the other for intellectual work

The Recovery Curve for Muscular Work

Illustrative of the first type of curve is Manzer's thesis [18]. He studied five different muscle groups: in the finger, the hand, the arm, the leg, and the trunk. The subject flexed these muscles repeatedly until a state of exhaustion was reached. He then rested 5, 10, or 20 minutes, at which time he was given a test to determine the degree of recuperation that had been reached by that time. The combined results for all muscle groups are shown in Fig. 6. The average work done in the test following each rest pause is expressed as a per cent of the average work done with unfatigued muscles. It can be seen

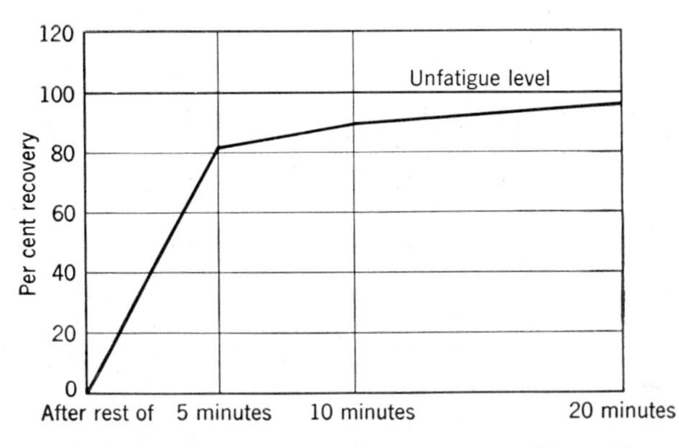

Fig. 6. Course of recovery from muscular fatigue. (From Manzer [18].)

that the average recovery after 5 minutes was 82 per cent; after 10 minutes, 90 per cent; and after 20 minutes, 95 per cent. The curve is negatively accelerated, with the greatest gain during the first 5 minutes. Longer rests gave diminishing returns in recuperative value.

The Recovery Curve for Intellectual Work

Methods for studying the recuperation curve for fatigue from mental work were developed by Kirby [15] for all three methods of approach, i.e., output, organic state, and feeling-tone. The mental work consisted of continuous solving of figure analogy problems, a type of material used in some intelligence tests, involving reasoning by analogy, but capable of being made highly homogeneous. A series of these problems is shown in Fig. 7. All subjects worked 30 minutes, then rested, and then were tested for degree of recovery by a 5 minute test. The rest period was varied systematically in length for different groups of subjects: one group rested 2 minutes, another 3, another 5, another 7, another 10, and another 20 minutes. Objective decrement was measured in terms of problems solved, number done correctly, and number of blocks. It was computed by subtracting the level of performance at the end of the work period from that obtained in a

5-minute test period the next day. With this value as a measure of 100 per cent decrement, the amount of recovery after a given length

[illegible]	[illegible]	1	[illegible]	[illegible]	37	[illegible]	[illegible]	73
[illegible]	[illegible]	2	[illegible]	[illegible]	38	[illegible]	[illegible]	74
[illegible]	[illegible]	3	[illegible]	[illegible]	39	[illegible]	[illegible]	75
[illegible]	[illegible]	4	[illegible]	[illegible]	40	[illegible]	[illegible]	76
[illegible]	[illegible]	5	[illegible]	[illegible]	41	[illegible]	[illegible]	77

Fig. 7. Section of work sheet illustrating figure analogy problems. (From Kirby's study [15].)

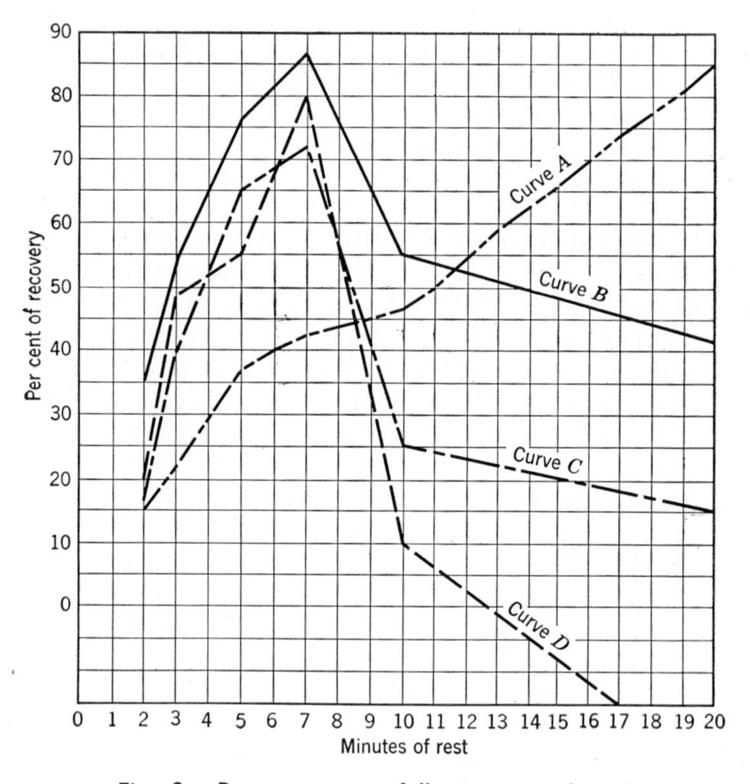

Fig. 8. Recovery curves following mental work.

Curve *A*. Skin-resistance changes. Curve *B*. Problems worked correctly. Curve C. Blocking tendency. Curve *D*. Feeling-tone changes. (From an unpublished thesis by T. Kirby, 1942, in the University of Cincinnati library.)

of rest could be computed as a percentage of it. Feeling-tone was measured by a scale of values ranging from 10 to zero, with descriptive statements for the upper and lower extremes to guide the subjects in their introspective reports. Recovery in feeling-tone with rest was computed in the same manner as recovery in objective performance level. Organic state was measured by the PGR, expressed in ohms resistance. This index rises under conditions of relaxation and drops during mental effort or attentional strain. Resistance was measured during a preliminary quiet period of 15 minutes before work was begun, during the 30 minutes of work, during the following rest period, and during the test period after rest. Figure 8 gives the curves of recovery for each of the criteria, i. e., skin resistance change, problems worked correctly, reduction in blocking, and improved feeling-tone.

It can be seen from Fig. 8 that skin resistance rose steadily during the rest period, regardless of how long it was, thus indicating a progressively increasing degree of relaxation. This very relaxation, however, apparently reached a point which made it difficult for the subjects to begin work again, because all the other curves show a reversal of the recovery tendency when the rest period is longer than 7 minutes. Output rises to a maximum recovery of 86 per cent at 7 minutes, then reverses its trend downward, so that at 20 minutes the recovery level is only 43 per cent. Recovery from the blocking tendency shows a similar rise and an even steeper drop. The reversal in subjective readiness for resumption of work, as indicated by feeling-tone, is even more drastic. These results agree with the discovery of a previous investigator that a worker's readiness to resume a task increases for a period of 5 to 10 minutes, then undergoes a decline before finally reaching the complete recovery stage. The optimal rest period, therefore, should terminate at the point where readiness to resume work is at a maximum.

Sleep as a Recovery Process

The methods of studying the recovery process outlined above do not cover the special problem of sleep as a recuperative process. Experimental findings about sleep have thus far been mainly negative. There is no certain method for determining the depth of sleep. Such methods as finding the strength of a sensory stimulus necessary to arouse the sleeper or recording the number of movements during sleep seem to give contradictory results, and it is not certain that the recuperative value of sleep is a function of its depth. Studies of the effect of loss of sleep, or voluntary insomnia, suggest that most mental work of a routine sort is performed as well or better after prolonged periods of wakefulness as after normal sleep [25]. That it is performed with no more expenditure of effort, however, is very doubtful. Probably the most fruitful approach to the problem is suggested by the experiment of Laird [16], who compared the amount of energy consumed in performing a stated task immediately after a normal night's sleep with that consumed by a person who had lost several hours of sleep. The loss of sleep resulted in greater energy expenditure.

THE INFLUENCE OF EXTRANEOUS FACTORS

The fourth major problem of efficiency, as outlined on page 471, involves the effect on work exerted by factors extraneous to the task itself, including (*a*) distractions and environmental influences, (*b*) physiological agents, and (*c*) suggestion and motivational factors. The past history of experimental work in this field shows that it is so difficult to avoid the influence of uncontrolled variables that much of the work already done is worthless and much more of doubtful significance. Let us first consider the problem of studying physiological agents, such as drugs, tobacco, alcohol, dietary factors, ventilation, and atmospheric conditions. What frequently neglected variables must be brought under control to insure significant results?

Studying Physiological Conditions

All physiological agents can be said to influence behavior in two distinct ways: first, by their direct effect on the organism through the blood stream and tissues; second, by the indirect effect which the subject's knowledge of their presence has upon his behavior. Since it is the first type of effect which is usually being investigated, the second must be controlled or eliminated in the following ways.

1. Concealing the presence of the agent. When the factor whose influence is being studied is introduced through the mouth, it is frequently possible to use a control dose, which is indistinguishable from the real dose, so that the subject never knows whether he is being given the control or experimental condition. Examples of this method are found in the Hull experiment [13] on pipe tobacco smoking, in which the blindfolded subject puffed warm air from a specially constructed pipe in the control condition, and in drug experiments in which a placebo, or neutral pill looking and tasting like the real pill, is used. An unavoidable loophole in the method, however, is

the fact that the experimental agent often produces secondary effects on the organism which warn the subject of its presence and thus influence his behavior by subtle suggestion. Moreover, it is impossible to conceal from a subject the fact that he has or has not gone without sleep or food.

2. COUNTER SUGGESTION. A striking example of this method is found in Dorcus's experiment [8] on the effect of cigarette smoking. He hypnotized his subjects and convinced them that they were smoking during a control condition in which an unlighted cigarette was held in the mouth. Ordinarily, one cannot be sure that the suggestion is really effective; but in this instance the subjects showed that it was by periodically shaking imaginary ashes from the ends of the unlighted cigarettes.

3. HABITUAL VERSUS OCCASIONAL USERS. The effect of continued use of drugs and other physiological agents is to build up tolerance, both organic and mental, for them. They therefore produce on habitual users effects quite different from those on occasional or nonusers. Results from these different groups must be interpreted separately.

4. TEMPORAL COURSE OF THE EFFECTS. Since the action of most physiological agents persists for a considerable time, the only adequate way to express their effects on performance is to plot a continuous curve indicating the entire course of efficiency through several hours. In some cases, effects do not appear until days later. There has been a tendency to investigate all such phenomena in too fragmentary a manner.

5. AMOUNT OR STRENGTH OF THE AGENT. A number of experimenters in this field have been motivated by the desire to answer some practical question, such as whether a person can get intoxicated on 4.4 per cent beer or whether two cups of coffee are harmful. The result is that they have failed to explore systematically the effects of all degrees of the agent. Sometimes a slight change in amount makes all the difference between a negligible and a marked effect on efficiency. Another problem is controlling the strength accurately, because this depends on the concentration within the body and not just the amount of intake.

6. THE PRACTICE FACTOR. The tasks used to measure efficiency should be well practiced. Otherwise improvement from learning is likely to be confused with improvement from the action of the agent. If the experiment is pursued for several days or weeks, cumulative effects are certain to appear, which may be due to practice or to the cumulative action of the agent.

STUDYING THE EFFECT OF ANOXIA. Illustrative of the problems

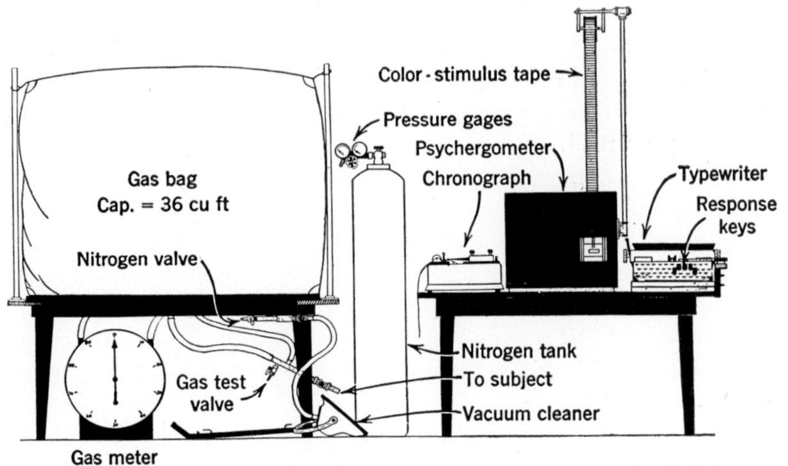

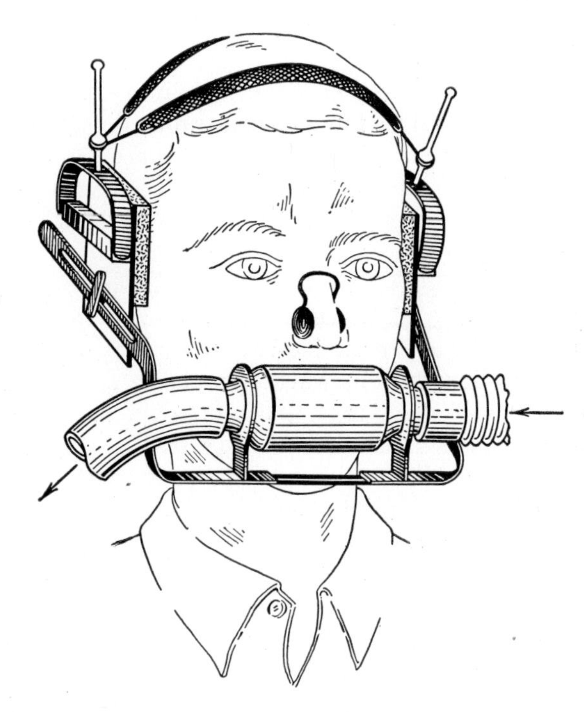

Fig. 9. Apparatus for studying mental performance under anoxemia.

(*Above*) Apparatus for presenting stimuli and recording responses, and for controlling the oxygen content of the inspired air.

(*Below*) Douglas double valve with headgear for breathing air from bag. (From an unpublished study by Geldreich and Bills.)

which arise in this field is the study made by Bills [4] of the effects of reduction in the oxygen content of inspired air on efficiency in the task of serial color discrimination. The method used was to prepare a large supply of air of a given desired oxygen content, before each experimental period, by mixing air with nitrogen in a chamber in the appropriate amounts. The subject then inhaled this mixture during the work period and exhaled through a separate exhaust valve. Six different concentrations of oxygen were used on different experimental days by each of the subjects: normal air or 20.9 per cent, 15 per cent, 12 per cent, 10.5 per cent, 9 per cent, and 8 per cent. The percentage of nitrogen used in diluting the air was controlled by a flow meter and checked by a chemical gas analyser. The subjects were equipped with a breathing apparatus, so that they inhaled only air from the chamber and exhaled into the room. Ten men and women acted as subjects, but only three of them tried the 9 per cent mixture, and only one was able to take the 8 per cent condition.

The breathing apparatus and the apparatus for responding and recording the responses are shown in Fig. 9. The subject sat facing the small window, through which the color stimuli were exposed, one at a time. He responded by pressing the keys corresponding to the colors exposed. The rate at which he responded determined the rate at which the color stimuli appeared, through an automatic electrical control. The recording of the responses was made on a wax kymographic paper tape, so that each separate reaction time could be later read in millimeters.

Each subject was first put through a series of four practice trials of a half hour each, on four separate days, in which he breathed normal air from the bag and responded manually to the colors. This practice series was designed to accustom the subject to the apparatus and to give him training in responding manually to the colors until further improvement from practice would prove negligible during the actual experimental sessions.

The conditions of the experiment are shown in the following chart. A control condition with normal air was run before the first experimental condition and again after the last one, so as to give a comparative basis for judging the degree of effect of the anoxia conditions. To avoid the effects of suggestion, the same apparatus was used for inhaling normal air during the control condition as for breathing the air of low oxygen content. The subjects were unable to tell the difference. Each subject went through the seven conditions in a different order, so that practice was equalized for all conditions in the group averages except IV and V.

No motive other than the desire to obtain true results was intro-

Condition	First Half Hour	Last 15 Minutes
Control I	Subject breathes normal air, while sitting at rest	Continues normal air while working
Experimental I	Subject breathes 15 per cent oxygen and rests	Breathes 15 per cent oxygen and works
Experimental II	Subject breathes 12 per cent oxygen and rests	Breathes 12 per cent oxygen and works
Experimental III	Subject breathes 10.5 per cent oxygen and rests	Breathes 10.5 per cent oxygen and works
Experimental IV	Subject breathes 9 per cent oxygen and rests	Breathes 9 per cent oxygen and works
Experimental V	Subject breathes 8 per cent oxygen and rests	Breathes 8 per cent oxygen and works
Control II	Subject breathes normal air and rests	Breathes normal air and works at task

duced into the work situation, since the subjects were sophisticated and mature enough to respond in a constant manner to this motive.

The results were both qualitative and quantitative. No subjective or objective effects appeared until the oxygen percentage was reduced below 12 per cent, and no marked effects showed above 9 per cent. At this point muscular rigidity of the fingers, tremors of hand and head, and loss of orientation and sense of time occurred. There was a tendency to perseverate at the task even when told to stop and also some giggling over nonsensical trifles, indicating a breakdown of emotional control. A narrowing of the field of attention was evident, and lapses of memory occurred. All but one of the subjects who tried the 8 per cent condition lost consciousness.

The quantitative criteria used were response time, number and length of blocks, and total block time measured in average reaction times. Errors were found to be so infrequent that they could be ignored. It can be seen from Fig. 10 that the 15 per cent oxygen condition was, in all respects, as efficient as the normal control; but that below this point there was a positively accelerated increase in frequency and length of the blocks for equal reductions in oxygen concentration. Response time, however, when corrected by eliminating block time from the calculation, remained constant. The effect of anoxia, therefore, is to exaggerate the blocking tendency and to lower efficiency in this manner. Figure 10 shows the increase in average total block time with successive reductions in oxygen content of the air.

Studying Distractions and Environmental Influences

The problems confronting the investigator of environmental influences on behavior are similar to those outlined for physiological agents, but the task of controlling them is even greater, because the subject's responsiveness to their influence is so much more dependent on attitude, suggestion, motives appealed to, and individual differences resulting from past experience. A good illustration can be taken from the work on so-called distractors.

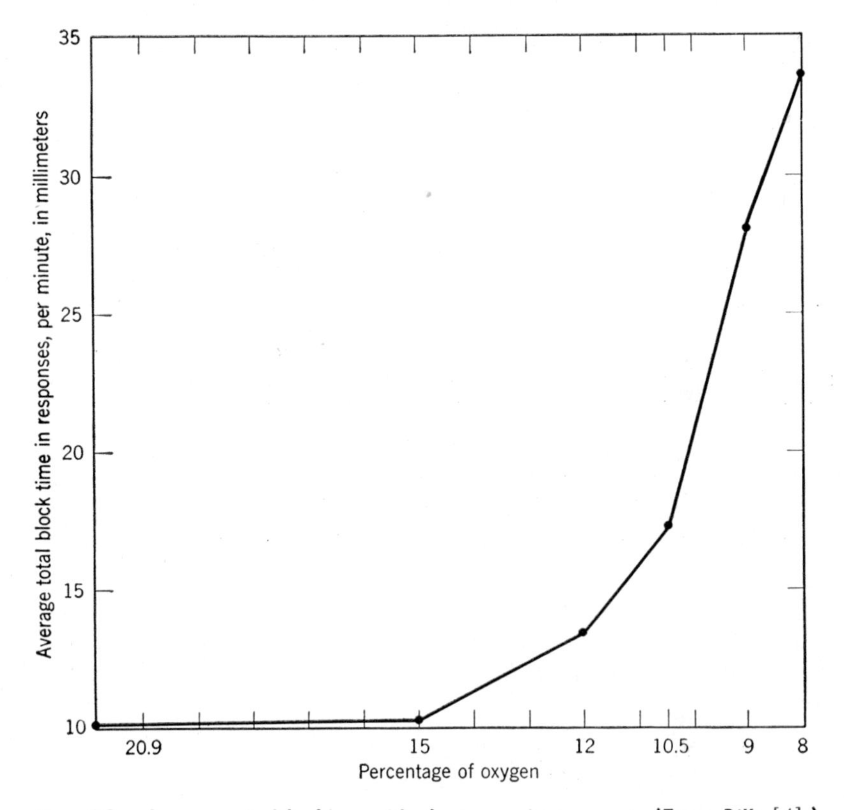

Fig. 10. Increase in blocking with decrease in oxygen. (From Bills [4].)

Under what conditions will an extraneous stimulus, introduced into a mental work situation, exert a detrimental effect on performance, and under what conditions will its effect be neutral or even beneficial? Studies of the effect of music played during working hours have produced highly ambiguous results, because of the complexity of the stimulus factors involved and the contradictory influences exerted. For example, a single discrete sound stimulus may exert a facilitative, neutral, or inhibitive effect on a response, depending on what fraction of a second beforehand it occurs. When continuous or intermittent distractors such as a metronome beat, a bell, or a continuously driven tuning fork are used during serial reactions, the effects will be facilitative or inhibitive, depending on whether the distractors are synchronized with the serial reactions. The strength of the distractor is important also, and the result will be further affected by whether the distractor acts on the same sense organ or organs as those involved in the task itself. Equally important is adaptation, because it has been found that even the most complex mechanical distractors will lose their effect after a short time [9]. Moreover, most persons display a tendency to exert extra effort to overcome the inhibitive effect of distractors in a work situation and thus to overcompensate, with a resultant facilitative effect on performance.

The problem of the long-time versus immediate effects of an agent is nowhere so important as in studying the influence of distractors, because the evidence from studies of metabolism, muscular tenseness, and other criteria of energy expenditure indicates that work under distractions requires a greater output of energy unless and until adaptation to the distractors has taken place. Such adaptation is more difficult with variable or intermittent distractors. Sooner or later, cumulative effects should appear in the objective performance level.

With music, two other elements besides sound and rhythm must be taken into consideration: affectivity and meaning. Persons fond of music are more definitely affected than persons who are indifferent to it. Familiar music exerts a greater effect than unfamiliar. The tempo and style of composition are important. Records of heart action and blood pressure indicate a heightened tonus accompanying the playing of martial tunes and a depressant effect of funeral music [14]. In the light of such complex results, no generalizations are safe, and no experiment designed to establish a general law of relationship could possibly be successful.

Studying the Influence of Motives and Incentives

The discussion of motivation in Chapter 13 makes unnecessary any further elaboration of the topic here, except to point out that it is an ever-present factor in every work situation, whether or not it is under control. Since it is impossible to eliminate this variable, the alternative is to control its strength and direction and if possible to measure and account for its influence. One very important point to recognize is that *motives* and *incentives* are distinct and independent variables. There is no assurance that, by supplying the appropriate incentive to workers, one can guarantee the presence of the corresponding motive and thus insure increased effort. The value of a reward differs with the individual; it may be zero in a person who lacks motives to which it can appeal. Is competition more effective than cooperation as a social incentive to workers? Maller [17] found that the answer depended on the kind of cooperating group, the degree of group solidarity. A situation designed to excite competition may fail to do so with some individuals. We hardly are justified in assuming that the relative strength of the competitive motive has been tested experimentally unless the incentive situation has actually had some appeal.

SUMMARY

The experimental study of efficiency in performance can be approached from two different angles, the analytical and the integrative. The first approach leads to experiments of the type exemplified by the quantitative study of the knee jerk, the simple, choice, and serial voluntary reactions, facilitative and inhibitive sets, and the ergographic record of isolated muscle groups. The second approach is concerned with the work of the integrated organism. It is mainly occupied with the effect of continuous performance on efficiency in the performance being studied and in related activities. These effects are studied at three levels: the objective output, the organic energy expenditure, and the subjective feeling-tone, and are expressed graphically in the curve of work. Recuperation from these effects is studied through the curve of recovery. Finally, the study of the influence of factors extraneous to the task itself, whether physiological or within the environmental setting, requires the use of special methods to overcome suggestion and the subtle motivational influences to which the human reactor is peculiarly susceptible.

REFERENCES

1. Bills, A. G. Blocking: a new principle of mental fatigue. *Amer. J. Psychol.,* 1931, *43,* 230–245.
2. Bills, A. G. *General Experimental Psychology.* New York: Longmans, Green, 1934.
3. Bills, A. G. Fatigue, oscillation and blocks. *J. Exper. Psychol.,* 1935, *18,* 569–70.
4. Bills, A. G. Blocking in mental fatigue and anoxemia compared. *J. Exper. Psychol.,* 1937, *20,* 437–452.
5. Bills, A. G., and W. McTeer. Transfer of fatigue and identical elements. *J. Exper. Psychol.,* 1932, *15,* 23–36.
6. Bowditch, H. P., and J. W. Warren. The knee jerk and its physiological modifications. *J. Physiol.,* 1890, *11,* 25–64.

7. Cathcart, E. P., and S. Dawson. Persistence, a characteristic of remembering. *Brit. J. Psychol.*, 1928, *18*, 262–275.
8. Dorcus, R. M. Effects of suggestion and tobacco on pulse rate and blood pressure. *J. Exper. Psychol.*, 1925, *8*, 297–309.
9. Ford, A. Attention-automatization: an investigation of the transitional nature of mind. *Amer. J. Psychol.*, 1929, *41*, 1–32.
10. Freeman, G. L. Facilitative and inhibitory effects of muscular tension on performance. *Amer. J. Psychol.*, 1933, *45*, 17–52.
11. Guilford, J. P. Fluctuations of attention with weak visual stimuli. *Amer. J. Psychol.*, 1927, *38*, 534–583.
12. Hersey, R. B. Emotional cycles in man. *J. Ment. Sci.*, 1931, *77*, 151–169.
13. Hull, C. L. The influence of tobacco on mental and motor efficiency. *Psychol. Monog.*, 1924, *33*.
14. Hyde, Ida. Effect of music on electrocardiograms and blood pressure. *J. Exper. Psychol.*, 1924, *7*, 213–224.
15. Kirby, T. K. *The Curve of Recovery from Fatigue.* Cincinnati: University of Cincinnati thesis, unpublished, 1942.
16. Laird, D. A., and W. Wheeler, Jr. What it costs to lose sleep. *Indus. Psychol.*, 1926, *1*, 694–696.
17. Maller, J. B. An experimental study of certain cooperative tendencies. *Relig. Educ.*, 1928, *23*, 361–363.
18. Manzer, C. W. An experimental investigation of rest pauses. *Arch. Psychol.*, 1927, *90*.
19. Morgan, J. J. B. Overcoming of distractions and other resistances. *Arch. Psychol.*, 1916, *35*.
20. Mosso, A. *Fatigue.* New York: Putnam, 1915.
21. Phillpots, S. J. A theoretical curve of fluctuations of attention. *Brit. J. Psychol.*, 1934–5, *25*, 221–255.
22. Poffenberger, A. T. The effect of continuous work on output and feelings. *J. Appl. Psychol.*, 1928, *12*, 459–467.
23. Robinson, E. S. Principles of the work decrement. *Psychol. Rev.*, 1926, *33*, 123–134.
24. Robinson, E. S., and A. G. Bills. Two factors in the work decrement. *J. Exper. Psychol.*, 1926, *9*, 415–444.
25. Robinson, E. S., and S. O. Hermann. Effects of the loss of sleep. *J. Exper. Psychol.*, 1922, *5*, 19–32.
26. Rounds, G. H., H. J. P. Schubert, and A. T. Poffenberger. Effects of practice on the metabolic cost of mental work. *J. Gen. Psychol.*, 1932, *7*, 65.
27. Schlosberg, H. A study of the conditioned patellar reflex. *J. Exper. Psychol.*, 1928, *11*, 468–494.
28. Sharp, L. H. Effects of residual tension on output and energy expenditure in muscular work. *J. Exper. Psychol.*, 1941, *29*, 1–22.
29. Stauffacher, J. C. The effects of varying amounts of induced muscular tension on the learning process. *J. Exper. Psychol.*, 1937, *21*, 26–46.
30. Stroud, J. B. The role of muscular tension in stylus maze learning. *J. Exper. Psychol.*, 1931, *14*, 606–631.
31. Thorndike, E. L. The curve of work. *Psychol. Rev.*, 1912, *19*, 165–194.
32. Vaughn, J., and E. Strobel. A colored light exposure apparatus. *J. Gen. Psychol.*, 1940, *23*, 443–444.
33. Woodrow, H. The measurement of attention. *Psychol. Rev. Monog.*, 1914, *7*, No. 76.

34. Woodworth, R. S. *Experimental Psychology.* New York: Henry Holt, 1938, pp. 305, 306–308.
35. Yochelson, S. Effects of rest pauses on work decrement. Quoted by E. S. Robinson, in *Handbook of General Experimental Psychology.* Worcester, Mass.: Clark University Press, 1934, pp. 580–584.

SUGGESTED READINGS

Bills, A. G. *The Psychology of Efficiency.* New York: Harper, 1943 (Chaps. I to IX).

Poffenberger, A. T. *Principles of Applied Psychology.* New York: Appleton-Century, 1942 (Chap. 20).

Robinson, E. S. Work of the Integrated Organism. In *Handbook of General Experimental Psychology.* C. Murchison, Ed. Worcester, Mass.: Clark University Press, 1934 (Chap. 12).

Woodworth, R. S. *Experimental Psychology.* New York: Henry Holt, 1938 (Chap. 14).

Chapter 17

Investigating and Appraising Intelligence and Other Aptitudes

Herbert S. Conrad[1]

There is no more hard-headed or practical question to be asked about an individual than, *"What can he do?"* In this connection the distinction must be recognized between *aptitude* and *achievement*. Aptitude refers to potential achievement, or the ability to acquire or improve proficiency upon exposure to appropriate opportunity and training; achievement, of course, refers to completed accomplishment. Wide differences exist among individuals in most (if not all) aptitudes or achievements; and definite differences exist also *within* an individual—thus, a person high in intelligence will not likely be equally high in, say, mechanical or musical aptitude. Especially in young people, the measurement of aptitudes is of tremendous practical importance; and it is with aptitudes, rather than achievement, that this chapter is concerned.

VARIETY OF METHODS

The problem of appraising intelligence and other aptitudes is as old as man himself. In general, of all the methods which may be employed for this purpose, the method of *tests* is the most practical, convenient, and widely applicable. Other methods, however, deserve at least passing notice. One obvious method is to give the individual an *extended trial on the job*—whether the job be that of studying in college or learning to be an airplane pilot. This method is usually too time-consuming and costly to recommend itself; it works well

[1] Technical Consultant, College Entrance Examination Board, Princeton, New Jersey.

only when the individual is successful. Another method sometimes used for appraising and investigating aptitudes is the method of *ratings based on observation of previous behavior.* Thus, an individual's aptitude for college work might be inferred from ratings obtained from his high-school teachers; the testimonial of a previous employer also belongs in this same class of appraisal. Such ratings or testimonials suffer from many drawbacks. Some raters or testimonial writers are accurate, but others are not—and one is hard put to know whether any particular rater is "on the beam" or off. One remedy for this defect is the "averaging out" of errors by the use of ratings from many raters; but even here there are difficulties. Thus, in ratings of students' intelligence, unpopular students are likely to be rated *down,* whereas "teachers' pets" are rated *up.* Another complexity lies in standards: the standards of rating used by urban teachers may not agree with those by rural teachers; the standards of public school teachers may not agree with those of private-school teachers; etc. Under favorable circumstances ratings can be a useful adjunct to tests, but not a practical and convenient substitute. The disadvantages and inconveniences of ratings appear also in connection with *records,* with the additional disadvantage that records too often fail to supply the specific, detailed, quantitative information that is needed. Probably the best records for the investigation and appraisal of intelligence are the records of students' grades or marks in school; these are sufficiently available and valuable to deserve recognition and use. The *experience check list* gives the individual an opportunity to indicate, by check marks on a systematic list, the nature and extent of his educational and occupational experience. The trouble with the experience check list is that it generally fails to provide reliable evidence concerning *how successful* the individual was in his education and experience. Finally, there is the method of the *interview.* This method is better adapted for the appraisal of social qualities than of intelligence and other aptitudes. Among other handicaps, the interview method is extremely expensive.

APTITUDE TESTS

Because tests are the principal method for the practical appraisal of intelligence and other aptitudes, it is to tests that this chapter is devoted. For purposes of broad overview, we shall first consider a general classification of aptitude tests according to (1) type of task, (2) type of response, (3) type of administration, and (4) type of scoring.

Type of Task

(*a*) The task can be novel or learned; thus, to try to match a pattern of red and green lights by manipulating two pedals and a "stick" (as in the Complex Coordination Test administered in the Army Air Forces) is a novel task; to prove that one can read, understand, and apply the content of a printed passage (as in a reading test) is a learned task. (*b*) The task can be apparently similar to the accomplishment one is aiming to predict or apparently dissimilar. Thus, the Complex Coordination Test (Fig. 9) seems to call for responses rather similar to those made by a pilot in flying a plane, and it has a useful degree of validity for the selection of airplane pilots; but this same test has also proved useful in helping to predict the success of airplane navigators, whose work, offhand, appears to call for reactions different from those in this test [11]. (*c*) The task may be of the paper-and-pencil variety, or it may require specially constructed apparatus. For several practical reasons, paper-and-pencil tests are generally preferable to apparatus tests. In the first place, it is generally expensive both to construct the apparatus and to prepare the duplicates needed to test a large number of individuals in a limited time; second, it is sometimes troublesome to maintain satisfactory comparability between different machines (this was a constant source of annoyance in the Army Air Forces psychomotor testing program); third, it is generally impossible for one person to administer the test to a large group of individuals at a time; and finally, special training or skill is frequently required in the scoring of responses to apparatus tests. If, however, the apparatus tests make a significant contribution to validity, the extra cost and inconvenience may be considered well justified. (*d*) The test may make heavy, small, or no demands upon speed by the testee, according to whether the time allowed for completing the test is brief, generous, or unlimited.

Type of Response

(*a*) In paper-and-pencil tests the individual's response is usually restricted to choosing among four or five "multiple-choice" alternatives. Sometimes the nature of the task requires that the individual be given greater leeway: e.g., a test of "fluency" requiring the individual to write as many four-letter words as he can that start with *p* and end with *r* (pear, poor, peer, purr, etc). (*b*) The response may involve recognition, recall, calculation, or special ingenuity. An example of the "ingenuity" type of item is as follows:

A mother sent her boy to the river and told him to bring back exactly 7 pints of water. She gave him a 4-pint vessel and a 9-pint vessel. Show me how the boy can measure out exactly 7 pints of water, using nothing but these two vessels and not guessing at the amount. You should begin by filling the 4-pint vessel first. Remember, you have a 4-pint vessel and a 9-pint vessel, and you must bring back exactly 7 pints.[2]

In the following item on arithmetical reasoning, the answer must first be "calculated" before it can be "recognized."

If 1 pound of oranges = 2 to 4 oranges, what is the least possible weight, in pounds, of 3 dozen oranges?[3]

(*a*) 6 (*b*) 9 (*c*) 12 (*d*) 16 (*e*) 18

(*c*) The response may be of the "performance" type, as in the Complex Coordination Test.

Type of Administration

Paper-and-pencil tests generally lend themselves well to *group* administration; apparatus tests cannot, in general, be administered to large groups at one time. Administration to large groups is, of course, faster and less expensive. The advantages of *individual* administration are that it permits closer control of the subject's attention and motivation and affords opportunity for detailed observation of the subject's behavior; these advantages are important in the testing of young children, of "problem" cases, and of persons examined at the order of a court. So-called "self-administering" tests require a minimum of supervision, the directions being quite simple and printed on the test.

Type of Scoring or Grading

(*a*) The scoring of responses to aptitude tests is typically objective, although occasionally more or less subjective. Thus, in the Wechsler-Bellevue test [23] the subject is asked to state orally what is meant by various words, such as "nuisance" or "armory"; the scoring here is only slightly subjective, since there is seldom any doubt or disagreement among examiners as to whether a given response should be

[2] From L. M. Terman, *Condensed Guide for the Stanford Revision of the Binet-Simon Tests*. Houghton Mifflin, 1920, p. 31.

[3] From *Bulletin of Information for 1946–1947*, College Entrance Examination Board, p. 11.

credited. On the other hand, the scoring of an English composition test (taken as part of a battery for college admission) is definitely subjective, since examiners, even under the best of conditions, rather frequently fail to agree on the scores or grades they assign. (*b*) Scoring can be done by hand or, with true-false and multiple-choice tests, by machine [14]. The scoring machine most widely used requires that the individual indicate his answers on a special answer sheet, with a special "electrographic" pencil; the marks by this pencil serve as conductors of electricity, which operates the machine.

CORRELATION, CRITERION, AND VALIDITY

The concepts of correlation, criterion, and validity are basic to this entire chapter. A positive *correlation* is said to exist between, say, intelligence test scores and college grades *if those who get high intelligence test scores also tend to get high grades, and, conversely, if those who get low intelligence test scores tend to get low grades.* "Perfect" or "complete" positive correlation exists if each individual's college grade falls at a point corresponding exactly to his intelligence test score. Perfect correlation is never found in actual fact, although it is occasionally approximated. The *degree* or *extent* to which correlation exists is expressed by the "correlation coefficient." Perfect positive correlation is expressed by a correlation coefficient of +1.00; complete absence of correlation—in which the individual's standing in one trait or characteristic is quite unpredictable from his standing in another—is expressed by a correlation coefficient of .00. Intermediate values of the correlation coefficient, such as .70, reflect intermediate degrees of correlation. An example of correlations of 1.00, .90, and .50 is shown in Fig. 1. The correlation coefficient is somewhat peculiar, in that a correlation of .70 does not mean seventy-hundredths of a perfect correlation; roughly and in general, .70 may be regarded as approximately $.70^2$ or .49 of a perfect correlation. Similarly, .60 may be regarded as approximately $.60^2$ or .36 of a perfect correlation; etc.

By a *criterion* is meant the ability or performance which the aptitude test aims to predict, and *validity* is the degree to which scores on the criterion are successfully predicted by the aptitude test. Validity is frequently expressed in terms of the correlation between the test and the criterion. Thus it has been found [8] that the validity coefficient (correlation coefficient) between college-entrance intelligence tests and freshman college grades is about .52, although the best tests, under favorable circumstances, reach a validity of .60 or even

.65. A distinction must be made between the pragmatic or *operational* criterion (the criterion actually employed in a validity study) and an ideal or perfect criterion, which may, of course, be expected to

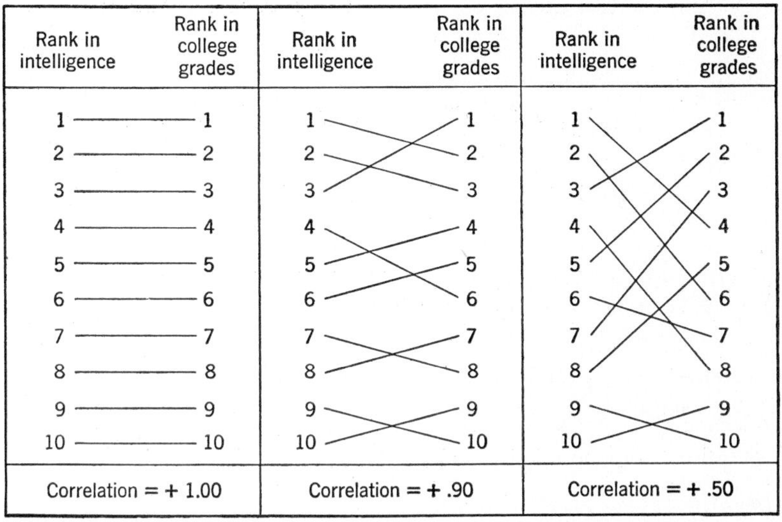

Rank in intelligence	Rank in college grades	Rank in intelligence	Rank in college grades	Rank in intelligence	Rank in college grades
1	1	1	1	1	1
2	2	2	2	2	2
3	3	3	3	3	3
4	4	4	4	4	4
5	5	5	5	5	5
6	6	6	6	6	6
7	7	7	7	7	7
8	8	8	8	8	8
9	9	9	9	9	9
10	10	10	10	10	10
Correlation = + 1.00		Correlation = + .90		Correlation = + .50	

Fig. 1. Correlation coefficients of various magnitudes. (After P. M. Symonds, *Measurement in Secondary Education*, 1929, p. 246; by permission of The Macmillan Co.)

differ to some extent from the operational criterion. The greater the difference between the operational and the perfect criterion, the less clearly interpretable a validity coefficient becomes.

ILLUSTRATIONS FROM PUBLISHED TESTS

Listed below are samples from several published tests. For greater familiarity with the wide variety of tasks found in aptitude tests, the student is urged to examine as many different tests as he can and to attempt to answer a fair proportion of the items in each test. Numerous additional illustrations from published tests are available in reference 10. Test bibliographies are furnished in references 3 and 13.

The following are some examples of items used to test **intellectual aptitudes:**

VOCABULARY:

1.[4] Do not *malign* him. rebuke eject slander molest support

2.[5] What does *fable* mean?

3.[6] Think of the word that fits the definition. Then mark the first letter of that word:

The theft of literary or artistic ideas of another is termed:

O P R U W

ANTONYMS:

4.[7] What *two* words below are opposite, or approximately opposite, in meaning?

resilient perspicacious salient inconspicuous

WORD FLUENCY:

5.[8] Write as many words as you can which begin with *con*.

6.[9] Each blank below is to be filled in by a word which, if used alone, would complete the sense of the sentence.

The horse pulled back ——— ——— ——— ——— ———

SIMILARITIES:

7.[10] In what way are a knife blade, a penny, and a piece of wire alike?

ANALOGIES:

8.[11] *Sawdust* is to *wood* as *flour* is to

(1) bread (2) grain (3) mill (4) ground (5) sand

9.[12] What words in a pair below are related to each other in the same way as the italicized pair of words at the beginning?

rest: fatigue	diploma: graduate	relaxation: recreation
	pinnacle: mountain	laziness: obesity
	praise: dejection	

[4] From I. Gansl, *Archives of Psychology,* No. 236, 1939, p. 49.

[5] From D. Wechsler, *The Measurement of Adult Intelligence,* Williams and Wilkins, 1939, p. 162.

[6] From L. L. Thurstone and T. G. Thurstone, *Psychological Examination for College Freshmen,* 1941 Edition, American Council on Education, p. 6.

[7] From *Bulletin of Information for 1946–1947,* College Entrance Examination Board, p. 9.

[8] From L. L. Thurstone and T. G. Thurstone, *Psychometric Monographs,* No. 2. University of Chicago Press, 1941, p. 73.

[9] From D. M. Johnson and F. Reynolds, *Psychological Record,* 1941, p. 184.

[10] From L. M. Terman, *Condensed Guide for the Stanford Revision of the Binet-Simon Tests,* Houghton Mifflin, 1920, p. 24.

[11] From L. L. Thurstone and T. G. Thurstone, *Psychological Examination for College Freshmen,* 1941 Edition, American Council on Education, p. 14.

[12] From *Bulletin of Information for 1946–1947,* College Entrance Examination Board, p. 9.

"Problem" question:

10.[13] My neighbor has been having queer visitors. First, a doctor came to his house, then a lawyer, then a minister (preacher or priest). What do you think happened there? (If response is simply "a death," check up by asking what the lawyer came for.)

Verbal absurdity:

11.[14] Mark *F* if the sentence is foolish; mark *S* if it is sensible.

S F Mrs. Smith has had no children, and I understand that the same was true of her mother.

Reasoning:

12.[15] Haste makes waste, and waste makes want. Therefore a man never loses by delay. True or False?

13.[15] Suppose that: All haystacks are typewriters.
All catfish are typewriters.
Then is it *true* or *false* that: All haystacks are catfish.

Directions test (measuring comprehension, memory, and speed):

14.[16] When I say "go," draw a line through every even number that is not in a circle and also through every odd number that is in a circle with a letter. Go! (Allow not over 25 seconds.)

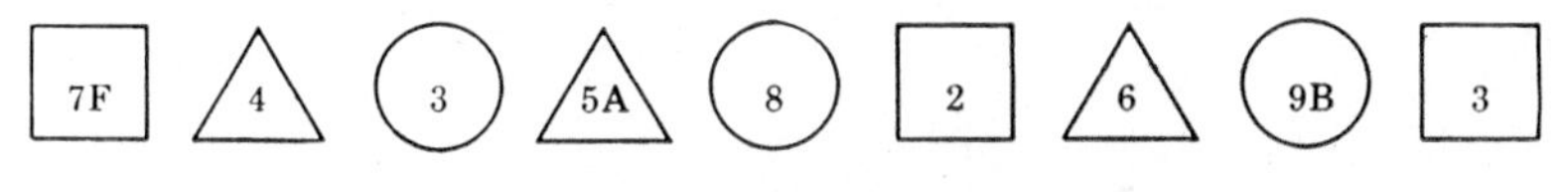

Fig. 2. Directions test.

Sentence completion:

15.[17] One of the most prevalent erroneous contentions is that Argentina is a country of.................. agricultural resources, and needs only the arrival of ambitious settlers.
(1) modernized (2) flourishing (3) undeveloped (4) waning (5) limited

[13] From L. M. Terman, *Condensed Guide for the Stanford Revision of the Binet-Simon Tests,* Houghton Mifflin, 1920, p. 25.
[14] From L. L. Thurstone and T. G. Thurstone, *Psychometric Monographs,* No. 2, University of Chicago Press, 1941, p. 47.
[15] From L. L. Thurstone, *Psychometric Monographs,* No. 1, University of Chicago Press, 1938, p. 48.
[16] From C. S. Yoakum and R. M. Yerkes, *Army Mental Tests,* Henry Holt, 1920, p. 59.
[17] From *Bulletin of Information for 1946–1947,* College Entrance Examination Board, p. 10.

PROVERBS (may be considered a variety of reading test):

16.[18] Which one of the six statements below explains the following proverb: A bird in the hand is worth two in the bush.

a. It is easier to carry eggs in two baskets than in one.
b. A man of action has a loud voice.
c. Tame birds are more expensive than wild ones.
d. It is better to be content with what you have than to lose it in gambling for more.
e. It is safer not to risk all on one venture.
f. What a man does is a better indication of his character than what he says.

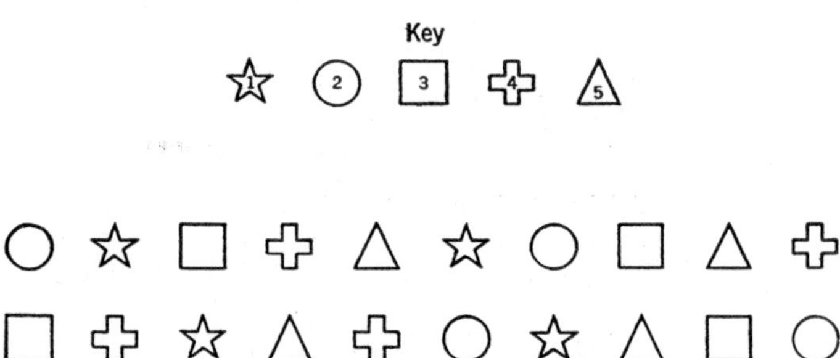

Fig. 3. Digit-symbol substitution test.

READING:

17. The typical reading test presents a full paragraph (or series of paragraphs), followed by multiple-choice questions. The examinee is usually allowed to refer to the reading material when attempting to answer the questions. The questions may refer merely to matters of fact, or may require application of the facts given in the paragraph, or may require inference, etc.

LEARNING TESTS:

18. Apart from paragraph reading, few brief learning tests have proved of value in intelligence testing. An exception is the "digit-symbol substitution" test.[19] In this test the subject records a number inside each geometrical figure, in accordance with the "key" at the top (see Fig. 3). This test may be given with a time limit, in which case the score is the number of geometrical figures correctly filled; or the score may be the time required to finish (with a deduction for errors).

[18] From A. S. Otis, *Otis Self-Administering Test of Mental Ability: Higher Examination, Form B,* World Book Company, 1922.

[19] From R. S. Woodworth and F. L. Wells, *Psychological Monographs,* Vol. 13, No. 5, 1911.

ARITHMETICAL OR NUMERICAL ITEMS:

19.[20] If a train goes 150 yards in 10 seconds, how many *feet* does it go in one-fifth of a second? ________

20.[21] What number is missing in this series?

15 ⅔ 15 ⅓ 15 ⅔ 15 15 ⅔ 14 ⅔ . . .

21[22]. $\frac{36 \times 18}{?} = 6 \times 3$

(*a*) ⅙ (*b*) 1 (*c*) 6 (*d*) 36 (*e*) 42

PERFORMANCE OR NON-VERBAL TESTS:

At the younger age levels, especially the preschool age levels, objects and pictures replace words and numbers as the vehicle for the intellectual processes in intelligence tests. At these levels what appears to the adult as mere motor manipulation requiring only a minimum of intellectual effort serves successfully for intelligence testing. The following are a few illustrations of some of the non-verbal or performance tests of intelligence. Some of these tests have a fair degree of validity at higher age levels up to and including the adult.

Drawing a man:

22. The child is requested to draw a man. This test has been standardized by Goodenough [9], who provides detailed directions for scoring.

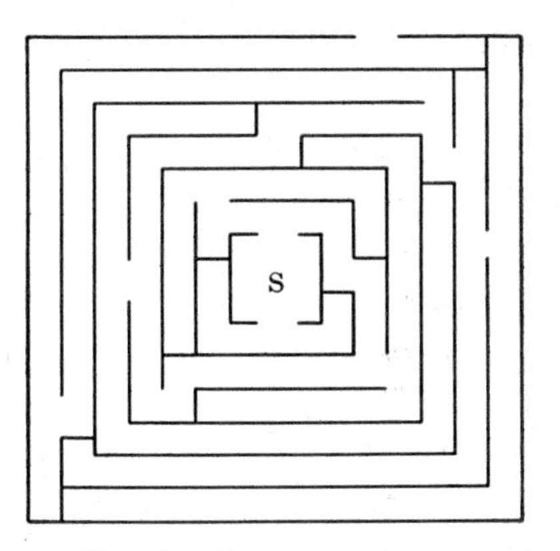

Fig. 4. Porteus maze test.

Maze test:

23.[23] The examinee places his pencil at S (see Fig. 4) and is told to show what "road" he would take to get out of the maze *without crossing any printed lines and without entering any closed "roads."*

20 From D. Wechsler, *The Measurement of Adult Intelligence,* Williams and Wilkins, 1939, p. 152.

21 From J. Tiffin and C. H. Lawshe, *Adaptability Test, Form A,* Science Research Associates, 1942.

22 From *Bulletin of Information for 1946–1947,* College Entrance Examination Board, p. 10.

23 From S. D. Porteus, *Guide to Porteus Maze Test,* Vineland Training School, Vineland, N. J., 1924.

Other performance tests:

24. The following are descriptions of two tests from the Performance Scale of the Wechsler-Bellevue test [23]. (*a*) In the "picture-arrangement test," the subject is presented with a disarranged series of pictures. The problem is to arrange the pictures in proper sequence so that they tell a story. (*b*) In the "block design test" the problem is to produce certain prescribed designs by arranging sixteen colored cubes.

It may be of interest to observe that the total score from the five "performance" tests of the Wechsler-Bellevue Intelligence Scale correlates with the total score from the five verbal tests of this scale to the extent of .67 [23, p. 126]. This is lower than usual for the correlation between two halves of an intelligence test; there is no doubt that the performance part measures somewhat different abilities from the verbal. In general, performance tests are less highly correlated than are verbal tests with the usual criteria of intelligence, such as grades in academic courses in school.

MEMORY:

25. Memory tests include such tasks as repeating a set of six numbers after hearing them once, repeating a set of numbers backward, repeating a sentence, and repeating the thought of a brief paragraph. Non-verbal memory tests include, for example, the reproduction of an asymmetrical geometric design after a brief (10- or 15-second) exposure. All these are examples of *immediate* memory. *Delayed* memory has not ordinarily been used in tests of intelligence; an exception occurs in the Babcock [1] scale for measuring mental deterioration in the aged.

The following sections will present (less extensively than for intellectual aptitudes) illustrative items or tasks from tests designed to measure perceptual, clerical, esthetic, psychomotor, and mechanical aptitudes. Below are given three tests of **perceptual aptitudes.**

IDENTICAL FORMS:

26.[24] In the test below, the task is to discover quickly the one figure in each row which is exactly the same as the first figure in the row.

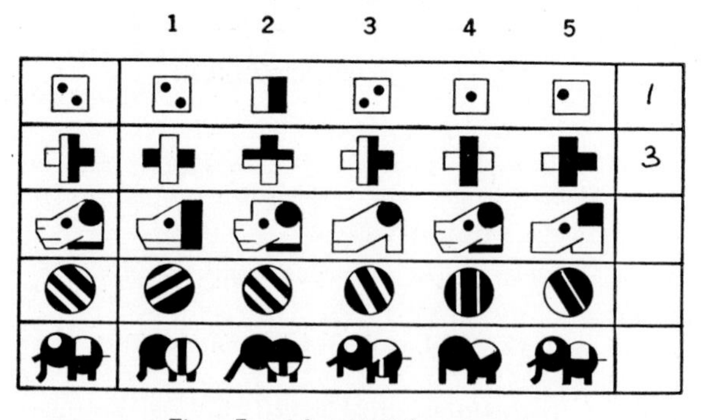

Fig. 5. Identical forms test.

[24] From L. L. Thurstone, *Psychometric Monographs,* No. 1, University of Chicago Press, 1938, p. 40.

Gottschaldt figures:

27.[25] The Gottschaldt figures test, though largely perceptual, is also related to intelligence.

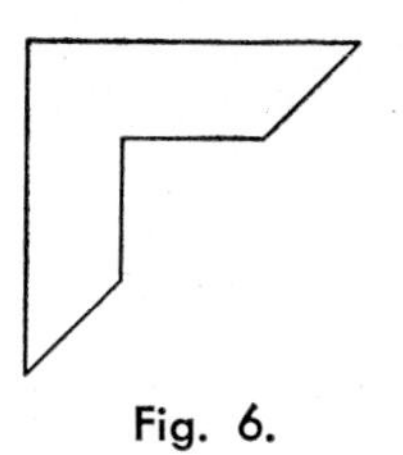

Fig. 6.

Look at the adjacent Fig. 6. This figure is contained in each of the drawings in Fig. 7. Find it in each drawing, and then mark it heavily in pencil. Mark only one figure in each drawing.

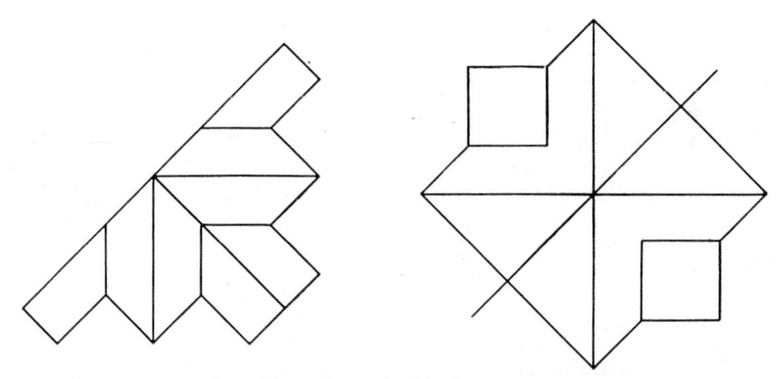

Fig. 7. Gottschaldt figures test.

MacQuarrie pursuit test:

28.[26] Figure 8 consists of ten lines which run across the diagram from left to right. Follow each line across from left to right. Record at the right the number

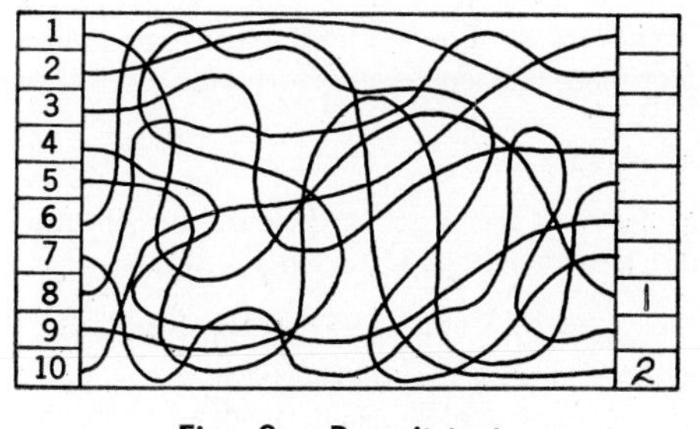

Fig. 8. Pursuit test.

[25] From L. L. Thurstone, *A Factorial Study of Perception,* University of Chicago Press, 1944, p. 75.

[26] Adapted from L. L. Thurstone, *Psychometric Monographs,* No. 1, University of Chicago Press, 1938, p. 41.

which belongs to the line. Lines 1 and 2 have already been done. Do each of the remaining lines.

In passing, it may be mentioned that tests of distance perception are needed in which the subject, while himself in motion, is observing one or more moving objects. Motion pictures provide a simple means for depicting the motion of objects; achieving simultaneous motion in the examinee during the test situation is more difficult.

Clerical aptitudes are reasonably well measured by tests of intelligence, except in the lower, more routine grades of clerical work. A common supplement to intelligence tests is the name- and number-checking test.

NAME AND NUMBER-CHECKING TEST:

29.[27] Compare the two lists of names or numbers, making a check mark when the two names or numbers to be compared are alike.

66273894	____	66273984
527384578	✓	527384578
New York World	✓	New York World
Cargill Grain Co.	____	Cargil Grain Co.

It is difficult to subclassify **psychomotor tests,** because such tests generally show low intercorrelations with each other (around .30 or below). A brief description of a few psychomotor tests follows.

FINGER-DEXTERITY TEST:

30.[28] The subject is provided with a tray containing small metal pegs, and with a board containing numerous small holes. The subject's task is to remove three pegs at a time from the tray, and place all three together into a hole in the board. This is repeated until all the holes have been filled.

TWO-HAND COORDINATION TEST:

31.[29] A metal stylus is grasped in each hand. The right and left hand simultaneously tap different areas of two metal plates, in a non-symmetric pattern. The score is based on speed of correct performance of the task.

COMPLEX COORDINATION TEST:

32.[30] The subject matches green and red lights, by simultaneous movements of feet (on pedals) and hand (on "stick") (see Fig. 9).

[27] From D. M. Andrew and others, *Minnesota Vocational Test for Clerical Workers,* Psychological Corporation, 1933.

[28] From J. O'Connor, *Personnel Journal,* 1926, pp. 379–382.

[29] From L. L. Thurstone, *A Factorial Study of Perception,* University of Chicago Press, 1944, p. 50.

[30] From *Psychological Bulletin,* by Staff, Psychological Research Unit No. 2, and Staff, Department of Psychology, Research Section, School of Aviation Medicine, 1944, p. 314.

Fig. 9. Complex coordination test. (Courtesy of Professor A. W. Melton.)

Most tests in the field of **esthetics** are measures of esthetic taste.

ART JUDGMENT:

33. In the Meier-Seashore Art Judgment Test,[31] the subject is asked which of two pictures (that differ only in some detail) he prefers; numerous pairs of pictures are presented, and the subject scores "high" if his preferences agree with those of a group of experts.

MUSICAL APTITUDE TESTS:

34. The musical tests prepared by Carl Seashore place the emphasis on aptitudes, rather than on esthetic taste. These tests are on phonograph records.[32]

[31] Published by the Bureau of Educational Research and Service, University of Iowa.

[32] Obtainable from C. H. Stoelting Company, Chicago, Ill.

Typical of others is the test for tonal memory, in which the subject is presented with two series of notes in succession. The task is to report whether the second series is identical with, or different from, the first. Numerous such tonal series are, of course, included in the test.

Mechanical aptitude tests are ordinarily classified as tests of spatial visualization, assembly tests, psychomotor tests, mechanical comprehension, mechanical information, and shop mathematics. The reading of paragraphs of technical material is also sometimes employed in measuring mechanical aptitudes.

SPATIAL VISUALIZATION: PAPER FORM-BOARD TEST:

35. The paper form-board test, as its name implies, is a paper-and-pencil means for measuring spatial visualization. In the test illustrated below,[33] the

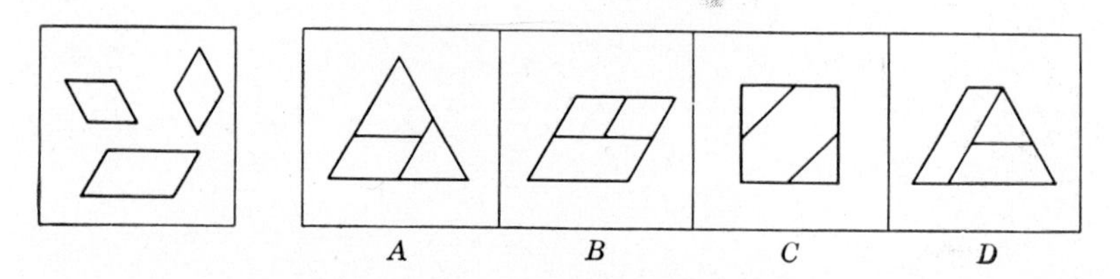

Fig. 10. Paper form board test.

task is to indicate which figure at the right could be formed by fitting together (without gaps or overlapping) the pieces at the left. The pieces may be turned around or turned over in any way to make them fit together.

SPATIAL VISUALIZATION: THREE-DIMENSIONAL FORM BOARD:

36. Crawford's Test for Tri-dimensional Structural Visualization[34] is an example of a three-dimensional form board for the measurement of spatial visualization. In this test, variously shaped parts are fitted into a base board containing various depressions and projections. A good score seems to demand rapid, accurate consideration of three dimensions at once. This test is reported to correlate highly (above .80) with grades in engineering drawing, but poorly with ordinary tests of intelligence.

ASSEMBLY TESTS:

37. (*a*) In the Minnesota Mechanical Assembly Test,[35] the subject is presented with the parts of a common mechanical device, e.g., a bicycle bell, and asked to put the parts together. Superior performance in this type of test appears to call for good spatial perception, and may be facilitated by general familiarity with common mechanical devices. (*b*) In the Purdue Mechanical Assembly Test, as reported by Tiffin, "the mechanisms involved are entirely new to all

[33] From *Specimen Questions from U. S. Civil Service Examinations,* United States Government Printing Office, 1945, p. 10.

[34] J. E. Crawford, *Journal of Applied Psychology,* 1940, pp. 482–492.

[35] Consult D. G. Pearson, and others, *The Minnesota Mechanical Ability Tests,* University of Minnesota Press, 1930.

testees" [21, p. 70]; this tends to eliminate the problem of differential familiarity with the test material.

MECHANICAL COMPREHENSION TESTS:

Tests of mechanical comprehension are typically pictorial or diagrammatic, requiring the application of physical principles to situations not specifically covered or emphasized in ordinary high-school physics courses. The following is an illustrative item:

38[36]. Which of the two illustrations is the more likely picture of a train wreck? *A B*

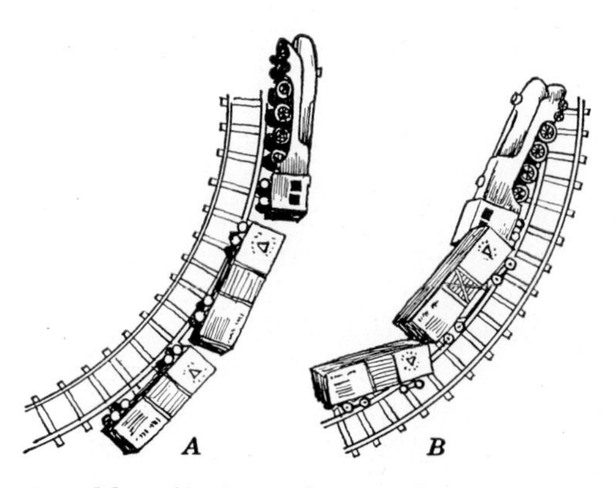

Fig. 11. Mechanical comprehension test item.

MECHANICAL INFORMATION TESTS:

Tests of mechanical information are included in measures of mechanical aptitude on the theory that those who pick up such information have more aptitude in mechanical matters than those who do not. This theory, however, probably does not hold very well for urban boys, among whom opportunities for mechanical learning may be limited. The following is an item that was used by the Army Air Forces in one of its tests:

39[37]. A metal band put around the handle of a tool in order to strengthen it is called a (*a*) ferrule, (*b*) shim, (*c*) casting, (*d*) node, (*e*) clevis.

SHOP MATHEMATICS:

40. Items in shop mathematics cover simple arithmetic, mensuration, and the reading of tapes, gages, etc.

It should be emphasized that the previous illustrations are merely a small sample of available types of test tasks. The interested student is referred to the text by Greene [10].

[36] From G. K. Bennett, *Mechanical Comprehension Test, Form AA,* Psychological Corporation, 1941.

[37] From *The AAF Qualifying Examination,* edited by Frederick B. Davis, United States Government Printing Office, 1947.

ESSENTIALS OF APTITUDE-TESTING METHODS

Job Analysis

The first requirement in aptitude testing is a careful functional analysis of the job or performance for which the test or set of tests is to be constructed. In many of its aspects this analysis is necessarily a judgmental affair, but it is by no means merely an "arm-chair" undertaking. When possible, information is obtained by first-hand observation of and participation in the job. Information is also obtained by interrogation of individuals on the job, especially those who are skilled or expert in performance; by consultation with others who have had opportunity for extended observation; and by study of the relevant scientific literature about the job or performance.

Because the specific functions involved in almost any performance—whether it be learning arithmetic, learning the details of a filing system, operating a lathe, or flying a plane—are quite numerous, it is helpful to organize these functions into various broad categories. A suggested set of categories, which conforms to current usage and thinking in the field of aptitude testing, is as follows:

1. Sensory abilities
2. Physical abilities
3. Perceptual abilities (including speed of perception)
4. Psychomotor abilities (including dexterities and athletic abilities)
5. Mechanical abilities
6. Clerical abilities[38]
7. Intellectual abilities (including memory)
8. Esthetic abilities (music, graphic arts, etc.)
9. Speed in different functions

In addition, it should be recognized that various personal-social characteristics, which are beyond the scope of the present chapter, may have an important bearing on the individual's success.

It may be observed, in the list above, that the *plural* form has been used consistently. The reason is that an individual is seldom characterized by a *uniform* level of aptitude within any given field. He may, for example, prove more dexterous in manipulating tweezers than in performing a complicated and delicate assembly job, or he may be much stronger in verbal intellectual functions than in mathematical.

[38] "Clerical abilities" are a composite or combination of sensory, perceptual, intellectual, and psychomotor functions. In addition, attitudes favorable to speed and accuracy in clerical work are very important. Separate listing is given to clerical abilities because the tests in this field are for the most part addressed to clerical abilities as such, rather than to the component functions.

Failure to recognize such differences within the individual is a serious mistake. "Intelligence" is probably more homogeneous than any of the other broad classes of ability mentioned above; but even here it is usually better to speak and think in terms of the components into which intelligence can be analyzed, than in terms of a single "intelligence." Statistical methods have shown that intellectual abilities can be classified into at least the following separate functions: verbal, numerical, spatial, verbal fluency, reasoning, and rote or "associative" memory. In addition, mental speed can be identified [7, 22], although it is not likely that an individual's speed in one type of function is very highly correlated with his speed in another. It must be added that analysis of the full register of human aptitudes is yet far from complete.

Planning the Test

A satisfactory test is fathered by planning and nurtured by experimental and statistical studies. Test planning is guided by many considerations, among which the following are clearly of dominant importance:

a. WHAT IS THE NATURE OF THE CRITERION? Is the criterion complex (divisible into several relatively independent components), or is it unitary? If complex, the test plan should either envisage a *battery* of tests or else aim definitely to measure only one specified aspect of the criterion; if unitary, the test plan can obviously be simpler. For example, flying a plane probably calls for a more heterogeneous, less highly intercorrelated group of aptitudes (intellectual, motor, and mechanical) than does, say, the study of social science; it follows that a wider variety of tests is probably needed for the selection of airplane pilots than of social-science students.

b. IS THE TEST TO SERVE AS PART OF A BATTERY OF TESTS? If so, it is important that the test should not duplicate, i.e., not correlate highly with, the other tests of the battery: for if it does, it will make no significant contribution of its own to what the other tests already accomplish. Thus the addition of another verbal test to a college-entrance test already containing many verbal tests would probably not be efficient.

c. WHAT KIND OF APTITUDE DOES THE TEST AIM TO MEASURE? Past experience indicates, for example, that intelligence tests should generally include a large proportion of verbal items or tasks,[39] whereas psychomotor tests generally require the use of apparatus of one sort

[39] Except in tests designed for very young children or for foreign-born adults who have not acquired facility in English.

or another (in this field paper-and-pencil tests alone are definitely not adequate).[40]

d. IS THE TEST TO BE USED FOR "DIFFERENTIAL PREDICTION"? Recently a healthy interest has developed in differential prediction—the use of test scores to predict whether, and to what extent, an individual can succeed *better* in one field than another, e.g., engineering versus business administration. *Any* prediction is fallible; but when *two* predictions are involved (one for success in engineering, the other for success in business administration), the difference between the two predictions is generally more fallible than either prediction alone. It follows that tests which are to be used in differential prediction must be *more accurate* than tests which will be put to less exacting use. If a "reliability coefficient" of .90 is set as the standard for ordinary aptitude tests, then a definitely higher coefficient, say .95, may be considered the minimum acceptable for an aptitude test to be used in differential prediction. (The "reliability coefficient" is discussed in a later section.)

e. IS THE INFORMATION FROM THE TEST TO BE CONSIDERED TENTATIVE AND AUXILIARY, OR FINAL AND EXCLUSIVE? If the former, a shorter and less elaborate test may be adequate, since presumably the test scores will be verified by a subsequent test (or by some other means) and interpreted in the light of supplementary information.

f. WHAT DEGREE OF IMPORTANCE ATTACHES TO THE USE OF THE TEST? Aptitude tests are, in general, used either for guidance or selection. The more important the decision involved, the more important it is that the test be carefully constructed, of adequate length, and thoroughly validated. Thus a test for college entrance has to be longer and more thorough than, say, a test for the sectioning of children into a "high" versus a "middle" group in reading.

g. TO WHOM WILL THE TEST BE ADMINISTERED? Paper-and-pencil tests are generally inappropriate for preschool children or seriously retarded adults. In general, group tests cannot be successfully administered to young children who have not yet learned to read well, to uncooperative or resistant "problem" children, or to adults who are seriously abnormal (retarded, deteriorated, or psychotic).

h. HOW MANY INDIVIDUALS WILL BE EXAMINED ON THE TEST? The Army and the Navy, during the last war, had to examine millions of men. As a result, it was necessary to select or construct reasonably short paper-and-pencil tests that could be administered in large groups.

i. HOW MUCH TIME CAN BE DEMANDED OF THE INDIVIDUALS WHO WILL TAKE THE TEST? Many aptitude testers, if given a free hand, would

[40] The best-known of the paper-and-pencil tests aiming to measure psychomotor functions is the MacQuarrie Test for Mechanical Ability [2, pp. 37–38].

require 2 or 3 days of testing time from each individual. In many school situations and in the armed forces during peacetime, this is both feasible and desirable. Ordinarily, however, the time available for testing is more limited.

j. HOW QUICKLY IS THE TEST NEEDED? Paper-and-pencil tests can generally be constructed and tried out much more rapidly than apparatus tests.

k. LASTLY, WHAT RESOURCES ARE AVAILABLE for test construction, test administration, test scoring, statistical analysis, determination of norms, and final interpretation of test results? If resources are limited, it may be better to plan a short "screening" test, rather than a more lengthy or definitive measure.

As mentioned in a previous section, the tasks presented by an aptitude test can be either novel or learned. The risk in using learned tasks is that some individuals, through no fault or lack of their own, may have suffered from severely limited learning opportunities. Despite this theoretical risk, learned tasks are frequently a successful part of an aptitude test, either because most individuals have enjoyed sufficient opportunity for learning, or because only individuals without aptitude fail to create or make use of opportunities for learning. Thus the vocabulary test can, in ordinary circumstances, serve successfully as part of an intelligence test. It is rarely desirable, however, to use *only* learned tasks in an aptitude battery: and the planners of an aptitude test must make a "working guess" to what extent learned tasks should be included.

Another problem in planning is to decide whether to measure (*a*) analyzed-out elements of ability, (*b*) whole functions, or (*c*) something in between these two extremes. As an example of a test measuring a whole function we might mention a test of paragraph reading. In such a test, the individual is not ordinarily measured separately for perceptual responses, knowledge of vocabulary, etc.: all the functions of reading are measured at once. The Complex Coordination Test (Fig. 9) is an example of a test measuring, not specific elements, and certainly not the whole function of flying an airplane, but something in between. The pitch-discrimination test, used in tests of musical aptitude, is an example of a test measuring a fairly narrow, elemental ability. The choice between the measurement of elements versus larger functions will depend on the comparative success of these two types of measurement in the hands of previous investigators, on the adequacy with which the larger function can be analyzed into its elements, on the degree to which the elements lend themselves to measurement, and on the intercorrelation between scores on the elements (the lower the correlation, the more important that each element be measured separately). An advantage of the measurement of elements is that it provides information sufficiently detailed to indicate *why* a person fails or succeeds; a disadvantage is that the measurement of numerous elements requires numerous tests and much time. Ideally, one would measure both elements and wholes. At the present time the measurement of elements is largely restricted to sensory functions and reaction time.

In paper-and-pencil tests containing more than one kind of item, e.g., an intelligence test containing vocabulary items, sentence-completion items, and arithmetical reasoning items, it is necessary to decide whether the items should be arranged in the form of *subtests* (each subtest containing only a single type of item), or in *spiral omnibus* form (one type of item following the other, in repeated cycles, with the items becoming more difficult as one progresses through the test). There is little empirical evidence concerning the comparative advantages of these two forms. If separate scores for the different kinds of items are desired, it is more convenient to organize the items into subtests.

Still other matters that require consideration in the planning of a test are:

a. FORM OF ITEMS OR TASKS. Mention has already been made of the differing suitability of apparatus versus pencil-and-paper tasks for measuring different aptitudes, and the important practical advantages of the paper-and-pencil form. In paper-and-pencil aptitude tests the multiple-choice item is the type most commonly employed.

b. DIFFICULTY OF THE TEST. In general, *most* of the items or tasks in an aptitude test should be of approximately "50 per cent difficulty"[41] for the group of individuals to whom the test will be

[41] A more exact statement would take into account (*a*) the factor of guessing, by which an individual executes some items or tasks correctly despite lack of knowledge or ability; and (*b*) the factor of speed, by which an individual may fail to reach some items or tasks which he could have executed correctly, had he been allowed sufficient time. The speed factor can be eliminated by lengthening the time limit sufficiently. This is not always practical, however, because of the limited time available for testing; moreover, it is possible that excessively long (as well as excessively short) time limits may adversely affect test validity. In multiple-choice items, the factor of guessing may be taken into account by a formula for "correction for chance":

$$\text{Corrected score} = R - \frac{W}{n-1}$$

where R = number of items answered right, W = number of items answered wrong, and n = number of alternatives in each item. For a test composed of two-choice items (such as a true-false test), $n = 2$, and the formula reduces to given; a few items or tasks should be harder, and a few should be easier. Some very easy items may be used at the beginning of the test in order to get the examinees off to a pleasant start; but in general, neither very easy nor very hard items serve efficiently in discriminating among the majority of the cases.[42]

c. LENGTH OF THE TEST AND NUMBER OF "SCORABLE UNITS." In planning the length of a test, two basic considerations are (*a*) the degree of accuracy of measurement that is desired, and (*b*) the time available for testing. When time is severely limited, it may be necessary to abandon the measurement of "wholes" (which provide relatively few scorable units) and resort to the measurement of elements; thus, a 15-minute reading test will generally yield unreliable results, whereas a 15-minute vocabulary test containing numerous separate items will generally yield highly reliable scores. Of course, a vocabulary test does not measure exactly the same aptitude as a reading test, and it is an open question whether the test constructor should insist upon getting the time needed for his original purpose. Frequently, however, the limitation of time is inherent in the situation and inescapable.

d. TIME LIMITS. If the test is to be administered by persons comparatively untrained in testing, it is desirable that the time limits be set in terms of large, familiar units, such as quarter-hours or, at the finest, 5-minute intervals. The shorter the time limit, the greater is the proportional error if somewhat too little or too much time is allowed by the test administrator. In general, the time limit for the *tryout* of a test should be longer than that for regular administration, because it is desirable, in the tryout, that all or nearly all individuals answer all items, including those at the end of the test. Although the time limit for the regular administration of the test can be kept the same as in the tryout, experience suggests that a shorter time limit results in more efficient use of the available testing time, in the sense that more tests can thus be crowded into a given testing period. Experimental study is needed to determine to what extent aptitude tests can be

---

$R - W$. Thus if, in a 100-item true-false test, the average individual answered 75 per cent of the items right and 25 per cent of the items wrong, the corrected average score (which in this case is also the corrected average difficulty of the test, or the corrected average item-difficulty) would be $75 - 25 = 50$ per cent. It should be noted that W in the formula refers to the number of items *actually answered wrong;* it does not include items that were omitted or never reached by the examinee.

[42] For certain special purposes a departure from the 50 per cent rule is desirable. Thus, in the examination of scholarship applicants, where the purpose is to differentiate only among the very superior, the test should contain a much larger proportion of difficult items.

"speeded" by short time limits without causing significant loss in test validity.

e. SCORING. The two chief problems under scoring are, first, whether to "correct for guessing" by penalizing individuals for wrong answers; and, second, whether to obtain one or more scores from the test. The current practice, in general, is to avoid true-false items, which are especially subject to guessing-effects, and to allow a reasonably ample time limit, so that a majority of the examinees can genuinely attempt each item, instead of being forced to make a series of quick guesses toward the end. Under these circumstances the quick and simple scoring procedure—based simply on number right, without any correction for guessing—becomes justifiable. Whether more than one score should be obtained from the test depends on whether the test is composed of homogeneous or disparate tasks.

Considerable space has been devoted in this section to the planning of the test, because in practice the *final* version of a test is generally rather closely similar to the *first*. The best tests are a product of sophisticated planning, clever and conscientious construction, and adequate trial. Each of these steps calls for knowledge, experience, and insight.

Test Construction

Test construction gives concrete expression to the test plan. The various steps in test construction are presented briefly below.

a. PREPARATION OF ITEMS OR TASKS. Apprenticeship, example, and experience seem to furnish the chief guides to aptitude-test construction. Detailed and explicit rules have been drawn up for the preparation of achievement-test items [12, 16], but these rules frequently require basic modification for aptitude-test purposes. Such aptitude items as are constructed must, of course, conform to the test plan, with respect to type of content, form, average level of difficulty, range of difficulty, etc. A moderate *surplus* of items is constructed in order to permit the selection of what appear to be superior items, and the replacement of items subsequently rejected in the process of editing or on the basis of actual trial.

b. ORGANIZATION OF ITEMS INTO SUBTESTS OR CYCLES If more than one kind of item or task is included in the test, the items are generally organized into subtests or cycles (see page 518). In any case the items are arranged in order of estimated difficulty, from easy to most difficult; this is essential, since otherwise an individual might spend a great deal of time working on difficult items that appear early in the test, while failing, through lack of time, to attempt later, easier items that he could have answered correctly. The number of items included in the test or subtest depends on several factors, which must be estimated either in advance or on the basis of previous experience: (1) the importance or value of the test, (2) the number of items needed to obtain a reliable, dependable score, and (3) the "attrition" due to rejection of items as a result of editing or actual trial.

c. EDITING. The purpose of editing is to examine the test critically, eliminate defects, and make improvements. Such questions as the following are considered in editing: (1) Does the item or task appear valid; i.e., will it measure what the test or subtest is intended to measure? (2) Is the item or task unambiguous? (3) Is the scoring key correct; i.e., is the supposedly correct answer or performance the only one which is justifiable or proper? (4) Does the test hit the appropriate difficulty level? (5) Is the test correct in all formal aspects (grammar, punctuation, spelling, and format)? Finally, all other aspects of the test are edited, particularly the directions for administration and the directions for scoring (see below).

d. PREPARATION OF TEST MANUAL. A motto of the Adjutant General's Office in World War II was: "The manual is part of the test!" The manual includes directions for administering, timing, and scoring the test. Unless these directions are clear and adequate, uniformity is impossible, with resulting injury to the validity of the test and injustice to individual examinees. A well-prepared manual insures that examinees will be (1) warned not to spend too much time on any one item, (2) advised to attempt items in consecutive order, (3) told whether to guess at items concerning which they are uncertain, and (4) given as clear an indication as possible of the relative importance of speed versus accuracy.

e. PREPARATION OF ANSWER SHEETS AND SCORING KEYS. In most modern paper-and-pencil tests answers are recorded not in the test booklet but on a separate answer sheet. The preparation of the test manual, answer sheets, and scoring keys constitutes the final "constructive" steps in the preparation of a test. Additional steps include preparing copy for the printer and checking printer's proofs to insure that the final test is free from error.

Tryout, Statistical Analysis, and External Validation

Once an aptitude test has been constructed, the prime question is: How can we be sure that the test is any good? If it is granted that the test was well planned, and the plan cleverly executed, the question still remains whether we have on our hands merely a well-planned and clever mistake. Evidence on the worth of a test is obtained by trial, statistical analysis, and external validation. These processes are described below.

TRIAL. The tryout of a test may be divided into three steps: (1) sampling, (2) administering, and (3) scoring. Under sampling, two essentials of method are: First, the sample subjects chosen for the tryout must, so far as possible, be *similar* to the group for whom the test is devised. Thus, if the test is devised for broad use throughout the country, it would be risky to select subjects from only one school system or only one region of the country, since such a selection might not be representative of the total group for whom the test is designed. Second, the sample must be *large,* if dependable findings are to be obtained. No uniform rule can be given for the minimum acceptable size of the sample, since this differs according to various technical considerations (such as the nature and extent of the subsequent statistical analysis of the data). Good practice frequently sets about five hundred cases as the minimum.

It goes without saying that the administration of the trial test must be as carefully and uniformly conducted as that of the final test. Uniformity in directions to the examinees is essential, and other conditions of the trial—such as seating, illumination, and acoustics—must be as consistent as possible. The administration of the trial test presents a good opportunity to observe whether the directions are easily and correctly understood, and whether the test stimulates interest and elicits cooperation. In order to obtain information regarding the proper time limit for the test (or time limits for the separate parts of the test), the examinees may be asked at stated time intervals to encircle the number of the test item on which they are working.

A special requirement of an *aptitude* test is that it be only slightly, if at all, affected by differences in practice or experience. For this reason it is desirable to *retest* at least a part of the tryout sample about a week or two after the original testing, in order to determine the degree to which practice effect operates. Practice effect on most verbal intelligence tests is generally practically negligible, but this seems less true for tests of psychomotor and mechanical aptitudes.

If it is intended to discover to what extent individuals are stable or consistent from one occasion to the next in their responses to the test, it is again necessary to *retest* at least a portion of the total sample, but this time at an interval that will discourage memory or practice effects (say 2 or 3 months). With an immature sample the interval must not be so long that growth effects become sufficiently great to obscure the findings on response consistency.

The scoring of a modern aptitude test is ordinarily a routine matter. In trial tests administered with a time limit, it is becoming more customary to note the point in the test beyond which the individual failed to attempt any more items. To the extent that this point varies from one individual to the next, it is likely that differences in *speed* among individuals played a part in determining differences in test scores.

STATISTICAL ANALYSIS. The data collected by the tryout are fair game for statistical analysis—an indispensable part of the method of appraising tests. Statistical techniques are used also in determining the "external validity" of the test: but more of that later.

The first step in the statistical analysis of test results is to prepare a frequency distribution of the test scores.[43] This is nothing more than a listing of the number of subjects earning each score on the test. Figure 12 is the graph of a frequency distribution of scores made

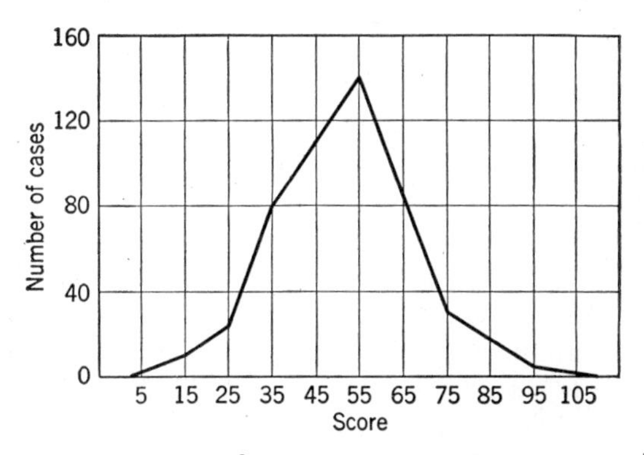

Fig. 12. Distribution of scores on general classification test.

by 500 naval recruits on the United States Navy General Classification Test [4]; the lowest possible score on this test is 0, and the highest possible is 100. It will be observed that: (*a*) the greatest concentration of cases in Fig. 12 occurs at the middle scores; and (*b*) the number of cases decreases as one proceeds from the middle to the extremes of the distribution. From the graph it is clear that (*c*) in the sample tested there is plenty of "top" or "ceiling" to the test, i.e., very few cases make perfect or nearly perfect scores; similarly, there is plenty of "bottom." All three of these characteristics are generally considered favorable in a mental test.

A fundamental requirement of a test is that it measure *consistently*

[43] If the test is composed of subtests, a frequency distribution is, of course, required also for the scores on each subtest.

whatever function it is measuring. There are generally two sources of inconsistency: (*a*) *response error,* i.e., fluctuations in the response of the individual to the same or equivalent items from one occasion to another; and (*b*) *content inconsistency,* i.e., lack of homogeneity in the content of the test. Thus a vocabulary test that included the words hemoglobin (from biology), trudgeon (from swimming), correlation (from statistics), and paradox (from general reading) would obviously be lacking in content homogeneity. Response error is comparatively seldom measured as such, mainly because this type of inconsistency is generally considered only a minor disturbing factor in most aptitude tests. The over-all consistency of measurement by the test is usually determined by means of the *reliability coefficient.* The simplest and most common method of determining the reliability coefficient is as follows: The individual is scored first on all the *odd-numbered* items of the test, and second on all the *even-numbered* items. The correlation is calculated between individuals' scores on the odd-numbered items and their scores on the even-numbered items. This odd-even correlation shows to what extent the odd-numbered half of the test yields results similar to those of the even-numbered half. To find out to what extent the *whole* test would agree with *another* (hypothetical) *similar* test, a statistical correction, called the Spearman-Brown correction, is applied.[44] A good aptitude test is generally expected to have a reliability coefficient of at least .90. The best intelligence tests, requiring an hour or somewhat less of working time, generally meet or surpass this minimum. Tests used in industry and business are frequently very brief (15–20 minutes) and are likely to fall definitely below .90 in reliability.

At least two other steps are carried out in the statistical analysis of a test. Usually a test is composed of two or more subtests, and the test itself may be part of a battery of other tests. The correlation must be calculated between the subtests, and also between the test and the other tests of the battery. In *subtests* designed to measure different facets of a given aptitude, it is generally considered desirable that the intercorrelation be fairly high (about .70–.85), but not so high that one subtest merely duplicates the other.[45] Correlations between different *tests,* however, should be as *low* as possible, so that

[44] This process is explained and illustrated in any standard textbook on psychological statistics. The student may refer to Reference 15.

[45] What seems wanted is a reliable total score, derived from measures of varying but not disparate functions. Thus a verbal score based on 100 opposites items would be reliable but narrow; a verbal score based on, say, 30 opposites, 25 sentence completions, 25 analogies, and 20 proverbs might be preferable. The ultimate check on the comparative merit of the two total verbal scores rests, of course, on the correlation with the criterion (see pages 525–529).

each individual test will make its own contribution to predicting subsequent performance, with a minimum of functional overlap or duplication between the different tests.

Finally, there is the task of studying the *individual items* in each test or subtest. For each item it is customary to determine (*a*) its difficulty (in the sample tested), and (*b*) the correlation between success on the item and score on the subtest of which it is a part. (If the test is not organized into subtests, the correlation is calculated between success on the item and score on the total test.) The difficulty (or rather the ease) of an item is usually determined simply by finding the percentage of persons who answered the item correctly. A slower procedure, preferred by some because of its probably greater validity, is to determine first the number of subjects who *attempted*[46] each item; the difficulty level is then defined as the percentage of successful attempts. Thus, if 400 individuals attempted an item, and 250 answered it correctly, the difficulty (or rather the ease) of the item would be at the 250/400 or 63 per cent level. The correlation between each item and score on the subtest of which the item is a part is usually determined by the statistical technique of *biserial correlation* (or some modification thereof). This is a technical procedure which cannot be discussed here (see reference 15). In selecting items for the final form of the test, those with a low[47] biserial correlation are rejected, on the ground that they are not measuring what the other items in the subtest are measuring.

Only a few items with very low or very high difficulty values are retained in the final test. In general, no item is retained which is passed by fewer than would be expected to answer it correctly by chance. Thus, in a four-choice item, where 25 per cent of the group could answer an item correctly by chance, no item would ordinarily be retained which is answered correctly by fewer than 25 per cent of those who attempt it.

External validation. The chief problem in gold mining is to find the gold, and the chief problem in the external validation of a test is to find good, valid, specific external criteria. "Success on the job" is seldom the best criterion, because no test can be expected to measure all aspects of success; moreover, such a general and usually ill-defined concept as success on the job is itself, in most cases, extremely difficult to measure objectively and adequately. Perhaps the first rule in test validation is that the test must be appraised in relation to the particular purpose for which it was designed. If, for

[46] An individual is considered to have attempted a given item if he answered it or if he answered any item beyond the one in question.

[47] The definition of "low" varies somewhat pragmatically, according as one has a large or a small supply of items with higher biserial correlations.

example, its purpose is to predict a student's average academic performance in college, it is no valid criticism of the test that it fails to measure the student's interest in his work, or his personal-social adjustments in college, or his money income 5 years after graduation. It would be fine, indeed, if some wonder test were devised which could measure "all things for all men." There is no such test. *Good testing means more testing,* in the sense that *many* tests are likely to be needed to make the various appraisals, diagnoses, and predictions that are wanted.

Besides asking the question, "Good for what?" it is necessary to ask, "Good for whom?" Thus, an intelligence test standardized on individuals who have had a "normal" educational and experiential background, would have only limited value or require special interpretation if applied, say, to canal-boat children not attending school, or to "submarginal" mountaineers with little schooling and seriously restricted intellectual experience. Similarly, the Minnesota Mechanical Assembly Test could not be validly applied to persons with unusual experience in the assembly or repair of common mechanical gadgets.

The external criterion usually employed in validating intelligence tests is either school grades in academic subjects, or scores on achievement tests in academic subjects, or both. In line with the current tendency to distinguish between verbal versus numerical or mathematical aptitude, it is desirable also to obtain *specific* measures of school achievement, such as grades in English and history (verbal subjects) versus grades in mathematics. Of course, both grades and achievement-test scores reflect a student's interest, effort, application in a course, as well as his intellectual aptitude; to this extent, grades and achievement-test scores must be considered inadequate as criteria. It would be more appropriate, in the validation of intelligence tests, to exclude students who, by their own admission and the testimony of their teachers, failed to apply themselves to their course work.

In general, the correlation between scores on a good, reasonably long intelligence test, requiring 1 or 2 hours for administration, and average college grades is about .50; when achievement is measured by good objective *tests* of adequate length, the correlation between intelligence-test scores and average college achievement rises to about .60. The correlation with achievement in elementary or high school is generally appreciably higher than with achievement in college.[48]

[48] One reason for the lower correlation with college achievement is the greater restriction in *range* of ability among college students. Such restriction in range tends to lower the validity coefficient of a test in somewhat the same fashion as

For tests of aptitudes other than intelligence, the criteria commonly used include quantity of output; quality of output (accuracy; freedom from errors, imperfections, or spoilage); freedom from accidents; job knowledge; trainability, learning ability, or "general aptitude" on the job; permanence in the position (as contrasted with discharge for inability); and rise in salary or rank. These criteria are obviously not of equal merit; for example, permanence in the position is not so valuable a datum as quality of output. Ideally, of course, one would make use of *multiple, specific, objective* criteria. In business and industry, supervisors' and foremen's ratings constitute the usual criterion; but such ratings tend to be of very uneven quality, depending on degree of familiarity with the individual's work, the standards of the supervisor or foreman, and many other factors. Sometimes the test scores of two *extreme groups* (one known to be definitely superior, the other definitely inferior) are compared; a large, reliable differentiation of the two groups is evidence that the test is valid. Sometimes, again, *another test* is employed as the criterion for a new test. Such "circular validation" is occasionally justifiable, especially if the test employed as a criterion has been well validated, and if a more direct criterion can be obtained only with long delay and great expense. Ultimately, test validity must rest on correlation with direct criteria which are themselves of acknowledged soundness and validity.

The best studies of test validity undertake to determine not only the correlation of a test with specific, well-defined aspects of the criterion, but also the *unique contribution* of the test. Thus, although a clerical test may be valid in itself, it may add little to what is already known about an applicant through inspection of his record in a well-managed commercial high school.

Another quality which is being increasingly required of an aptitude test is that it be serviceable for *differential* prediction. Educational advisers, personnel managers, and the Army and Navy all are in need of instruments which will validly indicate whether John Smith is better suited for course A or course B, position M or position N, specialty X or specialty Y.

The whole process of trial, statistical analysis, and external valida-

---

restriction in the range of differences among contestants at a beauty show tends to render the judges' decision more difficult and, in consequence, less valid. Probably another reason is the greater "specificity" of both intelligence and achievement at the college level, i.e., the fact that different intelligence subtests correlate lower with each other at the college level than at earlier levels, and similarly the fact that grades in different courses correlate lower with each other at the college level. Students interested in pursuing this subject are recommended to the works edited by Monroe and Conrad respectively. (See general references under Suggested Reading at the end of the chapter.)

tion has as its main purpose the collection of evidence answering the questions: Is this test *practical* (with respect to administration and scoring)? Is it *valid?* There is, however, one other important purpose: to achieve a better understanding of what the tests and their items measure, and also a better understanding of the nature and limitations of the criterion employed. In illustration of the latter point may be cited a study of grades in a certain trade school. Although the emphasis of the school was supposed to be on the actual operation and repair of equipment, it was found that an entrance test of arithmetical reasoning correlated higher with instructors' marks than either an entrance test of mechanical aptitude or one of mechanical knowledge. Further investigation showed that the instructors were allowing grades in shop mathematics to have an inordinate influence upon final term marks.

Lest it appear that the processes of trial, statistical analysis, and external validation represent merely formal requirements glorified by academic theoreticians, we present below a list of the items in the first and last published forms of the AAF Qualifying Examination (prepared for the preliminary selection of flying officer-personnel in the Army Air Forces [6]). It can be seen at a glance that the last test differs markedly from the first. As more validity data are accumulated and additional insights gained, it is quite likely that still further changes—in content, administration, timing, or scoring—will be made in this test. The following quotation on the validity of the AAF Qualifying Examination may be of interest at this point: " . . . in an experimental group of 1,003 essentially unselected applicants for pilot

	Number of Items	
Type of Items	Initial Test	Last Test*
General vocabulary	45	0
Technical vocabulary	0	5
Reading comprehension	15	15
Contemporary affairs	30	0
Pilot aviation information	0	20
Driving information	0	10
Flying information	0	10
Vocational and avocational information	0	5
Hidden figures	0	25
Mechanical comprehension	15	55
Practical judgment	15	5
Mathematics	30	0

*This was the last form published during the war. Seven types of items not listed in the table were employed in forms of the examination between the first and the seventeenth.

training, 35 per cent of the 598 who obtained at least a passing mark [on this test] graduated from advanced pilot training, while only 11 per cent of the 405 men who failed to attain a passing mark on the same test graduated from advanced pilot training" [6, p. 231].

Revision

At any point after the tryout the test may undergo revision. It is, of course, one of the main purposes of the tryout and subsequent statistical analysis to reveal the weak spots of the test and to suggest possibilities for improvement. Revision may affect the directions, the time limits, the individual items, the organization of items into subtests, the sequence of items within the subtests, the average difficulty of the test, the range of difficulty of items in the test. The test is usually shortened in revision through the exclusion of items or subtests shown to be inferior or defective.

Norms

Suppose that John Smith is informed that he has answered correctly 80 items of a verbal-aptitude test; he may fairly ask, "Is that good?" Such a question illustrates the need for *norms*. Norms are obtained by administering the test to a large sample of individuals similar to those for whom the test was devised. The most common type of norm for aptitude tests is the percentile norm; this simply states what percentage of cases (of a given age, or in a given group) falls below a particular score. If, for example, 90 per cent of graduating high-school seniors made a verbal-aptitude score below 80, then Smith's "percentile score" (in reference to graduating high-school seniors) would be 90, which is ordinarily considered quite good. Of course, Smith's percentile score in a group of *college students* would be lower than 90, because the competition is keener in the college group, i.e., the average verbal-aptitude score is higher. This illustrates the relativity of norms — which, incidentally, is one of the basic reasons for the necessity and usefulness of norms.

A type of norm which takes into account two variables at the same time is the *intelligence quotient*. Here the individual's performance on a mental test is expressed in terms of "mental age" (thus, a child whose performance is at the level of the typical 12-year-old would be given a mental age of 12); and the mental age is divided by the person's chronological age to yield the intelligence quotient or IQ. The formula for the IQ is:

$$IQ = 100\left(\frac{MA}{CA}\right)$$

where MA refers to mental age, and CA to chronological age. Thus, in our example, if the child with the MA of 12 were only 10 years and 2 months old, his IQ would be 100 (144/122 months), or 118. The *accomplishment quotient* (AQ), which compares educational achievement with intellectual ability, is obtained in a manner similar to the intelligence quotient. *Exceedingly accurate* measures of both educational achievement and intelligence are necessary if an accurate, dependable determination of the accomplishment quotient is to be obtained. In passing, it should be pointed out that not all IQ's (or AQ's) are comparable; an IQ of 120 on one test may not have the same meaning as an IQ of 120 on another test. The discrepancy arises mainly from differences in the detailed nature of the functions measured by the different tests.

At the present time it is fairly common to plot a graph of all the test scores made by an individual (the original or "raw" scores being first converted, ordinarily, to percentile scores). Such a graph is called a test "profile." In interpreting a test profile, not only the level of the individual's scores is taken into account, but also *differences* between scores. Norms of the *differences* between scores are rarely available. This appears to be a serious lack in our aptitude-test resources.

Combining Scores from Different Tests or Measures

It is common for the scores on a test to be combined with information from other sources, in order to obtain the best possible prediction of an individual's performance on the criterion. If properly executed, such a combination of measures is never less efficient than the most valid single measure in the combination, and sometimes is appreciably more efficient. If poorly executed, however, it is possible that the additional information, instead of supplementing or strengthening a good test, will serve merely to dilute or weaken it. The problem is one of weighting, i.e., of seeing that each test or measure is allowed to exert its proper influence or weight in the total or composite score. If all the data are quantitative, the technique of multiple correlation [15] is applicable, except in unusual circumstances, and supplies the proper weights. One then multiplies the score on each test or variable by its proper weight and obtains the sum of these weighted scores;

this weighted sum will correlate higher with the criterion than a sum obtained with any other set of weights. Sometimes, however, the data are not all quantitatively expressed. Thus, when an interviewer evaluates a person's test scores in the light of the subject's "background, education, training, and interests," formally quantitative measures of background, education, training, and interests are seldom available. The final outcome, ordinarily, is a net rating by the interviewer of the estimated over-all merit of the individual; this rating may be expressed on a three-point scale ("below average," "average," "above average"), on a five-point scale, or on a scale containing still more steps. In any event, it is highly important to *determine empirically whether the final, net rating yields results better than could be obtained by the quantitative test data alone.* In one well-authenticated study [5], based on 3496 cases, it was found that a combination of scores on an arithmetical reasoning and an electrical knowledge test correlated .50 with grades in a school for electrician trainees; whereas the interviewers' net ratings (based on the test scores, plus consideration of the individual's background, education, experience, and interests) correlated only .41 with grades. Evidently a good deal of effort was spent to *reduce* the validity of prediction! Nor did the interviewers' ratings seem to lead to the selection of men better qualified in personal-social characteristics. Such a study emphasizes again the importance of *empirical validation.*

STABILITY OF TEST SCORES

The longtime usefulness of an aptitude test is increased if individuals' scores on the test are stable from one year to the next. Thus, it is generally agreed that intelligence tests taken during the junior year of high school are as useful for predicting college aptitude as tests taken at the end of the senior year, and some authorities say the same for tests taken in the seventh grade of elementary school. Such longtime stability enables earlier planning. In general, the longtime stability of aptitudes other than intelligence has not been thoroughly investigated.

FACTOR ANALYSIS

The number of separate aptitude tests that have been constructed or that can be constructed is legion. Confronted with a bewilderingly large number of tests, one may on *a priori* or on "logical" grounds classify some tests as measuring intelligence, others as measuring spatial ability, etc. But *a posteriori* proof is required before such a classification of tests or aptitudes can be accepted. The identification and classification of aptitudes are properly experimental and quantitative undertakings.

Among quantitative methods "factor analysis" is only one—and not necessarily the most convincing one. Probably experiments which study the effect of specific training or of transfer of training are more convincing than factor analysis. Such experiments, however, are time-consuming; moreover, the results may sometimes themselves be best interpreted with the aid of factor analysis. Factor analysis is by no means opposed to other methods for the better identification and understanding of what a test measures.

The method of factor analysis is undeniably technical from a statistical point of view; in essence, however, the logic of the method is simple. The most natural way to determine what a test measures is to find out (*a*) with what variables the test is correlated, and (*b*) with what variables the test is uncorrelated. (Of course, correlation is a quantitative affair: it is not merely present or absent but can vary between +1 and −1.) If one determines the correlations among a number of tests, he is likely to observe some similarities and differences in those for the various tests—and thus to arrive at an improved understanding and classification of this group of tests. An early study by Schneck [17] may serve as an example. Schneck applied nine tests to 210 students in a college class in general psychology. The tests included (*a*) vocabulary, (*b*) opposites, (*c*) analogies, (*d*) sentence completion, (*e*) disarranged sentences, (*f*) arithmetical reasoning, (*g*) number-series completion, (*h*) equation relations, and (*i*) mental multiplication. Schneck observed that the *verbal* tests had an average intercorrelation, each with the other, of .49; the *numerical* tests had an average intercorrelation, each with the other, of .34; but the average "cross correlation" between the verbal and the numerical tests was only .14. From such results it is a fair "hunch," which Schneck verified by suitable statistical analysis, that (*a*) a verbal-ability factor underlies the first five tests; (*b*) a number-ability factor underlies the next four tests; and (*c*) a low degree of correlation prevails between the verbal and numerical factors.

Schneck's problem was a simple one. Had the number of tests been, say, 57, as it was in a study by L. L. Thurstone, a mere inspection or calculation of average intercorrelations could not possibly disentangle all the interrelations in such a large table of correlations. (With 57 tests, the number of correlations is (57 times 56)/2, or 1596.) Using statistical methods devised largely by himself, Thurstone [19] found seven clear factors among the 57 tests: *V* (verbal ability), *N* (facility in simple numerical operations), *S* (spatial visualizing in two or three dimensions), *W* (fluency in producing unconnected words that meet certain restrictions or requirements), *P* (perceptual speeds, or "facility in perceiving detail that is imbedded in irrelevant material"), *M* (rote memory), and *I* (inductive reasoning). Two other factors were also tentatively identified. No general-intelligence factor was found in this study, conducted with college students as the subjects. In a later study of a large sample of children in the eighth grade of elementary school, L. L. and T. G. Thurstone [20] did observe a general-intelligence factor, which they interpreted as accounting for the positive correlation prevailing among the other factors. A study of a sample of adults by the War Manpower Commission [22] also revealed a general-intelligence factor, besides most of the other factors identified by L. L. Thurstone.

It is impossible, within the limited space of a brief chapter, to discuss factor analysis at much greater length. The method, while uniquely valuable, is not a panacea. Certainly it does not replace shrewd observation and interpretation, nor does it in any way reduce the need for clever test construction. Three major limitations of factor analysis may be noted: (*a*) There is some disagreement concerning the best statistical methods to be employed in factor analysis; experimental, statistical, and mathematical studies are needed to settle this issue. (*b*) So far, it has not been possible to find or construct tests which provide pure measures of the factors; this leads to serious limitations and complications [18, pp. 102–129]. (*c*) Factor analysis yields *statistical* results, i.e., results which are true *on the average*, but which may not apply to any particular individual. This last objection would, of course, apply to practically all statistical findings. In defense, it may be pointed out that the average has its own intrinsic importance, and that the study of an individual proceeds most safely and judiciously if a background of the normal (as expressed in the statistical average) is kept in mind.

EFFECTUATING FACTORS

It would be a mistake to suppose that aptitudes exist or operate in splendid isolation from the rest of the personality. It seems obvious that interest, aspirations, effort, and persistence play a part in effectuating a person's aptitudes. Aptitude tests are useful in determining those who can; they are generally of negligible value for determining those who can but won't. In long-time follow-up studies of validity, another factor is the *opportunity* to make good. Opportunities are not always distributed with even-handed justice; and various personal-social skills are required in order to hang on to a favorable opportunity once it has been been gained. All these factors tend generally to blur the relation between aptitude-test scores and performance on the criterion. Obviously, some control of these "effectuating factors" is desirable in any validity study of aptitude-test scores.

USES OF APTITUDE TESTS

Aptitude tests are used in educational guidance and (at the college level) in educational selection; in occupational guidance and occupational selection; in recreational guidance (especially in the field of music); and in personal counseling. Numerous administrative uses are made of aptitude tests; thus, school superintendents expect a higher level of performance from schools in which the children are characterized by superior aptitudes. During World War II the Army and Navy made extensive use of aptitude tests, and devoted considerable effort toward producing additional tests especially suited to their needs. Aptitude tests also have a bearing on social issues, such as immigration and various social-class distinctions (the Hitlerian dogma of the superiority of an "Aryan race" was clearly disproved by the evidence from aptitude tests). Most important, fundamentally, is the use of aptitude tests for purposes of investigation or research. Aptitude tests are used in research on the nature of human abilities and in the study of motivation, learning, delinquency, and other psychological issues. Aptitude tests are also of basic or accessory importance in research on numerous educational, industrial, military, and social problems.

TRENDS

Certain trends in the investigation and appraisal of aptitudes are worth noting. The following discussion is limited to aptitude tests, rather than ratings, records, interviews, etc., because tests are generally the most useful and economical means of aptitude measurement.

In the first place, aptitude tests appear to be enjoying an increase in public recognition and acceptance. Concomitantly with this gain in status, the scope of measurement has expanded beyond the field of intelligence to include such areas as mechanical aptitudes, motor coordination, and administrative or executive aptitudes. In this process of expansion, the distinction between aptitude and achievement has not been so carefully respected as in the older field of intelligence testing. This seems a step backward.

An outstanding advance has been the increased recognition of the specificity or distinguishable components of intelligence and other aptitudes. The chief credit for this goes to the technique of factor analysis; the development of factor-analysis techniques has been an outstanding accomplishment. The use of factor analysis in the study of aptitude tests has continued to increase.

The adaptation of tests to machine scoring continues. However, some new tests are appearing which in their present form cannot be scored by machine; these are mainly tests of fluency in writing and in the production of ideas. Whether machine-scorable items can be devised that will be useful for the measurement of fluency-abilities remains to be seen.

A healthy emphasis has been growing on the importance of obtaining better external criteria for the validation of tests. The Army Air Forces made an outstanding effort to carry through long-term validation (from initial examination to performance in each of the successive training schools and finally to actual combat). It remains to be seen to what extent this splendid wartime example will bear peacetime fruit.

The statistical analysis of tests has improved considerably. Samples are larger; attention is being paid to the effect of the speed factor on measures of reliability and validity; and item analyses are being more widely and adequately conducted.

Taken altogether, the trends which have been noted add up to what may be termed an increasing institutionalization of aptitude-testing research. Research has become a longtime and expensive affair, which no ordinary individual is able to manage alone. In this respect aptitude-testing research is similar to medical research, atomic research, and industrial research. Although the individual is ever the source of original ideas, the execution of these ideas generally calls for the combined, coordinated resources of a complete organization. The day of the individual man, pitting his abilities against ignorance and falsehood, is gone. It would be well if this fact were more widely recognized and accepted.

SUMMARY

Aptitude refers to potential achievement. Tests, rather than ratings, interviews, or records, are the principal means for the practical appraisal of intelligence and other aptitudes. Pages 504–513 provide a few illustrations of the various types of tasks included in aptitude tests.

The preparation of an aptitude test is a lengthy process which starts with a job analysis, and proceeds through the steps of: planning the test; constructing the test; giving the test a trial in an appropriately drawn sample; analyzing the data obtained by the trial; revising the test; validating the test against a suitable external criterion (or against suitable external criteria); preparing norms; and determining the proper weights for combining the test scores with other measures.

The technique of factor analysis is uniquely valuable for the identification of basic aptitudes. Certain limitations of factor analysis were noted in the text.

It is important to realize that aptitudes do not exist or operate in splendid isolation from the rest of the personality. Aptitude tests are designed to discover "those who can," but are of negligible value for identifying "those who can, but won't."

Among the important trends in aptitude testing are: an increase in public recognition and prestige; a continuing expansion to fields beyond intelligence; improved statistical analysis; the development of factor-analysis techniques; emphasis on the distinguishable components of intelligence and other aptitudes; and emphasis on the importance of obtaining better external criteria for the validation of tests.

REFERENCES

1. Babcock, H. An experiment in the measurement of mental deterioration. *Arch. Psychol.*, 1930, No. 117.
2. Bennett, G. K., and R. M. Cruikshank. *A Summary of Manual and Mechanical Ability Tests* (preliminary form). New York: Psychological Corporation, 1942.
3. Buros, O. K. *The 1940 Mental Measurements Yearbook.* Highland Park, N. J.: Mental Measurements Yearbook, 1941.
4. Conrad, H. S. *A Statistical Evaluation of the Basic Classification Test Battery (Form I).* Washington, D. C.: Office of Scientific Research and Development, 1945.
5. Conrad, H. S., and G. A. Satter. *The Use of Test Scores and Quality-Classification Ratings in Predicting Success in Electrician's Mates School.* Washington, D. C.: Office of Scientific Research and Development, 1945.
6. Davis, Frederick B., Ed. *The AAF Qualifying Examination.* Washington, D. C.: United States Government Printing Office, 1947.
7. DuBois, Philip Hunter. A speed factor in mental tests. *Arch. Psychol.*, 1932, No. 141.
8. Durflinger, Glenn W. The prediction of college success: a summary of recent findings. *J. Amer. Assoc. Collegiate Registrars*, 1943, *19*, 68–78.
9. Goodenough, F. L. *Measurement of Intelligence by Drawings.* Yonkers, N. Y.: World Book Company, 1926.

10. GREENE, E. B. *Measurements of Human Behavior.* New York: Odyssey Press, 1941.
11. GUILFORD, J. P. New standards for test evaluation. *Educ. Psychol. Measurement,* 1946, *6,* 427–438.
12. HAWKES, H. E., E. F. LINDQUIST, and C. R. MANN, Eds. *The Construction and Use of Achievement Examinations.* Boston: Houghton Mifflin, 1936.
13. HILDRETH, G. H. *A Bibliography of Mental Tests and Rating Scales. 1945 Supplement.* New York: Psychological Corporation, 1946.
14. *Machine Methods of Test Scoring. Manual of Procedures.* New York: International Business Machines Corp. (590 Madison Ave.), 1940.
15. PETERS, C. C., and W. R. VAN VOORHIS. *Statistical Procedures and Their Mathematical Bases.* New York: McGraw–Hill, 1940.
16. RINSLAND, H. D. *Constructing Tests and Grading.* New York: Prentice-Hall, 1937.
17. SCHNECK, M. M. R. The measurement of verbal and numerical abilities. *Arch. Psychol.,* 1929, No. 107.
18. THOMSON, G. H. *The Factorial Analysis of Human Ability.* Boston: Houghton Mifflin, 1939.
19. THURSTONE, L. L. Primary mental abilities. *Psychometric Monog.,* No. 1. Chicago: University of Chicago Press, 1938.
20. THURSTONE, L. L., and THURSTONE, T. G. Factorial studies of intelligence. *Psychometric Monog.,* No. 2. Chicago: University of Chicago Press, 1941.
21. TIFFIN, JOSEPH. *Industrial Psychology.* New York: Prentice-Hall, 1942.
22. WAR MANPOWER COMMISSION, DIVISION OF OCCUPATIONAL ANALYSIS. Factor analysis of occupational aptitude tests. *Educ. and Psychol. Measurement,* 1945, *5,* 147–155.
23. WECHSLER, D. *The Measurement of Adult Intelligence.* 3rd Ed. Baltimore: Williams and Wilkins, 1944.

SUGGESTED READING

General

GREENE, E. B. *Measurements of Human Behavior.* New York: Odyssey Press, 1941.

BINGHAM, W. V. *Aptitudes and Aptitude Testing.* New York: Harper, 1937.

PATERSON, D. G., G. G. SCHNEIDLER, and E. G. WILLIAMSON. *Student Guidance Techniques.* New York: McGraw-Hill, 1938.

MONROE, W. S., Ed. *Encyclopedia of Educational Research.* New York: Macmillan, 1941. (Articles on Prognosis, Intelligence and intelligence tests, Adult intelligence, Norms, and Comparable measures.)

CONRAD, H. S., Chairman. Psychological tests and their uses. *Rev. Educ. Res.,* 1947, *17,* No. 1.

BUROS, O. K. *The 1940 Mental Measurements Yearbook.* Highland Park, N. J.: Mental Measurements Yearbook, 1941.

Intelligence

TERMAN, L. M., and M. A. MERRILL. *Measuring Intelligence.* Boston: Houghton Mifflin, 1937.

WECHSLER, D. *The Measurement of Adult Intelligence.* 3rd Ed. Baltimore: Williams and Wilkins, 1944.

Rapaport, D., with the collaboration of Merton Gill and Roy Schafer. *Diagnostic Psychological Testing,* Vol. 1. Chicago: Yearbook Publishers, 1945.

Predicting College Success

Crawford, A. B., and P. S. Burnham. *Forecasting College Achievement.* New Haven: Yale University Press, 1946.

Kandel, I. L. *Professional Aptitude Tests in Medicine, Law, and Engineering.* New York: Teachers College, Columbia University, 1940.

Manual and Mechanical Ability

Bennett, G. K., and R. M. Cruikshank. *A Summary of Manual and Mechanical Ability Tests* (preliminary form). New York: Psychological Corporation, 1942.

Industrial Applications

Stead, W. H., and C. L. Shartle. *Occupational Counseling Techniques.* New York: American Book Company, 1940.

Tiffin, Joseph. *Industrial Psychology.* New York: Prentice-Hall, 1942.

Military Applications

Stuit, D. B., Ed. *Personnel Research and Test Development in the Bureau of Naval Personnel.* Princeton: Princeton University Press, 1947.

Flanagan, J. C., Ed. *The Aviation Psychology Program in the Army Air Forces.* Washington: Government Printing Office, 1947.

Killinger, G. G., Ed. The psychobiological program of the War Shipping Administration. *Applied Psychol. Monog.* No. 12. Stanford University, Calif.: Stanford University Press, 1947.

War Department. Personnel classification tests. (*War Department Tech. Manual,* TM 12–260, April, 1946.) Washington: Government Printing Office, 1946.

Factor Analysis

Thurstone, L. L., and T. G. Thurstone. Factorial studies of intelligence. *Psychometric Monog.* No. 2. Chicago: University of Chicago Press, 1941.

Thomson, Godfrey H. *The Factorial Analysis of Human Ability.* Boston: Houghton Mifflin, 1939.

Chapter 18

Investigating and Appraising Personality

Saul Rosenzweig[1]

PSYCHOLOGY AND PERSONALITY

The definition of *personality,* as distinguished from other areas of psychological interest, has come to involve at least two indispensable ideas: integration and uniqueness. While other aspects of psychological research are directed to this or that segment of behavior, personality invariably has reference, for one thing, to the functioning of the whole man, and, for another, to those aspects of integration that distinguish any individual from his fellow. In studying personality the psychologist is therefore interested in knowing how the individual, in the expression of his needs and his relationships with other individuals, functions as a recognizable unit that possesses certain distinctive traits, drives, attitudes, and habits, and attains or fails to attain an adjustment to himself and to his environment.

It is useful, in thinking about personality, to distinguish it from certain other terms with which it is commonly connected. On the whole, personality does not refer to the goodness or badness of the individual in any moral sense and is thus distinguishable from the word *character,* which is more likely to have that significance. Similarly, the term *temperament* is sometimes used loosely as a synonym for personality. Technically speaking, temperament refers more commonly to certain consistent patterns in the affective or emotional life of the individual—patterns which make for a melancholy or optimistic outlook, an irritable or excessively mild way of taking things. It will thus be seen that temperament includes less than personality.

Psychologists differ in their conceptualization of the personality. To some the behavior of the individual in his immediate environment is all important, whereas to others the immediate environment is

[1] Chief Psychologist, Western State Psychiatric Institute and Clinic; Lecturer, University of Pittsburgh, Pittsburgh, Pennsylvania.

secondary to the effects of early life experience. Another difference consists in stressing relatively static units like trait and habit, on the one hand, or dynamic ones like need and drive, on the other. Closely related to both these differences in theoretical approach is a further, more general one concerned with choosing for emphasis between the conscious and readily verbalized aspects of behavior or the unconscious, implicit, and sometimes irrational parts of the personality. These distinctions are exemplified in the work of three contemporary leaders in personality theory—Allport [1], Lewin [17], and Murray [22]—a comparison of whom may be found elsewhere [26]. The reference is introduced here to bring out the fact that in this still relatively new field of psychology the particular aims and point of view of each investigator determine not only the concepts which he is apt to employ as appropriate to his objectives but also the methods that will be found cropping up in his investigations. Since it is our purpose to survey the entire range of personality investigation, such differences in point of view will be ignored, and instead an effort will be made to present a comprehensive picture of the various designs and devices which an average psychologist has at his disposal.

Although the preceding definition has implied that personality is to be understood as consisting of certain traits, drives, attitudes, habits, etc., all of which have a rather definitely non-physical reference, there are other aspects of personality which are presumed to have their basis in the physiology or physique of the individual. These latter topics are treated in Chapter 15 of this volume. Similarly, it should be noted that for a complete survey of personality the present chapter should be supplemented by Chapter 19 on clinical methods, Chapter 13 on motivation and emotion, Chapter 22 on social behavior, Chapter 21 on child development, and Chapter 17 on intelligence and aptitudes.

Even within the delimited area of this chapter, the treatment of methods for studying personality will not aim at being exhaustive. Instead certain representative devices will be discussed, so that the student may have an understanding of typical approaches rather than a long, lean list of techniques. In the selection to be made, regard for current trends will naturally play a part.

Methods of investigating personality may be conveniently divided on various bases. For the present purpose a division into *subjective, objective,* and *projective* methods has been adopted.

SUBJECTIVE METHODS

The subjective methods are those in which the individual is permitted to disclose what he knows about himself as he takes himself as an object of observation. The extent to which the statements made by the subject are used at face value by the examiner is variable, according to the particular method in question and the orientation of the particular psychologist. In every case, however, these subjective methods are based upon what the subject himself has to say about his traits, attitudes, personal experiences, aims, needs, and interests.

The Autobiography

One important subjective method is the *autobiography*—a narration by the individual, given either freely or according to certain subject headings provided by the examiner, of his experiences throughout life, of his present aims, purposes, interests, and attitudes. As a literary document, the autobiography has, of course, been known at least since Biblical times, but its systematic use by the psychologist is of fairly recent origin. At present it is employed mostly in rather extensive clinical studies of the individual, e.g., when a psychiatrist asks a patient to write such an account to aid in the more complete statement of the problem to be treated, and in such massive approaches to personality as may be found in the *Explorations in Personality* by Murray and his coworkers [22]. An obvious advantage of this device is the relative freedom which it leaves the individual in selecting those parts of his experience which seem to him of importance as a revelation of his personality—an advantage which is naturally increased when the examiner does not provide an outline for the subject to follow. A closely related disadvantage, however, lies in this very same factor of selection, since the subject is apt to pick out only those parts of his experience which he is willing to reveal, or, as with individuals like Rousseau [29], aspects which, while distinctly more private, are unduly emphasized because of some special satisfaction the individual derives from such self-revelation. Nevertheless, the method is of considerable value when it is properly employed and when its results are interpreted in relation to materials otherwise elicited. Even to know what the person thinks about himself or is willing or anxious to tell about his experience is, however partial, of great importance. For a discussion of the autobiography and related personal documents like the diary in the understanding of personality, Allport's monograph [2] may be recommended.

The Case History

The *life history* or *case history,* as employed in the study of personality, is almost invariably dependent to a greater or less extent upon the autobiography. Here, however, sources of information other than the subject's own account of himself are available. Even the autobiography need not be obtained in writing but may come from oral interviews. Interviews, moreover, may involve not only the subject but also his relatives or other close associates. The case-history method has its most common application in the study of abnormal personalities, where the information obtained has an important clinical bearing. The social worker and the psychiatrist employ the method characteristically in their orientation to a new case. Although the usual aim in such application of the life history is to obtain as comprehensive information of the individual's experience and personality as possible, a more recent point of view calls attention to the fact that many things in the life of the individual may have little bearing upon his present personality or upon the problems for which he needs psychological understanding. As a consequence, many psychiatrists and social workers limit the method of the case history to certain spontaneously produced aspects of the individual's experience. It is their opinion that aspects not so brought up by the patient himself are probably of little functional importance in the personality. Naturally, recognition is also given to the fact that complete freedom should be allowed the individual in revealing what he wishes to reveal about himself; in fact, it is precisely in order to make possible the individual's freedom and security in self-revelation that no attempt to probe comprchensively is made by the proponents of the view under discussion. While for research purposes this more specialized use of the life-history method may have less value in certain settings, the very existence of this emphasis brings to light an error that is often made in the use of life histories—the error of supposing that all the experiences of an individual have affected him equally or have, at least, left their mark. Here again, therefore, the method cannot be used without considerable critical interpretation and has its greatest value when employed in connection with information elicited from other sources.

The Interview Method

The *interview,* to which reference has been made in passing, is in itself a most important procedure for the study of personality. The face-to-face relationship in which the subject and the examiner carry on a conversation is so common that it may at first glance seem purely academic to label it as a technical method. Conversations of this sort occur everywhere, and everybody is involved in them every day. From this kind of experience, perhaps more than from anything else, comes the common belief that everyone is a psychologist. We are all continually evaluating the motives, attitudes, and traits of the people with whom we talk or have other living relationships. Actually, however, the method of the interview involves the possibility of great skill or of complete ineptness. The interview is indeed a far cry from the conversation between two friends—so much so that entire books have been devoted to the subject [4, 8]. Naturally, the purpose of the interview will determine to a large extent the technical aspects which will be emphasized, but even when the interview has a specific practical purpose, e.g., in the employment situation, it still represents a method for investigating or appraising personality, since there is hardly a practical relationship that one can think of in which the traits, needs, aims, and other characteristics of the subject would not have to be evaluated.

The chief dimension in respect to which the interview may vary is the rigidity or flexibility with which the interviewer holds to a predetermined outline of questions or topics. In some instances a definite list of points to be covered consecutively in the interview serves as a basis for the procedure. In that case the method requires considerably less skill than when more latitude is allowed the interviewer. Occasionally the topics to be covered are outlined with considerable freedom as to order. The examiner is then able to make a more natural experience out of the interview, the leads offered by the subject being taken as a basis for transition to other topics which the interview is intended to cover. There are, at the full extreme, interviews which are completely free situations—situations in which the examiner refuses to be tied by any set procedure and is more interested in the impact which occurs spontaneously between the subject and himself. As is obvious, an interview conducted in this fashion must depend for its success to a very great extent indeed upon the skill and experience of the interviewer. Closely related to this highly spontaneous type of interviewing is that in which the topics covered, whether predetermined or not, have relatively little to do with the traits that the examiner is attempting to assess. Frequently, in fact, the interviewer is consciously or unconsciously estimating the traits of the interviewee, not from the views the latter may express on a given topic, but by the dogmatism with which these views are stated, by the interest in people or a particular area of experience which the statements reveal, by vocabulary or incidental allusions which the subject employs unwittingly in his conversation. Naturally, the interview under these circumstances becomes a very subtle tool for revealing personality, but, as already said, it then requires a very astute examiner, one skilled in the observation and interpretation of material not anticipated.

Since even the best interview is apt to be influenced by the personality of the interviewer as well as by that of the subject, attempts have been made to provide more objectivity. One such device is to make the interview a matter not of two individuals but of a company in which the subject forms one, and the interviewers, two, three, or more members. Under these circumstances the board of interviewers is able to pool judgments and to bring to bear a variety of standpoints that reduces any personal bias in the interpretation of results. In a field like personality, where subjectivity of judgment is so prevalent and so dangerous, this modification of the interview method has distinct advantages. Once again, however, it cannot be overlooked that there is a closely related disadvantage—the extent to which a board of examiners introduces an atmosphere of greater formality and rigidity than does the sole interviewer.

It may also be mentioned, in order to illustrate the flexibility of the interview method, that a combination of the indirect method of interview (in which the examiner is interested less in the opinions of the subject than in certain implicit aspects of his statements and manner) and of the interview by board has recently been recommended by Freeman and collaborators [5] under the name *stress interview*. In this case the subject is brought before a group of interviewers and asked to perform certain complex tasks, presumably as a test of his intelligence or aptitude for the job. Actually the proficiency of the subject is of little significance, except in so far as his reactions to his own success and failure enable the judges to estimate certain important aspects of the subject's personality. The interviewers, moreover, "heckle" the subject by remarks either directed to him or made in a rather loud whisper among themselves. Each judge is responsible for noting certain features of the subject's behavior for the record. As can readily be seen, the naive subject in a situation of this type is being interviewed under very special circumstances, but at the same time the term interview, although rather distant in meaning from its ordinary conception, is clearly appropriate. The stress interview begins to partake very much of such miniature life situations as will be discussed under the objective methods.

The Inventory Method

Another very commonly employed method of personality study is the *inventory* or *questionnaire*. In this method the subject is presented with a series of statements or questions describing possible emotions, attitudes, or behavior in situations revealing personality, with the instruction to check or otherwise indicate his reaction to or judgment of the test items. One form of such inventories is the cross-out test, in which those remarks, comments, or characterizations which do not apply to the subject are crossed out by him and the remainder left standing. Another form gives optional modes of behavior in a described situation, with the instruction to the subject that he indicate the option appropriate to himself. Occasionally such questionnaires aim to reveal a rather complete picture of the individual's emotional and dispositional life, as is true, for instance, of the Bernreuter Personality Inventory [38]. More specialized uses of the device are also common, e.g., the Terman-Miles M-F Battery for the assessment of masculinity and femininity [39].

Below are five sample items from Guilford's Inventory of Factors *S T D C R* [9]. In this inventory the individual responds to each of 175 such items by encircling *Yes, ?,* or *No,* and a score is obtained on each of five factors: social introversion, thinking introversion, depression, cycloid disposition, and rhathymia.

S	Are you inclined to limit your acquaintances to a select few?......	Yes	?	No
T	Are you inclined to analyze the motives of others?...............	Yes	?	No
D	Are you sometimes so "blue" that life seems hardly worth living?	Yes	?	No
C	Do you have frequent ups and downs in mood, either with or without apparent cause?..	Yes	?	No
R	Are you inclined to act on the spur of the moment without thinking things over?..	Yes	?	No

If a person receives a high score on *S,* it indicates that he is shy and seclusive; *T,* is inclined to meditative or reflective thinking; *D,* is habitually gloomy, pessimistic in mood; *C,* has strong emotional fluctuations and unevenness of disposition; *R,* has a happy-go-lucky and carefree disposition.

It is natural that the inventory approach should have occurred relatively early to psychologists as a way of exploring the complex and diversified field of personality. Presumably the individual knows more about himself than does anyone else, and if he is willing to reveal his knowledge, the obvious thing to do in trying to find out about him is to ask him. Undoubtedly such an approach seems to provide a scope of information which other methods would find it hard to equal, but the validity of such results as are thus obtainable is open to very serious question. As has been pointed out by a number of investigators, the subject (*a*) may not be willing to reveal the facts about himself, and (*b*) may not even be in conscious possession of these facts. Even if the first difficulty could be overcome in certain cases where the confidence of the subject has been guaranteed on a therapeutic or other basis, the problem would still remain of overcoming the subject's ignorance of his own personality.

It is by now well understood that individuals often are unaware of the facts about themselves as regards complex characteristics unacceptable to the conscious ego. In other words, part of the personality is apt to be implicit or unconscious rather than explicitly available to the subject's scrutiny. In fact, an important part of the personality may consist in a certain defensiveness against a knowledge of defects and inadequacies which are painful to contemplate or to integrate with other traits and which can be discovered more readily by others than by oneself. The personality inventory or questionnaire is usually an inept tool for disclosing these obscure regions of the personality and, what is worse, is frequently invalid as a way of revealing even what the subject may know because these unaccepted aspects color the responses to other questions about himself.

The so-called "opinion errors" [25] which are thus involved in the inventory can sometimes be circumvented by indirect cross-checks which have recently been suggested by sophisticated investigators; compare, for example, the *lie* (*L*) score employed in the Minnesota Multiphasic Personality Inventory [14]. By this device it is possible, in this inventory, to evaluate the extent to which a person is falsifying his answers in order to appear more acceptable socially. There are fifteen items from which this control score is computed, e.g., "Once in a while I put off until tomorrow what I ought to do today." Since this illustrative statement has been found to be marked "false" by less than 7 per cent of normal persons, it is assumed that subjects marking this statement "false" for themselves are probably falsifying their answers. The *L* score thus becomes an index of the honesty of the responses to all the questions on the inventory. Corrective devices of this kind naturally increase the value of the inventory but have, up to the present, not succeeded in materially overcoming the basic disadvantages. Nevertheless, the approach remains an important one for the study of an individual's *opinion about himself,* right or wrong as this may be. The inventory or questionnaire can thus be reinterpreted as an instrument for eliciting verbal behavior which needs to be analyzed in relation to other data about the person instead of being accepted at face value as descriptive of what the subject is or does in life situations. This behavioral interpretation of the inventory will be mentioned again later.

A large number of inventories are devoted not only to personality traits and needs, but also to interests, e.g., the Strong Vocational Interest Blank [37]; attitudes, e.g., Harper's Social Study for liberalism and conservatism [10]; and values—economic, esthetic, religious—e.g., the Allport-Vernon Study of Values [42]. These more circumscribed devices share some of the advantages and disadvantages of the general personality inventory, although the disadvantages are perhaps less likely to play a part since one is actually attempting in these cases to study the individual's opinion (interests, attitudes, ideals) rather than more factual matters about his emotional life or behavior in life situations.

OBJECTIVE METHODS

As distinguished from the subjective approaches thus far discussed, the objective methods depend not upon the subject's own statements about himself but upon his overt behavior as revealed to others who serve as observers, examiners, or judges. At this point the methods of appraising personality approach those usually employed for the assessment of intelligence and other more specialized capacities. Proponents of these objective methods for studying personality point out that, just as one would hardly be satisfied with the subject's opinion of his ability in arithmetic and would wish actually to apply a test in which the subject had an opportunity to demonstrate the amount of his arithmetical skill, so in trying to understand personality it is necessary—perhaps even more necessary—to observe the subject in certain life situations where his particular traits, habits, needs, and other characteristics are brought into play and can thus be observed directly by the examiner.

Miniature Life Situations

A name that has been given to the most obvious application of the approach just described is *miniature life situations.* An excellent, and perhaps the earliest, statement of the point of view involved is found in a classical paper by Francis Galton [6], published in 1884. He wrote:

> Emergencies need not be waited for, they can be extemporised; traps, as it were, can be laid. Thus, a great ruler whose word can make or mar a subject's fortune, wants a secret agent and tests his character during a single interview. He contrives by a few minutes' questioning, temptation, and show of displeasure, to turn his character inside out, exciting in turns his hopes, fear, zeal, loyalty, ambition, and so forth. Ordinary observers who stand on a far lower pedestal, cannot hope to excite the same tension and outburst of

feeling in those whom they examine, but they can obtain good data in a more leisurely way. If they are unable to note a man's conduct under great trials for want of opportunity, they may do it in small ones, and it is well that those small occasions should be such as are of frequent occurrence, that the statistics of men's conduct under like conditions may be compared. After fixing upon some particular class of persons of similar age, sex, and social condition, we have to find out what common incidents in their lives are most apt to make them betray their character. We may then take note as often as we can, of what they do on these occasions, so as to arrive at their statistics of conduct in a limited number of well-defined small trials.

The reader will see at once how similar was Galton's idea to the stress interview which Freeman has recently devised and worked out in such great detail. Galton's method also recalls the procedures employed during the war by the Office of Strategic Services in Washington for the selection of special Army officers and used earlier by Simoneit [34] and other investigators in Germany.

Galton offers, among other specific suggestions, one which is so apt as again to deserve direct quotation:

The poetical metaphors of ordinary language suggest many possibilities of measurement. Thus when two persons have an "inclination" to one another, they visibly incline or slope together when sitting side by side, as at a dinner-table, and they then throw the stress of their weights on the near legs of their chairs. It does not require much ingenuity to arrange a pressure gauge with an index and dial to indicate changes in stress, but it is difficult to devise an arrangement that shall fulfil the threefold condition of being effective, not attracting notice, and being applicable to ordinary furniture. I made some rude experiments, but being busy with other matters, have not carried them on, as I had hoped.

In more recent years the method of miniature life situations has been extensively employed in the Character Education Inquiry conducted by Hartshorne, May, Maller, Shuttleworth, and others, whose results were published in 1928, 1929, and 1930 [11, 12, 13]. These investigators, working mainly with grade-school children, attempted to discover the moral knowledge of their subjects and—what is more relevant here—their actual behavior in situations involving honesty, cooperation, persistence, and similar traits. In a typical experiment (for measuring honesty) subjects were allowed to score their own papers on a test by means of a key provided them but were later retested under controlled conditions by means of equivalent tests which they were not permitted to score. The difference between the scores on the two tests indicated fairly reliably whether the examinee had copied answers from the key when he was allowed to use it. It is interesting to note that, although these investigators found a very high correlation (around +.70) between moral knowledge and intelligence, the correlations between moral knowledge and scores on behavioral tests of honesty, cooperation, etc., were extremely low (around +.25). These results clearly indicate what has been pointed out earlier: what the subject says about his behavior and personality is a very unsafe guide for prediction about his actual performance in life situations. In this case, of course, the subjects were not asked to judge what they would do in moral situations but rather what they might be expected to do, but the fact still remains that there is considerable discrepancy between behavior in life situations and predictions from an inventory.

Traits which have been frequently studied by methods of actual performance are suggestibility and hypnotizability. As is well known, individuals differ considerably in the extent to which they demonstrate suggestibility in either the waking or sleeping condition. It is easy to see why this particular trait lends itself naturally to objective life-situation measurement: it actually involves a relationship between two or more individuals, one of whom can become the examiner while the other is the subject. The examiner then actually attempts to get the subject to accept suggestions intended to produce a condition like swaying or to induce sleep of a hypnotic kind. The degree to which the individual responds to the suggestions of the examiner serves as a measure of suggestibility or hypnotizability [15].

Another area in which objective methods of measuring personality have been quite naturally employed includes reactions to success and failure or, in more general terms, *frustration* and *gratification.* Subjects can, for example, be given supposed tests of capacity, with the examiner actually interested not in their achievements but in their responses of an emotional kind on the basis of success and failure. Usually in experiments of this type the failure or success of the subject is prearranged, since measurements of capacity are of no importance, whereas the reactions to success and failure are. Naturally the subject is unaware of the artificiality of the situation, and precautions need to be taken to guarantee his naiveté. Investigations employing this methodology are well illustrated in the work of Lewin [17] and Rosenzweig [27].

Method of "Unobserved Observation"

While in the method of simulated success and failure the subject's behavior of a specialized kind is noted without awareness on his part of the examiner's objective, the same principle is employed even more patently in the procedure of *unobserved observation.* Here the subject is left in a room by himself with or without instructions to perform some task; he is then observed through a one-way mirror, screen, or other device and perhaps overheard by a concealed microphone setup, so that his behavior, uninfluenced by the presence of the observer, can be recorded accurately and completely. The method has been extended sometimes by having a stenographer take down in the observatory the exact verbalizations of the subject as these come through the speaker or headphones. It is often possible to take motion pictures of the subject if the arrangement has been properly installed and can be rationalized to him in advance. At the least, the method permits a verbal description of what the subject does while he is being observed. A recent extension of this approach has been its use for studying not only the behavior of the subject but also that of the examiner, as in the work of Rogers [23] and his associates who phonographically recorded verbatim records of therapeutic interviews and later analyzed them to reveal details of the behavior between examiner and examinee.

Although in this case the verbal behavior of the subject was of importance, other examples of the method where physical behavior, as well as verbal, plays an important part may be found in "time-sampling" studies, usually of children [40]. In these studies observers, concealed from their subjects or not, keep records of specific behavior during short selected intervals. These observations are treated as samples of the total behavior in time and are analyzed statistically to give an objective picture of the individual and his relationship to others in the situation observed. Further descriptions of uses of the time-sampling technique are found in Chapters 21 and 22.

Physiological Measures

In addition to the preceding objective methods for studying the overt behavior or language of subjects in actual life situations, there is a group of others in which characteristics of *physique* [32, 33] or such covert *physiological processes* as blood pressure or the galvanic skin response are investigated as expressions of personality. As has already been pointed out, this topic is treated in Chapters 14 and 15. It should, however, be noted here that not infrequently these methods are combined with studies of the subject's gross behavior or verbalizations, as in the Luria [19] technique which yields a simultaneous record not only of the galvanic skin reflex but also of the subject's word associations and involuntary muscle tremors.

Although all the objective methods thus far reviewed have involved some fairly well-defined area or areas of the individual's behavior, whether spontaneous or prearranged, other objective procedures are concerned with judgments made by individuals who are, by past association with the subject, in possession of information about him, although no systematic or experimental attempt has been made to provide that special knowledge. In other words, ratings, rankings, or matching of certain aspects of a subject's behavior by judges who are in some favored position for knowing about the variables in question may also be regarded as an objective approach to the investigation or appraisal of personality.

Rating Scales

Rating scales have long been used for the appraisal of individuals both in connection with personality traits of a general kind and with achievement or fitness for particular jobs. The variables may be marked by point values, e.g., on a five- or seven-point scale with the midpoint indicating the average for the trait; or each step in the scale

Avoids others	Tolerates others	Likes others	Likes others well	Seeks others

"Make a vertical mark crossing the above horizontal line to indicate the relative position the subject would hold in regard to his usual reaction to the company of others."

Fig. 1. A graphic rating scale.

may be defined in descriptive words which help the rater place the subject more concretely in relation to other individuals. See Fig. 1. A refinement of this latter procedure is the man-to-man rating scale, which requires that, before a group of individuals are rated, specific persons be chosen by the raters as typical of each of the various scale positions for each trait. In other words, a top, bottom, and middle man—and others according to the number of steps in the scale—are selected, and then the individuals to be rated are placed according to their difference from or similarity to these concrete examples of the points on the scale. It has been found from controlled experience that the number of steps on the rating scale must be at least five for reliable results to be obtained. As might readily be expected, the training and motivation of the rater are of crucial importance for valid results. The rater who is simply handed a sheet and asked to assign individuals grades on certain traits will ordinarily turn in a performance that is next to worthless and may, in fact, be extremely misleading. A common mistake made by raters consists in assigning estimates that cluster around the average point or veer, if at all, toward the favorable direction of the scale. Raters are ordinarily loath to commit themselves to the extremes on a rating scale and are likely especially to avoid very unfavorable ratings. It is essential, therefore, that raters receive adequate training in the definitions of the variables and of the steps in the rating scales, as well as in the method by which the ratings are to be made. Moreover, the raters must ordinarily be sufficiently motivated and unhurried to make their work dependable. If, as so often happens, ratings are given hastily and in spare moments snatched away from other work, the results cannot be trusted.

Even with the trained and well-motivated rater, other errors may readily vitiate personality ratings. The individual rater may have some special bias, whether favorable or unfavorable, to the subject rated. Sometimes such a bias appears in the form of a halo effect; a subject given a high or low rating for one trait will be found, where this effect has operated, to have been all-too-similarly rated high or low on the other traits to be estimated. To correct this and similar errors, it is well to employ a number of raters—three, four, or more if possible—so that the composite of the results can be relied upon instead of individually biased judgments. Multiple findings so reached are also useful in providing a range of ratings for a given subject on a given trait. Subjects who are found to have consistently low, high, or average ratings, as given by a number of investigators, are obviously different from those who may be rated over a rather wide range by different judges, and this difference in variability is often as significant as the average rating of a subject.

In general, ratings are notoriously unreliable and are not a valid method of appraising personality if used without supporting data. Nevertheless, the method is employed again and again in almost every type of personality investigation, although seldom relied upon exclusively. An interesting example of how the rating procedure can be employed with considerable validity almost because of its shortcomings is found in an investigation of Sears [30], who required subjects to rate both other individuals and themselves on the same traits, e.g., stinginess. Sears was interested in studying *insight* and *projection,* and he discovered from his work that subjects who are consistently rated high by others on such a negative trait as stinginess but who rate themselves low on this variable, thus indicating lack of insight, are very apt to rate other individuals high on the same trait, thus indicating the operation of projection. Individuals, on the other hand, who possess insight as defined in this experiment (agreement between self-ratings and ratings by others) are less apt to project. It should be noted, however, that on the basis of this study projection with respect to one trait does not necessarily warrant the expectation of projection for all traits.

The Matching Method

A related type of approach, in which judgments of both self and others are also employed, is exemplified in the investigations of Werner Wolff [43] on self-analysis and self-recognition. His characteristic procedure is to procure specimens of the subject's speech, handwriting, or gait without the subject's knowing that the specimen has been obtained; the specimen is then included with similar ones from other individuals, and the subject is asked to characterize the specimens, i.e., to describe the personality associated with each one. The results are frequently revealing and indicate that, although the individual may not consciously recognize his own forms of expression—a finding particularly true for voice, and for handwriting when presented in mirror image—the characterization, nevertheless, reveals that some unconscious self-recognition has occurred. For example, in a study of voice samples, it was found in one experiment that the unwitting self-judgment was more positive than the average characterization in 73 per cent of the cases, and more negative than the average in 20 per cent, only 7 per cent of the judgments falling into the neutral zone. Unconscious self-judgments were thus shown to be excessively favorable or, in a few instances, excessively unfavorable; scarcely ever are they neutral, as compared to the judgments made of others. Perhaps even more interesting is the fact that, although the subjects make these self-judgments without consciously recognizing their own forms of expression, they yet respond in a fashion that distinguishes self-judgments from judgments of others.

For some purposes it is an advantage to use the method of *ranking* instead of rating. The judge is, under these circumstances, practically coerced into adopting the advantageous man-to-man method previously mentioned. This procedure is, however, necessarily limited to smaller groups than it is possible to treat by ratings.

A variant of the rating (or judgment) method which has gained in popularity among personality investigators in recent years is *matching*. This procedure is to some extent an outgrowth of Gestalt psychology, in which emphasis has always been placed upon the total individual. It has long been known that the traits of the individual are seldom accessible to isolated study since the personality is an interacting unit. A judgment about any part is almost always affected by the judgment of the whole, and, inversely, a judgment of the whole is dependent upon a judgment of the parts. Some recent tests of personality have, in fact, been constructed with this point of view as basic, so that interpretations of results are always made not in respect to isolated variables, but with all the interdependent factors taken into account simultaneously. The Rorschach method, discussed on pages 558-560, is a clear example of such a test.

In order to make possible a comparison of individuals and at the same time have regard for the interdependence of the personality in its various aspects, the matching method was devised. Here, as opposed to the rating method, no attempt is ordinarily made to break down the personality into segments or parts regarded as more or less independently measurable. Instead, samples of the subject's gross behavior in two or more situations are compared in order to establish relationships which, if present, may be based on any or all aspects expressed in the samples. The method consists in offering judges several such samples derived from the behavior of a small group of subjects in two or more situations. The identity of the subjects is not given, it being the task of the judges to match the samples, if possible, and thus establish such psychological identity as may exist among them. The number of correct matchings in excess of chance serves as a measure of the extent to which the personality expressions in question reveal an underlying identity, which it then becomes the task of the investigator to analyze by whatever means he may have at his disposal. An example may again be gleaned from the studies of Werner Wolff [43]. See Fig 2. This investigator has taken various forms of expression from subjects—facial photographs, photographs of the hands, samples of handwriting or of the speaking voice—and has presented two or more series of these unidentified specimens in random order to be matched by neutral judges. In one experiment a group of subjects retold a story that was first read to them, and a verbatim typewritten record was made of each subject's version. Judges were then given three of these versions and a handwriting specimen of each of the same three subjects, with the instruction to discover which handwriting specimen went with which story version. The number of correct matchings obtained was one and one-half times greater than would have been expected by chance. Wolff points out that there must have been some similarity between the style of retelling the story and the handwriting of the persons being judged for such a result to have occurred. In similar fashion facial photographs and

I

III

Fig. 2. Illustration of the matching technique as employed in the investigations of Werner Wolff.

The above are musical notations to be matched with the names of three composers: A: Bach, B: Beethoven, C: Mozart. (Correct matchings are: I-B, II-C, III-A.) (Reproduced by permission of Harper and Brothers.)

specimens of recorded speech have been reliably matched. Naturally, it still remains to discover on what the correct matching judgments were based, but at least one cannot discard the forms of personality expression as having no relationship to each other, as more segmental and less adequate methods of investigation have so often done.

A statistical procedure which is often employed to evaluate measurements of personality, whether these measurements are in the form of ratings, test results, or data from other sources, is factor analysis. Although not a method of directly appraising or investigating a personality, factor analysis has become an important mathematical adjunct in studies of personality and thus deserves mention, at least, in the present account. In factor analysis quantitative data are treated mathematically to uncover the smallest number of basic variables to which the crude observations can be reduced and to throw light upon the relationships among these variables. Among the outstanding workers in this specialty may be mentioned Spearman [36] and Thurstone [41]. The inventory by Guilford, described on page 545, resulted from factor analysis.

PROJECTIVE METHODS

General Nature of Projective Methods

The projective approach, as distinguished from the subjective and the objective ones, attempts to achieve objectivity in the psychological sense by inviting the person under observation to be as "subjective" as possible. In other words, the examiner does not observe the overt behavior of the subject, as in the miniature life situations, to determine, let us say, aggressiveness or submissiveness; nor does he, on the other hand, ask the subject to state his opinion of his own behavior in certain situations or his feelings about certain experiences. Instead the subject is requested to behave in an imaginative way, e.g., by making up a story, interpreting ink-blots, or constructing some object out of plastic material. These techniques are therefore not objective in the sense of the objective methods previously discussed; they do not reveal directly what the subject does in actual situations. However, they are intended to reveal the underlying traits, moods, attitudes, and fantasies that *determine* the behavior of the individual in such actual situations and are therefore, if valid, more truly objective in their results than the objective methods themselves. Similarly, these projective techniques are definitely not subjective in the sense of the subjective methods above discussed; they do not instruct the subject to tell anything about himself. In fact, they are usually administered in such a fashion as to minimize as far as possible the subject's preoccupation with himself and to invite instead complete freedom from any sort of self-criticism. However, these methods, by emphasizing the individual's subjective life—in expressions of fantasy and imagination—capitalize upon subjectivity, although not upon self-criticalness.

This rather abstract way of describing projective techniques will become clearer from an example or two. It has repeatedly been noted that a person reveals himself—what his experiences have been, what his likes and dislikes are, what his problems and ways of thinking may be—even in purely imaginative productions. In fact, the freedom which an appeal to the imagination permits often tends to favor the projection of the real personality. Thus it sometimes happens that an author tells more about himself in his fictional works than in his consciously written autobiography—a fact that has been noted by discerning literary critics many times. The principle involved is actually a very general one: the individual reveals himself in all his behavior to a greater or lesser extent, but most in his less self-conscious moments, and the art of personality appraisal consists largely in the capacity to "read out" meanings which the individual "reads into" the world around him.

The projective techniques thus have in common the following characteristics: (1) The stimulus material is always neutral, ambiguous, or at least equivocal in its significance, and the subject is expected to supply meaning, significance, organization, or in some other way to leave the impress of his personality upon the undefined stimulus presentation. For such purpose ink-blots, incomplete stories, plastic materials, miniature life toys, meaningless auditory stimuli, and any number of other media may be made available to the subject. (2) The psychological reality, rather than the actual reality, of the subject's world is important in the projective techniques. The so-called facts of the individual's life may or may not have shaped his personality, may or may not now be determining influences in his behavior. The attitudes, opinions, ideals, conflicts, and fantasies which populate his private world, however, are inevitably important in his present adjustment or maladjustment, and it is to these aspects of psychological reality that the projective techniques turn their scrutiny. (3) Implicit or unconscious aspects of the personality are revealed, and psychodynamic principles therefore play an important part in the interpretations. Projective techniques are, in fact, derived historically from the free-association method employed in psychoanalysis. (4) Abuse of these techniques is readily possible, since it is easy for an untrained or immature examiner to project his own biases and fantasies into his interpretations of the subject's productions.

It is possible to classify the projective techniques in various ways—from the standpoint of the stimulus material employed, on the basis of the end product of the subject's reaction, or in terms of the particular aspects of personality which are most representatively revealed by each approach. For the present purpose the last of the three mentioned criteria has been adopted. The procedures are accordingly classified as *motor-expressive, perceptive-structural,* and *apperceptive-dynamic.*

Motor-expressive Methods

In the *motor-expressive methods* the subject expresses certain aspects of his personality by the manner in which adaptive acts are performed. Included here are the analysis of handwriting, gait, style of verbal expression, voice, and other motor activities in which not the end that the behavior serves but such dimensions as speed, amplitude, and intensity are relied upon for interpretation. Although this approach to personality, long considered significant in non-professional psychology, has been frowned upon by the academically oriented expert, more recently there has been a revival of serious interest in it. Not only Wolff but Allport and Vernon [3] and, in the area of handwriting analysis, Lewinson and Zubin [18] have contributed to this new interest. Even when the approach is not used exclusively for the interpretation of personality, it plays a part as an adjunct to the other methods in the present classification.

Perceptive-structural Methods

Of much wider present application is the *perceptive-structural* approach, in which the subject is permitted to organize perceptually such stimuli as ink-blots or meaningless auditory patterns, and from which the structural aspects of the personality—chief direction of interest (extraversion or introversion), impulsivity or self-restraint, and other aspects of temperament (as contrasted with the dynamics of motivation)—are readily derived.

The *Rorschach method of personality diagnosis* [24] is undoubtedly the best-known of these techniques and is, in fact, at present the most widely used of all the projective procedures. In this method ten ink-blots are shown to the subject, one at a time, with the instruction that he is to tell the examiner what he sees in them—what they remind him of or could represent. See Fig. 3. The responses given by the subject, as well as the answers to certain questions asked about these associations afterward, serve as the basis for scoring and interpretation. The responses are not scored chiefly according to content, as might be expected, but in relation to certain formal characteristics, such as whether the whole or parts of the blots are used by the subject

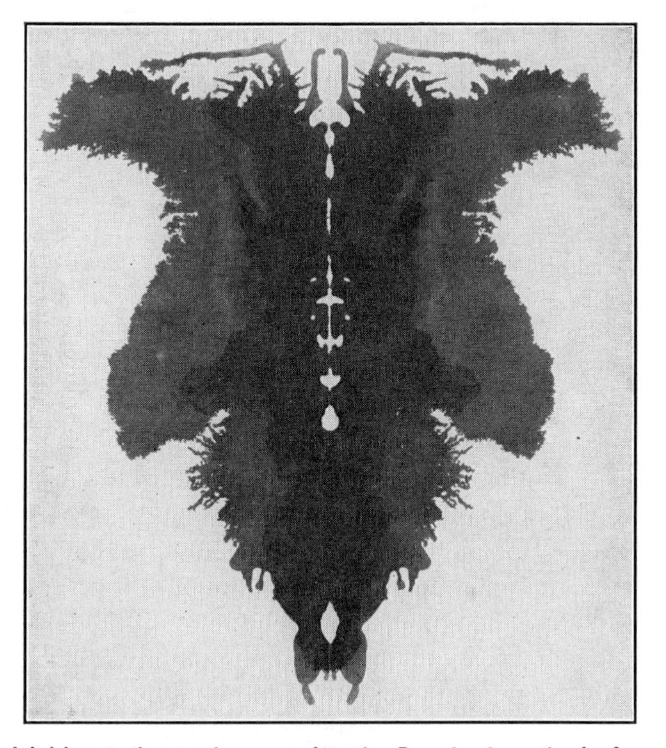

Fig. 3. Ink-blot similar to those used in the Rorschach method of personality diagnosis.

in his responses, whether and in what combination shapes and colors are used, and whether the movement of living creatures has entered into the associations. Content, e.g., the seeing of human figures, animals, or plants, is scored secondarily. The scoring categories of the test, such as movement and color, are interpreted as signifying different functions of the personality: intellectual creativity, outgoing emotions, practical-mindedness, and the like. Special attention is devoted to the manner in which various factors are related to each other in the expression of the total personality, since it has been found that the presence or absence of any degree of a particular scoring category may occur with widely different meanings, depending upon the context of other associated scores. From norms based upon work with subjects in various well-characterized groups—normal individuals, neurotics, and psychotics—the pattern of the subject's scores may be interpreted as belonging to one or another personality make-up. The findings throw light upon various kinds and degrees of intelligence (in the broad sense of the term), different types of temperament, neurotic tendencies, and psychotic trends.

The Rorschach method has continued to gain adherence since its introduction in 1921 and has been extended with certain modifications for group use. Great skill is required in the proper application of the method, since, as in all the major projective techniques, there are no right or wrong answers that can be looked up in a scoring key as a basis for mechanical interpretation. At the same time it should be noted that there are definite criteria for the scoring and interpretation of Rorschach findings and that further efforts to improve these standards are constantly being made. Although this method can be standardized, the simpler procedures that avail for the standardization of intelligence tests and personality questionnaires are not applicable to it because of its complexity and novelty and especially because it requires the consideration of many interdependent factors at the same time.

Another perceptive-structural technique that may be mentioned is the *tautophone,* a device introduced under the name of verbal summator by B. F. Skinner [35] and later rechristened in relation to the projective approaches by Shakow and Rosenzweig [31]. Here the subject is instructed to listen while a phonograph reproduces at low intensity various speech samples in a man's voice. The subject says what comes to his mind as he listens to each speech sample in much the same way that he might interpret ink-blots. This "auditory Rorschach technique" has as yet not been fully explored but seems to have promise as a supplement to the regular Rorschach method.

Apperceptive-dynamic Methods

The *apperceptive-dynamic* procedures require, instead of motor or perceptive activity, such complex or higher intellectual functioning as is involved in the production of fantasies or artistic representations (hence apperceptive) and are interpreted to reveal the themes, motives, drives, and urges fundamental to the behavior of the individual (hence dynamic). Some of these dynamic trends may not even be open to the subject's conscious recognition, although they are implicit in his behavior. These techniques are thus most obviously psychodynamic or psychoanalytic in their reference.

The most widely used is the *Thematic Apperception Test* [21], introduced by Morgan and Murray [20] in 1935. A series of pictures, arranged in appropriate groups for male and female adults and for children, are presented to the subject with the instruction to regard

Fig. 4. Picture similar to those employed in the Thematic Apperception Test. (Painted by Cordelia Knorr.)

each as an illustration for a story. See Fig. 4. The subject then tells the story by identifying the characters, explaining their relationship to each other, describing what preceded the situation shown in the picture, and stating an outcome. A verbatim record is made of each story told and this record is carefully analyzed according to the major themes revealed, e.g., sexual interests, vocational ambitions, family conflicts, and social status. It is naturally necessary to consider the frequency with which a particular story type occurs, and special importance is attached to deviations from the usual story or stories told. Of greater significance, however, is the recurrence of a given topic, i.e., the *thema,* that may appear within the record of a given subject as one proceeds in the analysis from story to story. Such themata project the implicit attitudes, habits of thought, ideals, and drives of the subject, as well as the characteristics of the chief inhabitants of his psychological world: mother, father, sister, brother, wife, or husband. Sometimes the formal characteristics in the telling of the stories shed additional light (in the manner of the motor-expressive techniques) upon the coherence or illogicality of thinking and the degree of creative ability. As with the Rorschach method, great skill, derived from broad clinical experience and from extensive use of this instrument, is required for the making of sound interpretations.

Of related interest, but with application primarily not to adults but to children, are various forms of *play techniques*. Here the subject is allowed to construct scenes by employing dolls, toys, blocks, and other building materials. Although frequently used for catharsis in the treatment of children's personality problems, the method is also important in the thematic diagnosis of personality.

Belonging in the area of the apperceptive-dynamic techniques but of considerably more limited scope than the Thematic Apperception Test or the various forms of play technique is the *word-association method*. This technique consists in presenting the subject with a list of words, one at a time, with the instruction to respond with the first word that enters his mind. The time required for giving each response and the responses themselves are noted. By the analysis of any departures from the average amount of time which the subject takes to give his responses, as well as from a study of the content of unusual associations, it is frequently possible to identify certain attitudes, anxieties, or sentiments. This method is of interest historically, since it may be reasonably regarded as the first of the formally set up projective techniques. Galton [7] and Jung [16] did the chief pioneer work. See also pages 596–602.

Among the most recent projective techniques may be mentioned the *picture-association method,* in which pictures of social situations are substituted for words as the stimulus material. In the Picture-Frustration Study [28], for example, the subject examines a series of twenty-four cartoon-like drawings, each of which depicts an everyday situation of frustration or stress involving two individuals, one of whom is usually shown frustrating the other. Facial expressions and features are purposely not sketched in. The frustrating person is shown saying certain words that either help to describe the frustrating situation in which the other person is involved or which themselves actually frustrate this second individual. It is the subject's task to write in the blank caption box above the head of the frustrated character the first association that comes into his mind as appropriate—not necessarily what the subject himself would say in the situation, but what first comes into his mind as possible for

Fig. 5. Four situations from the Rosenzweig Picture-Frustration Study. (Copyright, 1944, by S. Rosenzweig.)

the pictured character to say. See Fig. 5. As will be readily apparent, this approach shares with the other apperceptive-dynamic ones the assumption that the subject identifies himself with the character in the pictured situation for whom the association is produced, in much the same way that the heroes of the stories told in the Thematic Apperception Test are interpreted as identical in one response or another with the subject himself.

INTEGRATION OF THE METHODS

The three main approaches to the appraisal and investigation of personality—the subjective, objective, and projective—are actually less distinct when properly employed than might appear from the preceding exposition. Although it is true that the distinction is real in that it is possible to follow the subjective method and ask a subject for opinions about himself, to employ the objective procedures in which the individual to be studied is observed by others in his overt behavior, or to permit the subject to "project" himself into ambiguous or unstructured materials from which the implicit personality can then be read out, there are still ways in which each of these general methods can be employed so as to warrant its being classified under either or both of the other headings.

A brief reorientation with regard to the three main approaches will help in understanding their relationships better. The subjective methods are, in the last analysis, those in which the subject expresses opinions about himself. It might therefore be said that these methods reveal *opinion behavior.* Similarly, the objective methods are those in which the *overt behavior* of the subject is exposed to the view of the examiner. In this case, however, it needs to be borne in mind that the behavior of the subject, whether in the miniature life situation or in the life behavior to which a judge might have reference in giving ratings, is not open to direct interpretation. Overt behavior, although perhaps a more reliable index to underlying personality than opinion behavior, still involves covert personality factors that are not directly observable in the behavior itself. It is at this point that it becomes possible to appreciate how the *implicit behavior* of the projective techniques probes deeper than either of the other approaches. The determinants of both the opinion behavior and the overt behavior of the subject may thus be revealed if the projective procedures are successfully employed, and herein lies their peculiar advantage. The responses elicited in them, while in themselves seemingly trivial or even fantastic, are assumed to be representative of the underlying trends of the personality or of those implicit characteristics in terms of which the subject carries on his personal, social, and vocational life.

Nevertheless, as has already been stated, it is possible for any of the other two main approaches to approximate the projective techniques, provided that sophisticated methodology is employed. In fact, the preceding restatement of the subjective methods as involving opinion behavior already implies such a reorientation. Instead of regarding the responses in a personality questionnaire, for instance, as valid at their face significance, it is possible to think of them as the projection of the subject's own opinions about himself—opinion behavior—and to interpret the findings in relation to the results of other techniques as a criterion of insight or integration in a way that is far more meaningful. Not only the total scores from a personality questionnaire but also the answers to individual items must then be scrutinized. The interview may similarly be conducted so that it becomes not a matter of getting answers to specific questions but an opportunity for the subject to reveal himself spontaneously in much the same fashion that he might in responding to unstructured ink-blots. Such a spontaneous interview procedure has been discussed and contrasted with the more constrained type of question-and-answer method.

It may thus be concluded that all three of the main approaches can yield valuable data if properly employed, and that, although they may be distinguished quite validly for purposes of exposition, a more useful way of thinking about them is to emphasize the type of behavior—opinion, overt, or implicit—which each yields. It is then necessary to add that the opinion behavior of the subject, while highly superficial in some respects, is vital for a full understanding of him, since important self-critical defenses are here involved that are as much a part of the personality as anything else. The full understanding in question similarly requires that the somewhat more revealing overt behavior of the subject also needs to be taken into account; to know how the subject behaves in miniature or actual life situations is certainly of great value to a complete understanding of him. There still remains, however, those implicit determinative aspects of behavior that are hardly open to direct observation in the overt behavior of the subject but which the projective techniques can illuminate.

The meeting of the three main approaches becomes the more important in view of the interdependence of the total personality, which nearly every student of human nature now regards as a basic postulate. Although the projective techniques emphasize this point of view more completely than do other approaches, it is obvious that these other methods can contribute to the picture of the total individual aspects which may not be evident from the projective techniques alone. The necessity for the multiple study of a person is apparent whatever theoretical standpoint the investigator may adopt. The personality is so complex both in its facets and in the levels of its operation that to hope for any simple or limited tool which will yield all there is to know is fatuous. Both in clinical practice and in fundamental research, the appraisal and investigation of personality at the present time demand a composite plan of attack in which opinion, overt, and implicit behavior are all elicited and evaluated in a complementary fashion.

REFERENCES

1. Allport, G. W. *Personality; A Psychological Interpretation.* New York: Henry Holt, 1937.
2. Allport, G. W. The use of personal documents in psychological science. *Soc. Sci. Res. Coun. Bull.,* 1942, No. 49.
3. Allport, G. W., and P. E. Vernon. *Studies in Expressive Movement.* New York: Macmillan, 1933.
4. Bingham, W. V., and B. V. Moore. *How to Interview.* New York: Harper, 1941.
5. Freeman, G. L., G. E. Manson, E. T. Kalzoff, and J. H. Pathman. The stress interview. *J. Abn. Soc. Psychol.,* 1942, *37,* 427–447.
6. Galton, F. Measurement of character. *Fortnightly Review,* 1884, *36,* 179–185.
7. Galton, F. Psychometric experiments. *Brain,* 1879–1880, *2,* 149–162.
8. Garrett, A. M. *Interviewing, Its Principles and Methods.* New York: Family Welfare Association of America, 1942.
9. Guilford, J. P. *Personality Factors S T D C R.* Los Angeles: Sheridan Press, 1940.
10. Harper, M. H. Social beliefs and attitudes of American educators. *Teach. Coll. Contrib. Educ.,* 1927, No. 294.
11. Hartshorne, H., and M. A. May. *Studies in Deceit.* New York: Macmillan, 1928.
12. Hartshorne, H., M. A. May, and J. B. Maller. *Studies in Service and Self-Control.* New York: Macmillan, 1929.
13. Hartshorne, H., M. A. May, and K. Shuttleworth. *Studies in the Organization of Character.* New York: Macmillan, 1930.
14. Hathaway, S. R., and J. C. McKinley. *The Minnesota Multiphasic Personality Inventory.* Minneapolis: University of Minnesota Press, 1943.
15. Hull, C. L. *Hypnosis and Suggestibility: An Experimental Approach.* New York: Appleton-Century, 1933.
16. Jung, C. G. *Studies in Word Association.* New York: Heineman, 1919.
17. Lewin, K. *A Dynamic Theory of Personality.* New York: McGraw-Hill, 1935.
18. Lewinson, T. S., and J. Zubin. *Handwriting Analysis.* New York: King's Crown Press, 1942.
19. Luria, A. R. *The Nature of Human Conflicts.* New York: Horace Liveright, 1932.
20. Morgan, C. D., and H. A. Murray. A method for investigating fantasies; the Thematic Apperception Test. *Arch. Neurol. Psychiat.,* 1935, *34,* 289–306.
21. Murray, H. A. *Thematic Apperception Test.* Cambridge, Mass.: Harvard University Press, 1943.
22. Murray, H. A., *et al.* *Explorations in Personality.* New York: Oxford University Press, 1938.

23. Rogers, C. R. *Counseling and Psychotherapy.* Boston: Houghton Mifflin, 1942.
24. Rorschach, H. *Psychodiagnostics.* (Translation and English edition by P. Lemkau and B. Kronenberg; edited by W. Morgenthaler). New York: Grune and Stratton, 1942.
25. Rosenzweig, S. A basis for the improvement of personality tests with special reference to the M–F battery. *J. Abn. Soc. Psychol.,* 1938, *33,* 476–488.
26. Rosenzweig, S. Converging approaches to personality: Murray, Allport, Lewin. *Psychol. Rev.,* 1944, *51,* 248–256.
27. Rosenzweig, S. The experimental study of repression. In *Explorations in Personality,* by H. A. Murray, *et al.* New York: Oxford University Press, 1938.
28. Rosenzweig, S. The picture-association method and its application in a study of reactions to frustration. *J. Pers.,* 1946, *14,* 3–23.
29. Rousseau, J. J. *The Confessions of Jean Jacques Rousseau.* (Translated from the French with a preface by E. Wilson.) New York: Knopf, 1928. (Two volumes.)
30. Sears, R. R. Experimental studies of projection. I. Attribution of traits. *J. Soc. Psychol.,* 1936, *7,* 151–163.
31. Shakow, D., and S. Rosenzweig. The use of the Tautophone ("verbal summator") as an auditory apperceptive test for the study of personality. *Char. Pers.,* 1940, *8,* 216–226.
32. Sheldon, W. H., and S. S. Stevens. *The Varieties of Temperament.* New York: Harper, 1942.
33. Sheldon, W. H., S. S. Stevens, and W. B. Tucker. *The Varieties of Human Physique.* New York: Harper, 1940.
34. Simoneit, M. *Wehrpsychologie: ein Abriss ihrer Probleme und politischen Folgerungen.* Berlin: Bernard and Graefe, 1933.
35. Skinner, B. F. The verbal summator and a method for the study of latent speech. *J. Psychol.,* 1936, *2,* 71–107.
36. Spearman, C. *The Abilities of Man.* New York: Macmillan, 1927.
37. Strong, E. K., Jr. *Vocational Interests of Men and Women.* Stanford University, Calif.: Stanford University Press, 1943.
38. Super, D. E. The Bernreuter Personality Inventory: a review of research. *Psychol. Bull.,* 1942, *39,* 94–125.
39. Terman, L. M., and C. C. Miles. *Sex and Personality.* New York: McGraw-Hill, 1936.
40 Thomas, D. S., *et al.* Some new techniques for studying social behavior. *Child Develop. Monog.,* 1929, No. 1.
41. Thurstone, L. L. *Multiple Factor Analysis.* Chicago: University of Chicago Press, 1947.
42. Vernon, P. E., and G. W. Allport. A test for personality values. *J. Abn. Soc. Psychol.,* 1931, *26,* 231–248.
43. Wolff, W. *The Expression of Personality.* New York: Harper, 1943.

SUGGESTED READINGS

Allport, G. W. *Personality; A Psychological Interpretation.* New York: Henry Holt, 1937. (Part IV, The analysis of personality.)

Allport, G. W. The use of personal documents in psychological science. *Soc. Sci. Res. Coun. Bull.,* 1942, No. 49.

HUNT, J. McV., Ed. *Personality and the Behavior Disorders,* Vol. I. New York: Ronald Press, 1944 (Chaps. 4, 5, and 6).

LEWIN, K. *A Dynamic Theory of Personality.* New York: McGraw-Hill, 1935 (Chaps. I and VIII).

MURRAY, H. A., *et al. Explorations in Personality.* New York: Oxford University Press, 1938 (Chap. 6).

ROSENZWEIG, S. Converging approaches to personality: Murray, Allport, Lewin. *Psychol. Rev.*, 1944, *51,* 248–256.

ROSENZWEIG, S., L. E. BUNDAS, K. LUMRY, and H. W. DAVIDSON. An elementary syllabus of psychological tests. *J. Psychol.*, 1944, *18,* 9–40.

WOLFF, W. *The Expression of Personality.* New York: Harper, 1943 (Chaps. I and II).

Chapter 19

Methods and Techniques in Clinical Psychology

The Late Andrew W. Brown[1]

The term clinical psychology is used with two quite distinct meanings, which it is necessary to distinguish at the outset. The expression is frequently used to indicate a branch or subdivision of the total field of psychology, just as the term organic chemistry designates a branch of chemistry or physical anthropology delimits a certain area of the general field of anthropology. The term is also used to indicate a method of approach in the study of human behavior. In this chapter the term will be used in both senses. In most instances the context will make the meaning clear.

For the most part, however, this chapter will be concerned with clinical psychology as a method of approach. Most of the methods used in the investigation of human behavior can be grouped into three large categories: (*a*) the experimental approach, (*b*) the differential or statistical approach, and (*c*) the clinical approach. (See Chapter 1.) Each of these methods has its own peculiar advantages, and each has its limitations. No one of them is sufficient in itself to supply all the data necessary to construct a systematic body of knowledge which might be dignified by the term science. To be sure, these methods are not sharply differentiated, and in any particular investigation two or even all three methods might be employed.

In the statistical approach the experimenter starts with some hypothesis or with some assumption which it is his intention to investigate. He usually develops some instruments or tests of his own which can be treated quantitatively or uses those already available. With the aid of these instruments he collects samples of the behavior of a large number of individuals in relation to the problem under investigation. Then, with the aid of statistical devices and tools, he analyzes these data and arrives at some generalization or theory in

[1] Formerly Associate Professor of Psychology, University of Chicago.

regard to human nature. During the past 25 years this has been one of the most fruitful methods in psychological research. Such an approach has the advantage of clear, straightforward, inductive logic, precision of definition of concepts, and directness of interpretation. Its chief limitation lies in the fact that important areas of human behavior have not as yet been subjected to statistical study and analysis.

The experimental method too has its distinct advantages and also its limitations. A student pursuing this approach will set up his hypothesis, establish rigid controls, keep all variables constant except the one under investigation, use the most refined instruments available for the study of the phenomenon in question, record his observation, analyze his data with as much precision as possible, deduce his conclusions, and retest his hypothesis, and will make the whole process "public and repeatable." This is the time-honored scientific method, and in the long run all deductions must be submitted to this rigorous method of discovery and proof before they are admitted to the body of knowledge called science.

In the study of human behavior, however, this method has certain limitations. Often the behavior being observed in the experimental situation is isolated and out of context and may bear little causal relation to similar behavior as it occurs in an actual life situation, for the simple reason that in the actual life situation the factors conditioning the behavior are quite different from those set up in the laboratory experiment.

The clinical method of approach to the study of human behavior lacks the objective rigidity of either of the other two methods and to the extent that it lacks this rigidity may correctly be regarded as unscientific. This much, however, is true: it provides information which it is as yet impossible to secure by either of the other methods. In fact, it is fairly generally recognized that the "problems" of an individual case cannot be understood without the use of clinical methods. The nature of these methods will be made clear in this chapter.

Delineation of the Field

Two or three methods, none of which is definitive, have been used to determine the boundaries of an applied science. One method is to accept *a priori* definitions of the field. A second method is to survey the work being done by those in the field and from such a survey make a "job description" of the tasks performed. A third method is to investigate the type of training received by those engaged in the activities involved. All of these methods have been used. The difficulty with them is that one finds such wide ranges of opinion and practice that definitive conclusions are difficult.

If the boundaries are set by *a priori* definitions, then clinical psychology has a wide berth indeed. For example, the committee of the clinical section of the American Psychological Association recommends that the term clinical psychology "be used to denote that art and technology which deals with the adjustment problems of human beings." Again, Doll defines clinical psychology as "the science, technique, and art of employing psychological principles, methods, and procedures to promote the welfare of the individual person for purposes of optimum social adjustment and self-expression" [5]. There is substantial agreement in these definitions, which make clear that clinical psychology concerns itself with both the diagnosis and "treatment" of the psychological, i.e., non-medical, problems of human beings.

If the boundaries of the field and consequently the methods employed are empirically determined through a survey of the work actually being done by those who call themselves clinical psychologists, then again there is wide latitude. Such surveys [5, 6] have shown that the clinician is engaged in a very wide variety of activities, ranging all the way from simple psychometrics (usually under the direction of a superior) to independent consulting work where difficult problems of diagnosis and treatment are encountered.

Finally, if the limits of the field are to be determined by the type of problems which the clinician by right of his training and experience is prepared to handle, then the variety of tasks within the clinical field is even greater than if determined by either of the other methods. The difference in the training of psychologists in clinical practice is very great, ranging from the A.B. degree, with perhaps a major in psychology, to the Ph.D. degree, involving several years of graduate training and experience.

Whether the limits of the field are determined by *a priori* definition, by an empirical survey of the tasks performed, or by an investigation of the training the psychologist receives, it is clear that if he is to perform at the highest level he must be prepared to cope with a wide variety of problems. These problems range all the way from determining a Stanford-Binet IQ to analyzing complex personality problems and effecting an appropriate method of re-education. It is of course assumed in the foregoing statement that, when either medical or legal problems are involved, the psychologist works in cooperation with a qualified physician or psychiatrist.

The Problems Confronted by the Clinician

It is evident from what has just been stated that the problem of methods is inextricably associated with the problem of the delineation of the field. If, as is assumed in the previous section, the clinical psychologist is to perform the very serious and responsible task of giving technical advice on complex problems of human behavior and adjustment, he must be adequately prepared; otherwise he may do himself, his client, and his profession incalculable damage. In other words, the clinical psychologist, especially if he is to be a "general practitioner" or consultant, must be adequately equipped with a variety of techniques and methods for the analyses and treatment of a large variety of behavior deviations.

The problems of human behavior with which the clinician at one time or another may have to deal are complex and numerous. Ackerson [1] lists some 300 different personality and conduct problems for which children and young people have been referred to a guidance clinic. There is considerable overlapping in the notation of these problems, but with allowance for this overlapping his study indicates a wide range. The number of behavior deviations in any individual ranges from 1 or 2 to as many as 100 in extreme cases, with an average around 5 for personality problems and around 7 for conduct problems.

The most frequently appearing behavior difficulties and reasons for referring to the clinic, as noted by Ackerson [1] in 5000 consecutive clinic cases, are shown in Table I. The problems presented in Table I are those noted by psychiatrists, physicians, social workers, and psychologists and mentioned in the case record and tabulated by the research worker. The "per cent" column indicates the number of cases in which a given problem was noted in the record.

There are several factors which determine both the type of problem and the frequency of its occurrence. A publicly supported free clinic will have quite a different clientele from a private clinic. The "intake" policy is likewise a selective factor. Moreover, the problem recorded in the record will depend upon the particular biases of the professional workers in charge. The percentages therefore must be regarded as only a rough approximation of the true percentages in the general population.

It will be noted from Table I that a large number of problems seen in the clinic might be described as conduct or personality disorders, and the methods employed in dealing with them are those which have been found effective in diagnosis and treatment. It is important, however, to recognize that there are many other types of clinical

TABLE I

FREQUENTLY APPEARING CLINICAL PROBLEMS

Problems	Per Cent
Nervousness, restlessness, irritable temperament	41
Disobedience, incorrigibility, stubbornness, contrariness, defiant attitude	40
Retardation in school	37
Question of feeblemindedness or indequate intelligence	31
Temper display, "tantrums," irritable temperament	31
Dull, slow manner, listlessness, lack of initiative or ambition	30
Stealing	26
Immature childish manner or judgments, impaired judgment	25
Fighting, quarrelsomeness, violence, and threatening violence	25
Enuresis or bedwetting (beyond third birthday)	25
Lying, marked untruthfulness	24
Advice regarding placement, commitment, or institutionalization	24
Poor work in school	23
"Crying spells," crying easily	22
Truancy from school	19
Masturbation	19
Truancy from home	18
Sensitiveness or worrisomeness (general), sensitiveness or worry over some specific fact or episode	18
Bashfulness, shyness	17

problems which the psychologist is expected to handle either alone or in cooperation with a physician or psychiatrist.

For example, special methods and techniques are required in dealing with the many difficult social and psychological problems of the blind or partially blind, the deaf and hard of hearing, the physically and mentally handicapped, the spastic, the epileptic, the postencephalitic, the bright child retarded in school, the child with severe reading difficulty, the person with speech difficulties, and the individual who has difficulty in making an adequate vocational adjustment. All these require special, clinical methods and techniques which the psychologist must be equipped to employ. World War II has probably increased the number of problems and consequently the demand for trained clinical psychologists, but probably has not increased the variety of problems. War neurosis, battle fatigue, etc., are simply old problems with new names.

The Clinical Approach

It will be helpful at this point to recall the definition of clinical psychology stated at the beginning of this chapter and note now the implication for clinical methods. Clinical psychology was defined as "the art and technology of dealing with the adjustment problems of human beings." In this definition there are several implications for clinical methods: first, that the methods are applied to an individual case; second, that the individual has some "problem"; third, that both methods of diagnosis and treatment are employed in dealing with these problems; and fourth, that the clinical approach is an art as well as a science and a technology. It is important that these aspects be emphasized, as they give the clinical approach its uniqueness.

It is clear from this definition that clinical methods may include a wide range of techniques. In fact, any device, scheme, procedure, or instrument which a trained psychologist can use and which will give him a better understanding of human behavior or assist in its modification may rightfully be regarded as falling within the scope of clinical methods. If, for example, the operation of an electroencephalograph (see pages 448–451) is necessary for the understanding of the psychological problems of epilepsy, then this becomes a clinical instrument. If knowing how to give, score, and interpret the Rorschach test (see pages 558–560) provides the clinician with a technique for a better understanding of human motivation, then this too becomes a clinical device; if a mastery of the technique of psychodrama increases the psychologist's skill in treating behavior maladjustments, then this too falls within the scope of clinical methods.

METHOD OF DIAGNOSIS

It is obvious that the methods used in the analysis of any clinical case will vary with the problems involved. The approach in studying the problems of a juvenile delinquent will, for example, be quite different from that involved in examining a blind child to determine whether he should be sent to a school for the blind or to an institution for mental defectives. Although the details of the method may vary with the individual case, certain aspects of the approach are similar in their broad outline in all cases. These will be presented in the following sections.

Physical Examination

Every individual coming to a psychological clinic or being seen and "treated" by a psychologist should have a careful physical examination either by a physician in the clinic or by the family doctor. The psychologist should hold to this rule fairly rigidly, even though 70 to 80 per cent of the cases so examined by competent physicians are reported negative. It is important that the psychologist, in attempting to modify the behavior of any individual, should know whether the behavior exhibited is of a functional or of an organic basis. If the basis is organic, then the psychologist should work in close cooperation with a medically trained person. If, for example, the problem is truancy from school, the psychologist's first task is to rule out the possibility that the truancy is the result of postencephalitis, a brain injury, or some other physical defect.

The Case History

Perhaps the most important single instrument in the clinical examination is the case history. It is the only method by which the psychologist can gain an understanding of the development of the behavior. Psychological insight into the nature of any problem can be gained only by a knowledge of the forces, in their chronological relationships, which have acted upon the individual and to which he has reacted to make him what he is. These environmental "field forces" include not only those which constitute the cultural and community pattern, but also the subtle interaction in the immediate family group to which the individual has been exposed. Especially important are the forces to which the individual has reacted in the early years of his life, as these reactions form the habits of thinking and acting which become selective and contribute heavily to the determination of his later behavior. In many clinical cases the history alone not only gives an adequate diagnosis of the problem, but also suggests the methods of treatment.

The case-history method has frequently been criticized as unreliable and consequently unscientific as a method of approach in the study of human behavior. These criticisms have been based on two important observations. First, the report depends upon the memory or recall of past events of either the client or the informant, and recall is known to be inaccurate, especially when one is asked to recall events of several years ago. Second, any report is likely to be given either with a "halo effect" or with a bias, and consequently it may be either consciously or unconsciously distorted. These are sound objections and must be taken into account both in securing and in interpreting the case history. They are not, however, sufficiently pertinent to warrant the rejection of the case history as a scientific method. Instead, the psychologist should use every possible technique to minimize the chance of error.

In taking or recording the case history, the clinician recognizes that the recall of events is likely to be inaccurate, and he is constantly on guard and silently critical of data reported. He checks and examines them from as many different points of view as possible. He is on the watch for consistencies and inconsistencies in the report. The experienced historian is likely, during the initial stages of this fact-finding interview, to form hypotheses regarding the family, the parental relationship, the marital relationship, the sibling relationship, the economic status, or other possible causative factors. He holds these hypotheses tentatively and during the interview is in a continual process of revising and changing them. He skillfully directs the interview in such a manner as to test the hypotheses. In this process an error in the report of a single event is not a significant matter, as the test of the hypotheses depends not upon the veracity of a single statement but upon the relationship of a constellation of events, which it is difficult to falsify.

The historical data required for the understanding of any given case will depend, to some extent at least, upon the problem involved. For example, it is of little value to secure a detailed report of the mental and physical welfare of the paternal and maternal grandparents or the aunts and uncles of a young child referred to the clinic because of nail biting, thumb sucking, or enuresis. On the other hand, such information may be very necessary and pertinent if the child was referred because of mental retardation or some kind of seizure. Consequently, any outline for writing or reporting a life history is only suggestive. For some cases it may not be adequate; for others it may be in too great detail, and frequently much of the information it calls for will not be pertinent.

Space does not permit the inclusion in this chapter of a detailed schedule for taking a case history.[2] The following broad categories, with some of the details, indicate a few of the important lines of inquiry necessary for understanding most cases. A summary of the outline is presented in order to give an over-all view of the factors considered important in determining behavior patterns.

It will be observed that inquiry into three general areas is stressed: first, the organic, physical, and physiological; second, the environmental; and, third, the interaction between these two, including the influence of this interaction on subsequent behavior.

[2] The student will find two of these included in References 4 and 10.

Summary

of

Case-history Outline

I. Identifying data.

II. Statement of problem.

III. Congenital and physical factors determining behavior.

  A. Congenital factors.

  B. Physical factors (developmental).

IV. Environmental forces or situations which have influenced behavior.

  A. Factors in the home.

    1. Father.

    2. Mother.

    3. Siblings.

    4. Physical conditions.

    5. Method of control and supervision.

  B. Community and cultural factors.

  C. Educational factors.

  D. Occupational factors.

  E. Recreational factors.

V. Reactions to the congenital, physiological, and environmental forces, which may have in turn influenced present behavior.

  A. Reactions in early childhood.

  B. Reaction in later childhood and adolescence.

VI. Sources of information.

Case-history Outline

I. Identifying data.

Name, date of birth, age, sex, race, marital status, grade in school, occupation, names of members of family.

II. Statement of the problem.

Who is referring the case and why? What is the nature of the behavior disturbance? Who is being disturbed? Give specific examples. In some cases it may be helpful to give at this time a brief history of the evolution of the problem.

III. Congenital and physical factors.

A. Congenital factors.

Inquire regarding insanity, feeblemindedness, epilepsy, glandular disorders, alcoholism, "nervous breakdowns," instability, queerness, etc., in the maternal and paternal relatives, parents, and siblings.

B. Physical factors (developmental).

Inquire regarding condition of mother during pregnancy; nature of delivery; careful history of any birth injury; childhood diseases, (give course and any residual of each); accidents, convulsions, fainting spells, glandular disturbances; attitudes of parents toward health; age weaned, age of walking, talking, teething; inquire especially regarding diseases of the nervous system, encephalitis, chorea, "nervousness," nervous indigestion, prolonged sleeping spells; secure height and weight norms; secure report of medical or physical examination.

IV. Environmental forces or situations.

A. Factors in the home.

1. Father.

Inquire regarding his own childhood experiences, his education, occupation, and economic status, religion, and dominant personality traits. His attitude toward wife and siblings: kindly, sympathetic, dominating, democratic, etc. Hobbies, recreational interests, talents, physical characteristics, frustrations, and other important factors which may help to indicate his influence on the behavior of the client.

2. Mother.

Same as for father, and in addition inquire regarding the expression of the maternal relationship. Is it one of rejection or over-protection? Follow up, depending on the problem or the tentative hypothesis established.

3. Sibling interrelationships.

Attitude toward each other, their health, undue quarreling, rivalry, closely knit, schooling, present whereabouts, or occupations and activities.

4. Physical conditions in the home.

Secure a brief chronological account of home life from birth to present time, including changes in residence, foster-home placement, or the like. Inquire regarding orderliness, cleanliness, regularity, sleeping arrangements, facilities for recreation.

5. Methods of control and supervision.

Inquire if parents openly disagree in regard to discipline. Are they consistent? What kind of discipline, bribes, threats, deprivations? Are the parents indulgent, lax, repressive, cruel, just and sensible? Are there home duties or responsibilities?

B. Community and cultural factors.

Inquire regarding nationality and religious background; extent of participation in church activities; political activities; economic and social status of family in community; extent to which family has accepted the dominant community culture.

Inquire regarding neighborhood, if possible give delinquency or other rates, dominant nationality, economic status, types of dwellings, social controls, recreational opportunities.

C. Educational factors.

Inquire regarding age of entering, record schools attended, with location, grades repeated or skipped, any special difficulties in school subjects—reading, arithmetic, etc. Attitudes toward teacher, subjects liked most, extracurricular activities, evidence of leadership, rank in class; educational plans and ambitions.

D. Occupational factors.

Inquire regarding jobs held, reasons for changing jobs, dates of change, vocational interests and ambitions. What has determined them? Special skills.

E. Recreational factors.

Inquire regarding leisure-time activities. Are they solitary or with groups? Is subject sought out, tolerated, or rejected by others? Are there signs of leadership? Kinds of activities enjoyed? Do other members of family participate? Membership in gangs, clubs? Does subject have hobbies or special interests?

V. Reactions to the congenital physiological and environmental forces, which may have influenced present behavior.

A. Reactions in early childhood.

Emotional reactions, inquire regarding temper tantrums and how met by parents, signs of stubbornness, suspiciousness, sulking. *Fear reactions,* their origin and how handled by parents, any night terrors or sleep walking. *Love reactions,* attachment to parents, dependent, overaffectionate, shy, fearful. Thumbsucking, nail biting, masturbation, etc.

Is subject unusually sensitive, withdrawn, and secretive? Is he subject to crying or laughing spells? Does he laugh spontaneously and freely? Is he listless, distractable, hyperactive? Is he quarrelsome, impatient, selfish, cruel to other children or to animals? Is he inattentive, disinterested in surroundings, fussy, repressed, tense?

B. Reactions in later childhood and adolescence.

Inquire regarding freedom of expression, dependency on parents. Is subject becoming emancipated from parental control? Is he happy in group activities? Is he predominantly happy and carefree, outgoing, extroverted? Does he have many friends, is he a leader? Is he at ease with the opposite sex, does he date? What are his dominant recreational activities? Has he had any delinquency record or any contact with law-enforcing agencies?

VI. Sources of information.

List all sources of information in order of importance (amount of information received). Give name, address, and relationship to child of each person furnishing information. Statements of other than the main informant should be so indicated.

Impression of the informant: note appearance, intelligence, personality, insight, attitudes, and cooperation. Evaluate the reliability and adequacy of the information given. Evaluate the informant's capacity, intellectually and emotionally, to cooperate in a plan of treatment of the child.

List all social agencies who have had contact with the family (relief, medical, psychiatric, and other agencies) and the history of the contact of each. Include reports from agencies in the body of the case history under appropriate headings, indicating source in every case.

The Clinical Interview

Interviewing constitutes such an important aspect of clinical procedures that any treatment of it which can be given in a section of one chapter must of necessity be very inadequate. Yet such a chapter would be incomplete without some reference to this subject.

The interview is one of the clinician's most important instruments, because it is on the interview that he must rely for much of his data and it is through the interview that he must carry on much of his "treatment." It is highly important therefore that this art be carefully cultivated and refined. The clinician will find that a highly developed skill in this direction is indispensable to successful clinical practice. The student who wishes to become thoroughly acquainted with interviewing techniques will do well to read the excellent discussions provided by Bingham and Moore [2], Garrett [7], Rogers [15], Symonds [17], and Williamson and Darley [21].

As already indicated, there are two chief purposes for which the interview is used: first, to secure information, and, second, to impart information. In some instances both these functions are performed at the same time. There are many different purposes for which a clinician may wish to secure information, just as there are many different purposes for which he may wish to impart information, and the technique of the interviewer will vary with each occasion. Certainly the approach in public-poll interviewing or in a commercial survey is quite different from that used in securing the life history of a neurotic patient, yet in each case the interview is to secure information for a certain purpose. Again, the technique used in the final interview of a young man who has been referred for vocational guidance will be quite different from that in a non-directive therapeutic interview [15], yet the purpose of both is to impart certain information. Moreover, the interview will vary with age, sex, the nature of the problem, the personality of the client, and the attitude the client brings to the interview situation.

So many circumstances can alter the method used in securing or imparting information that it may seem hazardous to attempt any generalization. There are, however, some rules which are held inviolate. In clinical practice most of these become so much a part of the clinician's technique and manner that he is not conscious of using them.

First, the clinician must have a *genuine interest* in the welfare of his client. There must be a warmth of feeling and understanding which the client at once recognizes as real and sincere. It is not enough to smile blandly and talk sweetly; the client must have a feeling of acceptance and friendliness. If the conditions implied in this generalization exist, most of the other principles enumerated will, with some experience, follow naturally.

Second, the clinical interviewer must be a *good listener.* He must be willing to permit the client full and free expression without injecting his own opinions, wishes, or theories. This does not mean that he must be a passive robot. A good listener is one who can, by his manner and attitude, convince his client that he is genuinely interested and appreciative of what is being related.

Third, a good clinical interviewer is a *keen observer* of behavior and is skilled in the art of interpreting movements, verbal responses, and changes of expression. Although he must be keen, he must at the same time be cautious, as it is very easy with the lack of any objective evidence to make misinterpretations. It is only after careful study and much practice in the association of activities and language with certain meaning or symptoms and checking and rechecking his interpretation that the clinician can have any confidence in his conclusions.

Fourth, the good interviewer must have *insight* into the motivation of his own behavior. He must be aware of his own limitations as well as his own strengths and be able to compensate for them in some socially acceptable way.

A thorough analysis of interviewing technique is provided by Roethlisberger and Dickson [16]. Although the conceptual scheme which these authors develop is specifically directed toward interviewing in a large industrial plant, it is equally applicable to clinical methods and is briefly summarized here:

I. The interviewer should treat what is said in an interview as an item in a context.
   This rule has several important corollaries.
   A. The interviewer should not pay exclusive attention to the manifest content of the intercourse.
   B. The interviewer should not treat everything that is said as either fact or error.
   C. The interviewer should not treat everything that is said as being at the same psychological level.

II. The interviewer should listen not only to what a person wants to say but also for what he does not want to say or cannot say without help.

III. The interviewer should treat the mental contexts described in the preceding rule as indices and seek through them the personal reference that is being revealed.

IV. The interviewer should keep the personal reference in its social context.
   A. The interviewer should remember that the interview is itself a social situation and that therefore the social relation existing between the interviewer and the interviewee is in part determining what is said.
   B. The interviewer should see to it that the speaker's sentiments do not act on his own.[3]

The reader is referred to the text for an elaboration and interpretation of these rules. It is clear that several years' experience at actual interviewing is necessary for the mastery of these techniques.

The Appraisal of Aptitudes and Abilities

USE OF PSYCHOLOGICAL TESTS. The appraisal of aptitudes and abilities and the consequent diagnosis of strengths and weaknesses by means of objective tests are such important aspects of clinical methods that frequently they have been regarded as the only techniques a psychologist should use. As pointed out in an earlier section of this chapter, however, if in his analysis the clinician confines him-

[3] From Roethlisberger and Dickson [16].

self solely to the objective-test approach, large and important areas of any given behavior pattern will be left unexplored. Securing a history of the individual's development and an investigation of his own feelings and attitudes, neither of which can be adequately determined by objective tests alone, are important clinical procedure in the understanding of behavior. However, just as it is important not to lean too heavily on objective measurements, so is it important not to underemphasize them. The objective-test procedure is the one aspect of clinical method which may lay some claim to scientific accuracy. The other methods of drawing inferences from histories and interviews, although important, are those of the artist and depend upon experiential cues rather than upon objective evidence. The only reason the clinician resorts to this intuitive method is that psychology has not yet been able to develop tools which enable him to explore certain important areas of behavior scientifically. When the tools become available for a completely objective appraisal of human behavior, the clinician will be obliged to use them, and the methods of clinical psychology will then be much more in accord with the method of the exact sciences than they are at the present time.

Because the psychologist in his constant attempt to refine and improve his instruments has discovered some serious inadequacies in the "reliability" and "validity" of psychological tests, there has been a tendency on the part of a number of clinicians in recent years to discard them entirely or to minimize their use very greatly and resort almost completely to documentary evidence. They find it less disquieting to use instruments whose errors are not known than to use those who errors are known, even though the errors in the former may be much greater than those in the latter. In his excellent book, *How to Counsel Students,* Williamson [22] gives a clear expression of this point of view:

> This much may be said in defense of the testing method of analysis. The psychologist is one of the very few professional workers in the field of diagnosis who has studied his tools critically and scientifically to discover their weaknesses and strengths, quite apart from his own beliefs, prejudices, and hopes. For few other techniques has such a refined check been made of the accuracy of analysis. Possibly because of his naïveté, the psychologist has candidly published the results of research showing the limitations and errors of his tools. Since his are the only guidance tools presented with their errors listed, many people conclude that all other tools are free from error or that errors of other tools are negligible as compared with those of tests. This has led to the belief of uninformed counselors that there are no errors, few errors, or less serious errors in other techniques of analysis.
>
> This fallacy of abandoning one tool because its errors and limitations have

been discovered through research and clinical practice, and substituting another tool, the errors of which are as yet unknown or ignored, is characteristic of many present-day counselors. Many such counselors learn of the errors in tests and then proceed to avoid using them, preferring to use analytic techniques of self-analysis, tryout (work or school experience), or the reading of a book on occupational information, apparently blissfully ignorant of the many serious errors and limitations of these substitute tools.

THE INSTRUMENTS AVAILABLE. In so brief an account of clinical method as is necessarily contained in this chapter, no attempt can be made to survey the many instruments which psychologists and other scientists, through their constant and indefatigable research over a period of years, have made available for the appraisal of human behavior. There are many excellent manuals and textbooks giving detailed descriptions of these instruments and the methods of interpreting the results. The student is referred particularly to Chapter 17 of this book and to the books by Greene [8], Buros [3], Pintner [13], Terman and Merrill [18], and Wechsler [20]. The skill of the clinician will be directly proportional to his mastery of the intelligent use of these instruments. This, of course, does not preclude the necessity of other skills, but without skill in the use of the tools available for clinical practice he cannot expect to become an efficient clinician.

Psychological tests are available for a very great range of human problems covering a wide age span: infancy to senility. In fact, these instruments have become so numerous that mastery of the technique of administering and interpreting all of them has become almost impossible. The clinician has been forced to specialize either in some areas of investigation, such as educational problems, intellectual difficulties, or emotional difficulties, or in the problems of some age group, such as the preschool child, the elementary school group, adolescents, or adults. Even within any one of these areas the instruments and devices available for the objective evaluation and investigation of behavior are very numerous.

The following will illustrate some of the problems with which the psychologist in a typical child-guidance clinic is confronted and for which an objective evaluation is required:

A 7-year-old blind child has been temporarily refused admission to the state school for the blind. The superintendent wants to know his level of intelligence.

A child who is known to have average or superior ability is severely retarded in school. The principal wishes a diagnosis of the difficulty and suggestions for remedial work.

The judge wishes to know whether a 14-year-old boy who has been brought before him for breaking into a store should be sent to the state correctional school for boys or to the state school for borderline mental-defective delinquents.

A child had a brain injury at birth which has markedly affected his speech. The parents are concerned about his intellectual development.

A boy is ready for high school, and the parents would like to have an appraisal of his abilities and interests so that they can be more intelligent in their guidance.

These problems could be multiplied many times. All of them require a ready knowledge of the tests available for the age groups and problems involved. In a clinical situation the clinician will not have the opportunity to go to a test file or a yearbook to discover the most appropriate tests for the analysis of a given problem. He must have this information ready at hand as a part of his clinical training.

In general the psychological tests and inventories available for the appraisal of human behavior may be divided into the following categories:

- I. Tests of general intelligence.
  - A. Individual tests.
    - 1. Verbal.
    - 2. Performance.
  - B. Group tests.
    - 1. For the primary grades.
    - 2. For the intermediate grades.
    - 3. For high school.
    - 4. For college.
- II. Tests of school or academic achievement.
- III. Vocational tests and tests of special aptitudes.
- IV. Vocational-interest inventories.
- V. Character and personality tests and schedules.
- VI. Rating and attitude scales.
- VII. Tests for special disabilities.

In each of these categories a large number of tests or inventories are available by which the psychologist may obtain a quantitative rating of the individual's abilities and aptitudes.

The tests in some categories are much more reliable and valid than others. In general, the educational tests have the highest degree of predictability. Then follow the intelligence tests and the tests of special aptitudes. The character and personality tests have not proved particularly valid; i.e., they have not been very successful in predicting the situation as it actually exists.

A series of measurements which promise to be of particular value for clinical purposes are the tests of primary abilities developed by L. L. Thurstone [19]. Other things being equal, the more diagnostic an instrument is, the greater its clinical value, as it supplies the clinician with evidence of the subject's strengths and weaknesses and lets him know what abilities might be utilized in vocational training and what remedial measures should be applied. These tests of primary abilities are of this nature. Instead of an over-all rating in terms of an IQ or some other general index of brightness, the subject's intellectual capacity is described in terms of several independent factors. These are known as (*a*) the *space factor,* designated by the letter *S:* the ability to visualize in space flat or solid objects; (*b*) the *number factor,* designated by the letter *N:* the ability to do simple numerical tasks; (*c*) the *V* or *verbal comprehension factor:* the ability to deal with verbal concepts; (*d*) the *word-fluency factor:* the ability to produce words in a restricted context; (*e*) an *M* or a *memory factor* (which recent investigations seem to indicate as a composite of several memory factors): the ability to recall events and experiences; (*f*) an *I* or *inductive factor:* the ability to discover the rule or principle in the material one is working with; and (*g*) a *P* or *perceptual factor:* the ability to group things together into some form or consistent pattern. A number of tests are available which give fairly good indices of ability in each of these characteristics of a person's intellectual capacity. The clinical value of such a battery of tests over the single index for the analysis of intellect is fairly obvious. A more detailed description of these instruments is provided in Chapter 17.

In addition to these pencil-and-paper tests for the appraisal of the abilities, aptitudes, and interests of the more usual clinic case, there are a number of instruments available for the study of the physically and mentally handicapped with which the clinician must be thoroughly familiar. In general, such tests as have been briefly mentioned do not apply to the blind, the deaf, the spastic, the epileptic, the hard of hearing, the brain injured, or the individual with a severe reading handicap, yet the study of these problems constitutes a considerable part of the psychologist's work in a clinic. Frequently, special types of tests are necessary in order to make an adequate diagnosis. It may be that the psychologist is not skilled in the use of some of these instruments. He should know about them, however, and be able to refer the case to a competent authority in the field.

INTERPRETATION OF RESULTS. Although the most important purpose in giving a psychological test is to secure an accurate quantitative or objective evaluation of some aspect of behavior so that the individual in question can be compared with other individuals in the same group, nevertheless it is important that the psychologist make careful clinical observation of the client during the testing session. Often these observations contribute more to the understanding of the behavior than does the quantitative score. In fact, many psychologists regard the testing situation as a controlled interview in which the behavior of the client can be observed under standardized conditions.

The following outline has been found useful as a guide in interpreting the results of the Revised Stanford-Binet Examination:

OUTLINE

To serve as a guide in interpreting
results of the Revised Stanford-Binet Examination

School or institution............................Examiner.....................

Name...Date of examination..........

Date of birth...................................

Name of test....................................

CA ....Act. grade placement.........

MA...MA grade placement.........

IQ...TM classification ....

1. Observation of child's behavior during examination.
   A. *Approach to examination:* Is he resistant, passive, enthusiastic, reluctant?
   B. *Attitude during examination:* Is he spontaneous, inquisitive, impatient, irritable, interested in tests, aggressive, defiant, indifferent, shy, fearful, apprehensive, overpolite, cordial, distractable, persistent, suggestible?
   C. *Responses to directions:* Are they quick, slow, deliberate, careful, careless, impulsive, reflective, logical, irrelevant, rambling?
   D. *Physical activity:* Is he restless, lethargic? Does he exhibit specific mannerisms, such as nail biting, picking his fingers or other parts of his body or clothes, blinking, twitching, jerky movements, tremors, etc.?
   E. *Speech:* Describe defect, if any: stuttering, articulatory (record phonetically words mispronounced).
2. Analysis of test results.
   Give basal and scatter; mention any significant or consistent type of failures or success, language handicap, reading difficulty.
3. Evaluation of rating.
   Compare with previous ratings, if any (explaining discrepancies); compare MA grade placement and actual grade placement; compare MA grade with results of achievement tests, if any; describe any circumstance or condition which may have served to make the rating too high or too low.
4. Recommendations regarding (*a*) school placement, (*b*) tutoring, (*c*) institutional placement, (*d*) special help, (*e*) future progress.

One of the most useful devices in interpreting the results of the psychological examination is the *psychological profile,* which is simply a chart of equated scores, usually either percentiles or modified standard scores. The profile is a method of presenting these scores on a series of tests in a brief form, so that the reader can see at a glance where the subject stands in each of a number of traits and also any pattern of abilities.

The sample profile presented is that of a young unmarried woman 20 years of age. Her educational background included 1½ years at a college which she was attending at the time the profile was made. She reported one summer of experience working as a typist for her father's building and loan company. She stated that her high school and first-year-college work emphasized commercial and secretarial courses. However, she had had considerable difficulty with college economics and she had changed the emphasis of her schooling to the elementary teaching field.

The young woman came to the clinical laboratory because she was undecided about the type of work for which her interests and abilities were best suited. She was interested in obtaining a comparative measurement of her abilities, aptitudes, and interests to aid her in planning her future college work and her career.

Several of the test scores on the Bernreuter Personality Inventory, the Kuder Interest Inventory, and the Allport-Vernon Study of Values are omitted from the chart because of lack of space. A detailed interpretation of this profile will not be attempted, but even a superficial glance will enable the reader to make certain tentative inferences. First, it is clear that this woman's ability to carry college work was decidedly below that of the average student, and even though the correlation between scholastic aptitude and college success is not high, it is high enough to warrant the prediction that she will have some difficulty in completing her college work. Second, her pattern of abilities and interests was not fundamentally academic or scientific. Her vocabulary, her English aptitude, her reading, and her scientific interests were all low. These results, when combined with the brief history, make a reasonably consistent picture. The clinician might find it advisable, on further analysis, to encourage the young woman to accept some other course than the one she was pursuing. The reader will be able to make several other tentative deductions from the chart.

METHODS OF "TREATMENT"

Meaning of the Term

The term treatment, as it is used in present-day clinical work, is in many respects unfortunate, because it fails to reveal to the reader

Profile of Psychological Test Scores

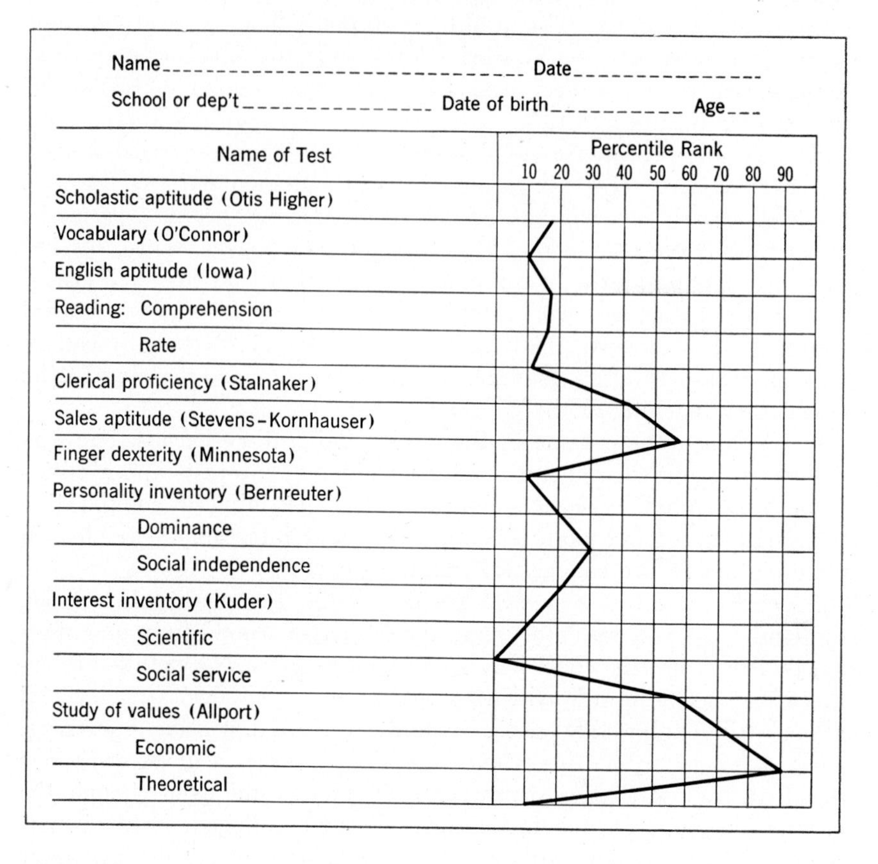

the nature of the process involved. In fact, the term actually conceals from many parents and guardians the essential characteristic of the remedial procedures in that it tends to imply that the process is something that can be superimposed from without, similar to giving a drug or performing an operation. The term therapy has similar objections. These terms, like the term clinical, have been borrowed from medicine and have unfortunately brought with them some of the same meaning they possess in that discipline.

Name
Date
School or dep't
Date of birth
Age
Name of Test
Percentile Rank
10 20 30 40 50 60 70 80 90
Scholastic aptitude (Otis Higher)
Vocabulary (O'Connor)
English aptitude (Iowa)
Reading: Comprehension
Rate
Clerical proficiency (Stalnaker)
Sales aptitude (Stevens-Kornhauser)
Finger dexterity (Minnesota)
Personality inventory (Bernreuter)
Dominance
Social independence
Interest inventory (Kuder)
Scientific
Social service
Study of values (Allport)
Economic
Theoretical

The term re-education, or even education, might describe the nature of the process more nearly than either treatment or psychotherapy. The essential psychological nature of "treatment" is the same as that involved in any other educative process. The chief difference between the education of the clinic, on one hand, and the education of the home, the community, and the school, on the other, is that in the clinic it is necessary to devise techniques and schemes to break down old habits as well as to establish new ones, whereas the teacher, parent, or guardian is concerned for the most part in establishing only new habits. Even this distinction does not always hold. Often the good parent or the good teacher is a good clinician, employing with skill and accuracy all the essential methods of treatment used by the good clinician. Very frequently it is the chief task of a parent or teacher to "re-educate" as well as to "educate," and often he does it well.

Treatment involves a change in behavior. The task of the clinician is so to arrange events and situations as to bring about this change. If the child has been brought to the clinic because he has been truanting from home and school, then the task of the clinician is to change this behavior pattern. If a client comes because he has a number of unexplainable fears and anxieties, the task of the clinician is to help him get rid of them. Treatment of any problem involves the acquisition of a new behavior pattern or the discarding of an old one or both.

The method of acquiring new patterns of behavior is a problem to which psychologists have given a great deal of attention. On one point there seems to be general agreement, namely, that behavior is acquired only through some kind of a reaction to a situation or a stimulus. This theory is known as the *reaction hypothesis,* which states that all forms of behavior, whether muscular, glandular, or mental, are reactions to definite stimulation.

The hypothesis has two very important implications for so-called treatment: First, that if a behavior pattern is to be changed, some stimulus or situation must be constructed to motivate the change; and, second, that the subject must be given some opportunity to practice or "exercise" the behavior in the making. These are essential elements in the acquisition of any behavior pattern. If this hypothesis is accepted, then no treatment can be effective without having inherent in it these two factors.

Many techniques and methods have been used by psychiatrists, psychologists, teachers, ministers, and priests in their attempt to change behavior patterns, and practically all methods from Couéism to psychoanalysis lay some claim to success, in terms of the individual case. The lame have walked, and the blind have seen. Little carefully controlled experimental work on the relative value of different methods of therapy, however, has been reported. The most thoroughgoing and systematic accounts of various treatment techniques have been reported by Rogers [14, 15], Kanner [11], Hunt [9], and the staff of the Illinois Institute for Juvenile Research [10].

In general, these treatment processes may be classified into two large categories: (*a*) those involving actual change of the environmental situation, and (*b*) those involving change of attitude toward the environment on the part of the client. The difference between these two is more apparent than real. As far as the psychological process which goes on within the individual is concerned, they amount to the same thing; i.e., they modify the stimuli which play upon the individual and thus modify his behavior. These two methods will be discussed in order.

Modifying the Environmental Forces

There are many ways which the psychologists have used to modify the environmental forces which play upon the individual. (1) If the situation demands it, the client may be physically removed from one situation and placed in another, e.g., moved from his own home and placed in a foster home or institution. Thus he is ostensibly forced to react to a completely new set of environmental situations in the hope that by so doing the desired changes in behavior will result. (2) The attitude of parents, siblings, teachers, and others toward the client may be changed. This effects a change in the "field forces" which act upon the individual and thus produces a change in behavior. (3) A change in the environmental forces may be brought about by providing more adequate recreation facilities and play activity. The client may be provided with membership in the YMCA, given a library card, sent to a camp, or, if he is older, advised "to get away from it all" for a while and take a vacation.

It is obvious that the methods of modifying the field forces could be almost indefinitely multiplied, depending upon the results of the diagnostic procedures. The three methods mentioned are those commonly used in clinical practice. The value of this type of treatment depends upon the skill and ingenuity of the therapist in providing situations which the client accepts, for it is only as he accepts them that they will have any re-educational value.

Modifying the Client's Attitude

In many instances the treatment cannot be carried out through the modification of the environmental forces alone. Often it is necessary to effect a change in the individual's attitudes toward himself, toward his associates, and, perhaps, toward society in general. Frequently, a complete reorientation of his concept of himself or his concept of the relationship between himself and his associates or of the relationship between himself and his immediate family is necessary. During the process of his development he has accumulated a number of faulty habits of thinking, feeling, and acting, and a complete modification of his philosophy of life is the only method by which his behavior can be altered.

This modification of behavior is always difficult and prolonged and often is impossible. If the client has developed fixed ways of feeling and acting, then he is likely to assume that same role toward the therapist and resent any intrusion into his "private affairs." Or he may attempt to prove to the therapist that his way of thinking and feeling is the only correct one, and everyone else should accept it. Such a person is likely to go through life making himself and everyone else with whom he associates unhappy and being dubbed a neurotic. In other instances, more severe and more pernicious ways of thinking and feeling may lead to what is called a "mental breakdown" or eventually to a psychosis.

Many techniques have been devised and developed in the attempts to modify the individual's ways of thinking, feeling, and acting. One of the best known is psychoanalysis. This is an elaborate theoretical psychological system, a detailed discussion of which does not belong in this chapter. As a technique of therapy, it involves a detailed report to the analyst (and under his direction) of the past experiences of the individual, especially of his early childhood—the relation to the mother, the father, the siblings, and the associates, and the influence of these upon his own development. This report, which may take several months, is interpreted to the client in accordance with psychoanalytic theory. The assumption in this method of therapy is that, once an individual has an intellectual understanding of all the forces that make him act the way he does, he will change his behavior to more socially acceptable patterns.

Another technique for modifying human behavior has been developed recently by Carl Rogers [15]. This has been called the nondirective or client-centered method of counseling and psychotherapy. The chief difference between this and the older psychoanalytic approaches, from which it is partially derived, is that in this approach the focus of attention in the therapeutic relationship is on the development and integration of the individual into a more consistent personality during the counseling process, and not on an analysis of his problems through a probing into his past history. It is assumed in this procedure that the client is capable of effecting this integration if he is given an opportunity to relate and consider his experience as well as his own thinking and feelings. The basic hypothesis is stated by Rogers [15] as follows: "Effective counseling consists of a definitely structured permissive relationship which allows the client to gain an understanding of himself to a degree which enables him to take positive steps in the light of his own orientation."

The relative value of these directive and non-directive methods of "treatment" will be determined by continued research in this relatively unexplored field.

CLINICAL METHODS IN INDUSTRY

The Selection of Personnel

In recent years the clinical approach to the understanding of human motivation and personality structure has been increasingly used in the selection of personnel in industry, especially for top management. The older approach, namely, using a battery of tests, has proved relatively sterile, and the assumption is that the more elaborate and more time-consuming clinical method will prove more successful. This assumption has not, however, been experimentally demonstrated.

The methods of the clinical approach in industry are essentially the same as those already described as in use in counseling centers, guidance laboratories, and clinics. In industry, however, the orientation and the problems to be solved are quite different. The clinician is not, as a rule, so much concerned with the problems of the individual as such as he is with predicting probable success in a given position. For the most part the methods are used in the selection of men for supervisory positions. Some of the questions the clinicians must be prepared to answer in the selection of personnel in industry are these:

Does the man think accurately and comprehensively?

Does he tend to make sound judgments?

Is he able to look ahead and make long-range plans?

Is he able to work rapidly with precision and accuracy?

Is he able to remain calm and objective under criticism?

Is he able to take orders without offense and give them with composure?

Can he lead others to accept his ideas without force or regimentation?

Can he give criticism frankly, honestly, and objectively?

Can he look ahead and plan an even flow of work throughout his department?

In selecting a man for a supervisory position, it is necessary to be able to answer these and many other questions dealing with the intellectual, emotional, and social characteristics of the client before making any prediction about his success in a given position.

The information which enables the clinician to attempt answers to these questions and to make a final recommendation to management is not secured from objective measurements alone. The amount of error in prediction will be considerably reduced if the clinician will follow the usual clinical procedure of integrating the test findings with information gathered from a personal history and an interview with the candidate.

The Developmental Interview and Upgrading

The therapeutic procedure, or developmental interview, as it is called in some organizations, follows along the same lines as that used in the usual clinical situation, except that as a rule the ultimate purpose of the interview is to increase a man's efficiency in a given position and prepare him for upgrading, rather than to develop his personality as an individual, although the two possible objectives are by no means incompatible. Very frequently greater efficiency on the job can be best achieved and preparation for upgrading be best accomplished by conducting the developmental interview with the purpose of helping the client to meet and solve some of his own individual problems.

The techniques of conducting these therapeutic interviews are well described by Roethlisberger and Dickson [16] and have been briefly mentioned in previous sections of this chapter.

REFERENCES

1. Ackerson, L. *Children's Behavior Problems.* Chicago: University of Chicago Press, 1931.
2. Bingham, W. V., and B. V. Moore. *How to Interview.* New York: Harper, 1941.
3. Buros, O. K. *The 1940 Mental Measurements Yearbook.* Highland Park, N. J.: The Mental Measurements Yearbook, 1941.
4. Carter, J. W. Manual for the psychodiagnostic blank: a guide for diagnostic interviewing in psychological clinic work. *Psychol. Rec.*, 1940, *20*, 251–290.
5. Subcommittee on Graduate Internship Training of the American Psychological Association and American Association of Applied Psychology. Graduate internship training in psychology. *J. Consult. Psychol.*, 1945, *9*, 243–266.
6. Committee on Professional Training in Clinical Psychology. Proposed program of professional training in clinical psychology. *J. Consult. Psychol.*, 1943, *7*, 23–26.
7. Garrett, A. *Interviewing, Its Principles and Methods.* New York: Family Welfare Association of America, 1942.
8. Greene, E. B. *Measurements of Human Behavior.* New York: Odyssey Press, 1941.

9. HUNT, J. M. *Personality and the Behavior Disorders,* Vols. I and II. New York: Ronald Press, 1944.
10. Illinois Institute for Juvenile Research. *Child Guidance Procedures: Methods and Techniques Employed at the Institute for Juvenile Research.* New York: Appleton-Century, 1937.
11. KANNER, L. *Child Psychiatry.* Springfield, Ill.: C. C. Thomas, 1935.
12. LOUTTIT, C. M. *Clinical Psychology.* New York: Harper, 1936.
13. PINTNER, R. *Intelligence Testing, Methods and Results.* New York: Henry Holt, 1931.
14. ROGERS, C. R. *The Clinical Treatment of the Problem Child.* Boston: Houghton Mifflin, 1939.
15. ROGERS, C. R. *Counseling and Psychotherapy.* New York: Houghton Mifflin, 1942.
16. ROETHLISBERGER, F. J., and W. J. DICKSON. *Management and the Worker.* Cambridge, Mass.: Harvard University Press, 1946.
17. SYMONDS, P. M. *Diagnosing Personality and Conduct.* New York: Appleton-Century, 1931.
18. TERMAN, L. M., and M. A. MERRILL. *Measuring Intelligence.* Boston: Houghton Mifflin, 1937.
19. THURSTONE, L. L. Primary mental abilities. *Psychometric Monog.* No. 1, 1938.
20. WECHSLER, D. *The Measurement of Adult Intelligence.* 3rd Ed. Baltimore: Williams and Wilkins, 1944.
21. WILLIAMSON, E. G., and J. G. DARLEY. *Student Personnel Work, An Outline of Clinical Procedures.* New York: McGraw-Hill, 1937.
22. WILLIAMSON, E. G. *How to Counsel Students.* New York: McGraw-Hill, 1939.

SUGGESTED READINGS

ALLPORT, G. W. *Personality; A Psychological Interpretation.* New York: Henry Holt, 1937, pp. 390–399.

LOUTTIT, C. M. The nature of clinical psychology. *Psychol. Bull.,* 1939, *36,* 361–389.

RICHARDS, T. W. *Modern Clinical Psychology.* New York: McGraw-Hill, 1946.

Chapter 20

Objective Studies of Disordered Persons

Joseph Zubin[1]

Nearly all the methods described in the foregoing chapters have dealt with people or animals whose behavior both during and after the experiments was understandable and to a certain extent predictable. In fact, the purpose of most of the investigations was to establish the basis on which future behavior could be predicted.

There are, however, some persons who are so odd or unusual that their behavior is not easily understandable, and an accurate prediction of their future behavior is not always possible. In dealing with this type of person we cannot always apply what we have previously learned about normal individuals. Careful observation and experimentation, however, reveal certain types of regularity in the behavior of these disordered individuals, but these regularities reveal themselves not so much in *what* the individuals do as in *how* they do it. This fact was first stressed by Emil Kraepelin, who pioneered in the application of experimental procedures to abnormal individuals.

For example, disordered individuals do not invariably do poorly on intelligence tests, but their disorder reveals itself in the particular combination of weaknesses and strengths which they exhibit. They fail easy items, pass difficult items, and in general exhibit a type of scatter in their performance which is very often diagnostic of abnormality. Although the actual score achieved by a normal individual on an intelligence test is usually the most important datum, the actual score achieved by a disordered person is not as important as the particular pattern of ability and disability which he displays. Another example of how abnormal persons differ from normal ones is in their greater variability in all measures. In general, group dif-

1 Assistant Professor of Psychology, Columbia University; Associate Research Psychologist, New York State Psychiatric Institute and Hospital.

ferences between normal and abnormal persons on tests or other measures are not nearly as large as differences in variability between the two groups.

Disordered persons do not differ markedly from normal individuals in their sensory acuity and responsiveness and in motor performance in everyday life as long as the task is short, is directed from without, and does not introduce emotional factors; but whenever sustained, self-directed tasks involving emotional factors are introduced, the disordered individual shows up to disadvantage. For this reason the usual laboratory experiments are not suitable for measuring or detecting the underlying difficulties of the disordered individual. Modifications must be introduced or new experiments conceived in which sustained, self-directed activity involving emotional factors as well as intellectual effort becomes the primary variable. Thus experiments involving volition, level of aspiration, and stress situations should prove quite fruitful in the objective investigations of disordered behavior.

There are three major groupings into which mentally disordered persons may be placed for convenience: (1) the outright insane, (2) the mentally defective, and (3) the peculiar or mildly disordered. The insane are persons "suffering from a real derangement of their mental life which is so severe that they do not respond to any of the usual methods of reason and logic which are sufficient to guide ordinary human beings" [15]. The mentally defective or feeble-minded are those "who from a very early age lack the ability to acquire knowledge or to profit from experience and training. They are unable to care for themselves adequately" [15]. The third group consists of a vast variety of individuals who, although not frankly disordered, nevertheless present some type of mental deviation (other than intellectual) and includes the neurotics, psychosomatic cases, and psychopathic personalities.

In the succeeding pages we shall give examples of work done with disordered persons in the following areas: (1) association tests, (2) memory tests, and (3) conditioning.

WORD-ASSOCIATION EXPERIMENTS

The systematic study of word associations was begun by Francis Galton (1885) with himself as subject. He exposed written stimulus words one at a time and noted with a stopwatch the time required for the response word, its general relation to the stimulus word, and the consistency with which the same response words occurred to a given stimulus. He concluded that the responses were not random in character but represented well-worn ruts of the mind in which thought continually traveled. Some 40 per cent of these associations dated back to his boyhood, 45 per cent to his manhood, and 15 per cent to recent events. The recent associations were the least stable.

Jung [12] utilized Galton's word-association technique to investigate the unconscious, which Freud had opened to psychological investigation. It was noticed that some stimulus words were responded to easily and readily, whereas others gave rise to very slow or very fast responses; some caused complete blocking of response; others were accompanied by various unusual behavior, such as repetition of stimulus word, misinterpretation of it, strange or apparent senseless reaction, such as laughing or rhyming of stimulus word with a nonsense syllable. Jung assumed that all this deviant behavior occurred because the stimulus word had touched off a deep conflict or complex. By following up these cues, Jung was sometimes able to bring to light conflicts and strivings of which the patient was often unaware. As further evidence of the emotional nature of such responses, Jung found accompanying changes in the psychogalvanic reflex, muscular movements, and respiration. A larger number of indications of complexes was found in the disordered groups than in normal persons. He also found that schizophrenics tended to give a larger proportion of subjective responses dealing with inner feeling and thoughts, whereas manic-depressive patients tended to give more objective responses dealing with outer objects. This tendency to respond with either subjective or objective responses later contributed to Jung's formulation of his introvert-extrovert hypothesis.

Kent-Rosanoff Word-association Study

The most extensive systematic study of word associations was conducted by Kent and Rosanoff [14]. In contrast with the stimulus words utilized by Jung, which had been selected for the specific purpose of arousing personal emotional associations, Kent and Rosanoff tried to avoid words that are especially liable to call up personal experience.

MATERIALS. The list of words which they used is given in Table I.

PROCEDURE. The subject sits with his back to the experimenter, who reads the 100 stimulus words from a list. The response word and the reaction time, usually to the nearest fifth of a second, are recorded in appropriate columns next to each stimulus word. The

TABLE I

KENT-ROSANOFF WORD LIST

1. Table	26. Wish	51. Stem	76. Bitter
2. Dark	27. River	52 Lamp	77. Hammer
3. Music	28. White	53. Dream	78. Thirsty
4. Sickness	29. Beautiful	54. Yellow	79. City
5. Man	30. Window	55. Bread	80. Square
6. Deep	31. Rough	56. Justice	81. Butter
7. Soft	32. Citizen	57. Boy	82. Doctor
8. Eating	33. Foot	58. Light	83. Loud
9. Mountain	34. Spider	59. Health	84. Thief
10. House	35. Needle	60. Bible	85. Lion
11. Black	36. Red	61. Memory	86. Joy
12. Mutton	37. Sleep	62. Sheep	87. Bed
13. Comfort	38. Anger	63. Bath	88. Heavy
14. Hand	39. Carpet	64. Cottage	89. Tobacco
15. Short	40. Girl	65. Swift	90. Baby
16. Fruit	41. High	66. Blue	91. Moon
17. Butterfly	42. Working	67. Hungry	92. Scissors
18. Smooth	43. Sour	68. Priest	93. Quiet
19. Command	44. Earth	69. Ocean	94. Green
20. Chair	45. Trouble	70. Head	95. Salt
21. Sweet	46. Soldier	71. Stove	96. Street
22. Whistle	47. Cabbage	72. Long	97. King
23. Woman	48. Hard	73. Religion	98. Cheese
24. Cold	49. Eagle	74. Whiskey	99. Blossom
25. Slow	50. Stomach	75. Child	100. Afraid

words are read distinctly, and the subject is asked to respond with the first word that comes to his mind. If the subject responds with more than one word or with phrases, he is reminded that he must give only one word. If the subject fails to give a response within a reasonable time (15 seconds), the examiner goes on to the next word.

The list of 100 words was administered to 1000 normal individuals selected from the general population and ranging in age from 8 to over 80 years, and in education from the lowest to the highest level, only a fair fluency in English being a prerequisite for inclusion as a subject in the experiment. The subjects covered a wide variety of socio-economic levels, but the authors gave no indication of how well their group sampled the general population. A table of norms, giving the frequency value of each response to each of the 100 stimulus words, is included in a manual [13] in which the frequency value of any response to a given stimulus word may be determined.

RESULTS. The first step in the analysis of the data is to determine the frequency value of each response; i.e., how often the given response occurred in the 1000 normal individuals whom Kent and Rosanoff tested. If the response word is not found in the norms, it is regarded as an individual response.

In order to provide a scale of equal units for presenting the frequency values, the normal distribution was utilized, and each frequency value was converted into its corresponding standard score in the normal distribution curve. These standard scores were then grouped so as to provide eight steps of frequency values, as shown in Table II. Some typical distribution curves obtained by using the

TABLE II*

INDEX NUMBERS CORRESPONDING TO FREQUENCY OF RESPONSE WORDS TO THE KENT-ROSANOFF WORD-ASSOCIATION TEST (Based on normal distribution curve)

Index Number	K-R Frequency per 1000
0	0–1
1	2–6
2	7–23
3	24–67
4	68–159
5	160–309
6	310–500
7	501–709

* This table applies only to the responses to the stimulus word *lamp,* which had a maximum frequency response of 650. Similar calibrations have been made for each of the 100 words in the Kent-Rosanoff list, and these are available in "Manual for Word-Association Test," New York State Psychiatric Institute (mimeographed), 1947.

transformation of frequencies to index numbers are shown in Figs. 1 and 2.

Kent and Rosanoff applied their word-association test to 247 individuals with various types of disorders: dementia praecox (108), paranoic conditions (33), epilepsy (24), general paresis (32), manic-depressive insanity (32), involutional melancholia (8), alcoholic psychosis (6), and senile dementia (4). The proportion of common and individual reactions given by the normal subjects and the 247 mentally disordered individuals is shown in Table III. The doubtful responses were those which varied slightly in grammatical form from the standard responses.

The outstanding differential between the normal and the mentally ill persons was the proportion of common or popular reactions which were found in the two groups. Although the normal individuals

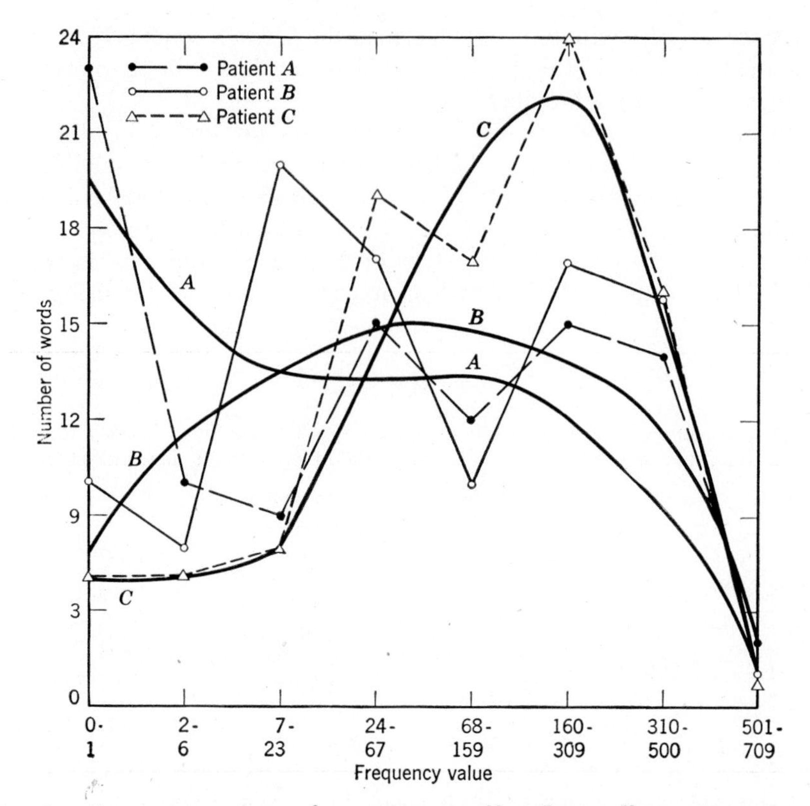

Fig. 1. Frequency values of responses to Kent-Rosanoff word-association test for three mental patients.

TABLE III

PERCENTAGE OF COMMON AND INDIVIDUAL REACTIONS GIVEN BY NORMAL AND DISORDERED PERSONS

Group	Common Reactions, Per Cent	Doubtful Reactions, Per Cent	Individual Reactions, Per Cent	Total *N*
Normal	91.7	1.5	6.8	1000
Abnormal	70.7	2.5	26.8	247

tended to give, in response to a particular stimulus word, one or another of a small group of common reactions, the mental patients gave a much larger proportion of highly individual responses. The percentage of common reactions given by each of the diagnostic categories is shown in Table IV.

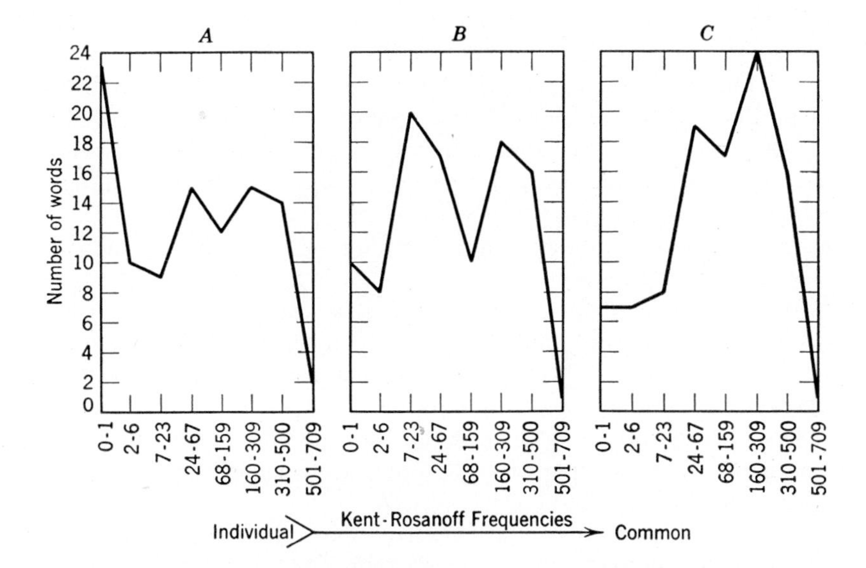

Fig. 2. Regrouping of material of Fig. 1 to show the types of word distribution found in the Kent-Rosanoff tests on patients at the Psychiatric Institute.

It will be noted that case *A* has a preponderance of responses in the lower frequency values, case C a preponderance in the higher frequency values (common), and case *B* falls in the middle between the other two.

TABLE IV

AVERAGE PERCENTAGE OF COMMON REACTIONS BY DIAGNOSTIC GROUPS
(Based on Reference 14)

Diagnostic Group	*N*	Percentage
Dementia praecox	108	58.9
Paranoic condition	33	71.3
Epilepsy	24	63.7
General paresis	32	71.8
Manic-depressive insanity	32	71.2
Normal individuals	1000	91.7

The clinical groups which deviate most from the normal persons in giving common reactions are those with dementia praecox and epilepsy, with only 59 per cent and 64 per cent of common responses respectively. Each of the three remaining clinical groups gives approximately 72 per cent of common responses.

On the basis of such analysis Kent and Rosanoff have concluded that "the one tendency which appears to be almost universal among normal persons is the tendency to give in response to any stimulus word, one or another of a small group of common reactions" [14]. This is not found to hold for abnormal individuals.

Kent and Rosanoff concluded that, in general, no sharp distinction can be drawn between normal and abnormal persons on the basis of frequency values alone. Individuals in some disease categories, however, especially dementia praecox, do reveal characteristic differentials, such as low proportion of common responses, neologisms (newly constructed words that have meaning only to the patient), and other types of deviating responses.

More recently attempts have been made to extend the study of word associations to normal individuals through the use of homographs, like the word *bat,* which may be interpreted in at least four different ways: (1) an animal, (2) a club, as for baseball, (3) to hit someone, or (4) to "go on a bat." Goodenough [7] has found that individuals differ in the type of interpretation that they choose and that their choice reflects their personality.

Another technique which utilizes free association to speech is the tautophone or verbal summator. In this technique the disordered individual is given auditory stimuli of low intensity—at the threshold of hearing—and is asked to tell what word or phrase is being said. The vocal stimuli are actually nonsense sounds, such as *uh-óh-ah-ée,* spoken so softly that even the normal individual can "hear a meaning into it" with some repetitions. These threshold stimuli are repeated several times so that their effect may summate and finally evoke a response. The responses given by disordered individuals have been analyzed according to various criteria, and correlations have been established between the patient's interpretation of the meaningless stimuli and his personality traits. See also page 560.

Similar techniques have been worked out in the visual field, such as the Rorschach test and the Thematic Apperception Test, which are described on pages 558–560 and 560–562. The interpretation placed upon the ambiguous pictures and ink-blots gives an indication of the subject's personality traits. Related to these projective procedures are analyses of handwriting and other expressive movements in disordered persons.

INFLUENCE OF ELECTRIC CONVULSIVE THERAPY ON MEMORY FUNCTIONING

One of the most prominent differences between normal and abnormal persons is found in memory functioning. A considerable amount of work has been done in this field, but most of it has been clinical rather than experimental. Unfortunately, the clinical and experimental approaches are quite far apart in this field. In contrast with intelligence, where for the most part the same concepts, same tests, and same techniques are utilized by clinicians and research workers, memory does not present such a united front. The greatest point of difference between the experimenter and the clinician is that the experimenter usually deals with implanted memories, whereas the clinician deals with "life" memories. Experimental psychologists naturally would also prefer to deal with life memories in their studies, but the genesis, history, and duration of such memories are usually obscure and defy scientific investigation. The few experimental results can be summarized briefly as indicating that mental patients, in general, take a longer time to learn new material but their retention of it seems to be no different from that of normal individuals. Certain types of patients, especially the Korsakoff, senile psychosis, and general paresis cases, however, are notoriously lacking in retention.

Usually a patient does not arrive at a clinic until he has sustained some injury or suffered some illness. It is too late then to obtain any experimental evidence of his premorbid memory functioning, and the clinician must resort to some shrewd guesses in deciding whether memory impairment has occurred. The recent introduction of shock therapy, however, has afforded experimentalists an opportunity to observe and study the alteration of memory functioning produced by the shocks. Since the patient's functioning is not altered too severely in any other respect than memory, the setting of the experiment is ideal for the investigation of memory functioning and impairment. Such investigations have been conducted at several institutions where shock therapy is administered, and the study that will be reported here took place at the New York State Psychiatric Institute and Hospital [1, 8, 19]. The most important question to be answered is: Does shock therapy permanently injure memory functioning? In answering this question, light was also thrown on the following problems: (1) what particular aspects of the memory process are affected? (2) are all types of memory materials affected equally? and (3) is material learned long before shock therapy also affected by the subsequent shocks?

It must be recalled that memory functioning depends upon three important elements: (1) learning or registration, (2) retention, and (3) testing or reproduction of remembered material. The final test of retention is influenced by the manner of original learning, the activity intervening between learning and retention, and the method used in testing retention. The experimental intervention of shock with its concomitant effects on memory offers an opportunity to study each of these three steps in the process of memory functioning.

Materials

For investigating memory changes in an objective way, "pure-culture" memories are needed—uncontaminated memories whose history and duration are known and to which presumably no special emotional attachments adhere. For this reason paired associates were used.

These paired associates consisted of specially prepared lists of two types, meaningful and semi-meaningful words. The meaningful lists consisted of fifteen pairs of common English two-syllable words selected from the highest frequency levels of Thorndike and Lorge's *The Teacher's Word Book of 30,000 Words* [17]. The semi-meaningful lists consisted of ten household commodities paired with ten pseudo-brand names composed of nonsense syllables and selected from Dunlap's *List of 43,200 Dissyllable Words and Paralogs* [4]. The pairs were constructed in such a manner that there was no apparent association between the members of each pair.

TABLE V

TYPICAL MEANINGFUL AND SEMI-MEANINGFUL CARDS USED FOR LEARNING, RELEARNING, RECALL, AND RECOGNITION

	Learning, Relearning, and Recall		Recognition	
Meaningful	EXPRESS	ADMIT	EXPRESS	PASSAGE ADMIT MANNER RIVER
Semi-meaningful	COFFEE	LUBEB	COFFEE	LUBEB PELIF MEDIG GUGOK

The paired associates were typed on individual cards as shown in Table V. The same card was used for learning, relearning, and recall. A second card was used for measuring recognition. This card, which is also shown in Table V, consisted of the first member of the pair followed by four choices, including the correct one. Care was taken to make the three incorrect choices as homogeneous as possible with the correct choice in form, level of difficulty, and general appearance.

Procedure

The patients were tested 30 to 60 minutes before treatment and the retesting was done 24 hours after treatment.[2] Every patient was taught a meaningful and a semi-meaningful list at each learning session up to the day when the confusion induced by the treatment impaired the speed of learning to too great a degree. Then he was given only one list each time, alternating the meaningful with the semi-meaningful material. The method of adjusted learning, as described by Woodworth [18] and Gillette [6], was used. A more detailed description of the method, as applied to our problem, will be given.

For the learning of the meaningful lists the subjects were directed as follows: "I want to see how quickly you can learn to associate two words so that when I show you the first word you will immediately read it and give me the word that was paired with it. On this card you will see two words in succession. Read them both aloud and try to connect them in your mind, so that whenever you see the first word, you will think of the second word."

During the first presentation of the list, both the first member and the second member of the pair were exposed for approximately 30 seconds, and the subject read them aloud in succession. Beginning with the second presentation, the experimenter exposed only the first member, the second being covered by his hand. A set interval of time, not exceeding 30 seconds, was allowed the patient in which to recall the second member.

The cards were shuffled before each presentation of a list. When the second member of the pair was correctly anticipated, the card in question was eliminated from the pack. By employing this method the factor of overlearning was eliminated, and all the pairs of the list could be regarded as learned to the same criterion of one correct repetition.

The same procedure was used in learning the semi-meaningful lists, in which the pairs consisted of a common household commodity paired with a nonsense syllable. In order to make the task of learning easier for the nonsense syllables, they were introduced as possible

[2] Because Saturday was a treatment day, and the patients were not available for testing Sunday, one list each week was relearned 48 hours after treatment.

brand names for the household commodities with which they were paired.

Retention

The retention test consisted of three parts: recall, recognition, and relearning. In testing retention by the recall method, each card was presented with the first member of the pair exposed, and the subject was asked to give the second member, which was covered by the experimenter's hand. After each exposure the patient was asked if he remembered learning the word before, if he was doubtful about it, or if he didn't remember learning it before. The second member of the pair was not exposed at any time during recall, regardless of whether the patient answered correctly.

In testing retention by the recognition method, the patient was handed the recognition cards and was asked which of the four words on the right he thought went with the one on the left. (See Table V.) If the patient protested that he had never learned the pair previously and, therefore, could not make a selection, he was asked to guess. After each response the patient was asked to indicate whether it was a mere guess, doubtful, or certain.

In testing retention by the saving method or relearning method, the learning cards were presented in the same way as for the original learning task, and the method of adjusted learning as described previously was utilized.

Learning difficulty was measured by the number of times each item card had to be exposed before it was correctly anticipated. This, of course, included the initial exposure, in which no correct anticipation was possible, but not the last exposure, which was, of course, the criterion trial and had to be correctly anticipated.

The relearning score was computed in the same way, but allowance was made for the correct recalls and recognitions that preceded relearning. If an item was correctly recalled, it was regarded as not requiring any relearning before correct anticipation; therefore, correctly recalled items were subtracted from the total score in the subsequent relearning.

If an item was not correctly recalled during the recall test, but was correctly recognized during the recognition test, however, such correct recognition was regarded as an extra repetition. Therefore, all correct recognitions were added to the score. This resulted in the following scoring formula for the relearning score: number of repetitions necessary to relearn a list (exclusive of last criterion repetition), minus items correctly recalled, plus items correctly recognized.

Results

The following questions are answered by an analysis of the results obtained on the individual patients:

1. How does learning ability vary before, during, and after the course of treatment?

2. How does retention, as measured by the saving method, change during the course of treatment?

3. Does electric convulsive therapy (ECT) affect meaningful and semi-meaningful material differentially?

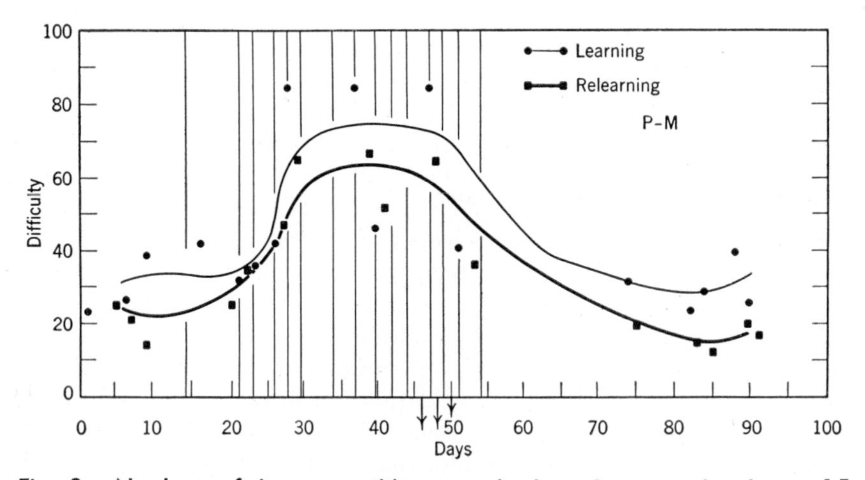

Fig. 3. Number of item repetitions required to learn and relearn 15 lists of 15 meaningful paired associates each before, during, and after ECT.

The day-to-day learning and relearning of one patient *P* is shown in Fig. 3. This figure reads as follows: On the first day of the control period (day 0) the patient required 22 item repetitions before learning the list to the criterion of 1 successful repetition. On the fifth day she relearned the same material and required 23 item repetitions to satisfy the criterion of 1 correct repetition. The other points on the graph are read similarly. The days on which shock was administered are indicated by a thin vertical line. Because the day-to-day record is so irregular, it is difficult to draw definite conclusions from it, except to note that there was a considerable increase in difficulty of learning with the introduction of shock.

In order to simplify the treatment of the data, the learning period was divided into four parts: (1) the control period, from the first to the twentieth day (including the initial shock-treatment day); (2)

the initial treatment period (twenty-first to twenty-seventh day); (3) the final treatment period (twenty-eighth to fifty-fifth day); and (4) the post-treatment period lasting 16 days.

The average learning and relearning scores for the four experimental conditions are shown in the second and third columns of Table VI. It will be noted that the average learning score increased considerably during the final treatment period. In order to determine whether the differences in learning induced by the treatment were statistically significant, the four means were compared with each other by the technique known as analysis of variance.[3] These means were found to differ significantly from each other, indicating a degree of differentiation on the .01 level of significance. Similarly, the means of the relearning scores were also found to be statistically significant.

It cannot be decided from the results of this analysis whether the shock treatments actually affected retention, since our measure of retention is dependent upon several factors: (1) difficulty of original learning; (2) difficulty of relearning; and (3) retention itself. Hence we must devise a method for keeping constant the first two factors if we are to determine the influence of shock on retention itself. To effect this, an analysis of covariance was undertaken [5, 16].

Analysis of covariance consists essentially of removing the influence of one factor while considering variations in another factor. It performs the same task in analysis of variance that partial correlation performs in the analysis of correlation coefficients. In the present problem analysis of covariance removed the influence of the original learning scores from the relearning scores and thus provided a measure of pure retention unaffected by the influence of variations in difficulty of initial learning. The first step was to predict by means of a regression equation the relearning score on a given day from a knowledge of the initial learning score. The difference between the predicted and observed relearning scores would be confined to chance fluctuations if shock did not alter retention.

Table VI shows the initial learning score, relearning score, and predicted relearning score for the four experimental conditions. In the next column are shown the deviations between the predicted and observed scores. These deviations must be investigated to determine whether they are due to chance before any significance can be attached to them. The means for the various conditions differ significantly from each other and are less than expected for the two control conditions (pre-treatment and post-treatment) and considerably larger

[3] This technique is merely an elaboration of the comparison of two means with their standard error of the difference. By means of this technique, statistical comparisons can be made of four averages all at the same time.

TABLE VI

LEARNING, RELEARNING, AND SAVING SCORES FOR MEANINGFUL PAIRED ASSOCIATES (Patient *P*)

Condition	Number of Lists	Learning	Relearning				Saving	Percentage Saving
			Observed	Predicted	Difference	Adjusted		
Control	5	35.0	20.4	29.2	−8.8	23.3	18.5	44.2
Initial treatment	3	35.7	38.3	29.5	8.8	40.9	1.0	2.4
Final treatment	5	67.2	56.0	42.9	13.2	45.3	−3.4	−8.1
Post-treatment	5	28.8	16.0	26.6	−10.6	21.5	20.3	48.5
Total	18	41.8	32.1	32.1	0.0	32.1	9.7	23.2
F ratio		7.62	26.26			12.60		
P		$<.01$	$<.01$			$<.01$		

than expected under the two experimental conditions. It may be concluded that, when shock is interpolated between learning and relearning, a considerable loss in retention occurs, in contrast with the saving which occurs under control conditions.

If it is assumed that the learning difficulty of each list was constant at 41.8 (the average learning score), the corresponding relearning score would be 32.1 (the average relearning score for the entire experiment). By algebraically adding to this expected mean performance the amount of deviation for each experimental condition, we obtained a new series of adjusted means, which are free of the learning difficulty level but which nevertheless reflect the differential effects of the control and experimental factors. These adjusted means and the corresponding percentages of savings are shown in the last three columns of the table. On the basis of this procedure the saving during the shock period vanishes completely, indicating that, when the effect of shock on learning ability is ruled out by statistical means, retention is found to be completely wiped out by shock.

It must, however, not be concluded that the absence of saving indicates a destruction of the memory traces. As was shown previously through a study of interference effects [20], the memory traces are not destroyed; they are simply disorganized and therefore cannot contribute toward the task of relearning.

The results for the semi-meaningful material were quite similar to those for the meaningful material with the exception that, although more effort was required to learn the semi-meaningful material, relearning proved to be considerably easier. Similar findings on this differential in retention between meaningful and semi-meaningful material have been reported by Hull [11].

RECALL. Thus far, we have dealt only with retention, as measured by the relearning method. How does ECT affect recall? On the 2 days before shock was administered (ninth and fourteenth days) 5 and 4 items respectively were recalled. After the introduction of shock, recall dropped out completely and did not reappear until after the shock treatments were ended. Then it gradually returned to its pre-treatment level. Similar results were obtained for the semi-meaningful material.

The data for the four experimental conditions, together with an analysis of variance for both types of material, are shown in Table VII.

TABLE VII

AVERAGE NUMBER OF ITEMS RECALLED IN MEANINGFUL AND SEMI-MEANINGFUL PAIRED ASSOCIATES BY EXPERIMENTAL CONDITIONS
(Patient P)

Conditions	Meaningful		Semi-meaningful	
	Number of lists	Mean	Number of lists	Mean
Control	3	3.0	2	0.0
Initial treatment	3	0.0	3	0.0
Final treatment	4	0.0	5	0.0
Post-treatment	5	2.4	5	3.2
Total	15	1.4	15	1.1
Number of items per list		15.0		10.0
F ratio	8.07		6.69	
P	$<.01$		$<.01$	

It is quite apparent that the interpolation of shock between learning and relearning caused recall to vanish completely and produced a significant decline below the amount of recall noted in the control and post-treatment periods.

Recognition

During the control period the patient was able to recognize correctly almost all the 15 items. With the beginning of shock, however, retention as measured by recognition dropped slightly. During the final treatment period it dropped even further, but after the end of treatment it returned to its preshock level. The corresponding data for the semi-meaningful material shows a similar pattern. The drop began in the initial shock period, descended further during the final shock period, and recovered to its pre-treatment level in the post-treatment period.

Table VIII shows the data for meaningful and semi-meaningful paired associates by treatment periods. It may be concluded that

TABLE VIII

AVERAGE NUMBER OF ITEMS RECOGNIZED IN MEANINGFUL AND SEMI-MEANINGFUL PAIRED ASSOCIATES BY EXPERIMENTAL CONDITIONS
(Patient *P*)

Conditions	Meaningful		Semi-meaningful	
	Number of lists	Mean	Number of lists	Mean
Control	5	14.6	4	10.0
Initial treatment	3	14.0	3	9.7
Final treatment	3	11.7	5	8.0
Post-treatment	5	14.8	5	10.0
Total	16	14.0	17	9.4
Number items per list		15.0		10.0
F ratio	2.33		3.89	
P	>.05		>.05	

there is a slight, but non-significant, loss in recognition during the treatment period in both meaningful and semi-meaningful paired associates.

Apparent Loss of Familiarity

Despite the resistance to impairment that recognition offers, closer analysis of the recognition process indicates that certain qualitative changes take place in it. In earlier experiments several cases were observed from the moment of shock to the moment when they were fully reoriented. The patient spends from 3 to 10 minutes in a state of complete disorientation. About 10 minutes after shock, however, when the patient is sufficiently reoriented to answer questions, he very often exhibits the phenomenon of *jamais vu*. Everything about him seems strange and new. He cannot remember ever having seen the examiner before nor the place he is in. He sometimes does not even remember his own name, and women will often give their maiden rather than married names. After a little while this *jamais vu* phenomenon seems to disappear, either of its own accord or through the patient's relearning by renewed contact with his environment.

When the recognition cards are shown to him soon after shock, the patient protests that he never saw them before. When urged to guess, however, he will guess correctly more often than would be expected by chance. This loss of familiarity despite the presence of the memory trace has been called "apparent loss of familiarity." If no relearning takes place, this apparent loss of familiarity is found to persist after the immediate confusional period following the shock is over.

Table IX shows the appearance of this phenomenon in the meaningful paired associates soon after the first shock, its continuance during the shock period, and its complete disappearance in lists learned after the end of therapy. Table IX also shows the data for the semi-

TABLE IX

PERCENTAGE OF CORRECT RECOGNITIONS ACCOMPANIED BY APPARENT LOSS OF FAMILIARITY

Conditions	Meaningful		Semi-meaningful	
	Number of lists	Percentage	Number of lists	Percentage
Control	13	00.0	12	00.0
Initial treatment	15	53.9	15	41.5
Final treatment	22	77.3	20	58.1
Post-treatment	14	00.0	12	00.0
Total	64		59	

meaningful material. A quantitative analysis of these data indicates that during the treatment period from 40 to 70 per cent of the correct recognitions are characterized by this loss of familiarity.

Thus far, it has been shown that recognition and familiarity will suffer when electro-shock is interposed between the learning and the testing period. But what happened to the material learned during the control week before shock was introduced? This material consisted of the oldest memories implanted, and no shock intervened between its initial learning and its testing 24 hours later. Did the treatments affect these memories also, and how long after treatment did the effects persist? In order to answer these questions, the lists taught during the control week were reviewed 2 weeks after the end of treatment, or some 60 days after their initial learning. Recall was still absent, and there was a slight decline in recognition, as compared to the original recognition test. The apparent loss of familiarity persisted. No such loss of familiarity has been observed in material learned after treatment, nor has it been observed in patients not receiving treatment.

It would seem as if that part of the recognition process which depends on the awareness of familiarity splits off from the memory trace during the treatment period and remains split off; but the basic memory trace on which the recognition process depends is not impaired, since the patient can recognize correctly even though he is unaware of the basis for his recognition.

This apparent loss of familiarity may perhaps play a greater role in the therapeutic process than is now appreciated. If the shock affects earlier personal memories in the same way that it affects the memories implanted in this experiment, it may tend to have a salutary influence on those perceptual cues in the patient's environment which tended in the past to evoke anxiety or irritation. If shock makes it more difficult to recall earlier memories spontaneously and if it causes loss of familiarity for objects and events that present themselves before the patient, this reduction in perceptual cues may help the patient resume his place in society. Thus far, however, there is no experimental proof that shock affects the feeling of familiarity for events occurring before the control week. Clinical impressions and observations have been recorded on the patients used in this study, however, which bear witness to the retroactive effect of these shocks on familiarity for earlier memories. Thus, one patient looked into her clothing closet and demanded to know who had put dresses in there which she herself had bought and placed in the closet several months previously. Another could not realize that the wristwatch in his dresser drawer in his apartment was his own and, although he assumed it must be, could not remember how he obtained it. It is at least plausible that, if he had not been reminded by his father (or in our terminology, relearned) that it was a gift, he would have continued to have a loss of familiarity for the origin of the watch.

Whether this loss of familiarity is itself a basic cause of improvement or whether it is merely a reflection of the lessened anxiety which the patient feels in general is difficult to estimate at this time. Further work is being continued with more personal memories whose presence can be determined before treatment begins.

Because free-association responses probably depend upon long-enduring memories and at least some of them seem to be emotionally charged, the free-association experiment is very suitable for investigating the influence of ECT on more personal, emotionally tinged memories. To this end the word-association test may be given before electric convulsive therapy begins, and the responses classified according to the degree to which they may be indicative of emotionality: (1) slow or very quick reaction time, (2) complete blocking of response, (3) clang association, like bell-rell, (4) phrase instead of a single response word, (5) proper name, (6) repetition or partial repetition of stimulus word, and (7) perseveration. After ECT is completed, the patient is retested with the same words to note whether his responses have changed and whether he gives fewer emotionally toned responses after treatment.

SENSITIVITY TO LIGHT IN HYSTERICAL BLINDNESS

The hysterical patient is sometimes characterized by the fact that he suffers from a loss or disturbance of bodily functions, such as sight, hearing, or touch. The symptoms of the hysterical patient seem at first glance to be due either to an organic cause or to malingering, but neither of these two suppositions is correct. No organic basis sufficient to explain these symptoms can be found, nor is the patient consciously misrepresenting or lying. In order to determine whether there is an actual loss of sensation or only an apparent loss, direct observation and measurement of the affected area are not suitable, because the patient fails to report any sensation whenever the affected area is involved. The following experiment indicates that, despite the fact that the patient suffering from hysteria does not "perceive" certain stimuli, he nevertheless can react to them even though he is unaware of this reaction. Two cases have been selected from the literature, one of hysterical blindness [2] and the other of genuine organic blindness (hemianopsia) [10], in order to contrast hysterical blindness with organic impairment of vision and to demonstrate the methods used. The hysterical patient was a 45-year-old male who became weak while attending a meeting, noticed feelings of numbness, and fainted. After admission to the hospital he began to complain of bilateral partial blindness and deafness of the left ear. His visual fields were plotted at this time and found to be asymmetrically restricted. On the basis of his clinical behavior and ophthalmological findings he was diagnosed as a psychopathic personality with hysterical symptoms. The case of hemianopsia was a 25-year-old woman who had been operated on to remove part of the left occipital lobe. Her visual fields showed a right homonymous hemianopsia.

Facilitation and Inhibition of Eyelid Reflex

First, a test was made of the blind area in the hysterical patient by presenting, in random order, light stimuli to the blind area and to the seeing area, with instructions to the patient to respond by tapping with his finger whenever he saw the light. He invariably tapped when the light fell on the seeing area and did not respond when it fell on the blind area. Apparently the direct approach of determining whether the patient was capable of consciously perceiving light in the affected area yielded negative results. A more indirect method, independent of conscious reporting, had to be found.

The method selected depended on the fact that stimulation in one modality may augment or inhibit the response in another modality. Hilgard [9] had reported that the normal reflex response of winking to a sudden noise can be modified by flashing a light into the eye before the sudden noise is heard. If the time interval between light and sound is extremely short (25 to 50 milliseconds), the normal reflex is augmented; whereas, if the time interval between light and sound is lengthened to 100 to 200 milliseconds, the normal reflex is considerably reduced. The apparent reason for this phenomenon is that light by itself will also produce a wink reflex of a rudimentary type. If the time interval between light and sound is such that the effects of the two stimuli can summate, the resulting response of the lid reflex is augmented considerably, even more than would be expected from mere arithmetical summation of the two responses. When the time interval is longer, the two responses interfere with each other, and inhibition results.

The method utilized in this experiment will detect the presence of an eyelid reflex to light even though it is too faint to produce actual lid movement. Furthermore, this method can be tested in the blind area and in the seeing area of the patient, the seeing area serving as a control for the blind area.

Figure 4 gives a diagram of the apparatus used. The movement of the eyelid was photographed by Dodge's shadow method [3]. The shadow was produced by attaching an artificial eyelash made of paper to the left eyelid. The sound stimulus, which was magnetically controlled, was produced by a wire hammer striking a wooden resonator. The visual stimulus was produced by suddenly illuminating a piece of white blotting paper. The film for photographing the movement of the eyelid was carried by a pendulum-photochronograph, which at the same time controlled the interval between stimuli.

Some sample records are shown in Fig. 5. The interval between the sound and the light stimuli which was intended to produce reinforcement of the eyelid reflex to sound was 45 milliseconds, whereas the interval which was calculated to inhibit the reflex was 120 milliseconds. In order to facilitate the successive illumination of the seeing field (on the left) and the blind field (on the right), a rotating mirror was utilized as shown in Fig. 4. When the patient was placed in position for the experiment, the entire field of vision subtended an angle of 10

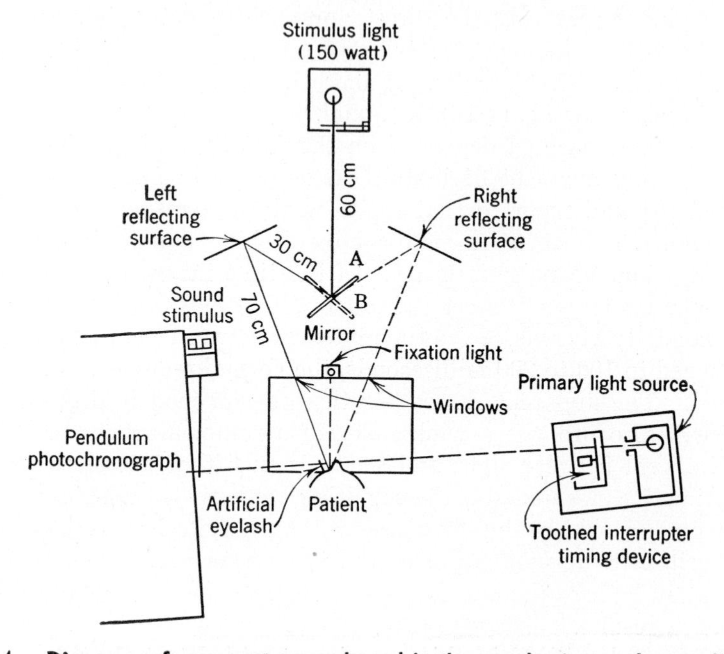

Fig. 4. Diagram of apparatus employed in the production and recording of conditioned eyelid responses.

degrees about the fixation points, ranging from 17 degrees of retinal arc to the left up to 27 degrees to the right of the fixation point. The white blotting paper used as the illuminating surface subtended 4 degrees in the vertical dimension. The choice of these positions was dictated by the need to avoid the blind spot and yet to be well within the visual field. The intensity of the sound stimulus was selected so that it was loud enough to cause a reflex wink and was held constant at this intensity throughout the experiment.

In order to force the patient to maintain a constant position, his head was placed against a forehead rest and a biting board placed between his teeth. The right eye was covered so as to exclude all light. Frequent rests were given to avoid discomfort. The breathing before each presentation of the stimulus was controlled by command, and no

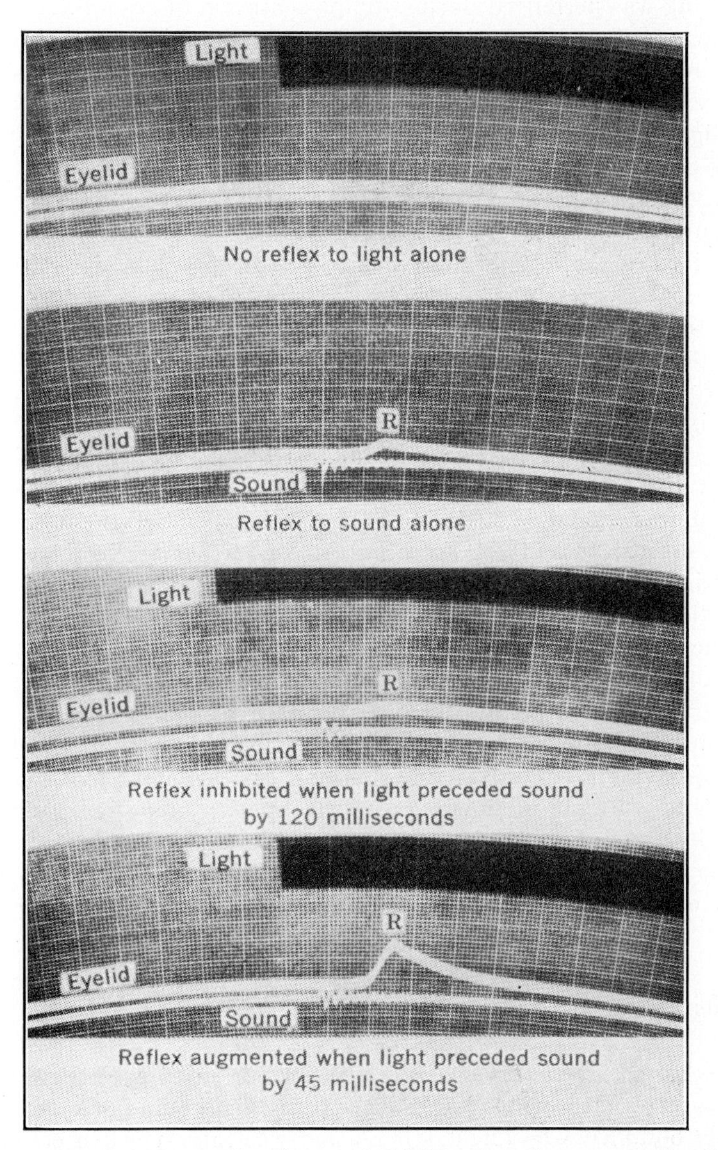

Fig. 5. Reproduced records of normal, inhibited, and augmented reflexes.

A rise in the eyelid shadow indicates lid closure. The occurrence of the light shows as a darkening at the top of the record. The sound shows as a break in the white line just below the lid shadow. Radial time lines read in units of 5 milliseconds. Every tenth line is emphasized, so that the larger units are 50 milliseconds. Each record represents about 0.8 second. Curved abscissae, due to the path of the pendulum, furnish base lines for reading amplitude, their spacing being 1 millimeter on records. (From Hilgard and Wendt [10].)

breathing was permitted during the presentation of stimuli. In order to acquaint the patient with the proper procedure, it was necessary to give several preliminary trials. The experimental design consisted of the presentation of the following four types of stimuli in random order: (1) light alone, (2) sound alone, (3) light preceding sound by 45 milliseconds (reinforcement), and (4) light preceding sound by 120 milliseconds (inhibition).

Figure 5 shows the responses obtained under these four types of conditions in the left (seeing) field. The results indicate that, when light alone is presented, the reflex lid movement never occurs. This holds true of the normal as well as of the blind part of the field. When light precedes sound by 45 milliseconds, a tendency to wink appears, but when light precedes sound by 120 milliseconds, this tendency to wink is partially inhibited.

The method described was used for the case of hemianopsia and served also for the hysterical patient with the following modification. A light was presented just above the fixation point in the area where the hysterical patient *could see* and again further above the fixation point in the area where he *could not see.* The stimulus was presented at a distance of 30 centimeters from the eyes and subtended an angle ranging from 5 degrees to 9 degrees above the fixation point. In the area of blindness the stimulus extended from 16 degrees to 20 degrees above the fixation point. The patient used binocular vision, and the stimulus consisted of patches of white bond paper illuminated from behind, giving an approximate brightness of 1 apparent foot-candle as measured with an illuminometer. The patient reported seeing the light by tapping with his finger. Whenever the light was presented to the lower (seeing) portion of the field, he tapped, but he never reported the light when presented to the upper (unseeing) field.

Results

Neither the seeing area of the eye nor the blind area was capable of yielding a measurable lid response to the light stimulus alone. The results obtained when light stimulation was introduced in conjuction with sound are shown in Table X.

For the hysterical patient, when light preceded the sound by 45 milliseconds, the reflex to sound was strongly reinforced. When the light preceded the sound by 225 milliseconds, there was almost complete inhibition of the reflex to sound. This reinforcement and inhibition were the same, regardless of whether the stimulus light was presented in the blind or the seeing area.

TABLE X

AMPLITUDE OF THE LID REFLEX TO SOUND IN HYSTERICAL BLINDNESS AND HEMIANOPSIA

Interval between Light and Sound	Hysterical Blindness					Hemianopsia				
	N	Mean, Millimeter	Deviation from Control	D/σ_D	P*	N	Mean, Millimeter	Deviation from Control	D/σ_D	P*
1. Control (sound alone)	6	3.7	—			8	1.5	—		
2. Reinforcement (45 millisecond interval)										
a. Seeing area	5	12.0	8.3	4.10	<.01	9	3.7	2.2	1.44	.07
b. Blind area	6	12.4	8.7	4.60	<.01	8	1.2	−0.3	−0.18	.43
3. Inhibition (120–225 millisecond interval)										
a. Seeing area	5	0.0	−3.7	−1.87	.03	8	0.8	−0.7	−0.44	.33
b. Blind area	5	0.2	−3.5	−1.76	.04	7	1.5	0.0	0.00	.50
Standard deviation			3.27					3.15		

* Since the direction of the deviation is established on the basis of previous experimentation, the value of $P/2$ is given to indicate how often the observed difference would lie in the positive or negative direction, depending upon the hypothesis under examination (reinforcement or inhibition).

The data for the patient suffering from hemianopsia are also presented in Table X. In this patient the visual defect was organically based, resulting from an ablation of a considerable portion of the left occipital area. Reinforcement and inhibition effects were quite apparent when light impinged on the seeing area but were absent when light was presented in the blind area.

When the sound was presented without being preceded by the light, the average amplitude of the eyelid in hysterical blindness was 3.7 millimeters, and in hemianopsia 1.5 millimeters. This control level may serve as a standard for comparing the amplitude under the two experimental conditions for the seeing and the blind areas. The deviation of the various amplitude measurements from this control level is given in the column in Table X headed "Deviation from Control." In order to obtain a good estimate of the standard error for these measures, separate analyses of variance were made for the data of the hysterical patient and that of the case of hemianopsia. The within-condition variance was obtained and converted into a standard deviation, which was found to be of the same magnitude in the two patients, 3.27 and 3.15. The case of hysteria showed a significant augmentation in eyelid reflex for the 45-millisecond interval between light and sound. Both the seeing area and the blind area showed the same magnitude of deviation, and the difference between the two areas was not statistically significant. Similarly, when the interval between light and sound was 225 milliseconds, the eyelid reflex practically disappeared in both areas.

The case of hemianopsia showed an augmentation of the eyelid reflex for the 45-millisecond interval and an inhibition for the 120-millisecond interval in the seeing area, but practically no change in the blind area. The close parallel between the behavior of the eyelid reflex from the seeing and blind areas in the hysterical patient was not found in the case of hemianopsia. Although the differences between the blind and the seeing areas in the case of hemianopsia are not quite statistically significant, the general direction indicates that the response of the blind area is uninfluenced by light, whereas that of the seeing area seems to be influenced by light. Subsequent data from another trial with the hemianopsia patient were found to show a statistically significant difference between the seeing and the blind areas.

Conditioning

Further experiments with the hysterical patient were conducted in an attempt to condition the eyelid reaction to light in the blind area. The unconditioned stimulus was a puff of air against the cornea, and the conditioned stimulus was the same visual stimulus as described above. The light preceded the puff by 400 milliseconds.

Although the patient never reported seeing the light, he gradually developed a tendency to close the lid when the light appeared. At the end of the experiment the closure to the light had increased to such an extent that he was closing his eyes completely to a light which he did not report as visible. As indicated by Table XI, the amplitude of the eyelid responses was practically the same for both the seeing and the blind areas, being 16.2 millimeters for the seeing area and 17.5 millimeters for the blind area, a difference well below statistical significance.

Verbal Conditioning

In the two preceding methods, the patient's sensitivity to light was determined by reflex and conditioned response methods. In the third

TABLE XI

CONDITIONED RESPONSES TO A LIGHT PRESENTED IN BLIND AND SEEING AREAS OF A HYSTERICAL PATIENT [2]

	Amplitude of Conditioned Response, millimeters	
	N	Mean
Seeing area	6	16.2
Blind area	6	17.5
F ratio		0.6
Probability		$>.05$

method to be reported, the patient was trained to shout "Light!" each time he heard a certain sudden sound. The sound was then repeatedly presented just after a light in the blind area. The problem to be examined is whether presentation of the light alone will cause the patient to shout "light" when the light impinges on the blind area.

In two instances the patient pronounced the word "light" even though he was unable to perceive it consciously, since it fell on the blind area. In thirteen other instances there was a sharp intake of breath in preparation for shouting, but no word actually came.

Summary

It was found possible to demonstrate that a hysterical patient can actually perceive light sensations in the part of the visual field which he consciously reports as being blind. This was demonstrated by showing that a light preceding a sudden sound will alter the normal wink reflex to sound, regardless of whether the light is presented to the affected or the unaffected area. This phenomenon could not be elicited in the blind area of a case of hemianopsia. Similarly, the hysterically blind area can be conditioned to give responses to light.

EPILOGUE

The three experiments reported in this chapter have exemplified the type of approach required for working with disordered individuals. These approaches by no means exhaust the field. The word-association experiment is the prototype of the group of techniques known as projective methods. These techniques have in common the following: (1) they are indirect approaches to the evaluation of personality; (2) they deal with material to which there is no right or wrong answer; (3) they deal with material so amorphous that the disordered person can project into them his own feelings, attitudes, fears, and insecurities. These techniques are powerful tools for probing personality and have proved their worth in the clinic. Not very much standardization has thus far been attempted, and a careful, rigorous experimental verification of the claims of the clinic now demands the attention of scientific research.

The memory experiments with patients receiving ECT illustrate the type of basic psychological research that can throw light on therapeutic procedures with disordered persons. The loss of memory was clinically observed long before it was measured by psychological techniques. The experimental results indicate what particular aspects of memory suffer under the treatment and pave the way for understanding, at least in part, the psychological importance of the memory changes that occur and their implications for recovery. Similar investigations into the psychological functioning of patients before and after frontal lobotomies, insulin therapy, and similar therapeutic procedures have been carried out and found to be useful in understanding both patient and therapy.

The third type of experiment dealing with functional and organic disorders gives an indication of how the psychologist, through such indirect methods as conditioning, can sometimes overcome the conscious or unconscious tendencies of a patient to interfere with the proper functioning of his own capacities and can determine whether the reported defect is on an organic or a functional basis. Other methods for attaining the same goal are the use of drugs and hypnosis, but these fields are so vast that only a passing reference can be made to them here. Conditioning studies in psychotics have indicated that, although it is more difficult to establish a conditioned response in them, once established it persists longer.

Other types of approaches that have been found useful in studying the disordered person are voluntary and involuntary behavior, level of aspiration, interrupted activity. Physiological studies utilizing the psychogalvanic skin response, respiratory and circulatory changes, and parotid-gland secretion have yielded interesting information, by means of which the different types of disordered persons can sometimes be differentiated for diagnostic purposes.

REFERENCES

1. COFFIN, JUDITH I. Unpublished master's essay. Columbia University, 1946.
2. COHEN, L. H., E. R. HILGARD, and G. R. WENDT. Sensitivity to light in a case of hysterical blindness studied by reinforcement, inhibition and conditioning methods. *Yale J. Biol. Med.*, 1933, *6*, 61–67.
3. DODGE, R. A pendulum-photochronograph. *J. Exper. Psychol.*, 1926, *9*, 155–161.
4. DUNLAP, K. *List of 43,200 Dissyllable Words and Paralogs Systematically Compiled and Arranged for Further Selection to Provide Adequate Lists for Experimental Work in Learning.* Division of Anthropology and Psychology, National Research Council.
5. GARRETT, H. E., and J. ZUBIN. The analysis of variance in psychological research. *Psychol. Bull.*, 1943, *40*, 233–267.
6. GILLETTE, A. L. Learning and retention: a comparison of three experimental procedures. *Arch. Psychol.*, 1936, *28*, No. 198.
7. GOODENOUGH, F. The use of free association in the objective measurement of personality. In *Studies in Personality, Contributed in honor of Lewis M. Terman.* McGraw-Hill, 1942.
8. HANSEN, H. Unpublished master's essay. Columbia University, 1946.
9. HILGARD, E. R. Reinforcement and inhibition of eyelid reflexes. *J. Gen. Psychol.*, 1933, *8*, 85–113.
10. HILGARD, E. R., and G. R. WENDT. The problem of reflex sensitivity to light studied in a case of hemianopsia. *Yale J. Biol. Med.*, 1933, *5*, 373–385.
11. HULL, C. L. The formation and retention of associations among the insane. *Amer. J. Psychol.*, 1917, *28*, 419–435.
12. JUNG, C. G., (Ed.) *Studies in Word Association.* London: William Heineman, 1918.
13. Kent-Rosanoff Free Association Test. Reprinted from *Manual of Psychiatry.* A. J. Rosanoff, Ed. John Wiley, 1927.
14. KENT, G. H., and A. J. ROSANOFF. A study of association in insanity. *Amer. J. Insanity,* 1910–1911, *67*, 37–96; 317–390.
15. LANDIS, C., and M. M. BOLLES. *A Textbook of Abnormal Psychology.* Macmillan, 1946.
16. SNEDECOR, G. W. *Statistical Methods.* 4th Ed. Ames, Iowa: Iowa State College Press, 1946 (Chap. 12).
17. THORNDIKE, E. L., and I. D. LORGE. *The Teacher's Word Book of 30,000 Words.* New York: Bureau of Publications, Teachers College, Columbia University, 1944.
18. WOODWORTH, R. S. *Experimental Psychology.* Henry Holt, 1938.
19. ZUBIN, J., and S. E. BARRERA. Effect of electric convulsive therapy on memory. *Proc. Soc. Exper. Biol. Med.*, 1941, *48*, 596–597.
20. ZUBIN, J. The effect of electroshock therapy on "interference" in memory (abstract). *Psychol. Bull.*, 1942, *39*, 511.

SUGGESTED READING

HUNT, J. McV. *Personality and the Behavior Disorders.* New York: Ronald Press, 1944.

Chapter 21

Methods of Studying the Behavior and Development of Young Children

Helen L. Koch[1]

The basic dynamics of child behavior is often not radically different from that in the adult. Since the differences that do exist between the young and the mature are chiefly in degree or emphasis, the methods employed in studying children have been directed toward many of the problems explored in adults. As might be expected, however, the greater the extent to which child subjects deviate in age from the adult, the greater are the necessary methodological adjustments, even when the same basic problems are approached. This being the case, in order not to overlap the material in other sections this chapter will focus mainly on the rather unique methods which have been used in the study of infants and preschool children. The chapter will also omit discussion of methods of investigating prenatal behavior, this topic having been treated in Chapter 15.

GENERAL PROBLEMS OF PROCEDURE IN RESEARCH WITH YOUNG SUBJECTS

Motivating, Contacting, and Directing Young Children

Studying young children offers many difficulties and challenges. An infant, or even a preschooler, cannot be expected to understand or follow most directions, much less respond with words. Young children

[1] Professor of Child Psychology, Departments of Psychology and Home Economics, University of Chicago.

are likely to be unwilling to cooperate and have to be courted at every step. The silence of the two-year-old who does not choose to talk would be baffling even to a prime minister, and the lack of ado with which the toddler removes himself from quarters that do not please him has punctured many an experimenter's vanity. Because the preschooler is a dependent creature, the investigator who deals with him is likely to find himself responsible for the child's physical care—something of a price to pay for the mere privilege of doing a little observing. And this is not the only price, for service must usually be given the child's mother in return for her cooperation. As a result the most imposing of our prolonged longitudinal studies of children have been made by workers in clinics or research stations which furnish gratuitous medical and psychological guidance for children. Most of the information we have about preschoolers has been acquired from the study of pupils in the nursery school. Surely this is unfortunate, for, since the home is the really important territory in the child's environment, we should know what is going on there.

Plotting Development

Investigators who aim to plot developmental change find they have many hurdles to clear, in addition to those of communicating with, motivating, and contacting young subjects. No completely satisfactory method of measuring is available. Although some efforts have been made to devise techniques for absolute scaling, we are still doing most of our measuring by systems which are comparable in their crudity to measuring length by using a ruler marked off in unequal units.

If, as is often desirable, the same children are to be studied over a period of years, the loss of subjects may be very great. Families move away, the cooperation of subjects is very difficult to sustain, and death, illness, and other casualties take their toll. The investigator may need to start with 1000 subjects in order to follow as many as 100 through a period of 15 years.

If, instead of following the same children for a long period of time, the experimenter uses different subjects at each age level, he is faced with the well-nigh insurmountable task of securing strictly comparable samples of the appropriate population for his various groups. At best, this normative cross-section method, with its description of successive age groups in terms of measures of central tendency and spread, portrays group trends, not the details of the progression of any one individual. Moreover, when several traits in the same population are measured, the method does not describe the details of either the relations or dynamics of the traits represented in any single person.

Because of the great complexity of development, an investigator usually contents himself with attempting to measure the course of change along only a limited number of dimensions. He has, hence, the further problem of locating or creating instruments suitable for use with children of different ages and measuring the same process or ability. Factor analysis is helping us to make progress with this quest. McNemar's factor analysis of the Revised Stanford-Binet test illustrates a promising approach [51].

THE HEREDITY-ENVIRONMENT PROBLEM

Control of Heredity

One of the problems on which child psychologists have focussed much attention is individual differences and the extent to which these derive from genetic or environmental sources. If it is desired to know merely whether environmental forces tend to produce differences, identical twins, triplets, quadruplets, and quintuplets are useful material, for these are individuals who develop from one zygote and therefore have the same heredity. With heredity thus held constant, the ways in which the members of a monozygotic group differ from each other must be the handwork of nurture. On the basis of the observation of a limited number of monozygotic groups, it is obviously unlikely, however, that one could gage the possible range of effects which environmental forces may produce, and certainly one cannot fathom just which environmental influences have been operative to create the differences noted.

The fact that individuals developing from the same germ cell are not born with labels, and their identicalness has to be determined, in itself presents a problem to the investigator. He can never be absolutely certain of a correct diagnosis, but a reasonably dependable one can be made if the individuals resulting from a multiple birth are alike in a considerable number of traits upon variance in which the environment has been shown to have relatively little effect. See references [49] and [54]. Among such traits are blood type, sex, pattern of iris and of finger, palm, and sole prints, hair color and form, shape of the pinna of the ear, and ability to taste phenylthiocarbamide. Note in Fig. 1 how similar the triplets are.

In those researches in which the effect of some one environmental influence is being studied, heredity is often held constant by subjecting the same individual to the selected variations of the experimental variable. A control group is usually needed in experiments of this design to furnish a check on the instruments used, as well as upon factors which may be affecting the subjects between their exposures to

Fig. 1. "Three of a kind." (Courtesy of The Children's Memorial Hospital, Chicago.)

the experimental variable in its various forms. To illustrate, a child may be studied before and after placement in a foster home in an effort to determine the impress of the home upon him. If the child's IQ increases, one may feel inclined to credit the change to the foster home.

He would do well, however, to consider carefully before he jumps to conclusions, since the foster home represents only one complex of influences which have been playing upon the child. Secondly, one must be sure his measures plumb what they are supposed to plumb. A child may score relatively better on his second intelligence test because, being older, he cooperated better, or because there were defects in the standardization of the test. A mental test in current use for preschoolers is so standardized that it tends to underrate two-year-olds and overrate four-year-olds. If used, this test may make it appear that a child during his stay in his foster home has added greatly to his intellectual stature, when in reality, perhaps, he has gained little or none at all.

Control of Environment

When we wish to keep environmental forces constant, while varying genetic ones, we are in much deeper water than when we attempt the reverse, for control of environment in any absolute sense is impossible. Even the best methods we have are treacherously defective. A few illustrations will suggest some common pitfalls. It is a mistake to maintain, as has been done, that up until the time of birth children are identically nurtured, because there is abundant evidence that the prenatal environments of individuals tend to vary in significant ways. The mother's nutrition, the extent to which she is host to diseases which can be transmitted to the fetus, and her possible possession of blood characteristics unfavorable to the child she is carrying are all important determinants of the development of the fetus.

Comparisons of the degree of resemblance between family members with the degree of resemblance of non-relatives usually yield no conclusive findings with respect to the force of genetic effects, because family members tend, on the average, to have more similar environments, as well as genes, than do non-related persons. A common type of study is that in which the degree of resemblance between foster children and their foster parents is compared to that between children and their biological parents. It is incorrect to assume that the small differences that have been frequently reported are evidence that the genetic similarity of children to their biological parents has little weight in determining the physical and mental likeness they have to each other. Since social agencies try to match in various ways a child with the people in the foster home in which he is placed, this selective placement may operate to cause foster children to show in some respects considerable similarity to their foster parents. This similarity is greater than would have obtained had the children been placed at random. The magnitude of twin dissimilarity in identical and fraternal pairs gives no certain clues as to the weight of genetic variables in the production of the variety we see in human beings, for the reason that the forces of nurture making for divergence between the pair members of identical and of like-sex fraternal twins are not essentially equal. By virtue of the fact, among others, that identical twins often look so much alike they cannot be told apart, they must receive more nearly similar attentions from their environments than do the pair members of like-sex fraternal twins.

PROCESSES AND PATTERNS OF MATURATION

Maturation Patterns

Closely related to the studies of the influence of heredity and environment are those concerned with the developmental sequence typical of human beings. No organism can develop in a vacuum, and the behavioral and structural unfolding characteristic of the members of a species must be mediated by both extra- and intra-organic forces which are almost invariably present. It seems reasonable, then, that the methods of studying human maturation should be focussed upon the discovery of what the essential details of the human developmental pattern are and of what forces within and outside the organism are significantly involved either in producing the pattern or in determining the rate at which it unfolds.

It may seem to the reader that the discovery of behavioral sequences typical of the development of human beings would be very easy, but, on the contrary, the discrimination of fine differences in behavior may necessitate long and painstaking observation. One way Gesell [27] aided himself in distinguishing the behavior patterns typical of infants differing slightly in age was to place two babies of the ages under consideration side by side before him. He would then observe them carefully and dictate to his secretary what he saw at the time he saw it, as well as take motion pictures of the subjects. After the babies were gone, Gesell would mull over the records and review his motion pictures many times, searching for differences. Progressions Gesell thought he observed he would then attempt to verify on many subjects before he made any claims for universality.

Below is a selection of items from a sequence of accomplishments that Gesell [27] offers as descriptive of progress toward walking. Because everything the child does is related to everything else, the behavior patterns listed have to be viewed as landmarks in his progress in growing up rather than any complete description.

Behavior	Approximate Median Age of Appearance, Weeks
Head sags	6
Legs extended briefly	6
Supports a fraction of weight briefly	12
Head steadily erect	12
Supports a large fraction of weight	20
Supports entire weight	32
Stands on toes	36
Stands, holding side rail	40
Lifts foot while supporting entire weight	44
Pulls to standing, holding side rail	48
Walks, two hands held	48
Lowers self, using support	48
Walks, one hand held	52
Attains standing independently	56
Stands alone momentarily	56
Walks alone a few steps, starts, stops	60

Photographic Dome and One-way-vision Screen

So that the infants would be relatively free from distraction while being photographed and observed, Gesell [27] placed them in a photographic dome. The walls of the dome were made of one-way-vision screen, in which were set runner tracks on which cameras could be moved up and down. This arrangement made it possible to photograph the babies from almost any angle desired.

The one-way-vision screen Gesell used was of very fine mesh and was painted white on one side, so that it reflected light chiefly toward the subjects inside the dome and thus prevented them from seeing through the wire, if the illumination inside the dome was higher than on the outside. Persons on the outside of the dome—on the side left unpainted—could, on the other hand, look through the screen.

Screens of this type are frequently used also in nursery schools and clinics. By this device it is possible to avoid having children influenced by persons who wish to observe them. Parents may be convinced of the efficacy of certain guidance methods they have been resisting by seeing their own children who baffle them handled successfully by a nursery-school teacher. Students may watch an expert test or interview a child by use of this device.

Methods of Mapping Actions

Halverson, one of Gesell's coworkers, did an especially fine piece of work in differentiating age differences in the pattern of reaching and grasping among babies [33]. Movies had been taken of the children in a standardized setting as they reached for blocks, pellets, and pieces of string. Halverson mounted the projector for the film so that it could be focussed on a piece of ground glass set in a table top. (See Fig. 2.) The projector was hand driven and provided with an adjustment for reversing. By these devices the film could be exposed at any

Fig. 2. Projection desk used for cinema analysis of infant behavior and sample film strip. (Courtesy of Professor A. Gesell. See reference [33].)

speed desired, and any section of it could be easily repeated. The time taken by any act could be computed merely by counting frames. To facilitate further the discrimination of behavior differences, maps were made of the course of certain actions. In plotting the route the infant's hand took in approaching a cube, the experimenter stilled each frame and indicated for it the position of the tip of the child's index finger by a dot on a map. The dots then outlined the course of the index finger. This map and the movies furnished data on the number of attempts the babies made to reach the cube, the number of failures in grasping, the extent of overreaching, the directness and height of advance of the hand, and the amount of hand rotation.

Kreezer and Glanville [46] similarly studied the action of hip, knee, and ankle joints in the walking of persons of various ages. These investigators mapped the course of marked parts of the subject's anatomy as shown in movies taken of the subject in a standardized position against a background that contained reference lines.

Method of Understimulation

The method of understimulation, in contrast to those just discussed, which yield descriptions, is useful for the analysis of factors influencing the tempo and pattern of developmental change. Although the method has been used more frequently and dramatically in the study of lower animals than in the study of children, child psychologists have employed it in spite of its risks. Dennis [22], who was interested in the effects upon the development of a child of depriving him of the usual social stimulations, isolated two fraternal twin babies from people other than their two keepers for most of a year. The twins were fed and kept clean but were not talked to, smiled at, played with, approved, or punished. Screened even from each other, they spent most of their day lying in their cribs. Despite this very low amount of social stimulation, the babies made progress in many infant skills about as do babies who are normally reared. Other examples of studies concerned with the effects of understimulation are those of individuals, who, after being without vision, have gained their sight as a result of an operation on their eyes [20]; Indian children who have been cradled and whose movements were restricted thus during much of their infancy [21]; and feral children [76].

Co-twin Control Method

The co-twin control method, which contrasts the effects of understimulation with systematic training along some line, has been popularized by Gesell and his students [26]. The method aims to reveal the effect upon the rate of learning of increased physical maturity. The design of the method is as follows: One of a pair of identical twins is trained in a specific skill, such as reaching or talking, and the other twin is prevented from having any experiences closely related to this skill. Then after a time the treatment procedures are reversed for the two individuals. If, as has usually been the case, the second twin acquires more rapidly the skill for which the two were trained, this fact is attributed to greater physical maturity. Since the twins are identical and demonstrated to be about equal in physical and behavior traits at the beginning of the experiment, heredity, native ability, and general experience seem eliminated as determinants of any differences that may appear between them in the course of the study. It is, of course, a question whether greater physical maturity, transferable experiences the second twin may have had during the period when the first was being systematically trained, or both, are responsible for the more rapid learning of the second twin. Gesell [26], Strayer [66], and others tend to believe the maturity factor the more important.

Method of Interspecies Comparison

To throw into relief the effect of gross gene differences on the tempo and pattern of development, Kellogg [41] reared with his own son a chimpanzee infant, treating the chimpanzee as if he were human. The ape and the human infant were tested periodically with the same tests, and the courses of their development thus compared.

Method of the Abnormal Case

The alert experimentalist often sees in a freak human being an "experiment" performed for him by nature or accident. Instances of this sort are the cases of puberty praecox. Here nature alters in an extreme fashion an internal process—in one type, for example, increases the secretion of the cortex of the adrenal glands. The result is that the secondary and primary sex characteristics appear abnormally early in the victims. Some children who are only a few years old become capable of procreation. The extent of the effects of very early sexual maturing upon other body tissues, as well as upon behavior and attitude, is an interesting problem into which considerable probing has been done. Nature or accident may also reverse the puberty-praecox type of experiment for us and offer us for study subjects deficient in some way, such as in sex hormones.

Prematurely born babies represent a case in which the usual environment is altered, instead of an internal process, as in puberty praecox. These babies help us to answer the question of whether the exposure of the infant very early in life to a more variable environment than the intrauterine one speeds the rate or alters the pattern of his development [35].

PERCEIVING, ABSTRACTING, AND GENERALIZING

General Methods of Analyzing Perception

Whether an individual's perception is being influenced by an object, quality, or relationship can be determined by noting whether he reacts differently when the object, quality, or relationship is altered or removed. It is of parallel interest whether a person, upon exposure to a variety of stimuli, reacts similarly to those stimuli which are alike. The question of children's ability to perceive various phenomena has, accordingly, been approached via these two procedures. The child may be: (1) exposed to two stimuli differing in only one respect, and his reactions to the two, whether learned or immediate, studied; (2) requested merely to express his preferences among stimuli differing in only one respect; (3) induced to verbalize on the differences he observes; (4) asked to match stimuli; (5) given the task of picking out the unlike item in a series the units of which are alike with one exception; or (6) instructed to copy or reproduce a stimulus.

Since the infant is lacking verbal skills and cannot follow directions, the first method is always employed to test his ability to discriminate. The really difficult task faced by experimenters dealing with the question of infants' discriminatory processes is to keep constant everything but the stimulus feature which is being systematically varied. As was explained earlier, the experimenter can never control all aspects of a situation. He will do well if he can keep the major constant and chance errors from befogging his findings.

Experimental Cabinet and Stabilimeter

To control as far as possible the stimulus situation of infants whose sensory abilities are being looked into, what has been called an experimental cabinet has often been used [23, 38]. See Fig. 3. The temperature in the cabinet can be kept virtually constant by means of a heater regulated by a thermostat. Since the cabinet closes out light, it is not difficult to keep the light from varying. The cubicles that have been used, unfortunately, have not been soundproof, but sound stimuli can be kept at a minimum by housing the cabinet in very quiet quarters. There can be no direct control over the tactual, kinesthetic, and visceral stimuli the baby receives.

The infant is placed in the cabinet on a platform supported so that it jiggles as the child moves. This platform, called a stabilimeter, is connected through switches and an electrical circuit with a polygraph pen, which records the platform's movements as oscillations on the tape of the polygraph. With a time marker the tape can be sectioned off into units representing constant intervals of time. A count of deflections on the tape, each representing a movement of

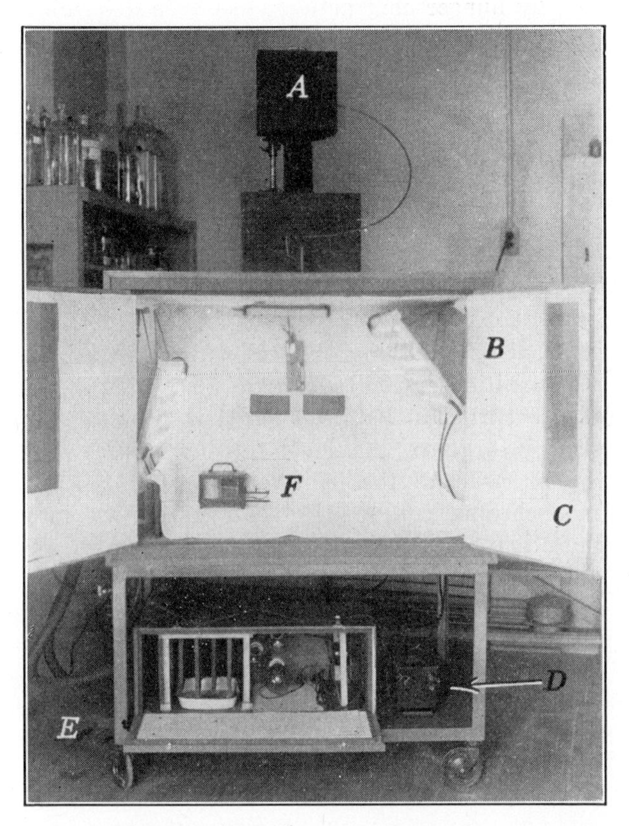

Fig. 3. Isolation cabinet for experimentation with infants.

A = camera, B = "cold lights," C = observation port, D = control for temperature and humidity, E = air tube, F = recording polygraph. (Courtesy of Professor F. C. Dockeray.)

some sort, in any chosen time interval can then be taken as a measure of movement frequency under a given condition of stimulation. If it seems desirable, the magnitude of the deflections can also be measured. Since the number of a child's movements and their magnitude tend to be highly correlated, usually the frequency is adequate to indicate differences between individuals as well as differences in behavior on the part of the same individual under diverse conditions. If, for instance, when a bell is rung, infants tend to increase or decrease their movements beyond what obtained during the previous quiet, it can be suspected that the sound effected the change in their behavior, i.e., that they hear. By the same general sort of comparisons, the sensitivity of infants to sounds and to lights of different intensities and to lights of different colors, as well as to internal stimuli such as those initiated by hunger contractions, has been determined.

It would be possible, although not likely, for an infant to fail to show his capabilities for discrimination in a setting such as has been described, because he is disinterested in the stimulus change. Hence, ideally, in experiments of the sort just outlined the test situation selected should be meaningful to the infant, and the adjustments he normally makes to the stimulus rather obvious.

A Method of Testing Color Discrimination in Infants

Peiper's method of studying the color discrimination of infants meets the two conditions suggested above [56]. Peiper noted that an eye-neck reflex occurred in babies when they were held upright and a light flashed just above the level of their eyes. By increasing gradually the intensity of the light sent through red, yellow, blue, and green monochromatic filters, Peiper recorded the intensity level for each color when the eye-neck reflex first occurred. These limen values for the four colors, he made evident, differed with photopic and scotopic vision. The brightness order from high to low of the colors in photopic vision was yellow, red, blue, and green, whereas when the child's eyes were dark-adapted, red and yellow decreased in brightness and green and blue increased. These changes are at least in the direction the Purkinje phenomenon would lead one to expect and therefore suggest that the same color mechanisms are operative in an infant's eyes as in an adult's. The student is referred to the works of Chase [15] and Smith [64] for other methods of studying color vision in infants.

Method of Equivalent Stimuli

When it is desired to discover whether children can readily learn to discriminate a difference, a sort of conditioning procedure has usually been employed. An illustration of this type of approach is Bing Chung Ling's investigation [48] of the ability of infants from 6 to 12 months of age to discriminate between such geometrical forms as a circle and triangle. Ling, furthermore, attempted to assess the capacity of the babies to form shape concepts, i.e., to react to circularity or triangularity, etc. Ling relied upon the tendency of young humans in their second half year to reach for almost everything in sight, to put into their mouths whatever they succeed in grasping, and to be partial to sweets. She pegged into a gray board which was placed before the baby in his crib a yellow square block and a circular block of the same color. The baby was trained to reach for the circular block as follows: The square could not be removed from the board, the circle could. The baby, if he removed the circular block and put it in his mouth, was rewarded by a sweet taste, for the blocks had been dipped in a saccharine solution. This reward apparently reinforced the success of dislodging the block. The babies learned to reach immediately for the form for which they were being trained. Then the position, size, and orientation of the key block were changed one at a time, and additional blocks were introduced to increase the difficulty of discrimination. It was assumed the babies had begun to abstract when they could readily recognize the discrimination object regardless of its position, size, or orientation and despite several confusion objects. Ling's method is known as the method of equivalent stimuli. It has been widely used, particularly with animals. A favorite problem to which it has been addressed is the determination of how obscure a quality can become before subjects fail in learning to recognize it.

Matching- and Discordant-items Procedures

The ability of older children to discriminate readily such small differences in form as are necessary if they are to learn to read without too much difficulty has been tested by some of the so-called reading-readiness tests, which usually employ either the matching- or discordant-item procedures mentioned earlier. The child is tested for his ability to perceive both likeness and difference. He is shown a letter and then told to cross out with a pencil the letter, in a series of two or more, like the one he has been shown. Or in a series of letters alike, with one exception, the child is asked to cross out the letter that is not like the others. It should be mentioned in passing that the typical reading-readiness test attempts to measure many kinds of readiness other than that in perceptual skill—readiness in general experience, language, and ability to think in abstract terms.

Preference Method

The method of expressed preference, referred to at the beginning of this section, was employed by Daniels [18] to discover whether preschoolers tend to have the ability to perceive differences in such esthetic qualities as balance. Since her young subjects would not have understood the directions had they been requested to indicate which of the presented compositions was the more balanced, Daniels asked the children to choose the one in each pair of block structures which they thought was the nicest. The youngsters were also told to build a structure like any one of the two exposed. Preferences thus expressed in a number of pairs of constructions, the two units of which differed in degree of balance but were alike in the number and color of the blocks composing them as well as in background, probably would disclose the subjects' sensitivity to balance. Any two compositions must, of course, have differed in ways other than in balance, such as in apparent size. Unless some constant errors were introduced, however, these differences need not vitiate the findings. It should be added here that the children did seem to prefer and did tend to copy more frequently the more balanced structures.

Method of Imitating or Reproducing

The method of reproducing is less satisfactory than the procedures for testing perceptual proficiency thus far explained, because subjects may fail more as a result of their lack of ability in manipulative skill than of ability in perceiving. Because one cannot paint as did Leonardo da Vinci does not prove he cannot discriminate between his own paintings and da Vinci's. Children's drawings have, accordingly, been of interest more for what they reveal of ability in drawing itself than for what they indicate concerning the children's perceptions.

A form of imitating in which the motor adjustments were kept sufficiently simple for the subjects studied, so that the perceptual components of the activity chiefly were determining of success, is represented in Williams' study [74] of the ability of preschool children to imitate a sound rhythm. Williams took motion pictures of his subjects as they tried to clap in time to music. These movies, taken with a wide angle lens, included not only the children but also a metronome oscillating before a white cardboard scale, and the pianist who was furnishing the music at the tempo dictated by the metronome. By studying the frames of the film, it could be determined whether the children clapped, i.e., their hands touched, at exactly the moment the metronome pointer or the pianist's posture indicated the beat was sounded.

Abstracting and Generalizing—Matching Procedure

It might be mentioned at this point that the use of a matching procedure to throw light on ability to abstract is somewhat different from its use to determine the ability of subjects merely to perceive a simple difference. In the studies of concepts the objects or structures to be matched, instead of being alike in all respects but one, may be alike only in one. This quality has to be abstracted out of the complex and responded to if the subject is to be successful. Horowitz [37], for example, showed white and Negro children cards containing at least two pictures—that of a Negro child of the sex of the subject and that of a white child of the same sex—and asked the subject, "Which is you?" In some instances pictures of non-human objects, such as a chicken or lion, were added to the series presented to determine whether the children were assigning themselves to the class of persons.

If subjects consistently identify themselves with the pictures of children of their own color, it can be assumed they have themselves correctly classified, at least as to pigment and species. They have the beginning of a concept of race.

Horowitz's study illustrates the type of investigation in which a test is made of a concept already learned. More frequent are inquiries like Ling's, described previously, in which the subject is motivated to learn to detect a given quality in whatever stimulus complex it occurs.

Method of Interviewing

The method of interviewing has been used to discover the content of many different sorts of child concepts: number, time, cause, God, death, life, thought, etc. Piaget [58] has employed it with excellent effect. The following protocol will illustrate how he proceeded in his effort to discover the details of certain moral concepts held by his subjects:

A little boy sees that his father's ink pot is empty. He takes the ink bottle, but he is clumsy and makes a big blot.—And the other one?—*There was a boy who was always touching things. He takes the ink and makes a little blot.*—Are they both equally naughty or not?—*No.*—Which is the most naughty?—*The one who made the big blot.*—Why?—*Because it was big.*—Why did he make a big blot?—*To be helpful.*—And why did the other one make a little blot?—*Because he was always touching things. He made a little blot.*—Then which of them is the naughtiest?—*The one who made a big blot.*

MOTOR SKILLS

Problems

So-called motor skills are merely those in which the muscular aspects of the adjustments are conspicuous. Like all adjustments they involve the total organism.

There are several classes of problems in the field upon which much attention has been centered: (1) rapid and accurate measurement of individual differences in motor adjustment and skill, (2) discovering why the differences in skill exist between individuals or in the same individual from time to time, (3) discovering the nature of the abilities that enter into so-called motor skills, and (4) methods for teaching or correcting or altering motor patterns of response, e.g., teaching writing or correcting stuttering.

Types of Measures

Some measures of motor skill that have been frequently used are (1) the time consumed for a unit of work; (2) the output in a unit of time; (3) assessments of the quality of the products, such as hand writing, resulting from motor activities; and (4) a count of the number of motor accomplishments, from among a representative list, which the individual possesses. Development in motor skill may be plotted roughly in terms of any one of these four criteria. Although the first measure is probably more discriminating than is the second, especially when the task is not of uniform difficulty throughout, the second is used more frequently because it is usually less cumbersome.

A Method of Measuring Hand Preference

The second measure was probably employed quite safely by Valentine and Wagner [71] in their study designed to throw light on the question of the nativeness of hand preferences. These investigators tied to each hand of newborn infants a light string which was then drawn over a pulley-counter arrangement. Any movement of the baby's arm activated the pulley wheel, which was connected so as to cause the counter to register. The final reading on the counter, then, indicated the total number of gross movements made in a known interval by the child's arm. Since similar assessments were made for each arm, it was possible to tell which member was the more active. Valentine and Wagner kept the babies under observation for the first 10 days of their lives.

For older children who have considerable manual skill and can be expected to follow directions, a parallel technique used by Goodenough and Tinker [31] gives a fairly satisfactory indication of the relative skill of the two hands, because usually the hand which is the more efficient in one difficult task performs the more ably in others. Goodenough had the children tap as fast as they could on key 1 on an adding machine. The machine thus automatically gave a count of the number of taps made in the 10-second time-unit chosen.

Time Sampling Procedures

The so-called time sampling procedure, popularized in child psychology by Thomas [67], may be cited as a special case of the constant-time, variable-output type of measure we have been discussing. This method has commonly been resorted to when individual motor characteristics, as well as social-emotional ones, are to be appraised. The general plan of the method can be illustrated for activeness as follows: If one wants to know whether a certain child is very active, he looks in on the subject at randomly distributed times for a number of days. A peek is probably enough to determine if the child is vigorously employed. If most frequently, when observed, the child is indulging in strenuous activity, he can be said to be an active person. Whether he is more or less strenuous than other children can be determined only if similar measures were made of others.

The units of behavior assessed in the time sample method are as a rule those provided in short intervals of time—a few seconds, a minute, or 5 minutes. The plan for describing the behavior in each time unit has varied in form from study to study. If the trait of activeness is the experimenter's interest, the description may be a rating, a pedometer reading, a tally of happenings, or a map of territory covered.

Since any description of behavior is necessarily an incomplete representation of it and of the situation in which it occurs, it is well to remember that gross distortion can proceed from this source. The observers' biases and lack of acuity may also introduce much error.

Methods of Estimating Observer Accuracy

The accuracy of the observer is a concern of great moment in the short behavior-sample method. The extent to which observer inadequacies render defective the appraisals made is usually estimated by having two independently working observers make evaluations of the same phenomena. After many behavior samples have been described independently in this way, the observers compare notes to determine to what extent their recordings agree. If there are disagreements, the observers try to determine why, to clarify the definitions that are guiding them, and to make decisions as to how certain types of situation should be recorded. Training is generally continued in this fashion until almost perfect agreement in reporting events is achieved.

It is well to determine periodically whether observers are adhering to the interpretations and procedures agreed upon in their initial training period, for subtle changes in method tend to creep in without the observers being aware of them. It should also be understood that observers may agree and yet be wrong in their diagnosis of what occurred. One way of checking more carefully on the observers' skill is to take a motion picture, as Thomas did [68], of a sampling of the happenings the observers are attempting to describe.

In the interests of facilitating the recording, it is well that as much of it as possible be done in code. The children's initials, for instance, can be used in place of their names, arrows to indicate the direction of an action, letters for various types of response, etc.

Duration and Distribution of Samples

The optimal duration and distribution of the behavior samples vary, of course, with the trait being studied and the purpose of the measurement. Generally speaking, the samples should have no greater duration than is necessary to make an accurate evaluation of the items being recorded or to give the significant behaviors a reasonable opportunity to occur. The units should be distributed systematically over the situations the behavior in which is of particular interest. Most investigators have limited themselves to observation in quarters where many children are assembled, such as the nursery school or the playground. It has also been common practice to observe subjects in activities in which their own inclinations are chiefly determining of what they do. The evaluations of a child made under these circumstances, it must be remembered, may not agree with appraisals made under other circumstances. A child's home and school behavior may be very different, or even his behavior in free and in directed play.

The total number of samples necessary to portray accurately the relative status of individuals varies with the fineness of the discriminations to be made and the variableness of the trait. Generally speaking, many short samples widely but systematically distributed are better than fewer long ones. It is well not to spread the samples over too long a period of time, however, if the quality measured is a changing one, because the final measure may then fail to represent the child at any time.

Limitations and Uses of Time Sampling

Most measures based on accumulated short behavior samples have limitations that stem from the inability of the experimenter to control the general meaning of the situation for the subject. A child may be less active than others at school because he is relatively new and is feeling his way, because some classmate cows him, or because the program bores him. If a quality independent of motivation or of certain specific motivations is the item of interest, the motivation variable should be either statistically or experimentally controlled. The achievement of this control has seldom been demonstrated.

Despite its limitations the method of time sampling has many uses [3, 9]. It lends itself readily to the measurement of individual differences in social-emotional qualities shown in natural group settings [43] and to the evaluation of materials or activities. If one wished to determine which pieces of play equipment are the most popular with children of various ages, he might give attention to the various pieces for a uniform number of appropriately distributed short intervals of time, noting how many children were playing with each piece. By keeping the subjects constant during the observation and by counting the children who used each toy or bit of apparatus in the time samples, he could estimate the appeal of each. Or, by noting the relative frequency of occurrence of certain types of behavior, such as nervous habits, in various settings, it might be possible to throw light on factors that contribute to the behavior. In this case settings must be sampled, and actors kept constant.

A Method of Describing Aspects of Walking

In contrast to devices for measuring motor skills directly, such as those just discussed, are the methods which give attention to the quality of "motor" products. The procedure used by Shirley in studying the walking of a young child is a good illustration of one yielding a detailed quantitative analysis of a motor product [63]. Shirley oiled the soles of her infant subjects' feet with olive oil and then had the children walk, either alone or supported if necessary, down a long strip of unglazed white wrapping paper, which promptly soaked up the oil as the child planted each foot. To make the oil

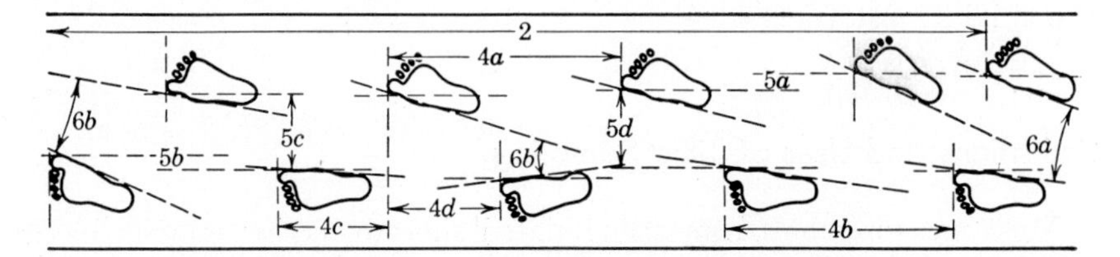

Fig. 4. Diagram showing the method of measuring footprints. (From Shirley [63], by permission of the University of Minnesota Press.)

2 total distance traversed.
4a right-right step length.
4b left-left step length.
4c right-left step length.
4d left-right step length.
5a right-right step width.
5b left-left step width.
5c right-left step width.
5d left-right step width.
6a standing angle.
6b stepping angle.

print clearly visible, Shirley dusted the paper with a powder mixture of graphite, acacia, and lampblack. This black powder adhered to the oil spots but could readily be brushed off the rest of the paper. To preserve the prints, the sheet was sprayed with a shellac spray. Shirley then measured the width, length, regularity, speed, and angle of the child's step. See Fig. 4.

Wolff [75], who was interested in determining the points of the foot which carry the greatest weight as the child walks, also used footprints. She dusted the child's foot evenly with chalk and then had him walk on a strip of black paper. It was readily evident from the white prints at which points on the sole the chalk dust was thinned down most quickly.

Product Scale

Another type of quality assessment of a more impressionistic type is made with the aid of product scales, such as those for handwriting [73], drawing [69], or block building [4]. In this case a bit of the child's handiwork is compared with the samples that constitute the scales. The value of the scale sample which the child's product most nearly resembles is the score the latter receives. The method of scaling products is discussed in Chapter 5.

Motor-development Scales

A motor-development scale contrasts with a product scale in that behavior items, rather than the products of behavior, constitute the scale content. A motor-development scale does not differ, in the skeleton of its construction pattern, from a general development or an intelligence scale. The usual problems of scaling and of subject and task sampling confront the worker who devises a motor scale. Since these are dealt with in Chapter 17, we shall merely describe here one of the more interesting motor-development scales for preschool children, e.g., that devised by Bayley [6], who, we might add, has also constructed a general development scale. By observing about sixty babies at uniform short intervals until they were 3 years old and making an inventory of their motor accomplishments, Bayley discovered achievements which virtually every child attains at some time or other during his first 3 years. She computed the average age of appearance of each such accomplishment among her subjects and listed the skills in the order of their time of development. The location of an item on the motor scale was expressed also in terms of absolute scale units. Below are listed about the first fourth of the items in Bayley's list.

Test Item	Absolute Scale Value	Age Placement, Months
Crawling movements	0.06	0.2
Postural adjustments when held to shoulder	0.13	0.5
Lifts head at shoulder	0.14	0.5
Lateral head movements	0.29	0.6
Retains red ring	0.34	0.7
Arm thrusts in play	0.75	1.7
Leg thrusts in play	0.78	1.8
Head erect — vertical	0.87	1.9
Dorsal suspension — lifts head	1.10	2.6
Head erect and steady	1.26	2.9
Turns from side to back	1.50	3.4
Prone — elevates self by arms	1.54	3.5
Sits with support	1.55	3.5
Hands predominantly open	1.62	3.6
Holds head steady	1.64	3.6
Beginning thumb opposition	1.88	4.1
Sits with slight support	2.14	4.6
Turns from back to side	2.34	5.0
Partial thumb opposition	2.42	5.1
Effort to sit	2.54	5.4

To determine a particular child's motor-development level by means of this scale, the experimenter stimulates the child to perform the activities listed on the inventory, or by inquiry determines which skills the youngster has had in his repertoire. The child's score is merely a count of the number of items passed. This simple point score is transmuted into a standard score in order to describe the subject's standing in his own age group. How representative of American children the subjects were on whom Bayley's norms are based is a question.

As motor skills become more diversified, differentiated, and complex, general motor scales, such as Bayley's, tend to become unsatisfactory. At later ages the so-called scales of motor ability are, as a rule, based on ability in sports: running, jumping, throwing, gripping, aiming, and balancing [11, 17, 24]. These abilities are not perfectly correlated with each other nor with such finer motor skills as playing the piano or typing. Hence, one would need to generalize cautiously from his test results.

LANGUAGE AND SPEECH

Recording Language

If samples of the spoken language of an individual are to be analyzed, a record of some sort generally has to be made. Mechanical recording is often desirable because it provides a more faithful reproduction of what is said than the human recorder can provide. It must always be remembered, however, that the record is not the analysis; it is merely the frozen product.

There are several common types of sound record, e.g., the phonographic, wire, and film. In each type mentioned, the sound waves which strike the diaphragm of the microphone alter the current through an electromagnet which, in turn, converts the variations in current into some sort of record. In the wire recorder the counterpart of the soundwaves is the degree of magnetization of the wire which passes slowly between the poles of the electromagnet as the record is made. The sound counterpart on the film, the "sound track," is the degree of darkness of a line, whereas in the phonograph it is the hill-and-dale pattern etched on a wax or plastic disk.

To the extent that physical forces, such as inertia, momentum, or friction, governing the recording mechanisms interfere with the production of a record pattern which has a one-to-one relationship with the pattern of sound waves which strike the microphone, or to the

upon. The ratio of action verbs to adjectives in a subject's speech offers some promise as an indicator of degree of extroversion or action interest.

Content Analysis

Language-content studies have been of many types. The following are a few of the content characteristics into which there has been some inquiry: the uses made of language; the affective tone of the content, the types of question asked; the time reference of the material; the number of vague terms, qualified statements, self-references, and negatives; the amount of hostile feeling expressed; and the incidence of specific themes, such as dependence, illness, and achievement. In the study mentioned above, McCarthy, by using an adaptation of a method developed by Piaget [57], probed the nature of the shifts that occur with age in the uses children make of language. She classified the remarks her preschool subjects made as follows: questions, answers, commands, requests, criticisms, simple information relative to the present, information about something not present, comments to the self, and comments perhaps stimulated by the presence of others but seemingly sent forth without much expectation of a response. The percentage of egocentric or self-directed remarks and the time reference of the comments tended to correlate with age, but several of the categories seemed more closely related to personality qualities other than maturity. The proportion of commands and requests in the total remarks is a case in point.

The thematic apperception, free-association, and a number of other projective tests represent language-content analyses directed toward the discovery of the subject's values, manner of mental functioning, and social-emotional attitudes. These tests have been used more with older children who have considerable linguistic skill. See Chapter 18.

SOCIAL-EMOTIONAL BEHAVIOR

Section Limits

Ratings, time sampling procedures, projective techniques, tests, inventories, autobiographies, guess-who methods, questionnaires, interviews, case studies, and various sociometric techniques, all of which have been used in the study of the social-emotional behavior of children, have received extensive exposition in various sections of this book. The present section, hence, will concern itself chiefly with illustrating a few techniques which have had their primary use in the study of young children.

Projective Methods

Projective methods have long been in informal use with young children because these subjects, lacking in verbal skill and understanding, have to be understood, in the main, in terms of their behavior and products. Fortunately not yet tutored in the concealment of feelings, values, and disapproved attitudes, young children reveal rather readily by their behavior the major color of their feelings. That toward which the feeling is directed and from which it stems has not always been equally obvious. It may take the whole household to decide why an infant is crying. In fact, the greater the gap in age and experience between the child subject and the investigator, the less successful the latter tends to be in inferring the reason for the child's feelings.

Projective methods, which aim to reflect both the feeling and its object, have been concerned with various characteristics of the structure and content of the subject's behavior and products. With older subjects verbal materials—interpretations given ink-blots, stories told in interpretation of a standard series of pictures, completions of stories, completions of statements expressive of values [61], free-association responses to homonyms [30]—have been the more frequently studied. With young children attention has been directed, as might be surmised, more to play behavior, products created, and choices expressed.

Amen and Dorkey [2] in their adaptation of the Thematic Apperception Test, provide an example of an important method. Their subjects were shown a series of pictures, each one of which lent itself readily to a variety of interpretations in terms of adult-child or child-child relations which a young individual might have experienced. See Fig. 5. The central figure in each picture was without a face. It was the subject's task to decide whether a happy or a sad face, between which he had to choose, would be the more appropriate for the child in the picture. The frequency with which the unhappy face was chosen, it was revealed, tended to be related to the degree of anxiety the child showed in his daily behavior at nursery school.

The Alschuler and Hattwick study of such creations of nursery-school children as paintings, drawings, modelings, block structures, and dramatic play themes is one of the most extensive investigations of the diagnostic value of child products [1]. Believing that children's choices of activity are of as much significance as the character of their fabrications, Alschuler and Hattwick made no effort to standardize the conditions under which their subjects' creations were obtained. For a school year the creations of 150 children in eight different nursery schools, serving both upper and lower class groups,

Fig. 5. Sample test item: "Neglect." (Courtesy of E. W. Amen. See reference [2].)

were collected and preserved for analysis. Those products, like block structures, which could not be preserved were photographed or sketched. Detailed records were made of the general conduct of the children both at home and at school, as well as of their preferences in materials and their behavior when using each medium. Case studies and group comparisons suggest, as significant for the diagnosis of certain personality qualities and attitudes, the choice of medium for creative expression, the child's behavior while constructing his product, and certain patterns of structure unique for the individual, as well as certain characteristics of more general occurrence.

The paintings, for instance, were analyzed for color, monotone or multicolored character, neatness, extent of overlaying of colors, amount of page covered, relative size, angularity and rhythm of stroke, presence or absence of certain features individual for the child, and relative size of the various parts of the objects represented.

The authors conclude, among other things, that children who emphasize color have strong emotional orientation, red being associated with the strongest feeling, and preference by a preschooler for blue being a sign of early socialization. The use of only a small part of the page for the painting suggests inhibitedness; roundness of composition, submissiveness; verticality, resistance; extensive overlay, repression; unusual lack of neatness, stress and confusion.

Play Interview

The play interview is still another technique centering around the play of children which is useful for unmasking the youngsters' feelings and attitudes. The play interview often, although not necessarily, is carried out when the child is playing with dolls. The investigator may question the child concerning the dolls' motives or feelings when he or the child causes them to behave in various ways. It is believed that, since the conversation is about the dolls' activities, the child will not feel self-conscious or spied upon, while at the same time he reveals his feelings concerning the persons, including himself, whom the dolls symbolize to him. Fite [25], for instance, aimed to discover how certain preschool children felt about fighting, e.g., their conflicts over their parents' prohibitions of physical assault and their urge to defend themselves by attack or to get what they wanted at any cost. Levy [47] has both asked questions about the dolls' behavior and interpreted it. Interpretations were given when it was thought the child needed and was ready to receive insight into his own and others' motivations, or when misinterpretations of adult practices and attitudes needed clarification.

Play Analysis

It can be seen from the comments on Levy's procedure that in this form of play therapy diagnosis tends to be formulated as the play proceeds, the interview being one of the chief diagnostic tools. Some therapists, however, object to any dictation of the play by the worker as well as direct questioning, believing these may bring about the self-exposure of the child more rapidly than he is ready to bear or that they may cover rather than disclose the child's attitudes. These workers, accordingly, base their diagnoses chiefly on the following:

the subject's spontaneous verbal and behavioral expressions in his play relative to his own and other people's feelings; the sequence of play events, especially those leading up to emotional displays, such as the beating up of the father doll or the crushing of a baby doll; the correlation of reported happenings outside the therapy session with what occurs in the session; the characteristics, especially in relation to the themes of his play, of the structure and manner of the child's speech as well as of the structure of other products.

There are several factors which should weigh against an unquestioned acceptance of the diagnosis made. Many interpretations which are made "on the spot" in a very rapidly moving drama are highly subjective. There is some likelihood of the examiner's determining the child's associations rather than tapping them, particularly if there is direct questioning and if interpretations are given at the time. Also there is often a lack of any precise normative framework for describing the feelings and attitudes revealed. That a therapist's theories concerning the dynamics of motivation may be strongly determining of the interpretations he emphasizes appears likely by virtue of the fact that the case material reported by a therapist belonging to a particular school usually tends readily to identify his affiliations.

It is important to appreciate the difficulty of the clinician's task, for whereas the experimentalist is trying to demonstrate principles and general relations, the clinician is trying to account for the unique pattern of the individual's value structure and reaction tendencies. Because no two persons are alike and because judging accurately the weight of pressures that are infinite in number is a task only the omniscient could perform, even the good clinician does well to sketch with some accuracy only a few of the major features and molding forces of the personality. He proceeds very tentatively, too, with his interpretations until he has a large body of supporting evidence.

Tests

Objective tests differ from the projective methods described thus far in that the behavior occurring in the standardized situations is accepted for its face value. Since it is difficult to control the meaning of the test situation for each child, even though the procedure is standardized, and what is being measured in social-emotional behavior is closely tied up with these meanings, personality tests, other than the pencil-and-paper type, have not been very popular. Adequate sampling of situations which would reveal how the child tends to act, not how he says he reacts, is difficult to achieve. In fact, it is doubtful whether, even in the sense in which is it accomplished in intelligence tests, adequate task sampling in tests of general social-emotional traits has ever been approached.

Two studies, those of Hartshorne and May [34] and of Murphy [53], represent about the peak of ambitiousness in sampling. Murphy tried to test the sympathy of young children. She framed eighteen situations which she thought would expose the readiness with which the child expresses concern for or prevents the discomfort of others. The children in one test, for instance, were led singly to quarters where a baby was confined in a playpen with his playthings lying out of reach outside the pen. It was noted whether the young subjects responded spontaneously to help the baby or whether, even after an interpretation was given of the infant's needs and feelings, any help was offered. In another test the child was shown a live mouse and was asked whether it should be given to a guinea pig to eat. In this case one might wonder whether fear or sympathy was responsible for what would be the socially approved behavior.

The susceptibility of the child to sympathy was described by Murphy in a number of other ways than in terms of his response to standardized tests. Appraisals were made in the form of teachers' ratings and of counts of the instances of sympathetic behavior noted in 160 hours of observation of the child in the nursery school. These two measures showed considerable agreement, but the results of the standardized tests did not correlate strikingly with either.

Time Sampling

It is in the area of social-emotional characteristics of young children that the time sampling methods have been most successful. Like the objective test, these methods permit study of the child in action. They differ from the test in that the environment in which the subject is viewed is not in any strict sense standardized; hence they yield no norms useful beyond the situation in which the observations took place.

Green [32], who was interested in the relative pugnaciousness of the members of a nursery-school group, tallied her subjects' quarrels in the time samples to which she gave attention. She also computed the ratio of the samples in which quarrelling occurred between each two classmates to the total opportunities each pair had for quarrelling. Caille [12] counted the refusals of her subjects to cooperate; Robinson and Conrad [60] counted the samples in which the child was seen talking to another; while Parten [55] rated the degree of social participation implied by the behavior she noted Reliable measures that are accurately descriptive of much of the child's social behavior in the environment in which he is studied are obtainable by the time sampling method if the procedure is pursued thoroughly. The motivation of the behavior, unfortunately, is not necessarily indicated.

Ratings

Ratings of one sort or other are an integral part of several of the methods already described in this section. Although no exposition will be given here of rating technique and evaluation, it is felt that the reader should be familiar with such systems of ratings as those of Conrad [16], Richards and Powell [59], Berne [7], and Champney [14]. An effort was made in the first three studies to set up a series of scales which would be descriptive of every social-emotional trait of any significance for preschool children, whereas Champney attempted to cover the attitudes and practices of parents thought to have an important bearing on the social development of children. The fact that Richards and Powell, after experimenting with descriptive systems of varying degrees of elaborateness, ended with 30 traits, while Conrad was not content with less than 133, indicates the arbitrary, pragmatic basis for the selection of traits to be evaluated.

Refinement of description, achieved by increasing both the number of traits dealt with and the number of degrees of magnitude discriminated in each trait, can go on almost indefinitely. Scales with five or fewer steps are, even so, more common than those with more. One problem, then, that becomes conspicuous, in addition to that of the limits of human discriminative powers, is how parsimoniously the raters can characterize the behavior complexes they think important. Richards and Powell, by a factor analysis of the intercorrelations between their ratings made on a sizable group of nursery-age children, found that most of the trait variance was due to three factors. After factoring, the investigator has the following questions to decide: (1) What is the nature of the common factors? (2) How can each of the factors best be measured in the individual? and (3) What is the magnitude of the uniqueness in each of the traits rated? By uniqueness is meant that which the trait involves which is not common to any of the other traits. If this uniqueness is of enough interest, it justifies the retention of the trait in the battery.

It must be made clear that the most parsimonious method of portraying social character may not for all purposes be the most useful. It should also be understood that factoring a table of inter-rating correlations may be helpful in other ways than through the simplification of the structure of the rating system it suggests; it may put the experimenter on the trail of basic causal forces. Baldwin's [5] factor analysis of ratings of parent attitudes and home atmospheres disclosed three major dimensions, tentatively diagnosed as democraticness, acceptance of the child, and indulgence. In terms of other things known of motivation, these dimensions make sense.

Sociometric Techniques

Although the techniques mentioned thus far in this section are focussed on individual diagnosis, sociometric methods are trained on group diagnosis, i.e., on the feelings of the members of a group toward each other. Because the work of Moreno [52], who was a pioneer with sociometric techniques, has been reported in Chapters 13 and 22, the discussion here will be limited to the paired-comparison procedure employed by Koch [42, 44, 45]. This investigator studied the classmate preferences of nursery- and school-age children by having every child in the class express his preference for one of a pair of classmates in every possible pair the class roster provided. Each child, then, in a class of 40 would express 740 preferences—780 minus the 40 pairs in which the judge himself was included. Younger children needed to be interviewed to obtain preferences, but children in the sixth grade and above at least are capable of giving their judgments by underlining the name of the favored classmate in each pair offered in a mimeographed or printed list. Koch presented the pairs of names in an order determined by a procedure for randomizing. It was Koch's hope to avoid position and grouping errors of various sorts. In the nursery school, each classmate pair was presented for judgment twice, the order of the names in the second presentation being the reverse of that in the first. A popularity score was computed for each child by a procedure consistent with the law of comparative judgment explained in Chapter 5. The popularity scores can furnish a scale against which the value placed by the group upon various human characteristics—sex, race, scholarship, pigmentation characteristics, social class, athletic skill, size, etc.—can be estimated.

By noting the percentage of times, in pairs composed of a boy and a girl of given race, the child expresses a preference for the boy, it is possible to estimate the strength of the subject's preference for the masculine sex. The same general sort of comparison for pairs in which children of the same sex but of different races are involved can be used to disclose the social distance between the racial groups in a classroom. Koch's method is probably more effective for portraying groups trends in social distance than for individual diagnosis, unless the group is large and the members of the classes compared numerous.

Although the method is laborious, it supplies a great wealth of detail concerning classmate relations. It permits, among other things, the determination of the status of each child with the various groups in his school class, the value order of each classmate for every child, the extent of each pupil's conformity to his peers in his likes and dislikes, the mutualness of liking and disliking among the members of the class, and the relation of subgroup leaders to each other.

EPILOGUE

The brief survey which the present chapter has furnished of the methods in child psychology should suggest the great variety of procedural detail which is the contribution of the psychologists who have worked with child subjects to the methodology of the science of psychology. Child psychology has been no parasite; it has given as well as received. The chapter should also have made clear the similarity in the basic methods employed by psychologists, whether they deal with children or adults.

REFERENCES

1. Alschuler, R. H., and L. W. Hattwick. *Painting and Personality: A Study of Young Children.* 2 vols. Chicago: University of Chicago Press, 1947.
2. Amen, E. W., and M. Dorkey. A continuation study of anxiety reactions in young children by means of a projective technique. *Genet. Psychol. Monog.*, 1947, *35*, 139–183.
3. Arrington, R. E. Time-sampling studies of child behavior. *Psychol. Monog.*, 1939, *51*, No. 2.
4. Bailey, M. W. A scale of block constructions for young children. *Child Develop.*, 1933, *4*, 121–139.
5. Baldwin, A. L., J. Kalhorn, and F. H. Breese. Patterns of parent behavior. *Psychol. Monog.*, 1945, *58*, No. 3.
6. Bayley, N. The development of motor abilities during the first three years. *Monog. Soc. Res. Child Develop.*, 1935, *1*, No. 1.
7. Berne, E. Van C. An experimental investigation of the social behavior patterns in young children. *Univ. Iowa Stud. Child Welfare*, 1930, No. 3.
8. Betts, E. A. An evaluation of certain techniques for the study of oral composition. *Res. Stud. Elem. School Lang.*, 1934, No. 1; *Univ. Iowa Stud. Educ.*, 1934, *9*, No. 2, 7–32.
9. Bott, H. M. Method in social studies of young children. *Univ. Toronto Stud., Child Develop. Ser.*, 1933, No. 1.

10. Brabant, L. L. A study of certain language developments of children in grades four to twelve inclusive. *Genet. Psychol. Monog.*, 1933, *14,* 387–491.
11. Brace, D. K. *Measuring Motor Ability.* New York: Barnes, 1927.
12. Caille, R. K. Resistant behavior of preschool children. *Child Develop. Monog.*, 1933, No. 11.
13. Champney, H. The variables of parent behavior. *J. Abn. Soc. Psychol.*, 1941, *36,* 525–543.
14. Champney, H. The measurement of parent behavior. *Child Develop.*, 1941, *12,* 131–166.
15. Chase, W. P. Color vision in infants. *J. Exper. Psychol.*, 1937, *20,* 203–222.
16. Conrad, H. S. The California behavior inventory for nursery school children. *Univ. Calif. Syllabus Series,* 1933, No. 244.
17. Cozens, F. W., *et al. Physical Education Achievement Scale for Boys in Secondary Schools.* New York: Barnes, 1936.
18. Daniels, P. C. Discrimination of compositional balance at the preschool level. *Psychol. Monog.*, 1933, *45,* 1–12.
19. Davis, E. A. Developmental changes in the distribution of parts of speech. *Child Develop.*, 1938, *9,* 309–317.
20. Dennis, W. Congenital cataract and unlearned behavior. *J. Genet. Psychol.*, 1934, *44,* 340–351.
21. Dennis, W. The effect of cradling practices upon the onset of walking in Hopi children. *J. Genet. Psychol.*, 1940, *56,* 77–86.
22. Dennis, W. Infant development under conditions of restricted practice and of minimal social stimulation. *Genet. Psychol. Monog.*, 1941, *23,* 143–189.
23. Dockeray, F. C., and W. L. Valentine. A new isolation cabinet for infant research. *J. Exper. Psychol.*, 1939, *24,* 211–214.
24. Espenschade, A. Motor performance in adolescence. *Monog. Soc. Res. Child Devel.*, 1940, *5,* No. 1.
25. Fite, M. D. Aggressive behavior in young children and children's attitude toward aggression. *Genet. Psychol. Monog.*, 1940, *22,* 151–322.
26. Gesell, A., and H. Thompson. Learning and growth in identical twins: an experimental study of the method of co-twin control. *Genet. Psychol. Monog.*, 1929, *6,* 1–124.
27. Gesell, A., and H. Thompson assisted by C. S. Amatruda. *Infant Behavior: Its Genesis and Growth.* New York: McGraw-Hill, 1934.
28. Gesell, A., *et al. The First Five Years of Life.* New York: Harper, 1940.
29. Gesell, A., and C. S. Amatruda. *Developmental Diagnosis: Normal and Abnormal Child Development.* New York: Hoeber, 1941.
30. Goodenough, F. L. The use of free association in the objective measurement of personality. In *Studies in Personality.* Q. McNemar and M. A. Merrill, Eds. New York: McGraw-Hill, 1942, pp. 87–103.
31. Goodenough, F. L., and M. A. Tinker. A comparative study of several methods of measuring speed of tapping in children and adults. *J. Genet. Psychol.*, 1930, *38,* 146–160.
32. Green, E. H. Friendships and quarrels among preschool children. *Child Develop.*, 1933, *4,* 237–253.
33. Halverson, H. M. An experimental study of prehension in infants by means of systematic cinema records. *Genet. Psychol. Monog.*, 1931, *10,* 107–286.
34. Hartshorne, H., and M. A. May *Studies in Deceit.* New York: Macmillan, 1928.

35. Hess, J. H., G. J. Mohr, and P. F. Bartelme. *The Physical and Mental Growth of Prematurely Born Children.* Chicago: University of Chicago Press, 1934.
36. Horn, E. The commonest words in the spoken vocabulary of children up to and including six years of age. *Yearbook Nat. Soc. Stud. Educ.*, 1925, *24,* (I), 186–193.
37. Horowitz, R. E. Racial aspects of self identification in nursery school children. *J. Psychol.*, 1939, *7,* 91–99.
38. Irwin, O. C., L. A. Weiss, and E. M. Stubbs. Studies in infant behavior, I. *Univ. Iowa Stud. Child Welfare,* 1934, *9,* No. 4.
39. Jersild, A. T., and R. Ritzman. Aspects of language development, the growth of loquacity and vocabulary. *Child Develop.*, 1938, *9,* 243–259.
40. Jones, H. E., and P. J. Moses. The adolescent growth study. VI. The analysis of voice records. *J. Consult. Psychol.*, 1942, *6,* 255–261.
41. Kellogg, W. N., and L. A. Kellogg. *The Ape and the Child: A Study of Environmental Influence upon Early Behavior.* New York: McGraw-Hill, 1933.
42. Koch, H. L. Popularity in preschool children: some related factors and a technique for its measurement. *Child Develop.*, 1933, *4,* 164–175.
43. Koch, H. L. An analysis of certain forms of so-called nervous habits in young children. *J. Genet. Psychol.*, 1935, *46,* 139–171.
44. Koch, H. L. A study of some factors conditioning the social distance between the sexes. *J. Soc. Psychol.*, 1944, *20,* 79–107.
45. Koch, H. L. The social distance between certain racial, nationality, and skin pigmentation groups in selected populations of American school children. *J. Genet. Psychol.*, 1946, *68,* 63–95.
46. Kreezer, G., and A. D. Glanville. A method for the study of human gait. *J. Genet. Psychol.*, 1937, *50,* 109–137.
47. Levy, D. Studies in sibling rivalry. *Amer. Orthopsych. Assoc. Res. Monog.* No. 2, 1937.
48. Ling, B. C. Form discrimination as a learning cue in infants. *Comp. Psychol. Monog.*, 1941, *17,* No. 2.
49. MacArthur, J. W., and N. Ford. A biological study of the Dionne quintuplets: an identical set. *Univ. Toronto Stud.; Child Develop. Ser.*, 1937, No. 11.
50. McCarthy, D. *The Language Development of Preschool Children.* Minneapolis: University of Minnesota Press, 1930.
51. McNemar, Q. *The Revision of the Stanford-Binet Scale: An Analysis of the Standardization Data.* Boston: Houghton Mifflin, 1942.
52. Moreno, J. L. *Who Shall Survive? A New Approach to the Problem of Human Interrelations.* Washington: Nervous and Mental Disease Publishing Company, 1934.
53. Murphy, L. B. *Social Behavior and Child Personality.* New York: Columbia University Press, 1937.
54. Newman, H. H., F. N. Freeman, and K. J. Holzinger. *Twins: A Study of Heredity and Environment.* Chicago: University of Chicago Press, 1937.
55. Parten, M. B. Leadership among preschool children. *J. Abn. Soc. Psychol.*, 1933, *27,* 430–440.
56. Peiper, A. Über die Helligskeit und Farbenempfindungen der Frühgeburten. *Arch. Kinderheilk.*, 1926, *80,* 1–20.

57. Piaget, J. *The Language and Thought of the Child.* New York: Harcourt, Brace, 1926.
58. Piaget, J. *The Moral Judgment of the Child.* New York: Harcourt, Brace, 1932.
59. Richards, T. W., and M. Powell. The Fels child behavior scale. *Genet. Psychol. Monog.,* 1941, *24,* 259–311.
60. Robinson, E. W., and H. S. Conrad. Reliability of observation of talkativeness and social contact among nursery school children by the short time sample technique. *J. Exper. Educ.,* 1933, *2,* 161–165.
61. Sanford, R. N. Pt. III. Studies of personality and development in physique, personality and scholarship: a cooperative study of school children. *Monog. Soc. Res. Child Develop.,* 1943, *8,* 125–501.
62. Seashore, R. H., and L. D. Eckerson. The measurement of individual differences in general English vocabularies. *J. Educ. Psychol.,* 1940, *31,* 14–38.
63. Shirley, M. M. *The First Two Years, A Study of Twenty-Five Babies.* Vol. 1, *Postural and Locomotor Development.* Minneapolis: University of Minnesota Press, 1931.
64. Smith, J. M. The relative brightness values of three hues for new-born infants. *Univ. Iowa Stud. Child Welfare,* 1936, *12,* No. 1, 91–140.
65. Smith, M. E. An investigation of the development of the sentence and extent of vocabulary of young children. *Univ. Iowa Stud. Child Welfare,* 1926, *3,* No. 5.
66. Strayer, L. C. Language and growth: the relative efficacy of early and deferred vocabulary training studied by the method of co-twin control. *Genet. Psychol. Monog.,* 1930, *8,* 209–319.
67. Thomas, D. S., *et al.* Some new techniques for studying social behavior. *Child Develop. Monog.,* 1929, No. 1.
68. Thomas, D. S., A. M. Loomis, and R. E. Arrington. *Observational Studies of Social Behavior.* Vol. I, *Social Behavior Patterns.* New Haven: Institute of Human Relations, Yale University, 1933.
69. Thorndike, E. L. A scale for general merit of children's drawings. *Teachers College Bull.,* 15th Series, 1923, No. 6, p. 5.
70. Thorndike, E. L., and I. Lorge. *The Teacher's Word Book of 30,000 Words.* New York: Bureau of Publications, Teachers College, Columbia University, 1944.
71. Valentine, W. L., and I. Wagner. Relative arm motility in the newborn infant. *Ohio Univ. Stud.,* 1934, No. 12, 53–68.
72. Wellman, B. L., I. M. Case, I. G. Mengert, and D. E. Bradbury. Speech sounds of young children. *Univ. Iowa Stud. Child Welfare,* 1932, *5,* No. 2.
73. West, P. V. *Manual for the American Handwriting Scale.* Chicago: A. N. Palmer, 1929.
74. Williams, H. M., C. H. Sievers, and M. S. Hattwick. The measurement of musical development. *Univ. Iowa Stud. Child Welfare,* 1933, *7,* No. 1.
75. Wolff, L. V. The development of the human foot as an organ of locomotion. *Amer. J. Diseases Child.,* 1929, *37,* 1212–1220.
76. Zingg, R. M. Feral man and extreme cases of isolation. *Amer. J. Psychol.,* 1940, *53,* 487–517.

SUGGESTED READINGS

Anderson, J. E. Methods of child psychology. In *Manual of Child Psychology.* L. Carmichael, Ed. New York: John Wiley, 1946. (Pp. 1–42.)

Arrington, R. E. Time sampling in studies of social behavior: a critical review of techniques and results of research suggestions. *Psychol. Bull.*, 1943, *40*, 81–124.

Barker, R. G., J. S. Kounin, and H. F. Wright. *Child Development and Behavior.* New York: McGraw-Hill, 1943.

Freud, A. Introduction to the technique of child analysis. (Translated by L. P. Clark.) *Nerv. Ment. Dis. Monog. Ser.*, 1928, No. 48.

Gesell, A. *Infancy and Human Growth.* New York: Macmillan, 1928.

Goodenough, F. L., and J. E. Anderson. *Experimental Child Study.* New York: Century, 1931.

Horowitz, R., and L. B. Murphy. Projective methods in the psychological study of children. *J. Exper. Educ.*, 1938, *7*, 133–140.

Monroe, W. S. *Encyclopedia of Educational Research.* New York: Macmillan, 1941.

Weiss, L. A. Rating scales: with special reference to the field of child development. *Psychol. Bull.*, 1933, *30*, 185–208.

(Various) Intelligence: its nature and nurture. *Yearbook Nat. Soc. Stud. Educ.*, 1940, *39* (Part 1).

Chapter 22

Studying Social Behavior

Theodore M. Newcomb[1]

The social psychologist, as scientist, sets himself the task of discovering the conditions under which individual behavior varies in response to social stimulation. No matter how complex the form of stimulation or how many persons involved, the social psychologist proceeds upon the basis of three assumptions: first, that individuals are responding to some form of social influence, direct or indirect, from one or more other individuals; second, that individuals' behaviors are not a matter of caprice or sheer chance, but correspond to certain conditions and vary in orderly manner with them; and third, that these conditions may be discovered if observations are properly made and conclusions properly drawn. Similar discoveries may also be made by studying the behavior of groups as wholes, but the social psychologist leaves this field of inquiry to sociologists, anthropologists, political scientists, and others. He often finds it necessary, however, to borrow from them.

Two obvious problems thus arise immediately. The social psychologist must devise means of observing response to social stimulation. He must answer the question, "What did the individual do?" in ways which can be demonstrated to be accurate and not merely impressionistic. Secondly, he must have an equally dependable method of knowing what social stimulation was involved. Since it is rarely feasible to consider all the possible social stimuli in a given situation, one of the best approaches to this second problem is to compare responses to two or more situations known to differ in one respect and to be alike in as many other respects as possible, as in an experiment.

There is also a third and less obvious problem. Human behavior, above the reflex level, is rarely so simple as to involve an invariable response to a given stimulation. Different individuals, or even the same one on different occasions, do not necessarily respond alike to

[1] Professor of Sociology and Psychology, University of Michigan.

conditions which are objectively standard. Certain psychological conditions, as well as conditions inherent in the objective situation, determine the individual's response to the situation. In many cases the social psychologist cannot discover the orderly conditions underlying behavior without knowing something about these psychological conditions, in accordance with which individual response is related to social stimulation. As we shall see, these processes, which have to do with the "meaning" imposed upon the situation by the individual, are ordinarily not directly observable; they must therefore be inferred, but always upon the basis of data which are directly observed.

In the following pages various investigations are cited to illustrate different ways in which these three basic kinds of problems have been met, and in this manner we shall survey some of the more representative methods of studying social behavior.

METHODS OF OBSERVING SOCIAL BEHAVIOR

The individual behaving in response to social stimulation does not present the observer with neat little units of behavior, each appropriately labeled. It is the observer who must apply the labels, and the manner in which he does so will depend upon the nature of his problem. Just as the chemist cannot simultaneously determine the specific gravity, the chemical purity, and the electrical resistance of a piece of metal but must investigate each problem separately, so must the social psychologist select a particular aspect of an individual's behavior which he wishes to observe at a given moment. The methodological problem with which we are here concerned is this: Quite apart from the question of what *produced* the behavior, what *happened*? The usual rules of empirical observation apply; in particular, the exact processes by which the observations were made must be recorded in such manner that they can be communicated to others. Thus it becomes possible to repeat the investigation and check the findings. These and other similar factors of importance are surveyed in Chaper 1.

Traits of Social Behavior

Sometimes the social psychologist is interested in a given kind of social behavior, such as generosity or dominance, considered as a more or less persistent trait of personality. Observations concerning such traits have meaning only as one individual's behavior can be compared with that of others. Such comparisons can be made either in terms of frequency or of degree—or preferably, both. In any case a given score, say of generosity, is significant only in terms of norms, i.e., scores made by others. It is also necessary to know the basis of selection of the others from whose scores the norm is constructed. This factor of *comparability* is of course important in all problems of measurement of behavior, and it is discussed in connection with mental tests in Chapter 17.

The short-sample observation technique, as described by Goodenough [13] and her associates, is one of the most satisfactory methods of determining frequency of a given type of behavior. It gets around such difficulties as whether to score a bullying episode of 2 minutes as representing twice as much aggression as a 1-minute episode, by the device of simply noting whether any aggression at all occurred during a brief period of time, say 2 minutes. The individual's aggression score is the number of observation periods in which he gets a positive score.

There are many varieties of such observation techniques, but most of them make no attempt to interpret the intensity or the significance of the behavior. Since, obviously, not all behaviors which can be regarded as sympathetic, for example, are equally so, it is common to rely upon the ratings of a trained observer who, interpreting the behavior in the light of all the relevant circumstances, expresses a judgment of its intensity. Since it is ordinarily neither feasible nor necessary to obtain a rating of every observed incident, such ratings are commonly obtained at intervals, say of a week, and represent summarized judgments of all observed behavior during that period. Under these conditions it is difficult to be certain that all individuals in a group have been under observation for equal amounts of time, and there is some evidence that the quieter and more retiring individuals may actually be seen less than others by observers. For discussions of techniques see Symonds [46, pp. 41–121], Allport [4, pp. 435–447], Jones [19, pp. 150–157]. These techniques are further analyzed and discussed in Chapter 21.

Self-judgments, too, represent a kind of observation tempered by judgment; the so-called personality tests best illustrate the use of this technique. For example, one of the thirty questions in the ascendance-submission inventory of F. H. and G. W. Allport [3] is: "Are you embarrassed if you have greeted a stranger whom you have taken for an acquaintance?" The respondent checks one of the three replies: *Very Much, Somewhat, Not At All.* Total score represents the respondent's preponderance of self-judged tendencies to behave ascendantly over tendencies to behave submissively, or vice versa, in a series of situations. Although self-judgments are often gravely at variance with those of outsiders, the former have their value—providing, of course, that respondents are motivated to be sincere. For example, a considerable majority of prospective store managers obtaining "submissive" scores on the measure just described turned out not to be successful on the job, whereas a large proportion of those making "ascendant" scores were successful, as judged by their superiors.

Response to Specified Forms of Social Influence

We now reverse our perspective. The previous problem was to observe variations in the behavior of single individuals in many situations; we turn now to observing variations among individuals in the same situation. The range of methods here is somewhat wider, since we are not limited to behaviors which may be thought of as individual characteristics.

Numerous studies of responses to various influences labeled "suggestion" illustrate the difference between the two kinds of problems. Among the frequently used measures of suggestibility are the following: (1) amount of body sway (as recorded by a kymograph connected by a thread to the subject's clothing, without his knowledge) in response to the experimenter's suggestion that the subject is swaying forward [8]; (2) the Binet progressive weights: the subject is presented with several weights, one at a time, each heavier than the preceding one, and then with several exactly like the heaviest in the preceding series; score is number of times the latter weights are judged to be heavier than the preceding one [9]; and (3) degree of hand rigidity in response to the experimenter's suggestion: "Hold out your hand—see, like mine—and fix your eyes on my hand. . . . While looking at my hand all the time, I want you to pay special attention to the feelings you get in your own. . . . You will probably feel a slight tingling or tightening or stiffening in your fingers. . . ." [6]. Two significant findings emerge from such investigations: (1) suggestibility in general is not an individual trait; individuals highly suggestible in one situation may show little or no suggestibility in others; and (2) degree of suggestibility tends to be normally distributed when the prestige of the experimenter is not the important influence, but to be distributed according to a U-shaped curve when it is the dominant influence; most individuals are either strongly influenced or scarcely influenced at all by prestige suggestion of this sort.

An example of a method for studying the degree of conformity to *institutional influences* arises in the analyses of the distribution of individuals' responses to a given situation, as contrasted to the variations of a single individual's responses in many situations. F. H. Allport and his students have for some years worked in this area [2]. For example, in certain regions of a city in which automobile parking was limited to 30 minutes, observers recorded the actual periods during which about 25,000 cars were left parked [1]. In this, as in many other situations involving social pressure toward conformity, it was found that, when behavior was charted according to degree of non-conformity (beginning with zero, which corresponds to complete conformity), the curve did not resemble the familiar "normal" distribution. Instead, it took a reversed-J form, somewhat resembling the right-hand half of a normal curve. Allport postulates several factors which would account for different degrees of conformity, as indicated by the distributions of such scaled behaviors in various situations.

Many of the very complex problems of social incentives (competition, working alone versus working in groups, etc.) have been studied in terms of the most easily measurable behaviors. Thus Dashiell [11] used, among other measures, simple multiplication problems in a series of experiments in which individuals worked now alone, now in groups, now spurred by rivalry, and now by conspicuous observation. The problem was to test the hypothesis that the greater productivity which is characteristic of most individuals when working in the presence of others, as compared to working alone, is a result of certain kinds of social stimulation, rather than of the mere presence of other people. It was found that most, but by no means all, subjects increased in speed at the cost of accuracy when observed or when competing; different kinds of social stimulation varied in their power to motivate or to distract different individuals. (See also page 673 of this chapter.) Maller [32], comparing effectiveness of group rewards and individual rewards in stimulating school children, found simple problems of addition to be the most satisfactory measure. Subjects chose to work for individual rewards 74 per cent of the time, on the average, producing more under such conditions than when working for a class prize. Strongest motivation, however, resulted when "teams" competed against each other. Such very simple means are not necessarily the best ways of measuring such complex phenomena; our information about them would be greater if a wider range of tasks, even though not so easily measurable, had been applied.

That rather intricate methods of observing behavior may be very rewarding is suggested in an experiment by Shaw [42], who, like Dashiell, had individuals perform similar tasks alone and in groups. Shaw's problems, however, were extremely difficult, involving a long succession of steps and complicated "moves"—so hard, in fact, that scarcely any of them were solved by individuals working alone, whereas in the group situation about half were solved correctly. Shaw had a note-taker record every suggestion by every individual in the group situation; whether the proposal was accepted or rejected, and by whom, was also noted, so that it was possible to reconstruct every step of the give-and-take process by which the group finally arrived at a solution. This sort of step-by-step recording of individuals' interactions to each other leads to conclusions consistent with the findings of other studies, but which emerged only from the very detailed observations of Shaw: that complex problems of this sort are more effectively solved by groups than by individuals, primarily because (1) a wider range of ways of looking at the problem is offered, (2) a larger number of solutions is proposed, and (3) each proposed solution receives more criticism than an individual, working alone, would be able to make of his own proposals.

Social Attitudes

An attitude is not a response, but a more or less persistent set to respond in a given way to an object or situation. The concept of attitude relates the individual to any aspect of his environment which has positive or negative value for him. It is not surprising, therefore, that social psychologists have spent so much time investigating social attitudes, as representing individuals' dynamic relationships to aspects of their social environment.

Systematic observations of attitudes have most commonly been made by the use of paper-and-pencil responses of subjects. (For present purposes we shall ignore other methods, such as content and symbol analysis.) It has been found both desirable and practicable to conceive of attitude toward any given thing, e.g., the U.N., as ranging along a scale, from the extreme of being very favorable to that of being very unfavorable, the midpoint being neutrality. Attitudes, so conceived, are subject to measurement, like temperature conceived of as above or below any arbitrary zero point. There are two major problems of measurement: (1) to make sure that each position on the scale is correctly placed in relation to other points (just as, on a yardstick, the point registering 8 inches must come between the points registering 7 and 9 inches, and not between any other points); and (2) to make sure that the intervals between any two adjacent points on the scale are equal (just as the distance on the yardstick between the points labeled 4 and 5 inches must be the same as that between any other two adjacent points).

The most successful attempts to make attitude scales as dependable as yardsticks are those of Thurstone and his associates [47, 49]. See also Chapter 5. (The serious student is referred to original sources, which can be only sketchily summarized here.) Both the major problems just mentioned are solved by recourse to a large number of judges, each of whom is presented in random order with a series of attitude statements, ranging from one extreme to the other, concerning a given issue. These statements are sorted by each judge into a number of piles (usually 11), according to degree of favorable or unfavorable attitude which the statement represents, *not* according to the judge's agreement or disagreement with it. Statements revealing contradictory judgments are discarded as ambiguous. The scale value of each remaining statement then becomes the median position assigned to it by all judges. Thus (to take an oversimple illustration), suppose statements concerning the U.N. had been sorted by 100 judges into 11 piles, the most extremely favorable being in the first pile, the most extremely unfavorable in the eleventh, and the most nearly neutral in the sixth. Suppose the statement, "I think most of the U.N. policies should be continued," had been put into the second pile by 10 per cent of all judges, into the third by 40 per cent, into the fourth by 40 per cent, and into the fifth by 10 per cent; its scale value would then be 3.5.

This procedure, known as that of "equal-appearing intervals," results in a series of statements (usually 20 or more) each of whose scale value is known. The "true" distance between any two points, i.e., statements, is the difference between their scale values, which also determine the proper sequence of the statements. Individual score on such an attitude scale is the mean or median of all scale values of the statements with which the subject expresses agreement.

All this, of course, is based upon the assumption that the original sorting of statements by judges has been done in about the same manner that the subject responding to the attitude scale would have done it himself. There are bound to be individual differences in such judgments, even after discarding the more ambiguous statements. Opinions concerning the issue involved, however, do not appear to be major determinants of differences in such judgments. Thus Hinckley [15], for example, has shown that two groups differing widely in attitudes toward Negroes express almost identical judgment concerning the scale value of statements of attitude toward the Negro. Altogether, Thurstone's procedure represents an immense advance in the direction of accurate measurement.

One of the shortcomings of Thurstone's scoring method, however, is that it does not provide adequately for differences in attitude intensity. A person extremely opposed to Russia, for example, would obviously agree with extremely stated anti-Russia statements, but he would also be likely to express agreement with some statements less extreme than his own position. His score thus becomes "diluted" with the scale values of less extreme statements.

This shortcoming, together with other considerations, has led Likert [28] to propose a scheme of responding to attitude statements in terms of degree of agreement, rather than all-or-none agreement. Likert's subjects respond to *all* statements in a scale, by checking one of the following: *Strongly Agree; Agree; Uncertain; Disagree; Strongly Disagree.* Each attitude statement thus becomes a scale within a scale. Careful statistical analysis showed that the simple device of scoring the foregoing responses 5, 4, 3, 2, and 1, respectively (if the statement is favorably worded) or 1, 2, 3, 4, and 5 (if it is unfavorably worded) resulted in scores equivalent to those obtained by more elaborate statistical devices. Final score is simply the sum of the values (1, 2, 3, 4, or 5) of each attitude response, so that the possible range of scores in a 20-statement scale would be from 20 to 100. Because it allows for greater extremes of intensity, the Likert technique has been reported to yield somewhat more reliable results than the Thurstone scoring system [29]. Although it is not necessary, in using Likert scales, to establish the scale values of each attitude statement (since it is not used in scoring), confidence in the Likert method is considerably increased because it yields results very similar to those obtained with Thurstone's methods.

The reader interested in the results of applying such measures will find a considerable body of evidence concerning social attitudes treated as response to situations, e.g., the kinds of experiences which give rise to or which modify them, and also concerning social attitudes as individual characteristics, e.g., personality traits associated with various attitudes, or with susceptibility to influences likely to modify them. See, for example, References 35 (Chapter 13) and 44. Attitude scales can be efficiently employed as dependent variables in investigations of many types of social behavior. Examples of this usage will be found in the following pages.

CONTROLLING SOCIAL STIMULATION

As the investigator seeks to discover the conditions under which individuals vary in their behavior, he must find ways of controlling social stimulation, i.e., knowing as much as possible about what influences are and what are not involved. Social stimuli are usually rather complex, and the individual commonly finds himself bombarded by many social influences at once. The investigator must have some means of knowing to which of these influences he can attribute observed changes in behavior.

Experimental Control

The most satisfactory, although often the most difficult method of controlling social stimulation is experiment, i.e., designed manipulation of conditions. The physicist interested in the problem of expansion under heat does not wait till he happens to find a given substance at various temperatures; he heats it to suit his experimental purposes. The social psychologist does the same thing when he can.

One of the problems most easily subject to experimental control is the effect of certain experiences upon social attitudes. For example, Thurstone [48] has shown that certain movies dealing with the treatment of criminals have an effect upon the attitudes of high-school children. As shown in Table I (in which low scores indicate attitude

TABLE I

MEAN SCORES OF ATTITUDE TOWARD TREATMENT OF CRIMINALS, BEFORE AND AFTER SEEING FILMS

Films Seen	Mean Score Before	Mean Score After	Mean Score Difference
None (control)	4.95	4.98	+.03
Film X	5.14	5.13	−.01
Film Y	5.23	5.27	+.04
Films X + Y	5.23	5.03	−.20
Films X + Z	5.14	4.97	−.17
Films Y + Z	5.23	4.95	−.28
Films X + Y + Z	5.22	4.83	−.39

of leniency in treating criminals), none of the three films, seen alone, has much effect, but any two are more effective than any one, and all three produce greater results than any two. Since the amount of attitude change varies consistently with the number of films seen, it is pretty certain that attitudes were influenced by the social stimulation of seeing the films.

In an experiment by Knower [21] the kind rather than the amount of stimulation was controlled. Attitudes toward prohibition (before its repeal in 1933) were measured before and after various types of appeals concerning the issue. Each of nearly 1000 students, as experimental subjects (in addition to 300 as controls), was subjected to both spoken and written appeals of one of the following types: dry logical, dry persuasive, wet logical, and wet persuasive. Oral presentation proved highly effective to all groups (with individual exceptions, of course), and mean scores of all groups subjected to written presentation were also significantly influenced, although to a lesser degree. There was no consistent superiority, for all groups, of either logical or persuasive appeal. Probably more significant is the experimenter's finding that, regardless of *direction* of initial attitude, i.e., wet or dry, least attitude change was shown by those whose attitudes were already definitely formed, and most by those whose initial attitudes were more nearly neutral. In this experiment we thus see the effects of social stimulation as it is controlled for three kinds of conditions: medium of presentation, mode of appeal, and previous attitude.

One of the persistent problems in social psychology has been *social facilitation,* as in the effect of various forms of social influence upon speed and accuracy of work done. Forms of social influence were controlled by Dashiell [11] as follows: (1) subjects working in a room alone, knowing that others were working simultaneously in other rooms, starting and stopping work by a buzzer heard by all; (2) in a room alone, by individual appointment; (3) seated together about a table, with instructions not to compete, since scores would never be compared; (4) seated together about a table, with instructions to compete, since scores would be compared; and (5) one individual working while conspicuously watched by two others. The material consisted of multiplication problems, mixed relations test, and free serial word associations. Directions were presented at the top of the work sheets, and five alternative sets of all materials were used, after it was first demonstrated that the five forms were equivalent. The subjects were told to work as accurately and as fast as they could.

By means of the controls described, Dashiell was able to show that increased speed (usually at the cost of accuracy) is found not when individuals merely work in the *presence* of others, but rather when individuals take a *competitive attitude* toward others. This attitude apparently characterized subjects in situation 1 above, since they worked faster and less accurately than those in situation 2. These results, however, represent group averages, with a significant number of individual exceptions. The evidence suggests that some individuals were hindered rather than stimulated by the competitive attitude. This factor, which is perhaps related to social extroversion, should also be controlled in future investigations of this kind. Another kind of experimental control is discussed in the section on social climates, pages 690–691.

Selection of Subjects of Different Backgrounds of Experience

Just as the astronomer cannot create an eclipse, but must wait till it occurs and then go where it can be observed, so the social psychologist cannot experimentally manipulate many of the experiences whose effects he wishes to study. He therefore selects individuals to whom such experiences have happened "naturally," taking pains to see that the individuals compared are as nearly as possible alike in other respects.

Thus Hall [14], wishing to study some consequences of unemployment during the 1930's, compared 300 employed with 300 unemployed professional engineers, matched for age, normal earning power, education, state licensing, nativity, and marital status. Four scales were employed, measuring attitude toward religion, attitude toward employers, "radicalism," and "occupational morale." It was found that the unemployed had much poorer morale than the employed and were much more critical of employers, but did not differ from them in radicalism or religion. By comparing various groups of those employed (according to financial resources, length of unemployment, etc.) it was shown that morale decreases steadily with lessened economic security. In this instance it was not possible to compare attitudes of the same individuals before and after unemployment, but comparisons of those subjected to different experiences with respect to employment yield results that seem to be dependable.

An investigation by Dodd [12] is an example of a method designed to test the effects of the various forms of social stimulation associated with religious affiliation. "Social distance" responses were obtained from 170 students of heterogeneous background in a Syrian University, representing 15 national and 11 religious groups. Each respondent recorded his attitudes towards members of several national, religious, economic, and educational groups, on a scale similar to those derived by the method of equal-appearing intervals. The actual steps of the scale used by Dodd, with the cultural backgrounds of the particular students in mind, were as follows:

1. If I wanted to marry, I would marry one of them.
2. I would be willing to have as a guest for a meal.
3. I prefer to have merely as an acquaintance to whom one talks on meeting in the street.
4. I do not enjoy the companionship of these people.
5. I wish some one would kill all these individuals.

X. I know nothing about this group; I cannot express an attitude.

The method of response was simply to check one of these scale steps for each national, religious, or other grouping referred to. The results were analyzed in terms of "intergroup distance," i.e., the scale value of the degree of acceptance of a Turk by an Armenian, for example, or of a Moslem by a Jew.

Among several other findings of interest, it turned out that the greatest variations in social distance (willingness to accept members of other groups) were those among religious groups. The investigator points out the dominance of religious forces in the Near East: residences, schools, legal codes, and even political representation are likely to be determined by religious affiliation. In short, the dominant interests of individuals are directly linked, partially in supposition and partly in fact, with their status as members of religious groups. In such investigations as this, social influences—whole clusters of them, in this instance—are controlled simply by selecting individuals who have been subjected to them.

Statistical Controls

Rather closely related to the preceding technique are various statistical devices by which one or more forms of social stimulation may be held constant while others are allowed to vary. When such methods are used, there is no initial selection of subjects on the basis of previous social stimulation; in fact, subjects may be selected by purely random means, provided they represent an adequate range in regard to the kinds of stimulation which it is desired to study. Since such methods are in common use in almost every area of psychological investigation, only one illustration will be presented, to save space for methods more uniquely characteristic of social psychology.

In an investigation of parent-child resemblances in social attitudes [40], scores were obtained from approximately 800 "children," ranging in age from 14 to 38 years, together with scores from one or both of their parents. Fairly consistent correlations were found between parents' and children's attitudes, regardless of sex, age, religious affiliation, or socio-economic status; the coefficients of correlation were in the neighborhood of .6, .5, and .4, respectively, for attitudes toward church, Communism, and war. The question then arose as to whether children closely resembling their parents in one attitude also resembled them in others; was the degree of relationship specific to a single attitude, or inclusive of all three? In order to answer this question, one group of families was selected in which parent-child differences in attitude toward church was .5 scale points or less; parent-child correlations were then calculated for both attitude toward war and attitude toward Communism. Similarly, another group of families was selected on the basis of close parent-child resemblance in attitude toward Communism, and parent-child correlations calculated for both of the other attitudes. The results, as shown in Table II, indicate only a

TABLE II

Parent-child Correlations in Attitudes toward Church and Communism

	N	Church	Communism
Group selected to correlate highly in attitude toward church	220	.96	.62
Group selected to correlate highly in attitude toward Communism	227	.74	.93
All cases, unselected	1090	.63	.56

slight tendency for children resembling parents closely in either attitude to resemble them in the other attitude more closely than do unselected cases (.74 as compared to .63, and .62 as compared to .56). The procedure here is that of controlling parental influence, as indicated by one variable, on the basis of a statistical criterion, while not controlling the other variable of individual differences.

Cultural Comparisons

Almost all the evidence so far submitted has been obtained from American subjects. To an unknown degree, the findings are therefore influenced by such cultural conditions as are peculiar to America; it would be totally unjustified to assume that the same findings would apply to all human beings everywhere.

Mead [33], impressed by such considerations, sought to compare in two contrasting cultures, American and Samoan, the conditions which appear to be related to the well-known phenomenon (in America) of adolescent storm and stress. To the extent that the phenomenon is a function of biological changes, it should appear among all human societies, regardless of cultural variations. To the extent that it is a function of the cultural variations, it should vary with them. The Samoan society was chosen because of certain indications that cultural circumstances apparently related to adolescent difficulties in America were not present in Samoan culture.

The major aspects of Samoan culture were ascertained by more or less standard ethnological procedures, especially through interviews (in the language of the natives) with selected informants, checked by other informants and by observation under varying conditions. For each household in three selected villages data were compiled concerning rank, wealth, relationship to other households, etc., together with a wide range of information concerning each individual in each village. For the specific study of adolescent behavior, all the girls between 9 and 20 years of age in the three villages were subjects. To these 68 girls were applied the methods of the clinician and the social worker: standardized (but informal) interviews were held, simple tests administered, and check lists concerning individual experiences and attitudes filled out by the investigator. The study may thus be said to be "scientific" in the sense that a hypothesis was checked by means of reasonably objective information concerning a known sample of the population, but not in the sense that all equally competent observers would necessarily have drawn the same conclusions from the data.

Mead has more recently presented [33] a comprehensive statement of objective means of recording the behavior of children. The interested reader will find many suggestions by means of which behaviors can be recorded with a minimum of subjective interpretation.

Mead's findings may be considered definitive in one respect: since adolescent storm and stress is much less frequent and less intense in Samoa, it must be to a considerable extent a function of culture (biological factors being assumed to be the same in both societies). As to the particular influences involved, her conclusions are more tentative, since it was not possible to isolate the many simultaneous influences with respect to which the two cultures differ. She points, however, to the following: Samoan children's careers are to a very large extent cut out for them, so that they have few weighty choices to make as they approach maturity; Samoan family arrangements are such that children develop very little emotional dependence upon any particular adults; and there is little social pressure for Samoans of any age to inhibit any expression of interest in sex, although there are, of course, approved and disapproved ways of expressing such an interest.

Within a society as complex as our own there exist, in effect, various subcultures, and contrasts among them may be quite as illuminating as those among totally different cultures. Thus Davis and his associates [10] have carefully observed the customs, particularly with regard to child training, shared by members of different social and economic groups of Negroes in America.

The several classes were distinguished according to methods originally devised by Warner [50]. Individuals are interviewed as to who their actual associates are, and these self-reports are supplemented by observations concerning visiting in each other's homes, membership in clubs and other groups, etc. The basic assumption is that individuals who associate freely together belong to the same class. The relative positions of the several classes are determined by direct questioning of individuals at all levels concerning the position of themselves and their associates relative to other groups recognized by them. It is asserted that "the members of all classes agree upon the relative status of each class." Behavior and attitudinal differences are ascertained by the systematic interviewing of both parents and children concerning themselves, other members of their families, their friends, and their associates.

By these means the investigators found, first, such strikingly different patterns of behavior as the following: middle-class Negroes, as compared with those of the lower class, are much more restrained in physical aggression, strongly disapprove of extramarital sex relations, take their church membership very seriously, and spend much more time with their children, in whom they attempt to create attitudes of restraint and inhibition, rather than controlling them by force, threats of beating, etc. Secondly (and more significantly for theoretical purposes), they show that these subcultural differences, which have obvious effects upon the developing personalities of children, are perpetuated by the social barriers between the two groups. Lower-class Negroes simply cannot acquire middle-class behavior, because they are excluded from intimate companionship with them, and middle-class Negro children are never allowed to lose sight of the awful fate in store for them if they allow themselves to descend to lower-class ways.

Such attempts to control cultural factors, while far less exact than those which are possible by experimental or statistical methods, are necessary supplements to these methods. It cannot be too strongly emphasized, in fact, that social psychological findings *within* a culture can be fully understood only in the light of comparable findings *outside* that culture.

RELATING INDIVIDUAL RESPONSE TO SOCIAL STIMULATION

Comparatively few social psychological problems can be solved simply by accurate observation of response to controlled stimulation. Solutions attempted by such means rarely go further than a distribution curve, i.e., a statement of what proportions of groups selected in a given manner make various degrees of response to the same stimulation, or to comparable stimulations. We are faced with the same limitation even in the attempt to account for the behavior of a single individual: at best, the investigator may conclude that individual X, confronted with social stimulation Y, shows a characteristic range, or distribution, of response, with greater frequency at some points within the range than at others.

Such limitations result principally from the fact that almost any social situation has many possible "meanings," either for the same individual or for different ones. For present purposes we shall define meaning simply as the manner in which the individual relates the situation to the direction of his own behavior. The notion of behavior direction implies selectivity on the part of the responding individual, both in his overt behavior and in his perceiving of the situation. Three aspects of behavior are thus interdependent: the goal toward which it is directed, the way in which the situation is seen to be related to the goal, and what the individual does about it. Any one of the three may determine both of the others. Thus, a pre-existing goal direction may determine both manner of perceiving and overt behavior; a particular manner of perceiving a situation (perhaps fixed by habit) may set a goal direction and initiate a course of action; or a given course of action, once begun, may reinforce or modify a goal direction with its corresponding manner of perceiving. In any case, these aspects of behavior, together with others, e.g., affective and cognitive, function together, pattern-wise, more or less harmoniously. For want of a better term, we shall refer to this over-all directionality of behavior at any given moment as a *motive pattern.*

This little essay on theory has been inserted into a treatise on method for two reasons: (1) no method is ever better than the theory upon which it is based; and (2) the more significant recent developments in social psychology, in the writer's judgment, have taken account of the fact that social stimulation affects behavior only as it influences a total motive pattern. The remaining pages will detail some of the conditions under which it is and is not necessary to deal with such problems, and some of the ways in which investigators have sought to meet them.

Sharply Defined and Weakly Defined Situations

In certain situations the manner in which social stimulation influences a motive pattern does not constitute a problem, because the possibilities are narrowly limited. Thus Landis [23], in studying facial expressions under strong emotion, presented his laboratory subjects with intense, well-defined stimulation, such as a strong electric shock or a live rat whose head was to be cut off with a dull knife. He found that, although certain individuals tended to favor certain muscle patterns and to neglect others, there were no standard patterns of facial expression on the part of all subjects which distinguished between one kind of emotional situation and another. Such a finding may be interpreted without further investigation of the nature of the individual motive patterns involved; it seems safe to assume that they were pretty standard, for all subjects. A more detailed description of Landis' important investigation has been presented in Chapter 13.

Some of Landis' situations involved little or no stimulation of a clearly social nature, but social stimulation may also be quite sharply defined. It is not necessary, for example, to inquire into the nature of the motive patterns involved in an intense panic situation, e.g., a crowd trapped by a fire from which there is no escape. Perhaps the nearest approximation to such a situation which has actually been investigated is Laird's study of "razzing" [22]. He arranged with the members of a fraternity to submit each fraternity pledge, one at a time, to a series of intensely humiliating experiences while performing certain motor tests (success in which was assumed by the pledges to be a condition of acceptance); each pledge thought himself to be the only one subjected to such razzing. In most tests the subjects performed less well than under control conditions. Here again, unless one is interested in making an intensive study of the individual subjects, it seems unnecessary to investigate individual motive patterns; for other purposes, the meaning of the stimulation may be assumed to be more or less standard.

Most kinds of social stimulation, however, provide many possibilities with respect to meaning. Hence methods of holding the stimulation objectively constant, no matter how accurate and rigorous, do not insure that individual motive patterns will be standard. The work of Razran [41] shows how such factors may become involved even in a "classical" laboratory experiment on salivary conditioning. He succeeded in obtaining a conditioned salivary flow to such stimuli as the beat of a metronome on the part of many of his human subjects. Careful analysis of his results, however, showed three distinct patterns of conditioning response: (1) the "normal" one, like that of Pavlov's dogs, (2) complete failure to establish the conditioned salivation, and (3) "reverse" conditioning, i.e., a smaller rather than a larger flow of saliva after the signal indicating food. The distinguishing factor turned out to be attitude toward the experimenter. Specifically, both the first and third groups sensed what the experimenter was up to; for various reasons the first group of subjects was motivated to "go along" with him, whereas the third group developed an attitude of resistance. Thus potent may social stimulation become even in laboratory situations, which have not commonly been thought of as involving social stimulation.

Failure to take such considerations into account may lead to doubtful interpretations of investigations otherwise well planned. Many investigators, for example, have somewhat naïvely obtained attitude measurements before submitting their subjects to some experience designed to modify the attitudes; when the attitude measurements are repeated after the experience, it is sometimes assumed that the observed change in attitude scores is a straightforward consequence of the experience. Startling examples of attitude shift have thus been reported as a result of a unit of school instruction. No matter how well controlled the objective stimulation, in such experiments, the suspicion remains that it is the subject's attitude toward the school or toward the instructor which may have set the dominant motive patterns, and thus determined the results.

Some of the more promising methods by which investigators have sought to observe or to infer the ways in which social stimulation is incorporated into motive patterns are noted below.

Projective Devices

All "projective" devices for investigating personality have in common the basic procedure of presenting the subject not with a situation already defined, to which he must simply make a choice among prescribed responses, but with a situation which he must define for himself. It is assumed that the manner in which he does so will determine his response. The reader is referred to Chapters 18 and 21 for more detailed description of these methods and is invited to note the frequency with which they involve social stimulation.

Frame of Reference Techniques

One of the reasons why a situation may have various meanings is that it may be judged by different standards. Sherif [43] has neatly demonstrated how social influences may operate to build up such standards. He made experimental use of the autokinetic phenomenon; i.e., a stationary pinpoint of light, if shown at an unknown distance in a completely dark room, is seen by all subjects to move. Since there are no objective standards in terms of which to judge the amount of perceived movement, subjects tend to build up standards or norms of their own, with repeated experience. Some of the subjects, working alone, made 100 successive judgments of the amount of perceived movement; by this time, each had established a characteristic range, e.g., 1 to 3 inches, or 8 to 10 inches. Other subjects went through the same procedure, working in small groups, each of which, similarly, established its own characteristic range, accepted by all members of the group. Conditions were then reversed: those who had first worked alone now working in groups, and vice versa. The significant finding was that norms established in the group situation persisted in the alone situation, but norms established alone were modified in the group situation, so that all members of the group came to make their judgments within the same range, regardless of what their previous, individually established norms had been. We have thus a demonstration of social influence at work in creating standards by which individuals judge weakly defined situations.

Some of Lewis' studies in political attitudes illustrate how suggestion operates, not as mere blind submission, but rather (when it operates at all) by way of shifting the standards by which judgments are made. In one study [27] she chose political slogans, e.g., "No peace without honor!" deliberately taken out of context, in order to study the contexts into which subjects placed them. Students whose political preferences were known were presented with rank order evaluations of these slogans, ostensibly by persons of prestige in their eyes, e.g., President Roosevelt for "liberals," or Browder for Communists. The stated order of preference, as presented to certain groups, was such that the alleged source of the evaluation was most improbable, and such that the subjects themselves would be certain to disagree with. For example, Republicans were told that ex-President Hoover had ranked very highly the slogan: "Workers of the World, unite!" Subjects were then asked to rank the slogans in order of approval. Later, in interviews, they were queried at some length as to the meaning of their responses.

In spite of the prestige of the stated authors of the evaluations, most subjects clung to their own opinions, although generally they accepted the authenticity of the evaluations presented, as indicated in interviews held later. In those cases where subjects changed their evaluations to agree with those of the admired figure, e.g., Roosevelt, reasons were elicited in interviews. For example, a Communist subject changed her formerly low evaluation of "No peace without honor!" to agree with the high evaluation attributed to Mr. Browder, explaining, "People are beginning to feel that way since Munich" (the Munich agreement, regarded by Communists as a conspiracy against Russia, had taken place only 2 months earlier). She had never thought of the phrase in this context before. The investigator gives abundant evidence for her conclusion: "If the suggestion . . . can cause a shifting of the particular opinion from one context to another, cause a reorganization of the subject's understanding . . . and if the new pattern thus created seems at least as clear and correct as the old, then a 'change of opinion' may take place, or rather a new opinion may evolve."

Methodologically, the important points here are: (1) the investigator should not be content with the mere conclusion that a majority of the subjects do or do not change opinions under a given influence; he must also explain the exceptions; and (2) only by careful attempts (in this instance by interview methods) to ascertain the meaning of the stimulation to the subject is it possible to discover why the same stimulation produces different effects upon different subjects.

Hyman [17], in a study of "subjective status" (defined as a person's conception of his own position relative to other individuals), has investigated the influence of varying frames of reference. He discovered, in preliminary interviews, that judgments of own status varied according to the reference group and according to the specific kind (or dimension) of status, in terms of which the judgment had been made. His experimental subjects were therefore asked to judge their own status in terms of 3 reference groups (total adult population in the United States, friends and acquaintances, own occupational group) and 6 dimensions (general, economic, intellectual, cultural, and social status, plus physical attractiveness). For this purpose 18 pairs of graphic rating scales were employed, 1 pair for each of 6 dimensions with reference to each of three groups. On 1 of each pair the subject indicated the percentage of the particular reference group whom he considered "higher" than himself in regard, e.g., to cultural status, and on the other the percentage of the same group considered "lower" with respect to the same kind of status. Each of the 18 indices of status was computed as the percentage of the reference group lower in the given status, plus half the percentage of that reference group in the same status.

The significant methodological contribution here is the obtaining of independent judgments under systematically varied frames of reference. By such procedures Hyman found that subjective status was altered considerably, for each kind of status, by shifts of reference groups; e.g., an individual might have high intellectual status in terms of the total American population, but low intellectual status in terms of his occupational group. Some subjects characteristically made use of one reference group, some of another; whereas others used more than one (as indicated in interview responses). Some subjects rarely or never thought in terms of some one specific status, whereas others were very important to them. As a further step in the experiment, subjects were therefore asked to rank the five specific kinds of status in order of importance to them; "general" status turned out to be a composite of specific statuses, particularly influenced by the most valued kinds of statuses. Interviews further demonstrated that these various subjective statuses had much to do with feelings of insecurity, with ego needs, with areas of striving, etc.

Such evidence as this, although it does not include overt behaviors, gives strong support to a hypothesis such as the following: there are many situations which inevitably involve judgments of own position relative to that of others; under such conditions social behavior will vary with the frame of reference in terms of which own status is perceived, which in turn determines the meaning which the situation has for the individual.

Intensive Individual Studies

It is a reasonable hypothesis, in view of all these considerations, that the persistence of traits and stability of personality organization, so often observed as characteristic of the individual, may be traced to persistent motive patterns in terms of which social situations are given meaning. Nothing short of prolonged and intensive studies of individuals in a wide variety of situations can serve to check such an hypothesis. The most ambitious attempt, so far, has been that of Murray [37], who relied heavily upon projective devices, supplemented by a wide range of other techniques, for observing and appraising individual personality.

In a more recent study, Murray and Morgan [38] have adapted similar methods to the investigation of individual sentiments or attitudes. Their various procedures have in common two characteristics not common to most methods of attitude measurement: (1) they are designed to circumvent "factors . . . which can interfere with the true avowal of a sentiment," such as variable understandings of the experimental situation, personal attitudes toward the investigator, and irrelevant motivations of the subject, and (2) they are designed to tap the dynamic aspects of attitudes, as related to other phases of personality.

This detailed, clinical study of the attitudes of 11 college men included 63 "foci of sentiments," or objects toward which attitudes are held; most of them had to do with war, religion, parents, and sex. The following methods are typical: (1) *aphorisms test:* the subject sorts out cards, on each of which is printed an aphorism relevant to one of the attitudes being studied, and indicates his degree of acceptance or rejection of it by placing the card in an appropriately labeled box; this procedure has "more of the quality of a definite commitment than making a pencil check on a sheet of paper"; (2) *sentiments examination:* the examiner reads off a list of words, to each of which the subject responds "by giving the most descriptive adjective he can think of," having been led to believe that his vocabulary is being tested; score is ratio of "appreciative" to "depreciative" adjectives; (3) *argument-completion test:* subjects are asked to "continue and finish" printed versions of interrupted arguments between two young men; subjects, who are led to believe that their powers of argumentation are being tested, usually make their own opinions clear, but if the examiner is in doubt he simply asks with which contestant the subject more nearly agrees.

It is not certain that such methods always yield quantitative scores of adequate reliability, but it seems quite clear that they are an improvement over other methods in respect to validity. Their chief virtue is that of getting at spontaneous expressions of attitude, as distinguished from forcing the subject to choose among prescribed alternatives.

Another study showing the necessity of this kind of approach is that of Murphy [36] on sympathy in young children. By means of ratings and objective observations, both in free playground situations and under controlled conditions, she established reliable measures of sympathetic behavior, showing that some children were very rarely sympathetic, others very frequently so. All children, however, were somewhat variable, in ways which did not correspond to objective situational changes. Such factors as the following, however, explained many of the apparent inconsistencies: One child, normally high in sympathy, abandoned such behavior when he felt that his position in the group was threatened. Another, normally not very sympathetic, became much more so when he felt insecure in the group. Obviously these two children had incorporated sympathetic behavior into quite different motive patterns; for the first, it was a more or less habitual and spontaneous way of expressing himself in social relations, whereas for the second it was a way of re-establishing his threatened security. Such an interpretation provides a key for understanding what would otherwise be incomprehensible inconsistency. Professor Koch has given a detailed description (page 656) of some of the other important aspects of Murphy's work on sympathy in children.

In an investigation of changes in political-economic attitudes of students, Newcomb [39] found it necessary to rely upon similar interpretations. In a small college community where the dominant attitudes were "liberal," although freshmen were characteristically very "conservative," nearly all prominent and popular students were conspicuously liberal, and nearly all who had attitudes of antagonism toward the college, or who were indifferent to college activities, were markedly conservative. Political attitudes, however, were not simply a matter of being assimilated into the college community in general, since some active and popular students remained conservative, and some who remained aloof developed liberal political attitudes. It became necessary to inquire into the manner in which students visualized their own relations to the college community.

Several methods were used in pursuing this inquiry. First, questionnaire responses were obtained, indicating quantitatively how students believed their own attitudes compared with those of freshmen, seniors, and faculty; these assumed attitude differences were compared with actual, obtained differences in attitude scores. (Two students whose attitude scores were identical might attach quite different meanings to them. For example, one conservative senior might consider her attitudes typical for her class, whereas another might be fully aware of her conservatism.) Second, a "guess who" technique of ascertaining community reputation was employed. Names were filled in by a cross-section panel of students in answer to such questions as the following: "What three students are most (least) absorbed in college community affairs? Most critical of student committees? Most anxious to be left alone to follow individual pursuits? Most resistant to community expectations?" Reputation scores were computed from these responses. Third, semistandardized interviews were held with each senior, in which she was encouraged to talk frankly and spontaneously, without being asked pointed questions, about such matters as the following: "In what respects have you changed most since coming to college? How about attitudes toward public issues? How do your present attitudes compare with those of other seniors? With those of student leaders? Have you felt that there is social pressure to 'liberalize' your attitudes?" Interview responses were not quantified, but classified into broad groups.

By these and other means it was discovered that some extreme conservatives, disappointed in their hopes for positions of college leadership, were consciously rebelling against what they recognized as social pressure toward liberalism. Other conservatives, having no such hopes, led such restricted lives that they believed their own conservatism typical of the entire community. Some extreme liberals were trying to conform, whereas others felt their own extreme attitudes to be a mark of intellectual superiority. The psychological processes by which such individuals adapted to the same community thus varied with the manner in which they fitted the social stimulation into their own motive patterns.

The methods by which such findings are arrived at are not simple. In Newcomb's investigation they included responses to attitude scales, personality ratings, individual case studies, controlled interviews, and objectively scored self-judgment of own relationship to the community. The method might be summarized as follows: comparable social stimulation for all subjects, together with objective records of behavior plus every possible approach, both objective and interpretative (providing only that all approaches are equivalent for all subjects), to the problem of how the social stimulation is seen by the subject to be related to his own motives. Findings obtained by such methods have significance beyond that for single individuals. Granting that, in the last analysis, each individual is unique, it will usually be found that many individuals reveal essentially similar patterns. For the purposes of any given problem, in other words, a limited number of patterns may be expected. There seems to be no substitute, however, for the method of intensive individual study in order to discover what the patterns are.

Psychiatric methods of studying individuals—methods chiefly interpretative rather than objective—must be mentioned in passing. Sullivan [45], for example, defines psychiatry as the study of interpersonal relations; the psychiatrist's diagnostic task thus becomes the discovering of the patterns in terms of which his patient perceives his own social relations. Horney [16] has more recently described the "basic conflict" of the neurotic in terms of "the fundamentally contradictory attitudes he had acquired toward other persons"—specifically, unsolved conflicts among patterns of "moving toward," "moving against," and "moving away from" people. Such contributions, although they must be accepted by the social psychologist as hypotheses rather than final conclusions, provide a supplementary source of data which are altogether congruent with other findings here reported.

Methods of analyzing "personal documents," such as letters, diaries, and autobiographies, have been summarized and evaluated by Allport [5]. One of the most promising techniques is symbol analysis, as outlined by White [51]. His basic assumption is similar to that which underlies all "projective" methods: "There is always a tendency for a person to think about what is related to his own needs or values, and to perceive his world in terms of those values." By White's method any free verbal expression, e.g., a speech, a therapeutic interview, or a diary, can be quantitatively analyzed in terms of values and agents (or objects) to which it is related. Having found that a comparatively few words serve to represent practically all the value judgments that are commonly put into words in our culture, White simply notes in the margin of the written material a standard symbol for the value referred to, together with another symbol for the object to which the value refers. For example, a sentence in which a writer states that he has little trust in Russians is summarized by three symbols: one for the value of truthfulness, one to indicate that the value is expressed negatively, and one for Russians. By counting and comparing the frequencies of different values thus expressed, it is possible to draw significant conclusions concerning meanings which many kinds of situations have for the individual under scrutiny. Systematic notation and classification of the writer's use of value-laden words lead to significant conclusions concerning the stimulus value which various persons and situations have for him.

Sociometric Devices

Group membership obviously provides an important source of social stimulation, but the same group may have widely different meanings to its component individuals. Moreno and his associates [34] proceed from the assumption that the nature of group influence is in large part determined by person-to-person relations within the group. The latter are ascertained by the simple device of asking group members to make spontaneous choices as to preferred and rejected individuals for specific purposes, e.g., living companions or team leaders. (There is reason to suppose that such choices have more validity if it is known that they will be acted upon, e.g., that one will actually be assigned to live with the chosen companion, but experimental evidence is lacking on this point.) The network of choices and rejections can thus be charted, either for the total group or for any given member. The meaning of the group for the individual can thus be understood in terms, for instance, of his total range of acquaintance, or of his own desirability, as viewed by others, in contrast with his desires for companionship with others. A description of the instructions and the diagrammed results of some of Moreno's work are given on pages 371–374.

A sociometric study by Jennings [18] has thrown some light on the social psychology of leadership. Using as subjects the members of a large industrial school for girls, she showed that girls chosen as leaders have widely divergent personality traits. A leader, in fact, cannot be defined in terms of the possession of certain traits, but only in terms of those various capacities of sharing and participating in the particular forms of interpersonal relations felt to be needed by members of the specific groups involved.

Group Influences on Individual Motive Patterns

Several recent investigations concerning changes of habits, or "re-education," have not only demonstrated that experimental procedures can be applied to real social situations, but have also thrown new light on the significant psychological processes involved in such changes. Thus Lewin [24], called upon to ascertain the conditions under which people were willing to change certain food habits, compared the effects of two procedures. It was found that response to formal lectures, replete with evidence, was slight. When groups were presented with the problem of using non-preferred foods, however, "group decision" after free discussion led to a determination by many individuals to try the new foods. Follow-up observations showed that in a large number of cases these decisions were actually carried out.

In a report of several similar investigations [25], the following are representative: (1) Key officials in a garment factory could not be shaken from their conviction that older women were inferior to younger ones at skilled jobs, in spite of overwhelming evidence to the contrary. Only after discussions among groups of leaders and subleaders was it decided to try the experiment of introducing more older workers; the experiment proved a conspicuous success, and the prejudices against them disappeared. (2) Confirmed alcoholics, whose individual attempts to "reform" have repeatedly failed, find that the craving actually disappears after membership in a group of other alcoholics, organized for the express purpose of supporting each other in their attempts to lead a satisfying life without alcohol, is established. See also Reference 7. From this and other similar evidence Lewin and Grabbe concluded that one of the outstanding means for producing acceptance of re-education is the establishment of a group in which the members have a feeling of belongingness. Under such conditions the individual seems to accept the new system of values and beliefs by accepting belongingness to the group, and this factor appears to be basic for re-education, in that the linkage between acceptance of the new facts or values and acceptance of certain groups or roles is a very intimate one.

An Experiment on Group Influences

In one of the most ambitious of recent social psychological experiments, Lewin [26] and Lippitt and White [30, 31] arranged to have several boys' clubs conducted under such conditions as to result in "social climates" labeled democratic, authoritarian, or *laissez-faire*. The problem was to determine variations in the behavior of the members of groups whose activities were systematically varied through different techniques of leadership. The experiment illustrates all three of the aspects of methodology with which this chapter has dealt.

1. *Control of social stimulation.* The several groups were equated as to intellectual, physical, and personality traits, including patterns of interpersonal relationship, as indicated by sociometric means. Individual personality factors were further controlled by subjecting each group to two or more sets of experimental conditions. Factors of leader personality were controlled by rotating the leaders among the different groups. Types of leader control, the major experimental variable, are summarized as follows:

Authoritarian	Democratic	*Laissez-faire*
Policy determined by leader.	Policy determined by group discussion, with assistance of leader.	Policy left free for individual or group decision; little leader participation.
Activities and techniques dictated by leader, one step at a time.	General procedures outlined by leader in advance, thus giving perspective. Various alternatives presented, when technical advice needed.	No help from leader, except to supply materials and to supply information when asked.
Work task and work companion of each boy dictated by leader.	Division of tasks determined by group; boys chose own work companions.	No participation by leader in assignment of work tasks or companions.
Leader "personal" in praise and criticism; remained aloof from participation except when demonstrating procedures.	Leader "objective, fact-minded" in praise and criticism; acted as participant group member.	No attempt by leader to appraise or regulate events; no comment on member activities unless questioned.

2. *Observing social behavior.* Observers, trained in preliminary experiments, made paper-and-pencil records of the following nature, five or more observers being assigned to each group of five boys: *social interactions,* in terms of frequency of directive, compliant, objective, resistant, and other types of behavior directed toward others; *group structure,* in terms of activity subgroupings, statements of nature and goal of activity, identity of the initiator of the activity, ratings of degree of group unity; *conversation,* recorded verbatim and

in entirety by stenographers; *interpretations*, including descriptions of incidents and notes on changes in tempo of activities, excitement, boredom, etc. It was found more satisfactory to assign each observer to a single type of behavior for all subjects, rather than to assign him to confine his observations to a single boy. All records by all observers were synchronized at 1-minute intervals, so that they could later be fitted together without error. Afterward these records were coded for various categories of behavior relevant to the hypotheses of the study; the reliability of the coding process proved satisfactory.

3. *Relating individual response to social stimulation.* This aspect of methodology has to do with the theory in terms of which experimental manipulations and behavior observations are made. Both must be such as to confirm or disprove hypotheses concerning motive patterns as intervening variables relating stimulation to response. In the present study one hypothesis was that adult controls tend to create egocentric rather than group-centered motive patterns. Hence the experiment was so planned that the following observations could be made.

In the autocratic groups, as compared with the others, there was a lower ratio of frequency of use of the word "we" to that of the word "I," a higher ratio of hostile to friendly behavior, more "restrictive" behavior by the leader, less casual sociability and spontaneous conversation among boys, more submissive behavior toward the leader, more competitive and more aggressive behavior toward other boys. (Quantitative evidence is presented for all these findings.) In the authoritarian groups, moreover, the proportion of time spent in "serious work" dropped sharply when the leader left the room, whereas it dropped scarcely at all when the democratic leader left. In the democratic groups, as compared with the others, there were markedly fewer expressions of discontent; there was more carefulness in work, a larger number of creative suggestions, and more pride in products of group effort. These and other findings serve to confirm the initial hypothesis. The methodology begins with the theoretical plan, which dictates the manner in which stimulation is controlled and behavior observed. In the actual planning of any investigation, this methodological step should be the first, not the last.

Such an experiment is valuable not only because it tells us *that* different individual behaviors result in predictable ways from varying leadership procedures, but also because it tells us a good deal about *why*. It could not have told us why, however, if controlled stimulation and accurate observation had not been so planned as to test a set of hypotheses concerning what happens between stimulation and response.

Such studies have little significance for methodology in the narrower sense, but have much to contribute to a wider understanding of method. No amount of methodological exactness or ingenuity will suffice if the problems which the methods are a means of solving are not adequately formulated. Methods of accurately observing response to social stimulation and of controlling social stimulation must be subservient to the major problem of explaining the psychological processes which determine behavior. Methods of observing response and of controlling stimulation are by no means perfected. Social psychology's most urgent present need, however, is better formulation of its problems, particularly in respect to the ways in which everyday forms of social stimulation are fitted into individual motive patterns.

REFERENCES

1. Allport, F. H. The J-curve hypothesis of conforming behavior. *J. Soc. Psychol.*, 1934, *5,* 141–183.
2. Allport, F. H. *Institutional Behavior.* Chapel Hill, N. C.: University of North Carolina Press, 1933.
3. Allport, G. W. A test for ascendance-submission. *J. Abn. Soc. Psychol.*, 1928, *23,* 118–136.
4. Allport, G. W. *Personality: A Psychological Interpretation.* New York: Henry Holt, 1937.
5. Allport, G. W. *The Use of Personal Documents in Psychological Science.* New York: Social Science Research Council, 1942.
6. Aveling, F., and H. L. Hargreaves. Suggestibility with and without prestige in children. *Brit. J. Psychol.*, 1921, *18,* 362–388.
7. Bales, R. F. *The Fixation Factor in Alcohol Addiction: An Hypothesis Derived from a Comparative Study of Irish and Jewish Social Norms.* Unpublished dissertation, Harvard University, 1944.
8. Baumgartner, M. The correlation of direct suggestibility with certain character traits. *J. Appl. Psychol.*, 1931, *15,* 1–15.
9. Binet, A. *La Suggestibilité.* Paris: Schleicher Fres., 1900.
10. Davis, A. Childhood training and social class. In *Child Behavior and Development.* R. G. Barker, J. S. Kounin, and H. F. Wright, Eds. New York: McGraw-Hill, 1943. See also A. Davis and J. Dollard. *Children of Bondage.* American Council on Education, 1940.
11. Dashiell, J. F. An experimental analysis of some group effects. *J. Abn. Soc. Psychol.*, 1930, *25,* 190–199. See also Experimental studies on the influence of social situations on the behavior of human adults. In *Handbook of Social Psychology.* C. Murchison, Ed. Worcester, Mass.: Clark University Press, 1935.
12. Dodd, S. C. A social distance test in the Near East. *Amer. J. Sociol.*, 1935, *41,* 194–204.
13. Goodenough, F. L. Measuring behavior traits by means of repeated short samples. *J. Juv. Res.*, 1928, *12,* 230–235.
14. Hall, O. M. Attitudes and unemployment. *Arch. Psychol.*, 1934, No. 165.
15. Hinckley, E. D. The influence of individual opinion on construction of an attitude scale. *J. Soc. Psychol.*, 1932, *3,* 283–296.

16. Horney, K. *Our Inner Conflicts.* New York: W. Norton, 1945.
17. Hyman, H. The psychology of status. *Arch. Psychol.,* 1942, No. 269.
18. Jennings, H. H. *Leadership and Isolation.* New York: Longmans, Green, 1943.
19. Jones, E. S. Subjective evaluations of personality. In *Personality and the Behavior Disorders.* J. McV. Hunt, Ed. New York: Ronald Press, 1944.
20. Katz, D., and F. H. Allport. *Students' Attitudes: A Report of the Syracuse University Reaction Study.* Syracuse: Craftsman Press, 1931.
21. Knower, F. H. Experimental studies in changes in attitudes. I. A study of the effect of oral argument on changes of attitude. *J. Soc. Psychol.,* 1935, *6,* 315–347. II. A study of the effect of printed argument on changes in attitude. *J. Abn. Soc. Psychol.,* 1936, *30,* 522–532. III. Some incidence of attitude changes. *J. Appl. Psychol.,* 1936, *20,* 114–127.
22. Laird, D. A. Changes in motor control and individual variations under the influence of "razzing." *J. Exper. Psychol.,* 1923, *6,* 236–246.
23. Landis, C. Studies of emotional reactions. II. General behavior and facial expression. *J. Comp. Psychol.,* 1924, *4,* 447–509.
24. Lewin, K. *The Relative Effectiveness of a Lecture Method and a Method of Group Decision for Changing Food Habits.* Committee on Food Habits, National Research Council, June, 1942 (mimeographed).
25. Lewin, K., and P. Grabbe, Eds. Problems of re-education. *J. Soc. Issues,* 1945, *1,* No. 3.
26. Lewin, K., R. Lippitt, and R. K. White. Patterns of aggressive behavior in experimentally created "social climates." *J. Soc. Psychol.,* 1939, *10,* 271–299.
27. Lewis, H. B. Studies in the principles of judgments and attitudes. IV. The operation of "prestige suggestion." *J. Soc. Psychol.,* 1941, *14,* 229–256.
28. Likert, R. A technique for the measurement of attitudes. *Arch. Psychol.,* 1932, No. 140.
29. Likert, R., S. Roslow, and G. Murphy. A simple and reliable method of scoring the Thurstone attitude scales. *J. Soc. Psychol.,* 1934, *5,* 228–238.
30. Lippitt, R. An experimental study of the effect of democratic and authoritarian group atmospheres. *Univ. Iowa Stud. Child Welfare,* 1940, *16,* No. 3, 43–195.
31. Lippitt, R., and R. K. White. The "social climate" of children's groups. In *Child Behavior and Development.* R. G. Barker, J. S. Kounin, and H. F. Wright, Eds. New York: McGraw-Hill, 1943.
32. Maller, J. B. Cooperation and competition: an experimental study in motivation. *Teach. Coll. Contrib. Educ.,* 1929.
33. Mead, M. *Coming of Age in Samoa.* New York: W. Morrow, 1928. Also, Research on primitive children. Chapter 13 in *Manual of Child Psychology.* L. Carmichael, Ed. New York: John Wiley and Sons, 1946.
34. Moreno, J. L. *Who Shall Survive? A New Approach to the Problem of Human Interrelations.* Nervous and Mental Disease Publishing Company, 1934.
35. Murphy, G., L. B. Murphy, and T. M. Newcomb. *Experimental Social Psychology.* New York: Harper, 1937.
36. Murphy, L. B. *Social Behavior and Child Personality.* New York: Columbia University Press, 1937.
37. Murray, H. A. *Explorations in Personality.* New York: Oxford University Press, 1938.
38. Murray, H. A., and C. D. Morgan. A clinical study of sentiments. *Genet. Psychol. Monog.,* 1945, *32,* 3–149; 153–311.

39. Newcomb, T. M. *Personality and Social Change.* New York: Dryden Press, 1943.
40. Newcomb, T. M., and G. Svehla. Intra-family relationships in attitude. *Sociometry,* 1937, *1,* 180–205.
41. Razran, G. H. S. Attitudinal control of human conditioning. *J. Psychol.,* 1936, *2,* 327–337.
42. Shaw, M. E. *A Comparison of Individuals and Small Groups in the Rational Solution of Complex Problems.* Master's essay, Columbia University Library, 1930. Also, A comparison of individuals and small groups in the rational solution of complex problems, *Amer. J. Psychol.,* 1932, *44,* 491–504.
43. Sherif, M. *The Psychology of Social Norms.* New York: Harper, 1936.
44. Sherif, M., and H. Cantril. The psychology of "attitudes." *Psychol. Rev.,* 1945, *52,* 295–319; 1946, *53,* 1–24.
45. Sullivan, H. S. Conceptions of modern psychiatry. *Psychiatry,* 1940, *3,* 1–117.
46. Symonds, P. M. *Diagnosing Personality and Conduct.* New York: Century, 1931.
47. Thurstone, L. L. Theory of attitude measurement. *Psychol. Rev.,* 1929, *36,* 222–241.
48. Thurstone, L. L. Influence of motion pictures on children's attitudes. *J. Soc. Psychol.,* 1931, *2,* 291–305.
49. Thurstone, L. L., and E. J. Chave. *The Measurement of Attitude.* Chicago: University of Chicago Press, 1930.
50. Warner, L. W., and P. S. Lunt. *Yankee City Series. Vol. I. The Social Life of the Modern Community.* New Haven: Yale University Press, 1941.
51. White, R. K. Black Boy: A Value Analysis. *J. Abn. Soc. Psychol.,* 1947, *42,* 440–461.

SUGGESTED READINGS

Cottrell, L. S., Jr., and R. Gallagher. *Developments in Social Psychology, 1930–1940. Sociometry Monog.* No. *1.* Beacon House.

Murchison, C., Ed. *A Handbook of Social Psychology.* Worcester, Mass.: Clark University Press, 1935.

Murphy, G., L. B. Murphy, and T. M. Newcomb. *Experimental Social Psychology.* New York: Harper, 1937.

Rusk, G. Y. The methodology of social psychology. *J. Soc. Psychol.,* 1931, *14,* 3–89.

Index of Names

Index of Subjects